PENGUIN REFERENCE

THE PENGUIN DICTIONARY OF AMERICAN FOLKLORE

Alan Axelrod taught at Lake Forest College and Furman University before becoming an editor, independent book producer, and author. His *Art of the Golden West* won the National Cowboy Hall of Fame's Western Heritage Award. He lives in Atlanta, Georgia.

Harry Oster is professor emeritus of English and American Studies at the University of Iowa. A winner of Guggenheim and Ford fellowships, he lives in Iowa City, Iowa.

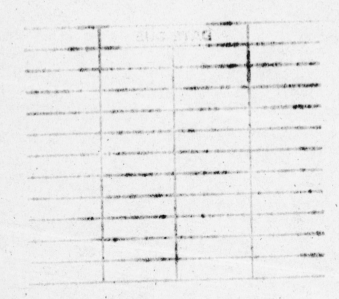

DATE DUE

THE PENGUIN DICTIONARY OF
AMERICAN FOLKLORE

ALAN AXELROD AND HARRY OSTER

WITH WALTON RAWLS

PENGUIN REFERENCE

PENGUIN BOOKS
Published by the Penguin Group
Penguin Putnam Inc., 375 Hudson Street,
New York, New York 10014, U.S.A.
Penguin Books Ltd, 80 Strand,
London WC2R 0RL, England
Penguin Books Australia Ltd, Ringwood,
Victoria, Australia
Penguin Books Canada Ltd, 10 Alcorn Avenue,
Toronto, Ontario, Canada M4V 3B2
Penguin Books (N.Z.) Ltd, 182–190 Wairau Road,
Auckland 10, New Zealand

Penguin Books Ltd, Registered Offices:
Harmondsworth, Middlesex, England

First published in the United States of America by Penguin Reference,
a member of Penguin Putnam Inc. 2000
Published in Penguin Books 2001

1   3   5   7   9   10   8   6   4   2

THE LIBRARY OF CONGRESS HAS CATALOGED THE HARDCOVER EDITION AS FOLLOWS:
Axelrod, Alan, 1952–
The Penguin dictionary of American Folklore / Alan Axelrod and Harry Oster with Walton Rawls
p.   cm.
ISBN 0-670-88752-8 (hc.)
ISBN 0 14 10.0240 9 (pbk.)
I. Folklore—United States—Dictionaries.   2. United States—Social life and customs—Dictionaries.
I. Oster, Harry.   II. Rawls, Walton H.   III. Title.
GR105.34.A94   2000
398'.0973'03—DC21   99–14073

Printed in the United States of America
Set in Sabon
Designed by Joe Rutt

For Anita and Ian, legends in their own time
—ALAN AXELROD

To my wife, Caroline, and son, Aaron, for their
loving support and unfailing encouragement
—HARRY OSTER

PREFACE

A dictionary is about definitions, and for a dictionary of American folklore this presents a problem. Folklorist W. Edson Richmond remarked in his introduction to Richard M. Dorson's *Handbook of American Folklore* (Bloomington, Ind., 1983): "It has long been a cliché that there are more definitions of folklore than there are folklorists." The *Standard Dictionary of Folklore, Mythology, and Legend* (New York, 1949) gave no fewer than twenty-one definitions, all quite different from one another. With a degree of realistic resignation, Richmond continued: the precise meaning of *folklore* "lies in the mind of its definer, not in the thing itself," and "the word *folklore* has come to be defined by some as whatever folklorists are interested in."

This presents a problem. Or it offers the opportunity of almost limitless license. For what we have included here are, indeed, the subjects that generally interest folklorists. But not just folklorists. We have defined our scope with even greater circularity: What we have included here are subjects that interest people who are interested in folklore.

Not that we have covered the field exhaustively. *The Penguin Dictionary of American Folklore* is a concise work of more than a quarter-million but less than a half-million words. So let us refine our circular mission statement: We have included the subjects we have reason to believe *most* interest *most* people who are interested in folklore. The point is that our choice of subjects proceeds less from any academic definition or set of definitions concerning folklore than it does from motives of practicality. We have aimed to include the information that will be of most use to most of our readers most of the time.

Who are our readers? Folklorists, students, students of American art, crafts, culture, and history, students in American studies programs, people interested in ethnic history and culture, those interested in popular culture, and, well, anyone who has any need, at any time, for information about American folklore. Like most modern students of folklore, we're none too particular.

All of this said, we should establish a few basic assumptions, if only to avoid creating disappointment.

Some students of folklore—we might call them folklore purists—hold that for a particular object, utterance, song, dance, or whatever to be deemed folklore, it must be the product of essentially oral transmission or informal demonstration, it must be identifiable as the product of tradition, and it must be capable of being shown to be a variation of some recognizable, traditional type. Moreover, the "purists" argue, folk artifacts are essentially anonymous in origin; even if the maker or speaker or singer can be identified, the product must be sufficiently formulaic to be, in effect, the original work of no single artist.

Increasingly, students of folklore have abandoned this "purist" point of view. That does not mean that it is outmoded or invalid, but that, as most recent scholars see it, it simply limits the field too severely. The purist would distinguish between *folklore* and *popular culture* in this way: Both folklore and popular culture are popular (that is, of the people, rather than of the academies or the institutions), but whereas popular culture is mass-mediated culture (commercial products transmitted through film, television, radio, recordings, and print), folklore is unmediated. It is essentially noncommercial expression. The problem with this distinction, most current students agree, is that it relegates folklore to the past—that is, to a past before the influence of mass media became pervasive. Our time (which takes in the relatively recent past) is saturated by mass communication, so that it has become difficult, even impossible, to distinguish between folk traditions, transmitted orally among small groups, and mass-mediated popular culture. Moreover, the mass media avenue is not a one-way street. Print, television, radio, and recording are all influenced by folklore, even as they in turn influence "the folk." Thus, while the reader will find in this book separate and distinct entries for both *folklore* and *popular culture,* he or she will also find a host of entries on subjects that smack, indiscriminately perhaps, of both. For example, there are entries on nineteenth-century Appalachian ballads, as well as entries relating to twentieth-century rock 'n' roll. While we have endeavored to cover the folklore of the past, when folklore really was orally transmitted among small groups (for many of our readers will be interested in precisely this), we also believe that folklore is very much alive today, albeit no longer "pure" and unmediated, and we have tried to encompass the present as well (again, anticipating the interests of our readers).

We readily admit that the foregoing hardly ties up all folklore's loose ends. (Most folklorists *like* loose ends, anyway.) But it does at least address them. (Tell a kid that his shoe is untied, and you'll rarely prompt him actually to tie it, but you might at least get a grudging response of "I know.") But we do need to "address" another loose end.

What is *American* folklore?

The organized collection and study of American folklore began in the second half of the nineteenth century, and the American Folklore Society was founded in 1888. It is no accident that institutionalized interest in collecting and preserving the artifacts of the "American" folk rose with the rising tide of immigration. Today, we tend to think of folklore study as reflecting essentially liberal and inclusive attitudes. In the United States, however, the origins of folklore study are to be found at least as much in a conservative impulse toward exclusion. For most American folklorists in the late nineteenth and even early twentieth century, "American folklore" consisted mainly of the ballads, oral narratives, and handicrafts produced by the New England and Appalachian descendants of seventeenth- and eighteenth-century emigrants from the British Isles. Added to this, but quite distinct from it, was an interest in collecting and preserving the songs and tales of African Americans living in the South. Again, this proceeded from no liberal impulse, but from a fear that the post–Civil War abolition of slavery would bring to an end certain distinctive black folk traditions. In effect, preserving African-American folklore and folkways would also preserve something of the antebellum status quo.

The evolution of American folklore studies has been, generally speaking, a broadening of these original assumptions and motives. For the noninvolved layperson—the proverbial man or woman on the street—the word *folklore* may still trigger images of aged Appalachian fiddlers and New England spinsters making straw brooms, but to the modern folklorist the term applies to the distinctive cultural products of almost any group that can be defined ethnically, nationally, regionally, socially, or vocationally. In the past, folklore study has been chiefly concerned with the cultural products of people past middle age (the bearers of tradition). Today, the work of people of all ages, including children, is studied. In the past, folklore was considered a rural phenomenon. Today, many folklorists do most of their collecting in America's cities.

This broadening trend has greatly enriched the field of folklore studies, but it makes the task of compiling a dictionary of American folklore far more daunting than it would have been a century, half a century, or even twenty-five years ago. Today's folklorists recognize that ours is a nation of immigrants, of course, which puts any comprehensive commentator on "American" folklore in the position of having to account for the folklore of Italian Americans, Greek Americans, Polish Americans, and so on. Is German-American folklore merely German folklore in America? Or does something happen to it to transform it into a distinctive German-American folklore? This dictionary does not pretend to answer these questions, nor to cover individual ethnic and national folklore in depth. However, it does offer brief survey entries for the major ethnic and national folklores as they are found in the United States.

Arguably, of course, the only *native* Americans are Native Americans, the people Columbus misnamed Indians. In this dictionary, we include an overview entry on Native American folklore and separate entries on certain aspects of Native American folklore, primarily where these aspects intersect with non–Native American folklore. The subject of Native American folklore is complex and deserves, doubtless, more than a few book-length reference works. Our book is no substitute for a full-scale work of this kind. That is especially unfortunate, since, although the anthropological literature on Native Americans is rich, there is as yet no single comprehensive encyclopedia or dictionary of Native American folklore.

And that brings us at last to the term *dictionary,* which we have used in preference to *encyclopedia.* In truth, neither term is wholly appropriate to this volume. An encyclopedia, to be deserving of its name, must be both comprehensive and thorough, covering a great many subjects and exploring each in reasonable depth. For this reason, an encyclopedia devoted to any large field must be a multivolume work. Our purpose and task was to create a single volume, by default a dictionary rather than an encyclopedia. And yet a dictionary, which favors comprehensiveness over thoroughness, typically offers many *brief* entries, usually written in telegraphically compressed prose devoid of personality. Such an approach runs contrary to the natural inclination of the authors, the spirit of folklore, and, most important, what we perceive as the needs and desires of our readers. So *The Penguin Dictionary of American Folklore* is a compromise between an encyclopedia and a dictionary, as it is a compromise between comprehensiveness and thoroughness. In each major entry, we have aimed at creating narrative prose that may be read for information, but without having to forego the pleasure of perusal. Yet we also recognize and admit that few of our entries are truly encyclopedic in depth. In all cases, we have tried to convey the essence of a topic, issue, or individual, but where the subject warrants it, we have directed the reader to more thorough and profound sources in a Suggested Reading section at the end of many entries. Fortunately, too, relatively few entries are required to stand wholly on their own. Most include cross-references to other relevant entries within the dictionary. Wherever possible, we have indicated these unobtrusively in small caps within the main text; in some cases, "see also" recommendations are found at the conclusion of an entry.

We have one final disavowal to make.

Nineteenth- and early-twentieth-century folklorists heartily embraced the role of arbiter, zealously culling "genuine" or "authentic" folklore from what Richard M. Dorson would later call "fakelore."

We explicitly disavow the role of arbiter. We are informed tourists in transit through the many realms and regions of American folklore and folklife, a territory, like the rest of the modern world, divided by fewer and fewer political, economic, and social borders. We invite our readers to travel with us.

ALAN AXELROD
Atlanta

HARRY OSTER
Iowa City

THE PENGUIN DICTIONARY OF
AMERICAN
FOLKLORE

A

Aaron, Jesse (1887–1979). Aaron was an African-American folk sculptor, who worked mainly with discarded wood, to which he added other "found" objects. Born in Lake City, Florida, Aaron was a professional cook until he was over seventy. At that time, his wife was temporarily blinded by cataracts, and Aaron stayed home to care for her. He opened a nursery on his modest property near Gainesville, Florida, but had to sell the business to pay for the operation that restored his wife's sight in 1968. Thankful, but out of work for the first time in his life, Aaron prayed to God to reveal a suitable occupation. Aaron reported that, at three o'clock on the morning of July 5, 1968, a spirit awakened him with the words "Carve wood." Aaron immediately rose out of bed and began carving some scrap oak. Aaron carved from that time until his death in 1979 at age ninety-two.

Aaron typically chose pieces of natural wood (especially cypress and cedar) that suggested human or animal forms and saw his task as bringing out of the wood the forms that God had put into it. He worked his materials with a chain saw, then finished them with chisels, knives, and drills. To many sculptures, Aaron added plastic eyes and such found objects as hats and antlers.

Aaron was born into a large family, part African American and part Seminole. He received little formal education and worked as a farmhand, baker, and chef before becoming an artist.

See also: WOODCARVING.

SUGGESTED READING: Jane Livingston and John Beardsley, *Black Folk Art in America: 1930–1980* (Jackson, Miss., 1982).

Aesop's fables. A collection of Greek ANIMAL FABLES, these works are almost certainly not the production of an individual author, but, rather, traditional tales from the sixth century B.C. attributed to a legendary figure named Aesop. (The Greek historian Herodotus said Aesop was a slave living in the sixth century B.C.; Plutarch dated Aesop similarly, but said that he was an adviser to Croesus, king of Lydia. Others have identified him as a Thracian, a Phrygian, or a freed slave living on the island of Samos and later becoming riddle solver to King Lycurgus in Babylon.) As with all animal fables, those of Aesop are

Nineteenth-century English book illustration of one of Aesop's fables.

An early twentieth-century American encyclopedia illustration of an imagined Aesop telling one of his fables.

most important for the morals they point rather than for the narrative per se.

Aesop's fables are known chiefly through a set of fables written by the Roman fabulist Phaedrus during the first century A.D. The seventeenth-century French poet Jean de La Fontaine was inspired by these to write a series of famous beast allegories. In America, the European tradition represented by Aesop–Phaedrus–La Fontaine was sometimes combined with the ANIMAL TALES of Native American and especially African-American folk traditions. This hybrid was given its most enduring expression by JOEL CHANDLER HARRIS in his UNCLE REMUS tales.

See also: DISNEY, WALT; WOLF.

African Americans. In 1888, the AMERICAN FOLKLORE SOCIETY identified African Americans (then called Negroes) as an American ethnic group with unique folk traditions that should be recorded, studied, and preserved.

African-American folk music traditions were brought to national attention before the Civil War through MINSTREL SHOWS. While the music in these presentations was variously adapted, modified, and/or bastardized, it did convey some of the flavor of traditional African-American music. But for most of white America, African-American folklore meant the folktales published by JOEL CHANDLER HARRIS at the beginning of the twentieth century in his UNCLE REMUS books. While Harris did not transcribe these tales verbatim, he did capture their essence, and the world came to know something of the TRICKSTER tale traditions of African Americans. Of greater interest to professional folklorists during the early twentieth century was the folklife of African Americans living on the Sea Islands of Georgia and South Carolina. This population had been isolated from "contamination" by mainstream culture, and many even spoke a unique GULLAH dialect.

Interest in African-American folk culture became general once again through the work of the African-American folklorist and novelist ZORA NEALE HURSTON, whose *Mules and Men* (1935) was a landmark collection of African-American folklore. In the meantime, the Harlem Renaissance inspired the African-American poet LANGSTON HUGHES to write a major study of African-American folklore, and the Depression-era Works Progress Administration (WPA) Federal Writers' Project, under the direction of BENJAMIN A. BOTKIN, sent a number of writers into the field to collect folklore from ex-slaves.

Throughout the twentieth century, African-American folk music forms have had profound and wide-reaching impact on American popular music. Spirituals, gospel, RAGTIME, BLUES, JAZZ, ROCK 'N' ROLL, and RAP are all popular (often highly profitable) musical styles that represent transformations of African-American musical traditions.

See also: ANANSI; BALL THE JACK; BLACK EN-

GLISH; BREAKDANCING; BRER FOX; BRER RABBIT; BUCK-AND-WING; CHRISTY, EDWIN P. "NED"; CRAFTS; AMERICAN FOLK GOSPEL MUSIC; HANDY, W. C.; HERSKOVITS, MELVILLE J.; JOHNSON, ROBERT; LEDBETTER, HUDDIE (LEAD BELLY); RICE, THOMAS "DADDY"; SHINE; SHOUT; SPIRITUALS, AFRICAN AMERICAN; STAGOLEE; TALLEY, THOMAS WASHINGTON; TAR BABY; TOASTS; VOODOO.

SUGGESTED READING: Daryl Cumber Dance, *Shuckin' and Jivin': Folklore from Contemporary Black Americans* (Bloomington, Ind., 1978); Richard M. Dorson, *American Negro Folktales* (New York, 1967); Alan Dundes, ed., *Mother Wit from the Laughing Barrel* (Jackson, Miss., 1990); William Ferris, *Afro-American Folk Art and Crafts* (Jackson, Miss., 1983); Gladys-Marie Fry, *Stitched from the Soul: Slave Quilts from the Antebellum South* (New York, 1990); Langston Hughes and Arna Bontemps, eds., *The Book of Negro Folklore* (New York, 1958); Thomas Kochman, *Rappin' and Stylin' Out: Communication in Urban Black America* (Urbana, Ill., 1977); Clarence Major, *Juba to Jive: A Dictionary of African American Slang* (New York, 1994); John W. Roberts, *From Trickster to Badman: The Black Folk Hero from Slavery to Freedom* (Philadelphia, 1989).

African-American vernacular English.
See BLACK ENGLISH.

AIDS tales. A subgenre of URBAN LEGEND, AIDS tales began to be told during the early 1980s, as public awareness of the burgeoning AIDS epidemic grew. The typical AIDS tale is ironic and moralistic: A man meets a beautiful woman in a singles bar, he "scores," they go back to his apartment, they make love. When he wakes in the morning, she is gone, and he finds a message written in lipstick on his bathroom mirror: "Welcome to the world of AIDS." As with other urban legends—and many folktales generally—the AIDS tale points an implied moral (in this case, don't be so quick to sleep around), in contrast to mere misinformation and superstition regarding AIDS (such as concerns that the virus may be transmitted by the most casual of contact or even through the air).

See also: GAY FOLKLORE.

Alamo. The Alamo is officially the Mission San Antonio de Valero, which was established at the new settlement of San Antonio, Texas, by the Franciscan Fray Antonio de Olivares and built beginning in 1716 by Indian converts from the Mission San Francisco Solano on the Rio Grande. Familiarly called "the Alamo" because of its proximity to a landmark cottonwood (in Spanish, *alamo*), the building became an American icon as the site of the battle fought between 179 Texas independence fighters, led by Jim Bowie, William B. Travis, and including DAVY CROCKETT, and a force of four thousand Mexican soldiers commanded by Antonio López de Santa Anna from February 23 to March 6, 1836.

Essentially abandoned by the Church early in the nineteenth century, the mission became a barracks for a company of Spanish cavalry, which gave it the Alamo nickname. After winning independence from Spain, the Mexican army occupied the Alamo from 1821 to 1835, when it was taken over by rebellious Texans at the outbreak of their war for independence from Mexico. When Santa Anna's army advanced into Texas to put down the rebellion, Travis, Bowie, and some

The Alamo, as seen when it was the headquarters of Brig. Gen. David E. Twiggs at the start of the Civil War. (From Harper's Pictorial History of the Civil War, 1866.)

145 Texans entered the Alamo on February 23, 1836. For the next thirteen days, the Alamo's defenders were held under siege by the vastly superior Mexican force. Travis called for reinforcements, but was joined by a mere thirty-two men from Goliad, Texas, who broke through the siege and into the Alamo on March 1. The Mexican troops stormed the mission-fortress on March 6 and killed everyone inside, including former Tennessee congressman Davy Crockett. (Some accounts say that Crockett and five or six others survived the battle, but were subsequently executed.)

The defenders of the Alamo were mourned and celebrated as martyrs to the cause of Texas independence, and the Texas rebellion was swiftly carried to a successful conclusion under the rallying cry of "Remember the Alamo!" Like the war cry "Remember the *Maine!*" which helped ignite the Spanish-American War some fifty-seven years later, the phrase entered the American popular consciousness and has survived far beyond the event that occasioned it.

Texas did not immediately dedicate the Alamo as a commemorative site, but granted the largely ruined structure to the Roman Catholic Church in 1841. The Church did not want the mission, and in 1848, after Texas was admitted to the Union, the Alamo was used as a U.S. Army supply depot. In 1878, after the army moved its supply depot to Fort Sam Houston, the property was acquired by Hugo Grenet, who used the convent as a retail store and the chapel as a warehouse. After Grenet's death in 1882, the convent remained in private hands, but the chapel reverted to the Roman Catholic Church, which sold the property to the state of Texas the following year, whereupon Adina de Zavala, granddaughter of the Mexican-born first vice president of the Republic of Texas, Lorenzo de Zavala, campaigned to raise money for the purchase of the convent. A loan from another San Antonio citizen, Clara Driscoll, made it possible to hold the convent until the Texas legislature appropriated additional funds for its purchase in 1905. The state entrusted administration and operation of the Alamo to the Daughters of the Republic of Texas, who maintain it to this day.

Most Americans have heard of the Alamo, which has been portrayed in many popular books and motion pictures, most notably *The Alamo*, a 1960 film produced and directed by John Wayne, who also played the part of Crockett, and the mission is the most-visited historic site in Texas. For many, the Alamo stirs more than casual emotion. Some are moved by it as the key symbol of Texas's fight for independence and statehood and the embodiment of a special "Texas sprit." Others respond negatively to the Alamo as a symbol of imperialist expansion and the cultural and political oppression of Hispanic Texas by Anglo-Texans.

See also: CUSTER, GEORGE ARMSTRONG.

SUGGESTED READING: Holly Beachley Brear, *Inherit the Alamo: Myth and Ritual at an American Shrine* (Austin, Tex., 1995); Walter Lord, *A Time to Stand* (New York, 1961); Lon Tinkle, *The Alamo: 13 Days to Glory* (New York, 1958).

Alger, Horatio[, Jr.] (1832–1899). One of the most popular American authors of the latter nineteenth century, Alger wrote more than a hundred rags-to-riches novels, almost always featuring a poor boy, who, through hard work, simple piety, cheerful perseverance, and a catalytic dash of good luck, earns substantial material rewards. For generations of readers, Alger's fiction defined the "American dream." Alger's working of the rags-to-riches formula was so pervasive in its influence that the phrase "Horatio Alger story" is customarily used to describe the life of any American man who rises from poverty to wealth through hard work.

The son of a Chelsea, Massachusetts, Unitarian minister, Alger graduated from Harvard University with Phi Beta Kappa honors in 1852, having concentrated his studies on the classics. Alger taught school and wrote for magazines, then enrolled in the Harvard Divinity School, taking his degree in 1860. Rejected for Civil War army service because of weak health, Alger was ordained in 1864 and became pastor of a church in Brewster, Massachusetts, but resigned two years later amid allegations of pederasty. Alger moved to New York City and published *Ragged Dick; or, Street Life in New York with the Bootblacks* (serialized, 1867; published in book form, 1868). This simple, sententious story of an impoverished shoeshine boy's rise to wealth created an immediate sensation. For the next thirty years, Alger continued to mine this vein, writing essentially the same story some one hundred times.

The appeal of his novels—despite wooden characters, stilted dialogue, and pasteboard plotting—may be explained as a literary expression of a folk belief in the universal availability of the American dream of material success. This sentiment was especially compelling in an age of burgeoning urbanization and industrialization, when great fortunes were being made on the backs of the working poor.

Alger's most popular series were "Ragged Dick," "Luck and Pluck," and "Tattered Tom." During his lifetime, his books sold in excess of twenty million copies.

See also: COMPUTER FOLKLORE; EDISON, THOMAS ALVA; FOLKLORE IN AMERICAN LITERATURE; FRANKLIN, BENJAMIN; MONROE, MARILYN; PRESLEY, ELVIS.

SUGGESTED READING: Edwin P. Hoyt, *Horatio's Boys* (New York, 1974); Gary Scharnhorst and Jack Bales, *The Lost Life of Horatio Alger, Jr.* (New York, 1985).

Alien abduction. Of all phenomena associated with purported UFO contacts, none is stranger or more controversial than reported abductions by UFO-borne aliens. A rich folklore has developed, in part built on stories disseminated through MASS MEDIA and UFO cultist literature, and in part on scientific (some professional, some amateur) investigation of abduction and associated phenomena.

During the UFO waves of the 1950s, five major "contactees" rose to national notoriety: George Adamski, Truman Bethurum, Daniel Fry, Orfeo Angelucci, and Howard Menger. In the words of one recent UFOlogist, these men "exhibited behavior consistent with the assertion that they fabricated hoaxes." Unlike most individuals during the 1950s who had simply seen UFOs and, fearing ridicule, shunned the spotlight, these contactees deliberately publicized their experiences, writing books and articles, giving popular lectures, and appearing on radio and television programs. They described riding in flying saucers and touring the planets, which they often described in great detail. Adamski claimed to have contacted a blond humanoid from Venus, who told him ("conversing" via telepathy) that

he had come to earth to stop atomic testing because of the danger of radioactive fallout posed to other planets in the solar system. Bethurum was awakened one night by eight to ten little men, who took him aboard their flying saucer, where he met a gorgeous female alien named Aura Rhanes from the planet Clarion. The other contactees had similarly implausible stories, and most declared that, following their experience, they felt compelled to impart various extraterrestrial messages and prophecies to their fellow earthlings. In the Cold War atmosphere of a world that seemed perilously close to nuclear armageddon, these preachments usually involved injunctions to promote world peace and global understanding.

Another class of abduction stories is more difficult to write off as hoax. The classic case of this type is that of Barney and Betty Hill (see HILL, BARNEY AND BETTY), a couple who reported a nighttime sighting in 1961 on a remote highway in New Hampshire. After the sighting, on their drive home, they both sensed that there were about two hours they could not account for. Following this incident, both began to experience nightmares, anxiety (Barney developed an ulcer), and depression. In the course of psychotherapy sought for these symptoms, both underwent regressive hypnosis, during which, independently of each other, they described their abduction by humanoid captors, who performed an invasive and traumatic quasi-medical examination of them. (Many recent authorities have criticized the regressive hypnosis technique as actually suggesting the alien abduction imagery. The point, however, is not so much whether or not the abduction was real, but that the "abductees" believe that it was.)

No formal census of similar abduction reports exists. However, one student of the subject, Budd Hopkins (see Suggested Reading), has personally reviewed "roughly five hundred" reports and believes that some "tens of thousands" of persons may have been abducted. The vast majority of reported cases follow strikingly similar patterns. Commonly, a young husband and wife with an infant or small child are driving late at night down a deserted highway. They see a bright light in the sky. It suddenly approaches the car. The light is soundless and maneuvers unlike any known aircraft, darting, hovering, and darting again. It passes over the car, then disappears behind the horizon or trees. At this point, the car's electrical system fails completely, and the vehicle stalls. The UFO then lifts off, reappearing at a slightly different position from where it had disappeared. The car's motor starts again, spontaneously. The occupants of the vehicle are uninjured, though mildly disoriented.

What they do not realize is that a period of time—usually about two hours—is "missing" from their lives. During this time, they have been inside the landed UFO and have undergone a quasi-medical examination, which has been somehow blocked from their memories. Typically, the abductees have no sense—or only the vaguest sense—of missed time. However, they may become aware of some unusual pain and physical marks—perhaps a red spot, which burns and is painful to the touch. In some cases, individuals report their sighting to a UFO investigator, who may elicit from them evidence of an abduction. He may then ask the abductees to undergo regressive hypnosis, during which the missing time is recovered. In other cases, chronic symptoms of emotional disturbance follow the sighting—nightmares, anxiety, depression—which prompts the individuals to seek psychiatric treatment, in the course of which the incidents of the abduction are gradually recalled.

Under regressive hypnosis, many subjects describe the extraterrestrial humanoids in remarkably similar terms: stature of a twelve-year-old child; disproportionately large head; eyes so big as to dominate other facial features; presence of nostrils rather than a full nose; pale, wrinkled, or mottled skin. What is the significance of these similarities? Believers cite them as "proof" of bona fide alien contact. More skeptical investigators point out that drawings of aliens have been widely disseminated, and they further point to the important ways in which cultural background seems to affect what alleged abductees report. Some English contactees and abductees report beings who are "Nordic" in appearance, tall and blond. In South America, aliens are sometimes described as hairy, simian creatures.

Typically, abductees describe a medical examination, usually invasive, often painful and even terrifying, involving probes of the body's orifices and the taking of blood and tissue samples. In the case of female subjects, the medical procedure resembles in some aspects a conventional gynecological examination. Some accounts even involve apparent artificial embryo implantation and/or removal.

See also UFO FOLKLORE.

SUGGESTED READING: John Fuller, *The Interrupted Journey* (New York, 1966; 1974); David Haisell, *The Missing Seven Hours* (New York, 1978); David Haisell, *The Missing Seven Hours Revealed* (New York, n.d.); Budd Hopkins, *Intruders: The Incredible Visitations at Copley Woods* (New York, 1987); Budd Hopkins, *Missing Time: A Documented Study of UFO Abductions* (New York, 1981); Coral and Jim Lorenzen, *Abducted!* (New York, 1977); Coral and Jim Lorenzen, *Encounters with UFO Occupants* (New York, 1976); Gordon Stein, ed., *The Encyclopedia of the Paranormal* (New York, 1996).

Allen, Barbara. See BARBARA ALLEN.

Allen, Ethan (1738–1789). Allen was a soldier in the French and Indian War (1754–1763), who later settled in what is now Vermont, and organized the Green Mountain Boys in 1770. This militia force helped take Fort Ticonderoga from the British on May 10, 1775. Allen was captured during an ill-fated attempt to seize Montreal (September 1775). Released in 1778, he became active in the cause of Vermont statehood. When this failed, Allen attempted to negotiate annexation of Vermont to Canada. But it is for his brief career as leader of the Green Mountain Boys that Allen passed first into Vermont folklore and then into national folklore. He was seen as an unbeatable, grassroots guerrilla leader—though his reputation and that of his militia unit far exceeded any effect they had on the outcome of the Revolution.

See also: REVOLUTIONARY WAR.

Statue of Ethan Allen by Larkin G. Mead in the rotunda of the U.S. Capitol.

The alligator was depicted as a dragonlike monster by early European visitors to the New World. This engraving is from Theodor de Bry's Collectiones peregrinationum in Indiam orientalem et Indiam occidentalem (1590–1634).

A long-current URBAN LEGEND holds that alligators inhabit the sewer system of New York City. The alligator population (according to the legend) sprang from an unwanted baby alligator (once a fashionable pet) flushed down a toilet. Stories have been told of alligators occasionally reemerging from Manhattan toilets—to the chagrin of the person seeking relief thereon. (New York City public works officials have repeatedly denounced the alligator stories as unfounded.)

See also: ANIMAL TALE.

Alligator. Found in the Southeast, alligators figure in Native American and African TRICKSTER tales, often as the butt of rabbit's tricks. One folktale holds that BRER RABBIT trapped an alligator in a dry field and set it ablaze—thereby giving it its scaly skin. Alligator teeth are prized among some African Americans and Native Americans as AMULETS to ward off witchcraft.

Almanacs. Books containing a calendar of the days, weeks, and months of the year; a record of miscellaneous astronomical and meteorological phenomena; long-term weather predictions; and sundry other information, as well as folk wisdom, folktales, and semiliterary sketches, American almanacs were a primary means of preserving and transmitting folk humor. The term *almanac* itself is of obscure origin, apparently related to the medieval Arabic word for weather. In Europe, the first printed almanac appeared in 1457, but the genre is rooted in ancient Egyptian and Greek calendars which showed festival dates and days deemed lucky or unlucky. By the seventeenth century, both in Europe and in America (the first book printed in America was an almanac by Capt. William Pierce, published in 1639 at Cambridge, Massachusetts), almanacs had evolved into a form of folk literature, replete with proverbs, folk-medical advice, and humor.

The most popular of the early American almanacs were *The Astronomical Diary and Almanack*, begun by Nathaniel Ames of Dedham, Massachusetts, in 1725 (and published through 1775), BENJAMIN FRANKLIN's *Poor Richard's* series of almanacs, begun in Philadelphia in 1732 (it was published through 1758), and *The Farmer's Almanac*, which was first published in 1792, by Robert B. Thomas, and has been in continuous publication ever since. By 1831 New York and Boston printers were grinding out pseudo-almanacs, which were humor and joke books, really, created by hack writers in imitation of the earlier, more folk-oriented almanacs. Within this fairly insipid body of popular literature, however, one notable series did evolve. Beginning in Nashville in 1835, the first of the DAVY CROCKETT almanacs appeared. The original series ended in 1841, but New York publishers began turning out Crockett almanac–joke books in 1836 and continued through 1856. The Crockett almanacs included tall tales about—and purportedly by—Davy Crockett and were rich with fantasy, frontier-style exaggeration, and elaborately grotesque coinages. The Crockett almanacs also printed a number of tales relating to MIKE FINK, the legendary keelboatman of the Ohio and Mississippi. By the end of the nineteenth century, the word *almanac* had come to describe a book of facts and statistics—minus the folklore—and the heyday of the traditional almanac was at an end, though it may be argued that the FOXFIRE series of magazines, started in 1966, which contain a wealth of folk wisdom and other folk material, have taken over some of the old almanac functions.

See also: AMES, NATHANIEL; BOWERY "B'HOY"; BROTHER JONATHAN; DIALECT STORIES; HUMOR, FOLK; URBAN LEGEND.

SUGGESTED READING: Robert K. Dodge, *Early American Almanac Humor* (Bowling Green, Ohio, 1987); Robb Sagendorph, *America and Her Almanacs* (Dublin, N.H., 1970).

By the early nineteenth century, Americans were reading temperance almanacs, anti-Masonic almanacs, and antislavery almanacs. This illustration is taken from one of the latter. It depicts a master or slave owner plying his whip against a woman who exclaims "Oh my child, my child." The child is visible at the right, struggling with a snake.

Ambrose, Ed (1913–). Ambrose is a carver, whose subjects range from mountain men to Indians to Miss Liberty to Uncle Sam, and to such three-dimensional political caricatures/cartoons as Richard Nixon hitchhiking and Jimmy Carter as a peanut. Born in Strasbourg, Virginia, Ambrose worked as a master carpenter, specializing in restorations. He started whittling when he was a boy and began selling his carvings at a highway truck stop in Stephens City, Virginia, in the late 1940s. Ambrose works mainly in basswood, which he paints and to which he may add metal fittings as necessary.

American Folklife Center. Established by Public Law 94-201 (American Folklife Preservation Act) in 1976 as part of the United States Library of Congress, the American Folklife Center is charged by Congress with preserving and presenting American folklife. The center has active publications and exhibits programs and maintains the ARCHIVE OF FOLK CULTURE, the largest and most comprehensive ethnographic collection of folk music, folklore, and folklife in North America. The center organizes and sponsors many field projects to document American folkcultural traditions.

Address: The American Folklife Center, Library of Congress, Washington, D.C., 20540-8100 (202-707-2000). The center maintains a site on the World Wide Web (WWW): lcmarvel @seq1.loc.gov.

American Folklore Society. Founded in Boston in 1888 by FRANCIS JAMES CHILD, WILLIAM WELLS NEWELL, Daniel Garrison Brinton, FRANZ BOAS, and other eminent students of folklore to promote the scholarly and "scientific" study of folklore, the American Folklore Society publishes the *Journal of American Folklore, The Centennial Index,* and *The American Folklore Society Newsletter,* as well as a distinguished series of book-length monographs. The society holds an annual meeting, which includes scholarly workshops, panel discussions, forums, and other presentations. The society's archives are housed at the Utah State University Library Special Collections Division.

Address: American Folklore Society, 4350 North Fairfax Drive, Suite 640, Arlington, VA 22203. On the Internet, log on to gopher. panam.edu to access American Folklore Society files and other materials.

See also: AFRICAN AMERICANS; BASSETT, FLETCHER S.

Ames, Nathaniel (1708–1764). Physician, almanac maker, tavernkeeper, and attorney, Ames created and published *The Astronomical Diary and Almanack* for 1726–64 (published 1725–63), with BENJAMIN FRANKLIN's *Poor Richard* series, the best of the early American ALMANACS. Ames was born in Bridgewater, Massachusetts. He was the son of an astronomer and settled in Dedham, where he earned a reputation as a cantankerous, eccentric intellectual. Ames's *Astronomical Diary,* begun in 1725, was highly successful, often selling some 60,000 copies a year. The historian of early American literature Moses Coit Tyler rated it higher in quality than *Poor Richard.* Although Ames included in the almanac his own essays, usually dealing with health or astronomy, and his satric verse (in the manner of Alexander Pope), he also was generous with pieces of folk wisdom and folklore. Even in his own compositions, Ames sometimes attempted to reproduce regional dialect—something quite rare in almanac writings of the period. Ames's *Astronomical Diary* inspired competitors, including Benjamin Franklin, and set the standard for American almanacs through the first third of the nineteenth century.

SUGGESTED READING: Marion Barber Stowell, entry on Ames in James A. Levernier and Douglas R. Wilmes, eds., *American Writers Before 1800: A Biographical and Critical Dictionary*, vol. 1 (Westport, Conn., 1983).

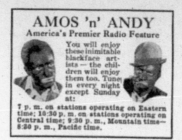

Newspaper ad for the Amos 'n' Andy *radio show, 1940s.*

Amos 'n' Andy. One of the the longest-running radio programs of all time, *Amos 'n' Andy* achieved even greater popularity when it was brought to television in the summer of 1951. Various civil rights groups, most notably the NAACP, protested that the series fostered racial stereotypes, as, indeed, it did. Both on radio and on television, the series is an excellent example of the propagation of what WILLIAM HUGH JANSEN called EXOTERIC FOLKLORE, traditional beliefs one group has of another group and supposes that group has of itself. While the series certainly played on stereotypes, it is an oversimplification to call it racist. The African-American actor who played Amos once remarked that he "didn't feel [the show] harmed the Negro at all. . . . Actually the series had many episodes that showed the Negro with professions and businesses like attorneys, store owners, and so on, which they never had in TV or movies before." Other supporters of the show have pointed out that the situations portrayed were really no different from those found in many conventional all-white television sitcoms. It is also true, however, that much of the humor of *Amos 'n' Andy* was based on a perception of African Americans as shiftless, lazy, and slow-witted.

The television series was produced by Freeman Gosden and Charles Carrell, the two *white* actors who had created and starred in the radio version. The show was set in Harlem and revolved around the get-rich-quick shenanigans of one George Stevens, "Kingfish" of the Mystic Knights of the Sea fraternal lodge. His levelheaded wife Sapphire, and her mother, the formidable Ruby Begonia, typically came into conflict with him over his schemes. Kingfish may be seen as the quintessential trickster—though his schemes never succeeded—and his lodge brother Andy Brown was the simpleminded, well-meaning confederate as well as victim of much that Kingfish did. When Kingfish's activities immersed both him and Andy in deep trouble, Kingfish would wail in histrionic dialect, "Holy mackerel, Andy! What is I gonna do?"—a phrase that gained great currency during the 1950s. Interestingly, the other title character, Amos, a hardworking and thoroughly sensible taxi driver, was no more than a minor character, who sometimes narrated the episodes.

The original television series ran nationally from 1951 to 1953, but was syndicated and rerun on local stations well into the 1960s. In 1964, when a Chicago station announced that it was broadcasting the reruns again, the protests were loud and bitter, and by 1968, the program was wholly withdrawn from sale. It has since enjoyed brisk sales in videocassette form and is relished by some as a bit of "forbidden" pop culture.

SUGGESTED READING: Tim Brooks and Earle Marsh, "Amos 'n' Andy," *The Complete Directory of Prime Time Network TV Shows: 1946–Present* (New York, 1992).

See also: ALLIGATOR; CHARMS; COLLEGE FOLKLORE; FINGERNAILS; HEX; KNOTS; MEDICINE, FOLK; ROOT WORK; TROLLS; WITCHES AND WITCHCRAFT.

Amulet. An amulet is a charm worn, carried, or placed in one's house as protection from danger. Amulets figure in the folklore of virtually all cultures, including the cultures of America. Amulets may consist of an animal part (such as the modern RABBIT'S FOOT charm), a plant, vegetable, or fruit (for example, garlic worn around the neck to ward off evil spirits—and vampires), figurines worn as jewelry (such as the Italian *cornicello,* suspended on the end of neck chain to ward off the EVIL EYE), or religious symbols (a cross, a Star of David, etc.). Some religious amulets are worn even by nonreligious people; many travelers habitually carry a medallion bearing the image of Saint Christopher, traditionally regarded as the protector of travelers. Some amulets contain writings of a sacred or magical nature. The mezuzah found on the doorways of many Jewish homes is inscribed with passages of Scripture or may contain a small strip of paper with scriptural passages written on it.

Traditional Native American culture makes much use of amulets, often consisting of such natural materals as stone, grass, animal parts, and even such human body parts as dried pieces of umbilical cord or placenta. Typically, amulets in Native American culture are associated with the wearer's helping spirits and are useful only to the person to whom the amulet belongs or for whom it was fashioned. Amulets may also serve ritual purposes; for example, Lakota grandmothers-to-be fashion amulets representing sand lizards and present these to their expectant daughters as protection for the unborn child.

Anansi. Alternatively spelled *Ananse, Anancy,* and *Nansi,* Anansi is a trickster spider who appears in tales from West and Central Africa and in tales brought to America by African slaves. Although, in his classic form, Anansi is a spider, he can appear as a human being or another animal, especially a fox or rabbit. BRER RABBIT, the trickster in JOEL CHANDLER HARRIS'S UNCLE REMUS nineteenth-century stories (many of them literary versions of African-American tales), may be seen as an incarnation of the Anansi character. (In one traditional Anansi story, a farmer catches the pilfering Anansi by means of a TAR BABY.)

The Anansi character figures in stories found throughout much of Africa, the Caribbean, northern South America, and the United States. In Haiti, the character is called 'Ti Malice; in the Bahamas, Boy Nasty and B'Rabby; in Curaçao, Nansi; and along the Carolina and Georgia coasts, Aunt Nancy or Miss Nancy.

In his spider form, Anansi is cunning and combines such human faculties as speech with arachnid abilities, such as web spinning and performing acrobatic feats on his silken thread. Anansi is sometimes portrayed as malevolent or simply mischievous, but he may also figure as a culture hero, who, like Prometheus, steals fire from the sun for the benefit of humankind.

See also: AFRICAN AMERICANS; CHRISTENSEN, ABBIE (ABIGAIL MANDANIA) HOLMES

SUGGESTED READING: William Bascom, *African Folktales in the New World* (Bloomington, Ind., 1992); Jean Andrea Purchas-Tulluch, *Jamaica Anansi: A Sur-*

vival of the African Oral Tradition (Washington, D.C., 1976); Robert S. Rattray, *Akan-Ashanti Folk-Tales* (1930; reprint ed., New York, 1983).

Anglo Americans. Historically, Anglo Americans have been the most numerous and influential force in American culture generally and American folk culture in particular. This was especially true during the period of American colonization, when most settlers were of English origin. Yet precisely because Anglo Americans for so long formed the dominant group in America, they tend to have less sense of their ethnic origins than many other groups. Indeed, in the years leading up to the Revolutionary War, many Anglo Americans strove to shed vestiges of their English heritage in order to identify themselves as Americans, period. Nevertheless, English folkways were imported into North America just as certainly as English laws and the English language. Like these basic features of culture, however, English folkways have been so thoroughly integrated into mainstream American life that they are difficult to identify with the "old country." For example, most of the "typical" American CHRISTMAS traditions are English in origin, but few Americans nowadays think of them as such. Indeed, watching one of several movie versions of the quintessential Christmas story, Charles Dickens's *A Christmas Carol,* is regarded as an *American* tradition—one of the things one does around Christmastime. So it is with most Anglo-American folkways.

For folklore scholars, the English BALLADS that flourished especially in APPALACHIA demonstrate most dramatically the ties that bind Anglo-American folk culture to England. Yet the singers of these songs do not think of themselves as paying homage to England as, for example, POLISH AMERICANS performing Polish folk music think

of themselves as celebrating their transatlantic cultural origins. This sense of the "invisibility" of Anglo-American folk culture also holds true for the many aspects of MATERIAL CULTURE and folk crafts of English origin. It should be observed, however, that much of the original impetus of scholarly interest in the folklore of Appalachia derived from a desire to preserve what had survived of the English heritage in American folk culture.

See also: "BARBARA ALLEN"; BASKETMAKING; BROADSIDES; CHILD BALLAD; CHILD, FRANCIS JAMES; CLOGGING; IMMIGRANT FOLKLORE; PARLOR BALLAD; PILGRIMS AND PURITANS.

SUGGESTED READING: Charlotte J. Erickson, *Invisible Immigrants: The Adaptation of English and Scottish Immigrants in Nineteenth-Century America* (Coral Gables, Fla., 1972).

Animal fable. The animal fable uses animal characters, endowed with animal as well as human characteristics (including the power of thought and speech) to point a simple, instructive moral. Originally an oral tradition, it is known today chiefly through literary sources, the best known of which are AESOP'S FABLES. The most famous American practitioner of the animal fable and the broader ANIMAL TALE was JOEL CHANDLER HARRIS.

Animal tale. Perhaps the oldest and most widely known form of folktale, the animal tale features animals as principal characters. Many animal tales concern the origin of some leading feature of the animal character in question—for example, the scaly skin of the ALLIGATOR was the result of having been tricked and set ablaze by

BRER RABBIT. Some animal tales, known as ANI-MAL FABLES, point simple morals. AESOP'S FABLES are typical of this genre. In American folklore, animal tales are found primarily in African-American and Native American folklore, although the genre has been frequently interpreted by writers of the Euro-American tradition, including JOEL CHANDLER HARRIS.

Appalachia. The mountainous region encompassing West Virginia and portions of Alabama, Georgia, Kentucky, Tennessee, Maryland, North and South Carolina, and Virginia has long been a mecca for folklorists because geographical and cultural forces conspired through the nineteenth century and much of the twentieth to keep the people of the region separate from the cultural mainstream. The result was a colorful develop-

ment and survival of folklore, folkways, music, and crafts, including highly distinctive examples of folk speech and FOLK-SAY, vivid examples of VERNACULAR ARCHITECTURE (particularly log houses), memorable (and quite attractive) FOLK MUSIC and folk dance, a variety of crafts, and a broad spectrum of folk practices relating to religion, and what might be called "folk justice." The folk-song researches of OLIVE DAME CAMPBELL and CECIL JAMES SHARP (published in 1917 as *English Folk-Songs from the Southern Appalachians*) and John C. Campbell's *The Southern Highlander and His Homeland* (1921) served to bring the region into sharp focus for folklorists early in the twentieth century. In the meantime, state folklore societies were established in Kentucky, North Carolina, Virginia, and West Virginia before the end of the nineteen-tens, and Appalachian folk festivals were founded in the twenties and thirties. GEORGE PULLEN JACKSON's *White Spirituals of the Southern Uplands* (1933) brought attention to Appalachian musical traditions beyond the English ballad, and ALLEN EATON's *Handicrafts of the Southern Highlands* (1937) laid the foundation for creation of the Southern Highlands Handicraft Guild, which served to introduce Appalachian handicrafts to the nation.

See also: ANGLO AMERICANS; BALLADS; CHILD BALLAD; CHILD, FRANCIS JAMES; CLOGGING; COPLAND, AARON; DULCIMER; FIDDLE; GRAHAM, MARTHA; HILLBILLY FIGURE; IRISH AMERICANS; REDNECKS; REGIONAL FOLKLORE; SPIRITUALS, WHITE; TOYS, FOLK; WEAVING.

SUGGESTED READING: John C. Campbell, *The Southern Highlander and His Homeland* (New York, 1921); Olive Dame Campbell and Cecil Sharp, *English Folk-Songs from the Southern Appalachians* (New York, 1917); Horace Kephart, *Our Southern High-landers* (New York, 1913); Cecil Sharp, *English Folk-Songs from the Southern Appalachians* (New York, 1932);

A magazine illustration of an Appalachian craftsperson carving an apple doll, about 1927.

David E. Whisnant, *All That Is Native and Fine: The Politics of Culture in an American Region* (Chapel Hill, N.C., 1983).

Appleseed, Johnny. Like PAUL BUNYAN, Johnny Appleseed is one of those vivid literary-legendary characters that seems a pure product of folklore and myth; however, Paul Bunyan was a commercial creation, and Johnny Appleseed is the byname of a historical person, John Chapman, who was born on September 26, 1774, in Leominster, Massachusetts, and died on or about March 18, 1845, near Fort Wayne, Indiana.

Chapman was an itinerant missionary and nurseryman, who, beginning about 1800, started collecting apple seeds from cider presses in western Pennsylvania and traveled westward, planting a string of apple nurseries from the Alleghenies to central Ohio and into Indiana. Although Chapman gave away thousands of seedlings to settlers—something that helped to transform the wilderness into a livable place—he also sold seedlings and expected to make his living from doing so. At his death—apparently from exposure—in 1845, Chapman owned 1,200 acres of planted land.

The peregrinations of Chapman, as Johnny Appleseed, have been told and retold many times, principally in books intended for children. He is usually described as unwaveringly cheerful and generous, a lover of nature, with a supernatural affinity for the wilderness and, like Saint Francis, for animals. In his orchard-planting wanderings, he carried a Bible, to which he was devoted, but he also had more than encyclopedic knowledge of medicinal herbs. Like many figures from nineteenth-century American folklore and literature, Johnny Appleseed had a special rapport with the Indians, among whom he lived and traveled in perfect harmony. Finally, Johnny Appleseed is always pictured as an eccentric, whose hair flows wildly from under the inverted mush pan he wears in place of a hat. His bare feet protrude from ragged trousers, and a worn old coffee sack, with holes cut out for his arms, serves as a rustic vest or surtout. Because of such characteristics, Johnny Appleseed figures as an American Adam, a primitive, natural man whose sensibilities, leavened by a dedication to Judeo-Christian tradition, bring him into harmony with God and nature.

See also: LINDSAY, (NICHOLAS) VACHEL.

SUGGESTED READING: Robert Price, *Johnny Appleseed: Man and Myth* (Bloomington, Ind., 1954).

April Fools' Day. Observed on April first in North America and Europe (where it is often called All Fools' Day), April Fools' Day gives children as well as adults license to play practical jokes on friends or to send them on purposeless "fools' errands."

The origin of this unofficial holiday is unknown, but it most likely came about as a result of the change, in France, from the Julian to the Gregorian calendar, which resulted (among other things) in New Year's being moved from March 25 to January 1. Traditionally, people had exchanged New Year's gifts on the "octave" of the new year, April 1. Those who persisted in doing so after the official adoption of the Gregorian calendar were called *poissons d'avril* (a folk belief held that "April fish" are easily deceived and caught) or April fools. (In France, the person who falls victim to an April fool is still called a *poisson d'avril*. In Scotland, the butt of the joke is called *gowk*—cuckoo, a bird that comes in April—and the day is called Huntigowk Day.)

On a more universal level, April Fools' Day may be related to the vernal equinox (March 21), when nature plays tricks on humankind with sudden, dramatic changes in weather. Finally, April Fools' Day seems to bear kinship with such festivals as the Hilaria of ancient Rome (March 25) and the Holi festival of India (ending March 31).

Most modern April Fools' Day pranks are harmless and include such stunts as affixing a "kick me" sign to someone's back or telling outrageous stories to the gullible. Popular journalists relish the day as an opportunity to publish elaborate hoaxes, and high school and college student newspapers have been known to put out all-hoax April 1 issues. With the advent of the personal computer and the Internet, some April Fools' Day jokes have turned ugly and have included the actual creation and transmission of "viruses" that may harm or destroy data as well as hoax announcements of the existence of such viruses.

SUGGESTED READING: Fran E. Challfont, "April Fool Jokes: A Look into the Heritage of WHIMSY," in Don L. Nilsen and Aileen Pace Nilsen, eds., WHIMSY V: World Humor and Irony Membership Yearbook (Tempe, Ariz., 1987); Alan Dundes, "April Fool and April Fish: Towards a Theory of Ritual Pranks," Folklore Matters (Knoxville, Tenn., 1989).

Aragon, José Rafael (ca. 1796–1862). Aragon was the most accomplished and popular religious folk artist in New Mexico during the first half of the nineteenth century. He drew on local craft traditions and late-Baroque Spanish sources to create painted and carved RETABLOS (altar screens) for Hispanic churches in New Mexico. Aragon's work was in such demand that he opened a workshop in which he trained apprentices to assist him and to carry on his style and technique. Aragon lived and worked at Pueblo Quemado, present-day Cordova, New Mexico.

See also: LOPEZ, JOSÉ DELORES; SANTO NIÑO SANTERO; WOODCARVING.

Archive of Folk Culture. The archive, founded in 1928 as the Archive of American Folk-Song under the aegis of the Music Division of the Library of Congress, became part of the AMERICAN FOLKLIFE CENTER in 1978. Two years later, it was renamed the Archive of Folk Culture, a name reflecting its expanded scope to various areas of ethnography.

As the Archive of American Folk-Song, the organization was first headed by Robert Winslow Gordon and, in the 1930s, by ALAN LOMAX. It was Lomax who expanded the archive's collecting activities beyond continental American folk music and included music from the Bahamas and Haiti. Lomax also took the archive's work beyond recording strictly musical examples; recordings made under his direction for the archive include oral interviews with folk-music artists and performers.

As part of the American Folklife Center, the archive has sponsored extensive ethnographic field projects and now holds more than a million items, including 600,000 manuscripts, 200,000 photographs, 50,000 sound recordings, and other materials.

For contact information, see entry on American Folklife Center.

See also: ARCHIVES, FOLKLORE.

SUGGESTED READING: Peter Thomas Bartis, A History of the Archive of Folk Song at the Library of Congress: The First Fifty Years (Ann Arbor, Mich., 1982).

Archives, Folklore. Folklore archives are depositories of folklore collections, which may include sound recordings, oral interview transcripts, video recordings, motion pictures, and documentary photographs, as well as artifacts of material culture, including examples of folk art and other folk objects. Typically, folk archives are organized by genre and/or region, and their content often reflects their locale. While the governments of some European nations established folklore archives in the nineteenth century, it was 1928 before the Library of Congress created the ARCHIVE OF FOLK CULTURE for the United States. Many other folk archives have been established throughout the country, typically affiliated with state governments and with universities. The archives function as safe and secure depositories of precious materials, usually identified, organized, and indexed according to some rational system. While a prime archive function is to protect collections, it must also make them available for study and, in many cases, for general public access as well. A number of major archives maintain access sites on the Internet's World Wide Web; for a list of some of the most important, visit http://eds.mounet.com/~folklore/linksarchivesandmuseums.html. A print list of archive sources may be found in Peter Bartis and Hillary Glatt, *Folklife Sourcebook: A Directory of Folklife Resources in the United States*, 2d ed. (Washington, D.C.: American Folklife Center, 1993).

Archuleta, Felipe Benito (1910–). Archuleta was a New Mexican folk carver best known for his colorful carvings of domestic and wild animals, some modeled from life, some from memory, and many from pictures in *National Geographic*. Archuleta received three years of elementary education in Santa Cruz, New Mexico, worked as an agricultural laborer and, during the Depression, as a line cook with the CCC (Civilian Conservation Corps). In 1939, Archuleta settled in Santa Fe, and worked as a cook at La Fonda Hotel, while also performing with a Hispanic dance band. He took up carpentry and worked as a union carpenter from 1943 to 1964, when, during a dispute with his union, the Lord appeared to him in a vision and commanded him to "carve wood." Archuleta confessed himself unworthy to be a *santero* (carver of sacred images), so he resolved to carve animals instead.

Archuleta's reputation spread rapidly, and by the 1970s his works were being exhibited at the Museum of International Folk Art in Santa Fe and were in high demand by collectors. Archuleta carved cottonwood, roughing out the work with a chain saw, then using hand tools for the fine work. The carvings were painted with latex house paint, and such materials as uncarded wool, hemp, rubber, marbles (for eyes), and so on were often added. Archuleta became identified with the "Santa Fe style" of carving. His son, Leroy Ramon Archuleta, has continued to practice his father's art.

Area 51. An aspect of UFO FOLKLORE and CONSPIRACY LORE, Area 51, also known as Groom Lake, has been described as "America's most popular secret military base," because it has given rise to much folklore and mass media attention. It is said to be a secret military facility about ninety miles north of Las Vegas. The designation "Area 51" refers to a six-by-ten-mile block of land surrounding an air base so secret, the government will not discuss its function. It may be used to test new, secret ("black budget") aircraft and was apparently used in the 1950s to test the U-2 spy plane. Most significantly for contemporary folklore, Area 51 has been popularly associated with UFO stories and stories of government UFO cover-ups since 1989, when a man named Bob Lazar claimed that he had worked with alien spacecraft at Papoose Lake, south of Area 51.

Area 51 has been the focus of much popular culture material, including movies (most notably the special-effects extravaganza *Independence Day* [1997]); television programs; novels, such as *Dreamland: A Novel of the UFO Coverup* by Ernest Hemingway's granddaughter Hilary Hemingway (New York, 1995); and rock music, including songs from bands called Area 51 and Dreamland. Various vendors have produced Area 51 "memorabilia," including Groom Lake and Area 51 T-shirts (bearing the warning "Deadly Force Authorized"), and there is at least one Area 51 nightclub (in Houston) in the United States. As of March 1997, there were nineteen "Area 51" trademarks registered for products ranging from jewelry to toys. The Internet's World Wide Web has spawned many sites devoted to Area 51; visit http://www.ufomind.com/area51/ for links to them.

people at the Berkeley Folk Festival. Lipscomb began a new life as a performer, which lasted until his death, fifteen years later.

Since this beginning, Strachwitz has gone on to record and produce a wide variety of authentic folk performers in several diverse traditions, including blues, WORK SONGS, JAZZ, COUNTRY MUSIC, CAJUN MUSIC, ZYDECO, TEX-MEX MUSIC, and KLEZMER MUSIC bands. Somehow, his notably uncommercial enterprise has survived into the present with a catalogue of hundreds of albums, including such rarities as reissues of the first MARIACHI recordings made in the 1920s, a variety of documentary films, and just about anything that appeals to Strachwitz's sense of what should be preserved and made known. He sells many of his releases through his retail store on San Paplo Avenue in El Cerrito, California (near Berkeley), which is also headquarters for his international mail-order business. In 1995, Arhoolie sponsored a three-day festival to celebrate its thirty-fifth year. Tex-Mex, Cajun, zydeco, jazz, blues, and gospel were heard.

See also: CHENIER, CLIFTON.

Arhoolie Records. During his 1960 summer vacation, Chris Strachwitz, a young German-born schoolteacher from Los Gatos, California, set out to record country BLUES singers in Texas. Lugging along a portable tape recorder, he made a major find when he turned up Mance Lipscomb, a sixty-seven-year-old retired sharecropper in the hamlet of Navasota. Lipscomb's exciting singing and playing were in a pure folk tradition and became the basis of the first release of Arhoolie Records, Strachwitz's fledgling company. Arhoolie soon grew into a modest success during the FOLK REVIVAL of the early 1960s. In 1961, Lipscomb, who had never left his hometown, was invited to perform for ten thousand

"Arkansas Traveler." This popular folk song is a question-and-answer dialogue between a lost traveler and a decidedly unhelpful squatter. The traveler asks the squatter, who is fiddling before his log cabin, for directions and lodging, but is met only with riddles and whimsical answers. Only after the traveler offers to play the rest of the tune on the squatter's fiddle is he accorded a welcome. The song is likely derived from various riddles and jokes current in the mid-nineteenth century and may have been modeled on any of a number of humorous verse and musical dialogues between innkeepers and travelers current in popular British publications of the period.

See also: CURRIER & IVES; FOLK MUSIC.

Arroyo Hondo Carver (working 1830–1850). Arroyo Hondo Carver was an anonymous *santero* (carver of SANTOS, Hispanic religious folk images) named for the village north of Taos, New Mexico, where most of his works are found. His carvings are strikingly frontal and static, like medieval sculpture, with schematic facial features that nevertheless convey considerable spirituality. Indeed, it is for their simple, frank spirituality that the works of this folk artist are most prized. He may have apprenticed with the ARROYO HONDO PAINTER.

Arroyo Hondo Painter (working ca. 1825–1840). One of the most celebrated of the New Mexican *santeros* (creators of SANTOS, religious folk images carved and/or painted in the Hispanic tradition), this anonymous painter is named for the village north of Taos, New Mexico, the location of his major work, the RETABLO (altar screen) for the church of Nuestra Señora de los Dolores de Arroyo Hondo. His art is prized for its great delicacy, sweetness, and refinement. Many consider his santos among the very best of the folk painting of New Mexico. His characteristic use of decorative patterns rather than solid areas for clothing, draperies, and background prompted one scholar to call him the "Dot-Dash Santero."

See also: ARROYO HONDO CARVER.

Asch, Moses (1905–1986). Asch founded FOLKWAYS RECORDS, the single most important and influential of the independent folk-music record labels.

The son of Sholem Asch, a very popular Yiddish author, Moses Asch was born in Warsaw, Poland, and was educated in France and in New York City, after the family immigrated to the United States in 1915. Asch dropped out of high school in New York, but returned for a time to Germany, where he studied electronics and radio technology for two years. He was back in New York by 1925 and worked in the emerging field of radio technology. He branched out into public address systems and, in 1941, commercial audio recording.

Beginning in 1941, Asch made records of cantorials (Jewish liturgical music), which he pressed and sold on his "Asch" label. Later that same year, he recorded HUDDIE LEDBETTER (LEAD-BELLY), the great African-American singer-composer, and, during the World War II years, made pioneering recordings of such American folk-song greats as WOODY GUTHRIE, Cisco Houston, PETE SEEGER, SONNY TERRY, and Josh White.

Asch enjoyed a degree of financial success with the jazz recordings he made during the war period, but Disc Records, successor to the Asch label, went bankrupt in 1947. Two years later, in 1949, he founded (with his secretary, Marion Distler) FOLKWAYS RECORDS, which he directed until his death in 1986, issuing some two thousand discs, which figured prominently in the folk-song revival beginning in the late 1940s.

See also: FOLK MUSIC.

SUGGESTED READING: Tony Sherman, "The Remarkable Recordings of Moses Asch," *Smithsonian* 18, no. 5 (1987): 110–21.

Ashby, Steve (1904–1980). Ashby was an African-American folk sculptor, who specialized in carvings and assemblages, usually of human forms, often costumed, always painted, almost always slyly humorous—and anatomically complete underneath the costume ("all man" and "all woman," as the sculptor proudly observed). Ashby lived his entire life in the Farquier County town of Delaplane, Virginia, earning his living as a farmhand and, for a time, as a waiter in a Marshall, Virginia, hotel. Throughout his life, Ashby made carvings, an activity to which he turned full time when he retired in his sixties. His preferred materials were plywood (at first cut by hand, but later with an electric saw) combined with tree trunks and branches, for life-sized figures. The sculptures were always painted, and often included photographs, hair, and clothing, as well as other found objects. The female sculptures he created were often adorned with the clothing and jewelry of his deceased wife. His subjects are typically rural, and animal subjects are almost as numerous as human ones. Many of his ideas came to Ashby in dreams.

SUGGESTED READING: Jane Livingston and John Beardsley, *Black Folk Art in America: 1930–1980* (Jackson, Miss., 1982).

Astrology. While mainstream science has long dismissed astrology as superstition, this ancient system of divination from the position and behavior of the stars, planets, and other heavenly bodies continues to be popular in the United States and elsewhere. Many books are devoted to the subject, as are newspaper columns and popular magazine features. During the 1960s and well into the 1970s, "What is your sign?" (referring to one's astrological sign) was a popular and much satirized icebreaker—or, more to the point, "pickup line"—in American bars and discos. Popular interest in astrology probably reached its

peak in the United States during the 1960s, when many people sought alternatives to rational Western thought and traditions. Then—and even now—many individuals based important decisions, including career and marriage choices, on astrological divination. It is also well known that the dictator Adolf Hitler employed astrologers during World War II (and so Winston Churchill employed them, too, in an effort to outthink his adversary), as did President Ronald Reagan, apparently encouraged by his wife, Nancy.

Astrology is believed to have originated in Mesopotamia about the third millennium B.C., but was most fully elaborated during the heyday of classical Greece. It was transmitted through the centuries to medieval western Europe not directly, but via Islamic tradition and was considered a science. While Christianity, opposing free will to determinism, is deeply resistant to astrology. The very story of the Nativity contains a strong astrological component in the Persian magi (the "wise men") following a celestial omen (the Star of Bethlehem) to the site of Christ's birth. Ultimately, however, it was not Christianity, but the post-Copernican view of a heliocentric solar system that deposed astrology as a science by the end of the sixteenth century.

Atomic bomb. It is understandable that something as ultimately powerful as atomic weaponry would give rise to a body of folklore, which has taken the form of jokes, art, speech, legends, and religious beliefs.

The paramount folk belief associated with atomic weaponry is that "the bomb" (as it is frequently called) will bring about the end of the world. This belief was ushered in with great suddenness in the wake of the atomic bombings of the Japanese cities of Hiroshima (August 6, 1945)

The mushroom cloud entered into popular consciousness as a powerful symbol of the atomic era. This is a U.S. Army Air Force photograph of the Hiroshima blast, August 6, 1945.

and Nagasaki (August 9, 1945), which ended World War II. Many religious apocalyptists see the advent of nuclear weapons as the fulfillment of divine prophecy. Some believers see the Book of Revelation as a crypto-prophetic description of nuclear apocalypse. During the height of the Cold War, some believed that only the conversion of "atheist" Soviet Russia to Catholicism could avert nuclear armageddon.

As extreme as the religious predictions of apocalypse are, they at least contain the hope of salvation in a divine plan. During the Cold War, secular beliefs about the bomb typically portrayed atomic scientists as indifferent geniuses whose obsession with forbidden knowledge would inevitably destroy the world. Among sec-

ular believers in nuclear apocalypse, gallows humor often prevailed. One of the most familiar jokes of the Cold War era—in which schoolchildren and others were routinely subjected to air-raid drills—was this instruction: "In the event of nuclear attack, put your hands over your head, put your head between your knees—and kiss your ass good-bye." Jokes related to genetic mutation caused by radioactive fallout were also prevalent. Atomic folklore has been less in evidence since the end of the Cold War in the early 1990s.

SUGGESTED READING: Spencer R. Weart, *Nuclear Fear: A History of Images* (Cambridge, Mass., 1988).

Aurora borealis. Also called the northern lights, the aurora borealis consists of luminous bands of light visible in the northern regions at night and caused by the ejection of charged particles into the magnetic field of the earth. The aurora figures importantly in Norse mythology, and in Native American cultures, among some Algonquian tribes and Eskimoes, the aurora borealis is believed to be the dancing spirits of the dead. Children are cautioned to be silent during the dancing of the lights, lest they be stolen by the spirits.

The aurora borealis as seen from space in a NASA photograph.

Austin, Mary Hunter (1868–1934). Austin wrote about nature and native cultures in the Southwest. A midwesterner by birth and upbringing, Austin grew up in Carlinville, Illinois, and moved to California in 1888. She was active in the western conservation movement and generally opposed the incursions of modern civilization into the pristine western landscape. As an antidote to the abominations of modern life, Austin looked to what she called "folk-life," a body of traditional beliefs and activities. Toward this end, in 1925, she was among those who organized the Indian Arts Fund and the Spanish Colonial Arts Society in Santa Fe, New Mexico. Austin wrote and lectured widely on many aspects of folklore and folk art, especially Native American song and poetry, which she saw as closely integrated with the natural environment—so much so, in fact, that the intimacy of this relationship typically escaped conventional and "scientific" folklore collectors and anthropologists. Understandably, Austin was looked on with doubt and suspicion by academic folklorists, yet, while her ideas about Native American culture are intensely romantic and, therefore, distorted, she did bring the Native American culture of California and the Southwest to broad public attention.

SUGGESTED READING: Mary Hunter Austin, *The Land of Little Rain* (Boston, 1903); Mary Hunter Austin, *The Land of Journeys' Ending* (New York, 1924); Augusta Fink, *I-Mary: A Biography of Mary Austin* (Tucson, Ariz., 1983).

Autoharp. Although typically used generically, "Autoharp" is the English-language trademark of the German *Akkordzither,* a kind of zither in which chords are played by pushing down chord bars, which may produce five to fifteen chords, depending on the instrument. The Autoharp was invented by C. A. Gütter of Markneukirchen, Germany, and was patented in the United States in 1881 by C. F. Zimmermann. Subsequently, Zimmermann sold out to Alfred

Dolge (1848–1922), a New York City maker of piano equipment. Beginning in the 1890s, Dolge widely marketed the instrument, door-to-door as well as through catalog sales. The latter was particularly effective in reaching rural consumers.

The best-known exponents of the autoharp was Ernest "Pop" Stoneman (of the Stoneman Family), who created the so-called Appalachian style of plucking and strumming the strings, which can be heard in recordings made as early as the 1920s. Maybelle Carter (of the CARTER FAMILY) revived the instrument after World War II in radio broadcasts of the *GRAND OLE OPRY.*

See also: FOLK MUSIC.

SUGGESTED READING: A. Doyle Moore, "The Autoharp: Its Origin and Development from a Popular to a Folk Instrument," *New York Folklore Quarterly* (1963; reprinted in Harry Tausig, ed., *Folkstyle Autoharp* [New York, 1967]); Mike Seeger, *Mountain Music Played on the Autoharp* (Folkways Records FA 2365, 1965).

This ad for an Autoharp appeared in Puritan: A Journal for Gentlewomen *in 1897.*

Autry, Gene (1907–1999). With Roy Rogers, Autry was the most famous of mass media's "singing cowboys," and although he was a polished commercial performer who did not sing folk material, he was responsible for introducing many to cowboy song. Autry was born Orvon Gene Aurry in Tioga, Texas, and was raised in Oklahoma, where his interest in music was sparked by singing in a church choir. Self-taught on a mail-order guitar, he began singing and recording in the 1920s, and, in 1933, released the hit single "That Silver Haired Daddy of Mine," which earned him the record industry's

Gene Autry promoted a wide variety of products, including Sparkies breakfast cereal from the Quaker Oats Company, from the late 1940s.

first-ever gold record. The following year, he sang two numbers for a Ken Maynard film, *In Old Santa Fe,* which launched Autry's movie career, which ran to ninety films. From 1939 through 1956, he was the star of radio's *Melody Ranch* musical variety show, and by the 1950s, he had moved into television as well. This extensive media exposure shaped the public's perception not only of cowboys, but of cowboy songs as well.

Autry parleyed his success as an entertainer into a wide range of highly lucrative business ventures, including ownership of the California Angels baseball franchise. In 1988, he founded the Gene Autry Western Heritage Museum (now called the Autry Museum of Western Heritage) in Los Angeles "to collect and preserve the cultural, artistic, and other evidence of the West from prehistoric cultures to the present." The museum's remarkable collections include materials ranging from prehistoric pottery to cowboy gear to modern artifacts and is especially valuable for covering the spectrum of the region's ethnic diversity with special sections on Asian, Mexican, African-American, European, and Canadian immigration and settlement. Students of material culture treasure the institution's unrivaled collection of cowboy gear from the 1700s to the present, and students of mass media and folklore are attracted to collections of art, advertising, Wild West show materials, film, literature, and radio and television recordings and artifacts.

See also: COUNTRY MUSIC; COWBOYS; COWBOY SONGS.

SUGGESTED READING: Gene Autry with Mickey Herskowitz, *Back in the Saddle Again* (Garden City, N.Y., 1978).

B

Babe the Blue Ox. The companion of PAUL BUNYAN, Babe was a giant ox that was turned from white to blue by the brutal "Winter of the Blue Snow" in the North Woods. Babe's eyes were set forty-two ax-handle-lengths apart, and the ox was so titanic that each step crushed through solid rock, ultimately creating the Great Lakes and other bodies of water. Prodigiously strong, Babe could clear an entire forest in one haul or straighten a winding river by giving it a good, hard tug. Babe was not immortal, however, and fell victim to his gargantuan appetite, inadvertently swallowing an entire blazing stove in his haste to consume a batch of hotcakes. As one story has it, Paul Bunyan buried his friend, creating the Black Hills of South Dakota to mark his grave.

Baca, Elfego (1865–1945). Baca was a southwestern law officer, politician, and lawyer, who became one of the best-known Hispanic figures of the West. His life was so steeped in legend that he became a feature of southwestern folklore well before he died in the mid-twentieth century. It is often impossible to tell where the facts of his life end and the legends begin, especially since Baca himself embellished his exploits in the course of various campaigns for public office.

Baca was born in Socorro, New Mexico, but moved to Topeka, Kansas, with his family, when he was only a year old. According to legend, while the Bacas were on their way to Topeka, the infant Elfego was kidnapped by Indians, who found him so wild a child that they returned him to his family four days later. After the death of his

Monuments to Paul Bunyan and Babe the Blue Ox at Bimidji, Minnesota, photographed in the 1930s.

mother in 1872, Elfego Baca was sent to live with relatives in southern New Mexico, where he found work as a cowboy. His father, Francisco, a wagon freighter in Topeka, soon joined his son in New Mexico, after the Atchison, Topeka and Santa Fe Railroad put him out of the wagon-freighting business. Baca senior became sheriff of Los Lunas, New Mexico, in 1878.

A typically violent cow town, Los Lunas saw more than its share of gunplay, and when Francisco Baca shot two popular cowhands during an 1882 saloon brawl, the Anglo-dominated establishment ordered his arrest and trial on charges of murder. He was found guilty and sentenced to a long prison term, whereupon Elfego Baca boldly broke his father out of the jail of the Socorro County Courthouse and spirited him away to the Indian pueblo of Isleta, where the senior Baca hid for seven years.

In 1884, at age nineteen, Elfego Baca became deputy sheriff of Frisco, New Mexico. He arrested an Anglo cowboy for assault and was pursued by a troop of eighty cowboys, demanding the man's release. Elfego Baca took refuge in a local *jacal* (a wattle-and-daub thatched-roof hut), from which he held off the cowboys in a running thirty-six-hour gunfight. In the course of the so-called Miracle of the *Jacal,* Baca killed two men, and managed to survive a fusillade of more than four hundred rounds. (Unknown to the cowboys, the dirt floor of the *jacal* was sunken below ground level, so that the bullets passed overhead.) Baca was rescued by a passing lawman, who brokered a cease-fire.

The self-educated Baca trained as a lawyer, was admitted to the bar, and served as county clerk, mayor, school superintendent, and, ultimately, district attorney of Socorro County. Early in the twentieth century, Baca moved to Mexico and set up as a border trader, engaging in legal as well as illegal cross-border trade. Baca espoused the cause of social outlaw and revolu-

tionary Francisco ("Pancho") Villa, the two becoming fast friends. After a short time, however, the friendship dissolved, and an angry Villa put a $30,000 bounty on Baca's head.

During the Mexican military revolution of 1911–1917, Baca had occasion to serve as lawyer for General José Inez Salazar, who was arrested and imprisoned in Albuquerque, New Mexico, for having violated the U.S. border. Baca was unable to secure his client's release by legal means, so he hired others to break Salazar out of jail. On his way out of town in a speeding automobile, the general shouted his thanks and farewell to Baca, who was enjoying a drink in a local saloon.

Such exploits and others—as a lawyer, border power broker, and newspaper publisher—continually enhanced Baca's legend-in-his-own-time reputation. In 1919, after gaining election to the post of sheriff of Socorro County, he mailed letters to a number of local fugitives, advising them to give themselves up or suffer the lethal—not *legal*—consequences. It is a testament to Baca's reputation that a number of the desperados did, in fact, surrender themselves to the new sheriff.

Baca died, at age eighty, at his home in Albuquerque in 1945. During the late 1950s, a generation of young television viewers frequently heard the name Elfego Baca on Walt Disney's Zorro series. The Disney Company also created a short-lived television series called *The Rousing Life of Elfego Baca.*

SUGGESTED READING: Kyle Crichton, *Law and Order Limited* (Albuquerque, N.M., 1928).

Baez, Joan (1941–). For many who came of age in the 1960s, Joan Baez was the quintessential folksinger. Although she was and is a commercial performer, she was a leading figure in the decade's folk-song revival movement, combining a liberal political sensibility, social consciousness, and a protest repertoire with a bell-like soprano that some critics have called "too pretty." However, it was in large part the beauty of her voice that helped bring the folk-song style to a wider, younger audience.

Baez was born on Staten Island, New York, the daughter of a research physicist. She was largely self-taught in voice and acoustic guitar, but quickly acquired a wide audience in the emerging coffeehouses of the 1960s, at folk-music festivals, and, finally, on television as well. During the height of her popularity, from 1960 through 1964, her record albums were best-sellers, and sales continued strong during the balance of the decade. Baez's repertoire ranged from traditional songs, especially traditional songs of labor and protest (such as "Joe Hill") to folk-style songs of her own composition. Baez's artistic life was always closely linked with the protest movement of the 1960s, and she was an early activist against the Vietnam War. In an act of civil disobedience, she withheld that portion of her 1964 income taxes she felt was going to finance the war in Vietnam and, in 1967, was jailed for three months as a result. Baez continues to perform and remains active in social causes.

See also: FOLK MUSIC; FOLK REVIVAL; HILL, JOE; HOPKINS, LIGHTNIN'; POPULAR CULTURE; RINZLER, RALPH CARTER.

SUGGESTED READING: Joan Baez, *Daybreak* (memoir) (New York, 1968); Joan Baez, *And a Voice to Sing With: A Memoir* (New York, 1987).

Balfa, Dewey (1927–1992). Dewey Balfa is a Cajun folk musician, who is also active in promoting Cajun culture. Balfa was the son of a sharecropper on Bayou Grand Louis in rural Evangeline Parish, Louisiana. He began playing the fiddle at age thirteen, and was influenced by local musicians, including his father and grandfather, as well as such professional entertainers as Bob Wills and the Texas Playboys. During the 1940s, Balfa and his four brothers played local dance halls. He achieved national recognition performing on guitar at the Newport Folk Festival in 1964. This event also triggered widespread interest in Cajun and other traditional Louisiana music. In 1974, Balfa helped organize a "Tribute to Cajun Music" in Lafayette, Louisiana. The event was so enthusiastically received that it became an annual event.

Ballads. A ballad may be simply defined as a stanzaic narrative song sung to a repeating tune. The ballad narrative is typically focused on a single episode and leading character, and it includes a beginning, a complication, climax, and a denouement. That is, a ballad tells a story. Ballads are generally sung by a solo performer, who may accompany himself or herself on an instrument or may sing a capella. Of the many forms of American folk song, ballads have drawn the most interest from students of folklore. Anglo-American folklorists typically define four general types of ballad: the CHILD BALLAD (which is based on medieval traditions), the BROADSIDE ballad, the BLUES BALLAD, and the PARLOR BALLAD.

See also: ANGLO AMERICANS; APPALACHIA; "BARBARA ALLEN"; BARRY, PHILLIPS; BELDEN, HENRY MARVIN; BLUEGRASS; BORDEN, LIZZIE; BRONSON, BERTRAND HARRIS; CAMPBELL, OLIVE DAME; CARTER FAMILY, THE; CHASE, RICHARD; CHILD, FRANCIS JAMES; CIVIL WAR; "CLEMENTINE"; CORTEZ, GREGORIO; COUNTRY MUSIC; "COWBOY'S LAMENT"; CRIME AND CRIM-

INALS; DAVIS, ARTHUR KYLE, JR.; EDDY, MARY O.; FOLK MUSIC; GAMES; GEROULD GORDON HALL; GRAND OLE OPRY; GUMMERE, FRANCIS BARTON; GUTHRIE, WOODY (WOODROW WILSON); IMMIGRANT FOLKLORE; JAMES, FRANK AND JESSE; JONES, CASEY; KITTREDGE, GEORGE LYMAN; LEDBETTER, HUDDIE (LEADBELLY); MACON, DAVID (UNCLE DAVE); MINUNG FOLKLORE; NILES, JOHN JACOB; POUND, LOUISE; RAILROAD FOLKLORE; REVOLUTIONARY WAR; RICHMOND, W. EDSON; SCOTTISH AMERICANS; SKILLET LICKERS, THE; TEX-MEX MUSIC.

American street ballad seller, about 1870. (Collection of Alan Axelrod)

Ball the Jack. An African-American dance originated some time before the Civil War, incorporated by white entertainers into MINSTREL SHOWS, and popular into the twentieth century, ball the jack features "snake hips," undulating movements while the feet and head remain still. Hand clapping and recitative accompany the dance, which is similar to dances performed in the Bahamas and along the Congo River. The name of the dance is derived from the traditional last line of the recitative verse stanzas that accompany the dance: "And I ball the jack on the railroad track." "Ball" is short for "highball," the railroad signal to proceed full speed ahead; thus the verse urges one to move fast and be reckless. Allusion to railroads and railroad-related activity is common in nineteenth-century African-American folklore, since the railroad symbolized the prospect of escape.

See also: AFRICAN AMERICANS; DANCE, FOLK.

Baltic peoples. The largest Lithuanian-, Latvian-, and Estonian-American communities are in New York City, Chicago, and Los Angeles. Lithuanian folklore recorded in America includes songs, tales, legends, and riddles. Material culture and foodways are also important; for example, meat preserved in aspic, and *klingeris*, traditional pretzel-shaped bread flavored with cardamom, colored with saffron, and decorated with almonds and powdered sugar, remain popular. Baltic holidays are celebrated in the ethnic communites. Estonian Independence Day is February 24; Latvian Independence Day is November 18; and Lithuanian Independence Day is February 16. Christmas and Easter, as well as Catholic Mardi Gras (for Lithuanians) are celebrated in ways traditional in the homeland. In addition, Midsummer night, June 23, is commemorated with bonfires and general celebration.

All three Baltic ethnic groups regularly stage performances of traditional songs using massive choirs; traditional musical instruments, including the zitherlike Estonian *kannel,* Latvian *kokle,* and Lithuanian *kankles,* are played in presentations and festivals of ethnic heritage.

See also: IMMIGRANT FOLKLORE.

Banjo. An extremely important instrument in American folk music, the banjo was brought to America by slaves during the eighteenth century. Until well into the nineteenth century, it was played exclusively by slaves. The banjo is a plucked string instrument related to the *halam* of the Wolofs and the *bania* or *banju* of the Mandingos. The banjo's body resembles a tambourine, with a hoop and a screw that secure a belly made of vellum to a frame. The tension of the vellum "skin" can be adjusted with screw stretchers. The banjo's strings pass over a violin-type bridge and are hitched to a tailpiece. During the early nineteenth century, the instrument lacked frets, but these were added by the end of the century. While early instruments had four gut strings, the modern banjo has five metal strings, four tuned C′-G′-B′-D″ from middle C, and a fifth, the chanterelle, or thumb string, fastened to a screw midway in the banjo neck and tuned to the second G above middle C. Also still in use is the plectrum banjo, which has no chanterelle and is played with a plectrum rather than the fingers. White people became interested in the banjo around 1840 with the rising popularity of blackface mistrel shows, and the complex rhythms made possible by combined downstroking and up-picking appealed to a very broad audience. The richness of the banjo's rhythmic possibilities made it an ideal

Banjos in action along the wharf at Long Beach, California, 1941.

BLUEGRASS instrument, as the duo of Lester Flatt and Earl Scruggs proved in the middle of the twentieth century.

See also: CARTER FAMILY, THE; FOLK MUSIC; GIBSON MANDOLIN AND GUITAR MANUFACTURING COMPANY, LTD., THE; HOEDOWN; MACON, DAVID (UNCLE DAVE); "OLD DAN TUCKER"; RAGTIME; RINZLER, RALPH CARTER; RODGERS, JIMMIE; ROUNDER RECORDS; SCRUGGS, EARL; SKILLET LICKERS, THE; "TURKEY IN THE STRAW."

SUGGESTED READING: Robert Lloyd Webb, *Ring the Banjar! The Banjo in America from Folklore to Factory* (Cambridge, Mass., 1984).

"Barbara Allen." Barbara Allen is the eponymous heroine of "Bonny Barbara Allen" (Child #84; see CHILD BALLAD), an English and Scottish BALLAD that was very widely disseminated in America, with more tunes, variations, and geographical distribution than any other transplanted ballad. First printed in Britain in 1740 and in the United States in 1830, the ballad tells of the beautiful but cruel Barbara Allen, who shows no pity to the swain dying for her love, then, upon his death, grows ill and dies of remorse.

See also: ANGLO AMERICANS; FOLK MUSIC.

Barbeau, Marius (1883–1969). Barbeau was among the most important and prolific of Canadian folklorists. From 1911 until his death, Barbeau was associated with Canada's National Museum. His wide-ranging contributions to the museum's folk collections include field recordings of Eskimo, Indian, French-Canadian, and English-Canadian songs. In addition, Barbeau studied and did fieldwork in virtually all branches of folklore as well as anthropology. His areas of expertise included Indian myths, language, ceremony, music, visual art, and culture; French-Canadian folktales, folk songs, visual art, sport and games, handicrafts, and vernacular architecture; and English-Canadian songs and art.

Barbeau published prodigiously. In addition to two novels based on Indian life, he wrote some fifty scholarly books (chief among which are *Totem Poles* [1950–51], *Haida Carvers in Argillite* [1957], *Huron-Wyandot Traditional Narratives* [1960], and three major volumes of French-Canadian songs, published in 1962, 1982, and 1984), another fifty pamphlets and monographs, and some seven hundred professional and popular articles.

A Fellow of the American Folklore Society, Barbeau was president and associate editor of the *Journal of American Folklore* and was founder of the Canadian Folk Music Society (1956). Whereas most folklorists work in quiet obscurity, Barbeau received wide recognition and many honors, including the Gold Medal of the Royal Society of Canada and honorary degrees from three major universities. He was awarded the Canadian government's highest civilian honor, the title of Companion of the Order of Canada.

See also: LACOURCIÈRE, LUC.

SUGGESTED READING: Entry on Barbeau in *Dictionary of Literary Biography* 92, pp. 13–16 (1990).

Barber pole. The red-and-white striped pole standing in front of barbershops was once a familiar sight in American cities and villages. Today, barber poles are far fewer in number and are regarded with a measure of nostalgia. The symbol is not peculiar to America, but was used wherever barbers served as surgeons as well as haircutters. During the eighteenth and nineteenth centuries, one of the barber's most common functions was the therapeutic bleeding of patients, and the red stripes against the white of the pole symbolize the blood on the bandage, while the pole itself suggests the wand that the patient held as his vein was opened. One aspect of the barber pole that did not survive into the twentieth century was the basin that topped the bowl; it symbolized the basin used to catch the flowing blood.

Barn dance. Social country dances, replete with SQUARE DANCES and other popular dance forms, were often held in barns and were presided over by a caller, who called the steps, and were accompanied by a fiddler or a small band. The barn dance was so thoroughly identified with country music that, when radio station WBAP broadcast the nation's first country music variety show in January 1923, it presented it in a barn dance format. In 1924, *The National Barn Dance*

The barber pole was once a common sight in America's big cities and small towns. Both photographs are from the 1940s.

premiered on Chicago's WLS radio station, and by 1932 was being carried on the NBC network, which distributed the program to some fifty stations coast to coast. During much of the thirties, barn dance radio acts were more popular than such musical giants as Al Jolson and Fred Allen. In 1925, WSM began regular broadcasts of *The Grand Ole Opry* from Nashville, imitating the barn dance format; the show continues to enjoy great popularity on radio as well as television.

See also: DANCE, FOLK; HONKY-TONK MUSIC.

Barnicle, Mary Elizabeth (ca. 1898–1979).
Barnicle was an educator and folklife collector specializing in Appalachian folk song. Trained at Bryn Mawr College as a medieval scholar (English literature), Barnicle taught at

New York University during most of the 1930s and 1940s. She became increasingly interested in folklore, taught the subject, and undertook field-recording expeditions to Georgia, Florida, and the Bahamas (1935). In 1935, Barnicle met Tillman Cadle, a Kentucky coal miner and union organizer. Cadle, who later married Barnicle, took the folklorist to Kentucky, where she engaged in several field-recording projects. Unfortunately, Barnicle's left-wing politics did not sit well with the conservative English faculty of the University of Tennessee, where she taught from 1949 to 1950, and she left that position. Worse, some two hundred of her field recordings, housed on campus, were reported as missing and were not returned to her. Dispirited, Barnicle made no more field recordings.

It was not until 1983 that folklorist Willie Smyth turned up 150 of Barnicle's 1938–49 Kentucky recordings, in forgotten storage at the University of Tennessee's radio station.

SUGGESTED READING: Norm Cohen, entry on Barnicle, in Jan Harold Brunvand, ed., *American Folklore: An Encyclopedia* (New York, 1996).

"Barnyard." Like the children's song "Old MacDonald Had a Farm," "Barnyard" is a humorous cumulative folk song that enumerates barnyard animals and imitates their meows, grunts, and other calls, each verse being added to the previous verses. The song originated in Appalachia.

Barrick, Mac E. (1933–1991). A collector of central Pennsylvania folklore, Barrick specialized in proverbs as well as folk beliefs, jokes, and traditional tools. He was educated at Dickinson College (B.A.), University of Illinois (M.A.), and University of Pennsylvania (Ph.D.).

In the 1960s, Barrick began collecting in central Pennsylvania, concentrating on proverbs, riddles, rhymes, legends, tales, anecdotes, poetry, language, games, folk medicine, and folk beliefs. Much of his collecting focused on material from the Pennsylvania Germans, and in 1987, he published a major volume on the subject, *German American Folklore*. He established an archive of central Pennsylvania folklore at the Center for Pennsylvania Culture Studies at Pennsylvania State University, Harrisburg.

In addition to his fieldwork, Barrick studied joke cycles and regional folk humor, as well as preindustrial (traditional) tools, including fishing spears, hay knives, corn knives, husking pegs,

and scrapers. His material culture studies extended to folk toys and vernacular architecture (log houses).

Barrick was best known for his regional work, but he was also an internationalist, publishing articles on Spanish folklore, on the use of proverbs in medieval Spain and Portugal, and on the role of folklore in the fiction of Miguel de Cervantes and in the works of other Spanish writers.

SUGGESTED READING: Simon J. Bronner, entry on Barrick in Jan Harold Brunvand, ed., *American Folklore: An Encyclopedia* (New York, 1996).

Barry, Phillips (1880–1937). A collector of American ballads, Barry developed the theory of communal re-creation, which has come to supplant the earlier communal theory of BALLAD origins.

Barry was educated at Harvard University under GEORGE LYMAN KITTREDGE, Kuno Franke, and Leo Wiener. Barry was in the forefront of the growing assault on the conclusions about ballad origins reached by FRANCIS BARTON GUMMERE, who held that ballads were the product of communal composition. While Gummere and others based most of their conclusions on studies of ballad collections in libraries, Barry devoted himself to fieldwork, through which he reached the conclusion that ballads are the work of individual composers but are communally re-created through the processes of transmission. But even these communal re-creative processes may be seen as the work of individual folksingers, who deliberately and for specific purposes alter the ballad material they perform. Thus Barry and those who followed him demystified the origins of the ballad.

In the course of formulating his theory of communal re-creation, Barry collected widely, beginning in 1903 and working mainly in northern New England and the Maritimes.

Barry founded the Folk-Song Society of the Northeast and published much of his collections (with commentary) in the *Bulletin of the Folk-Song Society of the Northeast* (1930–37).

See also: CHILD, FRANCIS JAMES; ECKSTORM, FANNIE HARDY; FLANDERS, HELEN HARTNESS.

SUGGESTED READING: D. K. Wilgus, *Anglo-American Folksong Scholarship Since 1898* (New Brunswick, N.J., 1959).

Bascom, William R. (1912–1981). Bascom was an important student of African and African-American folklore. His mentor was MELVILLE JEAN HERSKOVITS, with whom he shared an interest in the comparative study of religion, art, and folklore in Africa and the African diaspora.

Bascom did fieldwork in Nigeria in 1937. After World War II, he and his Cuban-born wife, Berta, embarked on studies of the Shango cult, *santeria,* and divination practices of Yoruba origin in Cuba and elsewhere in the New World.

After teaching at Northwestern University, Bascom founded and became the first director of the Lowie (now Phoebe A. Hearst) Museum of Anthropology at the University of California, Berkeley. Bascom was the author of several books and articles, including the standard reference *Continuity and Change in Africa Cultures* (coedited with Herskovits, 1959).

In addition to his fieldwork, Bascom was a theorist of folkloristics and was especially interested in the relationship among myth, narrative, and divination. He was also a major contributor to diffusion theory, and in his posthumously published *African Folk-tales in the New World* (1992), Bascom definitively demonstrates that North American folklore is rich with material of directly African origin.

SUGGESTED READING: William R. Bascom, *African Art in Cultural Context* (New York, 1973).

Baseball folklore. Organized baseball was created in the United States in 1845, when Manhattan's Knickerbocker Base Ball Club was founded, and its members formalized and wrote down the rules of a game traditionally called "rounder," "one o' cat," "base," or "baseball." Over the next two decades, the game surpassed cricket in popularity in the United States, and local teams soon became expressions of civic pride, while the game itself achieved the status of "our national pastime." By 1876, when team owners formed the National League of Professional Base Ball Clubs, the sport had become a business in which players were paid—albeit poorly—and team owners and investors grew wealthy. A rival American League was formed in 1901 and undercut the National League by charging twenty-five instead of fifty cents for tickets and also offering Sunday games, as well as beer for sale at the ballpark. The American League appealed to the working classes and to struggling immigrants. Neither league, however, permitted African-American players to join, and in the 1920s the Negro Leagues were organized. Scandal dogged professional baseball beginning as early as the "fixed" games of 1865 and reaching its zenith (or nadir) with the Black Sox Scandal of 1919, in which gangsters in New York and Boston bribed the Chicago White Sox (afterward branded the "Black Sox") to throw the World Series. Despite its urban origins and its growth as a

ABOVE: *The American National Game of Base Ball,
print by Currier & Ives, 1866. (Collection of Walton
Rawls)*

RIGHT: *The "great national pastime." U.S. presidents
have been throwing out the first ball of the
Washington team's season since Woodrow Wilson. In
a poster illustration for the 1937 All-Star Game,
President Franklin D. Roosevelt prepares to lob the
first pitch.*

big and sometimes corrupt business, baseball retained the aura of pastoral nostalgia.

If the game of baseball itself is entwined with myths of pastoral innocence, its players and managers have created and have become the objects of much folklore. Ernest Lawrence Thayer, whose 1888 poem "Casey at the Bat" became an instant and enduring classic, subtitled his work "A Ballad of the Republic." He understood that figures such as the fictional batsman Mighty Casey were invested with the hopes and dreams

Baseball has long been a pervasive part of American life. It was used as the basis of an 1860 political cartoon featuring Abe Lincoln ("The Railsplitter," with a rail for a bat). The caption runs: "The National Game. Three Outs and One Run. Abraham Winning the Ball."

of the game's fans. They were regarded as champions and heroes in the original sense of being the bearers of a community's spirit. When they succeeded, all felt ennobled; when they failed (as Casey did), "there was no joy in Mudville."

Baseball lore includes anecdotal legends, jokes, proverbs, superstitions, folk speech, and tall tales. Perhaps the single most famous tall tale is about the time GEORGE HERMAN "BABE" RUTH stepped up to the plate in the fourth inning of the third game of the 1932 World Series against pitcher Charlie Root. With two strikes against him, Ruth solemnly pointed with his bat to the centerfield stands, and hit the next pitch precisely to the spot he indicated. While eyewitnesses attest to the truth of this legend, Root claimed that Ruth was doing nothing more than taunting him, raising his bat (or his finger) and saying, "You still need one more, kid!"

Other stories are more straightforwardly tall tales, such as the account of Negro Leagues pitcher Satchel Paige having earned such a reputation for a superfast fast ball that he could strike out a batter without even throwing the ball. He would wind up, the catcher would slap his glove, and the umpire would call a strike—with nary a protest from the dazed batter. Another tale depicts fabled outfielder Honus Wagner, bow-legged and ham-handed, picking up whatever came his way. In one game (Wagner himself apparently said), he went after a two-hopper when a rabbit ran past him. Wagner scooped up both the ball and the rabbit and fired both at the batter. "I got the runner by a hare," Wagner remarked. (In another version, Wagner picks up a stray dog.)

Ritual and superstition also abound in baseball. No one questions the sanctity of the seventh-inning stretch, players develop a wide array of superstitious rituals, and they may carry with them various lucky charms. The game has also been productive of proverbs, the most famous of which may be "Nice guys finish last," universally but erroneously attributed to Leo Durocher. Phrases such as "Stick it in his ear," "Loosey goosey," "He struck out," or "He didn't even get to first base" have become so familiar in the language that they have all but lost their immediate connection to baseball. Words and phrases such as *rookie, southpaw, bush-league, pinch hit, pitch, step up to the plate, bunt, home run, out in left field, put one over, out of my league,* and *foul ball* have become commonplace figures of speech. A number of baseball figures have generated particularly colorful examples of FOLK-SAY, most notably YOGI BERRA, a font of fractured proverbs and truisms that are both absurd and right on target: "It ain't over 'til it's over" and "It's like déjà vu all over again."

See also: IRISH AMERICANS.

Baseball is played by children and by armies.

SUGGESTED READING: Tristram Potter Coffin, *The Old Ball Game: Baseball in Folklore and Fiction* (New York, 1971); Tristram Potter Coffin, *The Illustrated Book of Baseball Folklore* (New York, 1975).

Basketmaking.

Basketmaking. Among the earliest crafts practiced by humankind, basketmaking shapes natural material into container form either by plaiting, weaving, or coiling. In America, various groups, moved by religion, race, ethnicity, or regional traditions, have produced baskets cherished for their artistry. Among NATIVE AMERICANS, the basketmakers of the southwestern tribes are the most celebrated; indeed, the Anaszi, ancient ancestors of the Hopi and the Navajo, are often referred to as the Basketmakers. Among Euro-American groups, the Shakers are perhaps most widely admired for their baskets, which were beautifully crafted, well engineered, and manufactured in significant quantities to be sold outside of the community throughout much of the nineteenth century. Prized second only to the Shaker baskets are those of the Pennsylvania Germans. Among African-American baskets, those made in coastal South Carolina and Georgia of coiled sweet-grass have been greatly admired. Presumably, these baskets closely adhere to African prototypes. Other traditions are also recognized, including baskets from southern Appalachians and the Ozarks.

While American baskets typically show a rich exchange among diverse peoples, certain characteristics do tend to identify the culture of the maker. Native Americans usually use split reed, willow, and grasses for their baskets. This is true of African Americans as well, but they also incorporate distinctive colorings and designs into their work. Euro-Americans tend to use straight-grained hardwood stock for baskets, such as white oak and hickory. Native American as well as African-American baskets are usually highly ornamented, even playful, while the Euro-American examples are typically more austerely functional.

By the mid-nineteenth century, most baskets were being produced with the aid of machines, and culturally distinctive hand traditions were in danger of dying out. However, the craft revival movements of the 1920s and 1930s renewed interest in this traditional craft. There is a collectors' market for baskets made according to the traditional patterns of authentic basketry. Adult craft classes and recreational programs also foster basketmaking in the modern South, allowing one to learn to produce a basket under proper tutelage.

See also: ANGLO AMERICANS.

SUGGESTED READING: Virginia Harvey, *Techniques of Basketry* (New York, 1974); John Rice Irwin, *Baskets and Basket Makers in Southern Appalachia* (Exton, Pa., 1982); George Wharton James, *Indian Basketry* (New York, 1909; reprint ed., 1972); Jeannette Lasansky, *Willow, Oak, and Rye: Basket Traditions of Pennsylvania* (University Park, Pa., 1979); Gloria Roth Teleki, *Baskets of Rural America* (New York, 1975).

Basque Americans.

Basque Americans. Basque Americans come from the western Pyrenees and Cantabria, the southern coast of France and the northern coast of Spain. Many Basques were sheepherders, and much of their immigration to the United States came during the middle nineteenth century, when they tended flocks in the West or tried their hand at prospecting during the gold rushes of 1849 and the 1850s. Some Basques emigrated directly from Europe, while others came via the pampas of South America. By the end of the nineteenth century, Basque sheepherders were common in the West. Often, they were met with violent resistance from non-Basque sheepmen and cattlemen. Ironically, restrictive immigration laws created a shortage of experienced sheepherders in the West by the middle of the twentieth century, and in 1950, congressional legislation was introduced to recruit Basque herders on a temporary basis. After the sheep market became depressed in the 1970s, the presence of Basque herders declined, and relatively few now remain in the West.

In contrast, then, to most immigrant groups, the majority of Basques have been temporary residents and overwhelmingly male and single. Often, they made their homes in special Basque hotels near western rail lines. Well into the twentieth century, these hotels became the center of Basque-American social life. Beginning in the late 1940s and early 1950s, a few more formal Basque ethnic associations were formed, and in 1959, a national Basque festival was held in Sparks, Nevada, which encouraged the formation of several Basque clubs in the West. Typical activities in festivals and clubs include traditional dances, religious services conducted in Basque, contests of prowess and strength, and herding-related contests, including sheepdog trials. Food served combines traditional Basque fare with a western-style barbecue.

The celebration of Basque ethnic identity was furthered by the creation of a Basque studies program at the University of Nevada, Reno, in 1967, and in 1972, some of the Basque clubs formed over the years united in the North American Basque Organizations, Inc. (NABO). NABO sponsors a variety of activities, including music camps, in which children learn to play the *txistu* (Basque flute), and traditional games. NABO also sponsors American tours of traditional performing artists from the homeland. While the number of Basque Americans is quite small today, their cultural presence is felt in the West.

Many of the Basque hotels are now Basque specialty restaurants, popular with Basques and non-Basques.

See also: IMMIGRANT FOLKLORE.

SUGGESTED READING: William A. Douglass, entry on Basque Americans in Jan Harold Brunvand, ed., *American Folklore: An Encyclopedia* (New York, 1996); William A. Douglass and Jon Bilbao, *Amerikanuak: Basques in the New World* (Reno, Nev., 1975); Robert Laxalt, *The Basque Hotel* (Reno, Nev., 1957); Robert Laxalt, *Sweet Promised Land* (Reno, Nev., 1957).

Bass, Sam(uel) (1851–1878). The legend of Sam Bass became a part of Texas folklore almost before death ended his remarkable four-year criminal career. During that brief span, Bass robbed stagecoaches, trains, and banks with preternatural speed and efficiency. He worked so fast, that he seemed to be everywhere at once, from the Black Hills of the Dakota Territory to the Panhandle of Texas.

Bass was born in Mitchell, Indiana, near Woodville, on July 21, 1851. Orphaned early in life, he was consigned to the care of a mean-spirited skinflint uncle, David Sheeks, who kept Sam Bass from school and put him immediately to work on his farm. In 1869, to escape this grind, eighteen-year-old Bass, in a real-life adumbration of MARK TWAIN's Huck Finn, built a raft and floated down the Mississippi to St. Louis, thence to Rosedale, Mississippi, where he worked for a year. In 1870, employed as a teamster, Bass drove a cargo to Denton, Texas, and went to work for the local sheriff, W. F. "Dad" Eagan, who would later spend months in a vain effort to capture Bass when he turned outlaw. With his earnings, Bass bought a sorrel mare, which he raced successfully enough to enable him to quit working for Eagan.

Bass began frequenting the local saloons and befriended a bad element, including Henry Underwood. One day in 1875, Bass and Underwood bought melons. Bass dropped his when he tried to slice it, eliciting hoots and jeers from a group of young blacks standing nearby. Bass and Underwood hurled stones at their tormenters and were arrested (not by Eagan). The pair made a getaway, and, in this offhanded way, became outlaws.

Bass and Underwood quickly split up, Bass riding to San Antonio, where he met Joel (Joe) Collins, with whom he engaged in a successful cattle-driving venture, and then met cowboy and gunman Jack Davis. Davis, Collins, and Bass invested in a freight company, but soon sold out to invest in a mine, which failed. At this, Bass and Collins decided simply to take what they wanted.

They put together a gang of quick-on-the-draw rowdies, including Tom Nixon, Bill Heffridge, Jack Davis, and James Berry, and robbed seven Deadwood stages in the Black Hills area between 1876 and 1877. When guards opened fire on them, Bass and Collins shot back, killing the stage driver.

From stagecoach robbery, the gang graduated to train robbery, targeting a Union Pacific bearing gold from the Denver Mint. On September 19, 1877, they hit the train at Big Springs, Nebraska, netting more than $60,000 in newly minted $20 gold pieces, as well as an additional $1,300 from passengers, and $450 from the mail-car safe.

The gang split up following the robbery, going in pairs in separate directions to shake the posses they knew would bear down on them. Bass recruited a new gang, including Seaborn Barnes, Frank Jackson, Tom Spotswood, Henry Underwood, Arkansas Tom Johnson, all professional gunmen. In various combinations, they robbed trains. After three successful robberies, they attacked a Texas and Pacific express at the town of Mesquite on April 10, 1878. To the gang's dismay, the train was loaded with convicts on their way to prison, and heavily armed guards opened fire on the outlaws.

Despite the surprise, the gang got away, and the string of robberies so alarmed authorities that an army of lawmen assembled in the Dallas–Fort Worth area. A force that included Sheriff W. F. Eagan, Bass's former employer, located the gang on June 12–13, 1878, at their Salt Creek encampment. Bass escaped during an intense fusillade and he and his gang were reported to be in five different counties in a single day. At last, on May 21, 1878, James W. Murphy, who, along with his father, Henderson Murphy, had been charged with harboring the Bass gang, approached the lawmen with a proposition. He would deliver the Bass gang if charges against him and his father were dropped. The deal concluded, Murphy joined the Bass gang and, on July 19, 1878, led them into an ambush at Round Rock, Texas.

While all charges against Murphy were indeed dropped—and he was even given a large reward—he was regarded by the public as a Judas, much as Robert Ford would be condemned for assassinating the infamous Jesse James in 1882. Murphy committed suicide by swallowing poison on June 7, 1879.

SUGGESTED READING: Wayne Gard, *Sam Bass* (Boston, 1936); Bill O'Neal, *Encyclopedia of Western Gunfighters* (Norman, Okla., 1979); Helena Huntington Smith, "Sam Bass and the Myth Machine," *American West* (January 1970), pp. 31–35.

Bassett, Fletcher S. (1847–1893). Bassett is best remembered as the primary founder of the Chicago Folk-Lore Society, which first met on December 12, 1891. The Chicago Folk-Lore So-

ciety was an important alternative to the AMERI-
CAN FOLKLORE SOCIETY, which had been established 1888. Whereas the American Folklore
Society approached the study of folklore as a
branch of anthropology, the Chicago group approached it as literature.

Born in Adams County, Kentucky, Bassett
served in the Civil War with the 108th Illinois
Volunteers, then attended the U.S. Naval Academy and served as a naval officer for thirteen
years. Forced by health problems into early retirement in 1882, he became an independent
scholar based in Chicago.

He is the author of *Legends and Superstitions
of the Sea and of Sailors* (1885) and *The Folk-
Lore Manual* (1892). Unfortunately, the organization he created did not long survive his death.
The Chicago Folk-Lore Society folded in 1904.

SUGGESTED READING: W. K. McNeil, "The Chicago
Folklore Society and the International Folklore Con-
gress of 1893," *Midwestern Journal of Language and
Folklore* 11 (1985), pp. 5–19.

Baughman, Ernest Warren (1916–1990).

Baughman, an important collector of southwestern folktales, legends, jokes, rhymes, proverbs,
and superstitions, was born in Manson, Iowa, on
September 10, 1916. He did his undergraduate
work at Ball State Teachers College (B.A., 1938),
then moved to the University of Chicago (M.A.,
1939). He worked toward his doctorate at Indiana University under STITH THOMPSON, receiving his Ph.D. in 1953, specializing in folklore. His
dissertation, *A Type and Motif Index of the Folktales of England and North America* was published as Indiana University Folklore Series No.
20 in 1966.

Baughman's published regularly in scholarly

journals and periodically edited the *New Mexico
Folklore Record* between 1952 and 1979. Baugh-
man was named president of the New Mexico
Folklore Society in 1957.

Most of Baughman's scholarly career was
spent at the University of New Mexico, where
he amassed a large collection of some two thousand southwestern folktales and approximately
twenty thousand riddles, rhymes, proverbs, superstitions, jokes, and brief legends. (The collection is on deposit at the Special Collections
Department, Zimmermann Library, University
of New Mexico.)

SUGGESTED READING: Peter White and Kenneth B.
Keppeler, entry on Baughman in Jan Harold Brun-
vand, ed., *American Folklore: An Encyclopedia* (New
York, 1996).

Bean, Roy (ca. 1823–1903).

Judge Roy
Bean was the self-proclaimed "only law west of
the Pecos." For two decades, this uneducated,
colorful, harsh, and cantankerous man held court
(literally) from Langtry, Texas, earning a place in
western legend and lore during his own lifetime
and meriting celebration in a 1972 John Huston
movie, *The Life and Times of Judge Roy Bean,*
with Paul Newman in the title role.

Little is know about Roy Bean's early life other
than he was born about 1823 in a log cabin in
Mason County, Kentucky. As a teenager, Roy
Bean accompanied his older brother Sam to Mexico in search of fortune. Shortly after their arrival
in Chihuahua in 1848, the pair got into a scrape
with a liquored-up Mexican cowboy, who (it is
said) drew a knife on Roy Bean. The young man
responded by drawing his gun and shooting the
cowboy in the forehead. Local authorities
branded the shooting a murder, and Roy fled to

San Diego, California. There he worked for his other brother Josh, ran a saloon, and rode with the California Rangers. He went to Mesilla, New Mexico, in 1852, after Josh was slain in a gunfight. Roy, who consciously spun tales about himself, claimed that he had to leave San Diego because he had fought a duel on horseback, which resulted in the death of his opponent. Bean also claimed that he had stolen a beautiful Spanish girl from her Mexican lover near Mission San Gabriel outside Los Angeles and was lynched by the boyfriend and his comrades, who left him dangling from a noose. His sweetheart cut him down, and he fled, the rope burns vivid around his neck.

During the Civil War, Bean led a guerrilla band, The Free Rovers, who claimed to serve the Confederacy by robbing wealthy landowners; but there is no evidence that any of the loot ever benefited the Southern cause. After the war, Bean moved to San Antonio, Texas, where he worked variously as a butcher, a dairy operator, a saloonkeeper, and a freighter. Compulsively litigious, Bean became a fixture in the San Antonio courthouse and, in this way, learned whatever he came to know about the law.

Having made little enough of himself in San Antonio, Bean followed the advancing railroad west across Texas. At the town of Vinagaroon, a band of whiskey-soaked road-gang workers, impressed with Bean's ability to spout legal jargon, appointed him justice of the peace. Vinagaroon soon died, and Bean moved on with the Southern Pacific to Langtry, dusty and desolate, where he created a miniature empire, whose existence spread his fame across Texas and the West.

Bean secured an appointment as justice of the peace in Langtry on August 2, 1882, and set up in a twenty-by-fourteen-foot shack adorned with signs reading: "Judge Roy Bean, Notary Public," "Justice of the Peace," "Law West of the Pecos," and "Ice Beer." Another sign read: "The Jersey Lilly," a misspelled reference to the town's namesake, the popular actress Lily Langtry.

But it was for his actions as a judge that Bean became a western legend. When he found a body with forty dollars in gold and a pistol, he summarily fined the corpse forty dollars for carrying a concealed weapon—and pocketed the cash. Bean officiated at any and all occasions. He charged two dollars for coroner's inquests and five dollars each for weddings and divorces. (Bean had no legal right to grant divorces; when challenged on one of these, he replied, "I guess I got a right to unmarry 'em if it don't take.") Bean was also famous for concluding wedding ceremonies by fixing his gaze somberly at the groom and pronouncing, "And may God have mercy on your soul."

Bean's brand of justice was always dispensed with liquor, which sold "in court" at a handsome profit. A racist, he acquitted a railroad worker who had shot a Chinese laborer. After leafing through his single law book (a copy of the Texas statutes), he rendered judgment: "There ain't a damned law here that says it's illegal to shoot a Chinaman! Defendant is discharged." By the turn of the century, his legend had grown to such proportions that hundreds visited out-of-the-way Langtry just to get a glimpse of Bean rocking on his porch.

Bean died on March 16, 1903, after a prolonged drinking bout following a rousing cockfight in the Mexican quarter of San Antonio.

SUGGESTED READING: C. L. Sonnichsen, *The Story of Judge Roy Bean: Law West of the Pecos* (New York, 1943).

Beatty, Talley (ca. 1923–). One of the leading figures in African-American modern dance,

Beatty was born in New Orleans and was trained by ethnic dancer and choreographer KATHERINE DUNHAM. He was a member of Dunham's first dance troupe from 1940 to 1946, performing in such works as *Rites de Passage* (1941)—which many consider his greatest role—and *Tropical Revue* (1943). Beatty also studied with Martha Graham and with Aubrey Hitchins. After he left the Dunham company in 1946, Beatty performed as a freelancer, appearing in Lew Christensen's 1947 *Blackface*, Sylla Fort's *Procession and Rite* (1958), and Emily Parham's *Legend and Trajectories* (1958). After dancing in Maya Deren's *A Study of Choreography for the Camera* in 1945, he danced in a 1946 revival of Jerome Kern's musical *Show Boat*.

Beginning in 1948, Beatty was choreographing on his own, creating a series of folk-inspired dances for recital, including *Jim Crow, Blues, Sonatina,* and *Rural Dances of Cuba.* From this time and into the mid-1970s, he created many works, both for his own companies and for Alvin Ailey (most notably *The Black Belt,* 1968), the Boston Ballet, Birgit Cullberg Ballet of Stockholm, Bat-sheva Company of Israel, the Inner City Dance Company of Los Angeles, and New York's Ballet Hispanico.

See also: DANCE, FOLK.

Beck, Earl Clifton (1891–1977).

Beck, an important collector of Michigan lumberjack songs, began studying Michigan lumberjacks (loggers) during the 1930s and collected their songs, stories, and dances through the 1940s.

Nebraska-born Beck taught English and folklore at Central Michigan University. He published three lumberjack-related collections, *Songs of the Michigan Lumberjacks* (1942), *Lore of the Lumbercamps* (1948), and *They Knew Paul Bunyan* (1956). In 1934, he also formed and managed a musical performing group, The Michigan Lumberjacks, and participated in the production of the Library of Congress recording *Songs of the Michigan Lumberjacks* (1959). Beck edited the liner notes.

See also: LUMBERJACK FOLKLORE; WALTON, IVAN.

SUGGESTED READING: Earl Clifton Beck, *It Was This Way* (Ann Arbor, Mich., 1963).

Beckwith, Martha Warren (1871–1959).

Beckwith was an anthropologist and folklorist with a wide range of interests. Best known for her work in the field of Hawaiian mythology, she also studied the folklore of the Mandan, Hidatsa, and Oglala Sioux Indians; of Jamaica; of Portuguese living in India; of African Americans; of college students; and closer to home, the folklore of Dutchess County, New York.

Born in Wellesley Heights, Massachusetts (January 19, 1871), Beckwith was raised on Maui, Hawaii. She returned to Massachusetts for college, taking a B.A. in English from Mount Holyoke. She studied anthropology under Franz Boas at Columbia University, earning a Ph.D. in 1918 and, two years later, became research professor of the Folklore Foundation at Vassar College, serving in that position until she left Vassar in 1938.

Beckwith's fieldwork was extensive and wide ranging and included studies in Jamaica (1919–22), South Dakota (among the Sioux of the Pine Ridge Indian Reservation, 1926), and Goa, India (with Portuguese settlers, 1927). A translator of nineteenth-century Hawaiian writings, her most significant work was on Hawaiian creation chants and myths. Her *Hawaiian Mythology* was published in 1940. Beckwith was also deeply interested in the herbal folk medicine of Hawaii, and was among the first to study the subject, devoting her later years to collecting and classifying Hawaiian herbal remedies.

While Beckwith's book on Hawaiian mythology is considered her classic work, her 1929 *Black Roadways: A Study of Jamaican Folklife* was also well received as a pioneering ethnographic study. Beckwith served as president of the American Folklore Society from 1932 to 1933.

SUGGESTED READING: Martha Warren Beckwith, *Hawaiian Mythology* (New Haven, Conn., 1940); Katherine Luomala, "Martha Warren Beckwith: A Commemorative Essay," *Journal of American Folklore* 75 (1962), pp. 341–53.

Belden, Henry Marvin (1868–1954).
Born in Wilton, Connecticut, Henry M. Belden was an important collector and student of BALLADS and songs. After earning his B.A. from Trinity College (Hartford, Connecticut), he taught at a prep school before embarking on graduate work in English at Johns Hopkins University in 1889. In 1893, while he was teaching at the University of Nebraska, he met LOUISE POUND, with whom he would later do much of his work on the ballad.

After completing his Ph.D. dissertation in 1895, he began teaching at the University of Missouri. Here, in 1903, he discovered from his students that the ballad tradition, pronounced dead by pioneering ballad scholar FRANCIS JAMES CHILD, was very much alive in Missouri. He

began avidly collecting ballads and folk songs and, in 1906, founded the Missouri Folk-Lore Society. He served as president of the American Folklore Society in 1910 and 1911.

Unfortunately, Belden's plans to publish a comprehensive collection of Missouri ballads and folklore failed to come to fruition, in part because of disruptions caused by America's entry into World War I and also because of the death, in 1934, of MARY ALICIA OWEN, who was to be a major contributor to the volume, providing the African-American and Native American materials.

Belden was an earlier researcher into BROADSIDES and Native American ballads, and was never content with collecting texts apart from the music to which they were set. He also scrupulously collected information on singers and sources. An advocate of the theory that ballads are, first and foremost, the work of individual composer/singers, he argued against FRANCIS BARTON GUMMERE's pervasive theory of communal origin of ballads.

Belden published *Ballads and Songs Collected by the Missouri Folk-Lore Society* in 1940, and, with ARTHUR PALMER HUDSON, he edited the ballad and folk-song volumes of *The Frank C. Brown Collection of North Carolina Folklore* (1952).

SUGGESTED READING: Henry Marvin Belden, *Ballads and Songs Collected by the Missouri Folk-Lore Society* (Columbia, Mo., 1940; reprint ed., 1973).

Beliajus, Vytautas (1909–1995). "Vyts"
Beliajus was a Lithuanian-born American folk dancer, teacher, and the editor of *Viltis*, an important folk-dance magazine. He emigrated from

his native Lithuania to the United States in 1923, settling in Chicago. There Beliajus became interested in classical music and the stage, as well as in the folk life of the ethnically diverse city. He became deeply involved in Hasidic dance and soon was engaged by a local Zionist organization to present spectacles at the Civic Opera House. "Vyts," as Beliajus was affectionately called, started teaching folk dance under the auspices of the Chicago Park District in 1930 and, three years later, organized the world's first Lithuanian Folk Dance Club. In 1936, he organized the Chicago Park District's first large-scale folk-dance festival, held at the lakefront Soldier Field. During the 1930s and 1940s, he organized many other folk festivals, showcasing a wide range of traditions, including the eastern European, Hindu, and Israeli.

Beliajus published and edited *Lore,* the first folklore magazine devoted to dance, from 1936 to 1939. In 1942, he inaugurated *Viltis* (from the Lithuanian word for hope), a journal initially intended for U.S. military personnel serving in World War II. The journal proved popular and lasted well beyond the war years.

See also: DANCE, FOLK.

SUGGESTED READING: Betty Casey, *International Folk Dancing U.S.A.* (New York, 1981).

Benedict, Ruth (1887–1948).

Benedict, a student of FRANZ BOAS, was an influential anthropologist-folklorist, whose 1934 *Patterns of Culture* defined individual cultures as collective personalities ("personality writ large").

Benedict is important to the philosophy of folklore and anthropology because she stressed the interconnection of the humanities and anthropology (she was herself a student of literature and a published poet, writing verse under the pseudonym of Ann Singleton) and emphasized the importance of studying a culture holistically, always including folklore in any analysis. She demonstrated this latter approach in her 1935 *Zuni Mythology,* which concentrated on a body of folktales.

Benedict taught folklore and anthropology at Columbia University from 1926 until her death in 1948 and, from 1925 to 1939, edited the *Journal of American Folklore.* She was president of the American Ethnological Society (1927–29) and the American Anthropological Association (1946–47).

Her last major work was *The Chrysanthemum and the Sword* (1946), a study of Japanese national culture based on her wartime work for the U.S. Office of War Information.

SUGGESTED READING: Virginia Wolf Briscoe, "Ruth Benedict: Anthropological Folklorist," *Journal of American Folklore* 92 (1979), pp. 445–76; Judith Schachter Modell, *Ruth Benedict: Patterns of a Life* (Philadelphia, 1983).

Benét, Stephen Vincent (1898–1943).

Benét, a prolific American poet and novelist and author of some seventeen volumes of prose and verse, is best known for *John Brown's Body,* a 1928 narrative poem about the Civil War (transformed into a play by Charles Laughton in 1953) and for the 1937 short story "The Devil and DANIEL WEBSTER," a highly entertaining and provocative treatment of a TALL TALE about how the legendary orator duped the devil himself. Benét's short story has been dramatized for the stage and for film, and was also the basis for an opera by Douglas Moore.

Benét was a publishing prodigy, whose first book appeared when he was only seventeen. Educated at Yale University, he was deeply immersed in subjects drawn from American history and folklore. With his wife, Rosemary Carr Benét, he wrote *A Book of Americans* (1933), which told in verse the biographies of famous American historical figures and was widely read by schoolchildren. Benét wanted to render all of American history in epic verse, but had completed only Book I (of five projected books) of *Western Star* before he died.

See also: MORTON, THOMAS.

SUGGESTED READING: Stephen Vincent Benét, *John Brown's Body* (New York, 1928); Stephen Vincent Benét, *The Devil and Daniel Webster* (New York, 1937).

Berdache. *Berdache* refers to men in some Native American tribes who adopt the dress and social role of women; they are transvestites or homosexuals. Occasionally, the word also refers to Native American lesbians. Most tribes completely integrate berdaches into the social structure and incorporate them into various ceremonies and celebrations. Berdaches have been the object of much anthropological study, as well as much wonderment among non-Indians. The word is originally Arabic, denoting a boy sex slave or a male child used sexually by adults.

SUGGESTED READING: Walter L. Williams, *The Spirit and the Flesh: Sexual Diversity in American Indian Culture* (Boston, 1992).

Berk, Fred (ca. 1911–1980). An authority on Israeli folk dance, Berk founded and directed the Jewish Dance Division of the 92nd Street YMHA in New York City. He was born in Vienna and studied there at the State Academy of Dance. In Vienna, Berk performed with the Expressionist choreographer Gertrude Kraus and won a bronze medal in the 1934 Viennese State international dance competition as "the most promising dancer." With the outbreak of World War II, Berk came to the United States, where he performed with such notable dancers as Hanya Holm and Katia Delakova, whom he married and subsequently divorced. In 1945, Berk began teaching at the Jewish Theological Seminary, and from 1949 to 1954 directed the Stage for Dancers at the Brooklyn Museum, presenting programs and lectures by a host of modern dance figures, including Louis Horst, Glen Tetley, Daniel Nagrin, Merce Cunningham, and Alwin Nikolais. But Berk is best known for his commitment to the performance and study of Jewish and Israeli folk dance. He founded the Jewish Dance Division of New York's 92nd Street Y in 1950 and directed it until his death in 1980. In 1958 he also founded his own company, the Hebraica Dancers, edited an important Jewish folk-dance bibliography (*The Jewish Dance* [1959]), and wrote a variety of articles on the subject of Jewish folk dance. Berk also served as director of the Israeli Folk Dance Institute of the American Zionist Youth Foundation and was cofounder of the Merry-Go-Rounders dance company.

Bermuda Triangle. Also called the "Devil's Triangle," the Bermuda Triangle is an area in the Atlantic Ocean off Florida where a number of ships and aircraft have vanished. Neither the U.S. Coast Guard nor any government agency recognizes its existence as anything other than a popular belief. No official map exists of the Triangle's boundaries, though it is defined roughly by Melbourne, Florida, Bermuda, and Puerto Rico.

The legend of the Bermuda Triangle as a paranormal region began shortly after the "Flight 19 Incident," in which five U.S. Navy Avenger aircraft disappeared in a severe storm during a December 5, 1945, training mission. No trace of wreckage was ever found, and the rescue plane sent in search of the aircraft also disappeared without a trace. The label "Bermuda Triangle" seems to have been used first by a writer named V. Gaddis in a 1964 issue of *Argosy* magazine. Retrospectively, amateur investigators turned up "bizarre happenings" that had occurred for centuries in the area, beginning with a report that Columbus's compass had gone crazy and that his crew had seen strange lights in the sky. Another historical event retroactively attributed to the mysterious action of the Bermuda Triangle was the case of the *Mary Celeste,* which was found in 1892, mysteriously abandoned some 400 miles off its intended New York-to-Genoa course. (The appeal of the legend is such that it was applied to the case of the *Mary Celeste,* even though the ship was discovered nowhere near the Bermuda Triangle.) In all, at least two hundred incidents have been attributed to the Bermuda Triangle. Public interest in the "phenomenon" reached a zenith after the 1974 publication of Charles Berlitz's bestselling *The Bermuda Triangle,* a sensational account rather than a balanced investigation. Those interested in an "official" pronouncement on the Bermuda Triangle may consult the U.S. Navy Historical Department's World Wide Web site at www.history.navy.mil/faqs/faq8-1.htm. Another Web site, http://icarus.cc.uic.edu/~jdregel/toby/triangle/tri.html, offers links to a vast array of Bermuda Triangle information, speculation, and lore.

SUGGESTED READING: Larry Kushe and Deborah K. Blouin, *Bermuda Triangle Bibliography,* 3d ed. (Tempe, Ariz., 1975); Larry Kushe, *The Bermuda Triangle Mystery—Solved* (New York, 1975).

Berra, Yogi (1925–). Born Lawrence Peter Berra in St. Louis, Berra was a baseball player, manager, and coach, whose achievements in the record books—catcher's record for most home runs (313), most consecutive errorless games (148), most consecutive chances accepted (950), and most World Series games played as a catcher (75)—would have been sufficient to earn him a niche in baseball history; however, Berra is best known as a manager and coach who uttered seeming volumes of legendary malapropisms and gems of fractured sage advice and folk wisdom. Even those people who don't follow professional baseball seem to have a favorite Yogi-ism, and there are now Internet World Wide Web sites devoted to collections of his sayings. Among the most familiar and frequently quoted are "It ain't over 'til it's over," "It's like déjà vu all over again," "You can observe a lot just by watchin'," "If you can't imitate him, don't copy him," "Baseball is 90 percent mental, the other half is physical," "Nobody goes there anymore; it's too crowded," "You got to be very careful if you don't know where you're going, because you might not get there," and "It was impossible to get a conversation going, everybody was talking too much." When Phil Rizzuto remarked, "Hey, Yogi, I think we're lost," Berra replied: "Yeah, but we're making great time!" Which is thematically related to: "I knew I was going to take the wrong train, so I left early."

After playing organized ball with the YMCA and American Legion, Berra signed with the New York Yankees in 1942. His career was interrupted by naval service during World War II (1943–46), then, after less than a season in the minors during 1946, he was the Yankees' catcher through 1963. He was named the American League's Most Valuable Player—a rare honor for a catcher—in 1951, 1954, and 1955. Berra managed the Yankees in 1964. He won the pennant, but lost the Series and was fired. The New York Mets took him on as a coach (1965–72) and a manager (1972–75), after which he returned to the Yankees as a coach through 1983, when he was made manager of the team. He was fired in 1985. Berra was elected to the Baseball Hall of Fame in 1972. Berra received perhaps an even more significant pop culture accolade when television cartoon producers Bill Hanna and Joe Barbera named one of their most successful animated creations Yogi Bear (*The Yogi Bear Show*, 1960).

See also: BASEBALL FOLKLORE.

SUGGESTED READING: Yogi Berra, *The Yogi Book: "I Really Didn't Say Everything I Said."* (New York, 1998).

Big Dipper. For many people, the Big Dipper (Ursa Major) is the most readily recognizable "constellation." (Technically, the Big Dipper is not a constellation, but an asterism, a grouping of stars associated with a larger constellation. The Big Dipper lies within Ursa Major.) In several Native American cultures, it is the focus of vivid folktales of origin. For example, the Seneca tell a tale of six hunters. One is lazy and feigns illness so that the other five will carry him. The hunters encounter a bear and drop their companion in order to pursue him; however, the lazy hunter, having enjoyed the benefit of rest, quickly jumps to his feet and outdistances his fatigued companions, catching the bear and killing it. Intent on the chase, all of the hunters are unaware that they are ascending. By the conclusion of the hunt, they have reached the sky and remain visible as the stars of the Big Dipper.

Bigfoot. Popular name for Sasquatch (from Coast Salish Indian *se'sxac,* "wild men"), Bigfoot is a very large, very hairy, quasi-human creature known chiefly by his purported big footprints and believed by many to exist in the Pacific Northwest and in western Canada. It has been reported as between six and fifteen feet tall, and those claiming close encounters say that the creature exudes a foul odor. Footprints have measured up to twenty-four inches long by eight inches wide. Bigfoot is to North American folklore what the Abominable Snowman (Yeti) is to the folklore of the mountains of Nepal. The first sighting of Bigfoot tracks is usually credited to David Thompson, a British explorer who reported them in 1811. Since then, many sporadic sightings of the actual creature have been reported, and grainy still photographs as well as moving-picture footage have been produced. So far, none of this evidence is conclusive for determining whether Bigfoot is an actual creature, a strictly imaginative folk invention, or some combination (such as a familiar animal imagined to be the Sasquatch). Stories about Bigfoot sightings in particular abound among Pacific Northwest loggers and Indians. Although Bigfoot is said to look terrifying and is given to emitting eerie, high-pitched wails, it is apparently not a dangerous creature.

Bigfoot is one of the most familiar subjects of American regional folklore and has been made even more familiar by periodic coverage in supermarket tabloids and on popular television shows devoted to speculation about the "paranormal." Some recent stories have linked Bigfoot to UFO sightings.

See also: CRYPTOZOOLOGY; LUMBERJACK FOLKLORE; MOTHMAN.

SUGGESTED READING: Don Hunter, with René Dahinden, *Sasquatch! Bigfoot: The Search for North America's Incredible Creature* (Toronto, 1993); Linda Milligan, "The 'Truth' about the Bigfoot Legend," *Western Folklore* 49 (1990), pp. 83–98; H. H. Trotti, "Did Fiction Give Birth to Big Foot?" *Skeptical Inquirer* 18 (1994), pp. 541–42.

Big Sea Day. During the nineteenth and early twentieth centuries, Big Sea Day was celebrated along the coast of southern New Jersey on the second Saturday of August. Families traveled to the Jersey shore to bathe in the sea—wearing whatever clothes they had on—then sat in the sun to dry. The celebration was also, humorously, called Farmer's Wash Day.

Biker lore. At least since the 1954 appearance of the film *The Wild One,* starring Marlon Brando as the tough, black-leather-jacketed leader of a "motorcycle gang," biker folklore has been sharply divided between exoteric and esoteric components. In a famous exchange in *The Wild One,* Brando is asked, "What are you rebelling against?" He replies: "Whaddya got?" Nonbikers often regard the leather-clad figure with a mixture of envy, fear, and contempt. The biker is a social rebel, like the COWBOY, a free spirit, yet he (and she) is also regarded as a dangerous, irresponsible hoodlum, a member of a motorized marauding wolfpack, which may ride into a town and terrorize its "decent citizens" at will. For many, the image of the "motorcycle gang" is the Hell's Angels, which, by the 1960s, the decade in which the Angels became infamous for drug use and violence, had club chapters in many states other than California, where the organization originated. Some Hell's Angels chapters were communes, which the public saw as violent reverse images of the typical hippie commune of peace and love. Based on sensational news reports and on journalist Hunter S. Thompson's insider book, *Hell's Angels* (1966), the Hell's Angels communes appeared as havens for drug-fueled, psychotic, randomly violent antisocial behavior. That is the exoteric folklore associated with bikers generally.

Among bikers themselves there is a substantial body of esoteric folklore. People who identify themselves as bikers ride as often as possible. They do dress in leather or denim jackets and wear biker boots. Often, their jackets incorporate a club insignia (outlaw biker groups call these "colors") and souvenir patches commemorating rallies attended. Typically, they ride in groups and gather at rallies, races, rides, and runs. The overwhelming majority of bikers (at least six million in the United States) and motorcycle club members are law-abiding citizens, many of whom nevertheless cherish some aspect of the outlaw, rebel, or free-spirit image. Among themselves, the kind of bike owned and the experience of the biker are highly important, with Harley-Davidson machines generally held in highest esteem and Japanese imports derided as "riceburners." (Though the owners of sleek imports may in return criticize the Harleys as old-fashioned and mechanically unreliable.)

If there is one aspect of "outlawry" that even law-abiding bikers exhibit, it is contempt for state helmet laws. Instead of the high-tech full-face helmets now available, many riders wear small "token" helmets, abiding by the letter of the law while protesting its spirit. Other helmet styles may project the biker's attitude, which may or may not be self-ironic. Such helmets include Nazi or Wehrmacht styles or Wagnerian "Visigoth" helmets, complete with horns and fur trim.

Outlaw bikers traditionally sport an array of demonic tattoos, but even law-abiding or "straight" bikers often decorate their bikes with elaborate and symbolic painted motifs ranging from images of violent death, speed, Dungeons & Dragons–style fantasy, machismo, to, on women's bikes, symbols of femininity, such as bows and flowers. Bikes may also be adorned with portraits of children and spouse. Even most outsiders understand that bikers are highly protective of their machines. The bikers themselves observe rules of etiquette when "bike looking" at parked machines. They remain at least two feet away from unattended motorcycles and are careful not to lean over a bike, to avoid scratching it. When speaking to the owner about his or her machine, only admiration is expressed. It is bad form to criticize a stranger's machine. (While most bikers take great pride in their machines, some ride "rat bikes," the motorcycle equivalent of the automotive jalopy, the filthier and more thoroughly and obviously patched the better.)

See also: ESOTERIC FOLKLORE; EXOTERIC FOLKLORE.

SUGGESTED READING: Karen Baldwin, entry on bikers in Jan Harold Brunvand, ed., *American Folklore: An Encyclopedia* (New York, 1996); Lee Gutkind, "Hell on Wheels: The Outlaw Motorcycle Gangs," *Journal of American Culture* 6 (1983), pp. 58–64; Thierry Sagnier, *Bike! Motorcycles and the People Who Ride Them* (New York, 1974).

"Billy Boy." One of the most popular of question-and-answer folk songs, "Billy Boy" was brought to America by emigrants from the British Isles and exists in many variants on both sides of the Atlantic. The most familiar version begins "O where have you been, Billy Boy, Billy Boy? / Oh where have you been, charming Billy?" and goes on in question-and-answer form to detail the merits of a prospective bride ("Can she bake a cherry pie, Billy Boy, Billy Boy?" and so on).

See also: FOLK MUSIC.

Billy the Kid (ca. 1859–1881). The "most legendary" of the many legendary outlaws of the nineteenth-century American West, Billy the Kid was born Henry McCarty, possibly in Indiana, but most likely in the tough Irish ghetto of New York City. During the Civil War, the family moved to Kansas, and, following the death of his father, they settled in New Mexico, where Henry's mother married William H. Antrim in 1873. The boy took his stepfather's last name, but was later sometimes known as William H. Bonney, or Kid Antrim, or simply the Kid. He was not called Billy the Kid until six months prior to his death at twenty-one.

Billy's crime career began at fifteen, when he was jailed in Silver City, New Mexico, for petty theft. He broke out of jail and fled to Arizona, where, on August 17, 1877, he shot and killed one "Windy" Cahill, who had threatened and bullied him in a saloon brawl. On the run again, Billy returned to New Mexico, where he settled in Lincoln County, in the thinly populated southeastern corner of the territory. Billy, now calling himself Billy Bonney, became embroiled in the Lincoln County War of 1878–79, an extraordinarily violent conflict between rivals for commercial monopoly and federal contracts to supply the local fort and Indian reservation with beef. Billy went to work for rancher John Tunstall and became a vigilante, one of Tunstall's so-called Regulators. Billy demonstrated shooting skill and utter fearlessness in a series of gunfights with the rival forces of Lawrence G. Murphy and J. J. Dolan. He led an ambush that resulted in the deaths of the Lincoln County sheriff and his deputy on April 1, 1878, after the Murphy-Dolan faction had killed Billy's employer, Tunstall. In a final four-day gun battle during July 1878, Billy and others were cornered in the house of Tunstall's partner Alexander A. McSween in the hamlet of Lincoln. On the nineteenth, the house was set ablaze, and Billy led a desperate breakout.

Billy was arrested for the April 1 murder of Sheriff William Brady, but in March 1879, he made a deal with territorial governor Lew Wallace. In return for testimony against other Regulators, the governor agreed to drop the charges against Billy. Billy complied, but then began to doubt Governor Wallace's sincerity. He ran and, setting up at old Fort Sumner on the Pecos River east of Lincoln, he embarked on a brief career as a cattle rustler. Wallace responded by putting a price on Billy's head, and, in December 1880, after a shootout at Stinking Springs, lawmen led by Lincoln County's new sheriff, Pat Garrett, captured him. Tried and convicted of murder, Billy was sentenced to hang.

He was held under guard in the Murphy-Dolan store, which had been converted into the Lincoln County Courthouse. On April 28, 1881, he overpowered and killed his guard, fatally wounded another deputy, and fled Lincoln. It was at this point that territorial newspapers branded him New Mexico's most notorious outlaw and called him "Billy the Kid."

Garrett and his men tracked Billy to old Fort Sumner, where, on the night of July 14, 1881, Garrett stumbled on Billy in the darkened bedroom of one of the old military quarters. (Legend has it that Billy had come to Fort Sumner to see his sweetheart, Celsa Gutiérrez and that his pres-

ence was betrayed to Garrett by Billy's friend Pete Maxwell.) Billy, startled, unable to see in the darkness, called out "*Quien es? Quien es?*" ("Who is it? Who is it?"), whereupon Garrett, equally startled, drew and fired twice. The first bullet was fatal; the second missed. Billy the Kid was buried the next day in the Fort Sumner cemetery.

Billy's short, violent life became so quickly enmeshed with legend and lore, most of it commercial in origin, that historical information concerning him is often difficult to discover and assess. The legends grew out of exaggerated local newspaper accounts while he was still alive, as well as stories in such national publications as the *Police Gazette* and dime novels. Then, because he was bitterly criticized for having shot a "defenseless" Billy in cold blood, Pat Garrett authorized the self-serving and defensive *The Authentic Life of Billy the Kid* (1882), most of it the work of ghostwriter Ash Upson and most of it fiction. More than any other literary source, *The Authentic Life* gave rise to the enduring legends of Billy the Kid. In his 1926 *The Saga of Billy the Kid*, Walter Noble Burns polished and elaborated the legend, painting Billy the Kid as a misunderstood antihero, which is the image that has dominated such popular film treatments of Billy as *Billy the Kid* (1930), *The Outlaw* (1943), *One-Eyed Jacks* (1961), and the two most challenging, introspective film interpretations of the legend, Arthur Penn's *The Left-Handed Gun* (1958) and Sam Peckinpah's *Pat Garrett and Billy the Kid* (1973). The Billy the Kid story has also been the subject of a 1938 ballet commissioned by dancer-choreographer MARTHA GRAHAM from composer AARON COPLAND.

In its most essential form, the legend of Billy the Kid is rich with heroic motifs and archetypes, including a mysterious birth (Indiana? New York City?), a Robin Hood–like advocacy of the oppressed, and death through betrayal. Indeed, the legend also includes an element of resurrection, in that some believe Billy to have been Ollie L. "Brushy Bill" Roberts, who escaped, lived in Mexico and the Southwest, performed in Wild West shows, and died, peacefully, in 1950 in Hico, Texas.

What is beyond dispute is that the legends have greatly inflated Billy's criminal career. "Credited" with twenty-one kills, he actually killed four men by his gun alone, though he was present at or participated in the killing of others. Beyond his activity as a Regulator, Billy was never more than a small-time cattle rustler and horse thief. He never robbed a bank, store, stagecoach, or train.

See also: CRIME AND CRIMINALS; GUN-FIGHTER, WESTERN.

SUGGESTED READING: Stephen Tatum, *Inventing Billy the Kid: Visions of the Outlaw in America, 1881–1981* (Albuquerque, N.M., 1982); Robert M. Utley, *Billy the Kid: A Short and Violent Life* (Lincoln, Nebr., 1989).

Birthdays. In all cultures that regularly mark the passage of time, birthdays are specially recognized. In America, birthdays are generally recognized by the presentation of gifts and greeting cards (often humorous) by friends and family. Often, the occasion is also marked by a party, especially to celebrate the birthdays of young children. A specially decorated birthday cake is served, topped with candles corresponding to the child's (or adult's) age. The honoree is to make an unspoken, secret wish, then blow the candles out. If he or she succeeds in extinguishing them in a single try, the wish will come true.

Certain birthdays mark special milestones. For Jewish boys, the thirteenth birthday is celebrated as the *bar mitzvah,* a transition into adulthood (in the eyes of the religion); less frequently, Jewish girls celebrate their thirteenth birthday as the *bat mitzvah,* a similar rite of passage. Many American girls enjoy a special Sweet Sixteen party on their sixteenth birthday, and for boys as well as girls, the twenty-first birthday may be marked with a special celebration because it generally denotes the legal transition from minority to majority. Among Native Americans, birthdays of boys and young men are often marked by trials of strength, intended to demonstrate the honoree's progress toward manhood.

Black Bart (Charles E. Boles) (1832–ca. 1917). Black Bart earned legendary notoriety as a California stagecoach robber who often left doggerel verse penned on foolscap paper in the empty strongboxes he had looted. Black Bart emerged as an almost fabulous figure, the archetypal jokester, who managed to endear himself even to his victims.

Charles E. Boles was born and raised in upper New York State and moved to Illinois with his wife just before the Civil War, in which he served as a sergeant in the 116th Illinois Volunteer Infantry. After the war, he moved to California to seek his fortune. After failing at a number of occupations, including prospector, he began robbing stagecoaches. At first, he used his loot to invest in a number of legitimate businesses, but soon found he could not resist the urge to rob stages.

Bart struck his first coach, a Wells Fargo stage, at Funk Hill, four miles outside of Copperopolis, California, on July 26, 1875. Boles/Black Bart wore a long white duster and, over his head, a flour sack with holes cut out for his eyes. The driver surrendered the strongbox to Boles, who disappeared on foot. The driver turned back, only to discover a half dozen guns leveled at him from outlaws crouching behind boulders. Soon he realized that the "outlaws" were dummies—with sticks for guns. This would emerge as classic Black Bart. He worked alone, usually pretending to have a large gang supporting him.

Black Bart robbed twenty-nine stages during the next four years. His robberies were always marked by the extreme courtesy he showed to passengers, especially women. He refused to take the travelers' jewelry and cash: "I don't want your money, only Wells Fargo boxes." Soon, his fame spread as a "gentleman bandit."

On August 3, 1877, he struck a coach on the Russian River. He took the strongbox, which was later recovered, empty, save for a note:

I've labored long and hard for bread,
For honor and for riches
But on my corns too long you've tred,
You fine-haired sons-of-bitches.

The note was signed "Black Bart, PO-8." The letters and number apparently signifying "poet" (po-eight).

A year later, on July 26, 1878, Bart held up another stage, leaving behind another note:

Here I lay me down to sleep
To wait the coming morrow,
Perhaps success, perhaps defeat
And everlasting sorrow.
Yet come what will, I'll try it once,
My conditions can't be worse,
And if there's money in that box,
'Tis money in my purse.

Black Bart never used a horse, but always made his getaway on foot, disappearing into the

The legendary western stagecoach robber Black Bart, in a photograph taken some time after his release from San Quentin in 1888.

wilderness. Although he used a shotgun in his robberies, he never fired it—and could not have, since he never loaded it (or so he told arresting officers later).

Black Bart's last robbery occurred on November 3, 1883. In the course of the robbery, he was wounded in the hand. The handkerchief he wrapped around the wound was later found with a San Francisco laundry mark on it, and by means of this clue, detectives traced Bart. Tried and convicted, he served four years of a six-year sentence at San Quentin Prison, and was released on January 21, 1888.

Hounded by journalists, he made himself so scarce that it was thought he had returned to crime. A Wells Fargo stage was robbed on November 14, 1888. The bandit left doggerel in the empty strongbox:

> So here I've stood while wind and rain
> Have set the trees a'sobbin'
> And risked my life for that damned stage
> That wasn't worth the robbin'.

Jim Hume, one of the detectives who had captured Black Bart declared this new verse a hoax and said with certainty that Black Bart had "retired." A rumor was widespread that Wells Fargo had pensioned off Boles/Black Bart to keep him from preying on their stages.

Black Bart was reported to have died about 1917, though Hume had heard that he had died in the high California mountains while hunting game. The public refused to believe this, and newspapers periodically piqued an apparently insatiable appetite for Black Bart lore by reporting sightings in hundreds of different locations along the Wells Fargo lines. The reports stopped after Wells Fargo discontinued stage operations.

See also: CRIME AND CRIMINALS.

SUGGESTED READING: Bill O'Neal, *Encyclopedia of Western Gunfighters* (Norman, Okla., 1979).

Black Elk (1863–1950).

Nicholas Black Elk was a Lakota Oglala (Sioux) holy man, probably born in Wyoming, and is best known to the public as the subject of a lyrical biography by Nebraska poet John G. Neihardt (1881–1973), *Black Elk Speaks* (1932). Through Neihardt's book, Black Elk provides moving insight into the vision-driven religious life of the Lakota in conflict with the encroachment of white missionaries, government officials, and others. *Black Elk Speaks* opened up a world of Lakota folkways

and religion to a large audience. Although published in 1932, the book found many new readers during the revival of general interest in Native American life during the 1960s.

As a youth, Black Elk shared the hard fate of his people, who were pursued by the U.S. Army in the wake of GEORGE ARMSTRONG CUSTER's demise at the Battle of the Little Bighorn. While resident on the reservation, Black Elk had a great vision that haunted him for the rest of his life because the interference of missionaries and other elements of white culture prevented his acting on the vision as Lakota tradition dictated. While Black Elk suppressed his vision, embracing white Christianity, he never entirely abandoned the traditional beliefs of his people.

From 1886 to 1889, Black Elk performed in William "Buffalo Bill" Cody's famed Wild West Show. While the troupe toured Europe, Black Elk separated from the group and traveled for a time through France and Italy. Returning to the Pine Ridge Reservation in 1889, he witnessed the GHOST DANCE movement, a last collective gasp of the expression of traditional culture and religious belief.

Black Elk converted to Roman Catholicism and was baptized as Nicholas in 1904. By 1907, he was a Catholic missionary among the Indians. Neihardt met Black Elk in 1930 on the Pine Ridge Reservation and interviewed him extensively. In company with Neihardt, Black Elk visited the Black Hills (Paha Sapa), sacred to the Lakota, and prayed to the Great Spirit (Wakantanka Tunkasila): "Hear me, not for myself, but for my people; I am old. Hear me that they may once more go back into the sacred hoop and find the good red road, the shielding tree!"

Largely because of Neihardt's book, Black Elk became revered as a spokesman for the old Lakota ways, and his prayer before the Black Hills inspired, in the 1960s and 1970s, a Native American movement not only to secure civil rights from the federal government, but to recover the Black Hills, as well as fading spiritual traditions and folkways.

SUGGESTED READING: Raymond J. DeMallie, ed., *The Sixth Grandfather: Black Elk's Teachings Given to John Neihardt* (Lincoln, Nebr., 1984); John G. Neihardt, *Black Elk Speaks* (New York, 1932; reprint ed., 1961); Michael E. Steltenkamp, *Black Elk: Holy Man of the Oglala* (Norman, Okla., 1993).

Black English. Also called *African-American Vernacular English* (AAVE) and, more recently, Ebonics, Black English consists of a distinctive set of vocabulary, pronunciations, syntax, and grammatical forms used by some African Americans. The subject of Black English is complex and, sometimes, politically charged. It is complex because Black English varies widely among African-American speakers and is greatly influenced by socioeconomic and regional factors. Moreover, Black English has many features in common with rural white southern speech, although it is also influenced by its origins in West African languages.

Finally, Black English has been widely imitated by white entertainers (and even by black entertainers) on film and television and in music; these imitations, in turn, have doubtless affected both the use and perception of Black English among the general population of speakers. Black English also periodically surfaces as a sensitive political issue. For example, some educators and others hold that it should be treated and respected as a distinct dialect, while others argue that the schools should regard it as "substandard" English and that it should be eradicated because it is associated with economic disadvantage. Proponents believe that Black English enriches students' sense of their cultural heritage, while opponents insist that it perpetuates negative cultural stereotypes that block educational and vocational progress.

To the casual listener, pronunciation is the most distinctive feature of Black English. For example, *r* is rarely pronounced after a vowel or is pronounced "uh"; *th* may be pronounced "d" ("dis" for "this"), "v" ("bruvuh" for "brother"), or "f" ("bafroom" for "bathroom"). Other pronunciation features are common to southern folk dialects, white or black. The same holds true for many features of syntax and grammar. However, Black English is unique in its suppression of final consonants and especially consonant combinations, so that, for example, "hold" becomes "ho." This characteristic is so pervasive that it affects inflection. Possessive endings are frequently dropped, so that "his father's friends" becomes "his father friend," and "she runs" becomes "she run."

Linguists have long been interested in the way Black English treats verbs, especially *be*. *Is* and *are* are routinely eliminated, as in "he goin' home." And while Black English eliminates some verb forms, it adds others: the so-called habitual *be:* "he be makin' the same mistake over and over"; the perfective *done:* "she done tol' me already"; the remote-time *been:* "he been finish the job"; the double modals: "I might could do that," "We may can get together, but might can't settle everything." While some of these forms may be found in white southern folk speech, they are most closely and consistently identified with Black English.

The Black English of urban America has had even greater impact on American popular culture, slang, and general vocabulary outside of the African-American community. Book-length glossaries and dictionaries have been written on the subject. Most familiar are such terms as *bad* (meaning good), *cat* (meaning person), *cool* (meaning agreeable, admirable, pleasant, etc.), *fly* (stylish, attractive), *fox* (a sexy young woman), and *phat* (excellent), just to name a few.

See also: AFRICAN AMERICANS; FOLK SPEECH; GULLAH.

SUGGESTED READING: James Haskins, *The Psychology of Black Language* (New York, 1993); Selikoko S. Mufwene et al, eds., *African-American English: Structure, History, and Use* (New York, 1998); James Percelay, *Snaps* (New York, 1994); Theresa Perry and Lisa Delpit, eds., *The Real Ebonics Debate: Power, Language, and the Education of African-American Children* (New York, 1998); Geneva Smitherman-Donaldson, *Black Talk: Words and Phrases from the Hood to the Amen Corner* (Boston, 1994); Geneva Smitherman-Donaldson, *Talkin and Testifyin: The Language of Black America* (Detroit, 1986).

"Black Legend." The "Black Legend" is a loosely defined body of folk beliefs that portray Spain as the brutal, collectively sadistic exploiter of the Indians in the New World. The Black Legend found its first expression in *The Destruction of the Indies,* a book by Padre Bartolmé de Las Casas, a Spaniard, the first priest ordained in the New World, and a passionate critic of Spain's colonial policies. Las Casas's eyewitness accounts of Spanish cruelty toward the Indians were eagerly embraced by Spain's chief rival in the New World, the English, and were elaborated and diffused into a general dislike and distrust of the Spanish in the Americas.

The Black Legend survived the colonial centuries to inform and influence political and cultural relations between Anglos and Hispanics in the United States, especially in the Southwest. It was the Black Legend that deeply colored the Texas revolution of 1835–36 as a struggle between cruel, despotic, mongrel (mixed Spanish and Indian) barbarians, the Mexicans, and pure Anglo civilization, the Texans. (This ignored the reality that a significant number of the Texas revolutionaries were Hispanics.) The Black Legend played a motivating role in the Mexican War of 1846–48 as well, providing (for many Americans) ample moral justification for appropriating New Mexico, Arizona, and California to the United States.

Toward the middle of the nineteenth century, certain popular literary portrayals of the Spanish in America began to soften the Black Legend. WASHINGTON IRVING, Hubert Howe Bancroft, BRET HARTE and others cast Mexicans and other Hispanics in a more sentimental and romantic light. As the railroads pushed westward and tourism became a significant industry in the Southwest, the Black Legend receded further into the past.

SUGGESTED READING: Patrick H. Butler, III, "Black Legend," Charles Phillips and Alan Axelrod, eds., *Encyclopedia of the American West* vol. 1, (New York, 1996); Philip Wayne Powell, *Tree of Hate: Propaganda and Prejudice Affecting United States Relations with the Hispanic World* (New York, 1971).

Blacksmiths. Blacksmiths are artisans skilled in shaping iron and steel by heating them in a forge and pounding them into various shapes with a hammer and anvil and a variety of ancillary tools. The vocation of smith is ancient, reaching back before recorded history. In pre-twentieth-century America, as in most of the world, the blacksmith's craft was of central importance. Not only did he shoe horses, he created a wide variety of household and ornamental articles, repaired iron objects of all kinds, created and repaired agricultural implements, and cre-

A blacksmith shapes the clapper of a large bell. The photograph was taken in the late 1920s.

ated and maintained many of the tools other craftsmen used in their trades. The great importance of the blacksmith to preindustrial civilization is attested to by the fact that Smith is the most common of English names.

The work and level of skill among blacksmiths varied widely. Some were folk artists capable of creating tools and ornamental work, such as wrought-iron fences, of great beauty. Others did little more than shoe horses and perform simple repairs. Some blacksmiths, especially in remote rural areas, were generalists, creating or repairing whatever customers required. Others specialized. The farrier fitted horseshoes, the wheelwright built wagon wheels and fitted iron tires to them;

the wainwright or wagonwright built wagon bodies, fitted with iron parts. Toolmakers specialized in the creation and maintenance of tools for other tradesmen. Ornamental ironworkers designed and fabricated wrought-iron work. With the introduction of the automobile and the ascendency of mass-production manufacturing early in the twentieth century, the role of the general blacksmith shrank rapidly. Today, general blacksmiths are seen almost exclusively in outdoor folklife museums. Work is still being commissioned from ornamental ironworkers, however, since hand-wrought decorative grilles and gates are still desired.

See also: SIMMONS, PHILIP.

SUGGESTED READING: Frederick William Robins, *The Smith: The Traditions and Lore of an Ancient Craft* (London and New York, 1953); Alexander G. Weygers, *The Modern Blacksmith* (Princeton, N.J., 1974).

Blue Book, Project. The best known and most widely criticized of official U.S. Air Force UFO investigation programs, Project Blue Book was established on the crest of a wave of UFO sightings that swept the United States (and, indeed, the world) during the late 1940s and early 1950s. Project Blue Book was the successor to three earlier programs, Project Sign, Project Grudge, and Project Twinkle (an operation under the aegis of Project Grudge). Through the years, from its origin in Project Sign in 1947, until it was officially shut down in 1969, Project Blue Book was the subject of much UFO FOLKLORE and the source of much CONSPIRACY LORE. Believers in UFOs saw it as the nucleus of a government effort to cover up information about UFOs and even visitation and contact by extraterrestrials.

SUGGESTED READING: Jerome Clark, *The Emergence of a Phenomenon: UFOs from the Beginning through 1959* (Detroit, 1992); John Spencer, *The UFO Encyclopedia* (New York, 1991); Gordon Stein, ed., *The Encyclopedia of the Paranormal* (New York, 1996).

Bluegrass. Although BILL MONROE's Blue Grass Boys had been a featured act on the GRAND OLE OPRY from 1939, the group's name referred to the vegetation of Monroe's native Kentucky rather than to any particular musical style. It was not until two more stars who rivaled Monroe's brilliance, guitarist-singer Lester Flatt (in 1944) and virtuoso five-string BANJO picker EARL SCRUGGS (in 1945) joined the ensemble that Monroe's group began to evolve from old-time string band to bluegrass. The bluegrass they played was, like JAZZ, collectively improvised, centering on brilliantly and unbelievably fast syncopated solo performances by Monroe on MANDOLIN, Scruggs on banjo, Robert "Chubby" Wise on FIDDLE, backup by Flatt on GUITAR, and Cedric Rainwater (Howard Watts) on stand-up string bass. The modern bluegrass style crystallized between 1945 and 1948. On September 16, 1946, Columbia Records produced recordings that typified the modern style: Lester Flatt's composition "Will You Be Loving Another Man," in which Flatt sang lead, and "Blue Yodel No. 4," one of JIMMIE RODGERS's hits. Audiences, however, had heard the new sound earlier on WSM radio broadcasts and the tent-show tours Monroe produced. On some of their appearances, the band challenged their host communities to sandlot baseball games, events that helped publicize the nighttime concerts and also provided welcome diversion from the grueling tour schedule.

From 1945 to 1948, the banjo became more important in Monroe's band than it had been in any previous ensemble. (Traditionally, the instrument was associated with comic acts.) The bluegrass sound did not become widespread until other country bands started copying its instrumental and vocal traits. The first recording copying Monroe's style was the Stanley Brothers recording of "Molly and Tenbrooks" (1948), a BALLAD about a famous Kentucky horse race. While the Stanleys had heard Bill Monroe sing it in a live show, their recording preceded Monroe's by a year.

Flatt and Scruggs, weary of the exhausting road schedule, left Monroe's group, much to his annoyance, and later formed their own band, the Foggy Mountain Boys, named after a CARTER FAMILY song.

An endless stream of musicians passed through the Monroe group and went on to form their own bands, many of which recorded songs Monroe had drawn from his own family tradition. Often, these groups developed carbon copies of Blue Grass Boys performances.

See also: COUNTRY MUSIC; FOLK MUSIC; GOSPEL MUSIC; HAYS, WILL; HUNTING; MARTIN GUITAR COMPANY; ROUNDER RECORDS; SCOTTISH AMERICANS.

SUGGESTED READING: Robert Cantwell, *Bluegrass Breakdown: the Making of the Old Southern Sound* (New York, 1992); Neil V. Rosenberg, *Bluegrass: A History* (Urbana, Ill., 1993).

Blues. The blues is probably rooted in songs of lament during the days of slavery. Aged African Americans in New Orleans, some born in the 1860s, have attested, "The blues was here when I come." Little is known of the sad secular songs the slaves no doubt performed; no one wrote them down, except for a few fragments, and many slave owners discouraged mournful singing, since it might impair efficiency. Frances Kemble, who lived on a Georgia plantation from 1838 to 1839 wrote:

> I have heard that many of the masters and overseers prohibit melancholy tunes or words, and encourage nothing but cheerful music and senseless words, deprecating the effect of sadder strains upon the slaves, whose peculiar musical sensibility might be expected to make them excitable by any songs of a plaintive character and having reference to their particular hardships.

No doubt musical expressions of despair often resounded in the slave cabins out of earshot of the owners and overseers.

It is generally agreed that the principal ancestor of contemporary blues is the field HOLLER, which John W. Work has described as a "fragmentary bit of a yodel, half sung, half yelled":

> Approaching his house or that of his sweetheart in the evening, or sometimes out of sheer loneliness, a man would emit his holler. Listeners would say, "Here comes Sam" or "Will Jackson's coming" or "I just heard Archie down the road. . . ."

> In these hollers, the idiomatic material found in the blues is readily heard: the excessive portamento, the slow time, the preference for the flatted third, the melancholy type of tune. . . . Many . . . could serve as lines of blues.

The early blues drew on WORK SONGS as well as hollers. Robert Pete Williams's "Levee Camp Blues" is a significant example of how elements of hollers and work songs often combine to form blues. One of the stanzas runs:

> Oh, Captain, Captain, you better count yo'
>   men;
> Oh, Captain, you better count yo' men;
> Oh, some gone to the bushes [escaped], oh
>   Lord, an' some gone in.

Each verse begins with a long, drawn-out cry, which suggests the influence of the holler. There are frequent slurs, and usually at the ends of lines the last note tapers off downward into monotonal grunts—survivals of African style. The accompaniment consists of basically one chord. The ideas expressed and their sequence tend to follow the natural rambling pattern of the flow of thought and are characteristic of both work songs and blues.

Another form that originated early in the history of blues is the talking blues. In a nonliterate society, there is much less separation between speaking and singing than in a society more dependent on the written word. In all probability, then, a nineteenth-century slave field hand relaxing in his hut in the evening, plunking moodily on a banjo or thumping a rhythm on a drum or a barrel, would let his voice wander, sometimes speaking semirhythmically, sometimes slipping into a few lines of songs moving freely and naturally from one to the other with scarcely a perceptible break—as does Smoky Babe (Robert Brown) in his improvised "Workin' Blues," recorded in Scotlandville, Louisiana, in 1961 and here quoted in part:

> Spoken: Well, I always get up every mornin'
>   'tween five an', oh, six o'clock,
> Boy, I'm tellin' you it's a mess,
> You know it's a mess, oh, you know it's a
>   mess,
> Well, if you ain't got yo' wife aroun', you
>   ain't got no woman,
> She ain't at home, I'm tellin' you true, yo'
>   bed ain't made up.

Yo' floor ain't swept, an' everythin', I'm
* tellin' you true,*
It's rough, peoples, it's rough.
I gotta go out there an' feed my ole hogs,
An' fool aroun' ole cow an' everythin' . . .
You know out in the field, mean ole boss an'
* everythin' in the mornin' time,*
You know how you feel that mornin', don't
* wanna get up,*
But you gotta get up. . . .
I'm talkin' about how I got to go out here to
* work for my boss a while,*
To get some money for Saturday night you
* know,*
Have a good time then, hm . . .

Sung: Well, I'm gonna find my little woman,
* she lovin' somebody else.*
You know how you gonna find her?
Yeah, how she done left you all alone, see,
She done quit you done gone to another
* house.*
'Cause you ain't got nothin' but the cotton
* pickin' blues . . .*

The language and phrases in this example are not standardized. There are no tightly epigrammatic verses like those in "A Thousand Miles from Nowhere," a modern blues song on a similar theme:

I woke up early in the mornin', feelin' I'm
* 'bout to go out of my min', [repeat]*
I got to find me some kinda companion, if
* she dumb, deaf, crippled or blin'*

Smoky Babe's song is loose in construction. Although the guitar accompaniment maintains a precise beat, the poetic form of the text takes shape mainly from the natural conversational flow of his reactions. Before there was a large storehouse of traditional verses for singers to draw on for their improvisations, many of the early blues were essentially like Smoky Babe's "Workin' Blues."

By late in the nineteenth century, folk blacks were singing phrases essentially similar to those found in country blues of today. Although the following are taken from songs collected between 1905 and 1908, they were probably well known by folk blacks many years before:

Went to the sea, sea look so wide,
Thought about my babe, hung my head an'
* cried.*
O, my babe, won't you come home.

I got the blues, but too damn mean to cry,
Oh, I got the blues, but I'm too damn mean
* to cry.*

Got nowhar' to lay my weary head,
Oh my babe, got nowhar' to lay my weary
* head.*

I'm a po' boy, long way from home,
Oh, I'm a po' boy, long way from home.

Phonograph records began to play a vital role in the creation and dissemination of blues during the 1920s. On August 10, 1920, Mamie Smith, "contralto with Rega orchestra," cut Perry Bradford's "Crazy Blues" (Okeh Records 4169), a song with a chorus based on a twelve-bar structure, the first recording of a singer using a blues form. Although "Crazy Blues" was on the fringe of folk blues—described by Paul Oliver, in *Blues Fell This Morning*, as "half-vaudeville performances, which marked a late stage in the development of blues from simple folk music to a form of sophisticated entertainment"—the early sales of about 7,500 blues discs a week suggested that African Americans were eager to hear their own music on records. At the same time that blues recordings helped create a wider demand for the music, they also influenced the style of folk performers. Thus a basic pattern in blues development was established, in which the oral informant of a traditional society was often replaced by a disc, which exposed the listener to the style and repertoire of singers not in his immediate circle. The cycle of development then ran from folksinger to professional performer to record and back to folksinger. Both professional and nonprofessional performers built up a large reservoir of blues phrases and verses, which they would draw on, often by free association.

While in the earliest days of recording, the emphasis was on young women singing city blues, the record companies quickly discovered that there was also a considerable market for country blues singers. At first they brought the performers north to the studios; later, they took mobile units south. In July 1924, Paramount Records issued Papa Charlie Jackson singing the "Lawdy, Lawdy Blues," and in April 1926 Paramount advertised its first release by BLIND LEMON JEFFERSON, "Booster Blues" and "Dry Southern Blues": "Here's a real old-fashioned blues-singer—Blind Lemon Jefferson from Dallas.... With his singing he plays the guitar in real southern style." Lemon was indeed a genuine folk performer, and he had an enormous impact on African-American country blues artists. The great popularity of his records helped to harden the blues into a classic mold. Although he himself did not always consistently follow a twelve-bar form, Lemon did make use of a three-line form, which consisted of a verbal line, followed by an antiphonal guitar line form, which consisted of a repetition of the verbal line, followed by a response from the instrument, then a concluding verbal line—all of lengths varying freely from stanza to stanza.

The form Lemon used freely, amateurs and professionals began to use rigidly, until thousands of recorded and folk blues had essentially a standard structure and even similar GUITAR breaks. Also, when singers performed with several accompanying instruments, relatively standardized patterns of rhythm and harmony became necessary. Nevertheless, there continues to be a significant number of creative improvising blues poets and instrumentalists.

Although many blues songs express unrelieved gloom, a large number of songs are ultimately optimistic. While the texts may be mournful and bursts of moody feeling sound in the accompaniment, in the words of Richard Wright, blues songs "are not intrinsically pessimistic; their burden of woe and melancholy is dialectically redeemed through sheer force of sensuality into an almost exultant affirmation of life, of love, of sex, of movement, of hope."

See also: AFRICAN AMERICANS; ARHOOLIE RECORDS; BLUES BALLAD; BOLDEN, (CHARLES) BUDDY; CRIME AND CRIMINALS; DORSEY, THOMAS A.; FIDDLE; FOLK MUSIC; FOLK REVIVAL; FULLER, BLIND BOY; GIBSON MANDOLIN AND GUITAR MANUFACTURING COMPANY, LTD., THE; GOSPEL MUSIC; HARMONICA; HOOKER, JOHN LEE; HOPKINS, LIGHTNIN; HOUSE, SON (EDDIE); HURT, MISSISSIPPI JOHN; JACKSON, MAHALIA; JAZZ; JOHNSON, ROBERT; KING, B. B.; LEDBETTER, HUDDIE (LEADBELLY); LOMAX, ALAN; MASS MEDIA; McCOY, MINNIE ("MEMPHIS MINNIE"); MONROE, BILL; MUDDY WATERS; PATTON, CHARLEY; POPULAR CULTURE; RAINEY, MA; RODGERS, JIMMIE; ROUNDER RECORDS.

SUGGESTED READING: Alan Lomax, *The Land Where the Blues Began* (New York, 1994); Giles Oakley, *The Devil's Music: A History of the Blues* (New York, 1997); Paul Oliver and Richard Wright, *Blues Fell This Morning: Meaning in the Blues* (New York, 1994); Robert Palmer, *Deep Blues* (New York, 1995); John Wesley Work, *Folk Song of the American Negro* (Westport, Conn., reprint ed., 1974).

Blues ballad. Along with the BROADSIDE, the CHILD BALLAD, and the PARLOR BALLAD, the blues ballad is one the four types of Anglo-American BALLADS folklorists recognize. In contrast to the broadside and Child ballad, the blues ballad is not rooted in English and Scottish traditions, but is wholly American or, more correctly, African American. Blues ballad subjects are usually actual events with specific characters, but emotion and feeling take precedence over narrative, and the blues ballad tends to be highly selective and elliptical rather than richly narrative. It presents individual scenes rather than unfolding events. Like the Child ballad, the blues ballad makes generous use of repetition, formula, and formulaic imagery. To a degree greater than in any of the other ballad genres, the quality of the singer's voice, interpretation, emotion, and musicianship is of single importance. Often the performer is also an accomplished instrumentalist—typically on the GUITAR—and many blues ballads are performed with extended instrumental breaks between groups of stanzas.

See also: BLUES; FOLK MUSIC; FRANKIE AND JOHNNIE; McTELL, BLIND WILLIE.

SUGGESTED READING: David Evans, *Big Road Blues: Traditions and Creativity in the Folk Blues* (Berkeley, Calif., 1982); Alan Lomax, *The Land Where the Blues Began* (New York, 1993); Harry Oster, *Living Country Blues* (Detroit, 1969).

"Blue-Tail Fly." Composed about 1840 by DANIEL DECATUR EMMETT, "Blue-Tail Fly" was among the most popular of MINSTREL SHOW songs. It is likely that Emmett borrowed some aspect of the lyrics (which begin "Jimmie crack corn, and I don't care") and tune from an authentic slave song. The jaunty tune belies the dark irony of the lyrics, an expression of a slave's satisfaction at the death of his master.

See also: FOLK MUSIC.

Boas, Franz (1858–1942). Anthropologist and folklorist Franz Boas was an advocate of cultural relativism in anthropology. He taught generations of anthropologists and students of folklife to study a culture on its own terms, relative to the values it posits, and he insisted on the sovereign value of firsthand fieldwork and publication in the language native to the culture under study.

Born on July 9, 1858, in Minden, Westphalia, Prussia, Boas taught at Columbia University (New York City) from 1899 until 1942, creating the nation's leading department of anthropology. Boas himself specialized in North American Indian cultures and languages, but taught generations of anthropologists and folklorists who, in turn, laid the foundations of their areas of special interest. His best-known students include RUTH BENEDICT, Margaret Mead, and MELVILLE HERSKOVITS, among many others.

From early childhood, Boas was fascinated by the natural sciences, but while attending the gymnasium in Minden, he became interested in the history of culture. A polymath, he studied at the universities of Heidelberg, Bonn, and Kiel, taking a Ph.D. in physics and in geography at Kiel in 1881. After serving for a year in the army, Boas continued his studies in Berlin and embarked on a year-long scientific expedition to Baffin Island during 1883–84. This confirmed for him a career as an anthropologist, and he accepted a post in an ethnological museum in Berlin and on the geography faculty at the University of Berlin.

In 1886, returning from fieldwork among the Kwakiutl and other tribes of British Columbia,

Boas stopped in New York City and, deciding to stay, found work as an editor for *Science* magazine. In 1889, he was hired by the new and experimentally oriented Clark University in Worcester, Massachusetts, and later worked in Chicago, preparing anthropological exhibitions for the 1893 Columbian Exposition. He also served on the staff of the Field Museum of Natural History.

In 1896, Boas was named lecturer in physical anthropology and in 1899 professor of anthropology at Columbia University. From 1896 to 1905, he also served as curator of anthropology at the American Museum of Natural History in New York. For the museum, he directed the work of the Jesup North Pacific Expedition, which investigated relationships between the aboriginal peoples of Siberia and of North America.

Boas worked broadly in statistical physical anthropology, descriptive and theoretical linguistics, and American Indian ethnology, including the study of Native American folklore and art. Not only were his achievements as an original researcher extraordinary, his contribution as a teacher shaped the fields of anthropology and folklore. Boas founded the *International Journal of American Linguistics,* was a founder of the American Anthropological Association, and served in 1931 as president of the American Association for the Advancement of Science.

Among Boas's many books, *The Mind of Primitive Man* (1911) was accorded the honor of being burned by the Nazis in the 1930s. Boas's *Primitive Art* (1927) and *Race, Language and Culture* (1940) were also highly influential.

See also: AMERICAN FOLKLORE SOCIETY; HERZOG, GEORGE; HURSTON, ZORA NEALE; NEWELL, WILLIAM WELLS; PARSONS, ELSIE CLEWS.

SUGGESTED READING: Walter Goldschmidt, ed., *The Anthropology of Franz Boas* (Menasha, Wis., 1954).

Boasting. Boasting—extreme exaggeration—is often an element of American folklore, and is an especially important component of the TALL TALE. (Boasting is not synonymous with the tall tale, however, because it is not narrative.) Frequently, it is associated with frontier folklore and frontier humor, and especially with RINGTAILED ROARERS. In folk speech, boasting is not merely bragging, but the expression of elaborately outrageous hyperbole, usually concerning physical strength, endurance, and appetite and often focusing on such skills as marksmanship. Boasting is also associated with the folklore of a number of hypermasculine occupations, including those of the logger, the cowboy, the oil-field roughneck, and so on.

See also: SOUNDING.

SUGGESTED READING: Walter Blair, *Native American Humor, 1800–1900* (New York, 1937).

Boatright, Mody Coggin (1896–1970). This Texas folklorist took all of his academic degrees in Texas—B.A. from West Texas State Teachers College, M.A. and Ph.D. from the University of Texas—and taught English in Texas institutions, including West Texas State Teachers College, Sul Ross State Teachers College, and the University of Texas. He was secretary-editor of the Texas Folklore Society (1943–64) and was a Fellow of the American Folklore Society and of the Texas Folklore Society.

Boatright published the fruits of his Texas folklore research in *Tall Tales from Texas Cow Camps* (1934), *Folk Laughter on the American Frontier* (1949), *Folklore of the Oil Industry* (1963), *Gib Morgan: Minstrel of the Oil Fields* (1945), and *Tales from the Derrick Floor* (with William A. Owens, 1970). Boatright also wrote an analytical work, *The Family Saga* (1958), the first study of this narrative genre.

See also: PECOS BILL.

SUGGESTED READING: Ernest B. Speck, ed., *Mody Boatright, Folklorist: A Collection of Essays* (Austin, Tex., 1973).

American as well as Native American tradition. In many tribes, children are cautioned not to misbehave lest they be captured by the bogey. The word *bogey* is probably derived from *bugge,* a Middle English word meaning terror (as in "bugbear").

See also: FAIRIES; MILITARY FOLKLORE.

Boats, vernacular. Vernacular boats are built according to local traditions. The folk boatbuilder learns his craft through an informal apprenticeship with local boatbuilders, sometimes supplemented by more formal apprenticeship with professional shipwrights. American vernacular boat types are very numerous and range from craft produced by Native Americans (such as Alaskan skin boats and Indian bark canoes), to commercial fishing vessels (for example, the fish tug that sails Lake Michigan and the familiar lobster boat of coastal Maine), to recreational boats (jon boats, stumpjumpers, and the like). All of the craft are relatively small.

While the economic imperative to vernacular boatbuilding has diminished in the twentieth century, there is still much interest in the art and craft of wooden boats.

Bogey, bogeyman. This monster, generally called bogey in England and bogeyman in North America, is traditionally used by parents to frighten children into obedience and good behavior. The bogeyman is a shadowy figure, usually described as black and male, but not otherwise delineated. Leagued with evil and, perhaps, the devil, he is a creature of the night, who is powerless in daytime. The bogeyman figures in Euro-

Boggs, Ralph Steele (1901–1994). Boggs specialized in Latin American folklore and folkloristics. A native of Terre Haute, Indiana, he studied folklore with ARCHER TAYLOR at the University of Chicago, from which he earned a doctorate in Spanish (1930) with a dissertation on the folktales of Spain (published later in 1930 in *Folklore Fellows Communications*).

Appointed to the faculty of the University of North Carolina in 1929, he introduced the university's first folklore course. During the thirties, he worked with faculty members in diverse disciplines, all of whom were united by a common interest in folklore, to create the first graduate folklore curriculum in an American university. His collaborators included the sociologist GUY BENTON JOHNSON, professor of English ARTHUR PALMER HUDSON, drama scholar Frederick Koch, language professor Urban Tigner Holmes, musicologist Jan P. Schinhan, and professor of German Richard Jente.

Boggs left North Carolina in 1950 to teach at the University of Miami. There he worked within a network of Latin American folklorists and became director of the Hispanic American Institute, which grew into the university's International Center.

Boggs was a prodigiously prolific editor and author. He founded two important journals, *Folklore Americas* and *North Carolina Folklore,* and wrote some 150 books and articles on folklore and Spanish literature. For *Southern Folk-lore Quarterly,* he compiled its bibliography of folklore publications annually, from 1937 to 1959.

Boggs's voluminous correspondence with folklorists in the United States and Latin America is on deposit at the University of North Carolina library.

SUGGESTED READING: Beverly Patterson, entry on Boggs in Jan Harold Brunvand, ed., *American Folklore: An Encyclopedia* (New York, 1996).

Bolden, (Charles) Buddy (1877–1931).

Often called the father of JAZZ, Buddy Bolden was a New Orleans musician who was certainly among the very first to synthesize RAGTIME and BLUES into what would ultimately be called jazz. Born Charles Bolden in New Orleans to a drayman who died six years later, Bolden showed early musical talent and was playing cornet professionally at age seventeen. By the turn of the century, he was leading his own band in New Orleans, playing dance clubs, parties, and parades. He was locally famed for his ability to improvise and by 1906 was being called the "king of New Orleans jazz." By this time, too, Bolden and his band began traveling outside of New Orleans, although he never achieved a national reputation during his lifetime. In and about New Orleans, however, Bolden became something of a legend in his own time. His "way with women" seemed almost supernatural (it was believed that his romantic powers were hypnotic), and his capacity for drink was almost equally celebrated.

In the spring of 1906, Bolden began suffering from severe headaches accompanied by psychotic delusions. Seized by what was described as a fit, he attacked his mother and was arrested. He was soon released and resumed performing; however, Bolden was never the same. He quickly retreated into depression, which alternated with fits of rage. In September 1906, he was again arrested. Released, his condition deteriorated, and he was committed to the Insane Asylum of Louisiana. There he spent the remainder of his life. His condition was attributed to alcoholism.

Certainly, Bolden can lay some historical claim as one of the originators of jazz. His life and legend also partake of the same stream of folklore and legend that has produced stories of the poet, musician, or artist cursed by his own extraordinary creativity or even of the musician who sells his soul to the devil in exchange for phenomenal powers of virtuosity. Bolden seemed to set the tragic pattern that all too many short-lived jazz and, later, rock musicians would follow. One popular legend holds that Bolden once blew his cornet so hard that the tuning slide shot out twenty feet. He could achieve such volume, it was said, that his cornet could be heard across the Mississippi in Gretna, Louisiana.

SUGGESTED READING: Donald M. Marquis, *In Search of Buddy Bolden: First Man of Jazz* (Baton Rouge, La., 1993).

Boone, Daniel (1734–1820).

Boone was the quintessential American frontiersman, pioneer, and trailblazer, who was instrumental in opening the territory west of the Appalachians to white settlement. As early as 1784, when his purported autobiography was published in JOHN FILSON's *The Discovery, Settlement, and Present State of Kentucke,* Boone had already entered into American folklore. He had become, quite literally, a legend in his own time.

Unlike many heroes of legendary stature, the

Daniel Boone in a portrait by Chester Harding.

historical Boone did, indeed, perform prodigious deeds. He led the expedition that blazed an emigrant trail through the Cumberland Gap, near the juncture of Virginia, Tennessee, and Kentucky, and he defended the early Kentucky settlement of Boonesborough against Indian attack and throughout the American Revolution. In the process, Boone created the mold from which presidential candidates such as ABRAHAM LINCOLN and fictional characters ranging from JAMES FENIMORE COOPER's Natty Bumppo to any number of movie serial and television heroes would be struck. As an archetypal frontier hero, Boone's essential function was to make the wilderness hospitable to civilization. Perhaps ironically, then, Boone himself was little civilized, lacking in formal schooling and barely able to read and write. He was born in Berks County, Pennsylvania, but soon moved with his parents and siblings to the North Carolina frontier. All of his life, Boone would push steadily westward, in search of new land, supporting himself by hunting and trapping.

Boone first went to Kentucky in 1767, then spent from 1769 to 1771 hunting and trapping there alone. In 1773, he led his family and others into Kentucky, but their party was set upon by Cherokees, who killed his son James and another young man. Boone and his followers turned back, but Boone returned to blaze a trail through the Cumberland Gap in 1775. Planning to establish Kentucky as the fourteenth British colony in America, Boone and his companions built the Wilderness Road, which served as the principal route to what was then known as the West. Later in the year, Boone brought his wife Rebecca and their daughter to the new settlement of Boonesborough, Kentucky.

Like so many of Boone's plans, the scheme to establish Kentucky as a new colony failed, and the entire region became a frontier county of Virginia. Boone was made a captain of militia and led the defense of Boonesborough against the Indians. Captured by Indians in 1778, he was adopted by the Shawnee chief, Blackfish. Tribal adoption was not uncommon and was, in fact, a frequent feature of CAPTIVITY NARRATIVES during the eighteenth and early nineteenth centuries. In the case of Boone, tribal adoption set a pattern that fiction writers emulated in creating frontier heroes. Boone remained with the Indians for five months before escaping to warn Boonesborough settlers of an impending attack by British and British-allied Indians. Under Boone's leadership, the settlement withstood a ten-day siege in September 1778.

Like Cooper's Natty Bumppo, Boone did not prosper or profit by the civilization he helped bring into the wilderness. His many land claims could never be legally validated and, ultimately, came to naught. After the Revolution, Boone found work as a surveyor along the Ohio River, then settled for a time in what is now West Virginia, and finally, in 1799, followed his son Daniel Morgan Boone to Missouri—at the time in Louisiana Territory—where he once again took up hunting and trapping. His claim to 850 acres of Missouri land was invalidated after the Louisiana Purchase, but an act of Congress restored the land to Boone in recognition of his efforts in opening the West. Nevertheless, by this time, Boone was so deeply in debt that he had to sell the land, and he continued to hunt and trap until the end of his days.

See also: CULTURE HERO; DISNEY, WALT; GRAFFITI.

SUGGESTED READING: John Bakeless, *Daniel Boone* (New York, 1939); John Mack Faragher, *Daniel Boone: The Life and Legend of an American Pioneer* (New York, 1992).

Borden, Lizzie (1860–1927).

The sensational trial of Lizzie Andrew Borden in Fall River, Massachusetts, for the August 4, 1892, ax murder of her father and stepmother was nationally reported. Acquitted by a jury, Lizzie Borden never succeeded in clearing her name with the public, and the gruesome BALLAD "Lizzie Borden," usually sung to the tune of "Ta-ra-ra-boom-de-ay," became extremely popular, especially among children, not only during the balance of Borden's lifetime, but well beyond. The song expressed public sentiment concerning Borden's guilt: "Lizzie Borden took an ax / And gave her mother forty whacks; / When she saw what she had done, / She gave her father forty-one."

In 1948, choreographer AGNES DE MILLE staged *Fall River Legend,* a ballet based on the Lizzie Borden case, with a score by Morton Gould (1913–1996).

See also: CRIME AND CRIMINALS.

Botkin, Benjamin A. (1901–1975).

A pioneering student of oral folklore, Botkin coined the pervasive term FOLK-SAY in 1928 "to designate unwritten history and literature in particular and oral, linguistic, and floating material in general." Thus the material he studied, collected, and anthologized was folk-say.

Botkin was educated at Harvard and Columbia, and took his Ph.D. at the University of Nebraska in 1931. He was founder and editor of *Folk-Say,* a regional annual anthology of oral material. Four issues appeared, between 1929 and 1932.

Botkin received a Julius Rosenwald Fellowship in 1937 to study southern folk and regional literature in the Library of Congress. He went on to serve as national folklore editor of the Depression-era Federal Writers' Project and to help found the Joint Committee on Folk Arts of the Work Projects Administration (WPA). In addition to serving as chairman of the Joint Committee, Botkin was editor in chief of the Writers' Unit of the Library of Congress Project.

Botkin was named a Library of Congress Fellow in Folklore in 1941 (and remained an Honorary Fellow from 1942 to 1956). The following year, he became head of the library's Archive of Folk Song, resigning in 1945 to move to New York City as a full-time writer. He began to concentrate on urban folklore at this time.

Botkin's important, influential, and popular books include *The American Play-Party Song* (1937), a study of game songs on the frontier, and *Lay My Burden Down: A Folk History of Slavery* (1945), which was developed from WPA-sponsored interviews with ex-slaves. This book is regarded as one of the seminal examples of oral history documentation and technique.

Botkin also published annotated collections of regional and occupational folklore, based on oral as well as printed and archival sources. The most influential of these is *A Treasury of American Folklore* (1944).

See also: AFRICAN AMERICANS; KORSON, RAE ROSENBLATT; YARN.

SUGGESTED READING: Jerrold Hirsch, "Folklore in the Making: B. A. Botkin," *Journal of American Folklore* 100 (1987), pp. 3–38; Bruce Jackson, "Benjamin A. Botkin, 1901–1975," *Journal of American Folklore* 89 (1976), pp. 1–6.

Bottle trees. Once a common sight in the rural Southeast, bottle trees were made by stripping the leaves from a tree (typically cedar), then slipping bottles over the ends of upward-pointing branches. The practice was a feature of an African-American folk belief that spirits would enter the bottles and become trapped. They could be heard moaning when wind shook the tree. Sometimes paint was poured into the bottles before they were hung, presumably to help attract and trap spirits. It is believed that the tradition of the bottle tree is rooted in African totemism.

Bowery "b'hoy." This popular personification of the urban American street tough, from New York City's colorful Bowery district in lower Manhattan, was the creation of actor Francis Chanfrau and playwright Benjamin A. Baker. Baker wrote the extraordinarily successful *A Glance at New York* in 1848, which starred Chanfrau as Mose the Bowery "b'hoy," a dandified loafer tough guy and part-time volunteer fireman who is depicted as matching wits with any number of sharpers, swindlers, and con artists in the city. Chanfrau and Baker's character may have been based on a real volunteer fireman, Moses Humphries. *A Glance at New York* en-joyed such success that the Bowery b'hoy character soon appeared in such diverse locales as the goldfields of California, the sophisticated streets of Paris, and the deserts of Arabia. RICHARD M. DORSON reports that genuine "Bowery bums"—the hard-drinking down-and-outers who frequented the Bowery district when it had become Manhattan's skid row—told stories about Mose the Bowery b'hoy well into the twentieth century. Dorson also suggests that the Bowery b'hoy character was an urban incarnation of the DAVY CROCKETT–type character (as Crockett was depicted in American ALMANACS of the nineteenth century). Traces of the character may also be seen in the wisecracking urban tough guys of gangster fiction and films in the 1930s and early 1940s.

SUGGESTED READING: Richard M. Dorson, *American Folklore* (Bloomington, Ind., 1977).

Breakdancing. Also called "breaking," breakdancing is a dazzling genre of highly rhythmic, intensely athletic dance associated with young African-American men. Typical breakdancing moves include "baby swipes" (handstands executed while the legs scissor across each other and the hips spiral), "suicides" (forward flips executed "no hands," the object being to land on one's back), "hand glides" (spinning the body on the axis of one hand), "electric boogie" (a repertoire of robotic movements), "pop-locking" (locking joints between movements), *huevos* (walking on the toes of oversized shoes stuffed with newspaper), "moon walking" (shifting weight gracefully from one leg to the other while sliding backward—a move popularized by singer/dancer Michael Jackson), "uprocking" (simulated fighting), "top-rocking" (foot movements performed from a static position), and "shaming" (mimed insults) between dancers. The style developed in the 1970s and was often performed on the street for tips from passersby. By the 1980s, in such urban centers as New York and Los Angeles, breakdancing contests sometimes figured as an alternative to street violence.

Music for breakdancing may be improvised live percussion or recorded disco rhythms, and it may be accompanied by RAP lyrics. By the late 1980s, breakdancing had become largely commercial and had all but disappeared from the streets.

See also: AFRICAN AMERICANS; DANCE, FOLK.

SUGGESTED READING: Nelson George et al, *Fresh: Hip Hop Don't Stop* (New York, 1985).

A. B. Frost's illustration of Brer Fox, with Brer Rabbit, from Joel Chandler Harris's Uncle Remus: His Songs and His Sayings.

as an amalgam of African-American and European traditions.

See also: AFRICAN AMERICANS; DISNEY, WALT; FOX; TAR BABY.

Breakdown. A fast solo or group dance performed with a shuffling beat and common among rural African Americans in the nineteenth century. The breakdown resembled a JIG and included elaborate, improvised variations on the jig step, most characteristically stiff-legged shuffles and hops.

See also: HOEDOWN; JUBA; SKILLET LICKERS, THE.

Brer Rabbit. Brer ("Brother") Rabbit is a TRICKSTER character in folktales of African, African-American, and Native American cultures. He was popularized for a white American audience in the UNCLE REMUS tales of JOEL CHANDLER HARRIS. Brer Rabbit is the consummate trickster, who (in the Harris tales) typically matches wits with the wily BRER FOX, whom he almost always bests. Indian tribes of the eastern seaboard have a folktale tradition incorporating the Great Hare or the Master Rabbit, a figure strongly related to the African-American Brer Rabbit and similar to the COYOTE trickster figure who appears in many Native American folktales from the Plains.

See also: AFRICAN AMERICANS; ALLIGATOR; ANIMAL TALE; DISNEY, WALT; TAR BABY.

Brer Fox. Brer ("Brother") Fox is the adversary of BRER RABBIT in a cycle of TRICKSTER tales from African and African-American culture. Both Brer Fox and Brer Rabbit are wily tricksters, but Brer Rabbit usually gets the better of the fox. Brer Fox became known to a white American audience through the UNCLE REMUS tales of JOEL CHANDLER HARRIS, who fashioned the character

"If you don't lemme loose I'll knock you agin!"

A. B. Frost's illustration of Brer Rabbit and the Tar Baby from Joel Chandler Harris's Uncle Remus: His Songs and Sayings.

Brewer, J(ohn) Mason (1896–1975).

J. Mason Brewer was one of the nation's most prominent African-American folklorists. He was born in Goliad, Texas, and was educated in the segregated public schools of Austin. He received a B.A. in 1917 from Wiley College, in Marshall, Texas, then served as a French interpreter for the U.S. Army in Europe during World War I. After returning from the war, Brewer became a schoolteacher and a principal in Fort Worth.

Brewer published short stories and poetry, was a professor at Clafflin College (Orangeburg, South Carolina) and at Huston-Tillorson College (Austin, Texas). While he was teaching in Austin, he met University of Texas Professor J. FRANK DOBIE, who nurtured his interest in folklore and urged him to collect and publish African-American folklore. Brewer contributed material to the annual publications of the Texas Folklore Society and published several book-length story collections, including African-American slave tales in *Tone the Bell Easy* (1932), *The Word on the Brazos: Negro Preacher Tales from the Brazos Bottoms of Texas* (1954); *Aunt Dicy Tales* (1956), *Dog Ghosts and Other Negro Folk Tales* (1958), *Wiser Days and Better Times* (1965), and an anthology, *American Negro Folklore* (1968). In all of his works, Brewer scrupulously documented his informants and attempted to convey the nuances of dialect.

In 1950, Brewer earned an M.A. from Indiana University and, in 1951, was awarded an honorary doctorate from Paul Quinn College (Waco, Texas). His books received numerous awards, and he was regularly and universally praised by folklorists as the dean of African-American storytellers.

Brewer taught at Livingston College (Salisbury, North Carolina) and at East Texas State University (Commerce, Texas). He was the first African-American member of the Texas Folklore Society, the first to serve as vice president of the American Folklore Society, and the first African-American member of the Texas Institute of Letters.

SUGGESTED READING: James W. Byrd, *J. Mason Brewer, Folklorist* (Austin, 1967).

Brewster, Paul G. (1898–unknown).

Brewster was a student of folk songs and games. He was born in Stendal, Indiana, and earned a

B.S. degree at Oakland City (Indiana) College (1920) and an M.A. at the University of Oklahoma (1925). He taught chiefly at Tennessee Technological University.

Brewster published widely in the area of the American folk song and in other folk genres and practices (including folk medicine, riddles, jokes, rituals, snake handling, and fire walking). His most numerous and intensive studies deal with games, and *American Nonsinging Games* (1953) was his most significant publication in the field.

Brewster never completed his Ph.D., and he failed to advance in academic position. During the 1950s, he began to turn away from American folklore and collaborated with international folklorists on works about a wide range of European and Asian peoples and cultures.

Brewster's dropping out of the American folkore scholarly scene in the middle of his career has never been definitively explained. Some have attributed less than savory motives to his self-exile, possibly scandal. Assuming that Brewster has by now died, the place and date of his death are not known.

SUGGESTED READING: Janet M. Cliff, entry on Brewster in Jan Harold Brunvand, ed., *American Folklore: An Encyclopedia* (New York, 1996).

Bridger, Jim (1804–1881).

Best known of the "mountain men"—the long-distance fur trapper/explorers of the Far West—Jim Bridger was born in Richmond, Virginia. Orphaned at age fourteen after his family had moved to Missouri, Bridger answered William Henry Ashley's call for "enterprising young men" to enter the fur trade. In Ashley's employ, Bridger trapped in and explored the central and northern Rocky Mountains.

Mountain man Jim Bridger, photographed late in his life, probably during the 1870s.

One of the earliest stories attached to Bridger is of how he and John S. Fitzgerald had been assigned by Ashley's partner, Andrew Henry, to watch over another trapper, Hugh Glass, who had been severely mauled by a grizzly bear. Glass was not expected to live. After five days, Glass neither recovered nor died, and Bridger and Fitzgerald, believing he was as good as dead, abandoned him, reporting that he had died. By a feat of nearly superhuman strength and endurance, Glass managed to find his way to Fort Kiowa. He swore vengeance on Fitzgerald and Bridger, but once he confronted Bridger, he forgave him.

Bridger's travels took him from the headwaters of the Missouri River to the Spanish

Southwest. He took part in thirteen trappers' rendezvous (roughly annual gatherings, both for business and social purposes), was probably the first white man to see the natural wonders of what would become Yellowstone National Park, and, in 1824, followed the Bear River to its outlet into the Great Salt Lake. Although recent research suggests that others had encountered the lake before Bridger, legend persists in crediting him as its discoverer.

Beginning in the 1840s, as the fur trade diminished, Bridger hired himself out as a guide. During 1844–50, he guided emigrant wagon trains west, and, in 1850, outlined a trail for the U.S. Army Corps of Topographical Engineers. Much of Bridger's trail would be incorporated into routes for the Overland Stage and, later, the Union Pacific Railroad.

Bridger founded Fort Bridger on Black's Fork of the Green River in present-day Wyoming, a key wilderness outpost that supplied travelers along the Oregon and California trails all through the 1840s and 1850s. Bridger fell afoul of Mormon leader Brigham Young in 1853. Young accused him of inciting the Indians against the Mormon settlers, and he forced Bridger to vacate the fort. Two years later, the Mormons purchased the fort from Bridger, who nevertheless persisted in claiming that his ouster and the subsequent purchase were illegal. After the U.S. Army took over the fort during the so-called Mormon War of 1857–58, Bridger repeatedly petitioned the government for compensation. (His widow received a partial settlement.)

Bridger's presence is commemorated in a number of western town and place names, including Bridger, Wyoming; Bridger, Montana; Bridger Teton National Forest; Bridger Pass; and Bridger Lake.

Bridger was not only the subject of western folklore, he was also a source. His presence at the trappers' rendezvous was especially cherished because of his ability to tell a story well, though many of the stories attributed to him were almost certainly not his. Two famous tales associated with Bridger are the story of a petrified forest in which petrified birds sang songs that could not be heard, because they, too, were petrified, and the story of a stream, cool at the bottom but boiling on the surface, where one could catch a fish and, in the process, cook it. It is not certain whether Bridger actually told these tales and, if he did, whether he expected them to be taken as fact.

SUGGESTED READING: J. Cecil Alter, *James Bridger* (Salt Lake City, 1925; reprint ed., 1962); Fred R. Gowans, *Fort Bridger: Island in the Wilderness* (Provo, Utah, 1975); Stanley Vestal, *Jim Bridger, Mountain Man: A Biography* (New York, 1946).

Broadsides. With the CHILD BALLAD, the BLUES BALLAD, and the PARLOR BALLAD, broadsides are one the four types of Anglo-American BALLADs folklorists recognize. Broadside ballads appeared in Britain during the eighteenth century, typically printed on single sheets of paper ("broadsides") and hawked on street corners, markets, and fairs. The genre was also popular in colonial America and in the United States through the late 1800s. Subjects of broadsides were typically current events, especially sensational crimes and disasters, although sentimental subjects were also explored, principally courtship and love. Stylistically, the typical broadside ballad is a first-person narrative, which is often very specific in enumerating details of time and place. Broadsides are thus more "realistic"—or, at least, journalistic—than the earlier Child ballads, which tend to be stylized, generalized, and more formulaic.

Photograph of Brooklyn Bridge taken in 1905.

See also: ANGLO AMERICANS; BELDEN, HENRY MARVIN; CORTEZ, GREGORIO; EDDY, MARY O.

SUGGESTED READING: G. Malcolm Laws, *American Balladry from British Broadsides: A Guide for Students and Collectors of Traditional Song* (Philadelphia, 1957).

Bronson, Bertrand Harris (1902–1985).

Bronson was a student of the BALLAD, as well as a musicologist and a professor of English at the University of California, Berkeley. During his long career, spanning from 1927 to 1970, Bronson contributed to the scholarship on Middle English and eighteenth-century English literature, but he is best remembered for his work on the ballad. Bronson's chief objective was to reconnect the traditional ballads, most of which had been collected in text form only, with their associated tunes. Whereas FRANCIS JAMES CHILD and other pioneering collectors had tended to regard ballads as folk verse, Bronson collected and studied them as folk song.

Bronson exercised his detective work on the Child ballads themselves, publishing, between 1959 and 1972, a four-volume compilation titled *Traditional Tunes of the Child Ballads*. In this work, Bronson included texts, melodies, and discographical references. Remarkably, as early as the 1940s, Bronson employed computers in his musicological research in order to develop a new system of melodic classification.

By reuniting traditional texts and traditional melodies, Bronson not only increased the depth and scope of ballad studies as an academic endeavor, he contributed to the popular folk-song revival that began in the 1940s and 1950s. He also pioneered such approaches to folklore as performance study, a technique that steadily gained in importance during the 1960s and later.

SUGGESTED READING: Archie Green, "Bertrand Harris Bronson, 1902–1986," *Journal of American Folklore* 100 (1987), pp. 297–99.

Brooklyn Bridge. Spanning the East River from Brooklyn to Manhattan Island, New York City, the 1,595-foot suspension bridge was the longest bridge in the world when it was dedicated on May 24, 1883. An engineering marvel and a structure of extraordinary beauty, the bridge was begun in 1869 by master bridge-builder John Augustus Roebling, who died of injuries received early in the project. His son, Washington Roebling, saw the work to completion, but also nearly died in the effort, as the result of caisson disease (the bends), contracted when he was working in an underwater caisson in 1872. He was forced to supervise much of the rest of construction from his bed in an apartment in Brooklyn Heights overlooking the construction site.

The bridge was instantly regarded as a landmark symbolic of the city and symbolic, too, of all that nineteenth-century technology was capable of. It inspired poets (most notably Hart Crane, whose lyrical epic *The Bridge,* published in 1930, is widely regarded as a masterpiece), photographers (such as Alfred Stieglitz), and painters (especially Frank Stella, Sr.). The role of the bridge in popular culture has been even more pervasive. It has figured as a backdrop in countless movies and, since its completion, has also been the central prop in stories about the wide-eyed newcomer to the city swindled by a fast talker who proposes to sell him the Brooklyn Bridge. It has also drawn numerous stunt divers as well as scores of suicides. The leap into the East River has claimed numbers of both.

See also: CRANE, (HAROLD) HART.

SUGGESTED READING: David G. McCullough, *The Great Bridge: The Epic Story of the Building of the Brooklyn Bridge* (New York, 1983); Alan Trachtenberg, *Brooklyn Bridge: Fact and Symbol,* 2nd. ed. (Chicago, 1979).

Broonzy, Big Bill (1893–1958). Blues singer William Lee Conley "Big Bill" Broonzy was born, one of seventeen children, in Scott, Mississippi. He spent his childhood on a farm near Pine Bluff, Arkansas, where he learned fiddle from his uncle Jerry Belcher. He subsequently picked up the guitar and mandolin as well. By the time he was a teenager, Broonzy was earning money by performing at parties and picnics.

During World War I, Broonzy served in the army, and became a full-time musician after the war, first in black clubs in and around Little Rock, Arkansas, then, beginning in 1920, in Chicago. Here he met and performed in the city's blues clubs with many other musicians. He did not begin recording, however, until 1926, after which he recorded at least one session each year through 1957.

In Broonzy's early recordings, from about 1926 to 1936, the artist specialized in the humorous and bawdy hokum blues genre as well as rag songs. From 1936 to 1942, he recorded for the Bluebird label, creating a more commercial, even formulaic style. By the late 1940s, Broonzy shifted to the "folk" style and repertoire then emerging in New York City clubs frequented by college-age white audiences. Broonzy sang ballads, gospel songs, and traditional blues. Almost certainly because of exposure to this new audience, Broonzy gained wider renown than many of his blues contemporaries. In 1955, *Big Bill Blues,* his ghostwritten autobiography, appeared. He continued to perform, both in the United States and on tour in Europe, for the next two years, until he succumbed to cancer in 1957.

Broonzy is very well represented on record and is a unique bridge spanning rural and urban traditions.

See also: TERRY, SONNY.

SUGGESTED READING: Big Bill Broonzy, *Big Bill Blues* (New York, 1955); Samuel Charters, *The Country*

Blues (New York, 1959); Lawrence Cohn, ed., *Nothing But the Blues* (New York, 1993).

Brother Jonathan. As a nickname for and caricature of the American common man, "Brother Jonathan" appeared shortly after the end of the American Revolution. It was a pervasive stereotype through the middle of the nineteenth century, so much so that in the 1840s New York editor-writers Rufus Griswold and Park Benjamin named their popular literary weekly *Brother Jonathan.*

The Brother Jonathan figure developed from YANKEE DOODLE and was the precursor of UNCLE SAM. Like these earlier and later figures, Brother Jonathan was represented visually in many political cartoons and was a stock character in anecdotes and jokes found in almanacs, jest books, and especially in American theatrical comedies, beginning with ROYALL TYLER's remarkable 1787 stage comedy, *The Contrast.* (In that play, Brother Jonathan, an innocent from the backwoods of Tyler's Vermont, finds himself transplanted to New York City, where his solid, simple American naïveté prevails against the effete foppery of British officers and urban sophisticates.)

Popularized by literary expression in *The Contrast,* Brother Jonathan became most pervasive during the Jacksonian era, when the aggressive, open, hardworking, but shrewd character of the "western" democrat were particularly valued and celebrated.

The incarnations of Brother Jonathan were many. He was depicted as manservant, loyal to employer and nation alike. He was pictured as the rustic Yankee peddler, who invariably duped country bumpkin and urban sophisticate alike.

He was a cracker-barrel philosopher, whose image helped shape the popular perception of Abraham Lincoln (for example) as a dry, drawling, backwoods Solomon, whose disarming wit and wisdom always confounded conventional politicians. In adumbration of Uncle Sam, Brother Jonathan embodied national virtue. A lean, muscular frontiersman (much like Lincoln the "rail splitter"), shirtsleeves rolled up, he stood as a defiant challenge to any foreign power that might dare infringe upon the sovereignty and rights of the American nation. This image was particularly strong in nineteenth-century dramatic depictions of Brother Jonathan, and the War of 1812 gave special impetus and urgency to the character in this fiercely nationalist guise. The widespread popularity of Brother Jonathan during this period exposed American audiences to what became classic images of the country bumpkin in outlandish clothing and in exaggerated dialect speech. Established as a popular dramatic figure, Brother Jonathan became grist for the mills of political and satirical cartoonists, as well as the writers of almanac humor (see ALMANACS).

By the middle of the nineteenth century, Brother Jonathan was losing much of his regional New England tang and was becoming a generalized image of the "common" American. Increasingly, the figure was co-opted as the embodiment of conservative, even reactionary cultural and political points of view, especially a xenophobic abhorrence of immigrants and immigration. By the end of the Civil War, the figure was seen more often in the British popular press as a negative caricature of Americans and American attitudes.

See also: PAULDING, JAMES KIRKE.

SUGGESTED READING: Winifred Morgan, *An American Icon: Brother Jonathan and American Identity* (Newark, Del., 1988).

Brown, Frank Clyde (1870–1943). Brown was an important student and collector of North Carolina folklore. He was born in Harrisonburg, Virginia, and educated at the University of Nashville (A.B., 1893) and the University of Chicago (M.A., 1902; Ph.D., 1908). He spent his entire teaching career, as a professor of English and a teacher of folklore, at Trinity College (now Duke University) in Durham, North Carolina.

The great musicologist and folk-song collector JOHN LOMAX prompted Brown to create a local group to collect and publish North Carolina folklore. The North Carolina Folklore Society was established in 1913 with Brown as secretary-treasurer and guiding light of the society's collecting and publication program. The resulting collection is one of the largest of state collections, and Brown personally traveled North Carolina's back roads to record folk songs.

Brown repeatedly postponed publication of the collection as a whole, on the grounds that it was incomplete. After his death, however, *The Frank C. Brown Collection of North Carolina Folklore* (1952–1964) was published by Duke University in seven volumes. The Brown Collection itself resides at the Perkins Library of Duke University.

SUGGESTED READING: Newman Ivey White, "General Introduction," *The Frank C. Brown Collection of North Carolina Folklore,* vol. 1 (Durham, N.C., 1952).

Buck-and-wing. Also called a "buck dance," the buck-and-wing resembles CLOGGING in that buck dancers dance with their feet close to the floor and their arms hanging loosely by their sides. In contrast to clogging, however, the buck-and-wing is usually a solo dance. Buck-and-wing was most prevalent in the Appalachian Mountains, among blacks as well as whites. It is almost certainly based on the step dances of Scotch, Irish, Scotch-Irish, and northern English immigrants to the southern mountain region. Buck-and-wing also became a feature of MINSTREL SHOW dancing, and this, in turn, probably influenced the way the dance was performed in Appalachia. Some scholars have speculated that white buck dancers were also influenced by the toe-heel, toe-heel patterns of Native American ceremonial dances in the Southeast. The origin and precise significance of the term *buck-and-wing* are obscure.

See also: AFRICAN AMERICANS; DANCE, FOLK; RAGTIME; TAP DANCE.

Buffalo. The buffalo, or American bison, figures in Euro-American popular culture as an icon of the western plains and, as an animal nearly hunted to extinction in the nineteenth century, a symbol of the vanishing wilderness. An image of the buffalo once adorned the nickel.

For the midwestern and Plains Indian tribes, the buffalo was the most important of animals and remains the focus of many folktales, religious celebrations, and other ceremonies. For the Lakota Sioux, the buffalo is a spiritual presence responsible for giving game to the Lakota and is also responsible for female fertility.

See also: NATIVE AMERICANS; TAR BABY.

Buffalo Bill (William F. Cody) (1846–1917). Like so many American folk heroes, William F. Cody was born in a log cabin. His father, Isaac Cody, had settled the family near

One of many nineteenth-century images of William F. "Buffalo Bill" Cody.

LeClaire, Iowa Territory, where William was born, then moved farther west, to Missouri and Kansas. An abolitionist, Isaac was stabbed while making an antislavery speech in Leavenworth and never recovered. He died in 1857, leaving William to support the family. He did so by becoming a herder and a mounted messenger for Russell, Majors and Wadell, the freighters who organized the Pony Express. Possibly credible legend (perpetuated by Buffalo Bill himself) holds that the fourteen-year-old Cody rode for the Pony Express, but this cannot be independently verified. Cody also worked as a trapper and a Colorado prospector. Following the death of his mother, Mary, late in 1863, Cody joined the Seventh Kansas Cavalry, then, after the Civil War, in 1866, met and married Louisa Frederici, in St. Louis. The couple moved to Kansas and

raised four children, though Cody was rarely present. He drove a stagecoach for a time, but found his forte as a buffalo hunter. In an eight-month period from 1867 to 1868, he killed 4,280 buffalo to supply food to construction gangs pushing the Union Pacific westward. He earned a good living, as well as his famous nickname: "Buffalo Bill." He also impressed Gen. Philp Sheridan, who hired him as chief scout for the Fifth Cavalry in 1868. During 1868–72, 1874, and 1876, he compiled a legendary reputation as an Indian fighter and was awarded the Medal of Honor. His conspicuous gallantry was also well-timed. A month after GEORGE ARMSTRONG CUSTER fell at the Battle of the Little Bighorn in 1876, Buffalo Bill was hailed in newspapers for having killed a Cheyenne warrior in hand-to-hand combat. By this time, Buffalo Bill was already famous east as well as west of Mississippi. In 1872, Sheridan assigned him to escort the Grand Duke Alexis of Russia on a grand hunting expedition. Newspaper attention was lavished upon Buffalo Bill, who soon afterward appeared on the Chicago stage in *Scouts of the Prairie,* a melodrama by dime novelist Ned Buntline. This acting experience persuaded Buffalo Bill to develop his fabulously successful Wild West Show, which premiered on May 19, 1883.

For the next thirty years, until the show finally closed in 1913, Buffalo Bill toured the nation and the world with an outdoor spectacular featuring act after act that created the image of the American West in the popular mind. In shaping the world's perception of the West, the Wild West Show was among the first great interactions between folklore and MASS MEDIA. Dramatizations of Pony Express adventures, the wagon train, stagecoach robbery, "cowboy fun," scenes from Indian life (starring, for a time, SITTING BULL), battle reenactments, sharpshooting exhibitions (featuring Annie Oakley,

Two images of one of the star attractions of Buffalo Bill's Wild West Show, Annie Oakley: in a late-nineteenth-century photograph and in an early poster for the show.

"Little Sure Shot"), and trick riding fixed vivid western images forever—not only in the imagination of those who actually saw the show, but in those who told others about it, and, subsequently, in numberless scenes from western movies and television shows.

Cody enjoyed temporary financial success as a result of his shows, but overextended himself with investments in everything from mining to town building to speculation in early western film ventures. None of these panned out during his lifetime, and in 1916, an aged Buffalo Bill toured

as an attraction in Wild West shows staged by others. Within less than a year, he was dead. Newspapers nationwide lamented in his death the passing of "the Great West."

SUGGESTED READING: Joseph Rosa and Robin May, *Buffalo Bill and His Wild West* (Lawrence, Kans., 1989); Don Russell, *The Lives and Legends of Buffalo Bill* (Norman, Okla., 1960).

"Buffalo Gals." A favorite MINSTREL SHOW tune of the 1840s, "Buffalo Gals" was also a popular SQUARE DANCE and PLAY PARTY song. Performers, whether itinerant professionals or local amateurs, typically created impromptu versions to suit the locality: "Bowery Gals," "Pittsburgh Gals," and so on. The song remained popular well into the twentieth century.

See also: FOLK MUSIC.

Bulfinch, Thomas (1796–1867). Bulfinch, best known for his *Age of Fable* (1855), was an American collector of myths who brought the Greek and Roman myths to the attention of a broad public. He was born in Newton, Massachusetts, son of Charles Bulfinch, the first internationally recognized architect in the United States, and was educated at Phillips Exeter Academy and at Harvard (A.B., 1814). Bulfinch worked as a bank clerk while he pursued his passion for mythology. His books include *Hebrew Lyrical History* (1853), *The Age of Chivalry* (1858), *Legends of Charlemagne* (1863), and *Poetry of the Age of Fable* (1863), in addition to *The Age of Fable*.

Bultos. Three-dimensional representations of individual saints carved and painted by New Mexican Hispanic craftsman from the end of the eighteenth through the nineteenth century.

See also: LOPEZ, JOSÉ DELORES; MEXICAN AMERICANS; SANTO NIÑO SANTERO; WOODCARVING.

Bumper stickers. What LIZZIE LABELS were to the 1920s and 1930s, bumper stickers became from the 1960s on. Although as early as the 1930s roadside restaurants, tourist attractions, amusement parks, and other such establishments sometimes affixed advertisements to the bumpers of cars parked in their lots, so that the driver would more or less unwillingly spread the word, bumper stickers as deliberate displays of self-expression did not come into vogue until the 1960s. Often, they were political in nature, either supporting a particular candidate for office or expressing a certain point of view. Stickers protesting the Vietnam War became popular, as did stickers opposing war in general ("Suppose They Gave a War and No One Came" or "Make Love, Not War"), but so did "patriotic" stickers voicing support for the troops in Vietnam or simply bearing an image of the flag and proclaiming "Proud to Be an American." Environmental slogans were also seen frequently on stickers of the 1960s. With the end of the decade of protest, many bumper stickers became less overtly didactic and were simply humorous or expressive of an attitude, such as "I'd Rather Be Sailing." By the end of the century, bumper sticker messages were so numerous that only the outrageous attracted attention: "Mean People Suck." By this time, too, bumper stickers seemed almost to engage in a dialogue. The National Rifle Association (NRA) issued a series of bumper stickers opposing national gun control legislation, the best known of which bore the slogan "If Guns Are Outlawed, Only Outlaws Will Have Guns." Pro-control groups countered with: "If Guns Are Outlawed, Only Outlaws Will Accidentally Shoot Their Kids." And when any number of schools across the nation sold bumper stickers proclaiming "My Kid Is an Honor Student at [Such-and-such] School," some parents slapped the following on the bumper of the family car: "My Kid Beat Up Your Honor Student."

The enduring popularity of bumper stickers suggests the degree to which Americans personally identify with their automobiles, considering them as extensions of themselves or, at least, an extension of their personal space. The automobile has become a vehicle of self-expression.

See also: KOREAN WAR.

The bungalow style spread through new cities such as Los Angeles. This ad for a bungalow plan book appeared in National Geographic *in 1923.*

Bundling. This courting custom came to America during the eighteenth century, brought by emigrants from the British Isles and elsewhere; it persisted in New England, particularly in Connecticut, into the early nineteenth century. Lovers or engaged couples, fully or partially dressed, shared the same bed. It was also said that benighted travelers were sometimes invited to "bundle" with the eldest daughter of the house. The custom was the object of much moralizing and satire during the eighteenth and early nineteenth centuries, and it may well be the origin of the traveling salesman joke.

Bungalow. A development of VERNACULAR ARCHITECTURE, the bungalow is found in many regions worldwide, but is prevalent in the American Midwest (especially Chicago) and in Southern California (especially Los Angeles and environs), and is particularly identified with the

A BRICK - BUNGALOW

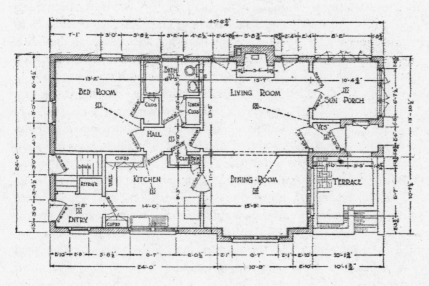

Floor plan for a bungalow, circa 1924.

South. The bungalow is prevalent in such cities as Nashville and Atlanta, though it is also widely found in other urban as well as rural areas of the South. The word *bungalow* is Hindustani in origin; *bangla* denotes a low house with surrounding porches. The typical bungalow is built on a single floor, is two rooms wide, and three or more rooms long. It has a simple gable roof with overhanging eaves and usually has a porch across the entire width of the front. During the early twentieth century, it was a style frequently used in tract housing.

See also: SHOTGUN HOUSE.

SUGGESTED READING: Clay Lancaster, *The American Bungalow, 1880–1930* (New York, 1985).

A woman in Bemidji, Minnesota, prepares "Paul Bunyan flapjacks." Oversized pancakes like these are still made in several Minnesota towns that stage Paul Bunyan festivals. The photograph is from the early 1940s.

Bunions and corns. The folk wisdom of many cultures identifies aching bunions and corns as a sure sign of rain. Folk medicine (see MEDICINE, FOLK) suggests numerous cures for corns, including stealing a small piece of beef and burying it; as the beef rots, the corn will disappear. A traditional African-American corn cure is to rub the corn with a kernel of corn, then feed it to an old rooster.

See also: WEATHER FOLKLORE.

Bunyan, Paul. Contrary to the impression many have, the Paul Bunyan tales are not the direct products of anonymous folklore, but the work of newspaperman James MacGillivray, who published the first Bunyan tale, "The Round River Drive," in the *Detroit News-Tribune* on July 24, 1910. The character immediately captured public interest, and during the next decade

and a half, a number of professional writers took up the Bunyan theme, rapidly transmuting the figure of the giant lumberjack into a national legend. The sources of MacGillivray's original character are not clear, but a Paul Bunyan did figure in oral traditions of lumbermen in Pennsylvania, Wisconsin, and the Pacific Northwest prior to 1910. After MacGillivray, the single greatest popularizer of the Paul Bunyan legends was W. B. Laughead, a Minnesota advertising man, who produced a series of pamphlets between 1914 and 1944, publicizing the products of the Red River Lumber Company and locating Paul in the north woods of Minnesota. Under the influence of the pamphlet series, Esther Shephard wrote a novel called *Paul Bunyan* in 1924. Another lumber-company ad man, James Stevens, embellished the growing legend in his own *Paul Bunyan* of 1925. Building on this foundation, many authors

Paul Bunyan Legend: Battle with the Big Swede, *1939 soft ground etching by Walter K. Fram.*

of books for juveniles produced versions of the Paul Bunyan legends, and various upper-Midwest communities introduced Paul Bunyan festivals to attract tourists to what they typically called "Bunyan-land." The Paul Bunyan tales also found their way into "highbrow" literature and art, through the poetry of such writers as Robert Frost, CARL SANDBURG, and Richard Wilbur and in an operetta with libretto by W. H. Auden and music by Benjamin Britten.

Paul Bunyan has been received as an occupational folk hero, the embodiment of frontier vitality, a symbol of largeness, might, a willingness to work hard, and a resolve to overcome all obstacles. Paul's exaggerated size is part and parcel of the western TALL TALE humor tradition, which populated the landscape with beings of gigantic proportions. Bunyan and his boon companions, BABE THE BLUE OX and Johnny Inkslinger, take in their stride rainstorms that last for months, mosquitoes of tremendous dimension, and formidable geographical obstacles. Indeed, geography

was no problem for Paul, who, godlike, created such physical features as lakes and rivers, not to mention Puget Sound, the Grand Canyon, and the Black Hills. Such prodigious creativity generates an enormous appetite, and, we are told, Paul's camp stove covers an acre and his hotcake griddle is so vast that it requires the service of men using sides of bacon for skates to grease it.

See also: APPLESEED, JOHNNY; CROCKETT, DAVY; FAKELORE; MORGAN, GIB; PECOS BILL; RUTH, BABE; SLAPPY HOOPER; SMITH, FRED

SUGGESTED READING: Daniel G. Hoffman, *Paul Bunyan: Last of the Frontier Demigods* (Lincoln, Neb., 1983).

Burchenal, Elizabeth (ca. 1876–1959).

Burchenal founded the American Folk Dance Society in 1916. She was a native of Richmond, Indiana, who grew up in an enthusiastically musical household. Educated at Earlham College, in Richmond, she earned an A.B. in English in 1896, then went to Boston, where she enrolled in Dr. Sargent's School of Physical Training, with the intention of becoming a physical education teacher—what today would be called a physical therapist. After graduation, Burchenal directed the Medical Gymnasium at the department of orthopedics in what would become Boston Children's Hospital. From 1898 to 1902, she taught physical education programs in Boston and Chicago. In 1903, Burchenal joined the faculty of Teachers College, Columbia University. During her stay in New York, she became increasingly interested in the folk-dance traditions represented by the city's huge immigrant population. In 1915, Burchenal had begun assembling what would become the Archive of American Folk Dance. She went to work for the city's Board of Education, creating dance-oriented physical education programs, and in 1916, introduced folk dance into the curriculum of the public schools. In that year, she also founded the American Folk Dance Society, serving as its president, then becoming the executive chairman and director of the Folk Arts Center, Inc.

SUGGESTED READING: Betty Casey, *International Folk Dancing U.S.A.* (New York, 1981).

Burroughs, Edgar Rice (1875–1950).
Edgar Rice Burroughs, the creator of TARZAN, was born and raised in Chicago, the son of a wealthy businessman. He was educated at private schools in Chicago and at Philips Academy, in Andover, Massachusetts, which expelled him. After this, he attended Michigan Military Academy, where he also briefly taught before drifting from one unsuccessful venture to another. In 1911, while working as an advertising copywriter in Chicago, he wrote a science-fiction short story titled "Under the Moons of Mars," which was so successful that he turned to writing fiction full time, publishing the first Tarzan story in 1912 and *Tarzan of the Apes* in 1914. Twenty-five more Tarzan novels followed, and the English nobleman abandoned as an infant in the African jungle where he was raised by apes attained the status of folk hero, not only in the United States, but worldwide. The Tarzan tales were translated into fifty-six languages and served as the basis for comic strips and a highly successful series of films, as well as radio serials and two television series. The films were so successful that, in 1919, Burroughs purchased an estate near Hollywood to be near the filming. The site of that estate is now the Los Angeles suburb of Tarzana. Burroughs published some sixty-eight novels, including works of science fiction, and served as a correspondent during World War II.

"Bury Me Not on the Lone Prairie." Also known as "The Dying Cowboy," this COWBOY SONG presents the dying cowpuncher's request not to be buried on the lone prairie "where the wild coyote will howl o'er me." The origin of the song may be traced to an 1839 song called "The Burial at Sea" (or "Ocean Burial").

See also: FOLK MUSIC.

C

Cajun music. Cajun music is a blend of Native American, Scotch-Irish, Spanish, German, Anglo-American, and Afro-Caribbean musical traditions with French folk traditions. After being expelled from Acadia (Nova Scotia) by the British in 1755, at the outbreak of the French and Indian War, many Acadians settled in Louisiana, where they soon became the culturally dominant group. They did not, however, simply impose their culture on those around them, but, in a rich give-and-take, absorbed as much as they bestowed, ultimately becoming the CAJUNS. Nowhere is this cultural cross-fertilization more apparent than in Cajun music, which borrows wailing styles and dance rhythms from Native American tradition; improvisational singing styles (and, much later, blues) from African Americans; fiddle tunes from the Anglo-Americans; and Spanish tunes and cadences from Spanish settlers. With the arrival of fugitive slaves from Santo Domingo at the beginning of the nineteenth century, Cajun music was enriched with a West Indian beat. Later in the century, Middle European immigrants brought the diatonic accordion, which quickly found favor among Cajun musicians. By the beginning of the twentieth century, black Creoles brought the rural blues to Cajun music.

Much of the traditional Cajun music began to disappear beneath the waves of commercial music broadcast during the 1930s and afterward. However, researchers and collectors such as ALAN LOMAX and Harry Oster worked to record the traditional sounds before they faded altogether. The traditional music was given national exposure in 1964, when the Newport Folk Festival featured performances by Gladius Thibodeaux, Louis "Vinesse" Lejeune, and Dewey Balfa, all practitioners of the unadorned, visceral Cajun tradition. By the 1970s, a cajun music festival became a regular, state-sponsored event in Louisiana.

See also: ARHOOLIE RECORDS; FOLK MUSIC; ROUNDER RECORDS.

SUGGESTED READING: Barry Jean Ancelet, *The Makers of Cajun Music/Musiciens Cadiens et Créoles* (Lafayette, La., 1984); Glenn R. Conrad, ed., *The Cajuns: Essays on Their History and Culture,* 3rd ed. (Lafayette, La., 1983).

Cajuns. *Cajun* is a "corrupt" pronunciation of *Acadian,* and Cajuns are descendants of French-Canadian residents of Acadia (present-day Nova Scotia) expelled by the British in 1755, during the early months of the French and Indian Wars. Cajuns are the refugees who settled in the bayou region of southern Louisiana. Through the course of the late eighteenth and nineteenth centuries, the Cajuns created self-contained communities made cohesive not only by certain general cultural features, but also by a distinctive patois combining archaic French with idioms borrowed from their English, Spanish, German, Native American, and African-American neighbors. Today, the principal Cajun communities are within southern Louisiana, though smaller communities are also found in east Texas and California.

Cajuns have been the subject of much EXO-TERIC folklore and ethnic stereotyping. By turns, they have been derided as backward, hot-tempered denizens of the swamps and fun-loving, passionate revelers in the good life. As portrayed in HENRY WADSWORTH LONGFELLOW's *Evangeline* (1847), the Cajuns were seen as simple, pious, and courageous—in effect, the French-Canadian equivalent of PILGRIMS AND PURITANS. A variety of LOCAL-COLOR STORY writers portrayed the Cajuns in a romantic light that combined many of the dominant stereotypes. Yet the Cajuns defy stereotyping. The exiles from Acadia were a heterogenous group, which included Mic-mac Indians, people from all regions of France, and even some Scots, Basques, and other Euro-peans. Once settled in Louisiana, they retained an ethnic identity even as they freely intermarried with their neighbors and borrowed from their traditions. Few of the MATERIAL CULTURE traditions manifested in Cajun Lousiana were brought from Acadia. Instead, they were borrowed and modified from traditions common among neigh-boring groups. Even Cajun FOODWAYS, which produced a cuisine enjoyed by non-Cajuns and Cajuns alike, combine traditions brought from Acadia with many others adapted from Native Americans and African Americans, including African Americans of Carribean descent. If Ca-juns are well known for their food, they are even more closely identified—at least by outsiders—with their music. Yet CAJUN MUSIC is a distinc-tive blend of German, Spanish, Scottish, Irish, Anglo-American, Afro-Caribbean, and American Indian traditions upon a foundation of European French and French Acadian traditions.

See also: FRENCH AMERICANS; MARDI GRAS, CAJUN.

SUGGESTED READING: Barry Jean Ancelet, Jay Ed-wards, and Glen Pitre, *Cajun Country* (Jackson, Miss., 1991); Carl A. Brasseaux, *In Search of Evangeline: Birth and Evolution of the Evangeline Myth* (Thibo-daux, La., 1988); Malcolm Comeaux, *Atchafalaya Swamp Life: Settlement and Folk Occupations* (Baton Rouge, La., 1972).

Cakewalk. Originally a strutting, high-stepping dance popular among African-American slaves and performed in the presence of their masters, the cakewalk (which did not get its name until much later) was actually a sly parody of white ballroom dances. By the end of the nine-teenth century, the cakewalk had become a stage dance for couples and was subsequently adapted as a ballroom dance. Couples formed a square, men on the inside, women on the outside. The couples strutted around the square and were eliminated, one by one, by a panel of judges. The final couple was presented with a fancy cake—hence the name of the dance and the origin of the expression "to take the cake" (i.e., to be the best). While the cakewalk soon disappeared from American ballrooms, it played an evolutionary role in dance steps accompanying RAGTIME and JAZZ.

See also: DANCE, FOLK.

This 1904 illustration from the British humor magazine Punch *is a caricature of the cakewalk.*

Calumet. Popularly called by non–Native Americans a "peace pipe," the calumet is a sacred smoking pipe used in ceremonies of peace as well as ceremonies of welcome. To smoke together, passing the pipe from person to person, is a symbol of kinship among several tribes, especially those of the Plains, for whom the ascending smoke symbolizes the Great Spirit. Inhaling and exhaling the smoke invokes the blessing of the Spirit. Pipe smoking is often accompanied by ritual dances, and the calumet is designed and decorated to distinguish it from everyday pipes.

Jonchonwit, an 1897 painting by E. Irving Couse, depicts the use of a calumet.

Campa, Arthur Leon (1905–1978).
Campa was a student of the cultures of the American Southwest. He was born in Mexico to a Methodist missionary family, but was raised, after his father was killed by Pancho Villa in 1914, on a ranch in west Texas.

Campa was educated at the University of New Mexico (B.A. and M.A.) and at Columbia University (Ph.D.), specializing in language, literature, and cultural anthropology. He taught at the University of Denver, where he was chairman of the Department of Modern Languages and Literature from 1946 to 1972. With LEVETTE DAVIDSON and JOHN GREENWAY, Campa was instrumental in bringing the American folklore program of the University of Denver to prominence during the 1950s.

Campa is best known for his monumental *Hispanic Culture in the Southwest*, published in 1979, the year after his death, and embodying a half-century of research. The unifying thrust of his work is the central idea that the traditional culture of a people consists of the products of a locale and a region.

In addition to *Hispanic Culture*, Campa wrote many articles in popular as well as scholarly publications. He also wrote *Spanish Folk Poetry in New Mexico* (1946) and *Treasure of Sangre de Cristos* (1962) and was editor of *The Brand Book* (1966).

SUGGESTED READING: Louie W. Attebery, entry on Campa in Jan Harold Brunvand, ed., *American Folklore: An Encyclopedia* (New York, 1996).

Campbell, Joseph (1904–1987).
Campbell was the best-known exponent of the Jungian school of myth and literary study, which identifies and analyzes plot patterning that is repeated and shared by heroic tales across diverse and otherwise unrelated cultures. His most important books, *The Hero with a Thousand Faces*

(1949) and the four-volume *Masks of God* series (1959–1968), continue to reach a wide popular audience. With journalist Bill Moyers, Campbell also appeared on a six-segment Public Broadcasting System television series that aired in 1988, *The Power of Myth,* which was accompanied by a book. Campbell taught as a professor of literature at Sarah Lawrence College (Bronxsville, New York) from 1934 to 1972.

Like Carl Jung, Campbell saw mythology as necessary for the successful existence of culture, and, further, saw mythology as the product of universal psychological processes and principles. When a culture neglected mythology—for example, by elevating "science" or "rationality" above it—the result, according to Campbell, was social and cultural dysfunction, typically manifested as violence, crime, and general unrest. Campbell himself saw no problem reconciling mythology with science. He rejected mythology as what it presented itself at face value—historical narrative—and instead embraced it as a singularly creative symbolic expression of the psyche. For Campbell, reconnecting with mythology could supply some or all of the spiritual benefits of religious faith, and he saw mythology as, perhaps, more acceptable than conventional religion to many moderns.

SUGGESTED READING: Joseph Campbell, *Myths to Live By* (New York, 1972); Joseph Campbell with Bill Moyers, *The Power of Myth* (New York, 1988); Robert A. Segal, *Joseph Campbell: An Introduction* (New York, 1987).

Hindman Settlement School in Caney Creek, Knott County, Kentucky, then at the Gander School in Letcher County, Kentucky, during the late 1920s and early 1930s. At Caney Creek, in 1926, she began collecting folklore, using her neighbors as her informants.

Campbell earned a B.A. in education at Southern Illinois University in 1932 and, in 1937, received an M.A. at George Peabody College. She taught English, folklore, and creative writing at West Georgia College, Peabody College, at Alabama Laboratory School, and at Carollton High School, Georgia, reserving her summers for trips to Kentucky on behalf of the Kentucky Crippled Children's Commission.

With the aid of a Guggenheim Fellowship, Campbell earned a Ph.D. in folklore and comparative literature from Indiana University (1956), then taught at Glassboro State College (New Jersey), Bowling Green State University (Ohio), and the University of Massachusetts (Amherst). She wrote articles in popular as well as scholarly periodicals, and compiled two collections of southern Appalachian folktales, *Cloud Walking* (1942) and *Tales of the Cloud-Walking Country* (1958). Her 1946 *Folks Do Get Born* was a groundbreaking study of southern African-American midwifery practices. She also wrote a novel, *A House with Stairs* (1950), about an African-American family in Alabama during the Civil War.

SUGGESTED READING: Margaret R. Yocom, entry on Campbell in Jan Harold Brunvand, ed., *American Folklore: An Encyclopedia* (New York, 1996).

Campbell, Marie Alice (1903–1980).
Marie Alice Campbell was a pioneering collector of the folklore of southern Appalachia. A native of Tamms, Illinois, she began teaching at the

Campbell, Olive Dame (1882–1954). A
prime mover behind the southern Appalachian folklore and folk-craft movement, Olive Campbell founded the John C. Campbell Folk School in

1925 at Brasstown, North Carolina, and co-founded the Southern Highland Handicraft Guild. She was also second executive secretary of the Council of the Southern Mountains. In the course of her work in Appalachia, Campbell discovered the Appalachian BALLAD and brought English folklorist CECIL JAMES SHARP to the region to collect ballads from this tradition.

Campbell herself was not a born southerner, but a native of Medford, Massachusetts, who came to the South in 1907, when she married folklorist John C. Campbell, who, in 1908, traveled to Appalachia on a Russell Sage Foundation grant to survey agencies operating there. Olive Campbell happened to hear a student at the Hindman Settlement School sing "Barbry Allen" and immediately became interested in balladry. She set about collecting and, after having secured some sixty ballads, communicated them to Sharp, asking that he come to Appalachia to embark on a systematic collection. During three tours from 1916 to 1918, he and Maud Karpeles combed the hills, finally producing the groundbreaking *English Folk Songs from the Southern Appalachians* in 1932.

After the death of her husband in 1919, Campbell succeeded to his position on the Council of the Southern Mountains and finished his book *The Southern Highlander and His Homeland*. The Southern Highland Handicraft Guild (a body she helped found), was instrumental in developing the southern Appalachian style of commercial handicrafts.

See also: APPALACHIA.

SUGGESTED READING: David F. Whisnant, *All That Is Native and Fine* (Chapel Hill, N.C., 1983).

Canals. Canals were being built in Europe since the end of the seventeenth century. In United States, a mere one hundred miles had been dug by the opening of the nineteenth century; however, by 1840, 3,326 miles were in operation. The most famous of all was the Erie Canal, 363 miles long with 82 locks from Albany on the Hudson River to Buffalo on Lake Erie, built by New York State between 1817 and 1825. It opened a freight and passenger route to the great midwestern prairies and was so successful that it ignited a canal-building fever. The Delaware and Hudson Canal, from Pennsylvania to the Hudson River in New York, was completed in 1828. The Mainline Canal, combining canal and railroad, was completed in 1834 and reached over the Alleghenies to Pittsburgh. The Ohio and Erie linked the Ohio River to Cleveland, and the Wabash and Erie linked Indiana's Wabash River to the

Passenger flatboat on the Erie Canal, about 1830. The drawing is from the 1940s.

Erie Canal. The Louisiana Purchase furnished the impetus for even more canals, including the Illinois–Michigan, connecting the Great Lakes and and triggering the first great growth of Chicago. By the 1850s, however, railroads were taking over much of the canals' business, and well before the end of the century more than half of the canals had been abandoned.

During their explosive but relatively short heyday, America's canals were the focus of a considerable body of folklore. For Americans of the early nineteenth century, the canals meant the adventure of distant places, and a host of colorful characters, especially the canal boatmen themselves, who were attracted to the hardworking but free-and-easy life of the canal. Typical canal lore includes work narratives, many of which were collected by professional folklorists during the waning days of the few remaining canals operating during the early twentieth century. Tall tales also flourished on the canals, with the emphasis on stories of superhuman strength and great feats of canal boat navigation. Superstition abounded as well, especially a belief in mischief (and worse) from the spirits of the dead. Nor is

Illustration from a New York City souvenir book of 1929 showing the grand opening of the Erie Canal in 1825.

oral folklore the only folk material associated with the canals. Fiddle music and song were frequent pastimes, and numerous BALLADS and folk songs were composed on the subject of canal activity, including "The Erie Canal," one of the nation's most familiar folk songs.

See also: NYE, PEARL R.; WORK SONGS.

SUGGESTED READING: Russell Bourne, *Floating West: The Erie and Other American Canals* (New York, 1992); George Korson, ed., *Pennsylvania Songs and Legends* (Baltimore, 1949).

Cansler, Loman D. (1924–1992).

Cansler was a collector and student of the folklore of the Midwest. He not only collected the folk songs of the region, but performed them.

Cansler was born into a family of singers and musicians in Dallas County, Missouri. He joined the U.S. Navy during World War II and, after the war, enrolled in the University of Missouri on the G.I. Bill, even though he had never finished high school. Enthralled by the university's library, he spent many hours exploring its shelves and was delighted to discover that songs published by H. M. Belden (*Ballads and Songs Collected by the Missouri Folk-Lore Society*) and Carl Sandburg (*The American Songbag*) included a good many his own family, friends, and neighbors sang. Thus inspired, Cansler set about collecting folk songs as well as folklore from his family and from fellow students at the university. Even more, he began researching the origins of the songs.

Cansler took his B.S. in 1949 and a master's in education the following year, then became a high school teacher and guidance counselor in rural Fayette, central Missouri, then in north Kansas City. During summers, beginning in 1954, he and his family traveled the back roads of Missouri (and, to a lesser extent, Kansas and Illinois), collecting and recording on tape traditional songs, as well as other folklore material. Cansler spent a summer of study at the Indiana University Folklore Institute (1962) and was Missouri's delegate at the National Folklife Festival in Washington, D.C. (1968).

For several Missouri songwriters who could be identified, Cansler documented their lives and compiled biographies. He wrote numerous articles for scholarly as well as popular periodicals and created two albums of songs for FOLKWAYS RECORDS, *Folk Songs of Missouri* (1959) and *Folksongs of the Midwest* (1973).

In 1982, Cansler retired from North Kansas City High School and devoted himself full time to transcribing and organizing the collection he had compiled for so much of his life. The collection resides at the University of Missouri Western Historical Manuscript Collection, Columbia, Missouri.

SUGGESTED READING: Rebecca B. Schroeder, entry on Cansler in Jan Harold Brunvand, ed., *American Folklore: An Encyclopedia* (New York, 1996).

Al Capone in the 1930s.

Capone, Al(phonse) ("Scarface") (1899–1947).

"Scarface" Al Capone symbolized the brazen crime and deadly violence of the Prohibition Era in the United States. To the public, he was the *archetype* of the czar of organized crime, the gangster; to writers, actors, and directors in Hollywood, he was the *prototype* after which the gangland villains presented on screen were modeled.

Capone was born in the slums of Brooklyn, New York, to an Italian-American family that included eight other siblings. Attending school sporadically to the sixth grade, Capone left after assaulting his teacher and receiving a humiliating beating from the principal in return. It is likely that, from that day on, Capone never spent an honest day in his life. He began running with small-time New York City street gangs, eventually graduating to the notoriously violent Five Points Gang of lower Manhattan. As a Five Pointer, Capone was schooled in extortion, robbery, and murder. For this education, he was an avid student.

Johnny Torrio gave Capone his first "adult" criminal job, at age sixteen, as a hired thug. Capone served as a brutal bouncer in Torrio's

Brooklyn saloon and brothel. He was frequently assigned to beat up those who got behind on payments to Torrio, who was, among other things, a loan shark. Later, Capone supervised Torrio's prostitution ring, personally punishing women suspected of holding back on Torrio's nightly take. Presumably, it was his early sexual experiences in Torrio's establishment that infected Capone with syphilis, which, untreated, would eventually debilitate and kill him.

By 1918, Torrio moved his operation to the wide-open city of Chicago. Capone would become closely identified with the Windy City as its chief crime boss, who had police and politicians, including the mayor, in his pocket. This popular and legendary perception of Capone was, in fact, largely true.

Capone continued working for Torrio in Chicago as a thug and hit man, cultivating a reputation for sadism. In particular, it became apparent that Capone enjoyed beating his victims to death. Torrio was working for his uncle, Big Jim Colosimo, Chicago's most powerful crime boss. But when Torrio suggested they begin reaping profits from the impending prohibition of alcohol, Colosimo, feeling that he was now sufficiently wealthy, begged off the new racket. Torrio realized that Colosimo was now an obstacle and commissioned Capone to kill him. The young man did the job in Colosimo's own cafe, afterward strolling calmly back to Torrio's club and upstairs into bed with a prostitute.

After Colosimo's death, Torrio convened a meeting of Chicago's gangland. They carved up the city among themselves, but Capone quickly infringed on the territory of the others, and the city witnessed its first full-scale gangland war. Intimidated after narrowly escaping a "hit," Torrio retired, leaving to Capone his entire operation. Having inherited from Torrio more than half the Chicago police force, as well as numerous aldermen, judges, and prosecutors, the gangster began

a ruthless program of extermination directed against his foes, in the process devoting little worry to the prospect of criminal prosecution. Typical of Capone's much-publicized behavior was an occasion on which he walked into a bar, put a gun to a man's head, coolly pulled the trigger, then just as coolly walked out. Of the only two witnesses in that crowded bar who said they saw Capone do it, one disappeared forever and the other "forgot" what he had seen.

At length, Capone had whittled his competition down to a single man, Hymie Weiss. The two waged spectacular urban warfare on each other, making frequent use of the Thompson submachine gun, developed for the army during World War I and, with the end of the war, sold in quantity as government surplus. The "Tommy gun" became a popular icon of Roaring Twenties gangsterism. After eliminating Weiss in an elaborately contrived hit, Capone turned his attention to Weiss's successor in the "North Side Gang," George "Bugs" Moran, masterminding another elaborate assassination. His plan was to kill Moran in the garage that the gangster maintained as a front for his operations. Two Capone men disguised as police detectives moved in, lined up the seven men they found in the garage, then pulled their Thompsons from beneath their coats. They sprayed the men with gunfire, nearly cutting several in two. This butchery, which took place on St. VALENTINE'S DAY, February 14, 1929, went down in gangland legend as the St. Valentine's Day Massacre and has been replayed in many movies and even commemorated in popular waxworks exhibitions.

While the massacre permanently etched Capone into legend, it also proved the turning point in his career. Before the bloody hit, Capone's criminal activities elicited surprisingly little public outrage. Indeed, he was, in the tradition of many of the outlaws of the Old West, something of a proletarian hero. In 1927, the public was delighted to read that he had amassed a personal fortune estimated at $100 million. But not only did the St. Valentine's Day hit fail to eliminate Moran (who was not present at the garage that day), its extravagant brutality mobilized public opinion against Capone. No longer regarded as a harmless bootlegger operating in the teeth of the much-hated Prohibition, he was seen now as a cold-blooded butcher. Nevertheless, Capone was so well insulated by his criminal organization and by his network of bribed officials that he evaded prosecution until federal authorities finally began probing his vast "business" interests with the object of prosecuting the gangster on multiple counts of income tax evasion.

Before the highly publicized tax investigation got under way, however, Capone learned that Moran had put a $50,000 price on his head. Deciding that prison was the safest place for him—at least for a time—Capone, the supreme user of "the system," arranged to have himself arrested in May 1929 for carrying an illegal firearm. He was sentenced to a year. But, following Capone's release, President Herbert Hoover personally pressed the Treasury Department to put Capone away for good. The IRS prosecuted Capone in 1931 for six years of tax evasion. Found guilty, he was sentenced to eleven years in prison and assessed $80,000 in fines and costs. By this time, however, the syphilis acquired from his years with prostitutes had resulted in paresis, progressively attacking Capone's central nervous system. Paralyzed and almost completely insane, he was paroled from prison in November 1939 and retired to his home on Palm Island, Florida, where he died of a massive brain hemorrhage on January 25, 1947.

See also: CRIME AND CRIMINALS; ITALIAN AMERICANS; NESS, ELIOT.

SUGGESTED READING: Laurence Bergreen, *Capone: The Man and the Era* (New York, 1994).

Captivity narratives. Narratives of settlers' captivity by Indians was the first form of mass literature produced in America, beginning with the first American "bestseller," published in Boston in 1682, *The Soveraignty & Goodness of God . . . , a Narrative of the Captivity and Restauration of Mrs. Mary Rowlandson.* The book went through two more editions in Cambridge (Massachusetts) and in London in 1682 and continued to be popular for the next century and a half, with major reprints in Boston (1720, 1770 [two editions], 1771, and 1773), New London (1773), and then variously throughout the nineteenth century. A later narrative, John Williams's *The Redeemed Captive,* an account of an English minister's captivity among the French-allied Indians of Canada, was published in Boston in 1706 and sold 1,000 copies in a single week. It was reissued in Boston in 1707, 1720, 1758, 1774, and 1776 and in New London in 1773. Between 1680 and 1716, captivity narratives dominated the list of frontier literature published in America. Indeed, during this period, three of the four most popular narrative works in the colonies were captivity accounts (the fourth narrative was the perennial favorite *Pilgrim's Progress* by John Bunyan).

Just what were captivity narratives, and why were they so popular with colonial readers? They were typically first-person accounts of an individual's experience of being captured and held by hostile Indians. The pattern characteristic of this folk-literature genre almost always included the suffering of hunger; pain; torture; the loss of a spouse, children (a frequent and heart-wrenching feature of these narratives is an episode in which an infant is snatched from his or her mother's arms and battered to death against a tree), and other relatives; and the patient endurance of all these things until the captive's "redemption" at the conclusion of the narrative. Mary Rowlandson's 1682 narrative remains, to this day, the best known of the New England captivity accounts. The word *redemption* (or *redeemed*) figures in the titles of many captivity narratives and is of particular significance. Captives were usually "redeemed"—that is, ransomed—from the Indians in exchange for money or other valuables. The word is also a pun on the religious significance of "redemption." Characteristically, these narratives depict Indian captivity as a trial ordained by God to test the victim's faith (and thereby strengthen it). The redemption that comes at the end of a string of travails—a metaphor of the sufferings to which the world subjects all men and women—is the reward of faith sustained. Thus, captivity narratives were in large measure religious parables meant to teach and to inspire. In addition, these narratives were also exciting tales about a subject of urgent importance to colonists clinging to the edge of a vast wilderness populated by "savages." Significantly, few of these narratives were about soldiers or solitary frontiersmen taken by Indians in combat. Most captivity narratives were written by or about women, who were taken from hearth and home. Throughout the most popular narratives, including those of Mary Rowlandson and Hannah Dustin (retold by COTTON MATHER in his *Humiliations Follow'd with Deliverances* of 1697), there runs a strong sexual undercurrent of a woman threatened with violent rape by a "heathen" of a different race. All of these elements—religious edification and a confirmation of faith, the dramatization of a common colonial danger and fear, the excitement of adventure, and sexual titillation—contributed to the enormous popularity of the captivity narrative, hundreds of which were produced. The genre both expressed and nurtured folk traditions · regarding the wilderness and Indian captivity and was America's first body of printed folk literature that could lay claim to mythic dimensions.

See also: BOONE, DANIEL.

SUGGESTED READING: Wilcomb E. Washburn, ed., *The Garland Library of Narratives of North American Indian Captivities* (311 titles in 111 vols.) (New York, 1976–78).

Carmer, Carl Lamson (1893–1976).

Carmer collected folklore from the South as well as from his native New York State. Educated at Hamilton College (Clinton, New York) and Harvard University, he collected upstate New York folklore and wrote verse based on it. From 1921 to 1927, he taught poetry at the University of Alabama in Tuscaloosa. It was here that he became interested in folk dancing and folksinging, and it was here that he discovered African-American oral traditions. Carmer observed life in Alabama in all of its dimensions, absorbing much from traditional storytellers and singers.

After he returned to New York, Carmer wrote *Deep South* (1930), a collection of verse, and *Stars Fell on Alabama* (1934), a narrative portrait of Alabama culture and history, which emphasized the more exotic or eccentric aspects of the state's folk life, especially on the plantation. Like many writers of his time, Carmer bathed the antebellum South in a romantic light, but he also looked unflinchingly at racial violence in the present (he witnessed and described a lynching), and he exhibited a vast and representative array of southern folklore and folkways.

Carmer's later books are devoted to the Hudson Valley folklore of his native state. He also collected and edited albums of regional songs, and he hosted a radio program, *Your Neck of the Woods,* which was devoted to folk heroes and myths of national interest.

SUGGESTED READING: Carl Lamson Carmer, *American Folklore and Its Old-World Backgrounds* (New York, 1956).

Carol. In its original sense, a carol was a traditional song type featuring a fixed stanza form with a chorus or burden, but by the early nineteenth century, the term was largely restricted to traditional Christmas songs. Christmas carols are very popular in the United States and are performed seasonally by ensembles both professional and amateur, neighborhood singing groups who serenade door to door, schoolchildren in pageants, and professional singers.

See also: FOLK MUSIC.

Carrière, Joseph Médard (1902–1970). Carrière was a collector and student of North American French language and customs and of the French folklore of the Midwest. He was born in Curran, Ontario, and studied French literature and romance languages at Laval University, Marquette University, the Sorbonne (Paris), and at Harvard University, from which he earned his Ph.D. in 1932. He taught at Northwestern University (Evanston, Illinois), and beginning in 1942, he taught at the University of Virginia, where he remained for the balance of his career.

Beginning in 1934, Carrière made a series of expeditions to Old Mines, Missouri, where he recorded folk songs and folktales among the six hundred French-speaking families living there. (His most important source of folktales was a barite miner named Joseph Ben Coleman.) Carrière published his collection of folktales in 1937, in the Creole dialect (the collection was republished in 1981 with English translations).

Carrière subsequently published phonological-historical analyses of the Missouri French dialect, a collection of Indiana French folk songs, and articles on French folk customs in the Midwest. Carrière was a leader in cross-cultural and cross-disciplinary studies.

President of the American Folklore Society from 1946 to 1947, Carrière was honored with many other appointments, including the Medal de l'Acadamie Française (1948), and the title of Chevalier de la Legion d'Honneur (1950).

SUGGESTED READING: Joseph Médard Carrière, *Tales from the French Folklore of Missouri* (Evanston and Chicago, 1937); Rosemary Hyde Thomas, *It's Good to Tell You: French Folktales from Missouri* (Columbia, Mo., 1981).

Carson, Christopher Houston ("Kit") (1809–1868). Among the many legendary names of the Old West, Kit Carson's is one of the most familiar. This Kentucky-born frontier scout, trapper, mountain man, Indian agent, and soldier fled an unhappy apprenticeship with a saddle maker in Missouri in 1826 to join a wagon train bound for Santa Fe, New Mexico. This marked the beginning of Carson's elevation into legend.

Carson's legend was in large part the result of his own skill, endurance, courage, and integrity, but it was also due to his friendship with the western explorer and politician John Charles Frémont (the "Pathfinder") and his wife, Jessie Benton Frémont, daughter of the powerful Missouri senator Thomas Hart Benton. The Frémonts were skilled and aggressive self-promoters, who, in turn, were eager to promote Carson as the western hero he did indeed become. Carson accompanied Frémont on several of Frémont's government-sponsored explorations of the far West in search of a suitable route for a transcontinental railroad. Carson served not only as a scout, but a trailblazer, who, always trusted and respected by the Indians, developed invaluable Indian contacts for Frémont as well as other explorers, hunters, and trappers.

From 1828 to 1831, Carson worked for

Photograph of Kit Carson late in life.

prominent fur trapper Ewing Young, ranging through much of the Southwest and California in search of beaver. In 1836, Carson was briefly employed by the powerful Hudson's Bay Company, and between 1841 and 1842, he worked out of Bent's Fort on the Arkansas River, in present-day Colorado. Accompanying Frémont's third expedition to California in 1845–46, Carson fought in the Bear Flag Rebellion for California's independence from Mexico and in the Mexican War. He also served as a courier and guide for General Stephen Watts Kearny, leading his forces from New Mexico into California.

By the end of the 1840s, Carson had married and settled with his wife on a sheep ranch in Taos, New Mexico. He trapped briefly in 1852, then, with Lucien Maxwell, drove his sheep herd to the new markets opening in California. Following this, Carson was appointed Indian agent in New Mexico, a post in which he served until the outbreak of the Civil War in 1861. In contrast to most Indian agents operating under the notoriously corrupt and inept federal Indian agency system, Carson was conscientious, efficient, caring, and respectful of his charges.

Carson first saw action in the Civil War at the Battle of Valverde, New Mexico, on February 21, 1862, after which he was promoted from lieutenant colonel of the First Regiment of New Mexico Volunteers to brigadier general. Although the union forces lost the battle, Carson's unit performed extremely well—the only New Mexico Volunteers who showed any degree of discipline. Most of Carson's duties during the Civil War did not involve fighting the Confederacy, but controlling hostile Mescalero Apache, Kiowa, and Navajo Indians. The assignment was one he faced with ambivalence, alternating considerable compassion (he had twice been married to Indian women) with utter ruthlessness. Nevertheless, his military operations against the Indians were far more successful than most, and they added to a reputation already legendary.

Carson himself contributed to the shaping of his legend by dictating (he was a lifelong illiterate) his autobiography, which his ghostwriter greatly embellished. Late in life, Carson and his third wife, Josefa, moved from Taos to Boggsville, Colorado (near present-day Las Animas). Josefa died there, and, a short time later, Kit Carson followed her.

SUGGESTED READING: Kit Carson, *Kit Carson's Autobiography,* Milo Milton Quaife, ed. (Chicago, 1935); Harvey F. Carter, *Dear Old Kit: The Historical Christopher Carson* (Norman, Okla., 1968).

Carson, Fiddlin' John (1868–1949).

Born on a hill country farm in Fannin County, Georgia, Carson became well known in North Georgia folk circles for playing his fiddle at political campaigns, at picnics, dances, and at the annual Georgia Old-Time Fiddlers' Association meeting in Atlanta. Beginning in 1913, he won the Old-Time Fiddlers' Championship almost every year to 1922. He reached a wider and more popular audience after 1922, playing on radio station WSB. RALPH PEER, innovator of field recording for commercial issue, captured Fiddlin' John singing and playing in June 1923. Peer found his old-time singing dreadful and wanted to issue only the fiddle tunes without the singing, but Polk Brockman, director of the phonograph department of Peer's grandfather's furniture store in Atlanta, which had built up a market for "race records" (as recordings of black music were called), persuaded Peer that there was a local audience of small farmers and mill workers who would warm to Fiddlin' John's singing as well as his fiddling. Brockman offered to buy five hundred copies as soon as they were pressed. Peer issued enough to fill the order, but without label or advertising—in short, exclusively for local circulation in and around Atlanta. Within a month, Brockman wanted another five hundred records, and Peer gave the issue a label number of 4890, thereby making it part of Okeh Records' popular catalogue and giving it wide distribution. Carson recorded twelve more sides in New York and agreed to record exclusively for Okeh. Fiddlin' John was the first southern white folk musician to have his material recorded and sold commercially, and his recordings were the first contribution to what became first the hillbilly music industry and, ultimately, the COUNTRY MUSIC industry.

See also: FOLK MUSIC.

SUGGESTED READING: Wayne W. Daniel, *Pickin' on Peachtree: A History of Country Music in Atlanta, Georgia* (Urbana, Ill., 1990); Gene Wigins, *Fiddlin' Georgia Crazy: Fiddlin' John Carson, His Real World, and the World of His Songs* (Urbana, Ill., 1987).

Carter Family, The. Among the dominant groups of early COUNTRY MUSIC history, the Carter Family came from humble origins. Alvin Plesant Delaney Carter (known as A.P.) was born in Maces Springs, Virginia, in 1891. As a youngster he sang in the local church choir, along with two uncles and an older sister. In 1918 he married Sara Dougherty, who was born in nearby Wise County, Virginia, and was an accomplished singer, guitarist, AUTOHARP and BANJO player. The third member of the group was Maybelle Addington, born in nearby Nickelsville, Virginia, in 1909, also a talented singer and player of the guitar, Autoharp, and banjo. She married A.P.'s brother Ezra in 1926.

The Carter Family was first recorded by the brilliant talent scout RALPH PEER, who set up the recording equipment of the Victor Talking Machine Company in Bristol, Tennessee, after announcing to the *Bristol News Bulletin* that he was auditioning local talent. Despite family opposition, the fact that Maybelle was seven months pregnant, and that the twenty-five miles to Bristol lay along rough dirt roads, the Carters piled instruments and the three children of A.P. and Sara (the youngest of whom was only seven months old) into their Model A Ford and made the trip to the recording session. The session was held on August 1, 1927, three days before Peer recorded another legend in the making, JIMMIE RODGERS. Peer was quite impressed by the Carter Family's commercial potential; they were the only group he recorded in Bristol who cut six sides, all accepted for release.

"When you recorded a session in those days," Maybelle later recalled, "you didn't get a second take because they had to scrape away several inches of wax, and it was simply unheard of." Peer had the songs copyrighted in A. P. Carter's name and published by Peer's own Southern Music Publishing Company. (There was a similar deal with Rodgers.) The six songs they copyrighted were not compositions of A.P., nor in fact were many other songs that bore his name. Peer was probably innovating the practice that still prevails in music publishing of claiming any song of unknown authorship. As the Carter Family reached wider and wider audiences, they soon ran out of well-known songs to record. A.P. would set out on song-hunting trips to find more material, a pursuit he carried out with impressive ability. While eventually the Carters did compose some of their own songs, many of A.P.'s finds were folk songs of the southern mountains.

Leslie Riddles, an African-American singer and guitarist from nearby Kingsport, Tennessee, taught the Carters several songs of his own, which they recorded. Riddles also accompanied A.P. on some of his collecting trips and later recalled A.P.'s efforts to find old sheet music and his insistence that people repeat songs enough times for him to write down the lyrics. When A.P. couldn't remember some of the tunes he had heard, Riddles could usually be depended on to retain them in his memory. He also had a significant influence on Maybelle's GUITAR style, and in some instances, she copied his accompaniments closely. The usual practice had been for the early country old-time musicians to make their instruments follow the melody. Since many of the older songs were in modal keys rather than the modern major and minor keys, and since often the songs in their traditional forms had been sung unaccompanied and with a free or irregular rhythm, the early commercial country singers simplified rhythm and melody, so that the songs could be accompanied by the three basic chords.

The Carters made their voices fit Maybelle's as she picked out the melody on the bass strings with her thumb and brushed the chords with her index finger on the treble strings—the reverse of the conventional practice. She also made skillful use of the embellishments of folk-style guitar, hammering-on, pulling off, and sliding. In some sessions she raised the nut of the guitar, tuned it to an open E chord, and played steel guitar lap-steel style. Usually, Sara played second guitar or Autoharp behind Maybelle's lead. Although the Autoharp was a form of zither, designed to be placed flat on a table with the left-hand fingers pressing down the chord buttons and the right hand strumming chord arpeggios, Sara developed a much more complex approach of holding the instrument on the left side of her chest, picking the melody with thumb and forefinger of the left hand and strumming back and forth with the right—a technique similar to what Maybelle did with her F-5 Gibson arch-top guitar. Sara, whose voice kept getting lower as the years passed, was the lead vocalist. Occasionally—reluctantly, and only at Peer's urging—she yodeled, and on one very special occasion, the Carters recorded with the Blue Yodeler himself, JIMMIE RODGERS.

Unlike typical country music stars of the day, the Carters appeared in public only intermittently, playing occasional shows in schoolhouses and churches in and around Virginia, Kentucky, and North Carolina. They avoided vaudeville tours, and their few concerts were informal events, publicized by handbills handed out by A.P. and maybe an ad in a local newspaper. A typical poster announced: "LOOK! Victor Artist A. P. Carter and the Carter Family will give a MUSICAL PROGRAM at . . . on . . . ," followed by the modest assurance that "The Program is Morally Good." Nor did the Carter Family make a serious attempt to reap a fortune from their records. There was never any formal written contract or a guaranteed minimum payment, and certainly no agents. While they did sell songbooks, they plugged or sold the records themselves. Only once did they appear on WSM's GRAND OLE OPRY. Moreover, the Carters made no attempt to keep up with the latest trends in the industry, but continued to perform in the same basic style—though they improved steadily in that vein.

They performed the songs they thought their

public would like: songs of home, death, mother, unrequited love, and the occasional novelty item. Typical songs included the BALLADS "John Hardy," "Sweet Fern," "Worried Man," "Mid the Green Fields of Virginia," "Hello Central Give Me Heaven," "Keep on the Sunny Side," and some revival spirituals, such as "Lonesome Valley," "Little Moses," and "I Wouldn't Mind Dying." They included a few Tin Pan Alley numbers, but modified them considerably. Their biggest seller was "Wildwood Flower," recorded in 1928, which had over a million sales.

After the divorce of Sara and A.P. in 1936, the Carter Family continued to work together as a group. They recorded for Decca, then moved to Texas, where they performed on various border stations. Other members of the family joined them: the daughters of Ezra and Maybelle, Anita, June, and Helen; and A.P. and Sara's children, Joe and Janette. The last recording sessions by the original Carter Family were held in 1941, and they disbanded in 1943. Maybelle then formed a group with her three daughters, and had a successful run on radio as well as at the Grand Ole Opry. A.P. died in 1960, ten years before the Carter Family was elevated to the Country Music Hall of Fame. After A.P.'s death, Maybelle and her daughters began to bill themselves as the Carter Family. Later, June went solo, joined Johnny Cash's road show as a singer and comic, and become Cash's supportive wife, helping him to recover from alcoholism and drug addiction.

See also: BLUEGRASS; FOLK MUSIC; GUTHRIE, WOODY (WOODROW WILSON).

SUGGESTED READING: Stacy Harris, *The Carter Family: Country Music's First Family* (New York, 1978).

Casey Jones. See JONES, CASEY.

Cassidy, Butch, and the Sundance Kid.

Butch Cassidy, whose given name was Robert LeRoy Parker (1866–1937?), and the Sundance Kid—Harry Longabaugh (1861–1908?)—were the nucleus of the Hole-in-the-Wall Gang, also called the Wild Bunch, which also included gunmen Ben Kilpatrick ("The Tall Texan"), Will Carver, and Harvey Logan ("Kid Curry"). A highly elusive, wide-ranging, and well-organized train- and bank-robbing gang, the Wild Bunch quickly earned legendary status and, in particular, earned that status for Cassidy and the Kid. The 1969 George Roy Hill film, *Butch Cassidy and the Sundance Kid,* starring Paul Newman and Robert Redford in the title roles, both capitalized on and revivified the mystique surrounding the two outlaws.

Robert LeRoy Parker was born in Beaver, Utah, one of thirteen children. He was raised in Circleville, Utah, and then on a small ranch, where, according to sister Lula Parker Betenson, he learned how to shoot (and how to rustle cattle) from a ranch hand and part-time outlaw named Mike Cassidy. At some time after he left home in 1884, Parker assumed Cassidy's name. (The "Butch" may have been acquired after Parker worked for a short period at a Rock Springs, Wyoming, butcher shop.)

Butch Cassidy roamed the countryside as a cowboy and a part-time rustler, but by June 24, 1889, he had begun robbing banks and trains. After robbing the San Miguel County Bank in Telluride, Colorado, on the twenty-fourth, Cassidy joined Harry Longabaugh (the Sundance Kid) and the others to form the Wild Bunch. They operated out of Hole-in-the-Wall, Wyoming, Robbers Roost, Utah, and Brown's Hole, Colorado, and were active all over the West, knocking over banks and trains.

Harry Longabaugh was born in Mont Clare, Pennsylvania, and raised in the East, but moved out west when he was a teenager. From August

1887 to February 1889, he served a term in the Sundance, Wyoming, jail for horse theft, and joined the Wild Bunch, as the Sundance Kid, almost as soon as he was released.

Although the Wild Bunch was highly successful, the group disbanded around 1900. Either together or separately, Cassidy and Sundance (the latter with his common-law wife, Etta Place, a schoolteacher and/or prostitute) fled to Argentina, where they set up as cattle ranchers. Sundance returned to Denver in 1907 when Etta Place developed appendicitis and required an operation. He subsequently rejoined Butch Cassidy in South America, and the two outlaws worked for a Bolivian mining company part time as they resumed robbing banks and trains on a grand scale, hitting targets in Argentina, Chile, and Bolivia.

In 1908, they pulled a payroll robbery and were run to ground in San Vicente, Bolivia, by government soldiers. Most believe that the Sundance Kid was killed in the resulting shootout, but that Butch Cassidy escaped, showing up in Michigan as William Thaddeus Phillips, a mechanical engineer from Des Moines, Iowa. Phillips died of cancer at the county poor farm near Spokane, Washington, in 1937. Some recent scholars have suggested that Sundance also survived the Bolivian shootout and returned to the United States.

See also: GUNFIGHTER, WESTERN.

SUGGESTED READING: Lula Parker Betenson, *Butch Cassidy, My Brother* (Provo, Utah, 1975); James D. Horan, *The Wild Bunch* (New York, 1958).

Cat's cradle. This traditional string game has long been popular in Europe as well as America.

It may be played solo or with two players, who manipulate a loop of string to create a number of evolving figures, the contours of which suggest a miniature cradle. In some cultural traditions, including, for example, those of Eskimos and of Australian aborigines, string-figure games assume great complexity and even ritual significance. In contrast, cat's cradle is simply a traditional amusement for children.

See also: GAMES.

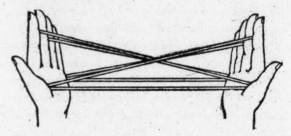

A simple, one-person cat's cradle. (Collection of Alan Axelrod)

Cemetery lore. The folklore related to cemeteries includes grave markers and the epitaphs often inscribed on them. Also subject to study is the siting of the cemetery itself. To begin with, the term *cemetery* enters common American usage relatively late, in the nineteenth century. Prior to this, burial places were known as burying grounds or graveyards. If this designation seems brutal to modern ears, even the "more polite" *cemetery* is yielding to *memorial park*, at least among the commercial operators of burial sites. However, "graveyard" or "burying grounds" aptly describes most colonial and early-nineteenth-century communal places of interment, which, typically, were plots of ground reserved just beyond the town limits. The early burying grounds are noteworthy for their lack of planning and pattern, in sharp contrast to mod-

Two traditional American "burying grounds": At Old Pennepack Baptist Church, Bustleton, Pennsylvania, and at the Mennonite Meeting House in Germantown (now part of Philadelphia), Pennsylvania.

ern cemeteries, which are usually attractively landscaped, with the graves and grave markers arranged in neat rows or even more complex, but regular, patterns. This was, in part, the result of a mid-nineteenth-century movement that tended to equate cemeteries with parks.

The most distinctive features of a cemetery are its grave markers or headstones. The urge to mark graves is ancient. The object is to mark the grave, housing a corruptible body, with a marker fashioned of a symbolically enduring material. Early American markers were slate. By the nineteenth century, marble predominated, giving way to polished granite by the twentieth century. Colonial New England artisans became highly skilled at fashioning grimly decorative grave markers, which are often carved with representations of winged skulls and other memento mori, such as coffins and hourglasses. Epitaphs carved into these early markers are generally admonitory, enjoining the passerby to think upon his own impending end.

With the passage of time—or by means of a journey away from New England—grave markers generally became less severe, featuring both iconography and epitaphs less focused on death than on hope. Instead of the winged skull, winged angels became commonplace, and epitaphs commented on the character of the deceased, expressed the love of his or her family, or expressed faith in a heavenly reward.

By the mid-nineteenth century, American cemeteries were increasingly influenced by the elaborate Victorian iconography of death, which included many motifs drawn from nature—weeping willows, representations of yews, garlands of vines and flowers—and from faith, such as hands brought together in prayer. Epitaphs became at once more personal—expressing a family's love—and conventional, drawn from hackneyed sheaves of Victorian funerary verse. Commercial twentieth-century grave markers tend to be monolithic, with simple designs and brief, highly formulaic epitaphs. The general sterility and monotony of modern cemeteries has added to the attraction of nineteenth-, eighteenth-, and seventeenth-century burying grounds, as well as rural cemeteries of more modern vintage, which often display more originality of craftsmanship in the carving of the markers and far more heartfelt sentiment in the epitaphs.

SUGGESTED READING: Alan Ludwig, *Graven Images: New England Stonecarving and Its Symbols* (Middletown, Conn., 1966); Richard E. Meyer, ed., *Cemeteries and Gravemarkers: Voices of American Culture* (Ann Arbor, Mich., 1989); Charles L. Wallis, *Stories on Stone: A Book of American Epitaphs* (New York, 1954).

Center for the Study of Southern Culture.

This institution for the interdisciplinary study of the American South was established in 1977 at the University of Mississippi under the directorship of William R. Ferris. An interdisciplinary curriculum is offered, drawing on the resources of history, English, anthropology, sociology, music, art, political science, Afro-American studies, and women's studies departments and programs. Among the center's most important activities is the publication of its newsletter, *Southern Register,* and the magazines, *Old Time Country, Rejoice!,* and *Living Blues,* as well as the scholarly journal *Crossroads.* In addition, the center sponsors cultural and folklife-related conferences.

Chanteys.

Also spelled *chanty* and *shanty* (from the French *chanter,* "to sing"), *chanteys* are the work songs of sailors from the era of sail. The chantey was intended to aid in the rhythmical coordination required for hoisting and manipulating heavy sails. A shantyman was positioned at the leading position on the rope, with the other sailors deployed behind him. The shantyman would sing a line of chantey, to which the group would respond in chorus, pulling together at a certain point in the melody. It was the shanty-man's job to select a song appropriate to the task at hand and to generate chantey lines as long as work had to be done. As actually sung, the lyrics of chanteys involved much more improvisation than printed texts suggest. Chantey subjects generally reflected the realities of the seafaring life, ranging from bawdy times ashore to stormy times at sea.

Musically, chanteys were a derivative form, founded chiefly on familiar ballad tunes that were adapted to three different types of work: short-haul, also called short-drag, which were short, simple ditties sung when a few pulls were required; halyard shanties, to accompany sail hoisting (the most famous of these is "Blow the Man Down"); and windlass chanteys, also called capstan chanteys, which aimed to synchronize footsteps for hoisting anchor ("Shenandoah" and "A-Roving" are the most familiar songs of this type). Among British sailors, the heyday of the chantey was the eighteenth century, while, for American sailors, chanteys were a nineteenth-century phenomenon.

See also: FOLK MUSIC; SAILORS AND SEAFARING LORE; "SHENANDOAH"; WHALING; WORK SONGS.

SUGGESTED READING: Stan Hugill, *Shanties from the Seven Seas: Shipboard Work-Songs and Songs Used as Work-Songs from the Great Days of Sail* (London, 1984).

Charlie Chaplin rhymes.

The silent-movie comedian Charlie Chaplin (1889–1977) had legions of fans and also inspired American children of the 1910s through the 1940s to create doggerel verses, mainly recited as skipping-rope rhymes. The most frequently heard rhyme is this: "Charlie Chaplin sat on a pin. / How many inches did it

Charlie Chaplin in his most famous guise: the Little Tramp.

go in? / One, two, three . . ." The count continues until the jumper misses. The First and Second World Wars occasioned a number of variations, including such lines as "Salute to the captain, bow to the queen, / And turn your back on the old submarine."

Charms.

Charms. Incantations and physical objects used to bring about desired results (for example, to create fertility, to attract a lover, and so on) or to promote general good fortune.

See also AMULET; COLLEGE FOLKLORE; HOODOO HAND; KNOTS; MEDICINE, FOLK; POWWOW; RABBIT'S FOOT; ROOTWORK.

Chase, Richard (1904–1988).

Chase, Richard (1904–1988). Chase collected and performed folk songs and dances, as well as JACK TALES, for which he is best known.

Born in New England, Chase grew up in Huntsville, Alabama, where his father owned a nursery. While attending Harvard University in 1924, Chase learned about the Pine Mountain Settlement School in Kentucky. He visited the school and there discovered the riches of the southern BALLAD tradition as well as the collecting work of British folklorist CECIL SHARP. Chase did not complete his Harvard degree. Instead, he devoted himself to collecting, performing, and teaching folklore in general and folk songs in particular. Both as a collector and a teacher-performer, he toured nationally.

In 1929, Chase took a B.S. degree in botany from Antioch College (Ohio) and subsequently traveled to Europe, where he established contacts with the English Folk Dance and Song Society. Returning to the United States, he was hired in 1935 to teach folk songs at a teachers' conference in Raleigh, North Carolina. In conversation with one of his students, he learned about the existence of Jack tales, fairy tales featuring a trickster (named Jack) as the protagonist. Fascinated, Chase collected and performed Jack tales, drawing on the Ward family of Beech Mountain, North Carolina, as his principal source. He published six in *Southern Folklore Quarterly* between 1937 and 1941.

Following up leads provided by the Wards, Chase collected additional Jack tales in Wise County, Virginia, then worked for the Works Progress Administration (WPA) Virginia Writers' Project to create a volume on Wise County folklore. Chase put the chief emphasis on folktales. Unfortunately, the book was never published, but Chase did include thirty-four Wise County tales, of which fifteen were Jack tales, in his three popular books, *The Jack Tales* (1943), *Grandfather Tales* (1948), and *American Folk Tales and Songs* (1956).

From 1934 to 1941, Chase worked with and performed at the White Top Mountain Folk Festival (North Carolina), then traveled widely as a performer. It is, however, for his work with Jack tales that he is best remembered.

See also: WARD, MARSHALL.

SUGGESTED READING: Charles L. Perdue, Jr., ed., *Outwitting the Devil: Jack Tales from Wise County, Virginia* (Santa Fe, N.M., 1987).

Chenier, Clifton (1925–1988). Chenier was the most famous exponent of ZYDECO music. He was born in Saint Landry Parish, Louisiana, and first imbibed zydeco south Louisiana musical traditions from his father, who performed on the accordion at local parties. Clifton Chenier and his brother Cleveland began playing together by the early 1940s. They formed the Hot Sizzling Band in the late 1940s and, through the early fifties, played the rough circuit of clubs along the Texas-Louisiana Gulf Coast that catered to oil workers.

In 1954, Chenier was discovered by a scout for Elko Records, and the performer made his first recordings. He and his band also began touring the Southwest, West Coast, and Chicago. By the early 1960s, Chenier had moved away from his zydeco roots, finding R&B more lucrative. But in 1964 he signed with ARHOOLIE RECORDS, which released a string of important zydeco albums, including *Louisiana Blues and Zydeco, Bon Ton Roulet, King of the Bayous,* and *Bogalusa Boogie.* Chenier soon found himself on the folk-revival circuit, appearing at the Berkeley Blues Festival in 1966 and the Newport Folk Festival in 1969 and touring Europe during 1967–69. By the early 1970s, Chenier was called (and was calling himself) the "King of Zydeco." He performed, often garbed in mantle and crown, with his Louisiana Hot Band throughout the Gulf Coast region as well as nationally until the end of his life.

Child ballad. With the BROADSIDE, the BLUES BALLAD, and the PARLOR BALLAD, the Child, or medieval, ballad is one the four types of Anglo-American BALLADS folklorists recognize. The nineteenth-century American scholar FRANCIS JAMES CHILD catalogued the medieval-style bal-

lad of the British Isles and recognized 305 distinct ballads, which he collected and documented in *The English and Scottish Popular Ballads* (1882–98). The medieval-style ballad genre, named in Child's honor, may be traced to Europe in the late Middle Ages, but its heyday extended from the late 1400s through the late 1600s, especially in Scotland. Although few new ballads of this type were composed after this period, the old ones continued to be popular and were brought to America by English and Scottish immigrants. Child ballads deal with four categories of topics, including the supernatural, the romantic and tragic, the historical and legendary, and the humorous. Romantic and tragic ballads are the most numerous. Stylistically, the Child ballad is somewhat remote, its story typically told in the third person, in contrast to the more modern broadside ballad, in which first-person narration predominates. Nor does the Child ballad editorialize, moralize, or otherwise direct the hearer's response to the story. It merely *tells* the story. Perhaps the characteristic that most distinguishes Child ballads from other folk-song and ballad genres is its formulaic nature. The Child ballads are replete with formulaic phrases, stock stanzas, and pat epithets, all in the manner of the heroic oral tradition. Metrical patterns are similarly formulaic, with ballads featuring four-line stanzas accented 4/3/4/3 or two-line stanzas accented 4/4.

See also: ANGLO AMERICANS; APPALACHIA; "BARBARA ALLEN"; DAVIS, ARTHUR KYLE, JR.; DUSENBURY, EMMA HAYS; FOLK MUSIC; "I GAVE MY LOVE A CHERRY"

SUGGESTED READING: Francis James Child, *The English and Scottish Popular Ballads* (1882–98; reprint ed., New York, 1965); MacEdward Leach and Tristram P. Coffin, *The Critics and the Ballad* (Carbondale, Ill., 1973).

Child, Francis James (1825–1896). One of the true pioneers of the American folklore movement, Child was, first and foremost, a collector and editor of the BALLAD. One of the founders of the American Folklore Society, he was also a highly respected literary scholar. Boston born, Child was educated at Boston Latin School and Harvard College, which employed him as a tutor in mathematics, history, and political economics. A promising scholar, he traveled to Europe for study at the universities of Berlin and Göttingen, then returned to Harvard as Boylston Professor of Rhetoric and Oratory. In 1876, he became Harvard's first professor of English.

In Germany, Child had been greatly impressed by the school of philology developed by the brothers Grimm, and he brought their linguistically grounded theories and methods of folklore collecting and study back to the United States. He approached the works of Edmund Spenser and of Geoffrey Chaucer as a linguist/philologist, editing *The Poetical Works of Edmund Spenser* and writing *Observations on the Language of Chaucer's* Canterbury Tales, a groundbreaking analysis of Middle English. An influential teacher of literature, Child counted among his students several who would later contribute to folklore studies, including GEORGE LYMAN KITTREDGE, FRANCIS BARTON GUMMERE, and PHILLIPS BARRY.

While literary scholars still prize Child's work on Spenser and Chaucer, he is best known for his monumental ballad collection, the five-volume *English and Scottish Popular Ballads* (1882–98). Not content merely to present a collection, Child applied the principles of German philology to his work. His extensive notes to each ballad discuss the narrative tradition from which the ballad arises and analyze narrative parallels from other countries. Furthermore, Child scrupulously reproduced his texts, exactly as he had found them,

so that they are valid documents for linguistic as well as folkloristic study.

By modern standards of folklore scholarship, Child does have his limitations. He was not a field collector. Instead, he collected almost all of his ballads from manuscript sources and based his classification (Child recognized and defined 305 ballad types) exclusively on these sources. Child paid no attention whatsoever to the musical content of the ballad; his focus was strictly textual. Further, while his scope was international, in that he drew thematic parallels between the English and Scottish ballads and the folklore of other countries, he defined the genre of the ballad strictly in terms of the English and Scottish examples he studied. Finally, Child assumed that he was studying an extinct tradition—that no new ballads were being created. Subsequent scholarship, based on actual fieldwork, has shown this to be the most serious of Child's mistakes. Whatever Child's shortcomings, however, it was he who established the foundations for all future study of the ballad. Many later scholars might have identified themselves in opposition to a number of Child's most basic assumptions, but at least he had provided something to define oneself against.

See also: AMERICAN FOLKLORE SOCIETY; ANGLO AMERICANS; APPALACHIA; BELDEN, HENRY MARVIN; BRONSON, BERTRAND HARRIS; CHILD BALLAD; FOLK MUSIC; GAMES; GEROULD, GORDON HALL; GUMMERE, FRANCIS BARTON; KITTREDGE, GEORGE LYMAN; KRAPPE, ALEXANDER HAGGERTY; POUND, LOUISE.

SUGGESTED READING: Francis James Child, *The English and Scottish Popular Ballads* (1882–98; reprint ed., New York, 1965); Sigurd B. Hustvedt, *Ballad Books and Ballad Men* (Cambridge, Mass., 1930).

Childbearing folklore. Childbirth has given rise to numerous folk beliefs and activities to predict outcomes and to protect mothers and their infants. Nowhere else in America are the beliefs, customs, and folk medicine (see MEDICINE, FOLK) associated with childbirth more varied than in the South. Native American, Afro-American, and Euro-American folk streams combine in this region.

Some folk beliefs revolve around determining at conception the sex of the child. For example, a father might keep a leather string on his person during intercourse to produce a boy. Some believed that if the mother turned on her left side following intercourse, the child would be a girl; lying on the right side produced a boy.

Other widespread folk beliefs concern the effect on the fetus of outside events. For example, the mother's suffering a fright would adversely affect the child. Some believed that the expectant mother should only look at beautiful things, lest the child be born deformed, ugly, or with bad habits. Some very specific sights were to be avoided altogether; for instance, if a pregnant woman sees a snake, her baby's ability to walk might be impaired. What an expectant mother eats has often been considered very important. Everything from birthmarks, to fussiness, to food aversions and allergies have been attributed to foods the mother ate or failed to eat.

The process of labor and birth have been attended traditionally by a variety of folk practices and folk medicines. Herbal teas were administered to hasten labor, and a knife, scissors, or other sharp instrument might be placed under the expectant mother's pillow "to cut the pain" of labor. In the South, various herbal teas and even Coca-Cola (which, prior to the 1903 Pure Food and Drug Act, contained cocaine) were frequently prescribed as painkillers during labor.

Among many groups, including people in the rural South, great importance was traditionally attached to the presence of a "caul," the amniotic sac membrane, covering the newborn's face. This is a sign that the child will possess psychic or spiritual powers. Beyond this, much emphasis was also traditionally placed on the manner in which the placenta, membranes, and umbilical cord were disposed of. Often, these were burned. Failure to dispose of these materials properly might adversely affect the child's future.

See also: COUVADE.

SUGGESTED READING: Marie Campbell, *Folks Do Get Born* (1946; reprint ed., New York, 1984).

Chinese Americans. This very large immigrant group is extremely diverse and dynamic, encompassing descendants of immigrants who established themselves during the gold rushes of the late 1840s and 1850s as well as new arrivals. Of the early wave of immigrants, most came to the West during the mid- to later nineteenth century and provided much of the manual labor that settled the country, most spectacularly in the building of the Central Pacific Railroad portion of the transcontinental railroad that was completed in 1869. The Chinese endured bitter racial discrimination, which, in many places, took the form of an organized anti-Chinese movement and legislation (including the Exclusion Act of 1882) to restrict Chinese immigration. In part as a defense against hostile white neighbors, toward the end of the nineteenth century many rural Chinese immigrants resettled in ethnically homogenous urban neighborhoods. Thus a number of major American cities, including San Francisco, Los Angeles, Chicago, New York, Boston, Philadelphia, and Washington, D.C., gained so-called Chinatowns. Within these urban ghettoes, native Chinese culture flourished, including the practice of traditional Taoist religion, foodways, art and ornamentation, and, to some degree, architecture, especially in the erection of temples.

Architecture and other aspects of Chinese MATERIAL CULTURE—such as features of ornament, costume, and the traditional queue (pigtail) worn by working-class men—became familiar to Occidentals who visited the Chinatowns. Chinese foodways, at least in modified form, also became familiar, as the inexpensive "Chinese restaurant" grew in popularity among non-Chinese urban Americans. Far less visible to outsiders, however, were the Cantonese folk songs immigrants brought with them. Most prominent among these were the *muk-yu* (wood-fish) cantefables, usually narrative songs on traditional mythic or historical subjects, but also devoted to contemporary immigrant sorrows and hardships. Few non-Chinese made any effort to learn about Chinese holidays and seasonal festivals, save for "Chinese New Year," which, in cities like New York and San Francisco, draw many curious non-Chinese visitors into Chinatown. For the Chinese themselves, New Year is both a social occasion and a time to drive away bad spirits with the noise of blaring instruments and firecrackers. Colorful parades occur in plenty.

For many years, well into the twentieth century, America's Chinatowns retained about them an air of somewhat sinister mystery. Beginning in the 1970s, a variety of Chinese-American cultural organizations have developed cultural and folklife programs designed to reach out to the non-Chinese community. Of particular interest to the non-Chinese has been Chinese opera, a form of theater that combines singing and acting with the martial arts.

See also: IMMIGRANT FOLKLORE.

SUGGESTED READING: Lani Ah Tye Farkas and Edward McAndrews, *Bury My Bones in America: The Saga of a Chinese Family in California, 1852–1996* (San Francisco, 1998); Ben Fong-Torres, *The Rice Room: Growing up Chinese-American from Number Two Son to Rock 'n' Roll* (New York, 1995); Dorothy Hoobler and Thomas Hoobler, *The Chinese American Family Album* (New York, 1994); Maxine Hong Kingston, *China Men* (New York, 1989); Ronald Takaki, *A Different Mirror: A History of Multicultural America* (Boston, 1994).

Christensen, Abbie (Abigail Mandania) Holmes (1852–1938).

This collector of the African-American folklore of the South Carolina Sea Islands was born in Massachusetts and moved with her abolitionist parents to South Carolina during the Civil War. There she transcribed the African-American dialect tales she heard, publishing them after the war. Among the tales she recorded were those in the ANANSI tradition involving BRER RABBIT. She correctly ascribed these stories, told to her by former slaves, as being of African origin. Christensen published "De Wolf, de Rabbit, an' de Tar Baby" in a Massachusetts newspaper in 1874, anticipating JOEL CHANDLER HARRIS's literary version by six years.

Christensen published other Sea Island dialect tales in the New York *Independent*. In 1892, she published a volume of dialect stories, *Afro-American Folk Lore Told Round Cabin Fires on the Sea Islands of South Carolina*, under the name Mrs. A.M.H. Christensen, the pen name she adopted after her marriage in 1875. Christensen was a member of the American Folklore Society and wrote a scholarly paper on African-American spirituals and shouts, which was presented at the 1893 World's Columbian Exposition in Chicago and published in the *Journal of American Folklore* in 1894. She donated profits from the sale of her book to the Port

Royal Agricultural School for African Americans, which she helped to found in 1902.

SUGGESTED READING: Monica M. Tetzlaff, entry on Christensen in Jan Harold Brunvand, ed., *American Folklore: An Encyclopedia* (New York, 1996).

Christeson, Robert Perry (1911–1992).

A fiddler since his boyhood days in Pulaski County, Missouri, Christeson also became an important collector and student of fiddle tunes. Raised in rural Missouri, Christeson taught himself to fiddle by watching fiddlers at local dances. He graduated from the University of Missouri and was employed as an assistant county agent, a county agent, and a resettlement administrator in rural Missouri, including the Ozarks region. While discharging his paid duties, he took time to observe and absorb the fiddling styles peculiar to different parts of the state. It would, however, be many years before Christeson made use of what he had learned. World War II military service and a job as statistician in the Livestock Reporting Section of the U.S. Department of Agriculture took him away from permanent residence in Missouri for nearly thirty years. Nevertheless, whenever he could, Christeson returned to Missouri to make field recordings, beginning in 1948 with recordings of Bill Driver, an African-American fiddler he had first heard in the late 1920s.

It was not until 1970 that Christeson returned to live in Missouri. He began to ready his fiddle-tune collection for publication, issuing a volume of fiddle tunes and field recordings in 1973 and following it in 1984 with a second volume.

SUGGESTED READING: Robert Perry Christeson, ed., *The Old-Time Fiddlers' Repertory*, vol. 1 (Columbia, Mo., 1973) and vol. 2 (Columbia, Mo., 1984).

Christmas.

In America, Christmas is both a Christian religious holiday commemorating the birth of Christ and a secular holiday, celebrated even by many non-Christians. Indeed, even in its religious aspect, Christmas has strong associations with non-Christian tradition. That it is celebrated on December 25 is almost certainly the result of a desire among early Christians to co-opt the pagan Roman Saturnalia, the seven-day celebration of the winter solstice beginning on December 17. Making merry and exchanging gifts were traditions of the Saturnalia that readily transferred to commemoration of Christ's birth and the presentation of gifts by the magi. Moreover, it is no accident that Christmas is celebrated so near to NEW YEAR's Day. The ancient Roman custom of decorating houses with greenery and lights to celebrate the New Year was, again, transferred to the Christmas celebration. As Teutonic tribes made their presence felt in the Gallic, British, and central European frontiers of the Roman Empire, German and Celtic Yule traditions entered into the celebration of Christmas as well. These included the burning of the Yule log, the making and eating of Yule cakes, "decking the halls" with greenery, and bringing into one's house a fir tree. The exchange of gifts and greetings were also features of the Germanic and Celtic seasonal tradition. The evergreen foliage and tree, symbolic of life everlasting, was readily adapted into the symbolic complex celebrating the birth of Christ, as were the midwinter fires (symbolized by the Yule log and Christmas lights), which also suggested life, the renewal of life, and hope. But not only does Christmas synthesize Christian and pagan traditions, it combines as its central symbols the newborn Christ child and SANTA CLAUS, a secularized version of St. Nicholas, patron saint of family and children.

In America, Christmas was almost certainly observed in the Jamestown, Virginia, colony in

As this late nineteenth-century chromolithograph suggests, Christmas in America has long been primarily a children's holiday.

Girls opening their Christmas stockings, Christmas morning, New Jersey, 1975.

1607, but was frowned upon (and for a time even outlawed) by the New England Puritans. Today, it is recognized as an official federal and state holiday, and few regional distinctions exist in the celebration of the holiday, although many southerners persist in shooting off fireworks and launching bottle rockets on Christmas Eve (a custom unknown outside of the South). The profusion of commercial ornaments, greeting cards, and gifts have further served to "nationalize" observance of the holiday. The Christmas tree, a feature of the holiday linked to the Celtic and Germanic past, may have been brought to America as recently as the Revolution. It is believed that Hessian troops introduced the custom of the decorated tree here. In 1856, President Franklin Pierce erected the first Christmas tree in the White House, a custom all other presidents have followed. In addition, many American cities erect an "official" tree, dedicating it at a public lighting ceremony.

Many people decorate not only the interiors of their houses, but the outsides as well. Especially in urban neighborhoods, brilliant (not to say gaudy) displays of lights on houses are common, as are Nativity scenes, Santa Claus figures, and effigies of such supporting characters as Rudolph the red-nosed reindeer and Santa's elfin "helpers." Within these festively decorated homes, traditional Christmas dinners (the main course is usually TURKEY or ham, rarely a goose, which is more popular in England) are served, as are alcoholic beverages, especially spiked punches and eggnog. Sometime during the days leading up to Christmas, many places of business throw "office parties," which not infrequently become sources of office folklore concerning (for example) the usually sober-sided CPA who has one too many.

See also: ANGLO AMERICANS; EASTER AND EASTER PARADE.

SUGGESTED READING: James H. Barnett, *The American Christmas: A Study in National Culture* (New York, 1954); J. M. Golby and A. W. Purdue, *The Making of the Modern Christmas* (Athens, Ga., 1986); Sue Samuelson, *Christmas: An Annotated Bibliography* (New York, 1982).

Christy, Edwin P. "Ned" (1815–1862).

Creator of the enormously popular Christy Minstrels, Christy was a pioneer of the MINSTREL SHOW, a nineteenth-century form of commercial entertainment founded, in part, on African-American folk traditions and catering to popular images of the South. Christy was born in Philadelphia and worked in New York as an office boy, a hotel clerk, and a traveling salesman. About 1840, he began performing on banjo and tambourine in hotels and barrooms in Buffalo, New York, and donned for performance what was perceived as "typical" African-American dress—so-called plantation clothes—and blackened his face with burnt-cork makeup. In blackface, he sang and danced at Harry Meech's Museum in Buffalo before forming his own company, the Virginia Minstrels, in 1842, in imitation of the group formed a few years earlier by DANIEL DECATUR EMMETT, the northern composer of "Dixie." When Christy expanded the group of four to seven in 1846, he renamed them the Christy Minstrels and performed throughout the country, spawning many imitators, until 1854.

If the Christy troupe had done nothing more than popularize the songs of STEPHEN FOSTER, it would deserve recognition, but the Christy company also was the troupe most responsible for giving the minstrel show the formal structure that became the convention of the minstrel genre: a company of performers seated in a semicircle, with an "interlocutor" at the center and "end men" at either end, one with a set of bones or castanets (he was called "Mr. Bones") and the other with a tambourine ("Tambo"). The interlocutor acted as the master of ceremonies and the straight man for the jokes that flew between Tambo and Mr. Bones. As Christy established it, the show was always performed in three sections. First, the players made an elaborate entrance, which culminated in the interlocutor's command, "Gentle-men, be seated." Next came the "First Part," consisting of songs, dances, and the comic repartee of Tambo and Mr. Bones, and then the "Olio," an assortment of individual specialty acts, which was the direct precursor of vaudeville. As Christy established the format of the minstrel show, all performers were white men in blackface, save for the interlocutor, who wore no makeup.

While Christy's minstrel shows were built upon, reinforced, and disseminated racial stereotypes, they also introduced to the public a host of popular stage dances, acquainting white audiences with at least facsimiles of African-American-inspired folk dance. Nourished by folk sources, Christy's minstrel show was the first important form of mass popular entertainment in America. Christy himself retired, a very wealthy man, in 1854.

See also: AFRICAN AMERICANS.

SUGGESTED READING: Russell Nye, *The Unembarrassed Muse: The Popular Arts in America* (New York, 1970).

Church, Henry (1836–1908).

Born in Chagrin Falls, Ohio, folk painter and monumental stone carver Henry Church received little formal education and apprenticed himself to his father, a blacksmith, who did not appreciate his son's evident artistic ability. Church set up his own smithy after he married in 1859 and pursued that trade until his retirement in 1886. It was, then, late in his life that Church began painting his hilarious still lifes. His typical subject was an arrangement of fruit set in various Victorian interiors, but always with an incongruous comic element. For example, his best-known work, *The Monkey Picture* (1895–1900?) shows two monkeys tearing up a lavish festive arrangement of fruit on a table while a policeman runs to stop them. Very different from the still lifes are Church's carvings on the rock walls of the Chagrin River. These carvings, which he titled *The Rape of the Indian Tribes by the White Man,* include life-sized animals, such as a mountain lion and eagle, and Indians. For many years after Church's death, the carvings were thought locally to be primitive carvings and did not become generally known until 1937, when Sam Rosenberg, a writer and photographer, documented them.

In 1888, Church set up a small museum to showcase his paintings. He charged ten cents admission, but had few takers. Worse, of the hundred or so paintings he completed before his death, all but twenty or thirty were burned by his daughter, Mrs. Jessie Sargent, in the late 1940s because she didn't have the room to store them.

Cibola, Seven Cities of.

The Seven Cities of Cibola—also called the Seven Cities of Gold—had basis in sixteenth-century colonial Spanish fact, rumor, imagination, and greed. "Cibola" referred to Zuni Indian villages located in what is today New Mexico. Early sixteenth-century Spanish conquistadors heard, cultivated, and embellished rumors that these villages possessed great wealth, and Alvar Nuñez Cabeza de Vaca, who had survived the calamitous 1520 expedition of Panfilo Narvaez, brought back tales of rich pueblos, though he never claimed to have visited them personally in the course of an eight-year sojourn in the Southwest. Another survivor of the Narvaez expedition, a black slave called Estevan, was part of an expedition Marcos de Niza led in 1539 to locate the Seven Cities. Zunis killed the unfortunate Estevan in a battle outside the Hawikuh pueblo, but Marcos returned to Mexico City and there rendered a vivid ac-

count of the pueblo and its treasures—although he had failed to gain entry into Hawikuh. This notwithstanding, Francisco Vazquez de Coronado mounted a bigger expedition to the pueblo in 1540 and quickly captured it, only to find that neither it nor the other Zuni villages he entered contained treasure, gold, or jewels.

With Coronado's disappointment, the legend of the Seven Cities of Cibola diminished, but did not die until well into the eighteenth century. It was revived as a deliberate popular metaphor during the 1849 California gold rush, when thousands of latter-day questers after riches trekked to the American West.

SUGGESTED READING: Stephen Clissold, *The Seven Cities of Cibola* (New York, 1961).

"Cindy."

This folk song is a popular SQUARE DANCE tune from Appalachia. Its lyrics celebrate a backwoods maiden.

See also: FOLK MUSIC.

Civil War.

Almost a century and a half after Appomattox, a great many Americans are still mesmerized by the Civil War. Since 1865, more than sixty-five thousand books have been published on the subject, and many Civil War movies, television shows, and even computer simulation games have been produced. Some twenty thousand men and women call themselves "reenactors," and invest substantial sums in historically accurate reproduction uniforms, arms, and other gear, and gather on the anniversaries of various battles for the purpose of re-creating them. Significantly, the movie that most film his-

A scene of Civil War camp life. (National Archives and Records Administration)

torians say marked the transition from the infancy of motion pictures to its early maturity was *The Birth of a Nation,* a Civil War epic by D. W. Griffith, which premiered on February 8, 1915. And one of the most successful movies of all time was based on one of the most successful novels of all time, *Gone with the Wind,* by Atlanta author Margaret Mitchell. The book has never been out of print, and the movie has been rereleased several times since 1939, always to great profit.

From a retrospective point of view, the Civil War may be regarded as a folklore object, for it is studied by thousands of amateur historians, reenactors, and others as a link to our collective past and a key to our national identity. From a contemporary point of view, the war produced a great deal of folklore, perhaps most abundantly in folk music and popular commercial music. Many familiar songs emerged from the war, including "Dixie," "Battle Hymn of the Republic," "Just Before the Battle, Mother," "Tenting Tonight," and "Battle Cry of Freedom." Less familiar today are the BALLADS, which often recounted momentous engagements, such as the clash between the ironclad *Monitor* and *Merrimac.*

Legends and oral anecdotes concerning battles and heroes abounded, of course, but perhaps the most enduring folkloric theme, on both sides of

Edmund Ruffin, sixty-seven-year-old rural Virginia newspaper editor and ardent defender of slavery, was generally credited with firing the first shot of the Civil War against Fort Sumter, South Carolina. Celebrated as a folk hero by the South during the war, he committed suicide when it was clear that the Confederacy would crumble. (National Archives and Records Administration)

the conflict, was the idea that this was a war of brother fighting brother. This emotionally charged motif continues to influence thinking about the Civil War to this day.

See also: JUNETEENTH; VIETNAM WAR; WORLD WAR II.

The McLean house at Appomattox Court House, Virginia, where Ulysses S. Grant accepted the surrender of Robert E. Lee's Army of Northern Virginia, effectively ending the Civil War. (National Archives and Records Administration)

SUGGESTED READING: Benjamin A. Botkin, *A Civil War Treasury of Tales, Legends, and Folklore* (New York, 1960); Irwin Silber, *Songs of the Civil War* (New York, 1960).

"Clementine." A popular American BALLAD, "Clementine" narrates the sad fate—death by drowning—of a forty-niner's daughter.

See also: FOLK MUSIC.

Cline, Patsy (1932–1963). Like the actor James Dean and the rock 'n' roll pioneer Buddy Holly, Patsy Cline died young (like Holly, in a plane crash), leaving behind a legion of devastated fans as well as a legendary status as a performer. Cline was a commercial singer, whose success straddled country and pop, but she embodied many of the qualities of a folksinger, including the ability to identify with and create a powerful intimacy with her audience and to create in her audience the conviction that she sang from her own experience.

Cline was born Virginia Patterson Hensley in Winchester, Virginia, and early on demonstrated a talent for music. A near-fatal bout with rheumatic fever during her teen years affected Cline's voice, imparting to it a deep, throaty, and plaintive alto quality. Cline was sexually brutalized by her father from age eleven until she was sixteen, at which time her father left home. Shortly after this, Cline began performing with Bill Peer and the Melody Boys, emulating the popular cowgirl singer Patsy Montana and even "borrowing" Montana's first name. In 1953, she married Gerald Cline and became Patsy Cline.

In 1956, she recorded "Walking After Midnight," a haunting song about a restless woman, which was destined to be a hit. Constrained by an exploitive recording contract with a fourth-rate label, however, Cline made little money from the recording, and, despite an appearance on Arthur Godfrey's popular *Talent Scouts* radio program, Cline's career languished until she signed with Decca Records. In the meantime, her marriage to Gerald Cline dissolved, and Patsy Cline married Charlie Dick, a man from her hometown. The two had a tempestuous relationship, the emotion of which found its way into Cline's singing. She recorded "I Fall to Pieces" in November 1960, and such Cline classics as "Crazy," "She's Got You," "Sweet Dreams," and "Faded Love" followed after Cline was nearly killed in a 1961 car wreck, which left her permanently scarred. She recovered, however, and enjoyed wide exposure on the *GRAND OLE OPRY*. Although her career was cut short by a March 5, 1963, airplane crash, Cline's posthumous fame became even greater than it had been in life. In 1973, she became the first female vocalist to be inducted into the Grand Ole Opry's Hall of Fame, and she has been depicted in such hit movies as *Coal Miner's Daugh-*

ter (1980) and *Sweet Dreams* (1985). Cline's *Greatest Hits* continues to sell strongly, and in 1995 she received a posthumous lifetime achievement Grammy Award.

SUGGESTED READING: Mark Bego, *I Fall to Pieces: The Music and Life of Patsy Cline* (Holbrook, Mass., 1995); Ellis Nassour, *Honky Tonk Angel: The Intimate Story of Patsy Cline* (New York, 1993).

Clogging. Clog dancing or clogging is a group dance that combines elements of the SQUARE DANCE with the BUCK-AND-WING. Clogging is of recent origin and is believed to have originated in western North Carolina during the 1920s or 1930s, perhaps in connection with the Asheville Mountain Dance and Folk Festival. Clogging gained national attention after a 1939 performance by the Soco Gap Dancers for President Franklin Roosevelt and British King George VI in Washington, D.C., James Kesterson, of Henderson County, North Carolina, and his Blue Ridge Mountain Dancers introduced precision clogging—highly choreographed patterned footwork—in the late 1950s. In contrast to precision clogging is freestyle, or traditional clogging, in which each performer on the team improvises steps as the team moves across the floor. Both precision and freestyle clogging are usually danced to traditional mountain fiddle tunes.

See also: ANGLO AMERICANS; APPALACHIA; DANCE, FOLK.

Clower, Jerry (1926–). Clower is a popular southern humorist who draws on the folk traditions of the rural southern storyteller. Clower performs in concert and on record albums, appears regularly on television, and has been a featured performer on the GRAND OLE OPRY. He is also the author of two volumes of humor. Clower also draws on the traveling salesman tradition, having worked as a fertilizer salesman for the Mississippi Chemical Company.

Clower was born in Liberty, Mississippi, and, after some years as a salesman, spoke on the banquet circuit. His tall tales, such as "A Coon-Hunting Story," delivered with a broad, boisterous, and convincing backwoods accent, were received with delight, and Clower graduated to the ranks of successful comic entertainers.

Cobb, Ned (1885–1973). Ned Cobb became a LOCAL LEGEND in Tallapoosa County, Alabama, after he and other members of the Sharecroppers Union, which he had helped form, were involved in a shootout with the county sheriff. Cobb and the others had tried to prevent the sheriff from foreclosing on a union member's livestock. In the resulting melee, Cobb was shot in the back but survived. Arrested the following day, he was tried and convicted of attempted murder, and sentenced to prison for twelve years. He repeatedly refused the parole that was conditional on his never returning to Tallapoosa County. After his release in 1945, he resumed farming and also making white-oak baskets, for which he became well known.

Cody, William F. See BUFFALO BILL.

Coe, Clark W. (1847–1919). Clark Coe, of Killingworth, Connecticut, created on his farmland a collection of fantastic life-sized wooden figures known as the *Killingworth Images*. Most of them were animated, driven by a water wheel system Coe had built. Work on the figures was begun about 1900 and continued until the artist's death. By the early 1910s, the *Killingworth Images* had achieved somewhat more than local fame. By trade Coe was a farmer, basketmaker, and maker of ax handles. Local lore holds that Coe began making the figures to amuse a disabled nephew or his grandchildren. Coe's land and animated sculptures were purchased in 1919 by a man who attempted to maintain them. However, by the close of the 1920s, many of the pieces had been dispersed.

Coe's subject matter was childlike and, if local lore is correct, was indeed intended to delight a child or children. Figures include (for example) a man riding a pig (sometimes called *Girl on a Pig*), a man with a lute on a Ferris wheel, a rustic preacher, and others. The animated figures had an aural element as well, their movement creating squeaks and squawks. Coe's favored materials were barrel staves, slats, driftwood, and tree stumps, cobbled together with nails and metal pieces, and painted. Although most of Coe's figures were built, they do include some carved elements as well. In addition, Coe added deft touches of whimsy and realism by dressing some of his figures in discarded clothing and bits of ribbon. Originally, some forty animated, articulated figures made up the total environment; only seven survive.

Cold War. The term *Cold War* was coined in 1947 by presidential adviser Bernard Baruch to describe the rivalry, always pregnant with the threat of all-out nuclear war, between the United States and its allies on the one side and the Soviet

Union and its allies on the other. The tenuous alliance with the Soviets that had endured against the Nazis in World War II quickly crumbled in the wake of victory in that war, and during 1948–53 escalated to something just short of armed conflict as the Soviets unsuccessfully blockaded the Western-held sectors of West Berlin, the U.S. and allies formed NATO, the Soviets tested their first atomic weapon, and the Chinese communists triumphed. The Cold War erupted into a bitter, albeit limited, armed conflict with the outbreak of the KOREAN WAR in 1950. Following an armistice in Korea in 1953, tensions eased for a time, but reached a nerve-racking peak in October 1962 during the Cuban Missile Crisis, when the United States and the Soviet Union were brought to the brink of nuclear armageddon in a confrontation over Soviet missiles secretly installed on the island of Cuba, just ninety miles from the U.S. mainland. While tensions ebbed and flowed throughout the 1960s and 1970s, they eased steadily during the 1980s, when Soviet premier Mikhail Gorbachev sought rapprochement with the West. In 1989, the Berlin Wall, the single most tangible symbol of the Cold War, was torn down, while the Soviet Union, near collapse, did nothing but watch. Three years later, the U.S.S.R. dissolved, and the Cold War came to an end.

On the U.S. home front, the creation of Cold War folklore was stimulated by an atmosphere of conspiratorial secrecy. The period coincided with McCarthyism and a sense that communist spies lurked everywhere. Winston Churchill had coined the term "Iron Curtain" to describe the military and ideological barriers that now separated communist Eastern Europe from the democratic West. This figure of speech was typical of the era's rhetorically charged climate, which promoted simplistic, polar, us-against-them thinking. Add to this the vague sense of impending nuclear doom, and it is understandable that people eagerly grasped at symbols to help them understand a situation that was both nebulous and fraught with danger.

During this period, the apparatus of technological warfare and science in the service of technological warfare dominated popular conceptions of what it meant to be a world power. At the other end of the spectrum, the 1950s were suffused with extravagantly bland images of domestic bliss: the ranch houses, the manicured lawns of suburbia, the Little League game, the family gathered about the dinner table. Television shows such as *Father Knows Best* (1954–63) and *Leave It to Beaver* (1957–63) served up portraits of the ideal family, stable and economically secure.

Turning from their television sets and venturing out onto the streets, Americans were confronted by yellow-and-black signs directing them to public bomb shelters—not very useful if one had excavated a private shelter in one's own backyard.

The counterculture movement that emerged during the middle 1960s deliberately turned away from the images of high-tech destruction and from complacent suburbia, embracing instead a combination of psychedelia and "folksy" themes: clothing that seemed to echo a world of homespun and calico, acoustic guitars, a desire to reconnect with nature, and, most of all, by fostering a folk-music revival. In effect, then, the Cold War produced a grassroots-level backlash and stimulated nostalgia for, as well as quite genuine interest in, "traditional" folklore, folkways, folk images, and folk music.

See also: EINSTEIN, ALBERT.

College folklore. American colleges are communities, often rather closely knit. Like other communities, they have developed recognizable patterns of folklore, including customs, folk speech, and LEGENDS.

For students, many aspects of the college experience are anxiety provoking. Major examinations, such as finals, are often faced with dread, and students commonly resort to a variety of good-luck CHARMS and AMULETS to see them through. Various ritual behaviors may also be observed, including, quite commonly, abstaining from sex the night before the exam. Beyond these academic customs are others relating more generally to campus life. These include a variety of drinking games and rituals and fraternity and sorority initiation rituals. Various institutions also have special places—often the site of a statue or gate—where benign rituals may take place. At the United States Military Academy (West Point), for example, Flirtation Walk is the place to be seen with one's girlfriend.

Probably the richest area of folklore in American colleges and universities is folk speech. Institutions of higher learning have long been generators of slang that has entered the popular mainstream. Terms such as *ace* (as in to *ace* an exam), *cramming, cut,* and *flunk,* long familiar in general speech, were coined on campuses.

Many institutions piously cherish tradition. Perhaps in response to this, students typically create a sizable body of legend and lore, which often relate to sexual prowess, drinking capacity, or spectacularly complex and successful schemes for obtaining answers to exams.

Academic folklore is not limited to students. Often, a sizable body of OCCUPATIONAL FOLKLORE is shared by faculty members, much of it involving students. Anecdotes professors tell as true include the male prof's retort to the pretty co-ed who says she'll do anything for an "A": "Would you try studying?" Or the reply to the student who complains, "I don't think my paper deserves an F!": "Neither do I, but it is the lowest grade I can give." Faculty members occasionally swap stories about cheating schemes, which range from the diabolically wily to the absurd.

SUGGESTED READING: Simon Bronner, *Piled Higher and Deeper: The Folklore of Campus Life* (Little Rock, Ark., 1980); Richard M. Dorson, "The Folklore of College Students," *American Folklore* (Chicago, 1959).

The Governor's Palace at the Colonial Williamsburg restoration.

Colonial Revival. A movement in architecture, the popular arts, and popular history that began around the time of the American Centennial Exhibition in Philadelphia in 1876 and that celebrated colonial folklife and material culture, albeit often in idealized form. The most ambitious expression of the Colonial Revival came with the commencement of the COLONIAL WILLIAMSBURG restoration in 1926.

See also: FORD, HENRY.

SUGGESTED READING: Alan Axelrod, ed., *The Colonial Revival in America* (New York, 1985).

Colonial Williamsburg. Begun in 1926, Colonial Williamsburg is a restoration of the early colonial capital of Virginia. The idea originated with Rev. William A. R. Goodwin, rector of Bruton Parish Church (1705–11), who interested John D. Rockefeller, Jr., and other philanthropists in financing the project. The restoration profoundly affected the popular view of colonial life, folklife, folk art, architecture, VERNACULAR ARCHITECTURE, and culture. Colonial Williamsburg has also sponsored important scholarly projects in the archaeology and MATERIAL CUL-

TURE of colonial America. Today, Colonial Williamsburg covers more than three thousand acres and encompasses some 150 buildings. It is a "living history museum," complete with period-costumed craftsmen, militiamen, reenactors, and docents. Although the Colonial Williamsburg Foundation is a private organization, part of the city is included within the Colonial National Historical Park.

See also: COLONIAL REVIVAL.

SUGGESTED READING: Alan Axelrod, ed., *The Colonial Revival in America* (New York, 1985); Philip Kopper, *Colonial Williamsburg* (New York, 1986).

Columbus, Christopher. Among many Americans, Columbus has been regarded as a CULTURE HERO, the figure who embodies the values of a nation or a people. This strikes any

Christopher Columbus as culture hero. Here he "reveals" to Spain's Ferdinand and Isabella that the world is round. This American book illustration is from the early 1920s.

number of historians as peculiar, since Columbus never set foot on the North American mainland and refused to believe he had even discovered a "New World." For a time, he clung to the belief that he had sailed to Asia (which was the original purpose of his voyage), and, after his final voyage, declared that he had discovered the site of Paradise or Eden. Indeed, he was not the first European to visit this hemisphere, the Norseman Leif Ericson having explored what he called Vinland (present-day Nova Scotia) about A.D. 1000. Furthermore, Columbus the culture hero, is popularly credited with the having "discovered" that the world is round, even though most educated Europeans had long conceded this fact.

Columbus was not always a culture hero, but he emerged as one soon after the Declaration of Independence, victory in the Revolutionary War, and the establishment of the new American republic. By the end of the eighteenth century, Columbus was the central figure in the nation's myth of origin. By this time, too, Columbus Day was officially observed, and monuments to the Italian navigator began to appear across the country. Moreover, Columbus proved a pliable hero. During the great waves of migration during the nineteenth century, both the Irish and the Italians claimed Columbus as an ethnic hero—the Irish on account of his Catholicism and the Italians because of his nationality as well as his religion.

While Columbus has always had his detractors, beginning with his contemporary Fray Bartolome de Las Casas (1474–1566), who catalogued the enormities Columbus and other Spaniards perpetrated against the Native Americans in *Historia de las Indias,* the most serious challenges came during the late 1960s and into the 1970s, when Native Americans (and whites espousing Native American causes) protested the paying homage to an invader, conqueror, enslaver, and (as some saw it) initiator of genocide. While Columbus Day is still observed as a federal holiday, reverence for the Great Navigator has perceptibly diminished since the 1970s.

See also: ITALIAN AMERICANS; MILLER, JOAQUIN.

SUGGESTED READING: Claudia Bushman, *America Discovers Columbus: How an Italian Explorer Became an American Hero* (Durham, N.H., 1992).

Combs, Josiah H. (1886–1960). Trained as a scholar of modern languages, Combs was also a folklorist, whose area of concentration was Appalachian dialect and folk music. Combs himself was a child of Appalachia, having been born in Perry County, Kentucky, as part of a large family fond of singing BALLADS and folk songs.

Combs received his undergraduate education at Transylvania University (Lexington, Kentucky), where he met Dr. Hubert Shearin, with whom he published *A Syllabus of Kentucky Folk-Songs* in 1911. In 1913, he wrote on his own *The Kentucky Highlanders from a Native Mountaineer's Viewpoint.* Two years later, Combs edited an anthology of Kentucky folk poetry.

During 1911–18, Combs taught languages and literature in high schools and colleges in Kentucky, Tennessee, Virginia, and Oklahoma. During this period, he also gave lecture-recitals on Kentucky folk music, accompanying his muscial illustrations on an Appalachian-style DULCIMER. Combs served in the U.S. Army at the end of World War I, then taught French and Spanish at West Virginia University (1922–24). He took his Ph.D. at the Sorbonne in Paris (1925). His dissertation *Folk-Songs du Midi des États-Unis* was translated (by D. K. WILGUS) and posthumously published in 1967 as *Folk-Songs of the Southern United States.*

While folklorists are most familiar with Combs's work on Kentucky folk songs, he also studied the relationship between American regional folk speech and earlier (Middle English and early modern English) forms.

Combs's last teaching position was at Texas Christian University (Fort Worth), where he taught literature and languages. Combs's collection of Kentucky folk songs and ballads is housed at Berea College (Kentucky), with the papers of his translator, D. K. Wilgus.

SUGGESTED READING: Josiah H. Combs, *Folk-Songs of the Southern United States* (Austin, Tex., 1967); D. K. Wilgus, "Leaders of Kentucky Folklore: Josiah H. Combs," *Kentucky Folklore Record* 3 (1957), pp. 67–69.

Come-all-ye. This type of folk song always begins "Come all ye" ("Come all ye jolly sailors," for example) and celebrates the exploits of rugged working people: sailors, loggers, miners, railroad men, and the like. The typical come-all-ye is spirited and emotional, often narrated in the first person, sung in double common meter, but with a degree of metrical irregularity in which syllables may be packed between accents. (Note that the term "come-all-ye" is also sometimes applied indiscriminately to almost any kind of ballad or street song.)

See also: FOLK MUSIC; LUMBERJACK FOLKLORE; "MICHIGAN I-O"; WHALING; WORK SONGS.

Comic strips. The modern comic strip, as published in newspaper "funny papers," began in the 1890s in rival newspapers published by William Randolph Hearst and by Joseph Pulitzer. The best known of the early strips include R. F.

Outcault's *Yellow Kid* (1896) and *Buster Brown* (1902), Rudolph Dirks's *Katzenjammer Kids* (1897), George Herriman's *Krazy Kat* (1910), Bud Fisher's *Mutt and Jeff* (1907), and George McManus's *Bringing Up Father* (1913). From the beginning, the comics have used themes and motifs recognizable as folklore, including the likes of the henpecked husband, the battling cat and mouse, and the underdog who wins out in the end. American folk types also always figured prominently: the hayseed, the he-man, the bully, the braggart who gets his comeuppance, and so on.

By the late 1910s and into the 1920s, comic strips became somewhat more sophisticated in content, and by the end of the 1920s, science fiction and adventure themes became popular with the introduction of such characters as TARZAN and Buck Rogers. Characters like these also gave rise to the comic book.

The American public was quick to incorporate the comics into mainstream popular culture. Such figures as Popeye the Sailor, Li'l Abner, and Mutt and Jeff became fixtures of everyday life, with characteristics instantly recognized by most people, even those who did not regularly read comic strips. Moreover, such characters have contributed to American folk humor and speech (FOLK-SAY). Popeye's "I yam what I yam" became a common expression, as did terms like "fall guy" (from *Mutt and Jeff*), and "heebie-jeebies" (from *Barney Google*). The SHMOO from *L'il Abner,* a ghostly creature in the shape of a blobby ham, lays eggs, gives both butter *and* milk (Grade A only), tastes like chicken when fried, steak when broiled, and pork chops when roasted, loves to be eaten, but reproduces itself so rapidly that it never dies. For these qualities, the Shmoo may properly be put in company with other fantastic creatures from fairy tales, myths, legend, and folklore. (He may also be seen as cartoonist Al Capp's [1909–79] bawdy in-joke,

Shmoo being derived from the Yiddish *schmo,* a euphemism for Yiddish *schmuck,* "prick," in the sense of penis.)

See also: SUPERMAN.

SUGGESTED READING: M. Thomas Inge, ed., *Anything Can Happen in a Comic Strip: Centennial Reflections on an American Art Form* (Oxford, Miss., 1995); Richard Marschall, ed., *America's Great Comic-Strip Artists: From the Yellow Kid to Peanuts* (New York, 1997).

Computer folklore. An emerging field of study for folklorists is computer folklore. The first fully electronic computer, ENIAC, was unveiled at the University of Pennsylvania in 1946. To most of the public, it was a mysterious "electronic brain," and folklore about the computer's omniscience emerged rapidly, driven in part by the perceived technological magnitude of the achievement, but also driven by fear of the unknown and anxiety over the machine eventually displacing human workers. By the 1950s and early 1960s, computers had assumed the status of Orwellian Big Brother, an all-seeing, all-knowing monolith with which one could not argue and against which one could not hope to prevail. Developing in parallel with this view of the computer was an opposite body of folklore portraying it as a dumb machine. It seemed that everyone had humorous anecdotes or horror stories about "the computer insisting I owed a million dollars on my phone bill" or the like. People frequently complained that such errors were almost impossible to rectify, since one could not speak to "a human being." Another popular anecdote concerned the Bureau of Vital Statistics or Bureau of Motor Vehicles computer that declared so-and-so dead and thereby nearly ruined his life.

With the advent of the personal computer in

the early 1980s, the "hacker" emerged as a folk-loric figure—the disaffected mad genius, a kind of cyber–TRICKSTER, who is able to break into the supposedly secure computer systems of great corporations or the U.S. Defense Department and wreak havoc upon them. A particularly sinister type of hacker creates computer "viruses," programs that contaminate computer software and hardware, creating effects from the merely annoying to the highly destructive, including "wiping out" all the data on one's computer.

Another body of emerging computer folklore concerns the creators of the personal computer industry, most notably Microsoft Corporation founder Bill Gates, the richest man in the world. Gates and others are sometimes seen as electronic-age HORATIO ALGER figures, who achieve great success through resourcefulness, pluck, and luck, and sometimes seen as evil, manipulative geniuses who seek to control the flow of information and, thereby, the world. In this view, the computer hacker is sometimes portrayed as a cyber–Robin Hood, who works counter to the monolithic powers that be.

As the twentieth century comes to a close, a body of folklore is coalescing around the so-called Millennium Bug, Millennium Bomb, or Y2K Problem (Y2K = Year 2000). Many older computer systems and software systems record years in two-digit form only: 1999 is 99 and 2000 is 00. The problem is that these computer systems will read "00" at the turn of the century as 1900, not 2000, and, we are told, large portions of government and industry may grind to a halt. *(You haven't paid your electric bill since 1900?! We're shutting you off!)* The Y2K problem smacks of CONSPIRACY LORE, but may well prove all too true.

See also: CRIME AND CRIMINALS.

SUGGESTED READING: Karla Jennings, *The Devouring Fungus: Tales of the Computer Age* (New York, 1990); Tracy Kidder, *The Soul of a New Machine* (New York, 1985).

Con artist and confidence man.

A confidence man or con artist or con man gains the trust of a gullible stranger and perpetrates a swindle upon him or her. Con men are stereotypically associated with the "big city," but the YANKEE TRADER OR TRICKSTER is a classic example of a rural con man. As a figure of folklore, the confidence man resembles the basic TRICKSTER figure.

The term *confidence man* was coined in 1847 in a newspaper story about a man who would approach a stranger on the street and ask the person if had enough "confidence" to trust him with his watch. The victim, assuming the confidence man was an acquaintance he didn't recognize, would give him the watch, and the confidence man would walk off laughing. HERMAN MELVILLE's strange novel of 1856, *The Confidence-Man: His Masquerade* was the first work of literature to use the term and to explore the type. While Melville's novel was a popular failure, the confidence man subsequently appeared many times in novels, plays, and movies—often as a folk hero rather than a criminal. Many students of folklore deem the con man the American version of Robin Hood. Certainly, the role of the confidence man in many American folktales or folklike anecdotes is to give the arrogant and self-righteous their comeuppance. The classic literary expression of this is Mark Twain's novella *The Man That Corrupted Hadleyburg* (1900).

See also: FOLKLORE IN AMERICAN LITERATURE; TWAIN, MARK.

SUGGESTED READING: Gary H. Lindberg, *The Confidence Man in American Literature* (New York, 1982); David W. Maurer, *The American Confidence Man* (Springfield, Ill., 1974).

Conjunto music. Also known as *musica norteña, conjunto* music is a FOLK-MUSIC style based on the accordion. It emerged during the late nineteenth century among Mexicans of the Texas-Mexico border region, then spread over a large part of Mexico and the American West. The *conjunto* style combines the diatonic button accordion and the Mexican twelve-string bass guitar, *bajo sexto*, with percussion often provided by the ranch drum (*tambora de rancho*), a folk instrument. The accordion was most likely brought to northern Mexico during the 1860s by German immigrants who settled in Monterrey, but some scholars believe that it was introduced by Germans or Czechs who settled in south Texas.

Conjunto music soon became identified with poor rural Mexicans on both sides of the border and was therefore shunned by wealthier Mexicans and MEXICAN AMERICANS. When the music came to the cities during the twentieth century, it retained its association with the working class. As *conjunto* music conjoins European and Mexican folk instruments, so it combines European and Mexican musical styles and forms. Such European forms as the redowa, schottische, mazurka, waltz, and, paramountly, the polka found their way into *conjunto*. The polka remained a signature of *conjunto* music well into the 1940s, by which time *conjunto* orchestras had been enlarged by the addition of string basses and trap drums. At about this time, too, singing was added, in the form of the *cancion ranchera* (country song), which had been made popular by mariachi performers. The *cancion ranchera* is analogous to the American country-and-western song, always focused on melodramatic themes of unrequited love. By the 1950s, the standard *conjunto* ensemble had evolved into a three-row button accordion, *bajo sexto*, electric bass, and drums.

Since the 1920s, *conjunto* has been essentially commercial music, but it has never lost its connection with its folk origins and with the rural poor and urban working class.

See also: JIMÉNEZ, FLACO; TEX-MEX MUSIC.

SUGGESTED READING: Manuel Peña, *The Texas-Mexican Conjunto: History of a Working-Class Music* (Austin, Tex., 1985).

Conroy, Jack (1898–1990). Conroy was a fiction writer and also a collector of industrial folklore. He was born and raised in a coal-mining camp near Moberly, Missouri, where he observed the folkways of ethnic Irish, British, and Italian coal miners.

Conroy became an apprentice mechanic in the shops of the Wabash Railroad, then, after the defeat of the 1922 Great Railroad Strike, he went to work in auto factories and steel mills until 1930, when the Great Depression put him out of work. In this crisis, Conroy began to write sketches and short stories for magazines, including H. L. Mencken's *American Mercury* and Mike Gold's *New Masses*. Conroy discovered his literary niche in adapting folk narrative to the literary sketch.

In the 1930s, Conroy founded and edited the *Anvil*, a periodical that published Nelson Algren, Erskine Caldwell, and Richard Wright. In Chicago, Conroy also worked with the Illinois Writers' Project of the WPA. In this position, he began systematically collecting industrial folklore. With African-American novelist Arna Bontemps, Conroy used some of the material he collected to create several successful and critically honored children's books.

SUGGESTED READING: Jack Conroy, *The Jack Conroy Reader* (New York, 1979); Douglas Wixson, "Jack Conroy and Industrial Folklore," *Missouri Folklore Society Journal* 6 (1984), pp. 61–68.

Conspiracy lore. Conspiracy theories are well entrenched in American popular culture and, in recent times, have abounded in such areas as UFOs, Hollow Earth (beliefs that the earth is hollow and world governments are suppressing this fact, often because extraterrestrial aliens are hidden there), the assassination of John F. Kennedy, government mind-control schemes, fluoridation of water (in the 1950s it was considered by many to be a communist plot), the power and influence of secret societies (such as the Illuminati and the Tri-Lateral Commission), the militia movement, the Philadelphia Experiment (claims that the U.S. Navy was able to render a ship invisible in 1943, but has kept the technology secret all these years), TWA Flight 800 (claims that the 1996 airline disaster was caused by a U.S. missile launch), Gulf War Syndrome (claims that the government is covering up what it knows about a mysterious illness among some Gulf War veterans), MIAs (claims that the government knows that many Vietnam War POWs are still alive), AIDS (claims that the AIDS virus was deliberately created), and so on.

The first widespread American conspiracy theories revolved around the activities of Freemasons. Captain William Morgan of Batavia, New York, published some of the secrets of Freemasonry in *Illustrations of Masonry* in about 1825. In an attempt to suppress the book, other Masons sought to bribe him to leave the country, offering him money and the prospect of a farm in Canada, but Morgan never made it to Canada. In 1827, a badly decayed body was found on the shores of Lake Ontario and was identified by Morgan's wife, his publisher, and others as the captain's remains. The Masons were accused of murder, and the next fifteen years saw waves of anti-Masonry sweep the United States. Masons were not only denounced from the pulpit, they were the target of politicians, and an Anti-Masonic Party nominated a candidate for president in 1832. (The party carried only Vermont.) In the 1930s, a Masonic investigator offered proof that Morgan had not died at all, but had sailed to Smyrna, where he took up life as a convert to Islam. Later in the nineteenth century, it was the Catholics who became targets of conspiracy theorists. In the early twentieth century—and again in the 1950s—the spotlight shifted to communism, which was seen as plotting not only against the United States government but against American culture. Conspiracy theories may be labeled examples of "folk history," attempts to explain the inexplicable and to gain some measure of control when certain individuals or groups feel powerless to control a given cultural situation.

See also: AREA 51; BLUE BOOK, PROJECT; COMPUTER FOLKLORE; CROP CIRCLES; HOOVER, J(OHN) EDGAR; LINCOLN, ABRAHAM.

Cooper, James Fenimore (1789–1851). The first American novelist to earn widespread international admiration, Cooper drew on his understanding of American wilderness folklore and myth to create his most enduring character, the frontiersman Natty Bumppo—better known by his various sobriquets, Leatherstocking, Deerslayer, and Hawkeye—the protagonist of the author's so-called Leatherstocking Tales, *The Pioneers* (1823), *The Last of the Mohicans* (1826), *The Prairie* (1827), *The Pathfinder* (1840), and *The Deerslayer* (1841).

Cooper was born in New Jersey and raised in upstate New York. Educated in an Albany private school, he attended Yale from 1803 to 1805. Expelled in his junior year because of a prank, he joined the U.S. Navy as a midshipman. After he married Susan De Lancy in 1811, he resigned his commission and did little of note for almost a decade. In 1820 (according to a possibly credible legend), Cooper read a popular novel and, throwing it aside in disgust, swore to his wife that he could do much better. She challenged him to do just that, and Cooper wrote a pallid imitation of Jane Austen called *Precaution* (1820). The following year, he published *The Spy* (1821), a far more successful imitation of another British author, Sir Walter Scott. *The Spy* was set against the backdrop of the Revolutionary War and developed distinctively rendered American character types.

The Spy was an international success, and Cooper went on to write the first of the Leatherstocking Tales, *The Pioneers* (1823). The novel introduced Natty Bumppo—Leatherstocking—an aged wilderness scout, whose character resonates with mythic and folk beliefs about the wilderness as a place that nurtures the kind of natural virtue associated in the European tradition with the NOBLE SAVAGE. Cooper based the Bumppo-Leatherstocking-Hawkeye character loosely on DANIEL BOONE, who had already achieved mythic stature by this time. Like Boone (as popularly portrayed), Natty Bumppo was brave, self-reliant, and at one with the surrounding wilderness, living in it and mastering it with the skill of an animal or an Indian. Beyond the Bumppo figure, *The Pioneers,* like the other novels in the Leatherstocking cycle, develop the myth of an American Eden on which the "march of progress" inexorably encroaches. Charged with such powerful mythic freight, *The Pioneers* is the first detailed fictional portrait of American frontier life, and it may be considered the first substantially original American novel. Cooper developed the Natty Bumppo character as well as the vision of the American wilderness in conflict with American civilization through the rest of the Leatherstocking novels, and Bumppo emerges as a moving, even elegiac hero, with neither wife, nor child, nor property, but wedded to a vanishing wilderness.

James Fenimore Cooper, as illustrated in Reuben Post Halleck's History of American Literature, *1911. (Collection of Alan Axelrod)*

Cooper wrote other fiction in addition to the Leatherstocking saga, including a series of sea novels, such as *The Pilot* (1823), *The Red Rover* (1827), and *The Sea Lions* (1849), as well as a nonfiction *History of the Navy of the United States of America* (1839). Cooper was also politically and socially active, founding the Bread and Cheese Club in the 1820s, which drew such luminaries as the poet William Cullen Bryant, painter and inventor Samuel F. B. Morse, and others. His 1838 *The American Democrat* is an acute political analysis of Jacksonian America. But it is for the Leatherstocking novels that Cooper is best remembered, and it is these that, despite often stilted language, most effectively tapped into the richly mythic sources that make so much of American literature, as well as American folklore, enduringly compelling.

See also: FILSON, JOHN; FOLKLORE IN AMERIcan Literature; Harte, (Francis) Bret[t]; Irving, Washington; Pocahontas; Squanto.

suggested reading: James Grossman, *James Fenimore Cooper* (New York, 1949); Donald A. Ringe, *James Fenimore Cooper* (New York, 1962).

Copland, Aaron (1900–1990). Often called the "dean of American composers," Copland successfully combined traditional American melodies and folk subjects with an expressive modern style to produce distinctive contemporary classical music with an American "feel" and identity.

The son of Russian-Jewish immigrants in New York City, he was educated in the local public schools and took piano lessons from his older sister. By age fifteen, Copland had determined that he would become a composer and took a series of correspondence courses in harmony. His first major breakthrough came in 1921, when he enrolled in the newly founded school for Americans at Fontainebleau, outside of Paris, where his principal composition teacher was the brilliant Nadia Boulanger.

Copland spent three years with Boulanger, then returned to New York City with an important commission from his teacher, to write for her an organ concerto she could tour with. Supporting himself as a pianist for a Pennsylvania resort hotel trio, he wrote *Symphony for Organ and Orchestra*, which was premiered at Carnegie Hall by the New York Symphony.

Copland's personality as a composer was protean. He absorbed the lessons of modernism, often tinged with jazz, and fell under the influence of Igor Stravinsky's neoclassical style, which led to such abstract, even austere compositions as *Piano Variations* (1930), *Short Symphony* (1933), and *Statements for Orchestra* (1933–35).

But Copland gradually came to feel that his new style was causing him to lose his connection with his audience. "It seemed to me that we composers were in danger of working in a vacuum," he observed, and decided to reach out to a more popular audience. This new approach not only changed the form and content of his music, it influenced his choice of performance venue as well. Copland began to write not just "absolute music" (symphonies, concerti, and so on), but music for the theater, as well as scores for films.

Copland's most important theatrical works are his ballet scores, all based on American folk material: *Billy the Kid* (1938), *Rodeo* (1942), and folklike *Appalachian Spring* (1944). His most important film scores include those for *Of Mice and Men* (1939), *Our Town* (1940), *The Red Pony* (1948), and *The Heiress* (1948). In addition, Copland wrote nontheatrical "program music," all of which was distinctly American in flavor. His *Lincoln Portrait* (1942), for speaker and chorus, on texts drawn from Lincoln's speeches, and *Letter from Home* (1944) were both inspired by patriotic urges during World War II. His *Third Symphony* (1946), although not program music in the strictest sense, is likewise full of patriotic passion and contains the famous "Fanfare for the Common Man," which had been composed and was regularly performed before it was incorporated into the symphony. It was regarded as a kind of anti-Fascist orchestral anthem.

While Copland consciously used folk material in composing some of his best-known music, he was certainly no folk musician. However, he felt that the American quality universally recognized in his music was as much the result of living and working in America as it was the product of the deliberate use of folk tunes, folktales, and popular legends.

Late in his career, Copland began exploring the twelve-tone or serial composition techniques of the modern Viennese composer Arnold Schoenberg. Such twelve-tone works as *Piano Fantasy* (1957), *Connotations* (1962), and *Inscape* (1967), dissonant and demanding, were not well received; this, however, did not return Copland to his earlier, folk-inspired approach. Instead, after 1970, Aaron Copland stopped composing, though he remained active as a lecturer and conductor into the mid-1980s.

Copland was much honored in his lifetime and universally regarded as the quintessential American composer. A prolific author, his books include *What to Listen for in Music* (1939), *Music and Imagination* (1952), *Copland on Music* (1960), and *The New Music, 1900–60* (1968). With Vivian Perlis, he wrote a two-volume autobiography, *Copland: 1900 through 1942* (1984) and *Copland: Since 1943* (1989).

See also: APPALACHIA; BILLY THE KID; DE MILLE, AGNES; FOLK MUSIC; GRAHAM; MARTHA; LORING, EUGENE; SHAKER FOLK ART AND CRAFTS.

SUGGESTED READING: Julia F. Smith, *Aaron Copland: His Work and Contribution to American Music* (New York, 1955); Arthur Berger, *Aaron Copland* (1953; reprint ed., New York, 1989); Neil Butterworth, *The Music of Aaron Copland* (New York, 1986).

Corn. Corn is an important crop for many Native Americans throughout most of North America and plays a role in mythology and ritual. Corn commonly symbolizes fertility and medicine (power). The crop is personified in many Indian cultures as a woman (Corn Woman), about whom many myths abound, including a tale of her being murdered, decapitated, and dragged through the fields, her blood fertilizing the ground from which the first corn sprang.

In Euro-American tradition, corn is associated with the values of rural "middle America," at once wholesome and nostalgic, but also laughably unsophisticated ("corny").

See also: MEDICINE AND MEDICINE MAN.

Corn dance. Among Native American groups for whom maize is a staple crop, the corn dance is a series of ceremonial dances relating to the spirit powers that govern the growth of maize. The corn dance cycle includes prayers for rain as well as thanks for the harvest. Understandably, the corn dance is most elaborately developed among peoples living in the desert regions of the American Southwest, where water is scarce and rain is a gift to be prayed for.

See also: DANCE, FOLK.

Cornett, Chester (1912–1981). Chester Cornett was renowned as an eastern Kentucky maker of chairs. Folklorists and collectors frequently cited him as a prime example of the dedicated folk craftsman. He was born in Letcher County and learned his craft from his maternal uncle, grandfather, and great uncle. His early life dealt him many blows: his parents deserted him, a fiancée jilted him, his first and second wives left him, and two years of military service during World War II left him with emotional and other health problems. Returning to Kentucky after the war, he worked a few odd jobs, then settled in the hamlet of Dwarf, Kentucky, where he began making distinctive eight-legged chairs, eventually using only an ax and drawknife. During the 1950s, he evolved a series of highly innovative and eccentric designs, which exaggerated the elements of traditional chairs. His work not only drew the attention of collectors, but that of folklorists as well, including Michael Owen Jones, who made an extensive study of Cornett's work in the 1960s. Cornett became the subject of numerous articles in national magazines and even of a 1981 film, *Hand Carved*.

SUGGESTED READING: Michael Owen Jones, "Chairmaking in Appalachia: A Study in Style and Creative Imagination in American Folk Art" (Ph.D. dissertation, Indiana University, 1969).

Corridos.

Corridos are Mexican folk ballads or male narrative folk songs, popular in Mexico and among MEXICAN AMERICANS in the American Southwest from about 1830 through the 1930s. The *corrido* lyric is composed in eight-syllable lines forming four-line quatrain stanzas. It is sung slowly in 3/4 or 6/8 time. Narratively, a typical *corrido* begins with an opening stanza that sets the scene and the issue at question, the middle stanzas develop and resolve the narrative, and the closing stanza comments on the events narrated and bids farewell to the audience. The subject of the *corrido* is usually something of importance or concern to the immediate community. While the *corrido*'s ancestry goes back to colonial Spain, the form developed distinctively in Mexico and in what is now the American Southwest during the nineteenth century.

Although the *corrido* folk-song tradition died out in the 1930s, the genre was adopted and adapted by professional singers. Whereas traditional subjects tended to exult heroic actions, local heroes, and social heroes, the commercial *corridos* focus on such issues as violent crime and drug-dealing.

See also: FOLK MUSIC; ROOSEVELT BALLADS.

SUGGESTED READING: José F. Limón, *Mexican Ballads, Chicano Poems: History and Influence in Mexican American Social Poetry* (Berkeley, Calif., 1992); Américo Paredes, "The Ancestry of Mexico's *Corridos*: A Matter of Definitions." *Journal of American Folklore* 76 (1963), pp. 231–35; Américo Paredes, "The Mexican *Corrido*: Its Rise and Fall," in Mody C. Boatright et al., eds., *Madstones and Twisters* (Dallas, Tex., 1958).

Cortez, Gregorio (1875–1916).

Cortez earned legendary status as a Mexican-American folk hero in south Texas during the early twentieth century. He was born on a borderlands ranch south of the Rio Grande on June 22, 1875. He moved with his family into Texas, settling near Austin in 1887. He and his older brother, Romaldo, worked together on farms in Karnes and Gonzalez counties, then, in 1900, the pair rented land to farm for themselves.

Cortez became a folk hero when he stood up to the Karnes County sheriff and the two deputies who had come to arrest him as a horse thief, a charge of which he was innocent. Knowing full well that Mexican Americans—derisively called "greasers"—could hardly count on a fair trial at the hands of the Anglos, Cortez had armed himself. Unaware that Cortez was carrying pistols, the sheriff shot Romaldo Cortez, severely wounding him. He then shot at Gregorio, but missed, and Gregorio returned fire, hitting the sheriff three times, and fatally wounding him. There followed an epic chase involving a number of posses ranging over five hundred miles. After ten days, Cortez was captured, betrayed by another Mexican American, who tipped off a Texas Ranger. During the chase, authorities killed more than two hundred Mexican Americans on the pretext that they were all members of the "Cortez gang."

Tried three times, Cortez was found guilty on each occasion, but the Texas Court of Criminal Appeals overturned the convictions. Subsequently, he was convicted for killing the sheriff and sentenced to life in prison. He entered the Huntsville Penitentiary in 1905, but was paroled by the governor of Texas in 1913. He died of natural causes three years later.

The Cortez story was widely publicized during the chase and trial, and he emerged as a Mexican-American folk hero who had the courage to take a stand against the oppressive Anglos. In the Mexican-American community, various legends developed around Cortez, and he and his story became the subjects of BROADSIDE ballads and folk BALLADS—or *corridos,* as hero-narrative ballads are called in Spanish.

SUGGESTED READING: Américo Paredes, "*With His Pistol in His Hand*": *A Border Ballad and Its Hero* (Austin, Tex., 1958).

Counting-out rhymes.

A childhood version of a magic rhyme or incantation, the counting-out rhyme is used to make decisions and choices and to determine who will be "It"—the child delegated to take (usually) some unwanted part in a game (for example, the seeker in hide-and-go-seek). A self-appointed leader recites the rhyme, pointing alternately to each child and him or herself on each word or syllable until he or she reaches the end. The one on whom the finger points is chosen. Sometimes the process is done repeatedly: each chosen child "falls out" at the end of each repetition of the rhyme until only one is left as "It." Counting-out rhymes are common in the United States and in Europe; their existence has been recognized at least as far back as the first century B.C. The rhyme most familiar to most Americans begins "EENY, MEENY, MINY, MO,"

but there are many others, often beginning with nonsense syllables or a mixture of nonsense syllables and actual words strung together without meaning.

See also: POETRY, FOLK; SKIP-ROPE RHYMES.

SUGGESTED READING: Charles Francis Potter, "Counting-out rimes," in Maria Leach, ed., *Funk and Wagnalls Standard Dictionary of Folklore, Mythology, and Legend* (1949; reprint ed., New York, 1984).

Country music.

Also called country and western, and until about 1949 called hillbilly music, country music originated among whites in the rural South and West. Today, as measured by the number of listeners, country music is the most "popular" of American popular music. A highly commercial genre, its roots run directly to the BALLADS and folk songs of the English, Scots, Irish, and Scotch-Irish settlers of the Appalachians and, to a lesser degree, other parts of the South.

Traditional string-band music was recorded in the 1920s, with FIDDLIN' JOHN CARSON scoring the first hit in 1923 and VERNON DALHART following the next year with the highly successful "WRECK OF THE OLD '97," a million-selling recording. Country music was also heard on the earliest commercial radio stations beginning during the 1920s. *National Barn Dance* was first broadcast in 1924, and the GRAND OLE OPRY began its epic run in 1925. From the beginning, these broadcasts were very popular, not only in rural areas, where radio quickly became the chief form of commercial entertainment, but in urban America as well, especially during the 1930s and the era of World War II, when many rural people migrated to the cities. Musicians such as the CARTER FAMILY and JIMMIE RODGERS brilliantly bridged the gap between folk music and commer-

A broadcast of The Barn Dance *radio program from* WLS Chicago *during the 1930s.*

plete with songs about poverty, lost love, and loneliness, appealed to listeners hard hit by the Depression (which affected rural areas well before the 1929 stock market crash) and those who had severed their country ties to seek opportunity in the city. Also during the 1930s, a more escapist appetite for nostalgia was satisfied by the emergence of cowboy singers such as GENE AUTRY and ROY ROGERS. This trend put the "western" in what came to be called country-and-western music. By the mid-1930s musicians like BOB WILLS had taken country-and-western to another level by combining it with the swing styles popular in mainstream big band dance music to create western swing.

Country music took another long stride away from its Appalachian string-band origins during the 1940s. HONKY-TONK MUSIC, the music of the country-oriented urban roadhouses and beer joints called honky-tonks, put a harder edge on country music, introducing themes of sexual passion and infidelity that appealed to a generation of country fans who had emerged from the era of World War II having lost their innocence and with a heightened degree of sophistication. HANK WILLIAMS and ERNEST TUBB were the early giants of this genre, which also spawned a nostalgic counter movement in the form of BLUEGRASS. This style, developed by BILL MONROE and his string band, with banjo virtuoso EARL SCRUGGS, reconnected commercial country music with its roots. While bluegrass never came to dominate country music, it has remained a popular and highly expressive subgenre.

By the end of the 1940s, country music had become a full-fledged entertainment industry, headquartered not in New York or Los Angeles, but in Nashville, Tennessee, home of the country studios and of the Grand Ole Opry, the genre's mecca and central venue. Into the 1950s and 1960s, such performers as Johnny Cash, Tammy Wynette, Buck Owens, Merle Haggard, PATSY

cial, popular styles, paving the way for the legions of musicians who followed. The demand for "hillbilly music" became so great that recording-company executives like RALPH PEER set up satellite recording studios in Bristol, Tennessee (1927), and elsewhere to find new talent at the source. This commercial outreach into the hinterlands was innovative, and perhaps unprecedented.

During country music's first two decades, the 1920s and 1930s, the ballad-style repertoire, re-

CLINE, Loretta Lynn, and Charley Pride (an African American, he was a rarity among country performers) became not just country stars but pop music stars. Most country musicians resisted the onslaught of ROCK 'N' ROLL during this era, many cleaving to the so-called Nashville sound of lush, polished instrumental arrangements. But in the 1970s, another of country music's counter movements emerged in the form of "outlaw" music. Willie Nelson and Waylon Jennings were the primary exponents of this style, which turned its back on the Nashville sound and embraced the amplified instruments and other aspects of rock. For the most part, since the 1970s, country music, while retaining an identity apart from rock, has moved closer to rock and pop styles and has appealed to audiences who enjoy all forms of popular music.

See also: ARHOOLIE RECORDS; FOLK MUSIC; GIBSON MANDOLIN AND GUITAR MANUFACTURING COMPANY, LTD., THE; HAYS, WILL; HUNTING; MACON, DAVID (UNCLE DAVE); POOLE, CHARLIE AND THE NORTH CAROLINA RAMBLERS; SCOTTISH AMERICANS.

SUGGESTED READING: Country Music Foundation, *Country: The Music and the Musicians* (New York, 1988); Bill Malone, *Country Music U.S.A.* (rev. ed., Austin, Tex., 1985).

Cousin Jack. "Cousin Jack" was the protagonist in jokes and brief humorous narratives revolving around nineteenth-century Cornishmen who immigrated to the United States as hard-rock miners. Cousin Jacks were miners inclined to hoist a few, despite the dictates of their Methodist religion and their temperance-leaning wives (known as "Cousin Jennies"). The characters in the narratives spoke in Cornish-inflected dialect, with the dialect often figuring prominently in the humor.

The name "Cousin Jack" may derive from the miner's habit of swearing—he was a "cussin' Jack"—or it may just allude to the fact that Cornishmen seemed always to have a "Cousin Jack" to recommend for work in the mines.

Cousin Jack stories were first documented and collected in Wisconsin's lead-mining district in the 1930s, but the stories have also turned up in Colorado, Minnesota, Montana, and in Michigan's Upper Peninsula.

SUGGESTED READING: Charles E. Brown, *Cousin Jack Stories: Short Stories of the Cornish Lead Miners of Southwestern Wisconsin* (Madison, Wis., 1940); A. L. Rowse, *The Cousin Jacks: The Cornish in America* (New York, 1969).

Couvade. A folk practice in which the husband of a woman in labor takes to his bed and emulates the process of labor. The purpose is for the male to take on some of the woman's pain, thereby providing relief. The practice is common in certain "primitive" cultures, but has also been found, rarely, in the American South. Somewhat more commonly, in the South, the husband or some personal article of his, usually clothing, is present in the labor room. The purpose is to transmit male strength to the woman to ease her labor.

See also: CHILDBEARING FOLKLORE.

Cowboys. The cowboy is almost certainly the most familiar of American folk-hero types. At the very least, the cowboy is the single most beloved, celebrated, talked about, and *sung* about worker in American history. Before the cowboy, generations of children read about and played at being knights in shining armor. Since the time of the cowboy, more American children—and many in Europe as well—have been raised on tales, songs, and images of the latter-day "knights errant" of the open range. The cowboy personifies a very powerful and distinctly American myth of freedom and self-sufficiency. Folklore also paints the cowboy as a white Anglo-Saxon, although, in fact, during the height of the range cattle industry (between the end of the Civil War and the blizzard of 1886–87, which brought the days of the great trail drives to an abrupt end), one out of five cowboys was African American and at least one out of five was Mexican American. Indeed, the cowboy's ancestors were the *vaqueros* (from the Spanish *vaca,* "cow"), originally Indians attached to the old Spanish missions of the seventeenth and eighteenth centuries and employed by them to handle their beef herds. The *vaqueros* roped steers with a loop of braided rawhide rope known as *la reata* (lariat) and wore *chaparreras* (chaps), leather trousers designed to protect their legs from brush and chaparral.

Before the Mexican War (1846–48), most cattle ranches were small, easily managed by a ranching family and a few hired hands. The war brought a sharp increase in the demand for beef to feed the U.S. Army. Once the cattle industry expanded, it did not contract. After the war, Texas ranchers started to drive their cattle beyond the confines of the ranch, pushing herds northward, where they could fatten on the grass of public lands before being shipped east. The Civil War threatened to bring the developing range cattle industry to an abrupt close as Union blockades kept Texans from shipping their beeves to market, and many cattle were left to run wild on the Texas plains as ranchers and ranch hands went off to fight for the Confederacy. For many returning Texas veterans, the ruin of war left some five million cattle freely ranging the state. Ex-Johnny Rebs became the first postwar cowboys, making it their business to round up and brand as many cattle as they could, then "trailing" these newly assembled herds to grazing lands, marketplaces, and railheads.

Although folklore was quick to depict the cowboy as a noble knight beholden to no one, looked at from the perspective of economic reality rather than folklore, cowboys were among the most miserably paid of the nation's laborers and were subject to brutal working conditions, which included prolonged exposure to the elements and work with large numbers of powerful and dangerous animals. On the ranch, the cowboy's principal job was to ride over an assigned stretch of range and tend the cattle, doing whatever needed to be done, including rough-and-ready veterinary work, rescuing animals from bog holes, dehorning rambunctious steers, castrating calves, fighting brush fires, and so on. Twice a year, the cowboys "rounded up" the stock for shipment to market or in preparation for a drive to other ranges. Young calves had to be roped and branded. The work ranged from tedious, to backbreaking, to extremely hazardous. Most demanding was the cattle trail drive, in which a herd of cattle—perhaps as small as five hundred head or as large (in one record-breaking instance) as fifteen thousand—was moved either to northern ranges for maturing or to market at railhead cattle towns like Abilene, Ellsworth, and Dodge City, Kansas; Pueblo and Denver, Colorado; and Cheyenne, Wyoming. Distances involved were often in excess of a thousand miles over four principal cattle trails: the Shawnee, from Brownsville, Texas, to Kansas City, Sedalia, and St. Louis, Missouri; the Chisholm, from various points in Texas to Abilene, Ellsworth, and Dodge City; the Western, from San Antonio, Texas, to Dodge City, and on to Fort Buford in Dakota Territory;

Two images of the American cowboy: in a painting by Frederic Remington, The Cowboy (1902) *and in an anonymous photograph from early in the twentieth century.*

and the Goodnight-Loving, from the middle of Texas to Cheyenne. Hazards of the trails were almost as numerous as the herds themselves: storms, floods, drought, stampede, rustlers, hostile Indians. Pay was about $100 for three or four months' work. And it was not unusual for a cowboy to blow his whole $100 stake during a few nights in the cattle town that lay at the end of the trail. The towns served as points of transfer from the trail to the rails. Here beef brokers shook hands on deals, and the cattle were loaded into railcars bound for the cities of the East. For the cowboy, a stay in town meant a bath, a shave, a woman (three hundred prostitutes plied their trade in the small town of Wichita), and plenty to drink (in many towns, saloons outnumbered other buildings two to one). Such towns were also home to professional gamblers, ready, willing, and able to part a cowboy from his cash. Like the mining camps of California in the 1850s, the cattle towns of the latter part of the century were rowdy, violent places. Gunfights were commonplace—though, alas, neither so frequent nor so violent as they are on the streets of many American cities today.

All of these elements—life on the trail, the hazards of the trail drive, and the hard-drinking, rough-and-tumble experience of the nearly lawless cattle towns—became delectable fodder for folktales, legends, songs, and BALLADS, as well as such commercial undertakings as dime novels, full-length fiction, stage melodrama, opera (most notably Giacomo Puccini's *La fanciulla del West* [*The Girl of the Golden West*] of 1910), and, later, movies, radio serials, and television series. One dangerous situation that formed a staple in dime novel, television, and other entertainment media, the conflict between "cowboys and Indians," did not exist in historical fact to any significant degree. If anything, cowboys and Plains Indians had more in common than either group had with the mainstream forces of white culture.

The folklore associated with the cowboy, especially COWBOY SONGS and cowboy poetry, did not appear until about 1870. The popular—and attractive—belief is that the songs began as rustic lullabies to help bed down restive herds at night on the trail. This may or may not have been the case. That songs were written to the gait of a horse is, for the most part, untrue, since more than half of the early cowboy songs extant were sung in 3/4 time, and very few four-legged animals waltz. Certainly, however, singing, story-telling, and verse recitation were popular pastimes around the campfire or, even more, in the ranch bunkhouse. But were these accompanied by the guitar that was depicted as inseparable from such twentieth-century singing cowboys as GENE AUTRY and ROY ROGERS? More likely, the FIDDLE, BANJO, and JEW'S HARP were the instruments of choice. The guitar was not a popular instrument in nineteenth-century Anglo America, but the fiddle and banjo were. Nor did many cowboys play the harmonica. Perhaps most of the bunkhouse singing was a cappella.

Doubtless, many stories were swapped among cowboys in the bunkhouse. The following, retold by Everett Dale in *Cow Country* (1942), is a prime example of the TALL TALE told in the dry, deadpan style associated with the cowboy:

"Hank Blevins [arrived in] Kansas City with a trainload of cattle [and] repaired to a swell restaurant for dinner. At the next table a girl and two men were giving their orders:

" 'Waiter,' said the girl, 'I want a thick steak, a rare steak please.'

" 'Bring me a steak, too,' said one of the men, 'and I want mine very rare.'

" 'I'll have a steak myself,' said the next man, 'but I want it extremely rare. Just sear the outside a little.'

" 'Waiter,' said Hank, when it came his turn, 'just cripple him and drive him in. I'll eat him.' "

If popular perception identifies the cowboy closely with song, it even more intimately connects him with a distinctive costume. The broad-brimmed, high-crowned hat marketed by John Batterson Stetson after the Civil War is most closely associated with the cowboy, although many wore variations on the Mexican sombrero as well, while others, working in the cold northern plains, wore fur caps. A bandanna or neckerchief was also standard and often colorful. It was essential in dry, dusty regions to keep dust and sand from going up the nose and down the throat. Over time, the bandanna (called a "wipe" in Texas and a "tuf rag" or "wild rag" in some of the northern plains regions) became as much decorative as utilitarian. When the work or the weather got particularly hot, however, the bandanna was rarely worn.

No form of footwear is more distinctive than the cowboy boot, which is immediately recognizable despite a bewildering array of variations. The early boots reached almost to the knee and soon evolved scalloped tops. Toes might be rounded, square, or pointed—the latter style useful for "finding" the stirrup quickly. Pegged soles and tall, underslung heels helped secure a rider's feet in the stirrups. Although many cowboys favored plain leather boots, top hands ordered custom-made creations with elaborate decorative cotton stitching—then, perversely, hid the decoration by wearing trousers over the boots rather than tucked into them.

Beyond hat, bandanna, and boots, cowboy shirts evolved from nondescript work garments to distinctively ornate styles with specially stitched yokes and pocket flaps. Britches were, for the most part, homespun woolens until Levi Straus introduced denim work trousers in the 1890s. In country overgrown with brush and chaparral, leather chaps were worn over trousers to protect the legs. Mexican and Mexican-influenced *vaqueros* wore tight leggings, while Anglo-Texan cowboys wore "bat wings," wide chaps with flaps of thick leather. In cold climates Angora goatskin or bearskin chaps were favored. When the Angora chaps became identified with "dudes"—noncowboys posing as cowboys—smaller chaps (called chinks) became popular. These covered the upper leg only and are still worn by many working cowboys.

The cowboy and his horse, according to popular belief, were inseparable, and dime novels as well as movies and television shows typically depicted a special relationship between a cowboy and his horse. In truth, cowboys rode many horses on the trail, because a cowboy's endurance outlasted that of a horse during the working day. While it behooved a good cowboy to respect his mounts and take care of them—as any worker respects and cares for his tools—few developed any deep or abiding affection for the animals and, in the twentieth century, readily took to transporting themselves by pickup truck or ATV (all-terrain vehicle) rather than aboard "Old Paint."

Is the cowboy of popular American belief dead? Better to ask if he ever existed, and even better to observe that the spirit of the cowboy, quite apart from the hard-working agricultural laborer with whom that spirit is associated, is as alive as it ever was.

See also: BIKER FOLKLORE; OCCUPATIONAL FOLKLORE; RAILROAD FOLKLORE; SHEEPMAN STORIES; TRUCKING AND TRUCKERS; WHALING.

SUGGESTED READING: David Dary, *Cowboy Culture: A Saga of Five Centuries* (New York, 1981); Teresa Jordan, *Cowgirls: Women of the American West* (Garden City, N.Y., 1982); Kathleen Jo Ryan, ed., *Ranching Traditions: Legacy of the American West* (New York, 1989); Fay E. Ward, *The Cowboy at Work: All about His Job and How He Does It* (Norman, Okla., 1987).

"Cowboy's Lament." Also known as "The Streets of Laredo," this BALLAD relates the death and the dying utterance of a young cowboy whose wicked ways with liquor, women, and cards brought about his death in a gunfight. The song may be traced to an Irish ballad from the end of the eighteenth century, "The Unfortunate Rake," which records the dying utterance of a soldier succumbing to venereal disease.

See also: FOLK MUSIC.

Cowboy songs. Evidence suggests that the songs most popular with working cowboys during the heyday of the range cattle industry (1865–87) were the sentimental popular songs and PARLOR BALLADS current in mainstream middle-class culture of the day. However, cowboys also created work songs of their own, to pass the time around a campfire on the trail or in the bunkhouse on the ranch. The trail drives produced such classics as "The Old Chisholm Trail" and "The Trail to Mexico," while "When the Work's All Done This Fall," "Little Joe, the Wrangler," and "Blood on the Saddle" acknowledge the dangerous nature of cowboy work.

The image of the singing cowboy was so pervasive by the end of the nineteenth century that Thomas Eakins, not known for painting western subjects, chose it as the subject of this study for The Home Ranch *(1888).*

Other songs, such as "That Gol Durn Wheel" (a "wheel" is a penny-farthing, "big wheel" bicycle), are tinged with the dry, sly humor long associated with the West; yet even these humorous songs typically present an edge of cool realism. BROADSIDES were especially popular, particularly those retailing sensational gunfights and the consequences thereof, such as "The Streets of Laredo," also called "THE COWBOY'S LAMENT" and derived from an eighteenth-century British broadside called "The Unfortunate Rake," about a soldier in the last stages of venereal disease begging for a military funeral. A select group of cowboy songs are original with the cowboys themselves. One of the best known is "The Sierry

Petes (Tying the Knot in the Devil's Tail)," by GAIL GARDNER, which is usually sung to the tune of "Polly Wolly Doodle."

By the beginning of the twentieth century, printed collections of cowboy songs began to appear, the first of which was NATHAN HOWARD ("JACK") THORP's *Songs of the Cowboys* (1908). In 1910, folklorist JOHN LOMAX published *Cowboy Songs and Other Frontier Ballads*. In the next decade, cowboy songs were being recorded and, soon after the introduction of commercial radio, were being broadcast as well. It was "When the Work's All Done This Fall," recorded in 1925 by Carl T. Sprague, that unleashed a steady stream of cowboy recordings, often by authentic cowboy singers, including Sprague himself, as well as Jules Verne Alien, The Cartwright Brothers, and Harry ("Haywire Mac") McClintock. Billie Maxwell, an artist of this period, was the first cowgirl singer. The Depression era added the film western to phonograph recordings. Not only did the cowboy movie hero emerge, but so did the classic "singing cowboys," among them GENE AUTRY, ROY ROGERS, and Tex Ritter. This era also ushered in commercial "cowboy songs" composed in New York City's Tin Pan Alley, and it further disseminated the image of the guitar-toting singing cowboy. Working cowboys were not likely to try to manage a guitar on horseback, and in any case, the guitar was not a popular instrument in Anglo America until well into the twentieth century. Most nineteenth-century cowboy singers sang unaccompanied or, perhaps, to a tune provided by fiddler, banjo player, or Jew's harper. As to Tin Pan Alley's idea of a cowboy song, it bore little resemblance to the traditional occupational cowboy folk songs; indeed, the kinds of songs sung by Ritter, Autry, and Rogers cannot be considered prototypes or precursors of any American popular or commercial country music.

See also: "BURY ME NOT ON THE LONE

Prairie"; Cowboys; Folk music; Work songs.

suggested reading: Hall Cannon, ed., *Old-Time Cowboys Songs* (Layton, Ut., 1988); Austin and Alta Fife, *Cowboy and Western Songs* (New York, 1969); John and Alan Lomax, *Cowboy Songs and Other Frontier Ballads* (reprint ed., New York, 1986).

Cox, John Harrington (1863–1945). A moving force behind the West Virginia Folk-Lore Society, Cox was a collector of folk songs and a professor of English philology at West Virginia University, Morgantown. He was educated at Illinois Normal, Brown University, and Harvard and became interested in American folk song through his study of medieval narrative poetry.

Cox was a principal founder of the West Virginia Folk-Lore Society in 1913, and under its sponsorship, Cox published *Folk-Songs of the South* (1925), the first major regional collection of American folk songs. With over four hundred songs, the volume remains one of the most comprehensive collections of American folk songs. It was supplemented and expanded in 1939 with the publication of *Folk-Songs Mainly from West Virginia* and *Traditional Ballads Mainly from West Virginia.*

Coyote. *Canis latrans,* the coyote, is a wild relative of the domestic dog and ranges throughout North and Central America. In the mythology and folklore of the Native Americans of the Central Plains, California, and the Southwest, the coyote is the figure who appears most often in stories. Coyote appears as a creator, a culture hero, lover, magician, and as a trickster. Coyote often figures as a demiurge (a creative force) or, especially among the Plains tribes, as a culture hero, a Prometheus-like figure who obtained for humankind such things as fire. In his negative aspect, coyote is sometimes seen as trickster—one who is, more often than not, ensared by his own devices. Among eastern tribes, the Great Hare, also called Master Rabbit, takes the place of the coyote trickster and is one source for the Brer Rabbit folk tales of southern African Americans—tales that became widely known to whites through the Uncle Remus tales of Joel Chandler Harris.

See also: Fox; Shape shifting; Tar Baby.

Crackers. An epithet used to describe poor white southerners, particularly those from south Georgia and north Florida, *cracker* is quite old, having been used as early as the mid-eighteenth century to describe Scotch-Irish residents of the Piedmont and southern frontier regions. The word was used in Scotland to denote a boastful person, but folk etymology finds the origin of the word either in the poor white farmer's pounding ("cracking") corn for food or in the relatively well-to-do plantation owner who used a horse-whip equipped with a "cracker" on the end to make a sharp report. *Cracker* is a pejorative example of folk-say; used by African Americans to describe southern whites, it is especially contemptuous.

See also: Etymology, folk; Rednecks.

Crafts, American folk. Constituting a vast area of folklore, crafts encompass handmade objects that use materials found locally and that embody the traditions and techniques of the craftsperson's community. While craft objects may be utilitarian, they serve, at least in part, an aesthetic purpose. Although craft objects continue to be made, they are most closely associated with preindustrial America, or, at least, an America before the age of mass production. Interest in the study and acquisition of craft objects as objects of art began well after the onset of industrialization and was stimulated in America by the Arts and Crafts movement, which was led in England by John Ruskin and William Morris, among others. Before the century was out, a variety of handicraft clubs and guilds and handicraft periodicals appeared in England as well as in the United States. Of particular interest in the nineteenth century were Native American crafts, including especially rugs, baskets, and pottery. By the end of the century, William Goodell Frost, president of Berea (Kentucky) College, recognized the aesthetic as well as commercial value of the crafts of Appalachia and, in 1893, created a work-study program at Berea called Fireside Industries. At the turn of the century, a number of Appalachian crafts organizations and industries began operation, most notably the John C. Campbell Folk School in North Carolina and the Hindman and Pine Mountain Settlement Schools in Kentucky. The Appalachian crafts movement went into full swing during the late 1920s, through the efforts of ALLEN EATON of the Russell Sage Foundation, who was instrumental in creating the Southern Highland Handicraft Guild in 1930.

What happened in Appalachia served as a model for crafts movements among various groups, including AFRICAN AMERICANS, PENNSYLVANIA GERMANS, and others. The Depression-era federal arts programs further fostered crafts movements, but by the 1950s, the handicraft traditions seemed to reach a low ebb or were swallowed up in a decade that embraced the comforting regularity of suburban tract housing, frozen TV dinners, and the mass production panacea. With the rise of the so-called counterculture of the 1960s and rejection of many of the values associated with the 1950s, interest in crafts was renewed in a general FOLK REVIVAL. It has not faded since.

See also: WOODCARVING.

SUGGESTED READING: Garry G. Barker, *The Handcraft Revival in Southern Appalachia, 1930–1990* (Knoxville, Tenn., 1991); Simon Bronner, *Grasping Things: Folk Material Culture and Mass Society in America* (Lexington, Ky., 1986); Edward Lucie-Smith, *The Story of Craft* (Ithaca, N.Y., 1981); David Whisnant, *All That Is Native and Fine: The Politics of Culture in an American Region* (Chapel Hill, N.C., 1981).

Crane, (Harold) Hart (1899–1932).

Crane combined a romantic sensibility and a passion to create living mythology with acutely modernist poetic techniques to create highly challenging lyric verse relating to American life in the industrial age. From the standpoint of folklore study, it is his epic masterpiece, *The Bridge* (1930), that is of most interest. Focusing on the BROOKLYN BRIDGE as its central subject and metaphor, Crane attempted to create a myth of the American experience. The poem that resulted is a kaleidoscope of folk speech and folktale fragments (including the story of Captain JOHN SMITH and POCAHONTAS).

Crane was born in Garrettsville, Ohio, and grew up in Cleveland. He was emotionally unstable, an alcoholic, and acutely uncomfortable with his homosexuality. His first book of verse, *White Buildings* (1926), was a critical success, and this, in addition to his subsequent poetry, gave him sufficient reputation to persuade philanthropist Otto H. Kahn to finance the composition of the fifteen-part *The Bridge*. After publication of this masterpiece, Crane received a Guggenheim Fellowship to finance a sojourn in Mexico City, where he planned to write an epic on a Mexican theme. He did not write the epic, and, returning by ship to the United States in 1932, he committed suicide by jumping overboard.

See also: FOLKLORE IN AMERICAN LITERATURE.

SUGGESTED READING: John Unterecker, *Voyager: A Life of Hart Crane* (New York, 1969).

Crane, Thomas Frederick (1844–1927).

Crane was a founder of the American Folklore Society and an important folklore scholar. He may be best remembered by American folklorists for his scholarly review of JOEL CHANDLER HARRIS's Uncle Remus tales, which provided evidence for the African origin of African-American folk narrative. Internationally, he was best known for his 1890 edition of *The Exempla of Jaques de Vitry*, which opened up the religious exemplum as a field for comparative folklore research and, indeed, provided a model for the comparative approach to folklore research. Crane was a member of the editorial board of the *Journal of American Folk-Lore* from 1888 to 1892.

SUGGESTED READING: Thomas Frederick Crane, "Plantation Folk-Lore: Review of Joel Chandler Harris' *Uncle Remus*," *Popular Science Monthly* 18 (1881), pp. 824–33; Thomas Frederick Crane, "Bibliography of the Writings of T. E. Crane," *Liber de Miraculis: Sanctae dei Genitricis Mariae* (Ithaca, N.Y., 1925).

Crazy Horse (ca. 1840–1877).

Crazy Horse was an Oglala Lakota (Sioux) war chief who earned fame among whites for having defeated in battle Gen. George Crook and, more infamously, GEORGE ARMSTRONG CUSTER, who died in the Battle of the Little Bighorn on June 25, 1876.

Crazy Horse was born near Butte, South Dakota, the son of an Oglala warrior and medicine man also called Crazy Horse and of Rattle Blanket Woman, a Minneconjou Lakota. After the young man demonstrated his prowess at arms, about 1861, he earned the name Crazy Horse. He was widely admired by his own people and was feared and admired by those he fought against. During the War for the Bozeman Trail, led by the Oglala chief Red Cloud against white incursions into Lakota lands in Wyoming and Montana, it was Crazy Horse who led warriors against Captain William Judd Fetterman at Fort Phil Kearny in 1866, killing Fetterman and the eighty soldiers under his command. Crazy Horse was also present at two other celebrated battles of the War for the Bozeman Trail, the Hayfield fight (1867) and the Wagon Box fight (1867). As a result of his success in combat, Crazy Horse acquired a large following among those Lakotas who refused to accede to the Treaty of Fort Laramie, which ended the Bozeman conflict in April 1868. In that year, Crazy Horse was chosen by a Lakota council convened in northeastern Wyoming as one of four young warriors to be a "shirt wearer," or head warrior of his people. Crazy Horse lost his shirt-wearer status in 1870, after a Lakota woman left her husband for him and the outraged husband shot Crazy Horse in the face with a pistol. Nevertheless, U.S. government officials and army officers continued to regard Crazy Horse as an important Lakota leader and perhaps the single most important leader of the Lakota resistance.

Crazy Horse was instrumental in fighting to retain for the Lakotas the Black Hills of South Dakota, which the Lakota held sacred, and the Lakota hunting grounds in the Yellowstone River basin. When gold was discovered in the Black Hills in 1874, the U.S. government abrogated treaty agreements that reserved the hills to the Lakota. Prospectors and others invaded the region, and, at last, in December 1875, the government ordered the Lakotas (and Cheyennes) in the Yellowstone River and Powder River region to retire to reservations in Nebraska or along the Missouri River. Crazy Horse and his nontreaty Lakota followers refused to move. After the army launched an offensive against a Northern Cheyenne village in March 1876, Crazy Horse and SITTING BULL (a Hunkpapa Lakota) emerged as the two principal leaders of a Lakota-Cheyenne alliance.

In what the U.S. Army called the Sioux War, Crazy Horse led some fifteen hundred warriors against thirteen hundred men under the command of Brig. Gen. George Crook in the Battle of the Rosebud on June 17, 1876. Crazy Horse checked Crook's advance, thereby scoring a significant strategic triumph. An even more celebrated victory came eight days later, when Crazy Horse defeated Lt. Col. George Armstrong Custer and elements of his Seventh Cavalry at the Battle of the Little Bighorn. In this, the legendary battle of the Indian Wars in the West, Crazy Horse was instrumental in leading a counterattack against Custer's cavalry, in which Custer and more than two hundred men under his immediate command were slain.

Crazy Horse's triumphs did not produce long-term results, however, and on May 7, 1877, the warrior-leader, realizing that further fighting would be fruitless, led his people to surrender at Camp Robinson, Nebraska, on May 7, 1877.

It was at this point that Crazy Horse fell victim to his own legendary status. Government officials as well as army officers vied with one another for an opportunity to meet with and talk to the great warrior. This aroused the jealousy of other war chiefs, who disseminated rumors that Crazy Horse planned to foment an uprising. Army officers ordered the arrest of Crazy Horse. On Sep-

tember 5, 1877, arrest was attempted at Camp Robinson, during which a soldier fatally bayoneted the chief.

He lived on in Native American folklore as one who was victorious against the white man. In white folklore and popular culture, his name became synonymous with the Plains warrior at his most fierce and skilled. He is remembered as the slayer of Custer in that folk hero's last and most famous battle.

Crazy Horse is the subject of a monumental sculpture begun in 1946 by Korczak Ziolkowski (1908–1982) on the face of Thunderhead Mountain in the Black Hills. The work was continued by others and is expected to extend well into the twenty-first century. The completed sculpture, 563 feet high and 641 feet long, will be larger than the Mount Rushmore presidential group.

See also: GERONIMO.

SUGGESTED READING: Mari Sandoz, *Crazy Horse: The Strange Man of the Oglalas* (New York, 1942); Richard Hardoff, *The Oglala Lakota Crazy Horse: A Preliminary Genealogical Study and an Annotated Listing of Primary Sources* (Mattiuck, N.Y., and Bryan, Tex., 1985).

Creighton, Helen (1899–1989). Creighton was a collector who specialized in the Anglo-Canadian folk song, especially the songs of the Martime provinces. A journalist by vocation, she was largely self-taught as a folklorist, though she attended Indiana University's Folklore Institute in 1942. She was the author of fifteen book-length collections of folk songs and folklore, as well as an autobiography. Her collecting method was recording in the field, and her independent work was recognized by the Rockefeller Foundation and by the National Museum of Canada (now the Canadian Museum of Civilization), which named her an adviser (1947–64).

Creighton was no mere dilettante collector. She was an aggressive promoter and popularizer of folklore, who inspired artists, writers, choreographers, and composers to create works based on Nova Scotian folklore. Her efforts also had a strong political effect, building provincial pride and a sense of identity. "Nova Scotia Song," a folk song she recorded and collected, was officially adopted by Nova Scotia as its provincial anthem.

SUGGESTED READING: Helen Creighton, *A Life in Folklore* (Toronto, 1975).

Crime and criminals. If folklore embodies expressions of social norms and communal values, it also often celebrates violations and violators of these. Crime themes permeate American folklore, especially in BALLADS and LEGENDS and in URBAN LEGENDS. The argot of criminality also figures in FOLK SPEECH, FOLK-SAY, and in popular speech generally. Only somewhat less directly, criminality figures in musical styles, most notably the BLUES (sometimes associated with prison) and PRISON WORK SONGS.

Many American criminals have achieved legendary status. This includes figures from the Old West, such as BILLY THE KID, BLACK BART, FRANK AND JESSE JAMES, and the like. Often, these westerners are portrayed as Robin Hood types and, indeed, are rarely called criminals, but, rather, "gunmen," "gunfighters," or "bad men." Of almost equally legendary status are lawmen such as WYATT EARP, who are often barely distinguishable from the bad men. In fact, the entire range of western figures from Billy the Kid to Wyatt Earp may simply be described as gunfight-

ers, skill with the Colt .44 being of greater importance than choosing one's side of the law. Close behind the western gunfighters in legendary status are the gangsters of the "Roaring Twenties" and the 1930s. The very term *gangster* or *mobster,* which shares a suffix with *monster,* suggests the emotional power of such figures as AL CAPONE and JOHN DILLINGER.

At least until the infamous gangland slaying known as the Saint Valentine's Day Massacre (February 14, 1929), gangsters, like the western gunfighters, were popularly regarded as Robin Hoods, robbers of banks and big business, not the man and woman on the street. Yet folklore has also been drawn to the most aberrant criminals as well, including alleged ax murders like LIZZIE BORDEN and more recent mass murders, such as Charles Manson (1960s leader of the "cult" that brutally murdered actress Sharon Tate and others) and Jeffrey Dahmer (Milwaukee's cannibal murderer). Less horrific than such as these, and less colorful than gunfighters and gangsters, are the "white-collar" criminals. These range from shady Wall Street traders to computer hackers (see COMPUTER FOLKLORE), who are celebrated for their ability to "game the system," to use financial institutions and their apparatus for their gain.

Most recently, a new type of criminal has entered the realm of American folklore: the political criminal. In this category is included terrorists and bombers, such as Timothy McVeigh, found guilty of having bombed a federal building in Oklahoma City on April 19, 1995, that resulted in the deaths of 169 persons, and Theodore Koczinski, known as the Unabomber, who killed or maimed several individuals over a sixteen-year period with bombs in packages sent through the mail.

SUGGESTED READING: Katie Hafner and John Markoff, *Cyberpunk: Outlaws and Hackers on the Computer*

Frontier (New York, 1991); Bill O'Neal, *Encyclopedia of Western Gunfighters* (Norman, Okla., 1979); Eleanor Wachs, *Crime Victim Stories: New York City's Urban Folklore* (Bloomington, Ind., 1988).

Crockett, Davy (1786–1836). Frontiersman, congressman from Tennessee, and one of the martyrs of the ALAMO, David (Davy or Davey) Crockett is also among the nation's most universally known folk heroes. In his own time, he published a successful almanac, which traded on, even as it enhanced, his popular heroic image. Protagonist in popular fiction, his adventures were the subject of a WALT DISNEY television series starring Fess Parker as Crockett, which gained a wide audience in the 1950s and prompted a generation of TV-addicted children to demand that their parents buy them a copy of one of Crockett/Parker's trademark "coonskin caps" (complete with bushy tail), which were offered for sale (it seemed) everywhere.

Crockett's actual life was, indeed, remarkable. He was born near present-day Rogersville, Tennessee, and grew up in the Appalachian backwoods. With little formal education, he joined the Tennessee militia and fought under ANDREW JACKSON during the Creek War, which coincided with the War of 1812. Crockett's military service gained him local recognition in Tennessee; he was appointed a justice of the peace, and then was easily elected to the Tennessee legislature in 1821. After serving two terms, he was elected to the U.S. House of Representatives as a Democrat.

Predictably, Crockett was an early supporter of the Jacksonian Democrats, but subsequently broke ties with Jackson. This rupture cost him his reelection bid in 1830, but, two years later, he was reelected as a Whig, a party that touted him as a potential presidential contender to defeat

Title page from Davy Crockett's Almanack *for 1836. (Library of Congress)*

Jackson's handpicked successor, Martin Van Buren. Crockett was defeated in his 1834 reelection bid, and, disgusted with Tennessee politics, offered this instantly famous farewell: "You may all go to hell and I will go to Texas."

Apparently hoping to revive his political career, he moved to Texas in 1835. He and a band of followers joined Col. William B. Travis and the other defenders of the Alamo, which was besieged for thirteen days during February–March 1836 by Mexican troops under Antonio López de Santa Anna, who were determined to crush the Texas war for independence.

Tradition holds that Crockett was killed within the walls of the Alamo, and Travis's diary attests to Crockett's steady heroism: He was everywhere in the Alamo, "animating the men to do their duty." While recent research has not contradicted the impression of Crockett's heroism, it does suggest that he, with five or six other survivors, was captured when the Alamo was finally overrun on March 6, 1836. Despite the pleas of a number of Mexican officers that the lives of the prisoners be spared, Santa Anna apparently ordered them bayoneted and then shot. This end is not to be found in any of the popular depictions of Crockett in books or on film. Instead, he is portrayed (as in John Wayne's 1960 *The Alamo*) as having fought to the finish, even using his rifle, ammunition exhausted, to club the Alamo's invaders, before he is cut down by a hail of bullets. One legend circulated that Crockett did, in fact, survive, only to be enslaved as a salt-mine laborer deep in Mexico.

To be sure, the Crockett legend was enhanced by his martyrdom at the Alamo. But, during his life, Crockett himself had worked to create the folk-hero image. In part, this was an effort to achieve political success, and, in part, it was an attempt to correct any number of stories that circulated about him. The most pervasive contemporary fictional version of Crockett's adventures was written by James Kirke Paulding (1778–1860). Nimrod Wildfire, the hero of Paulding's play *The Lion of the West* (1830), was transparently modeled on Crockett. In 1834, Crockett published *A Narrative of the Life of David Crockett of the State of Tennessee,* which served not only as a campaign biography, but as a corrective to a set of wholly fictional stories fraudulently printed under his name as the *Sketches and Eccentricities of Colonel David Crockett of West Tennessee* (1833).

After the successful reception of his *Narrative,* Crockett apparently abandoned any allegiance to the truth about his life and cooperated with some anonymous Boston-based writers who spun out tall tales for publication in the Crockett-authorized *Davy Crockett's Almanacks* (1835–56). As depicted in these tremendously popular almanacs, Crockett was an exemplar of heroic superlatives, who could "run faster, jump higher, squat lower, dive deeper, stay under longer, and come out drier, than any man in the whole country." In anecdotes that draw on the popular literary tradition of western exaggeration and that anticipate such wholly fictional heroes as PAUL BUNYAN, Crockett performs such superhuman and mythic feats as saving the world by unfreezing the sun and riding a pet gator up Niagara Falls.

Despite the elements of comic exaggeration, Crockett was and has remained a folk hero, the embodiment of all that Americans have liked to attribute to the frontiersman: bravery, strength, independence, and deep personal honor.

See also: ALMANACS; BOWERY "B'HOY"; CUSTER, GEORGE ARMSTRONG; FINK, MIKE; PAULDING, JAMES KIRKE.

SUGGESTED READING: Davy Crockett, *A Narrative of the Life of David Crockett of the State of Tennessee* (1834; reprint ed., Knoxville, Tenn., 1973); Michael A. Lafaro, ed., *Davy Crockett: The Man, The Legend, The Legacy,* 1786–1986 (Knoxville, Tenn., 1985); James A. Shackford, *David Crockett: The Man and the Legend* (Chapel Hill, N.C., 1986).

Crop circles. Crop circles are large areas of flattened crops, usually in grain fields, most often circular in shape, and often in elaborate patterns.

Crop circles were first reported during modern times in 1966, but those interested in the phenomenon claim evidence for the existence of crop circles as early as 1678 in Hertfordshire, England. By the 1980s, well-documented crop circle sightings became common, especially in England, but also in the United States and elsewhere. By the end of the 1990s, some five thousand crop circles had been photographed and documented.

Many attempts have been made to explain the phenomenon, including natural causes (such as the effect of magnetic fields) and extraterrestrial causes (communication by visiting aliens). In 1992, a pair of Britishers calling themselves Doug and Dave claimed to have been responsible for making many of the crop circles, and, following their confession, many people who had become fascinated by the phenomenon concluded that all circles were the work of hoaxers—which would certainly make crop circles a unique form of folk art. Others, however, believe that Doug and Dave's "confession" was the product of a conspiracy (see CONSPIRACY LORE) between the British government and the American CIA (Central Intelligence Agency), among others. Be that as it may, it does seem unlikely that Doug and Dave could have created five thousand crop circles worldwide, though other "copycat" hoaxers have emerged since the appearance of Doug and Dave.

Whether folk art on a large scale, a massive practical joke, a natural phenomenon, or the work of "folk" from another planet, crop circles have become a folklore phenomenon that has prompted the formation of various crop circle clubs and organizations and has spawned more than a dozen sites on the World Wide Web.

See also: UFO FOLKLORE.

Cryptozoology. Cryptozoology is the scientific study of hidden or unknown animals. This discipline meets folklore study in investigations of such subjects as BIGFOOT and the JACKALOPE.

An image (from the Internet) of crop circles at Chehalis, Washington. "Photo taken July 24, 1996, 6:30 P.M."

Culin, Stewart (1858–1929). Culin was an early student of traditional games, who concentrated on the Native Americans of North America and East Asian peoples. While his *Korean Games, with Notes on the Corresponding Games of China and Japan* (1895; reprint ed., 1958, as *Games of the Orient*), is still regarded as a key reference, it is for *Games of the North American Indians* (1907; reprint ed., 1975) that Culin is best known. Not only does Culin document and describe a broad range of Native American games, he classifies them and takes a comparative approach, pointing out important similarities to the games of Asian peoples.

In addition to his 1907 book, Culin published game articles in the *Journal of American Folklore* and in the *American Anthropologist*. Especially important are his essays on Hawaiian and Filipino games, as well as articles focusing on American urban games among adults and children.

Culin served as president of the American Folklore Society in 1897 and was a founding member of the American Anthropological Association (1902). From 1892 to 1903, he was director of the University of Pennsylvania Museum of Archaeology and Paleontology. Later, he was curator of ethnology at the Brooklyn Museum's Institute of Arts and Sciences.

Culture hero. The principal or key legendary figure of a tribe, people, culture, or other group, the culture hero is the figure who founds basic cultural values. The culture hero is usually male and may be a human being, an animal, or a wholly supernatural being. The folklore and mythic beliefs of Native American cultures are replete with culture heroes. For Anglo-American culture, such figures as GEORGE WASHINGTON (the father of his country), DANIEL BOONE (who pushed civilization into the wilderness), and even THOMAS EDISON (a modern Prometheus who gave humankind electric light) are often treated as culture heroes.

See also: COLUMBUS, CHRISTOPHER; DISNEY, WALT; EINSTEIN, ALBERT; FORD, HENRY; JACKSON, ANDREW; LEE, ROBERT EDWARD; LINCOLN, ABRAHAM; LINDBERGH, CHARLES A.; MEXICAN AMERICANS; SHAPE SHIFTING; SITTING BULL; SMITH, JOHN; TOBACCO; TURKEY; WOLF.

Curanderos. The *curanderos,* curers, are folk doctors among MEXICAN AMERICANS, especially in (but not confined to) the Southwest. The *curandero* (a *curandera* is a female folk healer) is believed to possess a God-given gift for healing and is the most highly respected folk healer among Mexican Americans. *Curanderos* may have local, regional, or even national reputations and clientele. Some are revered as holy men and women, veritable candidates for sainthood. Their knowledge ranges from herbal medicine to how to maintain good health or cure common ailments to combating witchcraft—the evil spells cast by a *bruja,* sorcerer or witch. Indeed, the *curandero* may be seen as the counterpart of the *bruja*. Both are believed to possess supernatural powers, but while those of the *curandero* are holy, the powers of the *bruja* come from allegiance to the devil. Although many Mexican Americans continue to make use of herbal remedies and folk healers, including herbal healers and lay midwives, few resort any longer to the *curanderos*.

See also: MEDICINE, FOLK.

SUGGESTED READING: Wilson M. Hudson, ed., *The Healer of Los Olmos and Other Mexican Lore* (Dallas, Tex., 1951); Ari Kiev, *Curanderismo: Mexican-American Folk Psychiatry* (New York, 1968).

Currier & Ives. Currier & Ives is the imprint of the best-loved American printmaker of the nineteenth century, whose prolific "Colored Engravings for the People" present an incomparable panorama of this country's coming of age. The firm began in 1834 when Nathaniel Currier (born in Roxbury, Massachusetts, 1813), set himself up as a job printer in New York City after apprenticeship in Boston with the first successful lithography business in the country and further training with a master printmaker in Philadelphia. Quite early he discovered an insatiable market for inexpensive "news" prints, particularly of maritime disasters and urban conflagrations, and soon he had branched out into numerous other bestselling categories, offering an active stock of "Popular Cheap Prints . . . which are in great demand in every part of the country." The name Ives was forever joined to his in 1857 when Currier offered a partnership to his artistically inclined bookkeeper James Merritt Ives, who was born in New York City in 1824. The firm went on to ever greater success for another three decades, but, ultimately, it failed to keep pace with technological and mechanical developments in printing and was closed down in 1907, its vast stock of old-fashioned prints sold off at pennies per pound. Currier had retired in 1880, after fifty-two years in the business, and died in 1888, while Ives was active until just before his death in 1895. Their sons had jointly managed the company until Edward West Currier sold his interest to Chauncy Ives, who presided over the liquidation of this great American institution, whose decorative product had made its way into practically every home in the country.

The firm's output, over a fifty-year period of prime activity, numbers in excess of 7,000 known prints in every possible category. Although often characterized as a form of folk art, Currier & Ives prints were mainly created by sophisticated artists and lithographers, some of whom, like Fanny Palmer and Louis Maurer, were full-time employees. Others, like Arthur Fitzwilliam Tait, the distinguished painter of outdoor life, and George Henry Durrie, the well-loved limner of New England farm scenes, sold paintings to the firm. Even though the subject matter of most prints tends to be based in fact, or on events unfolding at the time, there is often something in the very presentation that suggests legend or folklore. But much of this has to do with the firm's genius in anticipating and visualizing for future generations the fertile ground where America's kind of folklore was sure to grow: cowboys and Indians, the winning of the West, homesteading the prairie, building the railroads, the gold rush, whaling expeditions, rounding the Horn on clipper ships, steamboat races on the Mississippi, and Civil War battles. What *is* represented as folklore is often simply a conjuring up of story themes by such near-contemporaries as HENRY WADSWORTH LONGFELLOW and WASHINGTON IRVING, or the aphorisms of BENJAMIN FRANKLIN. Some prints do tend to couch actual events in trappings of folklore, as in *Last Gun of the Arctic,* which shows Stewart Holland, faithful to naval tradition, going down with his ship as, at his post, he continues to fire the distress signal. Another print, *The Arkansas Traveler,* illustrates an Ozark folktale from the 1840s in which a citified traveler is able to earn the log-cabin hospitality of a backwoods settler by playing him a tolerable HOEDOWN on his FIDDLE (see "ARKANSAS TRAVELER"). In examples such as these, Currier & Ives served as a transmitter of folklore and legend.

The tenure of this venerable firm coincided with the complex period of America's industrialization and its unsettling transition from rural to urban. Currier & Ives set out to serve both spheres by showing the latest developments in "lightning express" railroad trains and "walking beam" steamboats while not neglecting to re-

Home, Sweet Home *(1869) is a quintessential Currier & Ives print, evoking feelings of modest prosperity and domestic bliss. (Collection of Walton Rawls)*

mind people of the glorious history of their country. Many prints were copied from the paintings of well-known artists, such as *Declaration of Independence* and *Surrender of Cornwallis* by John Trumbull; and others showed legendary events such as the landing of the Pilgrims, the Boston Tea Party, and Washington taking leave of his officers.

Many of the prints touched themes already endowed with sentimentality for the passing scene, such as the old oaken bucket that hung by the well, the village smithy under the spreading chestnut tree, and the noble savage legend of HI-

AWATHA, all of which figured in often-recited poems by Woodworth and Longfellow. And finally there were numerous series of beautiful prints that recalled for nostalgic city dwellers the delights of the country life they had abandoned, things like skating on frozen ponds, maple-sugaring, cider-making, corn-husking, and haying: scenes that were both heartwarming for transplanted farm folk and educational for others, since they clearly evoked the stuff of legend, an idyllic America.

See also: SAMBO.

SUGGESTED READING: Harry T. Peters, *Currier & Ives: Printmakers to the American People* (New York, 1942); Walton Rawls, *The Great Book of Currier & Ives' America* (New York, 1979); Colin Simkin, *Currier & Ives' America* (New York, 1952).

Custer, George Armstrong (1839–1876).

Like DAVY CROCKETT, George Armstrong Custer was an actual person who rose to heroic and mythic stature partially through force of circumstance, timing, his own self-promotion, his inherent charisma and personal flamboyance, public yearning for a certain kind of hero, and the mass media's seizing on possibilities for exciting copy. He is one of the best known of American folk heroes, and the story of his death and apotheosis as a mythic figure is a vivid example of the processes by which legends are created.

Custer was born in New Rumley, Ohio, on December 5, 1839. He had an undistinguished career at West Point, graduating in 1861 at the bottom of his class, with ninety-seven demerits, only three short of dismissal. Custer's early military experience revealed a colorful character of mischievous high spirits—a figure others would find entertaining and the natural subject for stories—but once he entered the Civil War, he displayed the contradictory qualities of character that made him at once reckless and heroic. In his first battle (First Bull Run, July 21, 1861), he spied a classmate and cantered off, deserting his troops to talk to his friend. At that very moment, an emergency developed, and a leader was needed to reform panicked soldiers in order to march them over a bridge. Custer sprang to the fore and emerged a hero. He gained rapid distinction in a variety of dramatic situations. When an expendable man was needed to ascend in a hot-air observation balloon to scout enemy positions, General "Baldy" Smith called on Custer. The young officer made valuable reports, which soon drew the attention of Gen. George McClellan, then commanding the Army of the Potomac and soon to rise to command of the entire Union army. Later, Custer crossed a muddy stream on foot, behind enemy lines, and discovered a bend in the river that would be an excellent staging point from which a raiding party might launch an attack. McClellan was so impressed that he invited the lieutenant to join his staff as a captain and personal aide (June–July 1862). After a transfer to the staff of cavalry commander Gen. Alfred Pleasanton, Custer fought at Antietam (September 17, 1862), Fredericksburg (December 13, 1862), and Chancellorsville (May 2–4, 1863). He won a quick promotion to brigadier general of volunteers (June 1863) and was given the command of a Michigan brigade. He distinguished himself at Gettysburg (July 1–3, 1863) and was breveted a major of regulars. Transferred to Gen. Philip Sheridan's command, the Army of the Potomac, he fought at Yellow Tavern (May 11, 1864), Winchester (September 19), and Fisher's Hill (September 22). In March 1865, he was breveted brigadier general of regulars and given command of the Third Cavalry, which he led at Five Forks (April 1) and in pursuit of Robert E. Lee's Army of Northern Virginia, culminating in the surrender at Appomattox (April 9).

Everything about Custer's rise rang of myth and legend. A realistic-sounding account tells of Custer, during one skirmish, encountering a handsomely appointed riderless horse, on the saddle of which hung a superb straight sword, which was inscribed with the traditional motto: "Draw Me Not Without Provocation. / Sheathe Me Not Without Honor." Custer took the weapon, and it became his famed "Toledo blade." Another version of this story holds that Maj. Gen. George A. Drew of the Sixth Michigan presented Custer with the sword because Custer was the only man strong enough to arch the blade over his head. In either version, the echoes of literary myth are unmistakable, and in the latter version, the mythic motif distinctly echoes the legend of King Arthur and his acquisition of Excalibur. Excited by such tales—as well as by Custer's unmistakable dash and undeniable (albeit reckless) courage under fire—the media hailed him. The *New York Herald* dubbed Custer "the boy general" (a brigadier at twenty-three, he was, in fact, the youngest general officer in the history of the U.S. Army) and "the boy general with the flowing yellow curls." Not only did Custer wear his hair at an ostentatious length, he dressed in distinctive fashion, wearing a velveteen jumper with loops of gold braid on both sleeves, a star stitched on his shirt collar, and a bright red neckerchief.

Although Custer reverted to the rank of captain upon the reduction of the regular army following the conclusion of the Civil War, he was soon promoted to lieutenant colonel and given command of the Seventh Cavalry, stationed in Kansas. It was at this time that his impulsiveness, willfulness, and lack of judgment became increasingly apparent. The man who had been sorely lacking in discipline during his West Point days now became a martinet, driving his men unmercifully, including one forced march of sixty-five miles across a waterless tract of Colorado in 1867. When his men began deserting, slipping away a few at a time, Custer shouted to the officer of the day: "Stop those men. Shoot them where you find them. Don't bring in any alive." Shortly after this incident, Custer learned that cholera had broken out at Fort Riley, Kansas, and his beautiful wife, Elizabeth ("Libby") wrote him a terrified letter, begging him to return. Contrary to orders, and moving through hostile territory, Custer set out on a forced march with his already exhausted troops three hundred miles to Fort Riley. He was subsequently arrested and court-martialed for disobeying orders, moving without authorization, shooting deserters, and ordering excessive marches. He was sentenced to a year's suspension without pay. The sentence did not endure. General Sheridan recognized the killer in George Armstrong Custer, and it was killers that he needed in the army's ongoing war against the Indians. His first major campaign after being recalled to active duty was against the

George Armstrong Custer as a Civil War brigadier general, pictured in Library of Universal History *(1898).*

Cheyenne. On November 29, 1868, he attacked the village of Chief Black Kettle on the Washita River, cutting down warriors, women, children, and old men, including Black Kettle and his wife (never mind that Black Kettle had wished to make peace with the whites). Although the massacre raised some angry protests in liberal quarters, Custer remained a national hero. He nurtured this image with a best-selling memoir, *My Life on the Plains* (1874), written with the able assistance of his adoring wife.

Already a national hero, George Armstrong Custer rose to apotheosis—as did Crockett when he died a martyr's death at the ALAMO—giving his last full measure of devotion (in the popular imagination) by sacrificing his life in a battle against overwhelming hordes of Sioux warriors at the Battle of the Little Bighorn on June 25, 1876. Custer's "Last Stand" resulted in the deaths of 266 officers and men of the Seventh Cavalry. It can be persuasively argued that the debacle was due to Custer's characteristic recklessness; he not only led his troops into battle without first securing even rudimentary reconnaissance, he also divided his command into three columns, making an unsupported attack. At least three thousand warriors were massed against the 366 men of "Yellow Hair's" command.

George Armstrong Custer immediately became the most popular hero of the American people. This is not a subjective judgment, but is objectively evident from the fact that more paintings and illustrations have been devoted to the Last Stand than to San Juan Hill, Chateau-Thierry, D-Day, Iwo Jima, and Khe San combined. More than two thousand works of poetry and fiction feature the battle, and the character of Custer figures prominently in more than twenty motion pictures, including *They Died with Their Boots On, Bugles in the Afternoon, Sitting Bull, Two Flags West,* and *Little Big Man.* Long before he became president of the United States, actor Ronald Reagan played Custer in *Santa Fe Trail.* The story of Little Bighorn has also been featured on television, on such shows as *Custer, Branded, Time Tunnel,* and *Cheyenne.*

The process by which a preventable military catastrophe perpetrated by a reckless, perhaps incompetent, commander became a key icon in the national mythology provides valuable insight into how myth has functioned since mass media came into existence. First, Custer was a colorful, charismatic figure. The cavalry had an aura of romance at least as ancient as the horsemen of the Parthenon. Custer's personality inspired emotional extremes among his contemporaries, who either adored or despised him. Both camps wrote about him, and he himself wrote about his battle experiences, as did his ever-devoted wife. Libby Custer extolled her husband's bravery in a series of personal appearances, articles, and books over the remainder of her long life. Since 1876 was the Centennial Year, the nation was hungry for a national hero. The Battle of the Little Bighorn left no survivors to give an eyewitness account of what had occurred. The rescue party came upon Custer's body—"miraculously" unmutilated, in contrast to the corpses of the others—pierced by two bullets. One could only surmise what had actually happened, but the American people were eager for news of glory. Frontier newsmen filled in appropriate details from their active imaginations. Other writers copied these first accounts and added their own variations.

Another central cluster of factors rises out of the archetype of the hero who fights gloriously to the end against overwhelming odds. The archetype into which Custer has most often been cast is that of the hero who leads a small force against overwhelming odds. The hero and his unflinching followers make a stand, determined to fight to the death, convinced that they are defending their way of life against savage enemies, cultural inferiors, racial (or national) aliens sworn to destroy the hero's people. Determined to make their foe pay dearly for their victory, the hero and his men slay hordes of the enemy. Traditionally, the hero is the last to die. This pattern describes the stories of Davy Crockett at the Battle of the Alamo, the downfall of Roland in the *Chanson de Roland* during the reign of Charlemagne, the defeat of Sir Gawain in the *Mort d'Arthur* of 1360, the downfall of the Serbian King Kazar in the fight against the Turks, the death of the Scottish James IV and his troops at Flodden, King Leonides and the Spartans against the Turks at Thermopylae, and the defeat and death of Saul on Mount Gilboa as described in the first book of Samuel. There is, then, a cultural and emotional imperative to translate the Little Bighorn debacle

A Sioux warrior-artist named One Bull interpreted the Indian victory over Custer at the Little Bighorn.

into these archetypal terms as well. However, even after extensive recent investigation using modern archaeological techniques, little is known about the final crucial hour of June 25, 1876, when Lieutenant Colonel Custer and his command fell. Before modern scientific investigation was undertaken, details were even more scarce. What little was known was usually altered, and the gaps of knowledge of precise details was filled in imaginatively by folk tradition and the invention of artists, journalists, and biographers. Most of the thousand or so paintings and illustrations of the last moment show Custer with a sword, a weapon probably not used in battle since the Civil War, and even then only rarely. Unlike his depiction in artworks, Custer had shorn his long, flowing locks before the battle. Later interviews with the Indians who had taken part in the battle suggest that they had not even known who the opposing leader was, and their accounts report that the last surviving troopers made a desperate rush to escape to the Little Bighorn River. They were killed before they could get away. Custer died on the side of the hill some time before the fleeing cavalrymen. Capt. Frederick Benteen, who surveyed the scene of the battle shortly after the event, reported signs of

"panic and rout." Many stories of treachery flowered: Some blamed the army's Crow scouts, a highly unlikely eventuality, since the Crow Indians would hardly betray their soldier-employers to their hereditary enemies, the Sioux. Various officers of the Seventh were accused of incompetence or treachery, and, finally, the focus of the accusations became Maj. Marcus A. Reno, Custer's second in command.

Although Custer's body was found about fifty feet below the ridge—not dramatically on top of it, as his final moments are presented in most paintings—dead of two bullet wounds, and not mutilated or scalped like most of the others, a bloodier and more sensational finale entered print and tradition. The story developed that the Sioux warrior Rain-in-the-Face, avenging an alleged abuse of 1873, killed Custer or Custer's brother, Tom, and cut out his heart. Some versions have Rain-in-the-Face eating the heart. While it is true that certain eastern tribes practiced ritual cannibalism, eating the heart of an enemy in order to take on his valor, there is no evidence of this practice among the Sioux. Nevertheless, newspapermen, anxious to please a thrill-hungry readership, did much to disseminate this account. Yet there is no conclusive evidence that Rain-in-the-Face even took part in the Battle of the Little Bighorn, and, on October 27, 1906, a few months before his death, Rain-in-the-Face explicitly denied having killed Custer or his brother, let alone having cut out the heart of either. Yet no less a figure than HENRY WADSWORTH LONGFELLOW celebrated "The Revenge of Rain-in-the-Face" in verse: "And Rain-in-the-Face, in his flight, / Uplifted high in the air / As a ghastly trophy bore / The brave heart, that beat no more, / Of the white chief with yellow hair."

Another intriguing legend was based on the fact that Custer's body was found unmutilated. A story circulated that the corpse had been saved from the final indignity by a pretty Cheyenne maid, Mo-nan-se-tah, who (according to the tale) had borne Custer a child several years earlier, a child conceived when the girl served as an interpreter for the Seventh Cavalry at Black Kettle's ill-fated village in 1868. The legend held that, still in love with Custer, Mo-nan-se-tah protected his body from desecration. The story is a variation on the legend of Captain JOHN SMITH and POCAHONTAS—albeit, in the Custer variant, the maiden cannot save the white man's life, but must content herself with preserving his body and the memory of what he was in life. The archetype is an ancient one, illustrated as early as the episode of the *Odyssey* in which Nausicaa saves Odysseus, in Roman culture, by Lavinia's salvation of the outsider Aeneas, and in medieval romances in the story of "The Enamored Moslem Princess," in which a Moslem maiden saves the life of the Christian captive of her pagan father.

The death and apotheosis of George Armstrong Custer vividly illustrate the workings of the age-old mechanisms of myth creation in an era of MASS MEDIA. Given the appropriate circumstances, the stories woven around a significant incident are dictated less by individual imagination than by the imperatives of archetype and cultural need.

See also: BLACK ELK; BUFFALO BILL (WILLIAM F. CODY); CRAZY HORSE; PATTON, GEORGE SMITH; SITTING BULL.

SUGGESTED READING: Elizabeth B. Custer, *Boots and Saddles* (New York, 1885), *Following the Guidon* (New York, 1890), *Tenting on the Plains* (New York, 1887); General George A. Custer, *My Life on the Plains* (New York, 1874); David Humphreys Miller, *Custer's Fall* (1957; reprint ed., New York, 1996); Jay Monaghan, *Custer* (Boston, 1959); Bruce A. Rosenberg, *Custer and the Epic of Defeat* (University Park, Pa., 1974); Don Russell, *Custer's Last Stand, or the Battle of Little Big Horn* (Dallas, 1968); Robert M. Utley, *Custer and the Great Controversy* (Los Angeles, 1962); Frederick Whittaker, *Life of Custer* (New York, 1876).

D

Daddy longlegs. A long-legged arachnid of the order *Phalangidae,* the daddy longlegs is deemed beneficial because it eats insects harmful to crops. American folklore tradition holds that killing a daddy longlegs causes cows to go dry. The daddy longlegs can also help one locate missing cattle. Picking up a daddy longlegs by one of its legs, one recites "Granddaddy, granddaddy, where did my cows go?" and the arachnid will lift one or more of its free legs in the direction of the errant livestock. In New England, it was once common to wish on a daddy longlegs for good luck.

Dalhart, Vernon (1882–1948). Born Marion Try Slaughter on a northeastern Texas ranch in a one-story frame house on the western edge of the Old South, Dalhart grew up in a rich folk environment. One of his first jobs was cowpunching during a summer vacation. He learned to play the harmonica and to whistle melodies, and he also received formal instruction on the piano from a local teacher. Later, some time after his father had been fatally stabbed in a brawl, he and his mother moved to Dallas, where he studied at the Dallas Conservatory of Music. By 1910, when he had a wife and two children to support, he moved to New York City, where he hoped to pursue a career as a singer, but he began instead with a bread-and-butter job in a music store, probably selling and delivering pianos. While working in the music store, Dalhart had various gigs as paid soloist in New York churches and as a funeral vocalist for mortuaries. At the same time, he studied voice with opera instructors and auditioned for roles in grand and light opera companies. He may also have been singing in New York variety shows the black "Mammy songs" he knew from both his Texas environment and from popular recording artists such as Al Jolson and Eddie Cantor.

In 1912, Dalhart sang in his first professional role, a minor part in Giacomo Puccini's *La Fanciula del West* (*The Girl of the Golden West*), followed by leading roles in Gilbert and Sullivan's *H.M.S. Pinafore* as Ralph Rackstraw and as Lieut. Benjamin Franklin Pinkerton in Puccini's *Madama Butterfly.*

In 1914, during a low ebb in his fortunes, he auditioned for Edison Records, singing, "Can't Yo Heah Me Callin', Caroline," and was hired by no less than THOMAS ALVA EDISON himself. The same song was the first of Dalhart's to be issued on wax cylinder. It was the first of several hundred Edison would record by Dalhart, who used an apparently convincing southern black dialect. About his use of dialect he said to an interviewer in 1918: "I never had to learn it. When you are born and brought up in the South your only trouble is to talk any other way. All my childhood that was almost the only talk I ever heard because the sure 'nough Southerner talks like a Negro even when he's white. I've broken myself of the habit, more or less, in ordinary conversation, but it still comes pretty easy."

Edison continued to issue and reissue Dalhart's recordings of mostly light opera and classics until 1924, but then shifted primarily to county until the demise of the Edison recording firm in 1929. Dalhart's recording of "THE WRECK OF THE OLD '97" in 1924 was the first-ever smash hit country music recording. Dalhart persuaded Victor to issue it coupled with "The Prisoner's Song," and Dalhart became the first country music recording artist to become popular on a national and international scale.

From 1924 to 1928, Dalhart's most productive years, he recorded on all the major and minor labels and their subsidiaries under more than 110 individual and group pseudonyms. He cut his final takes for RCA Victor in 1938.

See also: COUNTRY MUSIC.

SUGGESTED READING: Country Music Foundation, *Country: The Music and the Musicians* (New York, 1988).

Dance, folk. The classic definitions of *folk dance* range from the traditional dances of a country or ethnic group to any form of dance that is nonprofessional. Yet not all folk dance is performed by nonprofessionals. Professionally trained troupes give staged performances of ethnic folk dance, and ballet and other professional troupes sometimes adapt folk dance steps to formal choreographic compositions. Furthermore, it is not always easy to distinguish between, for example, the POLKA as a folk dance and as a ballroom dance. Many authorities consider jazz dancing an American folk style, while others see it as commercial, professional dancing.

Many students of folk dance believe its origins are religious. The dancer is a celebrant or medicine maker, a key participant in a religious ritual. Many Native American dances still retain close ties to religious function, while, in non–Native

American folk dance, the religious elements are distant echoes, and the dance may be considered folk *art*.

However one chooses to define folk dance, the term, applied to American traditions, must take in a wide variety of dances, ranging from those of Anglo-American traditions (which many people identify as *the* American folk dance), African-American traditions, Native American traditions, and the traditional dances of a host of European immigrant groups. Beyond ethnic and national traditions are vernacular idioms, including, for example, BREAKDANCING, BUCK-AND-WING, and the SQUARE DANCE.

See also: BALL THE JACK; BARN DANCE; BEATTY, TALLEY; BELIAJUS, VYTAUTAS; CAKE-WALK; CLOGGING; CORN DANCE; DE MILLE, AGNES; DUNHAM, KATHERINE; FILIPINO AMERICANS; FOLK MUSIC; GRAHAM, MARTHA; GRECO, JOSÉ; HORNPIPE; JITTERBUG; LINE DANCE; LONGWAYS DANCE; MAZURKA; SCHOTTISCHE; SLAVIC AMERICANS; TAP DANCE; WALTZ.

Davidson, Levette Jay (1894–1957). An American folklorist and University of Denver professor, Levette Davidson was one of the prime movers of the university's folklore program, which, during Davidson's tenure at Denver, became one of the nation's most important centers of folklore study.

Davidson was born in Eureka, Illinois, and was educated at Eureka College (A.B., 1915), University of Illinois (A.M., 1916), Harvard University (A.M., 1917), and University of Michigan (Ph.D., 1922). He joined the English faculty of the University of Denver directly after taking his doctrate and rose steadily through the academic ranks, becoming chairman of the department in 1940 and acting chancellor of the university in 1953.

Davidson directed the Western Folklore Conference, an important annual event for American folklorists, and wrote many books and articles, including *Rocky Mountain Tales* (with Forrester Blake, 1947) and *Guide to American Folklore* (1951).

See also: CAMPA, ARTHUR LEON.

Davis, Arthur Kyle, Jr. (1897–1972).

Davis was a distinguished University of Virginia English professor specializing in Victorian literature and best known to folklorists as a scholar of the BALLAD.

A native of Petersburg, Virginia, Davis took his B.A. at Virginia (1917), as well as his Ph.D. (1924). He joined the university's English department directly after receiving his doctorate. His mentor, Prof. C. Alphonso Smith, founder of the Virginia Folklore Society (1913), steered Davis into folklore, particularly the collecting of folk songs. With Smith's death in 1924, Davis became president of the Virginia Folklore Society and set about editing the CHILD BALLADS in the society's possession. The result of this effort was *Traditional Ballads of Virginia* (1920), which was warmly greeted by folklorists for showing that the Child ballad tradition was very much a living thing in America.

Davis was responsible for creating a folklore curriculum at Virginia and produced two more volumes of Virginia folk songs, in 1949 and 1960.

Davis, Vestie (1903–1978).

Born Edward Davis in Hillsboro, Maryland, this folk painter of "naive" and lighthearted New York City scenes legally changed his name to Vestie Davis in 1940. He was personally a colorful man, who joined the U.S. Navy in 1921, serving through 1928, including a tour of duty in China. After his discharge, he settled in New York City, where he ran a newsstand, worked as a circus barker, and ran a concession stand at Coney Island. In 1932, he took up the embalmer's profession, working in this field until his retirement in 1960.

Davis began painting in 1947 and, during the early 1950s, began exhibiting at the outdoor art show in Washington Square Park in Greenwich Village. Morris Weisenthal, owner of the Morris Gallery, saw his work there and began to show him in his gallery. Davis's subjects are chiefly the familiar landmarks of New York City, along with an occasional image of Atlantic City. Typical scenes are recreational cityscapes, such as his *Coney Island Boardwalk* (1969) and his *Coney Island—Luna Park* (1970), in which the many figures represented exhibit individual character, yet are rendered in an almost cartoon style. Unlike many folk painters, Davis planned his works with great deliberation, usually taking photographs of the scene he wanted to depict, cutting and pasting the photographs into a composition that pleased him, then either beginning the painting or making pencil sketches first. Davis was a prolific painter, who created perhaps as many as eight hundred works.

Dead-man's hand.

In poker, a hand of aces and eights has been known as a dead-man's hand ever since WILD BILL HICKOK held such a hand when he was murdered in Deadwood Saloon Number 10 on August 2, 1876. The cards were pried from the gambler's dead fingers.

Death Valley.

Death Valley may be described physically as a desert basin in Inyo Count, southeastern California, 140 miles long and varying in width from 5 to 15 miles. It is a depression located between the Panamint Mountains to the west and the Amargosa Range to the east. Its dramatic name suggests that its significance in American popular culture goes beyond the geographical facts. The hottest and driest place in North America, it is also the lowest area of the Western Hemisphere, at 282 feet below sea level. The forty-niners—gold seekers of the 1849 California gold rush—found it a formidable barrier to their quest, and it was they who gave it its name. Here air temperatures have been recorded as high as 134°F (in 1913) and ground temperatures sometimes a baking 175°F. Because the Panamint Mountains block the incursion of moist air, the valley receives an average annual rainfall of only 1.5 inches. In the lowest areas of Death Valley, prehistoric lakes have left sterile, dead salt flats. Higher up, "survivor" vegetation (coarse grass, mesquite, cacti, and poppies) is found, as are such animals as coyotes, kangaroo rats, horned toads, bighorn sheep, wild burros, and ravens. The extreme conditions of Death Valley resonated powerfully with the tradition of

the western TALL TALE. Here was a western reality that more than matched the western storyteller's penchant for exaggeration.

While gold prospectors experienced Death Valley as a hellish portal through which they had to pass in quest of gold, later prospectors found another mineral of value in the valley. Borax, discovered in 1873 and used primarily as a basis for soap and detergent, was regularly hauled by "twenty-mule teams," which soon were transformed into a popular culture icon by their depiction on the trademark tins of the Boraxo powdered soap company.

The status of Death Valley as one of America's legendary or mythically potent places was enhanced in the twentieth century by tourism. After the borax deposits petered out, GHOST TOWNS, romantically forlorn and remarkably well preserved in the dry, sterile air of the valley, drew curiosity seekers. Tourism was further stimulated by the establishment of Death Valley National Monument (extending partly into Nevada) in 1933. Its area is 2,981 square miles, of which 550 square miles are below sea level.

SUGGESTED READING: Ansel Adams and Nancy Newhall, *Death Valley* (Boston, 1954); Ruth Kirk, *Exploring Death Valley* (rev. ed., 1981).

The shifting sand dunes of Death Valley, California. The photograph is from circa 1943.

De Mille, Agnes (1905–1993). One of the most influential figures in American modern dance, De Mille used folk-based choreography and classical ballet technique to create the "dance story" form of narrative dance theater. De Mille was born in New York City and studied with a variety of teachers, most notably Theodore Kosloff in Los Angeles and, later, Dame Marie Rambert in London. After graduating from the

University of California, Los Angeles, in 1927, she made her debut as a concert dancer that year and achieved a modicum of success with her solo dance work in the United States and in Europe, especially in England.

During the 1930s, De Mille danced in Rambert's company as well as in that of Antony Tudor. She also staged a Cole Porter musical, *Nymph Errant* in London in 1933. But it was on Broadway, as the choreographer of *Hooray for What?* (1937), *Swingin' the Dream* (1939), and the epoch-making Rodgers and Hammerstein musical *Oklahoma!* (1943)—hailed as the first musical to integrate all musical and dance elements into a cohesive narrative—that De Mille made her early reputation. While she was making history on the popular stage, she also created her unique style of story dance with the 1940 *Black Ritual* and the 1941 *Three Virgins and a Devil,* both written for Ballet Theatre (now American Ballet Theatre). A host of other major works followed, including *Rodeo* (1942), for the Ballet Russe de Monte Carlo and featuring a great folk-influenced score by AARON COPLAND, and *Fall River Legend* (1948), an extraordinary work based on the case of nineteenth-century Massachusetts' alleged ax murderer Lizzie Borden and still ranked by many as De Mille's single best work. In *Rodeo,* De Mille danced the lead, and both *Rodeo* and *Fall River Legend* are typical of her ability to combine elements of folk dance, social dance, modern dance, and ballet with an unerring instinct for spectacular theater.

De Mille always balanced her modern dance work with Broadway choreography, staging such hits as *Bloomer Girl* (1944), *Carousel* (1945), *Brigadoon* (1947), *Gentlemen Prefer Blondes* (1949), and *Paint Your Wagon* (1951). Although she continued to choreograph during her later years, creating such works as *The Four Marys* (1965), *A Rose for Miss Emily* (1971), *A Bride-groom Called Death* (1978), and her final work, *The Informer* (1988), to name a few, she increasingly directed her efforts toward the study and preservation of American folk dance. In 1973, she founded the Heritage Dance Theater at the North Carolina School of the Arts, in part to present the many forms of folk and popular dance and also to create a truly national dance company.

De Mille possessed great charisma and was in demand as lecturer. She was also a prolific author, whose works include several volumes of memoirs—*Dance to the Piper* (1952), *And Promenade Home* (1956), *Speak to Me, Dance with Me* (1973), *Where the Wings Grow* (1978) and *Reprieve* (1981), which records her struggle to overcome the effects of a 1975 stroke. She also wrote about other dance subjects, most notably in *Martha: The Life and Work of Martha Graham* (1991). De Mille received many awards (including Broadway's Tony) and some fifteen honorary academic degrees.

See also: DANCE, FOLK; GADD, MAY.

SUGGESTED READING: De Mille, Agnes, *Dance to the Piper* (New York, 1952).

Densmore, Frances (1867–1957). Densmore was a pioneering student of Native American music, who began collecting in the vicinity of her hometown, Red Wing, Minnesota, at the beginning of the twentieth century. Her training in music came at Oberlin College, and she also studied with great pianist Leopold Godowsky. Although Densmore enjoyed early acclaim as a piano recitalist and a popular lecturer on the music of Richard Wagner, she turned to the study of Native American music after 1892, when she attended a lecture on the subject given by John Comfort Fillmore. Densmore began field recording in 1901, among the Chippewas. Working from her home in Red Wing, she recorded among other Indian groups as well, eventually amassing some 2,400 songs, which are on deposit at the Smithsonian Institution.

Densmore published portions of her fieldwork early and to a primarily popular audience, but she approached her subject in a more scholarly way later, focusing on melodic analysis, exposition of the song's cultural setting, and the historic and social function of each song. She also tackled questions of method, particularly with regard to making valid transcriptions of melodies that are not in traditional Western tonality.

As was often the case during a period when folk-song collecting emphasized the gathering and analysis of texts rather than melodies, Densmore's work was at first more appreciated by musicologists than by folklorists and anthropologists. Her work bore artistic fruit in Alberto Bimoni's opera *Winona* and in several Indian-themed compositions by Charles Wakefield Cadman.

From 1907 until her death, Densmore was employed by the Smithsonian's Bureau of American Ethnology.

SUGGESTED READING: Charles Hofmann, *Frances Densmore and American Indian Music: A Memorial Volume* (New York, 1968).

Desliné, Jean-Léon (1928–). Born in Haiti, Desliné is a dancer, choreographer, and teacher who came to the United States to promote, present, and preserve the folk-dance heritage of his native country. Desliné was educated at the Ethnological Institute in Port-au-Prince and, while still in his teens, studied with Lina Mathon Blanchet, who founded the first professional Haitian folk-dance company. Desliné performed and toured in the United States with this troupe. Later, working as a staff reporter for *La Nouvelle* (a Port-au-Prince newspaper), Desliné returned to the United States with financial backing from the Rockefeller Foundation to study typography in New York City. He took the opportunity to pursue his dance training as well and was soon giving his own recitals. In the mid-1940s, Desliné returned to Haiti, where he joined a KATHARINE DUNHAM Bal Negre tour. From the late 1940s through the middle 1960s, he shuttled between Haiti and the United States to organize dance companies, make films, and stage folk-based recitals and festivals. In 1960, he began teaching Afro-Caribbean dance at the New Dance Group in New York, exerting a profound influence on folk-oriented dancers as well as dancers who use folk movement to broaden their own dance vocabulary. In 1975, Desliné became president of the Desliné Dance Foundation and has been a member of the faculty of New York University's School of the Arts. Both the United States as well as the government of Haiti have recognized Desliné's contributions to preserving and presenting the folk-dance heritage of Haitians in Haiti and the United States.

Devil, The. In the Judeo-Christian tradition, the devil is the personification of evil, a fallen angel who became the arch-opponent of God (the word is derived from an Arabic word meaning "adversary"), and as God rules heaven, the devil presides over hell. The devil seeks to thwart God's purposes by tempting human beings to evil, thereby winning their souls.

In folklore—as opposed to theology—the

devil is named by a variety of euphemisms, including Old Nick, the Duce, Clootie, and the Old Gentleman. He is often portrayed as mischievous rather than evil and is realized in popular iconic form as a red man with horns, a pointed tail, cloven hoofs, and a pitchfork in hand to prod the souls of the damned. Folklore and literature are replete with stories of intellectual contests with the devil, usually involving the solution to a riddle, with an individual's soul at stake. Also common are tales of bargains made with the devil, typically swapping one's soul for some supernatural power or knowledge as in the Faust legend.

See also: WEBSTER, DANIEL.

Dialect stories. Traditional tales that use distinctive dialects characteristic of certain ethnic or regional groups or members of a certain social class, dialect stories are generally humorous and revolve around recognizable stock characters. Such stories have a long history in America and appeared in print in colonial ALMANACS, which published anecdotes imitating Yankees, frontiersmen, Native Americans, and African Americans as well as Dutch, German, French, and Irish immigrants. The dialect story reached a height of literary expression in the works of LOCAL-COLOR STORY writers and especially MARK TWAIN and JOEL CHANDLER HARRIS. Later American writers frequently included dialect passages to suggest the speech of such immigrant groups as the Italians, Scandinavians, and Slavs. More than one generation of stand-up comics, "monologists," and storytellers have told jokes in YIDDISH-inflected dialects.

SUGGESTED READING: Walter Blair and Raven I. McDavid Jr., eds., *The Mirth of a Nation: America's Great Dialect Humor* (Minneapolis, 1981).

Dillinger, John (1903–1934). Perhaps the most famous of the Depression-era bank robbers, Dillinger entered into American folklore after J. EDGAR HOOVER branded him Public Enemy Number One. He was born in Indianapolis and, as a youth, became a petty thief. Arrested in the act of robbing a grocery store when he was twenty-one, Dillnger spent the next nine years of his life in prison, where he was schooled in more serious crime. On his release, he organized a gang of bank robbers who swept through the Midwest. Twice caught and incarcerated, he escaped both times and was the target of an FBI manhunt. In April 1934, he blundered into a combined FBI and police ambush at the Little Bohemia Lodge, in Wisconsin, just north of the Illinois State line. In a vicious gun battle, Dillinger fought his way out. Worse, FBI bullets cut down three innocent bystanders. Eager to redeem the bureau's reputation, Hoover made Dillinger his top priority. The director's highly publicized campaign transformed Dillinger into a legendary figure, the very incarnation of gangsterism.

The manner of Dillinger's death added to the growing legend. Hoover dispatched Special Agent Melvin Purvis to ambush the bank robber. Working with a "confidential informant" named Anna Sage, Purvis and his agents set up an ambush outside the Biograph Theatre on Chicago's Near North Side. On July 22, 1934, Sage, wearing a scarlet dress for maximum visibility— and instantly dubbed by press and public "The Lady in Red"—led Dillinger out of the theater (where they had just seen a gangster movie). The agents gunned down Dillinger (wounding two female bystanders in the process). Yet such was Dillinger's almost mythic stature that stories of the FBI's having killed the wrong man, leaving the "real" Dillinger very much alive, circulated for years. Another, even more enduring, popular legend holds that Dillinger enjoyed unfailing success with women and possessed a prodigiously large penis.

See also: CRIME AND CRIMINALS.

SUGGESTED READING: "Dillinger, John," in Alan Axelrod and Charles Phillips, eds., *Cops, Crooks, and Criminologists: The International Biographical Dictionary of Law Enforcement* (New York, 1996).

Dinsmoor, Samuel Perry (1843–1932).

Samuel Perry Dinsmoor was a folk sculptor who created *Garden of Eden* (1907–29), an environment of cement and limestone sculptures surrounding his eleven-room "Rock Log Cabin," which he built of limestone on his farm in Lucas, Kansas. The *Garden of Eden* environment includes sculptures of Adam and Eve, the serpent, Cain and Abel, as well as the goddess of Liberty, various flags, soldiers, Indians, animals, and birds, a collection of 150 works. Doubtless, Dinsmoor would have added even more, had cataracts not ended his career in 1929. The *Garden of Eden* as well as the Rock Log Cabin survive intact and continue to attract tourists to the little town of Lucas.

Dirty Dozens.

Late in the nineteenth century, a game developed in African-American communities in which members of a group engaged in verbal contests to determine who could come up with the most devastating and shocking insults. This process was variously called "the dirty dozens," "the dozens," "sounding," "signifying," "woofing," "joining," "screaming," "cutting," "capping," and "chopping." The terms generally refer to a ritualized series of insults

against relatives, often in the form of rhymed obscene couplets. The following are typical examples from various sources:

> I don't play the dozens, the dozens ain't my
> game,
> But the way I fucked your mama is a
> goddamn shame.

> I hate to talk about your mother, she's a good
> old soul.
> She got a ten-ton pussy and a rubber asshole.

> I fucked your mama on top of the piano.
> When she came out she was singin' the Star
> Spangled Banner.

> Fucked your mother in the ear,
> And when she came out, she said "buy me a
> beer."

> Iron is iron, and steel don't rust,
> But your momma got a pussy like a
> Greyhound bus.

This type of exchange was made into a song called "The Dirty Dozens," with words and music by J. Mayo Williams and Rufus Perryman (nicknamed "Speckled Red"), copyrighted by Leeds Music in 1929. The insults are considerably toned down here, though still coarse and suggestive. Speckled Red was a popular boogie-woogie pianist, who played all through the South and also toured in Europe. Born in Hampton, Georgia, in 1892, he recorded "The Dirty Dozens" in 1929 for Brunswick. His recording was a great success, and he followed it with another version for Brunswick in 1930. Various other performers and bands followed Speckled Red's lead and released numbers based on the dirty dozens, including the Alabama Rascals, Count Basie, Leroy Carr, Jed Davenport, Tommy

The Titanic, *source of much disaster folklore.*

Dorsey and the Clambake 7, Harlem Hamfats, Lonnie Johnson, Memphis Minnie, Sammy Price, and Tampa Red (Hudson Whittaker).

See also: GAMES; RAP.

Suggested Readings: Alan Dundes, ed., *Mother Wit from the Laughing Barrel: Readings in the Interpretation of Afro-American Folklore* (Jackson, Miss., 1994); Dennis Wepman and Ronald B. Newman, *The Life: The Lore and Folk Poetry of the Black Hustler* (Philadelphia, 1976).

Disaster folklore. Significant natural or human-made catastrophes, ranging from floods, tornados, earthquakes, and the like, to fires, shipwrecks, airline accidents, and so on, attack, disturb, and undermine the kinds of everyday routines and communal assumptions from which folklore springs. It is no wonder, then, that disaster events, destructive at physical as well as emotional and cultural levels, evoke much folklore themselves. Folklore is one way in which victims as well as outside witnesses cope with the emotional trauma of disaster.

Disasters typically spark anecdotal narratives, including TALL TALES of remarkable survivals and heroic rescues, but disaster folklore is not limited to words. In the aftermath of a particularly destructive disaster, such as a flood, survivors may permanently memorialize the high-water mark and may create what has been called "disaster shrines": deliberately arranged displays of remarkable debris, such as crushed automobiles. Survivors have been known to preserve and exhibit examples of freak acts of nature, such as a stalk of wheat or other plant thrust through a tree trunk or limb by a powerful wind.

Disasters also elicit jokes, both from outsiders and from survivors. A cycle of sick jokes followed the *Challenger* disaster (1986), in which all of the space shuttle's crew, including schoolteacher Christa McAuliffe, perished in a nationally televised fiery explosion: "What were Christa

McAuliffe's last words?" Answer (in a little-girl voice): "And what's this little red button for?" Also current was the query, "What's NASA stand for?" Answer: "Need Another Seven Astronauts." Gail Matthews-DeNatale and Doug DeNatale (see Suggested Reading) report that South Carolinians referred to Hurricane Hugo (1989) as a "four-billion-dollar blow job."

Depending on the scope and nature of the disaster, the folklore it elicits may long outlast the event and its immediate aftermath, either locally, nationally, or even internationally. The sinking of the great White Star liner *Titanic* in 1912, for example, continues to be commemorated in oral narratives as well as in books and movies, including the $200 million 1997 film directed by James Cameron.

See also: MINING FOLKLORE; SAILORS AND SEAFARING LORE; WEATHER FOLKLORE.

SUGGESTED READING: Gail Matthews-DeNatale and Doug DeNatale, "Disaster Folklore," in Jan Harold Brunvand, ed., *American Folklore: An Encyclopedia* (New York, 1996); Willie Smyth, "Challenger Jokes and the Humor of Disaster," *Western Folklore* 45 (1986), pp. 243–60.

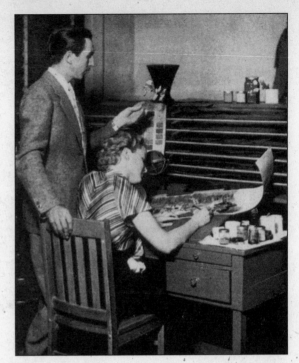

Walt Disney inspects an animation cel, about 1934.

Disney, Walt (1901–1966).

One of the giants of American popular culture, Walt(er Elias) Disney created MICKEY MOUSE, the single best-known character in the history of animation, and other familiar characters, including Minnie Mouse, Donald Duck, and Goofy. He also produced numerous live-action movies and television series dramatizing the lives of such American CULTURE HEROES as DAVY CROCKETT and DANIEL BOONE. And he sought to merge the worlds of fantasy and reality in Disneyland, his amusement park which opened in Anaheim, California, near Los Angeles, in 1955, and Walt Dis-

ney World, which opened near Orlando, Florida, five years after his death.

Born in Chicago, Disney was raised on a farm near Marceline, Missouri, which may have served him as a model for "Main Street U.S.A.," the idealized representation of the "typical" American town that is a central feature of Disneyland. After moving with his family to Kansas City, Missouri, Disney studied cartooning, at first through a correspondence course, then at the Kansas City Art Institute and School of Design. The family returned to Chicago in 1917, where Disney attended high school and continued to study cartooning. During World War I, he served as a truck driver for the American Red Cross in France and Germany, then returned to Kansas City in 1919, where he worked as a draftsman. In Kansas City, he met commercial artist Ub Iwerks, with whom he opened a small animation studio to create short advertisements to be shown on local movie-theater programs. Early efforts at longer cartoons were financial failures. Disney moved to Los Angeles and asked his brother Roy to serve as the business manager of a new animated cartoon venture with Iwerks. Their first successful character was Oswald the Rabbit, and was followed in 1928 by a mouse Disney wanted to call Mortimer until Disney's wife suggested Mickey. "Steamboat Willie," starring Mickey Mouse, was the first animated "talkie" (Disney provided the voice) and created a sensation.

Over the years, Disney produced numerous Mickey Mouse cartoons and added other characters. He also created adaptations of fairy tales, such as "The Three Little Pigs," and AESOP'S FABLES, which, for many children, became *the* versions of the traditional tales. In the mid-1930s, Disney began work on a spectacular feature-length version of "Snow White and the Seven Dwarfs," a project on which Disney successfully gambled the fortunes of his studio. *Snow White* (1937) was followed by *Pinocchio* (1940), and *Dumbo* (1941). Even more innovative was *Fantasia* (1940), an animated interpretation of music by Igor Stravinsky, Paul Dukas, Peter Ilich Tchaikovsky, and others. At this time, Disney also made movies combining animated and live action, including *Song of the South* (1946), a musical version of JOEL CHANDLER HARRIS's UNCLE REMUS tales. As with Disney's fairy-tale cartoons, for many children, Uncle Remus, TAR BABY, BRER RABBIT, and BRER FOX were creations of Walt Disney rather than Harris. Finally, while many other Hollywood studios feared and shunned the onslaught of television in the 1950s, the Disney studio embraced it, producing for TV series featuring such culture heroes as Zorro and Davy Crockett.

SUGGESTED READING: Richard Schickel, *The Disney Version*, (rev. ed., New York, 1985); Christopher Finch, *The Art of Walt Disney: From Mickey Mouse to the Magic Kingdoms* (New York, 1973); Frank Thomas and Ollie Johnston, *Disney Animation: The Illusion of Life* (New York, 1981).

Dixon, Willie (1915–1992).

Blues songwriter Willie Dixon was the composer of such songs as "Back Door Man," "Little Red Rooster," "Hoochie Coochie Man," and "Wang Dang Doodle," which became blues classics as performed by Chicago musicians Howling Wolf, Jimmy Reed, Muddy Waters, and Koko Taylor.

A native of Vicksburg, Mississippi, Dixon, like many African-American blues writers and performers, absorbed the rudiments of music from religious songs. Dixon became a quartet singer, a member of the Union Jubilee singers in Mississippi before moving up north to Chicago in 1936. There, he became a prizefighter while also performing in a number of blues-oriented musical groups, including The Five Breezes, The Four Jumps of Jive, and The Big Three Trio. Later in his career, Dixon showcased his songs with Memphis Slim and others.

Dixon was a talented singer and composer, but he was also a competent businessman and an able spokesman for the blues. His Blues Heaven Foundation was founded to promote and celebrate the blues.

SUGGESTED READING: Willie Dixon, *I Am the Blues* (New York, 1989).

Dobie, J. Frank (1888–1964).

Avid, eloquent, persuasive, and tireless in the collection, preservation, and promotion of Texas lore, Dobie was dubbed "Mr. Texas." He was educated at Southwestern University (Georgetown,

Texas) and at Columbia University (New York City), but his professional life was spent for the most part in and around the University of Texas at Austin, where, from 1914 to 1947, he was often on the faculty of the English Department. His signature course was Life and Literature of the Southwest.

In addition to teaching, Dobie was editor and secretary for the Texas Folklore Society (1922–42), though he drew the ire of many folklorists by his penchant for elaborating on and refining the raw materials he collected. Nevertheless, he succeeded in raising the public and professional consciousness about local history and local folklore. A prolific author, he published countless newspaper and magazine articles and twenty books, the most notable of which are *A Vaquero of the Brush Country* (1929)—a close-up look at the Texas cowhand—and *Coronado's Children* (1930), a collection of legends concerning buried treasure.

See also: BREWER, J(OHN) MASON; THORP, NATHAN HOWARD.

SUGGESTED READING: Lon Tinkle, *An American Original: The Life of J. Frank Dobie* (Boston, 1978).

Dr. Watts hymns. Isaac Watts (1674–1748) was an English theologian and writer of hymns, whose work appeared in colonial American editions of *Psalms of David Imitated* (Philadelphia, 1729) and *Hymns and Spiritual Songs* (Boston, 1739). Slaves showed an early enthusiasm for "Dr. Watts hymns" when missionaries exposed them to his music. They performed the hymns at slow tempos, with much wailing vocal ornamentation, and with each singer improvising his or her own variations. The complex effect is overwhelmingly mournful. Before long, slaves began to call all the songs performed in this style "Dr.

Watts hymns" or "Dr. Watts spirituals," regardless of the composer.

See also: SACRED HARP MUSIC; SPIRITUALS, AFRICAN-AMERICAN.

SUGGESTED READING: Selma L. Bishop, *Isaac Watts's Hymns and Spiritual Songs, 1707: A Publishing History and a Bibliography* (Portland, Ore., 1974); Isaac Watts, *The Psalms and Hymns of Isaac Watts: With All the Additional Hymns and Complete Indexes* (Nashville, Tenn., 1997).

Dogtrot house. An example of VERNACULAR ARCHITECTURE, the dogtrot is built around an open hallway that separates two rooms under a simple gable roof. The "traditional" dogtrot was built of logs, but timber or other materials may also be used. In the popular mind, however, the dogtrot house is made of logs, and that manner of building seems to have been one of the determinants of the form. The dogtrot style may be a vernacular adaptation of the Georgian Revival architectural models that predominated during the late eighteenth and early nineteenth centuries, when dogtrot houses were first erected in outlying settlements. Georgian practice emphasized symmetry, with the two sides of a facade mirroring each other. The dogtrot first appeared in the Southeast, then spread as far as the edge of the Great Plains from the end of the eighteenth century to about 1835. The dogtrot house is frequently identified with the poor rural South and is featured in much southern literature, most famously in the works of William Faulkner and Eudora Welty.

Dorsey, Thomas A. (1899–1993). A major figure in GOSPEL MUSIC and the BLUES,

Dorsey was born into the family of a country preacher near Atlanta, Georgia. As a boy, he yearned to play the piano, an ambition frustrated by his family's lack of a piano. He walked four miles each way four times a week for piano lessons. After only two years of training, he began to play professionally at local Saturday night dances. About 1919 he headed north to Gary, Indiana, finding work at first in the steel mills and later forming a five-piece dance band, which played parties in the black communities of Gary and South Chicago. In addition to getting practice in jazz arranging, Dorsey also earned enough money to attend the Chicago College of Composition and Arranging.

Between 1916 and 1932 he worked mostly in popular music, most notably blues, but he never abandoned his love for gospel songs, the African-American sacred counterpart of city blues, featuring improvisation with piano, guitar, and instrumental ensembles. Dorsey played with the Whispering Syncopators, which included several musicians who would later become famous in JAZZ circles, among them Les Hite and Lionel Hampton. He also put together a band for blues singer MA RAINEY and went on tour with her and he had had a four-year association with blues singer Tampa Red (Hudson Whittaker). One of the songs he wrote for Red, the suggestive "Tight like That," was such a hit that Dorsey's first royalty check from the recording was $2,400.19. During his popular music period, he was known as Georgia Tom, player and composer of blues.

But in 1932, Dorsey made a sudden and clean break with secular music and turned to writing sacred songs exclusively. Because of his past association with "the devil's music," he at first had difficulty gaining acceptance in gospel circles, but he eventually came to be recognized as the greatest African-American composer in the genre. He worked closely, in their early years, with Mahalia Jackson, Roberta Martin, and Salli Martin.

Over his career, Dorsey produced some five hundred sacred songs, the most popular of which have been "Precious Lord" "When the Last Mile Is Finished," "Wings Over Jordan," "If You See My Savior, Tell Him That You Saw Me" and "There Will Be Peace in the Valley."

SUGGESTED READING: Thomas A. Dorsey, *Great Gospel Songs of Thomas A. Dorsey* (New York, 1988); Michael W. Harris, *Rise of Gospel Blues: The Music of Thomas Andrew Dorsey in the Urban Church* (New York, 1992).

Dorson, Richard M. (1916–1981). One of the seminal figures of the academic study of folklore, Dorson was responsible for integrating folklore into the study of American civilization. It was in American civilization that Dorson earned his academic degrees, from Harvard University, where he also taught during 1943–44. He moved on to an appointment at Michigan State University (1944–57), then to Indiana University (1957–81), where he succeeded STITH THOMPSON as chairman of the folklore program. By 1963, he had created the Folklore Institute, of which he was director until his death.

Dorson believed that American folklore had to be interpreted in the context of the history and culture of the United States. His 1959 book, *American Folklore,* exemplified this. But Dorson was not primarily a theorist. He was a wide-ranging student of American folklore, who collected and wrote on African-American folklore (*Negro Folktales in Michigan* [1956]) and immigrant folklore (*Bloodstoppers and Bearwalkers: Folk Traditions of the Upper Peninsula* [1952]). Indeed, Dorson was especially interested in the preservation, transmission, and transformation of Old World folklore in the immigrant culture of the New.

Dorson's insistence on interpreting American folklore in the context of American history and culture put him at odds with advocates of the Jungian myth and archetype school; however, he was no parochial Americanist. He wrote a history of British folklore studies (1968) and edited important volumes of essays on Japanese (1963; 1972) and African (1972) folklore. He also wrote papers on folklore research worldwide.

Dorson was the author of a major folklore textbook in 1972 and the widely used *Handbook of American Folklore* (1983). Such works as these reached well beyond the professional folklore community, and indeed, Dorson was an ambassador on behalf of the value of folklore studies for other disciplines, such as psychology, history, sociology, and anthropology.

Dorson was editor of the *Journal of American Folklore* (1959–63), president of the American Folklore Society (1966–68), president of the Fellows of the American Folklore Society (1971–72), and founding editor, in 1963, of the *Journal of the Folklore Institute.*

See also: BOWERY "B'HOY"; FAKELORE; HUMOR, FOLK; MINING FOLKLORE.

SUGGESTED READING: Richard M. Dorson, *American Folklore* (1959; reprint ed., Chicago, 1977); Richard M. Dorson, *Handbook of American Folklore* (Bloomington, Ind., 1983).

Dowsing. A folk practice that seems to endlessly fascinate folklorists, dowsing is the use of a forked piece of hazel, rowan, or willow wood, or a Y-shaped metal rod, or a pendulum suspended by thread to detect underground water. *Dowser* is the term applied both to the rod and to the person who uses it. In addition to searching for water, dowsers may also use their techniques to search for valuable minerals, natural gas, oil, buried treasure, or even dead bodies. Dowsers have been employed in attempts to locate archaeological sites, and it is reported that U.S. Marines used dowsers (also called dowsing sticks, rods, or "divining rods"—though practitioners frown on this term) to search for the underground tunnels of the Vietcong. Dowsing was originally a European tradition and dates back at least to the late Middle Ages. The practice was brought to America by German and English immigrants, and it became widespread here by the beginning of the nineteenth century. It is sometimes called water witching, switching, water smelling, channel surveying, water finding, doodlebugging (in the oil industry), and water prophesying.

The dowser holds the rod by its two prongs, walks over the ground being searched, and waits for some force emanating from the object to deflect the rod downward. This indicates the presence of the water or other target object. Dowsers are often rural people who perform the service at the request of neighbors for little or no fee; however, a number of "professional" dowsers created the American Society of Dowsers in 1960, and many of these are city dwellers who perform their services over a wide area for fee-paying clients. There is no scientific evidence that dowsing actually improves the chances of finding water or other hidden targets, but believers steadfastly dispute the negative results of scientific tests.

SUGGESTED READING: E. Z. Vogt and Ray Hyman, *Water Witching U.S.A.* (2d ed., Chicago, 1979).

Drive-in movies. On June 6, 1933, Richard M. Hollingshead, Jr., sales manager for his fa-

A *drive-in movie theater in Alexandria, Virginia, in 1941.*

ther's Whiz Auto Products Company, and three investors opened the first drive-in theater, on Crescent Boulevard in Camden, New Jersey. Admission price was twenty-five cents for the car and twenty-five cents per person, to a maximum admission of one dollar total per carload. Hollingshead understood that the automobile had become more than a means of transportation. It provided the means of gathering the family before a movie screen. Hollingshead developed a system of miniature ramps for the front tires of the automobiles, strategically angled and spaced so that every car would have an unobstructed view of the screen. He obtained U.S. Patent 1,909,537 for the invention (declared invalid in 1950).

Hollingshead's drive-in movie theater proved highly successful, and theaters opened across the country, becoming familiar features of the American landscape. The facilities ranged in size from small lots capable of accommodating fifty cars to vast establishments, such as the Troy Drive-In in Detroit, which could serve 3,000. By 1954, there were 4,063 drive-ins nationwide. But with the growth of television, the numbers steadily diminished. By the end of the 1980s, fewer than 1,000 theaters remained open. On June 3, 1948, Edward Brown, Jr., a former U.S. Navy aviator, opened the first Fly-In Drive-In Theater, in Asbury Park, New Jersey, which accommodated 500 cars and 25 private airplanes.

Dulcimer. The term *dulcimer* is applied to two very distinct families of instruments. European dulcimers are stringed musical instruments re-

John Jacob Niles plays a mountain dulcimer. The photograph is from 1942.

lated to the psaltery and are played by striking the strings with small hammers rather than by plucking them. The modern piano may trace its ancestry to these instruments. In contrast, the Appalachian, or mountain, dulcimer is a small, narrow zither with three to five metal strings running over a fretted fingerboard. It is strummed with a stick or quill (or, today, a plastic guitar pick) held in the right hand while the left stops one or more strings to create chords and melody. Appalachian dulcimers vary widely in design and materials, although most include a sound box of hourglass or teardrop shape, with a belly usually made of pine, spruce, or other softwood and sides made of such hardwoods as cherry, maple, or black wal-

nut. The hardwood fingerboard mounts eighteen diatonic wire frets; in old instruments, the frets are under the melody strings only. The instrument is meant to be played on the musician's lap.

During the nineteenth century, dulcimers were built by a few families in the Appalachians and the instrument was essentially limited to the region. However, by the early twentieth century, such institutions as the Hindman Settlement School in Knott County, Kentucky, encouraged the spread of dulcimer music to the world beyond the mountains, and such folk musicians as JOHN JACOB NILES, Paul Clayton, Frank Noah Proffitt, and JEAN RITCHIE made the instrument nationally known by the 1930s. Today, a number of dulcimer builders offer their wares to the world, and teachers and performers are well connected through clubs, festivals, the quarterly *Dulcimer Players News,* and even the Internet.

See also: APPALACHIA.

SUGGESTED READING: Jean Ritchie, *The Dulcimer Book* (New York, 1963); Charles Seeger, "The Appalachian Dulcimer," *Journal of American Folklore* 71 (1958), pp. 40–51; David E. Whisnant, *All That Is Native and Fine* (Chapel Hill, N.C., 1983).

Dumb Dora jokes. A joke fad of the 1920s, Dumb Dora jokes always began "Dora was so dumb that . . ." (". . . she thought a subordinate clause was the son of Santa Claus," ". . . , she thought asphalt was a disease of the rectum," and so on). The Dumb Dora joke was the precursor of the LITTLE MORON JOKES of the 1930s and the POLACK JOKES of the 1960s.

See also: JOKE AND JOKE CYCLES.

Dunham, Katherine (1910?–). Of mixed African-American and Native American parentage, Katherine Dunham was a pioneering dancer, choreographer, anthropologist, and writer on ethnic dance theater. She was born in Joliet, Illinois, in 1910 (some sources give 1909, others 1912). Her mother was of mixed French-Canadian and Native American ancestry, and her father was an African American. Both parents were very musical, and young Dunham grew up in an atmosphere of music and with an intense interest in her ethnic roots. Dunham's dance career was long and may be divided into three phases: a period of training and anthropological research (1926–39), a period of international performance (1939–67), and, finally, a long period of service to the community (from 1967). Dunham's education began in the Joliet public schools and at Joliet Junior College. Her brother, a philosophy student at the University of Chicago, persuaded her to enroll there, and Dunham supported herself by giving dance lessons and by working as an assistant librarian while studying anthropology, with special emphasis on African-based ritual dance and the role of dance in popular culture. She secured a Guggenheim Fellowship in 1937 to do fieldwork in Haiti, Jamaica, Martinique, and Trinidad, work that became the basis of her Ph.D. dissertation, which was subsequently published in Spanish (1947), English (1957), and French (1983).

While pursuing her academic degree, Dunham also studied modern dance and ballet with Mark Turbyfill and Ruth Page of the Chicago Opera Ballet and with Ludmilla Speranzeva. She joined the Little Theatre Group of Harper Avenue, then founded the Ballet Négre in 1931, presenting her own *Negro Rhapsody* at the annual Chicago Beaux Arts Ball. In 1934, she appeared as soloist in Ruth Page's *La Guiablesse* at the Chicago Civic Opera. During the balance of the 1930s, Dunham continued her anthropological research and presented performances of ethnically inspired dance. Her first truly professional company was founded in 1939, supported in part by New Deal funding from the Federal Theatre Project. She presented her ballet *L'Ag'Ya,* based on the martial arts of Martinique. The company subsequently appeared in the Broadway production of *Cabin in the Sky* (1940), in which Dunham collaborated with George Balanchine as choreographer. During 1940–41, the show toured.

With the outbreak of World War II, Dunham appeared in the film *Star-Spangled Rhythm* (1942), a popular morale booster, and toured under the auspices of impresario Sol Hurok with her *Tropical Revue* during 1942–43. In 1943, Dunham established the Katherine Dunham School of Arts and Research in New York City, dedicated not only to the study of dance, but to acting, literature, and folk culture as well. Among her students were the actors Marlon Brando and James Dean. Her dance troupe proved a training ground for folk and ethnic performers, among them TALLEY BEATTY, one of the leading figures in African-American modern dance, and popular entertainer Eartha Kitt. Dunham's troupe performed and toured from 1940 to 1963, making its last appearance, at Harlem's Apollo Theatre, in 1965.

Dunham's many works of choreography, including the revues *Windy City* (1946–48), *Bal Négre* (1950–60), *Carribean Rhapsody* (1962–63), and *Bambache* (1964) were derived from ethnic folk dance and were, in turn, highly influential on other modern dancers, as well as on European fashion designers during the 1950s. From 1965 to 1967, Dunham represented the United States at the Festival of Black Arts in Dakar, Senegal, and she returned to the States to establish the Performing Arts Training Center of Southern Illinois University in the predominantly African-American town of East St. Louis, Illinois. Dunham is the author of several books, including *Journey to Accompong* (1946), *A Touch of Innocence* (1959), and *Island Possessed* (1969). She has received many awards and honors, including the University of Chicago Alumni Professional Achievement Award (1968), the *Dance Magazine* Award (1968), the Albert Schweitzer Music Award (1979), and the Kennedy Center Award (1983), among others.

See also: DANCE, FOLK; DESLINÉ, JEAN-LEON.

SUGGESTED READING: Joyce Aschenbrenner, *Katherine Dunham: Reflections on Social and Political Aspects of Afro-American Dance* (New York, 1981); Ruth Beck-ford, *Katherine Dunham: A Biography* (New York, 1979).

Dusenbury, Emma Hays (1862–1941).

Georgia-born Emma Hays moved with her family to Arkansas when she was ten years old. In Baxter County, she learned many traditional ballads and songs, and married Ernest Dusenbury, an itinerant worker, in the 1880s. Four years after her marriage, she suffered a severe fever that resulted in her becoming blind. Despite her handicap, she continued to sing and was discovered by Prof. F. M. Goodhue of Commonwealth College (Mena, Arkansas) and, during 1930–36, she sang for folk-song collector Vance Randolph, author John Gould Fletcher, composer and Arkansas Symphony director Laurence Powell, and folk-song collector JOHN LOMAX, among others. Twenty of Dusenbury's songs appeared in Randolph's *Ozark Folksongs,* and the recordings by Lomax (eighty-two songs) and Mrs. Sidney Robertson (forty-three songs) are housed in the Library of Congress folk-song collections. Her songs typify the traditions of the southern mountain region and include a number of CHILD BALLADS, but she also had many rare and unusual songs in her repertoire.

SUGGESTED READING: William K. McNeil, Introduction to *Ozark Folksongs Collected and Edited by Vance Randolph* (Columbia, Mo., 1980).

Dutch Americans. Dutch Americans are immigrants and the descendants of immigrants from the Dutch-speaking Netherlands, Flemish-speaking Belgium, Low German-speaking Germany, and Frisian-speaking Friesland. The term

is not to be confused with so-called Pennsylvania Dutch (see PENNSYLVANIA GERMANS). The Dutch settled in the Hudson River Valley, Long Island, and northern New Jersey beginning in the seventeenth century. A nineteenth-century migration was concentrated in the Midwest, most famously in Grand Rapids and Holland, Michigan. For many outside of the Dutch-American community, the stereotyped tulip festivals and windmills are Dutch folklore. In fact, these re-creations are a tourist industry. But, then, Americans have long been delighted by "quaint" Dutch folkways, as the popularity of WASHINGTON IRVING's A History of New York (1809) and The Sketch Book (1819–20), both replete with satirical sketches of Dutch-American character and customs, attests. Paradoxically, perhaps, the Dutch Americans of today do little to celebrate their ethnic heritage, beyond shows offered primarily to tourists. Most distinctive Dutch folklore, which includes folk songs, children's rhymes, and agricultural lore, faded by the end of the nineteenth century. The most enduring vestige of Dutch tradition is one most Americans do not readily recognize as Dutch: the association of Saint Nicholas, patron saint of Amsterdam (and of New Amsterdam, or New York), with Christmas. In the area of material culture, examples of Dutch VERNACULAR ARCHITECTURE—typified by stepped false-front roof gables—survive in parts of New York, New Jersey, Pennsylvania, and Delaware. Finally, a few fragments of EXOTERIC FOLKLORE survive in FOLK SPEECH. A "Dutch treat" is an outing in which no one is treated, because everyone shares the cost; a "Dutch uncle" is a stern adviser or brutally candid critic; "Dutch courage" is liquor; and to "get in Dutch" is to get in trouble.

See also: IMMIGRANT FOLKLORE.

SUGGESTED READING: David Steven Cohen, The Dutch-American Farm (New York and London, 1992); L. G. Van Loon, Crumbs from an Old Dutch Closet: The Dutch Dialect of Old New York (The Hague, 1938).

"Dying Californian." A religious ballad relating in the first person the dying utterance of a forty-niner. In 1855, it was published as a hymn.

See also: FOLK MUSIC.

Dylan, Bob (1941–). Born Robert Zimmerman in Duluth, Minnesota, this quintessential folksinger of the 1960s urban folk music revival adopted the name of the Welsh poet and playwright Dylan Thomas and traveled around the country, singing the Depression-era songs of his early idol WOODY GUTHRIE as well as composing and performing his own songs. In the early 1960s, he made appearances in the Greenwich Village coffeehouses of New York City, and released his first record album, called simply Bob Dylan, produced independently at a cost of $402. The album was mainly a collection of traditional songs and blues, all rendered in the nasal, somewhat raspy, rough-hewn, and ultimately sardonic style that has remained a Dylan trademark throughout his career. Subsequent albums made through 1964 brought Dylan the recognition and admiration of the rapidly growing folk-revival audience, and such songs as "Blowin' in the Wind" and "The Times They Are a-Changin'," became anthems of social protest generally and of the civil rights movement in particular.

Dylan developed richly as a composer during the 1960s. His lyrics, set to typically simple melodies, were often metaphorically elaborate and charged with a wry surrealism. It was not unusual for professors of university-level English courses to teach some of Dylan's songs as examples of contemporary poetry. But Dylan stunned his intellectual, folk-oriented following in 1965 when he introduced elements of ROCK 'N' ROLL into his music, including the hard back beat of rock and the use of electronically amplified instruments. While the albums *Highway 61 Revisited* (1965) and *Blonde On Blonde* (1966) drew protests from Dylan's original fans, their combination of folk styles, blues, rock, and intensely introspective lyrics opened up a new, vast audience. Dylan had transformed himself from a promising and popular folk-revival troubadour to one of the seminal figures of American rock music. Nor did he remain wedded to this style. He suffered a near-fatal motorcycle accident in 1966, retreated from performing for some time, then released a number of albums (most notably *Nashville Skyline*, in 1969), which drew back from the driving rhythms of 1965–66 and explored an elegiac, muted side of commercial country and country-folk styles. Dylan continued to explore new directions through the 1970s and 1980s, particularly after a religious conversion as a "born-again" Christian in 1979. His 1997 *Time out of Mind* was greeted as a profoundly moving and ambitious return to some of Dylan's earlier, more directly folk-influenced ballad compositions.

See also: FOLK REVIVAL; HARMONICA; HOPKINS, LIGHTNIN'; RINZLER, RALPH CARTER.

SUGGESTED READING: Clinton Heylin, *Bob Dylan: A Life in Stolen Moments Day by Day, 1941–1995* (New York, 1996); Patrick Humphries, *Complete Guide to the Music of Bob Dylan* (New York, 1995).

E

Eagle. In the folklore of many cultures, the eagle is the king of birds, and the American bald eagle was officially adopted as the U.S. national emblem in 1782. Eagles figure prominently in many Native American tales, often as symbolic representations of the chief or as figures who help or warn human beings in danger. Most tribes traditionally avoided killing eagles for food or sport (this was considered bad luck), but in California and on the Plains, eagles were trapped or ceremonially killed and their feathers and down used in ceremonial costumes and in ceremonial objects.

See also: WORLD WAR I POSTERS.

Earp, Wyatt Berry Stapp (1848–1929). When Wyatt Earp died, aged eighty, in his Los Angeles home on January 13, 1929, he left his first biographer, Stuart Lake, with these words: "The greatest consolation I have in growing old is the hope that after I'm gone they'll grant me the peaceful obscurity I haven't been able to get in life." There was to be no "peaceful obscurity" for Earp, however, who is remembered as the most notable lawman of the Old West. Earp has been the subject of dime novels and other popular fiction and has been the focus of a number of movies. He has also been the target of a small legion of revisionist historians who have sought to separate legend from historical fact, but have never succeeded in dimming the romantic legends associated with him.

Earp was born in Monmouth, Illinois, and spent his youth there and in Iowa with his four brothers, James C. (1841–1926), Virgil W. (1843–1906), Morgan (1851–82), and Warren B. (1855–1900) Earp. In 1864, the boys moved with their parents to San Bernardino, California, only to return to Illinois in 1868. On the way back, Wyatt and Virgil worked on the Union Pacific Railroad. The Earps soon left Illinois again and settled in Lamar, Missouri. Wyatt became well established in the town, was married in 1870, and gained election as constable. The death of his wife from typhoid, however, left him emotionally devastated, and he drifted through Indian Territory (present-day Oklahoma), through Kansas, becoming a police officer in Wichita (1875–76), and Dodge City (1876–77), before joining the gold rush in the Black Hills (1877–78). Failing to strike it rich, he returned to Dodge City as assistant marshal (1878–79). It was during these two years that Earp first earned a wide reputation as a lawman and as a gambler. He also befriended two legendary figures of the Old West, John Henry "Doc" Holliday (a tubercular dentist turned gunman) and Bat Masterson.

Earp left Dodge City with his second wife, and drifted through New Mexico and California, working for a time as a Wells Fargo guard, then settled in 1878 in Tombstone, Arizona. Tombstone was a wide-open town, rough and violent, but also offering considerable opportunity. Earp and most of his brothers settled there, buying real estate and businesses. Wyatt worked as a gambler and as a guard at the Oriental Saloon. Virgil Earp was the town marshal. In 1881, the Earps became involved in a public feud with a stagecoach-robbing gang, the Clantons. The feud came to its violent culmination in one of the most celebrated events of the "Wild West," the October 26, 1881, gunfight at the O.K. Corral. The Clantons shot it out with three of the Earp brothers, Virgil, Wyatt, and Morgan, along with Doc Holliday. Three of the Clanton gang were killed (the Clanton patriarch, Ike, and another gang member escaped).

In the wake of the gunfight, Virgil Earp was discharged as marshal, and a violent spree of retribution ensued. In March 1882 Morgan Earp was assassinated, and Wyatt and Warren Earp, together with others, killed at least two suspects in their brother's killing. Accused of murder, Wyatt fled to Colorado, then to a series of free-wheeling western towns, and even journeyed to Alaska during the Klondike gold rush at the turn of the century, before finally settling in California, where he worked as a policeman, gambler, prospector, and minor real-estate mogul. Earp's reputation, in part, lay in the remarkable coolness with which he handled his guns. He was not a fast-draw artist, but (according to eyewitnesses) calmly aimed and fired his weapon as bullets whizzed by him. He was never wounded. His reputation was enhanced by the appearance of Stuart Lake's 1931 biography, *Wyatt Earp: Frontier Marshal*. Earp was living in Los Angeles in 1929, when, a few months before he died, he collaborated with Lake on what was a highly romanticized biography. Earp has been the subject of numerous movies, most notably the 1946 John Ford masterpiece *My Darling Clementine*, with Henry Fonda as Earp, and television shows, including the long-running series *Life and Legend of Wyatt Earp* (1955–61), with Hugh O'Brian as Earp. The most famous episode of Earp's life, the O.K. Corral gunfight, has also been portrayed on film and even figured in a time-travel episode of the highly popular science-fiction television series *Star Trek* (1966–69).

While western historians have struggled to separate the facts from the legend of Earp's life, many have done so with the avowed purpose of debunking a legend and exposing Earp as an unsavory western killer and confidence man. That the Earp legend has drawn so many determined debunkers only attests to its continued attractiveness. The most balanced view of Earp's life is Casey Tefertiller's *Wyatt Earp: The Life Behind the Legend* (New York, 1997).

See also: CRIME AND CRIMINALS; GUNFIGHTER, WESTERN.

SUGGESTED READING: Glenn G. Boyer, *I Married Wyatt Earp: The Recollections of Josephine Sara Marcus Earp* (Tucson, Ariz., 1976); Stuart N. Lake, *Wyatt Earp: Frontier Marshal* (Boston, 1931); Casey Tefertiller, *Wyatt Earp: The Life Behind the Legend* (New York, 1997).

Easter and Easter Parade. Easter commemorates the crucifixion and resurrection of Jesus Christ. Easter retains more of its religious significance than CHRISTMAS, which, in America, has been significantly secularized. The non-Christian aspects of Easter are thoroughly separated from the Christian aspects. This solemn holiday celebrating the central miracle of the Christian faith is also marked by traditions clearly derived from pre-Christian fertility symbolism: the Easter bunny and Easter egg hunts and rolls. (The Easter egg roll is the closest Easter comes to being a federally recognized holiday. An "official" Easter egg roll takes place on the White House lawn.)

For observant Christians, Easter also marks the end of the Lenten season of self-denial and dietary abstinence. Members of various ethnic groups feast on special breads and pastries as well as Easter ham. Egg decorating also reflects eth-

Late nineteenth-century chromolithographed Easter greeting card. (Collection of Alan Axelrod)

nicity, as immigrants and their descendants color eggs in distinctive ways.

Other than the White House lawn Easter egg roll, the most famous "national" Easter celebration is the Easter Parade on New York's Fifth Avenue, an event celebrated by Irving Berlin in his song "Easter Parade" from the 1948 Fred Astaire movie of the same name. The Easter Parade custom began in the nineteenth century and is not a formal parade at all, but a group stroll along Manhattan's traditionally fashionable street. Originally, couples walked hand in hand or arm in arm, dressed in their finery ("Easter bonnets" for women); today, some of the costumes are more outlandish, and the event is "fun" rather than fashionable.

SUGGESTED READING: Hennig Cohen and Tristram Potter Coffin, eds., *The Folklore of American Holidays* (2d ed., Detroit, 1991).

Easter Parade, Fifth Avenue, New York, 1880s.

Eaton, Allen (1878–1962). Eaton was a moving force behind the United States revival of handicrafts during the fist half of the twentieth century. He worked with the Russell Sage Foundation and the American Federation of Art during the 1920s to create exhibits devoted to the arts and crafts of European homelands. His 1932 book *Immigrant Gifts to American Life* (1932) was based on this work and was the first important study of American immigrant handicraft traditions. Even better known is Eaton's work on the crafts of the southern Appalachians. He was instrumental in founding the Southern Highland Handicraft Guild, and his *Handicrafts of the Southern Highlands* (1937) remains a definitive work on the subject.

Eaton began his professional life not as a student of folk craft, but as a politician and educator. He was a four-term state representative in the Oregon House of Representatives and was on the arts faculty of the University of Oregon. In 1917, Eaton fell victim to wartime xenophobia and was forced to resign from the university because he was associated with an antiwar group and was accused of being pro-German. As a result of this injustice, Eaton became increasingly interested in the culture of America's immigrants, especially those groups that had been exposed to prejudice and injustice. In 1952, he published *Beauty behind Barbed Wire: The Arts of the Japanese in Our War Relocation Camps*, a study of the handicrafts produced by the Japanese Americans who had been interned during World War II.

See also: APPALACHIA; CRAFTS, AMERICAN FOLK; FOLK MUSIC.

Ebonics. See Black English.

Eckstorm, Fannie Hardy (1865–1946). Eckstorm was a student and collector of Native American lore and language, as well a collector of the folklore of Maine lumbermen and the folk songs of Maine. She was born in Brewer, Maine, and was educated at Abbott Academy and Smith College. The subject of her greatest interest were the Penobscot Indians of Maine, and she published *Indian Place Names of the Penobscot Valley and the Maine Coast* (1941), as well as many articles on the state's Native Americans. She is best known for her 1945 book *Old John Neptune and Other Maine Indian Shamans*.

Eckstorm's earliest works were not devoted to Native American culture, but to the lives of Maine lumbermen (*The Penobscot Man* [1904] and *David Libby: Penobscot Woodman and River-Driver* [1907]). She next turned her attention to collecting folk songs and ballads, contributing material to PHILLIPS BARRY's *Songs and Ballads of the Maine Lumberjacks* (1924) and his *Maine Woods Songster* (1939). Eckstorm and Barry collaborated on *Minstrelsy of Maine* (1927) and *British Ballads from Maine* (1929).

With Barry, Eckstorm founded the Folk-Song Society of the Northeast in 1930, and she published frequently in the society's *Bulletin* during 1930–37.

SUGGESTED READING: Jeanne Patten Whitten, *Fannie Hardy Eckstorm: A Descriptive Bibliography* (Orono, Maine, 1975).

Eddy, Mary O. (1877–1967). Eddy was an important collector of folk songs, BALLADS, and BROADSIDES. A native of Wayne County, Ohio, she was raised in Perryville, Ashland County, Ohio, and was educated at Wooster College. After earning her B.A. in 1898, Eddy taught high school in Canton, Ohio, and enrolled in the University of Chicago as a graduate student during 1915–17. Course work there with Albert H. Tolman prompted her to undertake collecting, beginning with family and friends in Perryville and then through her high school students in Canton. In 1939, she published *Ballads and Songs from Ohio,* an extraordinary presentation of material collected in a limited area, but representing many years of tradition and transmission.

SUGGESTED READING: Mary O. Eddy, *Ballads and Songs from Ohio* (Hatboro, Pa., 1939).

Edison, Thomas Alva (1847–1931).

Popularly known as the "Wizard of Menlo Park" (his laboratory/workshops were located in Menlo Park, New Jersey), Thomas Alva Edison was a very real figure who came to acquire the attributes of a folk hero and a CULTURE HERO. Edison was the very embodiment of that vague quality known as "Yankee ingenuity" or "American know-how." A culture hero in this sense, he may be seen as the champion or embodiment of the nation's cherished values. As the "modern Prometheus" (another epithet frequently applied to him in his own time), the inventor of the incandescent electric lamp was a culture hero in a broader and more ancient sense. More immediately, Edison was a "real life" HORATIO ALGER hero—a poor, misunderstood boy, who, through a combination of "pluck and luck," as well as genius and hard work, achieved a fabulous fortune.

Edison's achievements truly are of legendary proportions, suited to TALL TALES. By the time of his death in 1931, he held 1,093 patents. Much of the technology of the modern world may be traced back to his inventions, which include the phonograph, improvements to the telephone, the incandescent lamp, improvements to electric generators, the first commercial electric light and power system, the first electric railroad, and the elements of motion pictures.

Advertisement for a 1908 biography of Thomas Edison, twenty-three years before the inventor's death.

He was born in Milan, Ohio, and early in his life suffered hearing loss, which popular legend ascribes to beatings at the hands of his stern father. More likely, Edison suffered from chronic mastoiditis. After his father became a lighthouse keeper and carpenter near Port Huron, Michigan, Edison struggled through five years of elementary schooling. A dreamy, inquisitive boy, handicapped by poor hearing, he was judged backward by his teachers. He quit school in 1859 and worked as a "news butcher," selling newspapers and candy on trains between Detroit and Port Huron. In 1863, he worked for the railroad as an apprentice telegrapher, then became an itinerant journeyman telegrapher throughout the Midwest, South, Canada, and New England. He began tinkering with improvements to the telegraph, moved to New York City, and sold his first commercially successful invention, a stock ticker. In 1876, Edison established his laboratory/workshops at Menlo Park, New Jersey, about twelve miles south of Newark, and quickly produced a series of inventions, including the carbon-button transmitter, which greatly improved the quality of telephone transmission, a method for transmitting multiple telegraph messages over a single line, and, most significantly, the phonograph, which proved to be one of Edison's most financially successful inventions. Most spectacular of all was Edison's signature invention, the incandescent electric lamp, tested successfully on October 21, 1879. Just three years later, Edison started operation of the world's first permanent commercial central power system, on Pearl Street in lower Manhattan.

In 1886, Edison moved his home and laboratory to West Orange, New Jersey, and quickly produced a commercially viable version of the phonograph, created a motion-picture system and, indeed, helped create the motion-picture industry, and developed the alkaline storage battery. To the end of his life, Edison turned out invention after invention, generally clustered around five basic areas: electric light and power, the phonograph, the telegraph, the storage battery, and the telephone. As he seemed to fulfill the technological aspirations of humankind, so he was the fulfillment of the peculiarly American version of the technological dream: the ability to invent one's way from rags to riches.

See also: DALHART, VERNON; EINSTEIN, ALBERT; FORD, HENRY; GREENFIELD VILLAGE.

SUGGESTED READING: Neil Bladwin, *Edison: Inventing the Century* (New York, 1996); Matthew Josephson, *Edison: A Biography* (1962; reprint ed., New York, 1992).

Edmondson, William (ca. 1870–1951).

Edmondson was a Nashville, Tennessee, limestone sculptor who achieved fame as an African-American folk artist after twelve of his works were exhibited at the Museum of Modern Art in 1937. That the Modern should have given this artist a one-man show (he was the first black artist to be so featured by this museum) was due in part to the strikingly modern character of Edmondson's limestone sculptures, which may bring to mind the work of the modern Spanish sculptor Fernando Botero. Edmondson worked his limestone roughly, but roundly, creating generalized, abstract forms, typically in rigid, formalized poses. Like a number of African-American folk artists, Edmondson believed himself divinely inspired and had begun carving in obedience to a voice telling him to "pick up my tools and start to work on a tombstone." Thus Edmondson began his career as a tombstone carver, soon branching out into depictions of animals and people (preachers, teachers, brides, couples, and other figures), as well as such religious subjects as angels and crucifixes. This, too,

Mourning Dove, *limestone sculpture by William Edmondson, 1930s.*

Martha and Mary, *limestone sculpture by William Edmondson, 1930s.*

was at the behest of a divine voice. Edmondson's only medium was limestone, which he worked using chisels and files he himself made.

Edmondson was born near Nashville, the son of former slaves. He worked as a laborer, porter, and janitor, until he lost a job as janitor at Nashville's Women's Hospital (now the Baptist Hospital) and was inspired to carve. He worked under the auspices of the Depression-era WPA between 1939 and 1941. After his show at the Modern, he enjoyed several other major exhibitions of his work.

SUGGESTED READING: Jane Livingston and John Beardsley, *Black Folk Art in America: 1930–1980* (Jackson, Miss., 1982).

Eeny, meeny, miny, mo. The clergyman and part-time folklorist Charles Francis Potter (1885–1962) traced the origin of this popular children's counting-out rhyme back through nineteenth-century America and eighteenth-century New England, to "Druid times, about the

first century B.C." As a counting-out rhyme, "eeny, meeny, miny, mo" is used by children to make selections, decisions, or to determine who will be "It." For example: Who will get the last piece of candy?

> *Eeeny, meeny, miny, mo,*
> *Catch a nigger by the toe;*
> *If he hollers let him go,*
> *Eeeny, meeny, miny, mo.*

With each word, the reciter points alternately to himself and the others in the group. Whomever his finger indicates on the final "mo" is the chosen one.

There are many variations of the "eeny, meeny, miny, mo" rhyme, but at least since the mid-nineteenth century, almost all have included the now socially unacceptable "Catch a nigger by the toe," despite the efforts of generations of schoolteachers and mothers to insert such substitutes as "baby" (the most common), "rooster," "black cat," and others. During World War II, "Catch old Tojo by the toe" was common (Tojo Hideki [1884–1948] was Japan's prime minister and military leader during the war).

See also: COUNTING-OUT RHYMES; SKIP-ROPE RHYMES.

SUGGESTED READING: Charles Francis Potter, "Eeny, meeny, miny, mo," in Maria Leach, ed., *Funk and Wagnalls Standard Dictionary of Folklore, Mythology, and Legend* (1949; reprint ed., New York, 1984).

Einstein, Albert (1879–1955). By the COLD WAR era Albert Einstein had come to fill the popular culture stereotype of the scientific genius, a quaintly absentminded figure whose capacity for thought put him out on a plane far above mere mortals. He was the consummate "egghead," as scientists were often called at midcentury, and his rumpled appearance, baggy, sometimes torn sweaters, wild hair and bushy mustache became the elements of a cultural icon. His very appearance symbolized genius, and his name became a synonym for genius ("My son's a regular Einstein!"). To some, he was also a CULTURE HERO, the man who had given the world the "keys" to the universe—though few people understood his theory of the equivalence of mass and energy and the radically new ways he was describing space, time, and gravitation. The equation most basic to the Theory of Relativity, $E = mc^2$, is certainly the only mathematical equation that has ever entered into the realm of folklore—though, again, few people can explain just exactly what this equation expresses.

Einstein was born in Ulm, Germany, on March 14, 1879, and attended school in Munich, to which his family had moved. Like another culture hero, THOMAS EDISON, young Einstein fared poorly in school, which was harsh and conventional. Einstein left school at age fifteen without a diploma and moved to Milan, Italy, where his

Albert Einstein in 1922, at the height of his European fame and before he immigrated to America.

family had settled after financial reversals. He studied physics and mathematics at the Federal Polytechnic Academy in Zurich, graduating in 1900. He became a Swiss citizen, and supported himself as a patent examiner. Early in 1905, he published "A New Determination of Molecular Dimensions," which won him a Ph.D. from the University of Zurich. Following this was a series of papers that transformed physics and radically altered the scientific understanding of the universe. The most revolutionary of the papers was "On the Electrodynamics of Moving Bodies," which set forth the Special Theory of Relativity, postulating that for all frames of reference, the speed of light is constant and if all natural laws are the same, then time and motion are functions

Albert Einstein, American celebrity, with New York's colorful mayor Fiorello La Guardia, 1937.

relative to the observer. This was followed by "Does the Inertia of a Body Depend Upon Its Energy Content?" which set forth the equivalence of mass and energy, expressed as $E = mc^2$.

Following publication of these papers, Einstein held a series of teaching positions and, in 1916, published "The Foundation of the General Theory of Relativity," which wholly revised the Newtonian concept of gravitation by postulating that it is not a force, as Newton had said, but a curved field in the space-time continuum, created by the presence of mass. What is more, Einstein offered physical proof for this remarkable theory by measuring the deflection of starlight as it traveled close by the sun. When, in 1919, a Royal Society of London study of a solar eclipse verified Einstein's theoretical predictions, the physicist re-

ceived international acclaim as the greatest living genius and, perhaps, the greatest genius of all time. He was awarded the Nobel Prize for Physics in 1921.

Einstein became a visiting professor at Oxford University in 1931 and was finding himself an increasingly public figure as one of the world's foremost advocates of pacifism and world peace. With the rise to power of Adolf Hitler in 1933, Einstein renounced his German citizenship and came to the new Institute for Advanced Study in Princeton, New Jersey. He now turned against his pacifist ideals and urged free Europe to prepare for a fight against Hitler. Moreover, while he was in the States, Einstein became persuaded of the feasibility of building an "atomic bomb," and, fearing that Nazi scientists might build one first, he wrote a famous letter to President Franklin D. Roosevelt, recommending that the United States government fund atomic-bomb research. Such was Einstein's reputation that Roosevelt authorized the Manhattan Project, the monumental effort to create a nuclear weapon. While Einstein remained on the extreme periphery of bomb development, his name was popularly linked to the project and to the "atomic age" that the bombs of Hiroshima and Nagasaki inaugurated.

At the time of his death in the mid-1950s, the height of the Cold War and of nuclear paranoia, he was regarded as a giant of science, the iconic representative of all those scientists who had, in effect, let the genie out of the bottle, giving humankind unprecedented understanding and power, yet an equally unprecedented capacity for destruction and reason for fear.

SUGGESTED READING: Denis Brian, *Einstein: A Life* (New York, 1997); Jamie Sayen, *Einstein in America: The Scientist's Conscience in the Age of Hitler and Hiroshima* (New York, 1985).

Emmett, Daniel Decatur (1815–1904).

With THOMAS "DADDY" RICE and EDWIN P. "NED" CHRISTY, Emmett was one of the developers of the blackface MINSTREL SHOW, perhaps the earliest form of mass popular entertainment in the United States and one that featured commercially styled versions of "characteristic" African-American folk dance. Born of Irish immigrant parents who settled on the Ohio frontier, Emmett had little formal schooling and was apprenticed early on at his father's blacksmith shop. He later learned to read and write and was apprenticed to a printer, going to work at the *Huron Reflector,* a newspaper published in Norwalk, Ohio, and subsequently at the *Western Aurora* in Mt. Vernon, Ohio. At seventeen, Emmett left the printer's trade and enlisted in the army as a fifer. When he was stationed near St. Louis, he used leisure moments to study music and, in 1830 or 1831, composed "OLD DAN TUCKER," based on a folk tune his mother had taught him and which Emmett would popularize in 1843, when he organized his first minstrel troupe, the Virginia Minstrels.

Emmett was discharged from the army in 1835, and joined a circus troupe. Perhaps inspired by Daddy Rice's "Jim Crow" blackface dance performance, Emmett (playing fiddle and rendering the vocals) and three friends, Billy Whitlock (who played banjo), Frank Bower (who used animal bones as a rhythm instrument), and Dick Pelham (tambourine) organized the Virginia Minstrels in New York City in March 1843. Emmett designed the program, which included songs, dance, and comic patter, as well as the costumes—outlandish white trousers, striped calico shirts, and long blue calico swallowtail coats (known as "swallow-tail blues")—that would set an unchangeable pattern for the blackface minstrel show, which became a dominant form of popular entertainment in America for more than half a century.

Daniel Decatur Emmett near the end of his life.

Emmett's minstrel show was a commercial venture rather than a collection of African-American folk songs or African-American folk dances; however, much of the music and dancing were inspired by—or, almost as important, were claimed to have been inspired by—folk songs, folk dances, and long observation of "authentic" plantation slaves. In addition to "Old Dan Tucker," Emmett's musical compositions included the phenomenally popular "Dixie" as well as "The Road to Richmond," "Walk Along, John," and "Here We Are, or Cross Ober Jordan." Emmett toured Europe with the Virginia Minstrels, then, in 1857, joined another troupe, Bryant's Minstrels. From 1865 to 1878, he performed throughout the United States with his own troupe, living in Chicago until 1888, when he retired to a small farm near his boyhood home of Mt. Vernon, Ohio.

See also: "Blue-Tail Fly."

SUGGESTED READING: Russel Nye, *The Unembarrassed Muse: The Popular Arts in America* (New York, 1970); Constance Rourke, *American Humor: A Study of the National Character* (New York, 1931).

Empire State Building.

A 102-story Manhattan skyscraper completed in 1931, the Empire State Building is 1,250 feet tall (1,472 feet, including a 222-foot television antenna added in 1950) and was the tallest human-made structure in the world until 1954. Although both the World Trade Center (1977), in lower Manhattan, and the Sears Tower (1974), in Chicago, are taller (as of 1999, Petronas Towers, in Kuala Lumpur, Malaysia, is the world's tallest building, at 1,483 feet), the Empire State Building continues to occupy a special place in American popular culture as a symbol of the "Big Apple" and an expression of twentieth-century technology. This was recognized and exploited in the 1933 movie *King Kong*, in which the giant ape scales the brand-new skyscraper and terrorizes heroine Fay Wray.

A variety of jokes revolve around the Empire State Building as a Manhattan tourist magnet, including this one, which expresses the non–New Yorker's perception of the city's reputation for rudeness: Timorous midwesterner on Fifth Avenue to a passerby: "Excuse me, can you tell me how to get to the Empire State Building or should I go fuck myself?"

Ironically, this most famous of New York landmarks, completed in the depths of the Depression, failed for years to attract a sufficient number of tenants to become solvent and sur-

A meeting of two technological wonders of the 1920s and 1930s: artist's conception of how dirigibles were to use the top of the Empire State Building as a mooring mast. The mast was never used for this purpose, but did serve as a base for radio and television broadcast antennas. The illustration is from the 1930s.

vived for a long time on revenue from its observation decks. The building was completed in the final months of outgoing New York governor Al Smith's term, and the writer and critic Edmund Wilson reported that the new—and mostly empty—building, testament to an era of corporate wealth extinguished in the 1929 stock market crash, was widely mocked as "Al Smith's last erection."

SUGGESTED READING: Craig A. Doherty et al., *The Empire State Building* (New York, 1998); John Tauranac,

The Empire State Building: The Making of a Landmark (New York, 1997).

Emrich, Duncan B. M. (1908–1917).

Emrich was an all-around folklorist, who headed the Folk Song and Folklore Archives of the Library of Congress. He was educated at Phillips Exeter Academy, Brown University, Columbia University, Harvard University (where he was a student of GEORGE LYMAN KITTREDGE), and the University of Madrid. He began his teaching career at Columbia. He subsequently moved to the University of Denver, but during World War II, in 1943, he joined the U.S. Army as an intelligence officer and a staff officer to Supreme Allied Commander Dwight D. Eisenhower. In this capacity, he wrote an official history of the war in Europe.

After the war, Emrich did not return to Denver, but to the American Folk Song and Folklore Archives at the Library of Congress. He headed the department until 1955, leaving to become a cultural affairs officer at U.S. embassies in Greece and India. In his off-hours, he collected the local folklore.

Emrich went to work back in Washington in 1966 as an official with the United States Information Agency, then, three years later, was appointed to a teaching position in American folklore at American University (Washington, D.C.). In 1976, he endowed a fund to support a folklore lecture series.

Emerich was a popularizer of folklore rather than a strict theorist. His *American Folk Poetry* (1974) and *Folklore on the American Land* (1977), though deficient in intellectual rigor, are attractively written volumes that certainly introduced a substantial number of lay readers to the study of folklore.

See also: KORSON, RAE ROSENBLATT; MOSER, ARTUS M.

SUGGESTED READING: Duncan Emrich, *Folklore on the American Land* (Boston, 1972).

Environmental folk art.

Sculptural, typically large-scale works, usually built outdoors in gardens, yards, and parks, environmental folk art commonly uses recycled materials such as tin, glass, and found objects. One of the most celebrated works of environmental folk art is SIMON "SAM" RODIA's *Watts Towers* in Los Angeles.

See also: SMITH, FRED.

Esoteric folklore.

Esoteric folklore is the body of traditional beliefs one group has of itself and supposes others to have of itself as well. The term is one half of the "esoteric-exoteric factor" proposed by folklorist WILLIAM HUGH JANSEN in 1959 to enhance the understanding of the role of perception and image in folklore and in the study of folklore.

See also: BIKER FOLKLORE; EXOTERIC FOLKLORE; GAY FOLKLORE; HOBO FOLKLORE; IRISH AMERICANS; JAZZ; RAILROAD FOLKLORE

Espinosa, Aurelio Macedonlo (1880–1958).

Espinosa was a student of Spanish-American folklore, Spanish folklore, and Hispanic dialects. He was born in southern Colorado and took his Ph.D. at the University of Chicago in Romance languages and literatures, with additional work in Indo-European comparative philology. Espinosa was appointed to the Romanic Languages Department at Stanford University in 1910, where he taught through 1947. Throughout his academic career and even after retirement, Espinosa did fieldwork in northern New Mexico and southern Colorado, and (during 1911–19) in coastal California. He traveled to Spain for fieldwork in 1920.

In addition to working to develop the linguistic study of Spanish culture in America, Espinosa was an active folklorist and president of the American Folklore Society (1923–24). His most significant contribution to the study of Spanish folklore in America was his classification of folktales, which traced the origins of American folktales to their European roots and Asian influences. Espinosa also studied the material he collected in the context of other European and Native American traditions.

See also: FIFE, AUSTIN E.

SUGGESTED READING: Aurelio Espinosa, *The Folklore of Spain in the American Southwest: Traditional Spanish Folk Literature in Northern New Mexico and Southern Colorado* (Norman, Okla., 1985).

Estonian Americans. See BALTIC PEOPLES.

Ethnomusicology. The study of music in any world culture or subculture in its relation to that culture and in comparison with other cultures. The term was coined by Jaap Kunst, a Dutch student of Indonesian music, in the 1950s. The Society for Ethnomusicology was founded in 1955 and publishes the journal *Ethnomusicology*. Traditionally, the term has been applied to the study of non-Western music, but more recently its use has been extended to traditional music of all cultures.

See also: FOLK MUSIC.

Etymology, folk. A change in the form of a word or phrase that results from a commonly accepted but mistaken assumption about its meaning or composition. For example, etymologists point out that *shamefaced* is a corruption of the original *shamefast*, meaning "bound by shame." Through a process of repeated misunderstanding, the word was taken to describe the appearance of the person who was shamed and thus became *shamefaced*. Folk etymology may also apply to common misconceptions of the origins of words. For example, many people believe that *hooker*, a slang synonym for "prostitute," came from the profusion of camp followers attached to troops led by hard-drinking Union general "Fighting Joe" Hooker during the Civil War. Actually, the term was in current use, in England and the United States, well before the American Civil War, although its origin is murky. Some have suggested that the term is derived from Corlear's Hook, a district in New York City notorious in the nineteenth century for its abundance of prostitutes. More likely, however, the word simply refers to one who hooks—snares—clients: a prostitute.

See also: CRACKERS; YANKEE DOODLE.

Evil eye. Belief in the evil eye, the power to inflict harm merely by looking at an object or a person, is predominantly a European, North African, Near Eastern, South Asian, and Central American folk belief. It figures in American folklore primarily through traditions brought by immigrants. It may have been introduced to Mexican Indian and Central American Indian cultures by Columbus and the Spanish explorers and conquerors who followed him. The most common cause of evil eye is envy; therefore, those who hold traditional ethnic beliefs often seek to protect their possessions and their children by speaking disparagingly of them or by maintaining a public neutrality toward them. It is likely that the tradition of the bridal veil originated as protection from the evil eye.

AMULETS are often used to ward off the effect of the evil eye. Such "lucky charms" as four-leaf clovers and rabbit's feet were originally used for this purpose.

See also: GREEK AMERICANS; HEX; MISTLETOE.

Exaggerated postcard. "Photographs don't lie" was a widely accepted principle when, just after the turn of the twentieth century, American wit and ingenuity challenged this truism with a brand-new, visual twist on the TALL TALE. This clever phenomenon, the photographic postcard that outrageously stretched the truth or improved on reality through darkroom manipulation, flourished for nearly two decades at the begin-

ning of the twentieth century. Known as the exaggerated, freak, or tall-tale postcard, it originated in the Midwest, where, with agriculture the main source of wealth (and misfortune), farmers were prone to straight-faced exaggeration about the size of prize specimens of their livestock and crops, as well as their prowess as hunters and fishermen. To embellish achievements in outdoing the other fellow has long been a key element in the western tall tale tradition and America's folklore heritage. Farmers, long-suffering as the butt of traveling salesmen's jokes, were quick to embrace this visual outbreak of their kind of humor in tweaking the gullibility of city slickers about life in the countryside.

As with many a new phenomenon, this one could only have come about through the fortunate confluence of just the right elements. In the 1870s, the concept of a cheap, prestamped government-issue postcard was introduced to America from Austria, and a privately printed version was granted mailing privileges in 1898. In 1888 George Eastman had brought out the preloaded Kodak camera he had designed for amateur pho-

HICKEN'S FUR BEARING TROUT
Iceberg Lake

Photo by R. E. Marble, Belton, Montana

"Hicken's Fur Bearing Trout," as extracted from the very cold Iceberg Lake, near Belton, Montana. Example of an "exaggerated postcard" from early in the twentieth century. (Collection of Walton Rawls)

tographers, and by 1902 his company was producing postcard-size photosensitive paper on which images could be printed directly from hobbyists' negatives for a few cents each. This launched the possibility of limited-edition postcards, and many small-town photography studios began producing souvenir cards of the local sights. Given their darkroom facilities and growing skills in multiple exposure and combining negatives, many local photographers, notably Archer King of Table Rock, Nebraska, Walter T. Oxley of Fergus Falls, Minnesota, Alfred Stanley Johnson of Waupun, Wisconsin, and William H. Martin of Ottawa, Kansas, began to specialize in the exaggerated variety. Postcard collecting soon became a very popular hobby, and individual collections graced many a parlor table, mounted in handsome albums.

With communication by telephone and quick visits by automobile still rare in rural areas in the first decades of the twentieth century, the picture postcard began to serve a genuine neighborly function as the newly instituted Rural Free Delivery postal system spread throughout the land. And for showing the folks back East how smart you were to homestead in the Midwest and how successful you'd become as a farmer, there was nothing better than a picture postcard touting the kind of huge crops grown in your part of the country. A completely new form of folk expression had been born. From the far northwest where winters are so cold that fish would freeze if they didn't grow fur, to Maine where a single potato can overwhelm a flatcar, to Kansas where chickens grow so large that children saddle and ride them, the tall-tale postcard humorously captures many facets of everyday life in turn-of-the-century small-town America.

See also: JACKALOPE.

SUGGESTED READING: Hal Morgan, *Big Time/American Tall-Tale Postcards* (New York, 1981); Cynthia E. Rubin and Morgan Williams, *Larger than Life: The American Tall-Tale Postcard, 1905–1915* (New York, 1990); Roger L. Welsch, *Tall-Tale Postcards: A Pictorial History* (New Jersey, 1976).

Exoteric folklore. Exoteric folklore is the body of traditional beliefs one group has of another group and supposes that group has of itself. The term is one half of the "esoteric-exoteric factor" proposed by folklorist WILLIAM HUGH JANSEN in 1959 to enhance the understanding of the role of perception and image in folklore and in the study of folklore.

See also: AMOS 'N' ANDY; BIKER FOLKLORE; CAJUNS; DUTCH AMERICANS; ESOTERIC FOLKLORE; GAY FOLKLORE; GERMAN AMERICANS; HOBO FOLKLORE; IRISH AMERICANS; JAZZ; QUAKERS; REDNECKS; SAMBO; SCOTTISH AMERICANS; SITTING BULL; SLAVIC AMERICANS; TRUCKING AND TRUCKERS; URBAN LEGEND; VIETNAM WAR.

F

Fable. See ANIMAL FABLE.

Fairies. Supernatural beings, usually very small, even dolllike, who magically intervene in and often disrupt human affairs. Fairy lore is most common in Ireland, Cornwall, Wales, and Scotland, and is known in the United States chiefly through children's books; however, the folklore of Eskimos and other Native American groups include beings very much like fairies, and fairylike creatures are found in the folklore of many cultures worldwide.

The fairies most Americans know are harmless little creatures from children's stories. As late as Victorian times, however, fairies were often portrayed as malevolent or cruelly mischievous, and they were objects of considerable fear. In contrast to such supernatural creatures as the bogeyman, fairies were usually imagined as quite beautiful or handsome; however, they lack souls, and they have a disagreeable habit of carrying off children, leaving a "changeling"—a kind of clone—as a substitute. Fairies may also abduct adults to fairyland, from which there is no return once one has partaken of food or drink there. It is possible for human beings and fairies to be lovers or even to marry, but it is fatal to make love to some female fairies.

While most fairies are very small, around three inches tall, some are believed to be of human size. Much plant lore is devoted to means of warding off fairies.

A German book illustration showing the image of fairies popular in the late nineteenth century. (From Märchen und Sagen: Schatz, Theo. Stroefer's Kunstverlag, *1885)*

See also: BOGEY, BOGEYMAN; FAIRY RINGS; PLANTS AND PLANT LORE.

Fairy rings. Fairy rings are naturally occurring rings of mushrooms on a lawn or field. They result when the mycelium, or mushroom spore,

sends out an underground network of hyphae, fine, tubular threads that grow out from the spore evenly in all directions, thereby forming a circular network of hyphal threads from which the mushrooms grow, on the surface, in a ring pattern. Fairy rings formed by common field mushrooms typically measure about six feet in diameter, but those of the so-called fairy ring mushroom (*Marasmius oreades*) may grow in spectacular, if irregular, rings of up to 1,200 feet in diameter. Folk belief in America and in Europe holds that the fairy ring demarcates the dancing places of FAIRIES and that damaging the ring will bring great misfortune, including injury or blindness. An alternative folk belief is that the ring results from the birth of a foal on the spot.

Fakelore. A term coined by folklore scholar RICHARD M. DORSON to describe stories and characters that may resemble folklore, but are really the work of journalists and other "money writers." A prime example of fakelore is PAUL BUNYAN and associated characters.

See also: FOLKLORE.

Familiar. An animal or bird associated with a witch or wizard and believed to embody a demonic spirit associated with the powers of the witch or wizard. The familiar most commonly associated with a witch is a black cat.

See also: WITCHES AND WITCHCRAFT.

The Farmer's Almanac. *The Farmer's Almanac* or *Old Farmer's Almanac* was first published by Robert B. Thomas in 1792 for the year 1793 and has been in continuous publication ever since. It is a survival of the traditional American ALMANACS, which were repositories of folk wisdom, folklore, folk medicine, and folk humor. As always, the current *Farmer's Almanac* includes weather prognostications, planting schedules, astronomical tables, astrological material, sundry recipes, and rural-oriented anecdotes and lore.

Father Time. The personification of time, Father Time is typically pictured as an old man with a long white beard; often, he carries a scythe, so that he is identified with the personification of Death as the "Grim Reaper." The image of Father Time is probably founded on the mythical figure of Cronus (in Greek mythology) or Saturn (in Roman lore). In popular emblems associated with NEW YEAR's celebration, Father Time, representing the old year, is often contrasted with the figure of a baby, representing the new.

Woodcut of a mountain fiddler. (From Jim Harter, Music: A Pictorial Archive of Woodcuts and Engravings, *Dover Books, 1996*)

Fiddle. One of the most popular instruments in American FOLK MUSIC, the fiddle was prized not only for its sound, but for its portability. While radio, movies, and television have popularized the image of the singing COWBOY accompanying himself on guitar, it was actually the fiddle that was the bunkhouse instrument of choice. Folk-made fiddles range from crude instruments fashioned of hollow gourds and cornstalks to beautifully crafted instruments that bear comparison to the work of the great violin makers of Europe. Folk fiddlers also play on "store-bought" instruments, including, in the earlier part of the century, models ordered from the Sears, Roebuck catalog.

The fiddle was often used to accompany dances, and most traditional American fiddle tunes are based on eighteenth- and nineteenth-century English and continental dance forms,

such as the rent (a LINE DANCE tune in 4/4 or 2/4 time), the JIG (in 6/8 time), the HORNPIPE (4/4 time and often danced solo), and the REEL similar to the jig, but in 2/4 time). Later in the nineteenth century, the fiddle was also used to accompany the new couple dances, such as the WALTZ and the SCHOTTISCHE. The fiddle was also used to accompany singers and, because of its resemblance to the human voice, often replaced singers in so-called instrumental songs.

Folk fiddlers exhibit a range of performance styles, especially with regard to bowing technique. Some favor a style emphasizing separate strokes for each note, while others apply a more legato or slurring bow technique. In some rural traditions, especially those of the upper South, syncopated bowing techniques are favored. In contrast to classical violinists, folk fiddlers use little or no vibrato, and while many fiddlers are capable of producing a sweet, lyrical sound, the demands of the dance often call for a more percussive attack. Additionally, various ethnic groups contributed to the variety of American fiddling styles. It was African-American fiddlers who developed syncopated patterns that may be seen as the precursors of RAGTIME, JAZZ, and the BLUES. Irish immigrants as well as those from Germany and eastern Europe contributed their own folk styles.

The folk fiddler's repertoire is extensive and draws on tunes that may date to the eighteenth century. Relatively few contemporary fiddlers compose their own tunes, though most work improvisations on the traditional body of tunes. Contemporary fiddlers share and hone their art at various fiddlers' conventions.

See also: APPALACHIA; BLUEGRASS; CURRIER & IVES; HOEDOWN; "TURKEY IN THE STRAW."

SUGGESTED READING: Samuel Preston Bayard, *Dance to the Fiddle, March to the Fife: Instrumental Folk Tunes in Pennsylvania* (University Park, Pa., 1982).

also served with the U.S. Air Force as a historian and worked for the U.S. Department of Education. While folklore study remained for him an avocation, he was recognized as a distinguished expert and earned a Fulbright Fellowship to lecture on American folk music in France (1950), a Guggenheim Fellowship for the study of cowboy and western songs (1959), and a National Endowment for the Humanities Senior Award (1971). Fife founded the Fife Folklore Archive at Utah State University in 1972, the basis of which was his large personal folklore library and archive, which included field notes on Mormon folklore and on cowboy and western songs, audio recordings, and photographic documentation of material culture, with emphasis on characteristic fences, hay derricks, stone houses, mailboxes, and headstones.

See also: MORMONS.

SUGGESTED READING: Austin E. Fife, *Exploring Western Americana* (Ann Arbor, Mich., 1988); Austin E. Fife and Alta S. Fife, *Saints of Sage and Saddle* (Salt Lake City, Utah, 1956).

Fife, Austin E. (1909–1986). Best known as a student of Mormon folklore, Fife also studied cowboy and Western songs, and the material culture of the West. Fife was a Mormon raised in Utah and Idaho. Educated at Stanford and Harvard in French language and literature, most of his academic career was devoted to this field; however, at Stanford, Fife studied with the important scholar of Spanish-American folklore AURELIO M. ESPINOSA, an experience that sparked a lifelong interest in folklore, even as he continued to pursue his academic career.

Fife taught at Occidental College, Indiana University, UCLA, and Utah State University. He

Filipino Americans. Filipino Americans are immigrants and the descendants of emigrants from the Philippines, which became a U.S. possession in 1898, a U.S. commonwealth in 1935, and an independent republic as of July 4, 1946. Early in the twentieth century, many Filipino agricultural workers immigrated to Hawaii and California; later, the immigration became more general, and many Filipino Americans now live in cities. The Filipino-American community distinguishes between immigrants who came early in the century with those who arrived beginning in the 1960s. The former are sources of tales about the early struggles of migrant agricultural workers. More recent arrivals as well as the American-born descendants of first-wave immigrants greatly value the stories of the "old timers." Filipino communities are generally tightly knit, and social clubs play important roles in preserving such traditions as FOODWAYS, folk dances, and FOLK MUSIC, as well as traditional celebrations of Catholic holidays. In many cities, Filipino organizations plan parades, complete with symbolic floats and costumed marchers, as exhibitions of cultural heritage and cultural pride.

See also: DANCE, FOLK; IMMIGRANT FOLKLORE.

SUGGESTED READING: Carlos Bulosan, *American Is in the Heart: A Personal History* (New York, 1943); Fred Cordova, *Filipinos: Forgotten Asian Americans: A Pictorial Essay 1763–circa 1963* (Dubuque, Iowa, 1983); Herminia Q. Meñz, *Folklore Communication among Filipinos in California* (New York, 1980).

Filk music. If "filk music" looks like a typo for "folk music," that's because it is. It was a typographical error on the program for a science-fiction convention (nobody seems to know just when), and the term stuck. In what "filkers" (those who write and perform filk music) describe as the music's "earliest form," new, usually humorous words were set to old tunes. Parody was (and is) important to filkers, and the subject matter of the songs almost always relates to science fiction and fantasy, either directly (with songs about outer space, sci-fi books, movies, TV shows, creatures, and extraterrestrials) or indirectly (with songs about anything that interests sci-fi fans, from cats to computers and even the subject of being a fan). Filk is typically performed a cappella or with acoustic guitar accompani-

ment; however, it may also be performed with any combination of instruments, acoustic and electric. At the close of the twentieth century, several filk song conventions are held annually, a number of filking organizations exist, and a handful of World Wide Web sites are dedicated to filk music.

See also: FOLK MUSIC.

Filson, John (ca. 1753–1788?). Filson was the author of a single published book, *The Discovery, Settlement, and Present State of Kentucke* (1784), which presented not only the first history of Kentucky, but the first biography of DANIEL BOONE, thereby contributing to Boone's early and enduring reputation and helping to fashion him into a folk hero.

Filson came to the frontier from Chester County, Pennsylvania, where he had been born about 1753, the son of Davison Filson. Almost nothing is known of his early life, except that he probably attended West Nottingham Academy in Maryland, where he learned Latin, Greek, French, and surveying. He is known to have earned a living as an itinerant schoolmaster. Tradition holds that Filson's arm was wounded in the American Revolution and that after the war he returned to teaching but soon quit because his injury made it difficult for him to administer the paddle to recalcitrant students. It is, however, more likely that Filson spent the years of the Revolution quietly teaching in Wilmington.

Early in the fall of 1783, Filson made his first journey to Kentucky, where he acquired more than twelve thousand acres, surveyed the wilderness, and taught school at Lexington. It was near Lexington, in the house of Levi Todd, that he composed *The Discovery, Settlement, and Present State of Kentucke*. The book was based on

Filson's own travels as well as on interviews with Todd, Daniel Boone, and other Kentucky pioneers.

Why did Filson write *Kentucke*? Certainly, his primary motive was to attract settlers to the land in which he had heavily invested. The book is an example of the promotion tract, a most numerous early American literary genre, and like other promotional tracts, it depicts the territory that is its subject as a wilderness Eden. Seen in this light,

Filson's biography of Boone emerges as a purposeful effort to create a larger-than-life folk hero, the more to enhance the attractiveness of Kentucky. However, it is likely that Filson was also moved by a more disinterested desire to tell the dramatic story of settlement and to record remarkable phenomena of natural history.

The Boone narrative included in Filson's book is presented as a first-person autobiography dictated to Filson; however, its pedantic—indeed, schoolmasterish—language suggests that, while almost certainly based on interviews with Boone, the "autobiography" is mostly Filson's work. The Boone he presents foreshadows JAMES FENIMORE COOPER's Natty Bumppo, the stoic frontiersman whose affinity with the land goes beyond the stilted language in which it is framed. Like Cooper's Bumppo, Filson's Boone becomes an archetypal leader-savior figure, who makes the wilderness safe for settlement by suffering on behalf of civilization the depredations of savage Indians. It is Boone who transforms the "dark and bloody ground" of Kentucky into Filson's Eden.

Filson left Kentucky for Delaware in 1784 to have his book published in Wilmington, bringing with him the first map of Kentucky based on actual observation. The book and map sold well, though Filson abandoned plans for a second edition when George Washington declined his request for a public endorsement.

Filson taught school during the winter of 1784–85 in Wilmington and Philadelphia, then traveled west again in the spring. (Letters and manuscript notes concerning this trip to the Illinois and Kentucky country have been variously collected and published in the twentieth century.) In November 1786, Filson returned to Philadelphia, where he was embroiled in lawsuits and burdened by creditors' claims through 1787, when he left on a third journey to Kentucky. The following year, he became a partner in a venture

THE
DISCOVERY, SETTLEMENT
And present State of
KENTUCKE:
AND
An ESSAY towards the TOPOGRAPHY, and NATURAL HISTORY of that important Country:
To which is added,
An APPENDIX,
CONTAINING,
I. The ADVENTURES of Col. *Daniel Boon*, one of the first Settlers, comprehending every important Occurrence in the political History of that Province.
II The MINUTES of the *Piankashaw* council, held at *Post St. Vincents*, *April* 15, 1784.
III. An ACCOUNT of the *Indian* Nations inhabiting within the Limits of the Thirteen United States, their Manners and Customs, and Reflections on their Origin.
IV. The STAGES and DISTANCES between *Philadelphia* and the Falls of the *Ohio*; from *Pittsburg* to *Pensacola* and several other Places.
—The Whole illustrated by a new and accurate MAP of *Kentucke* and the Country adjoining, drawn from actual Surveys.

By JOHN FILSON.

Wilmington, Printed by JAMES ADAMS, 1784.

Title page to the first edition of John Filson's The Discovery, Settlement, and Present State of Kentucke, *which contains the first biography of Daniel Boone. (Courtesy Filson Club, Louisville, Kentucky)*

to found a city he wanted to call Losantiville but which came to be called Cincinnati. Filson disappeared while surveying the town site late in September or early in October 1788. His book, plagiarized during the early nineteenth century, has endured as the first and most-imitated story of Daniel Boone.

See also: FOLKLORE IN AMERICAN LITERATURE.

SUGGESTED READING: Alan Axelrod, entry on Filson in *Dictionary of Literary Biography* 37 (Detroit, 1985); John Walton, *John Filson of Kentucke* (Lexington, Ky., 1956).

Fingernails. In the folklore of various cultures, fingernail parings are used in AMULETS and charms and in witchcraft. Other beliefs relating to fingernails include the ability to predict the number of friends one will make in a given period by counting the white spots on the nail of the forefinger; the number of white spots on the middle finger is a prognostication of the number of one's enemies; white spots on the thumb portends the receipt of a gift; white spots on the ring finger means that a letter from your lover is coming. Various folk beliefs govern the cutting of fingernails. Some believe that if a baby's nails are cut before he is a year old, he will become a thief; cutting the nails improves eyesight; cutting the nails during a waning moon will cause them to grow back too rapidly; cutting them on Monday brings news, on Tuesday new shoes, on Wednesday portends travel, on Thursday brings illness, and on Friday toothache. Cut your nails on Saturday, and you will see your lover on Sunday. An old belief among some African Americans is that a dream of paring one's nails portends disappointment.

See also: WITCHES AND WITCHCRAFT.

Fink, Mike (1770/80–1823). The historical Mike Fink was born, probably, in the Fort Pitt (modern Pittsburgh) area and earned local fame first as a crack shot and then as a scout. Attracted to the developing keelboat commerce on the Ohio and Mississippi Rivers, he earned national fame as "king of the keelboatmen." His exploits quickly grew into the stuff of enduring legend and lore. His marksmanship was superhuman, as was his prowess with his fists, and, even in his own time, he became the embodiment of western frontier braggadocio and tall-tale spinning: a rough-and-ready man, whose speech and behavior were always bigger than life, and whose sheer exuberance could not be contained by civilization. Often identified in contemporary popular literature as a "roarer" or "RINGTAILED ROARER," Fink was, in effect, a white, backwoods version of the NOBLE SAVAGE archetype well known to Europeans since the eighteenth century.

Fink's actual life was brief. In 1822, he joined Gen. William H. Ashley's fur-trapping expedition to the upper Missouri River, and the following year was killed as the result of a personal feud.

Mike Fink tales were originally transmitted orally, but were quickly picked up by a variety of writers working from the 1820s until the beginning of the Civil War. After the war, Mike Fink's fame declined. *The Pedlar,* written in 1821 by the American playwright Alphonso Wetmore, contains the earliest known reference to Mike Fink, who is portrayed in the play as a crude and boastful river man. Subsequently, the character of Mike Fink appeared in scores of almanacs, sporting journals, and the like, including the DAVY CROCKETT almanacs (in which Mike is sometimes portrayed in encounters with Crockett himself). All who wrote yarns about Mike Fink claimed to have had the tales from eyewitnesses; doubtless, most of the printed stories were made up by individual writers, but it is also likely that at least some of the stories genuinely represent oral traditions.

Typical and recurring Mike Fink episodes include William Tell-like demonstrations of marksmanship, in which Mike shoots a cup of whiskey off the head of another boatman or his own wife. Sometimes the compliment is returned by another sharpshooter. (Popular accounts of Mike Fink's death portray the riverboat man as having killed someone—either accidentally or deliberately—by this stunt, after which he is killed in revenge by the victim's friend or relative.) Other typical anecdotes have Mike shooting the scalp lock off an Indian's head and "surgically" correcting the malformed protruding heel of a black man by a well-placed rifle shot.

As Mike Fink's popularity began to decline in the 1850s, portrayals of him were transformed as well. Fink stories from the decade before the Civil War frequently show him in defeat, his performance falling short of his brag. The character more or less disappeared during the Civil War and did not resurface until the early 1930s, when HENRY WHARTON SHOEMAKER, a Pennsylvania journalist and folklore popularizer, saw in Mike Fink the makings of a regional folk hero. Shoemaker claimed to have heard oral tales, in Pennsylvania, about Fink, but most folklorists dispute these claims as fabrications. Certainly, a sanitized Mike Fink has figured in more than a few twentieth-century children's books, but far less often and less elaborately than the likes of Davy Crockett and Daniel Boone.

See also: ALMANACS.

SUGGESTED READING: Walter Blair and Franklin J. Meine, *Mike Fink: King of Mississippi Keelboatmen* (New York, 1933); Walter Blair, *Half Horse, Half Alligator: The Growth of the Mike Fink Legend* (Chicago, 1956).

Finnish Americans. Immigrants and the descendants of emigrants from Finland proper and from Finnish-speaking regions of Russia, Norway, and Sweden. There have been Finns in America since the seventeenth century; a number of Finns were included in New Sweden (the Swedish colony in the Delaware Valley), whose VERNACULAR ARCHITECTURE legacy is a distinctive LOG CABIN style employing dovetailed corner construction. Finns were also active in early nineteenth-century Russian ventures in Alaska. Evidence of their work as carpenters still exists there in the form of vernacular architecture and the beautiful woodwork of the Sitka Lutheran Church. From Alaska, Finnish communities spread south into such cities as Seattle, Astoria (Oregon), and San Francisco. The next major wave of Finnish immigration to the United States spanned the mid-nineteenth century to 1924, tapering off with the enactment of stringent immigration restrictions. Approximately 700,000 persons of Finnish descent now live in the United States. In addition to communities in the Northwest, Finns are found in New England and upstate New York; New York City; the mining areas of West Virginia, western Pennsylvania, and northeast Ohio; Detroit and Chicago; the copper-mining region around Lake Superior; the iron-mining area of northern Michigan, Wisconsin, and Minnesota; west into the Dakotas; the Rocky Mountain states; and Southern California and Arizona. Most live in the Midwest.

The Finns have a strong nationalist tradition, intensified by their unique language, which is quite separate from other European languages, and by the fact that, for much of their history, the Finns were politically dominated by Sweden or Russia and did not achieve independence until 1917. This nationalism translated into strong institutions created by immigrants to preserve customs, strengthen communities, and foster folk arts. Finnish newspapers flourished, including handwritten papers circulated in small immigrant communities. In some communities, cohesiveness developed into communalism (as on Drummond Island in Lake Huron), and many early buildings in Finnish settlements were raised by cooperative effort. In some cases, substantial business ventures grew out of Finnish communalism.

Finnish Americans have developed a large body of oral folklore about the immigrant experience, which have been collected in a number of midwestern repositories, including Wayne State University in Detroit; the Immigration History Research Center, University of Minnesota; the Finnish Heritage Center, Suomi College, Hancock, Michigan; the Minnesota Historical Society, St. Paul; and the Iron Range Research Center, Chisholm, Minnesota. Yet because Finnish communities tended to be insular and even clannish, few features of their folk traditions, including a substantial body of folk music, have penetrated far beyond their communities. Exceptions include vernacular log construction, certain FOODWAYS especially the making of *rieska* (unleavened rye bread) and *pulla* (cardamom-flavored coffee bread), and, most familiar of all to outsiders, the sauna—the Finnish steam bath. Finns use the sauna for massage as well as a variety of folk medicine (see MEDICINE, FOLK) practices and even as a place for childbirth.

See also: IMMIGRANT FOLKLORE; SCANDINAVIAN AMERICANS.

SUGGESTED READING: Richard M. Dorson, *Bloodstoppers and Bearwalkers: Folk Traditions of the Upper Peninsula* (Cambridge, Mass., 1948); Yvonne Hiipakka Lockwood, "The Sauna: An Expression of Finnish-American Identity," *Western Folklore* 36 (1977), pp. 71–84; Yvonne Hiipakka Lockwood, ed., "Finnish American Folklife," *Finnish Americana* 8 (1990).

Finster, Howard (1916–).

Almost certainly the best-known living folk artist, Howard Finster combines religious inspiration with inspiration from the artifacts (and detritus) of popular culture to create paintings, sculptures, and artistic environments that are at once richly complex and naive. An extremely prolific artist, Finster has dedicated himself most intensely to his *Paradise Garden,* approximately two acres of swampland adjacent to his workshop in Pennville, Georgia, which he has progressively filled with an array of artwork fashioned from what Finster himself identifies as "other people's junk." Broken toys, dolls, tools, clocks, bottles—junk—is embedded in the concrete walls and paths surrounding a thirty-foot tower erected of bicycle parts. *Paradise Garden* also harbors other remarkable structures built of bottles and other cast-offs, as well as Finster's church, which he titles "The World's Folk Art Church, Inc." In addition to *Paradise Garden,* Finster turns out a staggering number of paintings. In the 1970s, he began numbering his works and, as of the late 1990s, they number well over fourteen thousand. The

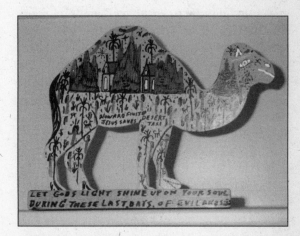

Howard Finster, Jesus Saves Desert Taxi; *Mixed media, "12:40 past midnight, November 11, 1990." (Collection of Charles Phillips and Patricia Hogan)*

paintings are often on biblical themes incongruously wedded to such icons of popular culture as Elvis Presley, Henry Ford, postcard imagery, and Coca-Cola bottles and generously interspersed with angels and saints. The paintings typically contain extensive quotations and original sayings (which collectors call "Finsterisms"), many of them enunciating apocalyptic messages.

Finster paints on plywood and heavy canvas obtained from a local rug manufacturer, but he has also painted on nail heads, gourds, bottles, mirrors, plastic, shovels, and an entire Cadillac. His preferred media is bicycle paint and house paint, in addition to crayon, pencil, and wax. Some of his images are stenciled.

Born in Valley Head, Alabama, and with about six years of formal education, Finster became an evangelical Baptist minister, preaching for some four decades at tent revivals and in various rural southern churches. In 1965, he retired as pastor of the Chelsea Baptist Church in Menlo, Georgia, and opened up a lawn mower and bicycle repair shop in Pennville, Georgia. Moved by divine command, Finster began at about this time to create his *Paradise Garden* and, subsequently, to create paintings and other smaller works to broadcast his spiritual messages to the world.

In 1982 the National Endowment for the Arts awarded Finster a Visual Artist Fellowship in Sculpture, which the artist used to enhance and improve *Paradise Garden*. By this time, he was gaining the attention of the mainstream art world and has had numerous shows and wide coverage in the mass media.

See also: VISIONARY ART.

SUGGESTED READING: Howard Finster, *Howard Finster: Stranger From Another World* (New York, 1989); John F. Turner and Howard Finster, *Man of Visions* (New York, 1988).

First Monday Trades Day. In many southern states, the First Monday Trades Day is an open-air market, usually held in front of the local courthouse, conducted on the first Monday of each month. All types of merchandise are sold, from livestock to produce to knickknacks of various sorts. The occasion is often quite social, complete with spontaneous music making and storytelling. Scottsboro, Alabama, and Canton, Texas, are well known for their First Monday Trades Days. When First Monday coincides with Labor Day, the festivities in these towns resemble a carnival. In some places, First Monday Trades Day is known as "Jockey Day" or "Court Day."

Fishing lore. Fishing lore falls into two categories, OCCUPATIONAL FOLKLORE pertaining to fishing as a commercial industry, and the folklore of fishing as a sporting and recreational activity. In either category, perhaps the folklore motif most commonly associated with fishing is the TALL TALE—the endless variations on the "one that got away." Fishing manifestly inspires exaggeration, stories about more and bigger and meaner.

Beyond this, commercial fishing has produced a rich body of occupational folklore, which has been influenced and fostered by the fact that commercial fishing is an often hazardous and, therefore, emotionally intense occupation and that commercial fishermen are typically members of fishing families and/or residents of more or less closely knit fishing communities. Commercial fishing requires great endurance, strength, judgment, and keen observational skills. Generally, the most successful fishermen are the most experienced; therefore, fishing depends on an informal apprenticeship and the communication of a great deal of lore and knowledge from one gener-

ABOVE LEFT AND RIGHT: *Fishing as a vocation: working through a rough sea and mending a net. Both photographs are from the early 1930s.*

ation to another. In addition to learning about the fish themselves, a fisherman must know how to navigate by landmarks and other means, must understand the significance of various weather phenomena, and must use the behavior of other animals, most notably birds, to judge the presence of fish. Often, fishermen also have a knowledge of boats and boatmaking (see BOATS, VERNACULAR) as well, and certainly must know how to manage their craft. Like other sailors, fishermen typically take great pride in a thorough knowledge of KNOTS. Additionally, fishermen tend to cherish certain routines and rituals (see SUPERSTITION), quite understandable when dealing with many variables and dangers.

Recreational fishing is deeply ingrained in American folklore, which has tended to view it as something of great spiritual value, on the one hand, and the ultimate negation of the American work ethic, on the other. As an activity that is

Fishing as cherished tradition: a photograph reproduced in The Puritan: A Journal for Gentlewomen, *1897.*

typically passed from parent or grandparent or uncle to child (but, most often, father to son), fishing is an ideal vehicle for the oral transmission of lore concerning technique, casting, locating the best fishing spots, baiting a hook, and so on. Moreover, the "older generation" has always valued fishing as a means of teaching the virtue of quiet patience to the "younger generation."

The degree of knowledge and the amount of equipment required for recreational fishing ranges from the ability to tie a string to a pole, bait a hook, and dunk it in the water, to the arcane techniques and expensive equipment (as well as remote and exclusive locations) associated with fly fishing, to the major investment of time, money, and equipment required for deep-sea game fishing.

Types of folklore associated with recreational fishing include ritual and superstition, WEATHER FOLKLORE, various beliefs concerning animal behavior, and, as already mentioned, a universal urge to lie about the volume and size of the catch and especially about "the one that got away."

See also: PORTUGUESE AMERICANS.

SUGGESTED READING: James M. Acheson, *The Lobster Gangs of Maine* (Hanover, N.H., 1988); Wayland Hand et al., *Popular Belief and Superstitions: A Compendium of American Folklore from the Ohio Collection of Newbell Niles Puckett* (Boston, 1981); Paula J. Johnson, ed., *Working the Water: The Commercial Fisheries of Maryland's Patuxent River* (Charlottesville, Va., 1988); Patrick B. Mullen, "*I Heard the Old Fisherman Say*": *Folklore of the Texas Gulf* (Austin, Tex., 1978); Michael K. Orbach, *Hunters, Seamen, and Entrepreneurs: The Tuna Fishermen of San Diego* (Berkeley, Calif., 1977).

Fisk Jubilee Singers. Formed in 1871 by a group of Fisk University students to help raise money for the Nashville-based black university, the Fisk Jubilee Singers toured nationally and internationally, bringing worldwide attention to the body of folk music now known as the spiritual or "Negro spiritual" (but at the time called "slave songs").

The original group consisted of eight singers and a pianist, all Fisk students, directed by George L. White. Within its first decade, the singers had toured the northern United States, England, and Europe and had sung for the president of the United States and for Queen Victoria. The Fisk Jubilee Singers continue to perform and tour today.

See also: FOLK MUSIC SPIRITUALS; AFRICAN-AMERICAN.

Flanders, Helen Hartness (1890–1972). Flanders, an important collector and editor of Vermont folk music traditions, began collecting the folk music of her state in May 1930, at the behest of the Vermont Commission on Country Life. Although Flanders was not a professionally trained folklorist, she met and learned from PHILLIPS BARRY, who acted as her mentor. She also worked with ALAN LOMAX, who recorded a number of her informants for the Library of Congress Folk Song Archives and for her growing Archive of Vermont Folk Music, which she housed at Smiley Manse, her estate in Springfield, Vermont. In 1941, she moved the collection to Middlebury College, establishing the Helen Hartness Flanders Collection there, which eventually encompassed some 10,000 items, including folk songs, BALLADS, and folk tunes.

Flanders published *Vermont Folk-Songs and Ballads* in 1931 and *The New Green Mountain Songster* in 1939, a more scholarly treatment than her first book. With musicologist Marguerite Olney, she wrote *Ballads Migrant in New*

England in 1953, a popular success, which included an introduction by Robert Frost.

SUGGESTED READING: Helen Hartness Flanders, *A Garland of Green Mountain Song* (Northfield, Vt., 1934).

Folk art.

The general definition of folk art is at least threefold: folk art may be any type of art created by people who are not formally trained in art and who live remote from urban, cosmopolitan centers; folk art may also be the art of social, racial, or ethnic minorities that have preserved certain aesthetic traditions apart from the dominant culture or "mainstream" culture; and as many define it, folk art may also be any native, spiritual, or religious art created by persons who lack substantial formal training (in this definition, location is unimportant—the artist may be a rural or urban dweller). Folk art encompasses literature, music, dance, and the visual arts, including painting and sculpture.

See also: MEXICAN AMERICANS; OUTSIDER ART.

Folklore.

A fairly new word to describe an old topic, *folklore* was coined in 1846 by William J. Thoms, a British antiquarian. He intended the term to replace "popular antiquities" and similar awkward phrases used to describe "the lore of the people" and including "the manners, customs, observances, superstitions, ballads, proverbs, etc., of the olden time." Thus "folklore" has been traditionally associated with the past in general and with the rural life of the past in particular, as well as with survivals of that "olden" time and place. Increasingly during the twentieth century, however, the term and the field of study it

describes has been broadened to take in the urban and contemporary as well. Many—but not all—folklorists do insist that, to qualify as an example of folklore, a tale or dance or song or belief or method of building or whatever must be the product of essentially oral transmission or informal demonstration, that it must be identifiable as the product of tradition, and that the item can be shown to be a variation of some recognizable, traditional type. Moreover, folk artifacts are essentially anonymous in origin; even if the maker or speaker or singer can be identified, the product must be sufficiently formulaic to be, in effect, the work of no single artist.

It should be observed that such strict criteria are probably rarely consistently applied in practice; for example, many so-called folk artists create works that are readily identifiable as theirs. Although it is also clear that they have not been academically trained, they are partaking of certain traditional motifs, and they are participating in certain traditions. Most students of folklore borrow selectively from the specifications of the traditional, strict definitions of folklore and apply what they borrow in varying degrees.

See also: FAKELORE; POPULAR CULTURE.

Folklore in American literature.

All students of folklore agree that it is important to distinguish between folklore and literature; however, the first major American writers to achieve significant literary recognition beyond the borders of the United States, WASHINGTON IRVING and JAMES FENIMORE COOPER, made their reputations in the age of Romanticism in Europe, when writers were making a conscious effort to use national folklore in their works. Thus, from the early major phase of American literature, folklore has often played a prominent role. While the works of some literary writers, such as JOEL CHANDLER HARRIS or ZORA NEALE HURSTON, blur the distinction between folklore and literature, it is often, but by no means always, clear that folklore serves as literary material, which is then transformed and expressed in more or less "artful" literary form.

In much of America's earliest literature, such as the work of Captain JOHN SMITH, SAMUEL SEWALL, and COTTON MATHER, folklore materials are reported or, in effect, transcribed. By the nineteenth century, America's emerging professional authors looked to Europe for models of composition, form, plot, and even subject; however, the most enduring of these writers also dug deeply into the folklore and folklife of America. In fiction, Irving and Cooper are prime examples of this. In poetry, HENRY WADSWORTH LONGFELLOW looked to such legends as that of HIAWATHA for distinctively American material, which he cast into the mold of venerable European patterns of verse and meter. By mid-century, HENRY DAVID THOREAU made ample use of wood lore, plant lore, and NATIVE AMERICAN folklore in his essays and extended works. NATHANIEL HAWTHORNE blended colonial history and folklore in such masterpieces as *The Scarlet Letter* (1850). HERMAN MELVILLE explored the rich lore of WHALING in *Moby-Dick* (1851) and, in *The Confidence-Man* (1857), he probed the allegorical ramifications of the CON ARTIST AND CONFIDENCE MAN, a rich folklore motif. In his poetry, WALT WHITMAN made no distinction between the rich mines of folklore he opened up and the sights and scenes of everyday life he transformed into literature. In his remarkable essay *Democratic Vistas* (1877), Whitman explicitly urged American writers to turn away from Europe and look to the nation's folklore for material. While there is no evidence that MARK TWAIN had Whitman's advice in mind (or even read *Democratic Vistas*), no American writer of the nineteenth century produced works that so satisfyingly capture, in literary form, the feeling of folklore. In turn, the characters and incidents of *The Adventures of Tom Sawyer* (1876) and *Adventures of Huckleberry Finn* (1884) have entered into American popular culture to such a degree as to be almost indistinguishable from folklore.

By the end of the nineteenth century, writers of the local color school made frequent, if often superficial, use of folklore, FOLK SPEECH, and LOCAL LEGENDS. In the twentieth century, William Faulkner seemed to tap the very roots of American folklore in such works as *The Sound and the Fury* (1929) and *Absalom, Absalom* (1936).

See also: ALGER, HORATIO; CRANE, HART; FILSON, JOHN; FRANKLIN, BENJAMIN; HARTE, BRET; LOCAL-COLOR STORY; MORTON, THOMAS; NASBY, PETROLEUM V.; PLANTS AND PLANT LORE; SANDBURG, CARL; THORPE, THOMAS BANGS; WARD, ARTEMUS; WHITTIER, JOHN GREENLEAF.

SUGGESTED READING: Steven Swann Jones, *Folklore and Literature in the United States: An Annotated Bibliography of Studies of Folklore in American Literature* (New York, 1984); Bruce A. Rosenberg, *Folklore and Literature: Rival Siblings* (Knoxville, Tenn., 1991).

Folkloristics. The comparative study of folklore, folkloristics seeks to identify elements common to folklore, irrespective of geographical or social origin, and also to examine the specific geographical, social, and other variations on these common elements.

See also: JANSEN, WILLIAM HUGH.

Folk music. At least two definitions of folk music are important today. The first is lyric and melody that is central or at least germane to the culture of a nation or ethnic group and that is transmitted by oral tradition, that is learned through hearing rather than reading. Secondarily, the term *folk music* describes a style of popular, commercial music inspired by or emulating "genuine" folk music traditions; such music became especially popular during the FOLK REVIVAL of the 1960s.

In its primary sense, folk music is chiefly rural in origin and is the music of the "common people" rather than the elite; however, in contrast to so-called popular music, it does not depend on recordings or radio broadcast for dissemination. It is shared within families or communities. It must be observed, however, that folk music rarely exists in this "pure" form any longer. The penetration of MASS MEDIA is so thorough and pervasive that many distinctions between folk music and popular music are blurred.

See also: APPALACHIA; "ARKANSAS TRAVELER"; ASCH, MOSES; AUTOHARP; BAEZ, JOAN; BALLADS; BANJO; "BARBARA ALLEN"; "BILLY BOY"; BLUEGRASS; BLUES; BLUES BALLAD; "BLUE-TAIL FLY"; "BUFFALO GALS"; "BURY ME NOT ON THE LONE PRAIRIE"; CAJUN MUSIC; CAROL; CARSON, FIDDLIN' JOHN; CARTER FAMILY, THE; CHANTEYS; CHILD BALLAD; CHILD, FRANCIS JAMES; "CINDY"; "CLEMENTINE"; COME-ALL-YE; CONJUNTO MUSIC; COPLAND, AARON; CORRIDOS; COUNTRY MUSIC; "COWBOY'S LAMENT"; COWBOY SONGS; DANCE, FOLK; "DYING CALIFORNIAN"; EATON, ALLEN; ETHNOMUSICOLOGY; FIDDLE; FILIPINO AMERICANS; FILK MUSIC; FISK JUBILEE SINGERS; FOLKWAYS RECORDS; FOSTER, STEPHEN; "FRANKIE AND JOHNNIE"; GIBSON GUITAR AND MANDOLIN COMPANY LTD., THE; GOSPEL MUSIC; GUTHRIE, WOODY (WOODROW WILSON); "I GAVE MY LOVE A CHERRY"; IVES, BURL; JACKSON, GEORGE PULLEN; JACKSON, MAHALIA; JAZZ; JEFFERSON, BLIND LEMON; JEW'S HARP; JIMÉNEZ, FLACO; "JOHN HARDY"; KLEZMER MUSIC; LEDBETTER, HUDDIE (LEADBELLY); LOMAX, ALAN; LOMAX, JOHN; "MADEMOISELLE FROM ARMENTIÈRES"; MANDOLIN; MARTIN GUITAR COMPANY; MEXICAN AMERICANS; "MICHIGAN I-O"; NILES, JOHN JACOB; OCARINA; "OLD DAN TUCKER"; "OLD SMOKY"; PARLOR BALLAD; "POP GOES THE WEASEL"; PRISON WORK SONGS; RAGTIME; RAP; REVIVAL SONGS; ROCK 'N' ROLL; ROOSEVELT BALLADS; SACRED HARP MUSIC; SAINTE MARIE, BUFFY; SANDBURG, CARL; SHAPE-NOTE SINGING; SHARP, CECIL JAMES; "SHENANDOAH"; SLAVIC AMERICANS; SPIRITUALS, AFRICAN-AMERICAN; SPIRITUALS, WHITE; TAMBURITZA MUSIC AND ORCHESTRA; TEX-MEX MUSIC; "TURKEY IN THE STRAW"; WORK SONGS; "WRECK OF THE OLD 97, THE."

Folk revival. Beginning in the late 1950s, Appalachian musicians—among them Doc Watson, BILL MONROE, and the Stanley Brothers—as well as such BLUES musicians as Sonny Terry, Brownie McGhee, Mississippi John Hurt, and MUDDY WATERS, began touring American universities, offering concerts of traditional music to often idealistic and always enthusiastic student audiences. Among those excited by the "new" old music were the likes of Dave Von Ronk, John Koerner, BUFFY SAINTE-MARIE, JOAN BAEZ, Phil Ochs, Tom Paxton, and BOB DYLAN. By the early 1960s, these as well as a host of lesser musicians were performing in small urban clubs, especially in New York's Greenwich Village and on the West Coast, in such college towns as Berkeley. Soon, the clubs invited the older traditional musicians who had played—and still played—the college circuit, and, by the mid 1960s, the folk revival was in full swing and gave rise to the Newport Folk Festival. The Festival of American Folklife, inaugurated by the SMITHSONIAN INSTITUTION in 1967, was not a product of the folk revival, but certainly benefited from it and, in turn, fed continued interest in the genre. By this time, however, many of the younger folk-oriented musicians were combining traditional blues and folk with ROCK 'N' ROLL to produce a relatively short-lived, but influential "folk rock" style. Leading musicians and groups included Donovan (a Scottish import), Cher, the Buffalo Springfield, the Mamas and the Papas, Janis Ian, Joni Mitchell, Loudon Wainwright III, and, most significantly, Bob Dylan—who outraged the hard-core folk revivalists in 1965 when he started to use amplified instruments. This, it was felt, heralded the end of the folk revival and signaled a sell-out to what "purists" regarded as commercial rock 'n' roll. In fact, the folk revival continued as a major force in popular music at least through the end of the decade, and it sparked a substantial renewed interest in traditional folk music as well as commercial folk-style music that continues to this day.

See also: ARHOOLIE RECORDS; CRAFTS, AMERICAN FOLK; FOLK MUSIC; HARMONICA; HOPKINS, LIGHTNIN; "I GAVE MY LOVE A CHERRY"; JAZZ; KING, B. B.; RINZLER, RALPH CARTER; SCOTTISH AMERICANS; "SHENANDOAH"; TOYS, FOLK.

Folk-say. Folk-say is a term coined by folklore scholar BENJAMIN A. BOTKIN in the title of a series of folklore anthologies he edited during 1929–32. He explained the term in "Folklore and Folk-Say" (*American Speech* 31 [1931], pp.

404–6) as a description of literature of the folk, the "oral, linguistic, and story-telling . . . aspect of folklore and its living as well as anachronistic phrases."

See also: APPALACHIA; BASEBALL FOLKLORE; COMIC STRIPS; CRACKERS; CRIME AND CRIMINALS; FOLK SPEECH; OPOSSUM; SHEEPMAN STORIES; WAMPUM.

Folk speech. Folk speech encompasses vernacular pronunciations, grammar, expressions, and figures of speech associated primarily with rural or old-fashioned speakers—though many folklorists would also include in folk speech examples of speech peculiar to various urban ethnic groups. Regional variation plays a central role in folk speech; for example, even casual listeners recognize certain speech patterns as characteristic of "hillbilly talk" or the "Down East" speech of the oldtimer from Maine. Most folklorists exclude slang from the definition of folk speech, because slang tends to be used by the young, is limited to groups with special interests, and is typically short-lived.

See also: BLACK ENGLISH; CRIME AND CRIMINALS; DUTCH AMERICANS; FOLKLORE IN AMERICAN LITERATURE; FOLK-SAY; FOLKWAYS; GAY FOLKLORE; GRAFFITI; HOEDOWN; HUNTING; MASS MEDIA; MENCKEN, H[enry] L[ouis]; MEXICAN AMERICANS; MILITARY FOLKLORE; MONROE, MARILYN; OCCUPATIONAL FOLKLORE; RAILROAD FOLKLORE; THOREAU, HENRY DAVID; TWAIN, MARK; VIETNAM WAR.

Folkways. Coined in 1906 by the American sociologist William Graham Sumner, *folkways* has come to encompass manners, customs, mores, and even values that are habitually used and repeated by culturally, regionally, or ethnically definable groups. Folkways may include distinctive patterns of FOLK SPEECH, distinctive patterns of VERNACULAR ARCHITECTURE, distinctive familial relationships and practices, and distinctive FOODWAYS among other things.

See also: FOXFIRE; MEXICAN AMERICANS; PORTUGUESE AMERICANS.

SUGGESTED READING: William Graham Sumner, *Folkways: A Study of the Sociological Importance of Usages, Manners, Customs, Mores, and Morals* (1906; reprint ed., New York, 1960).

Folkways Records. Folkways Records was the foremost commercial enterprise devoted to recording FOLK MUSIC and the music of the FOLK REVIVAL from 1949 to 1986. The label was founded by MOSES ASCH and Marian Distler in 1949, and, in thirty-seven years of production issued more than two thousand LP titles (including early 78-rpm disks reissued as long-playing albums). Folkways Records both participated in and helped to spark the folk-music revival that began in the late 1940s and reached its peak in the 1960s.

Folkways Records recorded the work of anthropologists, folk-song collectors, and amateur as well as professional folk musicians. Ethnic music figured prominently in the label's catalogue, but was never limited to any particular ethnic group. Well represented were African music, Appalachian music, Native American music, and much else, including such nonfolk genres as avant-garde and experimental music by such composers as John Cage. During the 1950s and 1960s, the label became well known for issu-

ing the work of blacklisted (those branded as Communists) performers, including the great PETE SEEGER. Nor was the Folkways catalog limited to music. It was an important label for spoken-word albums, many of which were oral histories relating to current events of social significance, especially the civil rights movement.

Folkways albums were always distinguished by their documentation, which went far beyond traditional album liner notes. Many albums were accompanied by extensive pamphlets documenting and explaining the recorded material.

Although Folkways was a commercial enterprise, economics rarely entered into Asch's editorial decisions. He kept costs to a minimum and published work that seemed of value and significance to him.

As an independent commercial enterprise, Folkways eventually fell victim to the folk revival it had helped create. As folk-oriented and folk-inspired music became increasingly popular, major labels signed many of the singers who might otherwise have recorded for the label. In 1987, the company's catalogue was acquired by the SMITHSONIAN INSTITUTION, which has made a commitment to keep all of the recordings in print.

See also: CANSLER, LOMAN D.; MOSER, ARTUS M.; NILES, JOHN JACOB; RINZLER, RALPH CARTER.

Foodways. A specialty within folklore studies devoted to food and artifacts and customs associated with food as a medium through which communal, ethnic, national, or other distinctive group values are expressed, affirmed, and communicated. Folklorists interested in foodways study such relationships as food and the informant's age, ethnicity, gender, region, occupation, and religion.

See also: CAJUNS; FILIPINO AMERICANS; FINNISH AMERICANS; FOLKWAYS; GERMAN AMERICANS; GREEK AMERICANS; ITALIAN AMERICANS; JAPANESE AMERICANS; KOREAN AMERICANS; MATERIAL CULTURE; MEXICAN AMERICANS; PENNSYLVANIA GERMANS; SLAVIC AMERICANS.

SUGGESTED READING: Charles Camp, *American Foodways* (Little Rock, Ark., 1989); C. Paige Gutierrez, *Cajun Foodways* (Jackson, Miss., 1992).

Foo-fighters. During WORLD WAR II, Allied bomber pilots reported that strange balls of light and disk-shaped objects sometimes followed them as they flew missions over Germany and Japan. The pilots called these "foo-fighters," apparently after a pun on the French word *feu* (fire), which appeared in "Smokey Stover," a popular comic strip of the period ("Where there's foo, there's fire," Smokey was wont to declare).

Foo-fighters appeared to dance off the bombers' wingtips or kept pace with the aircraft in front and in back. Sightings were not limited to pilots. Naval personnel, on board warships at sea, reported seeing foo-fighters maneuvering overhead. Explanations offered at the time ranged from static electricity charges to Japanese and German secret weapons, intended either to foul the ignition systems of the bombers or (since the foo-fighters never committed a hostile action) merely to inspire psychological terror. After a cursory investigation, the U.S. Eighth Air Force dismissed the phenomenon as "mass hallucination." Perhaps because the sightings ended with the war, no further effort was made to explain the phenomenon.

Interestingly, after the war, German and Japanese pilots revealed that they, too, had encountered foo-fighters, which they had believed were secret weapons of the Allies.

See also: UFO FOLKLORE.

Ford, Henry (1863–1947). Everyone identifies Henry Ford with the early development of the automobile, but contrary to popular belief, he did not invent that vehicle. He created or improved the systems of mass production and assembly-line process that enabled production of the famous Model T on a large scale and put the automobile within the reach of most Americans. In so doing, Ford became a CULTURE HERO comparable in stature to his close friend THOMAS ALVA EDISON. His mass-produced Model T transformed the American landscape, American MATERIAL CULTURE and POPULAR CULTURE, and generally revolutionized American life. Both Ford and his automobiles also directly affected American folklore. The widespread availability of private transportation made the hinterlands, including folklore-rich Appalachia, more generally accessible. Moreover, the automobile created a demand for destinations, and these came to include sites of historic as well as folkloric interest. Ford himself became passionately interested—some would say obsessed—with recreating the American past in general and the more or less idealized world of his childhood in particular. With John D. Rockefeller, Jr., he was one of the prime movers behind the creation of COLONIAL WILLIAMSBURG. A restoration of the early colonial Virginia hamlet begun in 1926, Colonial Williamsburg was part of a COLONIAL REVIVAL movement that had started with the American Centennial of 1876 and did much to shape popular perceptions of colonial American folklife. Even more important to Ford was the creation of

GREENFIELD VILLAGE in 1933, in his birthplace, Dearborn, Michigan. Greenfield Village is, in effect, an outdoor museum of history and folklife, albeit as seen through the lens of Ford's idealized image of an idyllic America before it was transformed by the industrialization he himself had been so instrumental in bringing about. Ford's consuming interest in the world of the past seems paradoxical in light of what is perhaps his most famous saying: "History is more or less bunk."

Ford was born on a farm near Dearborn, just eight miles west of Detroit. He went to work as a machinist in Detroit when he was sixteen and became interested in the internal-combustion engine. At the end of 1893, Ford became chief engineer at the main Detroit Edison Company plant, which gave him the time and money to experiment with improving the internal combustion engine, which, in 1896, he adapted for use in a "horseless carriage" of his own design. He worked tirelessly on improving and refining his vehicle and built several race cars at the turn of the century. His most famous, "999," was driven by the legendary Barney Oldfield to a number of speed records. In 1903, he organized the Ford Motor Company, and, in 1908, introduced the Model T, the mass-produced "Tin Lizzie," proclaiming it "a motor car for the great multitude." Over the next two decades, 15.5 million of the model were sold in the United States, another million in Canada, and 250,000 in Great Britain.

By 1913–14, Ford and his engineers had perfected a super-efficient assembly-line system and were paying workers $5 a day (other auto manufacturers paid $2.34). This enhanced his stature as a culture hero and a popular hero, a friend of the working man. Moreover, the cost of a Model T was steadily reduced, from $950 in 1908 to $290 by 1927, thereby making it a truly democratic machine.

In the meantime, Ford became obsessed with

Industrialist Henry Ford transformed American popular culture with the mass-produced automobile, yet sought to preserve a romantic, nostalgic American past in Greenfield Village.

the concept of vertical integration, the control of all materials and processes that went into the production of his cars. He acquired a railroad, sixteen coal mines, some 700,000 acres of timberland, a fleet of Great Lakes freighters, and a glassworks. Operations were innovatively integrated at his new River Rouge plant in 1927. Ultimately, however, Ford's thinking became as monolithic as his company. He declined to develop his automobiles in response to consumer needs, and he lost valuable ground to other automakers. As sales declined, Ford's attitude toward his workers became less benignly paternalistic and increasingly dictatorial. He used a private police force and hired thugs to squelch unionization efforts in the 1930s. During World War I, he worked vigorously, if idiosyncratically to bring about peace and understanding, while at the same time publishing anti-Semitic tirades in *The Dearborn Independent,* a newspaper he owned. (In 1927, he formally retracted his rants against what he had called the "International Jew.") The Ford Foundation, established in 1936, not only perpetuated the family's control of the company, but as the richest private foundation in the world, it became a major international philanthropic force, underwriting, among many other projects, numerous folklore and folklife programs.

See also: LONGWAYS DANCE.

SUGGESTED READING: Alan Axelrod, ed., *The Colonial Revival in America* (New York, 1985); Reynold M. Wik, *Henry Ford and Grass-Roots America* (Ann Arbor, Mich., 1972).

Fort, Charles (1874–1931). Often called the father of UFOlogy, Charles Fort was the author of a series of speculative books about what might be described as weirdness. In 1915, he began two manuscripts, one called *X,* which explored the idea that life on earth was or had been controlled by events or beings from Mars, and another, *Y,* which built a case for the existence of a sinister civilization based at the South Pole. Neither manuscript has been found, although Fort's friend, the American novelist Theodore Dreiser, read *X* and wrote that "It was so strange, so forceful, so beautiful that . . . it was certainly one of the greatest books I have ever read in my life." In addition to several unpublished novels

and one that did receive publication, Fort wrote *Book of the Damned* (1919) and *New Lands* (1923), the first of which is an encyclopedic speculation on extraterrestrial life and visitations to earth, and the second a satirical attack on hidebound astronomers. *Lo!* (1931) introduced his idea of teleportation. His *Wild Talents,* dealing with psychic abilities, was published after his death, in 1932.

Fort might be dismissed as an eccentric author who deliberately blurred any distinction between science fiction and rational speculation were it not for the fact that his works have become the nucleus around which a community of those interested in the weird, the occult, and in UFOs have formed. Indeed, the word *Forteana* has been coined to cover a host of miscellaneous strange and supernatural subjects and phenomena.

Fort was born in Albany, New York, and left home at the age of eighteen, mainly to escape the brutality of his father. He became a reporter in New York City, then hitchhiked through Europe. Returning to New York in 1892, he married Anna Filan (or Filing), an English servant girl in his father's house, and the two lived in extreme poverty in the Bronx and in Manhattan's Hell's Kitchen neighborhood. Fort was a compulsive and omnivorous reader, who took voluminous notes and wrote lengthy manuscripts, only to burn most of them in disgust. In 1921, Fort and his wife moved to London, where Fort attempted to absorb all that the British Museum had to offer. He formed the opinion that space travel was inevitable, and he wrote letters to *The New York Times* detailing his opinions. He also spoke on the subject at London's Hyde Park Corner. Fort returned to New York in 1929. Already friendly with Theodore Dreiser, he met and befriended another novelist, Tiffany Thayer, who was fascinated by Fort's collection of mounted specimens of giant spiders and objects Fort said had fallen from the sky. Fort become progressively ill, and died of an undiagnosed disease that was most likely leukemia.

See also: UFO FOLKLORE.

SUGGESTED READING: Damon Knight, *Charles Fort: Prophet of the Unexplained* (New York, 1970); Charles Fort, *The Complete Books of Charles Fort* (New York, 1975).

Fortier, Alcée (1856–1914). Fortier collected Louisiana French folklore. A native of St. James Parish, Louisiana, Fortier was the son of a well-to-do sugar-planting Creole family. He left the plantation, however, to become a professor of French at the University of Louisiana—modern Tulane—in 1884. He published *Louisiana Folk-Tales* in 1895, which contains tales reported by Creole-speaking African Americans. Fortier published them bilingually. Fortier also published books on Creole customs and superstitions.

He founded the Louisiana Association of the American Folklore Society in 1892 and served as president of the national society in 1894.

SUGGESTED READING: De Caro, F. A. "A History of Folklife Research in Louisiana," in Nicholas R. Spitzer, ed., *Louisiana Folklife: A Guide to the State* (Baton Rouge, 1985).

Foster, Stephen (1826–1864). Born and raised in what is now Pittsburgh, Pennsylvania, Foster grew up on the very edge of the western frontier. With no formal training in music, he began to write songs as a boy, imbibing such

Stephen Foster: his commercial songs were so popular and so naturally American that they are readily confused with folk songs.

influences as the Victorian PARLOR BALLAD tradition, African-American church music (he attended black church meetings with his family's servant Olivia Pise), MINSTREL SHOW music, and African-American WORK SONGS heard at the Pittsburgh warehouse where he worked for a time. He published his first song, "Open Thy Lattice, Love," in 1842, but could not support himself as a song writer and moved to Cincinnati in 1846, where he worked as a bookkeeper.

Foster wrote "Oh, Susanna" in 1848 and, the

next year, contracted with Firth, Pond & Co., New York music publishers, with whom he made a financially disadvantageous deal. In 1851, EDWIN P. "NED" CHRISTY commissioned songs from Foster for his famous minstrel show. The best known of these, "Old Folks at Home" ("Swanee River"), appeared originally under Christy's name. "Old Folks at Home" and Foster's other minstrel show tunes caused him to be identified as a southern writer of folk songs, although he was neither a southerner (he visited the South only once, in 1852) nor a folk musician. Yet many of his songs are so evocative of the romantic-nostalgic vision of the South purveyed in the minstrel shows that the twin misconceptions are quite understandable. Certainly, Foster, who declared an ambition to be recognized as "the best Ethiopian [that is, minstrel] song writer," was inspired to a significant degree by African-American folk music. Nevertheless, Foster's output was by no means exclusively in this vein. He was also a composer of sentimental parlor ballads, such as "Jeanie with the Light Brown Hair" and "Beautiful Dreamer."

Foster's music was popular in his own time and continued to be so universally popular that it is often branded indiscriminately as "traditional music." Foster himself enjoyed slim reward for his genius. Plagued by depression, alcoholism, and poor business judgment, he sold all rights to his future songs to his publisher for about $1,900 in 1857. He moved to New York City in 1860, and the next year, his wife left him. Although he continued to turn out sentimental ballads, Foster sank deeper into melancholy and drink. He died, deeply in debt, having written some two hundred songs, usually both the words and music, among them "Camptown Races," "Nelly Bly," "My Old Kentucky Home," "Massa's in de Cold, Cold Ground," and "Old Black Joe."

See also: FOLK MUSIC; GREENFIELD VILLAGE; HAYS, WILL.

SUGGESTED READING: Ken Emerson, *Doo-Dah! Stephen Foster and the Rise of American Popular Culture* (New York, 1997); Steven Saunders and Deane L. Root, *The Music of Stephen C. Foster: 1844–1869: A Critical Edition* (2 vols.; Washington, D.C., 1990).

Fox. In Euro-American folktales, the fox often appears as a wily TRICKSTER and is especially well known as BRER FOX in the UNCLE REMUS tales of JOEL CHANDLER HARRIS. Brer Fox is an amalgam of African-American and European traditions. Among western Native American tribes, the fox is often the lesser companion of the trickster COYOTE. In Eskimo traditional tales, the fox is a beautiful woman who steals into a hunter's house, cooks for him, then sets up housekeeping with him—until he complains of her musky odor, whereupon she dons her fox skin and leaves the house.

See also: OPOSSUM.

Foxfire. A series of book-length magazines devoted to practical articles on folklore and FOLKWAYS, the first *Foxfire* book was published in 1967 as a project of Eliot Wigginton's high school English class at the Rabun Gap–Nacoochee School, in the Appalachians of northwestern Georgia. In some ways, *Foxfire* was an ordinary student magazine—except for extensive material on local folk beliefs and folk medicine (see MEDICINE, FOLK). *Foxfire* sold out its first two printings, and Wiggonton's students put together a second issue, which included more folklore, both of a practical nature (recipes, soap making, etc.) and of a more "escapist" variety (ghost stories). Soon, *Foxfire* began to appear quarterly and by the early 1970s achieved national circulation and recognition, prompting emulators and also the publication of *The Foxfire Book* anthology, as well as other, more specialized collections of folk material. A Foxfire record label was briefly active, as was a Foxfire String Band.

See also: ALMANACS.

SUGGESTED READING: John L. Puckett, *Foxfire Reconsidered: A Twenty-Year Experiment in Progressive Education* (Urbana, Ill., 1989); Eliot Wigginton, ed., *The Foxfire Book: Hog Dressing, Log Cabin Building, Mountain Crafts and Foods, Planting by the Signs, Snake Lore, Hunting Tales, Faith Healing, Moonshining, and Other Affairs of Plain Living* (Garden City, N.Y., 1972).

Fraktur. In Rhenish Germany, *Fraktur* were illuminated manuscripts characterized by ornate calligraphy (or "decorative writing") and used for certain legal and family documents, such as baptismal and marriage certificates. The art of creating *Fraktur* was brought to America by German immigrants during the late seventeenth century and throughout the eighteenth. Examples of American-made *Fraktur* may be found in the Delaware Valley among the PENNSYLVANIA GERMANS and in other places to which Germans and Pennsylvania Germans migrated, including Maryland, Virginia, North Carolina, and South Carolina.

Fraktur is a German word denoting a sixteenth-century German typeface. As applied to such items as birth, baptismal, and marriage documents, the word denotes ornate hand lettering and embellishment with such watercolor illustrations as colorful borders replete with stylized hearts, tulips, birds, and other imagery. Typi-

cally, *Fraktur* was the work of ministers and schoolmasters. *Fraktur* were produced well into the nineteenth century. Among Mennonites in Lancaster County, Pennsylvania, and the Shenandoah Valley of Virginia, *Fraktur* were called *Zierschrift.*

"Frankie and Johnnie." Also known as "Frankie and Albert," this is a BLUES BALLAD, with origins dating to the end of the nineteenth century and relating the story of a "sporting woman" (Frankie) who shoots her lover (Johnnie) for having "done her wrong." Any number of incidents have been suggested as the "true-life" inspiration of the song, but, of course, the shooting of one lover by another is not an uncommon occurrence. There are many variations of the song, with different names for the two principals.

See also: FOLK MUSIC.

Franklin, Benjamin (1706–1790). One of the most remarkable and colorful of the Founding Fathers, Benjamin Franklin is important to American folklore both as an early collector and transmitter of folk wisdom (in his *Poor Richard's Almanac*) and as a subject of folklore himself. In his *Autobiography* (partially published in 1789; published in full in 1868), Franklin offers his formative experiences as a kind of typical American story and himself as the archetypal American. As he presents himself in the *Autobiography*, Franklin is a real-life anticipation of a HORATIO ALGER hero.

Franklin was born in Boston, Massachusetts, and at age twelve, he was apprenticed to his brother James, a printer. After a dispute with

Benjamin Franklin's kite experiment, illustrated here in a Currier & Ives print from the nation's centennial year, 1876, is part of the nation's folklore. From the perspective of the nineteenth century, "stealing" electricity from the heavens made Franklin, already honored as a Founding Father, a full-fledged culture hero. (Collection of Walton Rawls)

his brother, he traveled to Philadelphia to make his fortune. His entrance into the city, as described in the *Autobiography*, has long been an American icon: the callow youth walks the streets of Philadelphia with "three great Puffy Rolls," two tucked under each arm, the third being munched. After a sojourn in London, where he worked as a printer, Franklin returned to Philadelphia and his trade and, by 1728, set up as a printer, scoring a financial coup when he secured a contract to print Pennsylvania's currency. He also became public printer of New Jersey, Delaware, and Maryland, and launched a newspaper, the *Pennsylvania Gazette,* and his famous ALMANAC, *Poor Richard's,* which appeared annually from 1732 to 1757. The almanac contained a wealth of short folk narratives, WEATHER FOLK-

The composing stick Franklin used when he was a young printer in Philadelphia. It is now enshrined in that city.

LORE, and many, many PROVERBS. Doubtless some of what Franklin included was original with him and some was American folklore he collected, but the overwhelming majority of the proverbs were copied from English almanac sources. In this way, much British proverbial lore was imported, as it were, wholesale, into America.

During the years before the Revolution, Franklin became involved in a variety of projects for the public good and also dabbled in the study of natural science. In the winter of 1746–47, Franklin and three friends experimented with weather-related electrical phenomena. Another folkloric image portrays Franklin flying a kite in a thunderstorm, a brass key attached to his end of the string and grounded in a primitive battery known as a Leyden jar. The experiment—which might well have proved fatal—demonstrated the electric properties of lightning. Franklin published his work in 1751 and became world famous as a "natural philosopher." Moreover, his experiments prompted him to suggest that tall buildings be protected from the "electrical fluid" of lighting by means of lightning rods.

In 1753, Franklin became deputy postmaster general for all the northern colonies. With the approach of the French and Indian War, he proposed a "Plan of Union" for uniting the colonies and was very active in the affairs of Pennsylvania government. Franklin was instrumental in the independence movement and, during the Revolution, performed brilliantly as a diplomat, winning the support of France in the colonies' war with Britain, then helping to negotiate the treaty that ended the war and gave the United States its independence. He stayed on in France for two years after the war, concluding a series of trade agreements, then returned to the United States as the new nation's first elder statesman.

See also: AMES, NATHANIEL; CURRIER & IVES; FOLKLORE IN AMERICAN LITERATURE; TURKEY.

SUGGESTED READING: Frances M. Barbour, *A Concordance to the Sayings in Franklin's "Poor Richard"* (Detroit, 1974); Benjamin Franklin, *Autobiography* (many modern editions); Benjamin Franklin, *Poor Richard's Almanac* (many modern collections).

French Americans. French Americans include immigrants and the descendants of immigrants who either came to the United States directly from France or via Canada or the West Indies. Thus French Americans make up an extremely diverse group.

The French arrived in North America in the seventeenth century and vied with the English for domination of the continent, ultimately losing their bid for supremacy as a result of their defeat in the French and Indian War (1754–63). Nevertheless, the strong French influence in the territory that is now the United States is revealed in the many place names of French origin, ranging from major cities like Detroit and St. Louis to natural features such as Sault Ste. Marie to midwestern suburbs, such as Des Plaines, Illinois. Of special interest to an earlier generation of folklorists was the folklore, folklife, and WORK SONGS of the *voyageurs,* the early explorers and fur trappers of the West, Upper Midwest, and Canada. As late as the mid-nineteenth century in and about Detroit, folktales were told about the voyageurs, and folklorists working under the auspices of the Depression-era WPA collected voyageur tales in the 1930s in Vincennes, Indiana. The SHIVAREE, a raucous wedding custom, was brought to America by French settlers and is still practiced in some remote areas, including rural Michigan.

In contrast to the English settlers of the eighteenth century, the French voyageurs and other trappers freely intermarried with Native American women, producing so-called Métis. Métis folklore is more common in French Canada than it is in the United States, although Métis folktales have been recorded in Michigan's Upper Peninsula.

The descendants of early French settlers and the Métis people were joined during much of the second half of the nineteenth century and through the first quarter of the twentieth century by French-Canadian emigrants from Quebec, many of whom found work in the lumber camps of New England and the Upper Midwest. These "new" immigrants brought with them many of the old voyageur songs and tales, but also added TALL TALES typical of loggers and usually concerning the feats of men who were stronger and bigger than anyone else. Not all of the French-Canadian immigrants became lumbermen. Many settled in the mill towns and industrial cities of New England, creating ethnic neighborhoods and enclaves known as Little Canadas (Petits Canadas). Today, many New Englanders are of French-Canadian descent.

See also: CAJUNS; IMMIGRANT FOLKLORE.

SUGGESTED READING: Dennis Au, The Lingering Shadow of New France: The French-Canadian Community of Monroe County, Michigan, in C. Kurt Dewhurst and Yvonne Lockwood, eds., Michigan Folklife Reader (East Lansing, Mich., 1987); Theodore Christian Blegen, Voyageurs and Their Songs (St. Paul, Minn., 1966); Marie Caroline Watson Hamlin, Legends of le Détroit (1884; reprint ed., Detroit, 1977); Brigitte Marie Lane, Franco-American Folk Traditions and Popular Culture in a Former Milltown: Aspects of Ethnic Urban Folklore and the Dynamics of Folklore Change in Lowell, Massachusetts (New York, 1990).

Friday the Thirteenth. The belief that a Friday falling on the thirteenth of any month is a "bad luck" day is probably the most pervasive superstition among Americans. The origin of the SUPERSTITION is rooted, in part, in the Christian belief that Friday is inherently a bad day because Christ was crucified on Good Friday. In most Western cultures, the number thirteen is also deemed unlucky. This belief is so pervasive that many skyscrapers lack a thirteenth floor, progressing from the twelfth to the fourteenth. While certain individuals are afflicted with triskaidekaphobia (irrational fear of the number thirteen), something of this phobia affects many aspects of American popular and material culture; however, many folklorists believe that dread of Friday the Thirteenth is fostered by the MASS MEDIA, which tends to feature news stories about misfortunes occurring on this day.

Fuller, Blind Boy (1903–1941). A BLUES musician born Fulton Allen (contracted to Fuller) in Milledgeville, Georgia, in 1903, moved with his parents to Rockingham, North Carolina. In that area he mastered the guitar and began to perform, singing to his own accompaniment at dances and suppers. His repertoire leaned heavily on RAGTIME and dance music. It is said that he was blinded in his early twenties when, during an argument with a woman he was living with, she poured lye in the basin in which he was washing his face. As was true of many talented blind performers, singing and playing in the streets became his only way of making a living. He moved to various tobacco-producing towns, most importantly Winston-Salem, North Carolina, and played for handouts from shift workers leaving the curing sheds and factories. City ordinances clamped down on what the authorities thought of as begging, so he and other blind musicians moved on from town to town along Highway 70, including Greensboro, Graham, Burlington, and Hillsboro. Fuller's strong rhythmic guitar and projective gritty voice attracted other blues artists to him. He probably learned some of his guitar techniques from Blind Gary Davis, who was some years older. Sung over his ragtime guitar, his blues themes tended toward comments on life and bawdy songs in a genre that has been labeled "party blues." He paired up with SONNY TERRY, a virtuoso HARMONICA ("harp," in folk parlance) player, who had been blinded in an accident. The two blind men became such good friends that Sonny Terry moved in with Fuller and his wife for an extended stay.

J. B. Long of Bullerton, North Carolina, who managed a furniture store in Durham, heard Terry and Fuller performing together and persuaded Fuller to hire him as his manager. Long brought him to audition in New York for the American Recording Company. ARC liked Fuller's style and he recorded twelve blues numbers in 1935. "I Don't Have to Worry" and "Looking for My Woman" were issued on the Vocalion label in September. Fuller's efforts caught on well, and he recorded about every six months for the next two years, all for ARC, except for two Decca sessions in 1937. Fuller performed best in a duo; he would let his partner handle rhythm while he played brilliant melodic variations on the upper strings, using a steel-bodied National resonator guitar, which had a vigorously projective sound. Fuller recorded frequently over the ensuing years, principally with Sonny Terry and alternatively with the washboard player Oh Red (George Washington).

Brownie McGhee became part of Fuller's circle and eventually teamed up with Blind Sonny Terry. When Fuller died of a kidney ailment in 1941, Brownie, who inherited Fuller's National guitar, recorded a moving tribute, "The Death of Blind Boy Fuller," on Okeh (06265).

G

Gadd, May (1891–1979). Gadd was an Anglo-American expert on Anglo-American folk dances. English by birth, she was sent to New York City in 1927 under the auspices of the English Folk Dance and Song Society to assist with a summer dance program being presented by the organization's American branch. Once in the States, Gadd became so interested in Appalachian dance forms and their relation to their English roots, that she remained in America permanently. In 1937, partly under her influence, the American branch of the EFDSS officially became the English Folk Dance and Song Society of America and, later, the Country Dance and Song Society of America, with Gadd as national director.

As a performer, the indefatigable Gadd danced through 1976, when she was well into her eighties, but she was even better known as a teacher who imparted the steps of well over a thousand English and English-derived folk dances. AGNES DE MILLE frequently called on Gadd for information on folk sources for the dances she staged in *Brigadoon* and *Oklahoma*.

Games. Folklorists began to study games by the middle of the nineteenth century, collecting traditional games much as other folklorists collected BALLADS and folktales. The first landmark publication in the field was WILLIAM WELLS NEWELL's, *Games and Songs of American Children* (1883). In 1907, Edward B. Tylor and Stewart Culin published *Games of North American Indians*. The early work on games, through the first years of the twentieth century, concentrated on games of the past; that is, collectors approached adults to ask questions about the games they had played as children. It was not until the 1930s, with the work of Dorothy Mills Howard, that collectors turned their attention to the children themselves. The collection of ongoing, contemporary game lore is the prevailing direction in this area today. Remarkably, most of these more recent studies suggest that traditional games, such as ring-around-a-rosy, hide-and-go-seek, and so on, have a very high degree of survival. Unlike so many other folk practices, they seem to be in little danger of disappearing.

Thus far, no scholar has attempted to classify games in the way that FRANCIS JAMES CHILD classified ballads. Nevertheless, traditional games tend to fall into such categories as singing games, counting-out games, chasing games, catching games, seeking games, follow-the-leader games, daring games (such as truth or dare), guessing games, fortune-telling games, dueling games (see DIRTY DOZENS), play-acting games, pretending games (for example, cowboys and Indians, or doctor and patient), ball games, jump rope and other rhythmic games, games of chance, parlor games (such as charades), games of skill (often requiring minimal equipment, such as jacks or CAT'S CRADLE), and board and card games. To what degree folklorists will admit for study recent technology-driven games (computer games and video arcade games) and Dungeons & Dragons fantasy role-playing games remains to be seen.

SUGGESTED READING: Elliott M. Avedon and Brian Sutton-Smith, *The Study of Games* (New York, 1971); Brian Sutton-Smith et al., eds., *Children's Folklore: A Sourcebook* (New York, 1994).

Gardner, Emelyn Elizabeth (1872–1987).

Gardner was an important collector of immigrant (Armenian, Italian, Polish, and Finnish) folklore in Detroit, which she used as the basis of the Folklore Archives at Wayne State University in 1939.

Gardner first became interested in folklore when she was a girl growing up on her family's New York state farm. She was fascinated by the tales told by one of the farmhands. After teaching high school for five years, Gardner took an A.B. degree from the University of Chicago (1902) and there developed an interest in folklore scholarship. She went on to earn a master's degree at the University of Michigan (1915), writing a thesis that was subsequently published as *Folklore from the Schoharie Hills, New York* (1937). After teaching at Ypsilanti State College, Gardner joined the Wayne State University faculty in 1918, teaching folklore and children's literature. Her Detroit folklore was collected in *Ballads and Songs of Southern Michigan* (1939), which she compiled with her student Geraldine Jencks Chickering.

See also: JAMES, THELMA GREY.

SUGGESTED READING: Emelyn Elizabeth Gardner, *Ballads and Songs of Southern Michigan* (1939; reprint ed., Hatboro, Pa., 1967).

Gardner, Gail I. (1892–1988).

Gardner was a cowboy poet, who was born in Prescott, Arizona Territory, and educated at Dartmouth College (1911–14). He operated a small ranch in Prescott until 1960, also serving as the town's postmaster from 1936 to 1957.

Gardner wrote his first poem, "The Sierry Petes, or Tying Knots in the Devil's Tail," in 1917, which was set to music by another cowboy, Bill Simon. This first-person narrative is the story of how Gardner and another cowboy tangled with the devil in Prescott. Gardner sang his lyric at an annual rodeo on Jimmy Minotto's ranch near Prescott in the 1920s. He performed again ("The Moonshine Steer") at the rodeo the following year, and from then on, his annual premieres of new poems were eagerly anticipated events at the rodeo. Gardner published a dozen of his verses in 1935 as *Orejana Bull for Cowboys Only*, which was popular enough to see seven editions. "The Sierry Petes" remains Gardner's best-known poem, especially among working cowboys.

See also: COWBOY SONGS.

Gatto, Victor Joseph (1893–1965).

Gatto was born in New York City's "Little Italy" section. He was orphaned early and spent several years in a Catholic orphanage and school. There his artistic ability was recognized and encouraged, but he did not develop an art-related career. After leaving school, Gatto drifted from one menial job to another and even did a stint as a professional featherweight boxer (1913–18). He joined the U.S. Navy toward the end of World War I, but was dishonorably discharged and then served ten years in a New York state prison (1920–30). After his release, Gatto, without family, found whatever work he could to support himself. In 1938, he visited a Greenwich Village outdoor art show and, learning that there were people willing to pay as much as $600 for a painting, he stopped calling himself Joe Gatto, became Victor Joseph Gatto, and took up his brush. He worked almost exclusively in oil, painting either on Masonite or canvas (not always properly stretched, which gives many of his works a distinctly out-of-plumb look). In 1943, he had a well-received one-person show at the Charles Barzansky Gallery in New York, and he began to sell paintings.

For his subjects, Gatto rarely drew on his gritty life, but, instead, delved into his imagination, producing gentle works of fantasy, many, such as *Eve and the Serpent* (1940s), on naive religious themes. He also painted horse and dog races, landscapes, jungle scenes, and a few portraits.

Despite widespread recognition for the colorful complexity of his fantasy work, Gatto never enjoyed substantial financial success from his art. His abrasive, sometimes violent personality repeatedly defeated him.

Gay folklore.

The study of folklore relating to gay men and lesbian women is an emerging field. Much gay folklore is humorous, including "camp"—basically a humorous exaggeration of the superficial attributes of homosexuality—jokes, FOLK SPEECH, and costume. Camp behavior includes, among men, dressing in outlandish drag, and most gay folklore has sexual overtones. "In-jokes" among gay men and lesbian women often deal with the anxiety of "coming out"—that is, proclaiming one's sexual orientation. In recent years, much gay folklore, both esoteric and exoteric, revolves around AIDS (see AIDS TALES).

The folk speech relating to gay men and lesbian women is rich. Most dramatic has been the manner in which such gay rights groups as Queer Nation have co-opted the straight world's term of derision, "queer," and adopted it as a term of pride. The word *dyke* has undergone a similar, if less dramatic, transformation.

Among gay men as well as lesbian women, coming-out stories are a common form of personal narrative concerning a central life event. Frequently, this narrative is told early in a relationship or a potential relationship.

Beginning in the 1970s, the "gay pride" movement has encouraged not only public celebrations of "gay-ness" and gay culture, but has fostered formal festivals, including many relating to the arts as practiced by gay men and lebian women.

See also: ESOTERIC FOLKLORE; EXOTERIC FOLKLORE.

SUGGESTED READING: Barry Adam, *The Rise and Fall of a Gay and Lesbian Movement* (Boston, 1987); Michael Bronski, *Culture Clash: The Making of a Gay Sensibility* (Boston, 1984); Wayne Dynes, *Encyclopedia of Homosexuality* (New York, 1990); Joseph P. Goodwin, *More Man Than You'll Ever Be: Gay Folklore and Acculturation in Middle America* (Bloomington, Ind., 1989).

Gayton, Anna Hadwick (1899–1977).

Gayton was both an anthropologist and folklorist who studied Native American mythology in California. She was also a student of textiles, California ethnography, and Peruvian archaeology. Educated at the University of California, Berkeley (Ph.D., anthropology, 1928), she carried out ethnographic fieldwork during 1925–30 on the Yokuts and Mono Indians of the southern San Joaquin Valley, publishing nine essays (1929–48) concerning Yokut and Mono myth. In all, Gayton collected more than 200 separate myths and analyzed them not only with regard to their content, but also for their distinctive narrative style.

In 1948, Gayton joined the faculty of the Department of Decorative Arts at Berkeley and published articles on textile analysis. During this period, she also worked in the University of California folklife program, where she championed the comparative approach to folklore studies. In her own work, this resulted in studies of religious festivals among Azorean Portuguese in Gustine, California.

SUGGESTED READING: Ruth M. Boyer, "Anna Hadwick Gayton, 1899–1977," *Journal of American Folklore* 91 (1978), pp. 834–41; Anna Hadwick Gayton, "Folklore and Anthropology," *Utah Humanities Review* 2 (1947), pp. 26–31.

German Americans. German immigration to America spans the colonial period, through the nineteenth century, and into the war-torn twentieth, making German Americans the nation's largest immigrant and immigrant-descendant group. Many of the early German immigrants were members of Protestant religious groups in search of religious freedom. Among the most prominent of these were the Mennonites and Quakers who settled in Pennsylvania toward the end of the seventeenth century, so that, by the middle of the eighteenth century, one-third of the colony was German. (See PENNSYLVANIA GERMANS.) Others sought to escape oppressive governments in the fragmented Germanic states, and still others came in search of economic opportunity after decades of ruinous war during the era of Napoleon.

During the remainder of the nineteenth century, many German immigrants were political refugees and, perhaps for this reason, formed strong and influential political blocs in U.S. towns and cities. In many places, German solidarity was fostered by the *Turnvereine,* German athletic and social clubs. The Germans not only actively cultivated and preserved their political identity, but perpetuated separateness by resisting assimilation into the American "melting pot." In German communities and neighborhoods, German art, song, literature, and general culture was actively encouraged, as was the use of the German language. Anti-German feeling has often run high in various American communities, typically during times of war. During the Civil War, most German Americans who fought, fought on the side of the Union, and in response, many Southerners castigated the German Americans among them by recalling the participation of Hessian mercenaries on the side of the British during the Revolution. During World War I—but less so during World War II—German Americans were often actively persecuted. Aside from outright prejudice, German Americans are sometimes the victims of EXOTERIC FOLKLORE, in particular portraying an overfondness for large quantities of beer and an underappreciation of humor.

German customs maintained by descendants of the immigrants are varied and rich, especially in the areas of language and FOODWAYS. A host of festivals and religious celebrations also abound, including traditions relating to the observance of Lent, Easter, and Christmas. Easter, for example, may be celebrated with traditional Protestant religious ceremonies as well as special bonfires that suggest pagan traditions. St. Nicholas Day, December 6, a traditional holiday, has been conflated with Christmas in some German-American communities.

German culture is celebrated and promoted in many German-American communities by a variety of organizations; however, most German-American cultural organizations tend to emphasize German high culture, especially literature and classical music, rather than folk culture.

See also: IMMIGRANT FOLKLORE.

SUGGESTED READING: Mac E. Barrick, *German-American Folklore* (Little Rock, Ark., 1987); Albert Bernhardt Faust, *The German Element in the United States* (Boston, 1909); La Vein Rippley, *Of German Ways* (1970; reprint ed., New York, 1980).

Geronimo (ca. 1823–1909). This Chiricahua Apache war leader had a reputation as a "wild man" among his own people and, among whites, earned a reputation as a brilliant guerrilla fighter who eluded vastly superior American and Mexican forces during the Apache Wars. With such Native Americans as CRAZY HORSE and SITTING BULL, he is among the legendary Native American figures of the Old West.

Geronimo, whose Apache name, Goyahkla, means "He Who Yawns," was born on the upper Gila River in present-day Arizona or New Mexico. He gained early and enduring renown as a skilled, courageous, and absolutely dauntless warrior. Married seven or nine times, he lived with several Chiricahua bands, depending on which band his current wife was a member of.

Following Chief Mangas Coloradas, young Geronimo and his family settled in Chihuahua, Mexico, where, in a surprise attack on March 5, 1851, Mexican troops killed twenty-one Apaches, including Geronimo's mother, wife, and three children. From this point, Geronimo swore vengeance on the Mexicans and engaged in intensive raiding along the U.S.–Mexican border region. His periods of raiding alternated with relatively quiet periods on the San Carlos (Arizona) reservation. Except for these reservation intervals, Geronimo was a guerrilla and a fugitive from 1865 until his surrender in 1886.

It was in the late phase of the Apache Wars (a phase of the conflict often called Geronimo's Resistance), from about 1881 to 1886, that Geronimo reached the height of his renown. Typically leading fewer than a hundred warriors, Geronimo raided in the American Southwest and in Mexico, repeatedly eluding large army task forces numbering as many as five thousand men. He surrendered at last on September 4, 1886, after leading his latest pursuers on a two thousand-mile, four-month chase. His capitulation to Gen. Nelson A. Miles marked the end of the Apache Wars, and Geronimo, with other Chiricahuas, was sent to prisons in the East. Geronimo was first incarcerated in Florida, then Alabama, and, finally, confined to a reservation attached to Fort Sill, Oklahoma.

Even in his own lifetime, Geronimo was celebrated by the white American public as a warrior hero of legendary proportions. Theodore Roosevelt invited him to appear in his 1905 inaugural parade, with five other Indian leaders. Indeed, Geronimo made numerous public appearances, including at the St. Louis World's Fair of 1904, where he exploited the potential for profit his fame had earned by selling autographed pictures of himself, along with other memorabilia.

Although charismatic and brilliant as a guerrilla leader, Geronimo accomplished little of enduring strategic significance. Certainly, his raiding did not improve the lot of the Apaches, though it did gain legendary status for himself and, perhaps, created respect for the fighting prowess and endurance of the Indian warrior. Curiously, the name of Geronimo was commemorated during World War II, when U.S. Army paratroopers adopted the exclamation "*Geron-*

imo!" as a jumping cry. Geronimo died on the reservation, in 1909, of pneumonia.

SUGGESTED READING: Angie Debo, *Geronimo: The Man, His Time, His Place* (Norman, Okla., 1976).

Gerould, Gordon Hall (1877–1953).

Gerould was the author of two books that exerted significant influence on the study of folklore. *The Grateful Dead: The History of a Folk Story* (1908) was read by students of literature as a model for how to use folklore in the study of literature. It was a landmark in the development of the historic-geographic method of analyzing folktales. *The Ballad of Tradition* (1932) was even more influential. It outlined the theory of communal re-creation, the method by which FRANCIS JAMES CHILD had studied the BALLAD, but which he himself never fully discussed. *The Ballad of Tradition* remains a standard work in the field.

Born in Goffstown, New Hampshire, Gerould took an A.B. at Dartmouth College (1899) and a B.Litt. at Oxford University (1901). He held academic positions at Bryn Mawr College and at Princeton University, where he became Holmes Professor of Belles Lettres and, from 1942 to 1946, chairman of the Department of English. In addition to his two major books on folklore, he wrote a study of medieval saints' legends and translated *Beowulf* and *Sir Gawain and the Green Knight*. He wrote two textbooks, *How to Read Fiction* (1934) and *The Patterns of English and American Fiction* (1942), and four novels.

SUGGESTED READING: Gordon Hall Gerould, *The Ballad of Tradition* (1932; reprint ed., New York, 1974); Gordon Hall Gerould, *The Grateful Dead* (1908; reprint ed., Folcroft, Pa., 1973).

Ghost Dance.

The Ghost Dance was a movement of religious and cultural revitalization, which occurred first among tribes in the Great Basin, Oregon, and California during 1870 and then recurred among the Bannock, Shoshone, Arapaho, Cheyenne, Kiowa, Lakota, and Paviosto. The first Ghost Dance movement began with the vision experience of a Paviosto man named Wodziwob (Gray Hair), who foresaw the coming of a messianic ruler who would transform the world into a paradise, bring eternal life, and eliminate strife between the races. The second Ghost Dance movement, inspired by the first, originated in the vision of a Paviosto named Wovoka (Jack Wilson), who preached a messianic belief in which generations of dead warriors would rise and the white invaders would perish from the earth. This second Ghost Dance movement alarmed many white settlers, citizens, and officials, who acted to extinguish its spread. This ultimately led to the 1890 Massacre at Wounded Knee Creek.

See also: BLACK ELK; NATIVE AMERICANS; SITTING BULL.

Ghost stories.

A ghost is the spirit of the dead returned and made manifest in some form to the living. Folklorists sometimes refer to ghosts as REVENANTS. Ghost stories are very common in folklore and are told by and among children as well as adults. Literary versions abound as well. Typically, when a ghost story is related as true, it is not presented as a firsthand experience, but as something that happened to a friend of a friend. Typically, too, the ghost story is strongly rooted in a particular place—often an old, dilapidated house (a "haunted house"), cemetery, or battlefield, or along lonely highways or ships (there are many tales involving the unquiet spirit of a hapless workman, who had been trapped inside the double hull of a ship under construction, haunting the vessel). Generally, ghosts do not randomly appear, but manifest themselves for a purpose, including redress of some injustice, completion of business left unfinished in life, or, sometimes, to reveal the whereabouts of a hidden treasure. Usually, the ghost appears to someone with whom he or she had a connection in life. The spirit of a loved one returns from the dead: A spouse returns to visit—or haunt—the surviving spouse, a mother or father appears to a child. A murder victim returns to haunt and punish the murderer. Virtually all ghosts are spooky, but most, however disquieting, are relatively harmless; a minority are malevolent and terrorize their victims.

See also: GREEK AMERICANS; MEXICAN AMERICANS; MILITARY FOLKLORE.

SUGGESTED READING: Jean Anderson, *The Haunting of America: Ghost Stories from Our Past* (Boston, 1973); Eliot Wigginton, ed., *Foxfire 2* (Garden City, N.Y., 1973); Fred Siemon, *Ghost Story Index: An Author-Title Index to More Than 2,200 Stories of Ghosts, Horrors, and the Macabre* (San Jose, Calif., 1967).

Ghost towns. The boom-and-bust economy of the nineteenth-century West produced entire settlements rapidly founded in remote locations to exploit a single resource—usually gold, silver, or other mineral—which vanished just as quickly when the local resource was exhausted. Far from established communities and major transport routes, such towns, when abandoned, sometimes became forlorn ghosts—if they weren't obliterated entirely by decamping residents dismantling buildings and salvaging what they could. The bulk of abandoned town sites left faint traces, a few artifacts and the outlines of structural foundations. However, a small number of ghost towns retained a core population of residents who recognized that their communities held an irresistible appeal for western tourists. In places such as Virginia City, Nevada; Central City, Colorado; Tombstone, Arizona; and Calico and Nevada City, California, residents and outside entrepreneurs restored saloons, shops, hotels, and the like expressly to attract visitors. To some degree, these ghost towns are genuine collections of MATERIAL CULTURE artificats and VERNACULAR ARCHITECTURE, but many have been "restored" by dubious means based on doubtful information, and they are more properly called tourist attractions than real ghost towns.

The greatest variety of ghost towns are to be found in Arizona, California, Colorado, Montana, Nevada, New Mexico, and Utah.

See also: DEATH VALLEY.

SUGGESTED READING: Robert Silverberg, *Ghost Towns of the American West* (Athens, Ohio, 1994).

Gibson Mandolin and Guitar Manufacturing Company, Ltd., The. The son an English immigrant, Orville Gibson (1856–1918) began to revolutionize GUITAR and mandolin design in his shop at 114 South Burdick, Kalamazoo, Michigan, in 1896. He believed that the earlier practice of bending flat strips of wood for guitar and mandolin bodies was not as acoustically productive as carving out arches from solid slabs. The approach was a continuation of centuries-old traditions of making bowed instruments in the violin family; the tops were hollowed out of solid pieces of wood; the bridges were high and held in place only by friction, and the strings were attached to a tailpiece, which was anchored to the end block. He did, however, initially prefer an oval sound-hole to f-holes. He also invented the arch-top guitar.

On Ocober 11, 1902, the Gibson Mandolin-Guitar Manufacturing Company, Ltd. was established by an agreement among five Kalamazoo financiers. This "Partnership Association Limited" was created "for the purpose of manufacturing, buying, selling, and dealing in guitars, mandolins, mandolas, violins, lutes, and all other kinds of stringed instruments." Ironically, it was this group of men, not Gibson, who achieved fame for the Gibson name. Gibson himself was not a partner, but signed a contract in which he committed his name and single patent (for a mandolin design) to the company for a fee of $2,500, and also agreed to be advisor to the management and to train workers in the techniques of tuning tops and carrying out other steps in instrument making. When the firm incorporated in 1904 with $12,000 capital stock, Gibson himself was not one of the twenty-four charter stockholders and apparently never became an officer or a shareholder in the company. On April 12, 1915, Orville Gibson negotiated an agreement to get paid a monthly royalty for the rest of his life.

Orville's spirit, however, continued to be felt as a missionary zeal in the proud young company, which proclaimed, "The Reckless Indifference of Some Teachers to the Gibson Is Because the Gibson Is So Far Advanced of Some Teachers' Ideals."

During World War I the company thrived with the production of low-priced Army and Navy Special mandolins. Lloyd Loar joined the firm in 1919. He was a gifted acoustic engineer, mandolinist, and composer—in short the Stradivarius of Kalamazoo. He created the great F-5 mandolin, later used brilliantly by BILL MONROE and a host of other virtuoso mandolinists. Though Loar's signature appears from 1922 to 1924 only on the Style 5 instruments, he is given credit for important innovations actually devised by his staff—the elevated fretboard, the elevated finger rest, the intonation-adjustable bridge, the f-hole design, and the floating head, ball-bearing rim, and tone tube of the Mastertone BANJO.

Between the world wars, ukuleles and banjos continued to be popular, but the guitar became an increasingly essential instrument among singing cowboys, who tended to play flat tops with round sound holes. The arched-top f-hole guitar suited dance needs, however, because it could cut through the loud sounds of horn players. Guitars began to take on more importance in popular music of all kinds. During the Depression the company introduced a lower-priced line, the Kalamazoo—plain but well made.

In 1944 the Chicago Musical Company acquired control of the company and invested heavily to enable large scale expansion. Already a world leader, Gibson was on the verge of doubling and redoubling its output in the guitar-hungry market after World War II. Since then, the company has survived all the changes in needs for special guitars, like the hollow-body arch top with pick-ups favored by JAZZ and some BLUES players, the solid guitars preferred in rhythm and blues and ROCK 'N' ROLL, and the large boomy guitars for COUNTRY MUSIC. It has also weathered changes in ownership, competition from Japan and Korea, economic ups-and-downs (including a long downward slide from the late sixties to the eighties). It is now the most diversified and admired guitar company in America.

See also: FOLK MUSIC.

SUGGESTED READING: Walter Carter, *Gibson Guitars: 100 Years of an American Icon* (New York, 1996).

Gordon, Robert Winslow (1888–1961).

Gordon was an important early folk-song collector. Educated at Harvard, he taught at the University of California, Berkeley, then returned to Harvard for graduate study. Backed by a Sheldon Fellowship, Gordon collected southern folk songs during the early 1920s, using portable recording equipment he himself had designed and assembled. Operating out of Asheville, North Carolina, Gordon recorded some 1,000 cylinders. In 1926, he settled in his wife's hometown of Darien, Georgia, and set about recording the narratives of ex-slaves and African-American spirituals and chants.

Gordon's relatively brief teaching experience at Berkeley had left him with some negative impressions of the academic study of folklore and folk songs. When he published, he chose popular outlets rather than the scholarly journals and, from 1923 to 1927, edited a column called "Old Songs Men Have Sung" in *Adventure* magazine.

Gordon served as the first archivist of the Archive of American Folk Song at the Library of Congress, beginning in 1928 and using his own collection of several thousand songs as the core of the collection. Within a few years, however, Gordon was dismissed as director of the archives because of his unscholarly ways. Gordon maintained an association with the American Folklore Society and participated in folk-song festivals, but he continued to shun publication in professional journals. As a result, he is remembered chiefly for the songs he collected and recorded, rather than for any analysis or discussion of them.

SUGGESTED READING: Debora Kodish, *Good Friends and Bad Enemies: Robert Winslow Gordon and the Study of American Folksong* (Urbana, Ill., 1986).

Gospel music.

Gospel music developed from conventional Protestant hymnody during the nineteenth century among evangelical groups emphasizing a personal and emotionally charged approach to religion. Thus gospel hymns are typically first-person lyrics dealing in a direct and personal way with the singer's relationship to Christ and his feelings about salvation. Structurally, gospel hymns consist of verse and chorus set to strongly contrasting tunes.

By the end of the nineteenth century, American gospel music tended to divide at the Mason-Dixon line. Northern gospel composers such as Fanny Crosby conceived the songs along the lines of contemporary sentimental commercial songs. In the South, SHAPE-NOTE SINGING traditions predominated, often influenced by African-American camp-meeting songs. It is the southern tradition that survived into the twentieth century, not only among Baptist and Pentecostal denominations in the South, but in the repertoire of BLUEGRASS and professional gospel groups.

It was not until the twentieth century that African-American composers, such as THOMAS A. DORSEY, began writing gospel songs. The gospel style has continued as a vital performing tradition in African-American communities, in church as well as in popular entertainment venues. Many African-American BLUES and soul musicians trace their roots to gospel.

See also: AFRICAN AMERICANS; FOLK MUSIC; JACKSON, MAHALIA; KING, B. B.; MACON, DAVID (UNCLE DAVE); VAUGHAN, JAMES D.

SUGGESTED READING: Don Cusic, *The Sound of Light* (Bowling Green, Ohio, 1990); Bernice Johnson Reagon, *We'll Understand It Better By and By: Pioneering African American Gospel Composers* (Washington, D.C., 1992).

Graffiti. Most of the public calls these writings, symbols, and other inscriptions chalked or painted on exterior walls and other surfaces (including subway cars, railroad cars, and trucks) vandalism. A minority, including some folklorists, consider it admirable self-expression, at its best a kind of folk art. Certainly, a number of recent "fine artists," including the late Keith Haring, have taken inspiration from graffiti. But the point of graffiti is not artistic self-expression, but *illicit* self-expression, sometimes artfully contrived, but always created at the risk of getting caught and punished. Graffiti is, therefore, an inherently subversive activity.

The range of graffiti is extremely varied. One might classify as graffiti the drawings on prehistoric cave walls or the petroglyphs found in such Native American sites as the Canyon de Chelly in Arizona as well as the inscriptions on rest-room walls. Indeed, it was lavatory "folk epigraphy" that first captured scholarly attention (the folklorist Alan Dundes called it "latrinalia"). While scholars such as Walker Read (*Lexical Evidence from Folk Epigraphy in Western North America,* 1935) studied lavatory inscriptions as examples of FOLK SPEECH, others have collected it as examples of folk humor.

Some graffiti is territorial, such as the inscriptions one finds on trees or rocks at some popular natural attraction or in the middle of nowhere. Perhaps the most famous single piece of graffiti in American history is DANIEL BOONE's inscription on a Tennessee tree: "D. Boon Cilled A. Bar in THE YEAR 1760." Other territorial graffiti includes "tagging," usually inscribing a sign, symbol, or stylized initials on walls or on the outsides of subway cars using spray paint or a broad-tipped felt marker. The figure "belongs" to a "tagger," who, if he or she is persistent and sufficiently artful, becomes known to other taggers. Tagging may also be a street gang-related activity, a means by which gang members stake out their "turf."

Graffiti may also spark dialogue. Close examination of the graffiti in many public rest rooms often reveals a pattern of one writer answering another. If those who abhor graffiti classify it as an antisocial activity, it nevertheless has often served a very social purpose. During WORLD WAR II, the simple figure of the top of a head,

Native American petroglyphs are among the earliest forms of graffiti. This photograph was taken in South Mountain Park, Phoenix, Arizona, during the 1940s.

Graffiti has influenced artists of all kinds. Jeff Short poses in front of one of his wall paintings, Tucson, Arizona, 1996.

with eyes and nose, peering over a line representing a wall, accompanied by the inscription "Kilroy was here," became almost ubiquitous—a sign of some kind of solidarity.

A highly specialized form of graffiti was developed by American hoboes (see HOBO FOLKLORE). Using chalk, hoboes would inscribe messages of guidance (for example, "generous homeowner") and warning ("mean dog") on fence posts and walls. The messages consisted of arcane symbols, supposedly intelligible only to other members of the hobo fraternity.

For most of the twentieth century, at least, graffiti was almost universally regarded as vandalism; however, in New York City, beginning in the 1970s, elaborate, highly stylized, often very skillful spray-painted graffiti appeared on subway cars and on building walls. The so-called New York Style became a subject of controversy; some artists and art critics, as well as urban sociologists, praised the work as an extraordinary combination of daring self-expression (decorating a subway car is very dangerous work) and urban folk spirit, while city authorities declared war on what they perceived as an epidemic of vandalism.

See also: JAZZ; KOREAN WAR; POETRY, FOLK; ROCK 'N' ROLL.

SUGGESTED READING: Crag Castleman, *Getting Up: Subway Graffiti in New York* (Cambridge, Mass., 1982); Robert Reisner, *Graffiti: Two Thousand Years of Wall Writing* (Chicago, 1971).

Graham, Martha (1894–1991). One of the giants of twentieth-century American dance, Graham drew on Native American traditions for some of her best-known work and on general American folk material for her *Appalachian Spring,* the music for which she commissioned from AARON COPLAND in 1944.

Graham was born in Pennsylvania and grew up in Santa Barbara, California. She studied at the Los Angeles Denishawn School of Ruth St. Denis and Ted Shawn, where she was exposed to a range of dance traditions, including folk traditions and those of Native Americans. Graham performed with the Denishawn company from 1916 to 1923, then left for New York in 1923 and taught at the Eastman School of Music, in Rochester, New York, from 1924 to 1926. She performed in New York beginning in 1926 and was at first well-received, but her more experimental works, which she created during the late 1920s and through the middle 1930s, were often scorned by public and critics alike.

While much of Graham's most characteristic choreographic work uses elements of classical mythology and Greek tragedy, she also created dances from American folk life and frontier life,

Martha Graham dances in Aaron Copland's Appalachian Spring, *1944.*

the most famous of which was *Appalachian Spring*. By 1970, Graham retired, but continued to create dances and teach.

See also: APPALACHIA; DANCE, FOLK; TAMARIS, HELEN.

SUGGESTED READING: Don McDonach, *Martha Graham* (New York, 1973).

Grand Ole Opry. The mecca of COUNTRY MUSIC, the Grand Ole Opry is both a performing venue (now just outside of Nashville, Tennessee) and a longtime national radio and television broadcast from that venue. The radio program (at first called *WSM Barn Dance*) began weekly broadcasts in December 1925, playing what was then called hillbilly music. By 1926, it was called *The Grand Ole Opry*, a name that distinguished

it from *The National Barn Dance*, broadcast from WLS radio in Chicago. The Nashville show was originated by radio announcer George Dewey Hay, who had been the announcer for *The National Barn Dance*. For *Opry* broadcasts, Hay assumed the persona of "the Solemn Ol' Judge" and acted as the program's master of ceremonies.

The Grand Ole Opry soon became the most popular country music radio show and was also successful, later, on television. Exposure on the show could make a country career. In its earliest days, *The Grand Ole Opry*'s single most important star was UNCLE DAVE MACON, singer of rural BALLADS, but the program soon showcased a wide range of hillbilly music, including string bands, cowboy music, western swing, and the progressively more commercial country genres of the 1940s through the present.

Beginning in 1941, *Opry* broadcasts originated live, before an audience, at the Ryman Auditorium in downtown Nashville. The show moved to the vast Opryland amusement park in 1974. It was largely because of the influence of the Grand Ole Opry that Nashville became the center of the popular country music industry.

See also: AUTOHARP; BLUEGRASS; CARTER FAMILY, THE; CLINE, PATSY; CLOWER, JERRY; MONROE, BILL; SCRUGGS, EARL; TUBB, EARNEST; WILLIAMS, HANK.

SUGGESTED READING: The Country Music Foundation, *Country: The Music and the Musicians* (New York, 1988).

Great Diamond Hoax. One of the most impressive swindles in the history of the American West, the Great Diamond Hoax quickly assumed a place in popular nineteenth-century lore. The scam was the work of two con men from Kentucky, Philip Arnold and his cousin John Slack. Early in 1872, posing as legitimate, if naive, prospectors, they brought a bag of uncut diamonds to the Bank of California in San Francisco and attempted to deposit it as if it were cash. Bank director William C. Ralston and other California financiers quickly learned of the two rubes and determined to gain control of what was apparently a western diamond field. Such a prospect was difficult to resist, especially for bankers and financiers. The year 1872 was not a hopeful one: a broad-based economic depression was impending, and the major gold rushes had petered out. The focus of people all over the world had turned from the gold fields of the American West to the news of fabulous diamond discoveries in South Africa. The popular reasoning was that, if the West had already yielded so much mineral largesse in the form of gold, why not diamonds, too?

Arnold and Slack took a representative of Ralston and the other potential investors, had the man blindfolded, and escorted him on a circuitous journey by train and on horseback to a remote location in northwestern Colorado. There the blindfold was removed, and the representative was shown a "natural" deposit of diamonds as well as rubies. The representative obtained samples, and the prudent San Franciscans had them examined by Tiffany and Company, which certified their authenticity and value. At this, the tycoons formed the San Francisco and New York Mining and Commercial Company, capitalized it to the tune of $10 million, and paid Arnold and Slack some $600,000—surely, they reasoned, a bargain.

Word of the enterprise soon leaked, touching off an avalanche of rumor and speculation. Guides purporting to know the location of the di-amond fields sold their services to all comers. A number of the "guides" were employed by the new mining company in an effort to deliberately deceive would-be prospectors. Nevertheless, no fewer than twenty-five mining companies were formed, representing $200 million in capital, all determined to extract precious gems from the western soil.

During this period, Clarence King was leading the United States Geological Exploration of the Fortieth Parallel. Intrigued by the rumors of diamonds, he was able to identify the site of the field, and, being a geologist, was also able to prove that the site had been "salted," deliberately strewn with the gems. The San Francisco and New York Mining and Commercial Company was forced to admit that it had been duped. Ralston and the other syndicate organizers eventually repaid their stockholders' losses, and the ever-ingenious Arnold and Slack escaped prosecution. Arnold returned to Kentucky, where he spent his share of the $600,000 lavishly, though he did make a $150,000 settlement with his victims. In 1878, he was badly wounded in a duel, recovered, then succumbed to pneumonia shortly after his convalescence. Slack sunk into increasing obscurity, ultimately becoming a coffin maker in the town of White Oaks, New Mexico.

The public—at least the noninvesting portion of it—was hardly outraged by the Great Diamond Hoax. If anything, easterners and westerners alike took pleasure in contemplating the tweaked noses of big-moneyed San Francisco tycoons. Even more, people relished a real-life incarnation of the western TALL-TALE tradition, which had always thrived on exaggeration, confidence scheming, hot air, and the ready greed of listeners eager for wealth and enchantment.

SUGGESTED READING: Bruce A. Woodward, *Diamonds in the Salt* (Boulder, Colo., 1967).

Greco, José (1918–). Greco popularized Spanish folk dance—especially flamenco—in the United States. He was born in Montorio nei Frentani, Italy, and was raised briefly in Seville, Spain, before his family moved with him to Brooklyn. There he studied with Helene Veola and worked as a specialty dancer in New York nightclubs. The famed ethnic ballet dancer La Argentinita saw one of his performances and engaged him as a partner for two years, until she died in 1945. With her, Greco appeared in such modern ballets as *El Amor Brujo, Bolero,* and *Pictures of Goya.* After La Argentinita's death, Greco performed in Spain with her sister, Pilar Lopez, in the Ballet Español of Madrid. He subsequently formed his own company, the Ballets y Bailes de España, in 1949, and then the José Greco Dance Company, with which he toured Europe, Asia, and the Americas.

World famous by the early 1950s, Greco's popularity was greatly enhanced by appearances in several Hollywood films and on television. He began a gradual retirement from performance in the 1960s and, in 1971, formed the Foundation for Hispanic Dance, an educational institution to preserve and present Hispanic folk dance. Although most widely known as a performer, Greco was a prolific choreographer as well.

See also: DANCE, FOLK.

SUGGESTED READING: José Greco, *Gypsy in My Soul: The Autobiography of José Greco* (New York, 1977).

Greek Americans. Greeks are relatively recent immigrants to the United States, first arriving in significant numbers during the 1910s, and settling for the most part in eastern and midwestern urban areas. Few national groups have a deeper background of folk tradition and mythology than the Greeks. Greek Americans give expression to their heritage through FOODWAYS, dancing, and folk music played on traditional instruments, including the *bouzouki,* a mandolin-like instrument that has lent its name to the style of dance music made familiar to non-Greeks through such popular channels as the 1964 film *Zorba the Greek.* At Greek ethnic festivals, traditional musicians often accompany group dancers, who perform traditional circle and chain dances.

SUPERSTITION plays an important part in Greek folklife, especially among older Greek Americans. Belief in the EVIL EYE is common, as are methods of warding off its ill effects, including the wearing or eating of garlic and the avoidance of looking too admiringly at anyone or anything, lest the evil eye be inadvertently cast and harm come to the object of one's attention.

Greeks traditionally relish oral narrative and enjoy telling stories and listening to them. Among the traditional cycle of folktales still told by Greek Americans are those concerning the TRICKSTER Nastradin Hodja. More ominous are GHOST STORIES involving *vrykólakas,* a corpse that periodically walks about us, perpetrating poltergeist-like annoyances as well as acts of outright violence.

See also: IMMIGRANT FOLKLORE.

SUGGESTED READING: Robert A. Georges, *Greek-American Folk Beliefs and Narratives* (New York, 1980); Robert A. Georges, "Greek Americans," in Jan Harold Brunvand, ed., *American Folklore: An Encyclopedia* (New York, 1996).

Greene, Madelynne (1908–1970). Greene was active in the San Francisco Bay area as a teacher, scholar, and advocate of folk dancing. Trained in traditional ballet, she turned to folk forms in 1942, after she saw a performance by the Changs International Folk Dancers in San Francisco. She founded and directed the International Dance Theater in San Francisco, and spent her career traveling extensively, especially in the United States and Canada, giving classes in folk dance performance and forms. She researched the folk dances of Spain, Mallorca, Portugal, France, China, Hawaii, Novarra, Ukraine, Canary Islands, Italy, Poland, and Japan, notating, studying, documenting, and performing a host of diverse forms. For some forty years, she was regarded by many folk-dance enthusiasts and professionals as the nucleus and driving force of the folk-dance community in the United States.

Greenfield Village. An outdoor "living history museum" consisting of approximately one hundred historic buildings on two hundred acres in the Detroit suburb of Dearborn, Michigan,

The workshop in which Henry Ford tinkered together his early internal combustion engines and automobiles is one of many historical buildings that was transported to Greenfield Village.

HENRY FORD founded the village in 1933, near where he had been born. There he relocated or reconstructed important buildings from all over the United States, including the birthplaces of individuals Ford deemed quintessential Americans, among them William Holmes McGuffey, Noah Webster, Luther Burbank, and Orville and Wilbur Wright. The village also includes THOMAS A. EDISON's New Jersey and Florida laboratories, the home of STEPHEN FOSTER, and the courthouse where ABRAHAM LINCOLN argued cases when he was a Springfield, Illinois, lawyer. Also on-site is the Henry Ford Museum.

Greenfield Village is in large part an expression of Ford's idiosyncratic, biased, and even xenophobic vision of the American past; however, it remains an important center for the study and exhibition of American MATERIAL CULTURE and nineteenth-century folklife.

SUGGESTED READING: Alan Axelrod, ed., *The Colonial Revival in America* (New York, 1985); Reynold M. Wik, *Henry Ford and Grass-Roots America* (Ann Arbor, Mich., 1972).

Greenway, John (1919–1991). Born John Groeneweg in Liverpool, England, Greenway immigrated to the United States and was naturalized a U.S. citizen. He took his Ph.D. at the University of Pennsylvania, writing a dissertaion that was subsequently published in 1953 as *American Folksongs of Protest*. Greenway taught English at Rutgers University and the University of Denver, then secured an appointment in anthropology at the University of Colorado.

The range of Greenway's intellectual interests was staggering. He published nineteen books on such diverse topics as James Joyce's *Ulysses*

(1922), *Folklore of the Great American West* (1969), and works on the aboriginal people of Australia. He was also editor of *Southwestern Lore* from 1959 to 1963, *Western Folklore* (during 1960–61), and the *Journal of American Folklore* from 1964 to 1968. For a period late in the 1950s and early in the 1960s, Greenway earned a measure of fame as a folksinger specializing in protest songs.

See also: Campa, Arthur Leon.

Gremlins.

Imps or demons that cause problems with (primarily military) aircraft, gremlins were widely discussed among military aircrews during World War II, and mechanical failures and other difficulties that could not be otherwise explained were regularly attributed to them, tongue in cheek, but with an unmistakable edge of seriousness, too. By the middle years of the war, U.S. and British aircrews even provided descriptions of gremlins, which were depicted as about twenty inches tall and looking like a jackrabbit crossed with a bull terrier. Some descriptions clothed the gremlins ("green breeches and red jackets, ornamented with neat ruffles" as well as spats and top hats). Other descriptions depict them more frankly as demons: six inches tall with horns and black leather suction boots. Gremlins were not seen as primitive beings, but as technically proficient and expertly versed in flight mechanics. They also possessed superhuman strength.

While the heyday of the gremlin was World War II, there is evidence that it was talked about by the aircrews of World War I as well. The origin of the word *gremlin* is itself obscure; etymologists conjecture that it derives from a blend of *gruaimin,* an Irish word meaning a bad-tempered little fellow, and the modern word *goblin.*

Groundhog Day.

Groundhog Day occurs on February 2. Neither a sentimental nor an official holiday, its observance consists of watching a groundhog (woodchuck) come out of its burrow, presumably to check the weather. If the sun is shining and the groundhog sees its shadow, one can be sure of six more weeks of winter. If the day is overcast, and the groundhog therefore fails to see his shadow, winter is bound to end early.

Groundhog Day is a quaint (or kitschy) tradition in the United States, kept alive largely by national television and radio news "fluff" coverage of the emergence of "Punxsutawney Phil," the official Groundhog Day groundhog, who makes his home in Punxsutawney, Pennsylvania, where he is feted as a celebrity and his emergence is part of a townwide festival. There are local variations in the observance of Groundhog Day. In parts of Missouri, Arkansas, and Illinois, observance takes place on February 14 (despite a resolution of the Missouri Legislature fixing February 2 as the official day of observance). Nor is Groundhog Day an original American holiday. It apparently evolved from European Candlemas Day (February 2) traditions, which mark the vernal equinox and the beginning of the growing season. The French Candlemas belief is that a bear returns to its cave for forty days if the sun shines when it emerges on February 2. Germans look for the emergence of the badger and whether or not it sees its shadow.

Groundhog Day, like its European Candlemas parallels, is an aspect of WEATHER FOLKLORE, and, while it is a trivial occasion now, it was at one time regarded as a predictor of the quality of the planting season. If the animal prognosticator indicated a speedy end to winter, prospects for planting were good.

SUGGESTED READING: Hennig Cohen and Tristram P. Coffin, eds., *The Folk-lore of American Holidays* (Detroit, 1987).

Guitar. The six-string acoustic guitar appeared in the late eighteenth century, developing out of the five-course double-string Renaissance instrument. The usual tuning, from high to low, is e, b, g, d, a, e, and the instrument can be played with a plectrum, with thumb and forefinger, or in the classically derived style of thumb and three fingers, often in folk music and jazz with a pick on each finger.

At the turn of the century THE GIBSON MANDOLIN AND GUITAR COMPANY, LTD. developed a style of arch-topped guitar with several features modeled on the cello: an angled neck, a high bridge, a tailpiece, and, in the early models, bracing of the top that roughly corresponds to the bass bar and sound post of bowed instruments. Jazz musicians and some old-time performers like Maybelle Carter (see CARTER FAMILY, THE) found this style congenial, picking a Gibson L-5.

The round hole flat-top continued to be the favorite until beginning in the 1930s, when pickups on acoustics and solid-body electrics began to make inroads into the guitar scene. Fascinated by the music of Hawaiian guitarists in vaudeville, many American folk guitarists adopted their slide guitar approach in which the guitar is tuned to an open chord stopped by a metal sliding bar, while the guitar is held flat on the performer's lap. With the advent of amplification, a simpler form appeared, the lap steel, a fingerboard on a solid wooden base with a pickup. The slide bar continued as before.

In the 1920s, the Doypera brothers invented the Dobro, a hollow-body in which the bridge rests on an internal metal resonator hidden by a metal cover plate. The result is a much more projective sound, and the instrument lends itself either to slide or fretted chord playing. The wooden-body Dobro appealed to white country musicians, whereas African Americans favored the all-metal instrument. The latter group of performers also developed a much more versatile slide style called "bottleneck" (originally using the neck of a Coca-Cola bottle), in which a slippery, hollow object such as a bottleneck, thimble, or automobile bushing is fitted on the little finger of the left hand, the guitar is held diagonally across the body in the traditional way, and the performer can fret with his fingers part of the time and at other times use the slide. This is a technically brilliant approach, which greatly appealed to many BLUES performers of the Mississippi Delta.

As electrified instruments became more popular, slide guitar evolved into a much more technically elaborate instrument, the pedal steel, with up to three fingerboards with ten strings on each and an elaborate network of foot pedals, with which the player could slide pitches upward or downward and achieve complex effects. The instrument has been a favorite of commercial country bands since the 1950s.

See also: BLUEGRASS; GUTHRIE, WOODY (WOODROW WILSON); RODGERS, JIMMIE.

SUGGESTED READING: Walter Carter, *Gibson Guitars: 100 Years of an American Icon* (New York, 1996); George Gruhn and Walter Carter, *Accoustic Guitars and other Fretted Instruments: A Photographic History* (New York, 1997); Tom Wheeler, *American Guitars: An Illustrated History* (New York, 1992).

Gullah. Linguists believe that this Creole dialect, based on English as spoken by former African-American slaves and their descendants living on and near the Sea Islands of South Carolina, is a significant influence on BLACK ENGLISH. The name *Gullah* comes from the West African tribal name of the people who came to live on the Sea Islands, the Gullahs. Also present on the islands are descendants of the Geechee tribe. The Gullah dialect is built on pidgin English that is based on the speech of seventeenth- and eighteenth-century British colonists and that is combined with vocabulary and some grammatical forms from such West African languages as Vai, Mende, Twi, Ewe, Hausa, Yoruba, Ibo, and Kikongo. Gullah is characterized by unique features of phonology, grammar, syntax, and vocabulary. In general, Gullah simplifies English words and syntactical and grammatical structures. Speakers do not have the characteristic southern drawl, and their intonation echoes African origins more strongly than English influences. A few Gullah words have passed into mainstream English, including goober ("peanut"), GUMBO (which means "okra" in Gullah, okra being a key ingredient in gumbo), juke (as in jukebox or juke joint), and voodoo (the Gullah interpretation of the Ewe *vodu,* Fon *vodun,* and Louisiana French *voudou*).

See also: AFRICAN AMERICANS.

Gumbo. One of the most interesting of folk foods, gumbo is a soup thickened with okra or filé. Filé is powdered dry sassafras leaves and was introduced to Cajun and Creole cuisine by the Choctaw Indians, who traded it at the French Market in New Orleans. Gumbo is derived from *ngombo,* the Bantu word for okra. On the foundation of okra or filé (or both) are laid a variety of herbs, spices, vegetables (the "holy trinity"—onion, celery, and bell pepper), seafood, and meat. Gumbo is a southern dish, particularly identified with Louisiana, where it is prepared in characteristic (and different) ways by Creoles and Cajuns. Creole gumbo is less hotly spiced than Cajun gumbo and is not as thick.

The word *gumbo* has been borrowed to denote Mississippi mud and as the name of the patois of French and African languages formerly spoken by New Orleans blacks.

See also: GULLAH.

Gummere, Francis Barton (1855–1919). Gummere was a distinguished literary scholar and philologist, who, despite his achievements as a scholar, is best known in folklore circles as the chief apostle of the now generally repudiated theory of communal origins for the traditional BALLAD. His *Germanic Origins* and *The Beginnings of Poetry,* both of which deal with the origins of poetry and of the ballad, are based on a flawed reading of the Grimm brothers' philological writings about fairy tales and hold that all poetic expression is rooted in everyman rather than in the work of individual writers or composers. This concept misinformed ballad scholarship from the turn of the century through much of the 1930s.

Gummere was a native of Haverford, Pennsylvania, and was educated at Haverford College (A.B., 1872; A.M., 1875) and at Harvard College, where he was a student of FRANCIS JAMES CHILD. After further study at the universities of Strasbourg, Berlin, and Freiburg, he took his Ph.D. at Freiburg. He was professor of English at Haverford College from 1887 to 1919. His work on the origin of the ballad was part of his lifelong interest in the origins of literature generally.

See also: BARRY, PHILLIPS; BELDEN, HENRY MARVIN.

SUGGESTED READING: Francis Barton Gummere, "The Ballad and Communal Poetry," *Child Memorial Volume, Harvard Studies and Notes in Philology* 5 (1897), pp. 40–56; Francis Barton Gummere, *The Popular Ballad* (Boston and New York, 1907).

Gunfighter, western. The oral folklore relating to the gunfighters of the "Old West" was quickly co-opted by such MASS MEDIA vehicles as dime novels (in the nineteenth century), movies (by the early twentieth century), and television (by the mid-twentieth century). All of these media tended to reflect popular sympathy for the western outlaw (who was often perceived as a latter-day Robin Hood), who stole from the institutions ordinary folk, especially westerners, hated: big, heartless, banks and the even bigger and more rapacious railroads. While some gunfighters, such as John Wesley Hardin (1853–95) were depicted as simply bad men, in effect homicidal maniacs, most were portrayed as "good bad men," hardened outlaws who nevertheless followed their own code of justice and who were often chivalrous to the weak, the poor, and to women and children. More specific stereotypes can be discerned in the folklore and popular tales associated with gunfighters. In addition to the homicidal maniacs and the "good bad men" are the peace officers who sometimes used their office to exact personal vengeance (Wild Bill Hickok and WYATT EARP) and the strong but peaceable marshal, who seldom resorted to his guns (Bill Tilghman and Bear River Tom Smith, for instance).

Not surprisingly, exaggeration characterizes much of the lore surrounding gunfighters. First is the notion of the quick draw and the idea that gunfights were "showdowns" or duels in which opponents faced each other from opposite ends of a dusty western street and vied to draw and fire first. In reality, very few western gunfights were duels; most were murders from ambush. Moreover, nineteenth-century handguns were notoriously inaccurate weapons, and gunfighters prized accuracy over speed; indeed, few gunfighters carried their weapons in a hip holster, but, instead, tucked them into a hip pocket, a coat pocket,

Gunfighter folklore in a B-movie: Warner Baxter (left) *with his stunt stand-in on the set of* Robin Hood of El Dorado, *1936.*

belt, or waistband. The speed of the draw was, for the most part, irrelevant.

The second area of exaggeration concerns the number of kills attributed to the legendary figures. BILLY THE KID supposedly killed twenty-one men ("not counting Mexicans"); in fact, he killed four in sixteen gunfights, although he may have assisted in the killing of another five men. Jesse James, perhaps the most famous of all outlaws, killed only one man in nine gunfights and may have assisted in the killing of three more, while Wyatt Earp killed none in five gunfights, though he may have assisted in the killing of five men. Indeed, while nineteenth-century mining and cattle towns were certainly raucous and often virtually lawless, they were less violent places, on the whole, than certain neighborhoods in many modern American cities.

Finally, as is true of many figures who assume near-mythic proportions, gunfighters inspire survival legends. Rumors that Billy the Kid was still alive were circulated well into the twentieth century, as were stories about the survival of Jesse James. Interestingly, belief in the survival of Butch Cassidy is probably justified. While it is probable that his partner, the Sundance Kid, was killed in a 1908 shootout in Bolivia, most historians believe that Butch Cassidy escaped, surfacing in Michigan as William Thaddeus Phillips, a mechanical engineer from Des Moines, Iowa. Phillips died of cancer in 1937.

See also: JAMES, FRANK AND JESSE; CASSIDY, BUTCH AND THE SUNDANCE KID.

SUGGESTED READING: Bill O'Neal, *Encyclopedia of Western Gunfighters* (Norman, Okla., 1979).

Guthrie, Woody (Woodrow Wilson) (1912–1967).

Itinerant folksinger and composer, Guthrie was born in Okemah, Oklahoma, where his upbringing was economically impoverished but rich in folk tradition. He absorbed a diverse array of folk songs and BALLADS from his parents and others. Seized by a wanderlust early on, he traveled the Southwest doing odd jobs. When he picked up some basic GUITAR chords from his Uncle Jeff in Pampa, Texas, the two joined forces as a hillbilly band to entertain at local events. Woody's restlessness brought him to California in 1937, where he was one of a large crowd of Okies escaping from the Dust Bowl. He got a job singing on a Los Angeles radio station with his cousin Jack, and in a short time, Lefty Lou (Maxine Crissman) joined their group. In the early part of his career, Guthrie was essentially a

hillbilly singer, his guitar playing much influenced by Maybelle Carter's pick-and-scratch technique. He depended heavily on the songs of the CARTER FAMILY, JIMMIE RODGERS, and standard commercial hillbilly singers. When he composed his own songs, it was generally a matter of new wine in old bottles, setting his own original lyrics to existing tunes. For example, he designed "Oklahoma Hills" to be sung to the tune of "The Girl I Loved in Sunny Tennessee"; and "The Philadelphia Lawyer" was set to the tune of "The Jealous Lover." His most famous song, "This Land Is Your Land," was set to the melody of "Little Darling of Mine."

As his sympathies were aroused for homeless, suffering migrant workers, Okies like himself, Guthrie became a radical, pouring out his indignation at social injustice in a series of great passionate protest songs, "Talking Dust Bowl Blues," "I Ain't Got No Home in This World Anymore," and one of the greatest American songs, his eloquent tribute to the migrant pickers of fruit, "Pastures of Plenty," which ends on a note of lyrical affirmation:

> It's always we've rambled, that river and I.
> All along your green valley I'll work till I die.
> My land I'll defend with my life if it be,
> For my Pastures of Plenty will always be free.

When he moved to New York in 1940 he was widely accepted as a great singer and composer of protest songs—over a thousand of them—including numerous classics like "Tom Joad," a tribute to the protagonist of John Steinbeck's *The Grapes of Wrath*; "This Train Is Bound for Glory"; "Union Burying Ground"; and "Blowing Down This Old Dusty Road." He had a lasting effect on a generation of songwriters such as BOB DYLAN, PETE SEEGER, Tom Paxton, and Phil Ochs. His son Arlo has carried on Woody's tradition, most notably in the brilliant song "Alice's

Restaurant." And Woody's own "This Land Is My Land" has become our unofficial national anthem:

> This land is your land, this land is my land,
> From California to the New York island,
> From the redwood forest to the Gulf Stream
>   waters,
> This land was made for you and me.

In 1954 Woody was hospitalized for Huntington's chorea, a hereditary wasting nerve disease (of which his mother had died). The end came in 1967, by which time he could no longer walk, talk, focus his eyes, or feed himself.

See also: ASCH, MOSES; FOLK MUSIC; HILL, JOE; LOMAX, ALAN; TERRY, SONNY.

SUGGESTED READING: Woody Guthrie, *Bound for Glory* (reprint ed., New York, 1995); Janelle Yates, *Woody Guthrie: American Balladeer* (Staten Island, N.Y., 1995).

H

Hair of the dog that bit you. In Great Britain and North America, this phrase is used to describe curing a hangover by taking a small drink of whatever made one drunk in the first place. In this sense, the phrase may be traced to the sixteenth century (it occurs in John Heywood's *Proverbes* of 1546). "Hair of the dog" has also been used in folk medicine (see MEDICINE, FOLK) to cure an actual wound inflicted by "the dog that bit you."

Halloween. Halloween, also known as All Hallow's Eve, is celebrated on October 31, the eve of All Saints' Day. In the United States, since the early twentieth century, Halloween has become largely a children's holiday, a time for dressing in costume and walking door to door "trick or treating"—soliciting a treat (usually candy) in return for not playing a trick (which may be a prank or even a minor act of vandalism). In recent years, the holiday has also become popular with young adults as an occasion to attend costume parties. American Halloween has its origin in the festival of Samhain eve, observed on October 31 to celebrate the end of summer and to usher in the New Year in pagan Britain and Ireland. On Samhain day, November 1, the ordinarily invisible world of gods and spirits was believed to be made manifest to humans, the spirits of the dead walked the earth, and the pagan gods on this day played tricks on people. It was a festival fraught with fear and apprehension, and people customarily lit great bonfires to ward off unwanted spirits.

Something of the Samhain tradition was kept alive in Ireland, and it was the Irish immigrants of the mid-nineteenth century who introduced into the United States what had by then become Halloween—the pagan celebration adapted to the eve of the Christian All Saints' Day. Throughout much of the nineteenth century, Halloween was taken as a license for often destructive mischief-making, which would be classified as malicious mischief and vandalism under most modern laws: window breaking, the overturning of outbuildings such as chicken coops, doghouses, sheds, and outhouses, and so on. Although by the end of the first third of the twentieth century, most of this behavior had softened to pranks played by young children, in some places serious vandalism persisted. Even today, the night *before* Halloween is faced with dread in Detroit as Hell Night, an evening on which arson becomes a widespread and serious problem.

Halloween can be a time for great inventiveness with "homemade" costumes, and in some communities or in schools, prizes are awarded for the most imaginative or elaborate or most frightening outfits; however, increasingly, parents purchase inexpensive ready-made costumes for their children. The most familiar symbol of Halloween is the jack-o'-lantern, a hollowed-out PUMPKIN carved in the appearance of a (usually) demonic face. A lighted candle is placed inside the pumpkin, which is usually displayed on one's porch or windowsill.

SUGGESTED READING: Leslie Pratt Babbatyne, *Halloween: An American Holiday, An American History* (New York, 1990); Jack Santino, *Halloween and Other Festivals of Death and Life* (Knoxville, Tenn., 1994).

SUGGESTED READING: Jane Livingston and John Beardsley, *Black Folk Art in America: 1930–1980* (Jackson, Miss., 1982).

Hampton, James (1909–1964). James Hampton, a reclusive African-American folk artist who lived in Washington, D.C., is best known for his monumental assemblage called *The Throne of the Third Heaven of the Nations Millennium General Assembly* (begun ca. 1950). A labor of religious devotion as much as of art, *The Throne* is made mainly of old furniture and other found objects covered in gold and silver foil and purple kraft paper. Some 180 pieces are assembled in a celebration of the Second Coming, a vision loosely based on Hampton's reading of the Book of Revelation. Hampton created *Throne* in a small garage he rented in northwest Washington. It is now on permanent display at the National Museum of American Art, Washington, D.C.

Hampton did not identify himself as an artist, but called himself Saint James, appointed himself pastor of a self-created church, and titled himself "Director of Special Projects for the State of Eternity."

Hampton was born in Elloree, South Carolina, and moved to Washington, D.C., when he was nineteen, working there as a short-order cook. He served in the U.S. Army during World War II, then returned to Washington, where he worked as a janitor for the General Services Administration—a job he held for the rest of his life. He rented a garage in 1950 and there began work on *The Throne*. It was discovered there after the artist's death.

Hand, Wayland D. (1907–1986). Hand was trained primarily as a scholar of German literature, but shifted his concentration to the literature of German folklore when he was working toward his Ph.D. at the University of Chicago (1936). His dissertation was published as *The Schnaderhüpfel: An Alpine Folk Lyric*. Hand taught German at the University of Minnesota, then at UCLA, where he developed the Center for the Study of Comparative Folklore and Mythology as well as the university's folklore research library. With ARCHER TAYLOR, he founded the California Folklore Society in 1941 and was editor of the *Journal of American Folklore* from 1947 to 1951 and of *Western Folklore* from 1954 to 1966. He served as president of the American Folklore Society (1957–58) and of the California Folklore Society (1969–70).

Hand's folkloristic interests were wide ranging, but he is especially well known for his work in popular belief and superstition and was responsible for compiling the UCLA Archive of Popular Beliefs and Superstition. He developed a system of classifying this body of material, which he applied in works that he edited: *Popular Beliefs and Superstitions from North Carolina* (1961–64), *Popular Beliefs and Superstitions: A Compendium of American Folklore from the Ohio Collection of Newbell Niles Puckett* (1981), and *Popular Beliefs and Superstitions from the Anthony S. Cannon Collection of Utah Folklore* (1984). Hand was also an avid student of folk medical practices, which he compiled in *Magical Medicine* (1980).

See also: SUPERSTITION.

Handcox, John L. (1904–1992). Handcox was an African-American agrarian union organizer for the Southern Tenant Farmers Union (STFU) in Arkansas and Missouri during the 1930s and wrote such labor protest songs as "We're Gonna Roll the Union On" and "There Is Mean Things Happening in This Land." He became known as "The Share-cropper Troubadour." He recorded in 1937 for the Library of Congress Folk Song Archive.

Handcox was inactive as an activist after 1937, but resumed writing and performing labor-related poetry and songs in 1980 and continued doing so until shortly before his death.

SUGGESTED READING: H. L. Mitchell, *Mean Things Happening in This Land: The Life and Times of H. L. Mitchell, Cofounder of the Southern Tenant Farmers Union* (Montclair, N.J., 1979).

Handy, W. C. (1873–1958). William Christopher Handy was an African-American composer who is often called the "Father of the Blues" (which is the title of his 1941 autobiography). He was, in fact, a commercial popularizer of the blues, injecting the blues idiom into ragtime and making it palatable to black as well as white audiences. In this, he also paved the way for the popular acceptance of jazz. His single best-known work is the "St. Louis Blues," which he published in 1914.

Handy was the son of a minister, and was educated at Teachers Agricultural and Mechanical College (Huntsville, Alabama). He taught school and organized a band, eventually leading his own commercially successful orchestra (1903–21). Handy had a genius for taking traditional vocal blues melodies and adding formal European harmonies and orchestral arrangements to create a transitional music between ragtime and jazz. Yet while "Memphis Blues" (1911), "St. Louis Blues" (1914), and other early compositions were forward-looking, they also embodied an appealing nostalgia, strongly evocative of southern black traditional music.

In contrast to many musicians, black and white, Handy was an excellent businessman, who was able to build on the growing popularity of his music. When no white publisher would issue his "St. Louis Blues," Handy founded his own publishing company, which he directed until very late in his life. Not only did he publish his own compositions, but he issued those of other African-American composers, and he also issued anthologies of African-American spirituals and Latin music. In 1917, Handy made his first commercial recordings as a band leader, and he issued a number of recordings through the 1930s.

Folklorist DOROTHY E. SCARBOROUGH interviewed Handy in the 1920s, relying on him as her chief informant concerning the history of the blues—a dubious, though understandable choice, since Handy published an anthology of his own and other songwriters' blues compositions in 1926 (as well as a survey of African-American composers in 1938); Handy, however, was not a blues musician, and was certainly not a folk musician. If anything, after his early commercial success, Handy became increasingly associated with "high culture" and was a leading figure of the Harlem Renaissance of the 1920s. Of course, it is ridiculous to blame Handy for not being a folk artist. He used—and, in using, celebrated—folk traditions in his commercial music, and, in all of his enterprises, he honored the spirit, dignity, and beauty of African-American folklore and folk music.

See also: AFRICAN AMERICANS.

SUGGESTED READING: W. C. Handy, *Blues: An Anthology* (New York, 1926; rev. ed., 1949); W. C. Handy, *Father of the Blues* (New York, 1941).

Harmonica. Also known as the mouth organ, the harmonica was invented by Friedrich Buschmann in Berlin in 1821 and was called the *Mundäoline*. Technically, the harmonica is a free-reed wind instrument, consisting of metal reeds set into slots in a small wooden frame that is enclosed with metal. The tones of the diatonic scale are produced by alternately blowing and sucking, since the reeds are positioned to sound by alternate directions of wind flow. The tongue is used to cover the wind channels not required for a particular note. Harmonicas are also available in chromatic—twelve-note—versions. On such models, a finger-operated stop is used to select either of two sets of reeds tuned a half tone apart. Harmonicas typically range from two to four octaves. Bass harmonicas are available, but are rarely played as solo instruments; they are used in harmonica ensembles or harmonica bands.

While a few harmonica virtuosos, most notably Lawrence Cecil "Larry" Adler (1914–), have inspired classical composers to write for the instrument, the harmonica is chiefly played, by ear, by amateurs and folk musicians. It has been particularly favored by many engaged in outdoor occupations, such as cowboys and soldiers, who like the instrument's extreme portability. The harmonica has long figured in BLUES, typically as an accompaniment to vocals. (Blues musicians often call the instrument a "harp.") The harmonica enjoyed a particular renaissance during the FOLK REVIVAL of the 1960s, when it was popularized by such musicians as BOB DYLAN.

See also: FULLER, BLIND BOY.

Harris, Joel Chandler (1848–1908). Harris was journalist and writer, who is best known for his "Uncle Remus" tales, told in black dialect. Harris first became acquainted with the folklore and dialects of ex-plantation slaves while he was working as an apprentice on *The Countryman*, a weekly paper. Throughout his career, Harris wrote for newspapers in Macon, Georgia, New Orleans, and Forsyth and Savannah, Georgia, finally joining the staff of the *Atlanta Constitution* in 1876. He wrote for that paper for almost a quarter century. During this entire period, he established a national reputation as a humorist, beginning with his 1879 story, "Tar-Baby," which was published in the *Constitution*. Most likely, "Tar-Baby" was inspired by William Owens's "Folk-lore of the Southern Negroes," which had appeared in *Lippincott's Magazine* in December 1877. The popular reception accorded "Tar-Baby" led Harris to write a series of dialect stories narrated by UNCLE REMUS, the wise, gentle, and genial ex-slave. Later students of folklore have recognized in Uncle Remus's tales of the trickster Brer Rabbit and his dealings with Brer Fox and other animals parallels with the ANANSI folktales of Africa and the African diaspora. *Uncle Remus: His Songs and His Sayings* was published in book form in 1880, and other Uncle Remus volumes followed in 1883, 1889, 1892, 1905, and 1907, with posthumous volumes appearing in 1910, 1918, and 1948. From 1907 until his death, Harris also edited *Uncle Remus's Magazine.*

Although he is best known for his Uncle Remus stories, Harris wrote other books dealing with African-American life in the South: *Mingo, and Other Sketches in Black and White* (1884), *Free Joe and Other Georgian Sketches* (1887), *Sister Jane, Her Friends and Acquaintances* (1896), and *Gabriel Tolliver* (1902). All of these explore facets of life in the post–Reconstruction South. He also edited a number of popular col-

Three images of Joel Chandler Harris: a dust jacket engraving, the industrious writer, and relaxing on the veranda of the Wren's Nest, the author's home in Atlanta.

lections of literature and folk literature, including *American Wit and Humour* (1907) and the seventeen-volume *Library of Southern Literature* (1909–23).

In his introduction to *Uncle Remus: His Songs and Sayings,* Harris wrote that the tales were recollected from his childhood on a Georgia plantation. He also noted that they were still in oral circulation. Interestingly, he claimed that only the Uncle Remus folktales were current; others, no longer heard, he used in books that did not feature Uncle Remus, including the "Thimble-finger Series" of juvenile books. A master of dialects, Harris wrote books that featured numerous African-American dialects, as well as white Georgia dialects, and Gullah dialects.

While Harris's interest in folklore was not scholarly, it was deep and genuine, beyond the commercial success it brought him. He was a member of both the (British) Folk-Lore Society and of the American Folklore Society, which he joined as a charter member in 1888. Moreover, he had more than a nodding acquaintance with folktale scholarship. His use of folklore in his writing was conscious and deliberate, and he was very interested in ensuring that the folklore heritage of the South was published and preserved.

See also: AESOP'S FABLES; AFRICAN AMERICANS; ANIMAL FABLE; ANIMAL TALE; BRER FOX; BRER RABBIT; CHRISTENSEN, ABBIE (ABIGAIL MANDANIA) HOLMES; COYOTE; CRANE, THOMAS FREDERICK; DIALECT STORIES; DISNEY, WALT; FOLKLORE IN AMERICAN LITERATURE; FOX; LOCAL-COLOR STORY; SAMBO; TAR BABY; TRICKSTER.

SUGGESTED READING: Florence Baer, *Sources and Analogues of the Uncle Remus Tales* (Helsinki, Finland,

1980); Bruce R. Bickley, *Joel Chandler Harris: A Reference Guide* (Boston, 1978); Bruce R. Bickley, *Joel Chandler Harris* (Athens, Ga., 1987); Joel Chandler Harris, *On the Plantation* (autobiography; New York, 1892).

Bret Harte as a prosperous popular author.

Harte, (Francis) Bret[t] (1836–1902).

Harte was the best-known American practitioner of the western LOCAL-COLOR STORY, the professional literary version of the LOCAL-CHARACTER STORY. His short fiction set in the Gold Rush–era West was tremendously popular and was accepted by many as "authentic" regional "folklore." Harte was, in fact, no westerner, having been born in Albany, New York, and raised in New York City and Brooklyn. Many people associate Harte with a single work, "The Luck of Roaring Camp" (1870), a local color story set in a California mining camp, and for that reason, Harte is often thought of as a denizen of the rough-and-tumble camps. In truth, he visited the mining country only briefly after coming to California in 1854, then worked as a journalist in rural northern California during the late 1850s, until his support of the rights of local Indians made him unpopular and prompted his removal to San Francisco. Here he worked for a periodical called *The Golden Era,* which published the first of his *Condensed Novels,* hilarious parodies of the fiction of JAMES FENIMORE COOPER, Charles Dickens, and others. Working part time in the U.S. mint, he became editor of the *Californian,* and gave frequent assignments to the young MARK TWAIN. After Harte was named editor of the *Overland Monthly,* he wrote "The Luck of Roaring Camp" and "The Outcasts of Poker Flat," the two local color sketches that made him world famous. Although these and other of Harte's western local color pieces strike modern

readers as conventional and overly sentimental, to nineteenth-century sensibilities they came as an invigorating revelation, full of the language and character of the far West. They seemed nothing less than skillful transcriptions of western life and lore. Harte's reputation was further advanced by an 1870 poem he called "Plain Language from Truthful James" (1870), but which was subsequently retitled "The Heathen Chinee." This balladlike verse narrative satirically recounts the backfiring duplicity of one Truthful James and Bill Nye who try to swindle Ah Sin in a euchre game, and combines the dry humor typical of western folktales with a sophisticated verse form in imitation of Swinburne's *Atalanta in Calydon.* In 1877, Harte collaborated with Mark Twain on *Ah Sin,* a play based on the poem.

Harte achieved great financial success with his

local color tales, signing a contract with *Atlantic Monthly* for a dozen stories a year at an annual fee of $10,000—the most money any magazine had ever paid an American writer up to that time. Harte moved to New England, where he reveled in the plaudits and companionship of the likes of HENRY WADSWORTH LONGFELLOW and Oliver Wendell Holmes, Sr. However, Harte's creativity ebbed, and in 1878 he became U.S. consul in Crefeld, Germany, then Glasgow, Scotland, retiring in 1885 to live the rest of his life in London.

See also: FOLKLORE IN AMERICAN LITERATURE.

SUGGESTED READING: Henry Boynton, *Bret Harte* (New York, 1972); Bret Harte, *Selected Stories and Sketches* (New York and Oxford, 1995); Patrick Morrow, *Bret Harte* (Boise, Idaho, 1972).

Nathaniel Hawthorne as pictured in Reuben Post Halleck's History of American Literature, *1911. (Collection of Alan Axelrod)*

Hawthorne, Nathaniel (1804–1864). One of the greatest writers of the so-called American Renaissance (which included the likes of Ralph Waldo Emerson, HENRY DAVID THOREAU, HERMAN MELVILLE, WALT WHITMAN, Edgar Allan Poe, and Emily Dickinson), Hawthorne was a novelist and short-story writer who consciously used aspects of the folklore (as well as the history) of his native New England to create fiction of universal allegorical and symbolic import. In turn, many of his best-known works have the "aura" or "feel" of received folklore and legend rather than professional storytelling.

Hawthorne was steeped in the history of Salem, Massachusetts, the town of his birth. His seventeenth-century ancestor John Hathorne (it was Nathaniel himself who inserted the "w" into the family name) was among the three magistrates who presided over the infamous Salem witchcraft trials of 1692, a fact that seemed to haunt Nathaniel Hawthorne (who half believed his family cursed) and that probably influenced his principal masterwork, *The Scarlet Letter* (1850). Hawthorne was educated at Bowdoin College (Brunswick, Maine) and published a first novel, *Fanshawe*, at his own expense when he graduated in 1828. He soon tried to collect and destroy all copies. Within the next five years, however, Hawthorne discovered his great subject in the look, feel, heritage, history, and legends of colonial New England. He began to write a series of short stories, including "My Kinsman, Major Molineux," "Roger Malvin's Burial," and "Young Goodman Brown," which, with others, were collected in *Twice-Told Tales* of 1837. These stories foreshadow the elements prized by readers and critics alike in Hawthorne's more mature works: finely wrought form and architecture, expressive language, a brilliant command of allegory and symbol, and an evocation of a time and place rendered magical, mythic, mysterious, and legendary. Based on local legends, the short stories of *Twice-Told Tales* have the form of art and the feeling of folktale.

While Hawthorne's *Twice-Told Tales* was well received, he could hardly afford to live off his literary income, and took a job in the Boston Custom House (1839–40), then took up residence in the utopian cooperative experiment, Brook Farm, in West Roxbury, Massachusetts (1841)—an experience that would find its way into his novel *The Blithedale Romance* (1852). In 1842, Hawthorne married Sophia Peabody, with whom he lived in the Old Manse at Concord, Massachusetts. Here he met Emerson, Thoreau, Bronson Alcott, and other Transcendentalist thinkers, though he remained somewhat aloof from them. He published another successful short-story collection, *Mosses from an Old Manse,* in 1846, which became the subject of a penetrating and admiring critical essay (by another aspiring American writer, Herman Melville).

Again in need of a steady income, Hawthorne obtained an appointment as surveyor of customs in Salem in 1845, a political patronage job he lost when President Zachary Taylor assumed office in 1849. Released from the mundane labor of the Salem custom house, however, Hawthorne quickly wrote *The Scarlet Letter* (1850), a book that combines the appeal of a tragic love story with the romantic and mythic setting of Puritan colonial New England. With exquisite art, Hawthorne fashions an intriguing and emotionally powerful allegory while again evoking the feeling of folk legend. The novel brought Hawthorne immediate fame and has endured as one of the great American works of fiction. It was followed by *The House of the Seven Gables* (1851), which, like *The Scarlet Letter,* was loosely based on a blend of local history and local legend. It is the story of the cursed Pyncheon family, who are ultimately redeemed by love.

Hawthorne's third novel, *The Blithedale Ro-mance* (1852) was not well received. In 1853, he moved with his family to Liverpool, England, having been appointed U.S. consul by his former Bowdoin classmate, President Franklin Pierce. This marked a curtailment and diminishment of Hawthorne's creative life. *The Marble Faun,* an 1860 novel set in Italy, which Hawthorne toured extensively after his consulship was terminated in 1857, lacked the force of his American works. On his death, he left fragments and sketches for four novels, *Septimius Felton, The Dolliver Romance, Doctor Grimshawe's Secret,* and *The Ancestral Footstep.*

See also: FOLKLORE IN AMERICAN LITERATURE; MAYPOLE OF MERRY MOUNT; MORTON, THOMAS; POCAHONTAS; SALEM WITCH TRIALS.

SUGGESTED READING: Arlin Turner, *Nathaniel Hawthorne: A Biography* (New York, 1980); Terence Martin, *Nathaniel Hawthorne* (New York, 1983); Edwin Haviland Miller, *Salem Is My Dwelling Place: A Life of Nathaniel Hawthorne* (Iowa City, Iowa, 1991); Hyatt H. Waggoner, *Hawthorne: A Critical Study* (rev. ed., New York, 1963).

Hays, Will (1837–1907). A popular songwriter of the nineteenth century, Hays did not achieve the enduring reputation of STEPHEN FOSTER, but, like Foster, he blended folk traditions with the Victorian PARLOR BALLAD and MINSTREL SHOW conventions to create a number of enduring songs, including "The Drummer Boy of Shiloh" (1862), "I'll Remember You, Love, in My Prayers" (1869), "Mollie Darling" (1871), and "The Little Old Cabin in the Lane" (1871).

Hays was born in Louisville, Kentucky, and was skipper of the Mississippi steamer *Grey Eagle* as well as "river editor" of the Louisville

Democrat. He later worked on the Louisville *Courier-Journal* and the Cincinnati *Enquirer*. A poet who favored sentimental verse, he composed more than five hundred songs and, in his time, was perhaps the nation's most successful songsmith. His tunes were popular both on the minstrel stage and in the Victorian parlor. In the twentieth century, some of Hays's old songs were revived by COUNTRY MUSIC artists, including Eddy Arnold, who had a 1948 hit with "Mollie (spelled "Molly") Darling." Hays's tunes continue to be popular among BLUEGRASS musicians.

SUGGESTED READING: Bill C. Malone, *Southern Music—American Music* (Lexington, Ky., 1979).

Henry, John. See JOHN HENRY.

Henry, Lorenzo ("Len") (1852?–1946).
Len Lorenzo was an Idaho teller of tall tales. At his death, his reputation as a western Münchhausen figure was well established in the region, but his stories were not collected in quantity until well after his death. (Karl Friedrich Hieronymus, Baron von Münchhausen [1720–97] was a German raconteur of tall tales whose name became a byword for anyone who tells fantastic stories incorporating grotesque exaggeration.) In the early 1960s, Jan Harold Brunvand and his students at the University of Idaho recorded 116 versions of 67 stories from 28 informants. The tall tales related to hunting, fishing, farming, and similar activities. The narratives are first person and told from the perspective of a trickster persona.

Henry may have been born in Kansas City of Pennsylvania German stock. He probably came to Idaho in the 1860s, and was married to a Nez Percé woman.

SUGGESTED READING: Jan Harold Brunvand, entry on Lorenzo Henry in Jan Harold Brunvand, ed., *American Folklore: An Encyclopedia* (New York, 1996).

Henry, Mellinger Edward (1873–1946).
Henry was an avid amateur collector of folk songs and ballads in the Blue Ridge, and was a founding member of the Southeastern Folklore Society. A native of Mount Pleasant, Pennsylvania, Henry was educated at Brown University, Harvard, and Columbia. During 1906–37, he was a high school English teacher in Paterson and Jersey City, New Jersey. It was while vacationing in the North Carolina mountains in 1923 that Henry and his wife, Florence Stokes, attended a lecture on balladry given by C. Alphonso Smith. The experience inspired the couple—enthusiastic hikers, both—to collect songs from people they met during summer trips to the Blue Ridge and Great Smoky Mountains. Henry transcribed the lyrics, while his wife notated the tunes.

Acting on his own initiative, Henry corresponded with established folk-song scholars and was thus able to put his work in perspective while making it known to the academic folklore community. Henry was also active in lobbying local and national government to develop the Blue Ridge Mountain region for vacationers and hikers.

Much of the Henrys' collection was published in the *Journal of American Folklore* (1931 and 1932), and in *Songs Sung in the Southern Appalachians* (1934) and *Folk Songs of the Southern Highlands* (1938). Henry's papers and ballad collection are on deposit at the John Hay Library of Brown University.

SUGGESTED READING: Florence Henry, "The Ballad-Hunting Henrys," *North Carolina Folklore* 7 (1959), pp. 32–34.

Herskovits, Melville Jean (1895–1963).

Herskovits was an anthropologist and eminent student of African and African-American folklore. He pioneered the field of African-American studies, becoming the first head of an African-American studies department, at Northwestern University in 1961. His interest in African-American culture extended well beyond the realms of folklore and anthropology. He studied the social problems of African Americans, and he systematically attacked the prevailing white misconceptions about blacks in his highly influential *The Myth of the Negro Past* (1941). In the twilight of European colonialism, he opposed the assumption that Africa must remain under the direction of Europeans.

Herskovitz was educated at Hebrew Union College, at the University of Chicago (Ph.D., 1920) and at Columbia University, (M.A., 1921; Ph.D., 1923), where he was an anthropology student of FRANZ BOAS. Herskovitz taught at Howard University (Washington) and then, for the balance of his long career, at Northwestern University (Evanston, Illinois). An entire generation of distinguished folklorists and anthropologists considered him their mentor.

The broad spectrum of Herskovits's interests are suggested by his major writings, which include *The Economic Life of Primitive Peoples* (1940; second edition, *Economic Anthropology*, 1952); *Man and His Works* (1948; abridged as *Cultural Anthropology*, 1955); and *The Human*

Factor in Changing Africa (1962). While primarily known as a theorist, Herskovitz did extensive fieldwork in Suriname, sub-Saharan Africa, Haiti, Brazil, and Trinidad, producing two works on African folklore, *Suriname Folk-lore* (1936) and *Dahomean Narrative: A Cross-Cultural Analysis* (1958). Herskovits and his wife, Frances S. Herskovits, also recorded extensively throughout Suriname, Dahomey Ashanti, Nigeria, Togoland, Trinidad, and Brazil, and they documented dance and drumming in Haitian voodoo practice and Trinidadian *shango*.

See also: AFRICAN AMERICANS; BASCOM, WILLIAM R.

SUGGESTED READING: George E. Simpson, *Melville Herskovits* (New York, 1973).

Herzog, George (1901–1983).

Among American folklorists, Herzog is best remembered as the scholar who did most to establish ethnomusicology as a discrete discipline. He did this chiefly by fusing the methods of research into Hungarian folk music developed by the great Hungarian musical nationalist Bela Bartók with the comparative methodology of the Berlin ethnomusicologists and the principles of cultural anthropology imbibed from his Columbia University mentor, FRANZ BOAS.

Herzog was born in Hungary and was educated chiefly in Berlin, before immigrating to the United States in 1925. In New York, at Columbia University, he studied under Boas and received his Ph.D. Herzog undertook numerous recording trips among the Pueblo, Pima, Yuman, Comanche, and Navajo in the Southwest. During 1930–31, he traveled to Liberia to study the language and linguistic signaling systems of the Jabo. Herzog taught at Columbia from 1932 to

1948, then at Indiana University from 1948 until illness forced his retirement in 1958.

SUGGESTED READING: Bruno Nettl and Philip V. Bohlman, eds., *Comparative Musicology and Anthropology of Music: Essays on the History of Ethnomusicology* (Chicago, 1991).

Hex. Most Americans understand *hex* as synonymous with a curse or spell; however, it may also refer to a person who is a wizard or witch. The word has special significance among Pennsylvania Germans (also called Pennsylvania Dutch), who traditionally employed hex doctors to effect cures for a variety of ills and, more specifically, to counteract the spells put on one by malevolent hexes. Hex doctors combine magic formulas, AMULETS, and rituals to effect cures and to defeat spells and hexes. In Pennsylvania German country, "hex signs"—bold, colorful, and often quite beautiful geometric designs—still decorate barns; they are said to protect farmers and their livestock from spells and the EVIL EYE. The word *hex* is of German origin, and *hexerei* is used to denote collectively the practices and beliefs associated with hexes.

See also: PENNSYLVANIA GERMANS; WITCHES AND WITCHCRAFT.

Hiawatha. The name and character of Hiawatha were made famous among American as well as European whites by HENRY WADSWORTH

Thanks in large measure to Longfellow's poem, Hiawatha entered into non-Native American folklore. The Milwaukee Road appropriated his name for its crack passenger trains between Chicago and Minneapolis. This 1945 advertisement promoting the railroad's service in World War II begins "The Milwaukee Road's Hiawathas are on the warpath."

Hex signs on a Pennsylvania-German barn in Lancaster County, Pennsylvania.

LONGFELLOW's immensely popular narrative poem in metric imitation of the Finnish *Kalevala,* the *Song of Hiawatha* (1855). The poem is based, in large part, on HENRY ROWE SCHOOLCRAFT's pioneering collection of Ojibwa folklore, *Algic Researches* (1839). Hiawatha—an Ojibwa name meaning "He Makes Rivers"—was, however, revered as a legendary chief by the Iroquoian tribes long before the advent of Longfellow's verse. About 1450, this Onondagan chief is said to have laid the foundation for what became the Iroquois Confederacy, a grand union of the Mohawk, Oneida, Onondaga, Cayuga, and Seneca tribes (and, after 1722, the Tuscarora as well), that was very powerful during the seventeenth and early eighteenth centuries and that continues to exist today.

The legendary figure Longfellow borrowed was a creator and civilizing force. He taught agriculture, navigation, medicine, and the arts. Through his potent magic, he subdued the powers of nature that menace humankind. After performing an array of mythic feats, Hiawatha, both as portrayed in Iroquoian tradition and by Longfellow, assumed leadership among his people, married the beautiful maiden Minnehaha, then, at the end of his life, departed to the Isles of the Blessed.

See also: CURRIER & IVES; FOLKLORE IN AMERICAN LITERATURE.

Hicks, Edward (1780–1849).

One of the most familiar among early nineteenth-century American folk painters, Hicks specialized in portraying the pastoral landscape of Pennsylvania and New York, but is best known for his multiple versions of *The Peaceable Kingdom.* Some twenty-five of these variations are known, but it is believed that Hicks painted as many as one hundred. This charming painting is founded on Isaiah's prophecy (11:6–9):

One of the many versions of Edward Hicks's The Peaceable Kingdom.

The wolf will live with the lamb,
the panther lie down with the kid,
calf, lion and fat-stock beast together,
with a little boy to lead them.
The cow and the bear will graze,
Their young will lie down together.
The lion will eat hay like the ox.
The infant will play over the den of the
*   adder;*
the baby will put his hand into the viper's
*   lair.*
No hurt, no harm will be done . . .

The prophecy harmonized with Hicks's pacific QUAKER philosophy, and, in many of the paintings, William Penn and other Quakers are depicted concluding their famous treaty of peace with the Indians.

Hicks was a coach and sign painter by trade, and a preacher by conviction. He did not begin to create easel paintings until he was well into middle age, despite his concern that the creation of paintings for pleasure was, perhaps, contrary to holy commandment.

SUGGESTED READING: Alice Ford, *Edward Hicks: His Life and Art* (New York, 1985).

Hill, Betty and Barney.

Perhaps the most famous account of a "close encounter of the third kind (CE-III)" (i.e., physical contact with an extraterrestrial being) and ALIEN ABDUCTION is that of Betty and Barney Hill, who, on the night of September 19, 1961, were returning to their Portsmouth, New Hampshire, home after a visit to Niagara Falls. They were driving south on Route 3 through the White Mountains, when, at 10 P.M., near Groveton, some seventy miles south of the Canadian border, Betty noticed a bright star or planet just below the moon. An hour later, when the Hills were just south of Lancaster, a companion object appeared near the planet. Betty Hill later described the sighting to officials at nearby Pease Air Force Base, where, in fact, radar had confirmed the presence of a UFO in the area at 11 P.M.

The Hills stopped their car and observed the object through binoculars. It had red, amber, green, and blue flashing lights. It appeared to have a fuselage shape, but no wings, and it flew in what Barney Hill described as a "steplike flight pattern, dropping vertically, leveling off, tilting upward again." It was absolutely silent.

The Hills resumed driving, the object keeping pace with their car. South of Indian Head, the object approached closer, and Betty saw a change to a steady white glow in the pattern of flashing multicolored lights. When it stopped to hover about 100 feet above the ground, the Hills stopped their car. Barney got out and walked nearer to the object, which now appeared to be a huge glowing disc with a double row of windows curved around its perimeter. Fifty feet from the object, using his binoculars, he could see eight to eleven humanoid creatures through the windows. They stood still at first, then began to scurry about within the ship, apparently manipulating controls on the wall. One of the figures remained at the window, gazing at Barney Hill.

At this point, two finlike projections, a red light on the tip of each, slid out of the sides of the ship as Betty, waiting in the car, heard Barney yell, "I don't believe it. . . . I don't believe it. . . . This is ridiculous."

Barney ran back to the car, shouting that they were going to be captured. He put the car into gear, stepped on the gas, and took off down the highway. Strange beeping sounds, apparently coming from behind the car, made the vehicle vibrate. Both Betty and Barney Hill were overcome by a peculiar sensation of "tingling drowsiness."

A while later, the beeps resumed. Then the Hills continued home without further incident—except that they arrived at 5 A.M., about two hours later than they should have.

Following the encounter, both Hills were uneasy, at first disturbed by the conviction that they had "lost" two hours out of their lives—two hours of which they had no conscious memory. Then they began to be plagued by nightmares, unbearable feelings of anxiety, insomnia, and, in Barney's case, the development of duodenal ulcers.

The Hills sought psychiatric help from Dr. Duncan Stephens, who, after a year of treatment that produced no positive result, referred them to Boston psychiatrist Dr. Benjamin Simon, a specialist in hypnotic therapy. In the course of six months of regressive hypnosis therapy, the Hills apparently recovered the two missing hours. Under hypnosis, Betty related how a group of humanoids approached their stopped car, opened the door of the vehicle, and pointed a small device at her. ("It could have been a pencil," she reported.) Independently, both of the Hills described being taken aboard an alien ship and given quasi-medical physical examinations. Betty recalled:

> Most of the men are my height. . . . None is as tall as Barney, so I would judge them to be 5′ to 5′4″. Their chests are larger than ours; their noses were larger than the average size although I have seen people with noses like theirs—like Jimmy Durante. Their complexions were of a gray tone; like gray paint with a black base; their lips were of a bluish tint. Hair and eyes were very dark, possibly black.
>
> In a sense, they looked like mongoloids . . . this sort of round face and broad forehead, along with a certain type of coarseness. The surface of their skin seemed

to be a bluish gray, but probably whiter than that. Their eyes moved, and they had pupils. Somehow, I had the feeling they were more like cats' eyes.

Barney Hill's description differed in some significant details, particularly concerning the hair and nose of the extraterrestrials:

> The men had rather odd-shaped heads, with a large cranium, diminishing in size as it got toward the chin. And the eyes continued around to the sides of their heads, so that it appeared that they could see several degrees beyond the lateral extent of our vision. This was startling to me. . . . [The mouth] was much like when you draw one horizontal line with a short perpendicular line on each end. The horizontal line would represent lips without the muscle we have. And it would part slightly as they made this *mumumumumm*ing sound. The texture of the skin, as I remember it from this quick glance, was grayish, almost metallic looking. I didn't notice any hair—or headgear for that matter. I didn't notice any proboscis, there just seemed to be two slits that represented the nostrils.

The beings, according to the Hills, communicated among themselves through audible language ("*mumumumumm*ing sound"), yet communicated with the Hills through telepathy *in English* (according to Betty, "with an accent"). "I did not hear an actual voice," Barney Hill reported. "But in my mind, I knew what he was saying. It wasn't as if he were talking to me with my eyes open, and he was sitting across the room from me. It was more as if the words were there, a part of me, and he was outside the actual creation of the words themselves."

One of the more remarkable aspects of the

Two images of the hillbilly from the late nineteenth century exemplify pejorative exoteric folklore. Both are from John B. Gough's Platform Echoes, *1884.*

Betty and Barney Hill sighting is that Betty reported that the alien "captain" showed her a "star map" while she was on board the vessel. Under hypnosis, Betty Hill was able to reproduce the star map in great detail, from which researcher Marjorie Fish determined that the aliens had come from Zeta Reticuli I or II, about thirty light years from our sun.

Following regressive hypnosis therapy, the emotional state of both Betty and Barney Hill improved markedly.

Barney Hill succumbed to a stroke on February 25, 1969. Betty Hill, seventy-seven in 1997, continued to claim her story as true. Moreover, she has been what UFO investigators call a "repeater witness," who has reported numerous subsequent encounters with UFOs, but no further abductions.

The Betty and Barney Hill sighting has provoked a great deal of controversy. Dr. Simon believed that the abduction portion of the UFO experience was a neurotic fantasy. Others, most notably abduction researcher Budd Hopkins,

have treated it as a classic and richly documented instance of a CE-III.

See also UFO FOLKLORE.

SUGGESTED READING: John G. Fuller, *The Interrupted Journey* (New York, 1966; 1974).

Hillbilly figure. The word *hillbilly* is of surprisingly recent coinage, having first appeared in print in 1900 in the pages of the *New York Journal,* which defined the term to mean "a free and untrammelled white citizen of Alabama, who lives in the hills, has no means to speak of, dresses as he can, talks as he pleases, drinks whiskey when he gets it, and fires off his revolver as the fancy takes him." Push the boundaries of the original definition to cover any mountainous region in the South, and you have an accurate expression of the hillbilly figure stereotype that endured into the first quarter or so of the twentieth century. With the Depression, the stereotype became harsher. The hillbilly was still portrayed as poor and lazy, but also dirty, disease-ridden, and given to incest or, at least, marriage within the extended family. Running counter to this grim image were popular depictions of hillbillies as poor but decent, good-humored, naively hilarious salt-of-the-earth types, such as Ma and Pa Kettle, characters in Betty MacDonald's best-selling novel *The Egg and I,* which was made into a film in 1947. This spawned a series of nine "Ma and Pa Kettle" movies (1949–55) staring Marjorie Main and Percy Kilbride in the title roles. The Kettles raise a dozen or so rambunctious youngsters and good-naturedly battle neighbors and the law. In the 1960s, the Ma and Pa Kettle stereotype made the transition from big screen to small in the highly popular *Beverly Hillbillies* (1962–71), a situation comedy exploiting the conflict between hillbilly backwardness and city slicker sophistication. (The hillbillies always came out on top.) But by far the most popular depiction of the hillbilly figure came in 1934, with the premiere of the *L'il Abner* comic strip by Al Capp. L'il Abner was the hillbilly as NOBLE SAVAGE, uneducated and naive, but also unspoiled and humane.

See also: APPALACHIA; SKILLET LICKERS, THE.

SUGGESTED READING: John C. Campbell, *The Southern Highlander and His Homeland* (1921; reprint ed., Lexington, Ky., 1969).

Hill, Joe (1879–1915).

Hill was an extraordinary figure in the American labor movement, in the creation of the protest song, and in the folklore of labor. He was born Joel Emmanuel Hägglund in Gävle, Sweden, and, after immigrating to the United States in 1902, he sometimes called himself Joe Hillstrom. He became involved in radical union politics and, largely because of his ability as a songwriter and performer, he became a moving force within the Industrial Workers of the World (IWW), the radical labor party founded in 1905 by Utah mine-labor organizer William "Big Bill" Haywood. Hill composed numerous protest songs, dealing with migratory laborers, sweatshop workers, and railway employees, all marked by dark humor and elementary Marxism. The most enduring of the songs are "Casey Jones: The Union Scab" and "Pie in the Sky." The latter song was originally titled "The Preacher and the Slave," but became popularly known by the phrase Hill coined within the song—"pie in the sky," which is the reward promised the exploited worker: "You will eat, bye and bye / In that glorious land above the sky; / Work and pray, live on hay, / You'll get pie in the sky when you die."

Joe Hill became most famous, however, as a martyr to the cause of labor. After he came to the United States, he drifted from job to job before joining the San Pedro (California) local of the IWW in 1910. In January 1914, Hill was arrested and charged with the robbery and murder of a Salt Lake City grocer and his son. The prosecution based its case almost entirely on Hill's having sought treatment for a gunshot wound some hours after the murders. Hill testified that he had been shot in a quarrel over a woman, but he refused to identify her on the grounds of protecting her good name. He was found guilty, and despite legal appeals as well as mass demonstrations and specific protests from public figures including Samuel Gompers, Helen Keller, and even President Woodrow Wilson (who appealed directly to Utah's governor), Hill was executed by a firing squad on November 19, 1915. It was widely assumed that Hill had been found guilty and executed largely because of his radicalism. On the night before his death, he telegraphed Big Bill

Haywood: "Goodbye Bill. I die like a true rebel. Don't waste time in mourning. Organize."

Hill was celebrated in the ballad "Joe Hill," written in 1925 by Alfred Hays. This, as well as other songs about Hill, have been performed by WOODY GUTHRIE, PETE SEEGER, and JOAN BAEZ.

See also: MINING FOLKLORE.

SUGGESTED READING: Gibbs M. Smith, *Joe Hill* (Salt Lake City, Utah, 1984).

Hirshfield, Morris (1872–1946).

Hirshfield was a New York painter of women, often nudes portrayed against backgrounds of rich and intricate fabrics (Hirshfield was in the garment business), and cats, dogs, lions, tigers, and zebras. His work, especially his naive portrayal of animals, has been often compared to the paintings of the French primitivist Henri Rousseau (1844–1910). Hirshfield painted in oils on canvas, usually working from large preliminary drawings, which he traced onto his canvas. Typically, his work consumed him, and he worked many hours a day on each painting, often returning to individual works years later to modify them. By the 1940s, he became recognized as one of the most important of American folk painters.

Hirshfield was born in 1872 in Lithuania and immigrated to New York City with his family when he was eighteen years old. He went to work in the city's garment district, became a coat maker with his brother, then started the highly successful E. Z. Walk Manufacturing Company, specializing in women's slippers. Stricken by illness, Hirshfield retired from business in 1937.

Since childhood, Hirshfield had shown artistic ability, but he began to paint only after his retirement. He was discovered in 1939 by the prominent New York gallery owner Sidney Janis, who

The cover of an automobile industry magazine from 1929 featured this image of the American hobo. Footsore, the seated hobo, a Rolls-Royce brochure under his arm, disdains the Ford literature proffered by his companion.

invited Hirshfield to exhibit in "Contemporary Unknown American Painters," a show he was curating at the Museum of Modern Art. In 1943, Hirshfield had a one-man show at the museum. After this came widespread recognition, though, the artist complained, paltry financial reward.

Hobo folklore.

Alongside the work ethic most Americans profess to value there exists a romantic fondness for the free and easy life of the hobo—the nomad without employer, without home, without wife and children, who rides the rails (stows away on railroad boxcars) for free and lives in the great outdoors. He is the man without responsibilities.

The figure of the hobo or tramp or bum has been popular since the nineteenth century and flourished particularly in the early twentieth century, until the harsh realities of the Depression made it difficult to maintain an idealized picture of the supposedly unfettered hobo life.

Outsiders—the respectable citizen and the American working stiff—believed that hoboes chose their way of life. They believed that there was a more-or-less secret brotherhood among hoboes, a kind of underground society. This belief was fostered by the evidence of "hobo signs," usually chalked symbols that were used to communicate among the "brotherhood." Certain signs indicated a generous household, other signs warned of a mean sheriff or a bad dog. To some degree, this EXOTERIC FOLKLORE coincided with the ESOTERIC FOLKLORE. Some hoboes actively professed preference for the rootless life and for the companionship and camaraderie of other bums. Some saw themselves as living the *real* American dream: not a dream of material prosperity, but of untrammeled liberty.

See also: GRAFFITI; RAILROAD FOLKLORE.

SUGGESTED READING: Roger Bruns, *Knights of the Road: A Hobo History* (New York, 1980); Charles Elmer Fox, *Tales of an American Hobo* (Iowa City, Iowa, 1989); Adolph Vandertie and Patrick Spielman, *Hobo and Tramp Art Carving: An Authentic American Folk Tradition* (New York, 1995).

Hoedown. Sometimes used as a synonym for SQUARE DANCE and the music accompanying a square dance, a hoedown is, more generally, a rural group dance or dance gathering and the music that accompanies it. In this sense, *hoedown* is used interchangeably with BREAKDOWN and is a style influenced by African-American rural dance traditions, including the breakdown and the JUBA. Hoedowns are danced to a variety of traditional FIDDLE tunes, with fiddle and BANJO prominent.

The origin of the term hoedown is uncertain. It may refer to a work stoppage, a break in work during which the hoes are thrown down and everyone dances. It may refer to hoe-wielding movements that may have been part of these dances. It may be related to the FOLK SPEECH expression "hoe it down," hurry up, thus suggesting the speed with which the dance was performed.

See also: CURRIER & IVES.

Hogan. The hogan is an example of Navajo folk architecture. It is a generally circular structure built of logs and mud and, rarely, of stone. Logs are stepped to create a dome-shaped roof. The hogan has no windows or interior room divisions, but does have a circular opening in the roof, which allows smoke to escape. The structure of the hogan is a model of the Navajo vision of the world, its four main supports identified with the four cardinal directions, and its wood-framed, blanket-covered entrance oriented eastward, toward the rising sun.

See also: NATIVE AMERICANS; SANDPAINTING.

Hollers. In a form of expression of African derivation, weary African-American field-workers on their way home would let their voices wander

A Native American hogan (at the left) on display with a teepee and a Northwest Coast lodge building at the World's Columbian Exposition, Chicago, 1893.

in a wail, often into falsetto, and often embodying most of the elements of BLUES: slow, melancholy tunes, the use of a flatted third, occasional repetition of a simple verbal line, portamento. In short, the holler may be thought of as blues without the rhythm and European harmony. Numerous hollers have been recorded for the Library of Congress's Archive of American Folk-Songs and are among the archive's earliest releases.

See also: RODGERS, JIMMIE.

Honky-tonk music. Honky-tonk is "hard" COUNTRY MUSIC, born during the Depression in rural roadhouses and beer joints. By the late 1940s and well into the 1950s, honky-tonk was the mainstream country sound. While ROCK 'N' ROLL began to transform the country sound beginning in the later fifties, the honky-tonk style persists as a subgenre within country music.

Honky-tonk came about for at least two reasons. To begin with, it expressed the mood of the postwar years, which was harsher and had

a harder core than the earlier, more nostalgic country styles of the early 1930s and 1920s. On a more immediate level, country performers needed a music that could be heard and felt above the raucous din of a beer joint. This was no PLAY PARTY or BARN DANCE.

See also: TUBB, ERNEST; WILLIAMS, HANK.

Hoodoo hand. A bag in which various CHARMS and MOJOS are kept to perform specific functions; for example, a "curing hand" contains material to heal a specific disorder, a "love hand" contains the necessary ingredients to bring your lover to you, and so on. The hoodoo hand is generally worn on one's person and may contain such items as a RABBIT'S FOOT, fish scales, snakeskin, and so on. Hoodoo hands may be used for malevolent purposes as well. A "killing hand" typically contains hair or fingernail parings from the person one wishes dead, together with such items as needles and pins and graveyard soil.

Hooker, John Lee (1917–). The Mississippi BLUES musician called "The King of the Boogie" was born to a sharecropper in Clarksdale, Mississippi. He imbibed the local traditions of sacred and secular music, then moved to Memphis and, in 1943, to Detroit, where he wrote "Boogie Chillen," his first important song. Hooker is among the most idiosyncratic of blues performers, combining an intense vocal technique with a rhythmically spontaneous guitar technique. Unlike many of his contemporaries, he resisted the influences of mainstream popular music throughout his career.

Hoover, J(ohn) Edgar (1895–1972). Longtime director of the Federal Bureau of Investigation (FBI), Hoover not only achieved legendary status within the world law enforcement community, but came to occupy a niche in popular culture and folklore. Born in Washington, D.C., he took night-school law degrees at George Washington University in 1916 and 1917, then joined the U.S. Department of Justice as a minor functionary in 1917, becoming within two years special assistant to Attorney General A. Mitchell Palmer during the so-called Red Scare that followed Russia's Bolshevik Revolution. Hoover assisted Palmer in a series of raids to round up suspected Bolsheviks. His zeal earned Hoover the post of acting director, then director of the Bureau of Investigation (later called the Federal Bureau of Investigation) in 1924. The bureau Hoover had inherited was riddled by corruption and inefficiency, and Hoover set out to reorganize and reform it. Not only did Hoover recruit agents of great aptitude and professionalism, he also built a fingerprint file (soon the world's largest), a crime-detection laboratory (soon recognized as state of the art), and the FBI National Academy (which trained G-men and other law enforcement agents).

If Hoover was a genius of administration, he was also a master at creating a legendary public image. During the depression-plagued early 1930s, when gangsters were gaining facile popular reputations as latter-day Robin Hoods, Hoover engaged them in highly publicized battles. He created the FBI "Ten Most-Wanted List" and the label of "Public Enemy Number One," which he affixed to the target of whatever FBI manhunt was current. By the late 1930s, President Franklin D. Roosevelt redirected Hoover's focus from gangsters (who had, in any case, lost their public glamour) and assigned his bureau to investigate espionage in the United States as well as the activities of communists and fascists. After World War II, during the Cold War and the communist witch-hunting era of Senator Joseph McCarthy, the FBI engaged in widespread surveillance not only of communists, but anyone else Hoover deemed too far to the left—or, for that matter, the right. Hoover investigated Martin Luther King, Jr. (as well as other black activists of the 1960s), and the Ku Klux Klan. Hoover increasingly regarded the FBI as his personal agency and used surveillance to effectively blackmail politicians (usually with sexually compromising material) in order to maintain his own absolute power. No president dared challenge his authority—though Hoover fell under increasing popular criticism during the 1960s, not only because of his autocratic direction of the FBI, but also because of his hands-off policy with regard to the Mafia and organized crime. Nevertheless, it was death alone that ended his forty-eight-year tenure as FBI director. He had outlasted eight presidents and eighteen attorneys general.

While Hoover focused much publicity on his bureau, he shunned the spotlight himself. Even as his G-men became the subjects of popular lore, legendary for straight-arrow ideals and incorruptibility, Hoover managed to live the life of a bachelor, maintaining a close relationship with Deputy Director Clyde Tolson, who lived in an apartment near Hoover's home and with whom Hoover took two extended vacations a year for some thirty years, yet avoiding public accusations of homosexuality. He could not avoid, however, a body of rumor as well as folklore concerning his apparent transvestism, on the one hand, and on the other, an ever-growing body of CONSPIRACY LORE, which painted Hoover as the "real power" behind any number of presidents and elected lawmakers.

See also: DILLINGER, JOHN; WINCHELL, WALTER.

SUGGESTED READING: Richard G. Powers, *Secrecy and Power: The Life of J. Edgar Hoover* (New York, 1986); A. G. Theoharis and J. S. Cox, *The Boss* (New York, 1988).

Hopkins, Lightnin' (1912–1982). BLUES

singer Sam "Lightnin'" Hopkins, born in Centerville, Texas, was playing a homemade cigar-box instrument by age eight; he learned some guitar chords from his brother Joel and sang in the church choir. During the 1920s, he drifted around Texas, picking up odd jobs as well as the musical traditions of agricultural laborers. He performed itinerantly in Texas through the 1930s and early 1940s. Hopkins was playing in Houston in 1946 when a California talent scout arranged a recording session at Aladdin Records in Los Angeles. It was the Aladdin company that dubbed him Lightin' Hopkins (and his pianist Wilson Smith, Thunder Smith). Hopkins continued to record and tour, then, in 1955, was approached by folklorist Mack McCormick, who booked Hopkins on the folk music circuit during the FOLK REVIVAL of the early 1960s. It was in this context that his national reputation was built, with performances that included New York's Carnegie Hall on a bill with BOB DYLAN and JOAN BAEZ. He recorded widely and toured the folk and college circuit until his death.

Hornpipe. A clog-and-shuffle solo dance imported to America from England and Scotland and popular among sailors, including riverboatmen, the hornpipe often includes elements of maritime-related pantomime (such as hauling the anchor or hoisting the sail) counterpointed to traditional Scottish toe steps. The name derives from the hornpipe (an old reed instrument with bell and mouthpiece fashioned of horn), which traditionally accompanied the dance.

See also: DANCE, FOLK; FIDDLE.

House, Son (Eddie) (1902–1988). Born in

the Delta, near Clarksdale, Mississippi, seminal Delta BLUES musician Eddie "Son" House was raised in strict Baptist tradition where he heard a great deal of music but was taught that the blues was sinful. He recalled for an interviewer after his "rediscovery" in the 1960s that "Just puttin' your hands on an old guitar, looked to me like that was a sin." Nevertheless, in 1927, House began singing and playing blues. Within only three years, he had become skilled enough to join the Charley Patton–Willie Brown ensemble, performing in the basic Mississippi Delta style, playing at Saturday night juke joints and parties, and entertaining at the bootleg whiskey parties common in the early Depression.

In the hard-driving, intense Delta style, his first recordings in 1930 were "My Black Mama," "Preachin' the Blues" (one of several of his blues that influenced ROBERT JOHNSON), "Dry Spell Blues," "Clarksdale Moan," "Mississippi County Farm Blues," and "What Am I to Do Blues." During this 1930 session, Son House and Willie Brown greatly enjoyed working together, stimulated by each other's company and artistry. They became a team and were accepted as kings of the blues for the next thirteen years, until Brown's death in 1942. House then moved to Rochester, New York, and gave up music for many years.

In 1964, blues researchers rediscovered Son House and persuaded him to resume performing. He sang and played around the United States, mostly at folk and blues festivals and at colleges, as well as in Europe, where he impressed a large public. A spell of bad health forced him to end his revived career after only a few years. He died in a rest home in Detroit.

SUGGESTED READING: Lawrence Cohn, ed., *Nothing but the Blues: The Music and the Musicians* (New York, 1993).

Howard, Dorothy Mills (1902–). Howard was an early student of children's folklore. Her 1938 Ph.D. dissertation, "Folk-Rhymes of American Children," was unique in that she collected her material directly from children, rather than from adults recalling their childhoods. It was this focus on the children themselves that distinguished her work and that set the standard for subsequent work by other researchers.

Howard taught in public school and, as an English professor, at Frostburg State College (Maryland). After her retirement in 1967, she worked with the Tri-University Project in playlore conducted by the University of Nebraska, New York University, and the University of Washington. Howard published widely in professional jour-

nals and wrote three books, *Dorothy's World: Childhood in Sabine Bottom, 1902–1910* (1977), a recollection of her own childhood; *Folklore for Children and Young People* (with Eloise Ramsey, 1952), a bibliography and resource guide for teachers; and *Pedro of Tonala* (1989), a book documenting the life of a boy growing up in a Mexican village.

SUGGESTED READING: Sylvia Ann Grider, "Dorothy Howard: Pioneer Collector of Children's Folklore," *Children's Folklore Review* 17 (1994), pp. 3–17.

Hudson, Arthur Palmer (1892–1978). Hudson was a southern folklorist best known as an excellent editor of collections. His *Folksongs of Mississippi and Their Background* (1936), *Humor of the Old Deep South* (1936), and *Folklore in American Literature* (1958) are all important collections. With HENRY MARTIN BELDEN, Hudson also edited the two volumes of song texts in *The Frank C. Brown Collection of North Carolina Folklore*. Hudson succeeded Frank C. Brown as secretary-treasurer of the North Carolina Folklore Society and served as editor of the organization's journal, *North Carolina Folklore*. He was also head of the curriculum in folklore at the University of North Carolina (1950–63), and part of his own collection became the foundation of the important Southern Folklife Collection of the University of North Carolina.

Born in Attala County, Mississippi, Hudson was educated at the University of Mississippi (B.S., 1913; M.A., 1920), the University of Chicago (a second M.A., 1925) and the University of North Carolina (Ph.D., 1930). He taught folklore and British romantic literature at the University of North Carolina.

See also: BOGGS, RALPH STEELE.

SUGGESTED READING: Hudson, "An Attala Boyhood," *Journal of Mississippi History* 4 (1942), pp. 59–75, 127–55; Beverly Patterson, entry on Arthur Palmer Hudson in Jan Harold Brunvand, ed., *American Folklore: An Encyclopedia* (New York, 1996).

Hughes, (James Mercer) Langston (1902–1967).

An African-American poet, Hughes made extensive use of black folklore as the basis and inspiration of much of his work. Born in Joplin, Missouri, Hughes was raised by his mother and grandmother after his father and mother separated. When his grandmother died, Hughes wandered from city to city before settling in Cleveland. There he attended high school, and his poem "The Negro Speaks of Rivers" was published in 1921, shortly after graduation. He moved to New York, where he attended Columbia University during 1921–22, before finding work as a steward on a freighter bound for Africa. He returned to the United States in 1925 and gained further recognition for his poetry while supporting himself as a busboy in a Washington, D.C., hotel. Recognizing the poet VACHEL LINDSAY in the dining room, Hughes put three of his poems beside his plate. Almost immediately, stories ran in the newspapers that Lindsay had discovered "a Negro busboy poet," and Hughes was awarded a scholarship to Lincoln University, from which he graduated in 1929—but not before publishing *The Weary Blues* (1926) and *Fine Clothes to the Jew* (1927). In 1930 came *Not Without Laughter,* a novel.

During the 1930s, Hughes became increasingly political and served as a correspondent during the Spanish Civil War in 1937. He wrote a collection of short stories, *The Ways of White Folks* (1934), and an autobiography (to age twenty-eight), *The Big Sea* (1940). (His later years would be covered in *I Wonder as I Wander,* 1956.) Two anthologies, *The Poetry of the Negro* (1949) and *The Book of Negro Folklore* (with Arna Bontemps, 1958) followed. Hughes also wrote for the stage, and translated the Spanish poetry of Federico García Lorca and Gabriela Mistral.

See also: AFRICAN AMERICANS.

SUGGESTED READING: James Emanuel, *Langston Hughes* (New York, 1967); Langston Hughes, *The Langston Hughes Reader* (New York, 1966).

Humor, folk.

The systematic collection of American folk humor—humorous traditional tales—began in the early twentieth century, when the tales were collected and classified according to motif in the manner of general folktales. Less systematic interest in American folk humor came before the middle of the nineteenth century, when folk humor was increasingly identified as the "soul" of American literature. This assertion was explored in scholarly detail by CONSTANCE ROURKE in *American Humor* (1931), which analyzed the great comic figures and forms of American folk humor and showed how these shaped American literature. Following in the footsteps of Rourke, RICHARD M. DORSON published examples of American humor in *Davy Crockett: American Comic Legend* (1939) and in *Jonathan Draws the Long Bow* (1946). Dorson regarded American humor as the product of a national mythology that developed during an age of unbelief. In such an age, he argued, mythology is not elevated to the realm of the superhuman, but reduced to the stage of the comic.

The folklorists of the generation of Rourke and Dorson looked principally to rural America, and especially the nineteenth-century western frontier, for orally transmitted humor (or versions of that humor as published in ALMANACS, newspapers, and other subliterary sources). The TALL TALE is frequently cited as the example par excellence of American frontier humor. More recent folklorists, such as Alan Dundes in the 1980s, have studied urban humor, typically from a psychoanalytic perspective. Dundes has studied and catalogued a variety of contemporary joke cycles, including elephant jokes, Polish jokes, Jewish American Princess jokes, dead-baby jokes, and the like, interpreting such cycles as outlets for socially unacceptable thoughts and sentiments.

SUGGESTED READING: Mody C. Boatright, *Folk Laughter on the American Frontier* (New York, 1946); Richard M. Dorson, *America in Legend: Folklore from the Colonial Period to the Present* (New York, 1973); Alan Dundes, *Cracking Jokes: Studies of Sick Humor Cycles and Stereotypes* (Berkeley, Calif., 1987); Constance Rourke, *American Humor: A Study in the National Character* (New York, 1931).

Hungarian Americans.

Persons of Hungarian descent often refer to themselves as Magyars, the ancient tribal name for Hungarians. Immigrants and their descendants form a relatively small group in the United States of fewer than two million, mostly in urban areas. The earliest immigrants were primarily refugees from the anti-Hapsburg revolution of 1848. From about 1870 until World War I, more immigrants arrived, mainly in search of economic opportunity. By the beginning of the twentieth century, most Hungarian immigrants made their living as laborers in heavy industry, with significant populations developing in midwestern industrial cities such as Detroit and Cleveland, as well as the smaller industrial centers of Ohio and Indiana. With the end of World War I, a substantial number of professionals—physicians, scientists, teachers—immigrated. Another wave of immi-

grants from the professional classes followed the collapse of the struggle against Communist rule in 1956.

Despite the small but heterogeneous composition of this immigrant group, the Hungarian community established solidarity during the late nineteenth and early twentieth centuries through a variety of social and religious organizations, which, rather than emphasizing the folklore practices of the peasantry, stressed demonstrations and displays of Hungarian nationalism, combined with American patriotism. With the new wave of immigration after 1956, interest in ethnic folk identity revived. Traditional dances, songs, and crafts were exhibited in various festivals. In addition, interest grew in collecting and preserving the folklore of the earlier immigrants and of the immigrant experience.

See also: IMMIGRANT FOLKLORE.

SUGGESTED READING: Linda Dégh entry on Hungarian Americans, in Jan Harold Brunvand, ed., *American Folklore: An Encyclopedia* (New York, 1996); Emil Lengyel, *Americans from Hungary* (Philadelphia and New York, 1948).

Hunting.

Hunting has given rise to much folklore, including songs associated with the hunt, TALL TALES, SUPERSTITIONS, and FOLK SPEECH. Hunting metaphors, such as being "hot on the trail" of an idea or having "picked up the scent" of trouble, abound in everyday speech. "Old-timey" musical traditions, as well as COUNTRY MUSIC and BLUEGRASS, frequently allude to hunting. In modern, urban-dominated America, the activity of hunting itself is called a sport, but it is probably more properly considered a ritual effort to reconnect with nature through animals. In this ritual, the quarry animal serves as a worthy adversary, while the hunting dog serves as an aid to

The Life of a Hunter / "A Tight Fix," *print by Currier & Ives, 1861, after a painting by A. F. Tait (Collection of Walton Rawls). Hunting could certainly be a hazardous occupation in the mid-nineteenth-century West; however, it was also a source of exciting tall-tale narratives.*

the hunter. With both animals, however, the hunter forges a bond. The significance of the contest with the quarry may be found in recalling Native American beliefs such as, by killing a worthy animal, the hunter may acquire some of the qualities of that animal—the cunning of the fox, the strength of the bear, or the swiftness of the deer. Partaking of the flesh of the animal reinforces this exchange, and some Indian hunters made it a point to eat the heart of the slain animal. Such identification of hunter and hunted may, in attenuated form, be an impetus behind the modern sport-ritual of hunting. Indeed, committed hunters would dispute the term "attenuated." While few people in our day pursue hunting as a means of livelihood, many insist that it is nevertheless a way of life, an activity from which they not only derive pleasure and satisfaction, but emotional and cultural validation. Among avid hunters, the lore and ritual of the hunt are cherished as cultural heirlooms to be passed to their children—traditionally to boys, although hunting is also a family sport and many women become enthusiasts as well. In some regions and among some people, killing one's first buck is still a rite of passage into (typically male) adulthood.

See also: WHALING.

SUGGESTED READING: Barbara Allen and Thomas J. Schlereth, *Chaseworld: Foxhunting and Storytelling in New Jersey's Pine Barrens* (Philadelphia, 1992); Stuart Marks, *Southern Hunting in Black and White: Nature, History and Ritual in a Carolina Community* (Princeton, N.J., 1992).

Hurston, Zora Neale (1891? 1903?–1960).

Hurston was an African-American folklorist and writer, a key figure in the Harlem Renaissance, whose works explore black culture of the rural South. She was born in Eatonville, Florida; while all sources fix her date of birth as January 7, they vary as to year, either 1891 or 1903. She was educated at Howard University in 1918, then moved to New York City in 1925, where she became a part of the Harlem Renaissance movement and entered Barnard College. After taking her B.A. from Barnard (1928), she studied with FRANZ BOAS at Columbia University and did fieldwork on voodoo in Haiti. At Boas's urging, she also collected folklore in the South, writing *Mules and Men* (1935), which presented materials collected in Florida and Alabama during 1929–31. Her 1937 novel *Their Eyes Were Watching God* contained much African-American folk material, including folk beliefs, manners, and speech. This, her second work of fiction, was greeted both with acclaim and criticism, principally from African-American commentators, who objected to the book's essentially celebratory tone. Hurston celebrated black southern culture instead of portraying her characters as the abject victims of white beliefs in the inferiority of the black race. In 1938, Hurston published a collection of Jamaican and Haitian folktales, *Tell My Horse,* which includes much of what she had gathered about voodoo and spirit possession.

Hurston published her last novel, *Seraph on the Suwanee,* in 1948, then retired into increasing obscurity. She worked as a librarian and as a maid, suffering a stroke in 1959, from which she never recovered. She died the following year at the Saint Lucie County Welfare Home, Fort Pierce, Florida, and was buried in an unmarked grave.

See also: AFRICAN AMERICANS; FOLKLORE IN AMERICAN LITERATURE.

SUGGESTED READING: Zora Neale Hurston, *Dust Tracks on the Road* (autobiography; New York, 1942); Zora Neale Hurston, *I Love Myself When I Am Laughing and Then Again When I Am Looking Mean and Impressive* (anthology; New York, 1979); Robert E. Hemenway, *Zora Neale Hurston: A Literary Biography* (Urbana, Ill., 1977).

Hurt, Mississippi John (1893–1966). A Delta BLUES singer and guitarist from Teoc, Mississippi, Hurt made his local reputation performing in Avalon, Mississippi. He recorded a number of sides for the Okeh label beginning in 1928, including "Candy Man," "Spike Driver Blues," and "Stagger Lee Blues." He was little known nationally until his appearance at the 1963 Newport Folk Festival, after which he continued to record and began touring. His belated national discovery was cut short by his death in 1966.

Hyatt, Harry M. (1898–1978). Hyatt was an amateur collector of American folklore, with particular emphasis on superstition and the supernatural. By vocation an Episcopal clergyman, Hyatt grew up in Quincy, Illinois, studied theology at Oxford University, and produced, in 1928, a study of the Coptic Church of Abyssinia. Hyatt began collecting folklore along the Mississippi River near Quincy, amassing some 16,000 items, which were included in *Hoodoo-Conjuration-Witchcraft-Rootwork: Beliefs Accepted by Many Negroes and White Persons,* five volumes published during 1970–78. Much of this material concerns superstition, and during 1936–40, he collected in the East and South, concentrating on hoodoo, conjuration, witchcraft, and divination. The exhaustive hoodoo collection concentrates on African-American beliefs and remains the most thorough ever undertaken. In 1972, the American Folklore Society officially recognized Hyatt's massive contribution to folklore fieldwork.

SUGGESTED READING: Richard M. Dorson and Michael Bell, eds., "Harry Middleton Hyatt," *Journal of the Folklore Institute* 16 (special issue, 1979).

I

"I Gave My Love a Cherry." This American folk song was a staple of the FOLK-REVIVAL movement of the 1960s. A charming love song, it is derived from "Captain Wedderburn's Courtship," a CHILD BALLAD.

See also: FOLK MUSIC.

I house. The "I house" got its name when a student of VERNACULAR ARCHITECTURE identified this house type as typical of Indiana, Illinois, and Iowa (all states beginning with *I*); however, the I house is actually much more widely distributed throughout much of the United States. The I house is built on a plan that is basically two rooms wide, one room deep, and two rooms tall ("two over two"). The structure's gable roof has eaves running to the front and rear. This basic pattern was subject to much architectural variation.

Immigrant folklore. As the cliché puts it, America is a nation of immigrants, and many American folklorists study the folk traditions of those who have immigrated to the United States or who identify themselves as descendants of immigrants. Folklorists study the degree to which imported folk traditions survive intact, change, or disappear. They observe which traditions seem the most important—that is, which survive most

tenaciously—and why. They consider how imported folklore functions to preserve and affirm ethnic identity. Conversely, a number of European students of folklore have seen America as a place of survival of folk traditions. For example, the British folklorist CECIL SHARP came to the Appalachians to collect examples of British BALLADS that had all but disappeared from their place of origin.

See also: ANGLO AMERICANS; BALTIC PEOPLES; BASQUE AMERICANS; CHINESE AMERICANS; DUTCH AMERICANS; FILIPINO AMERICANS; FINNISH AMERICANS; FRENCH AMERICANS; GERMAN AMERICANS; GREEK AMERICANS; HUNGARIAN AMERICANS; IRISH AMERICANS; ITALIAN AMERICANS; JAPANESE AMERICANS; KOREAN AMERICANS; MEXICAN AMERICANS; PENNSYLVANIA GERMANS; POLISH AMERICANS; PORTUGUESE AMERICANS; SCANDINAVIAN AMERICANS; SCOTTISH AMERICANS; SLAVIC AMERICANS; WELSH AMERICANS.

Irish Americans. The first major American immigrant group, Irish Americans met with much prejudice and even persecution in the nineteenth century, yet, of all national immigrant groups in this country, they are now regarded with perhaps the greatest affection and interest from non-Irish Americans. Excluded from many vocational and social venues during the nineteenth century, the Irish community in America is now more than willing to invite outsiders into the many public aspects of Irish heritage, including song, dance, and strong drink. SAINT PATRICK'S DAY, nominally the feast day of Ireland's patron saint, has become an unofficial *American* national holiday.

As early as the seventeenth century, the first Irish immigrants came to America to escape English oppression and to find not merely economic opportunity, but survival. The great Irish potato famines of the mid-nineteenth century were devastating to the Irish economy and to the subsistence of the Irish peasantry. Subsequent immigration was motivated by a somewhat less urgent quest for general economic opportunity. The nation the Irish left is very rich in folklore and especially folktales (that the Irish are "natural" storytellers is a cliché), yet little of the rural folk traditions were brought to America, except in the commercially sanitized form of leprechaun and shamrock decorations seen everywhere on Saint Patrick's Day and at all times in such places as Irish bars. The rich oral tradition of the old country has been distilled on this side of the Atlantic into a handful of witty "old Irish" toasts, sayings, proverbs, and blessings, such as "May the wind be always at your back and God hold you in the hollow of His hand." While some Irish Americans perform traditional Irish music—popular in certain urban bars ("Irish pubs"), even among non-Irish patrons—few celebrate Irish folk culture in the way many other European immigrant groups do, with traditional foods and costume. Instead, they tend to honor the spirit of the Irish homeland ("the old sod"), for which even Irish Americans several generations removed from immigration have reverence. (It should be noted that various American organizations do exist to foster the preservation of ethnic traditions; The Irish American Cultural Institute, St. Paul, Minnesota, is the leading national organization of this kind.)

Today, to think of Irish Americans is to think principally of urban dwellers; however, through much of the eighteenth century, so-called Scotch-Irish immigrants (Ulster Presbyterian Irish of Scots ancestry) settled primarily in the southern colonies, and many of them migrated to the Appalachian frontier, where they developed one of the richest regional folk cultures in America (see APPALACHIA). It is in this region that rural Irish folk culture has made itself most strongly felt in American folklore.

Beyond Appalachia, however, both esoteric and exoteric Irish-American folklore tends to be centered either in the city or in industrial and construction laboring groups. In the cities (especially New York, Boston, and Chicago), the Irish, at first the social and political underdogs, often rose to rough-and-tumble political prominence. Irishmen occupied high urban political office (many were mayors) as well as rank-and-file municipal offices: cop, firefighter, streetcar conductor. Irish politicians were the heart and soul of American urban machine politics. By the late nineteenth and early twentieth centuries, traditional Irish songs and popular songs composed along traditional lines (such as those by George M. Cohan) were popular among Irish and non-Irish audiences alike. In the meantime, Irish laborers became celebrated as the muscle behind such titanic undertakings as the Union Pacific portion of the transcontinental railroad and the construction of such urban wonders as skyscrapers and the Pennsylvania Railroad tunnels under the Hudson River. Irish physical prowess also manifested itself in professional sports. Early BASEBALL and boxing history was dominated by the Irish, with the prizefighter John L. Sullivan (1858–1918) emerging not only as the first boxer of national renown, but as an Irish-American folk hero. Indeed, Sullivan was viewed by Irish and non-Irish alike as the transformation of the stereotypical "fighting Irishman" from a street brawler to a grand sportsman and athlete. That "fighting

Irishman" image is only one of several Irish stereotypes. Like the others, however, it is less a product of exoteric folklore and stereotyping by others than it is a form of ethnic self-portrait and even self-parody. Irish Americans have freely transformed such stereotypes as the combative Irishman, the boastful Irishman, the corn beef-and-cabbage-eating Irishman, and the hard-drinking Irishman, as well as such symbols as the leprechaun and the shamrock, into public badges of ethnic pride.

See also: ESOTERIC FOLKLORE; EXOTERIC FOLKLORE; IMMIGRANT FOLKLORE.

SUGGESTED READING: Bob Callahan, *The Big Book of American Irish Culture* (New York, 1989); William D. Griffin, *The Book of Irish Americans* (New York, 1990); Lawrence J. McCaffrey, *Textures of Irish America* (Syracuse, N.Y., 1992); Kerby A. Miller, *Emigrants and Exiles: Ireland and the Irish Exodus to North America* (New York, 1985).

Irving, Washington (1783–1859).

With JAMES FENIMORE COOPER, Irving was the first American writer to gain an international reputation. His most successful, popular, and highly admired works, the short stories in *The Sketch Book of Geoffrey Crayon, Gent.* (1819–20), which includes "Rip Van Winkle" and "The Legend of Sleepy Hollow," strike the reader as having been founded on folktales—as, indeed, they were, albeit from a mixture of local and European sources. In turn, certain of Irving's characters, such as Diedrich Knickerbocker (fictional author of Irving's satirical and parodic *A History of New York* [1809]), Rip Van Winkle, and Ichabod Crane have some of the qualities of folk characters and mock folk heroes, while the Headless Horseman is a mock folk monster. These charac-

Washington Irving, as illustrated in Reuben Post Halleck, History of American Literature, *1911. (Collection of Alan Axelrod)*

ters have all entered into the pantheon of popular culture, and even people who have not read Irving know of Rip Van Winkle and of Ichabod Crane and the Headless Horseman.

Irving was born in New York City and grew up, a frail and highly favored child, in a large family. He was early on steeped in the lore of his native place, especially its Dutch heritage. "Rip Van Winkle" is set in New York State's Catskill Mountains, while "The Legend of Sleepy Hollow" takes place in the vicinity of Tarrytown, just north of New York City; however, the folktale-like quality of both works derives mainly from German rather than native sources. The roots of the "Rip Van Winkle" tale may be traced to a tale about one Peter Klaus (published in Otmar's *Volksaagen*), and the origins of the Sleepy Hollow tale may be found in *Der wilde Jäger* by Bürger, as well as Johann Karl August Musaeus's *Volksmärchen der Deutschen*. Nevertheless, while Irving did not make extensive use of local folklore, he did imaginatively realize vivid local Dutch stereotypes, and he was clearly fascinated by folklore, engaging in correspondence with the

Etching by F.O.C. Darley of Ichabod Crane and the Headless Horseman from Washington Irving's "The Legend of Sleepy Hollow."

German folklorist Karl Böttiger and drawing inspiration from the great British novelist Sir Walter Scott, whose works make extensive use of folkloric materials.

Irving was early on apprenticed to a lawyer, Josiah Ogden Hoffman, to whose daughter Matilda he became engaged. After a European tour and the newspaper publication of sketches later collected as *Letters of Jonathan Oldstyle* (1802–03; 1824), Irving passed the bar examination (1806) and opened a law office; but he became far more interested in collaborating with his brother William and JAMES KIRKE PAULDING on the Addisonian-style essays of the *Salmagundi* series (1807–08). In 1809, Irving published the delightful *History of New York,* in which the fictional author, Diedrich Knickerbocker, emerges as the archetypal pedant, and in which the Dutch burghers of the colony's early years are comically fabulous antiheroes. In this same year, Matilda

Hoffman died suddenly, leaving Irving brokenhearted. He was to remain a lifelong bachelor.

Although Irving pursued his family's business interests for some years, the death of Matilda left him adrift until 1815, when, in Liverpool on business, he met Sir Walter Scott. At the great writer's urging, Irving brought out *The Sketch Book of Geoffrey Crayon, Gent.,* his most enduring work. Now launched in full earnest on a literary career, Irving produced a sequel to the *Sketchbook, Bracebridge Hall* (1822), and traveled widely. He wrote a biography of Christopher Columbus (1828) and another historical-biographical volume, *The Companions of Columbus* (1831), followed by two books steeped in legends of Spain's Moorish past, *Conquest of Granada* (1829) and *The Alhambra* (1832). When he returned to New York in 1832, after seventeen years in Europe, he was lionized as a great writer. Having spent so many years in the lap of Old World civilization, Irving turned westward, making a journey through the American West and producing *A Tour of the Prairies* (1835), *Astoria* (1836), and *The Adventures of Captain Bonneville* (1837), all of which contain rich pictures of life on the frontier and in the far West.

For four years, from 1842 to 1846, Irving served as U.S. minister (ambassador) to Spain, then retired to "Sunnyside," his Hudson River estate in Tarrytown, New York.

See also: CURRIER & IVES; DUTCH AMERICANS; FOLKLORE IN AMERICAN LITERATURE; LOCAL-COLOR STORY; LONGFELLOW, HENRY WADSWORTH; MORTON, THOMAS; RIP VAN WINKLE; THORPE, THOMAS BANGS.

SUGGESTED READING: Henry A. Pochmann, "Irving's German Sources in *The Sketch Book*," *Studies in Philology* 27 (July 1930), pp. 489–94; Stanley T. Williams, *The Life of Washington Irving* (New York, 1935); Philip Young, "Fallen from Time: Rip Van Winkle," in Philip Young, *Three Bags Full: Essays in American Fiction* (New York, 1972).

Isolate art. A term used to describe the highly personal, idiosyncratic work of artists who are isolated, physically, emotionally, or both, from the cultural mainstream.

Italian Americans. As many Italian Americans are quick to point out, the first Italian in the New World was no less than CHRISTOPHER COLUMBUS, and it is true that Italian explorers, trappers, and traders were active in North America throughout the period of exploration and set-tlement; however, the period of the greatest immigration of Italian Americans came at the turn of the nineteenth century and into the first two decades of the twentieth century. Italian immigrants from the period prior to 1880 were, for the most part, from northern Italy, the nation's wealthier region; after 1880, southern Italians formed the majority of immigrants, many of them quite poor, who, like the nineteenth-century Irish, immigrated to escape economic destitution and political oppression. While the earlier group of immigrants settled throughout the country, forming small communities in the cities and working on their own farms elsewhere (in Northern California, Italian Americans started a prosperous wine industry), the later immigrants settled mostly in the cities of the Northeast, forming large ethnic neighborhoods known as Little Italies. The remarkable cohesiveness of these neighborhoods reflects the village culture of southern Italy. The solidarity and ethnic identification of Italian Americans is reinforced in no small measure by FOODWAYS; Italian cuisine, in both its homelier and more elegant forms, has long been popular in the United States among Italians and non-Italians alike.

In predominantly Italian urban neighborhoods, ethnic activity is typically centered in the church. Street festivals on certain saint's days (such as the San Gennaro Festival in Manhattan's Little Italy) offer food, entertainment, and religious processions that attract neighborhood residents and people from all over the city and of all ethnic backgrounds.

While maintaining strong ethnic identity and affiliation, Italian Americans assimilated well and successfully into the American cultural mainstream. What prejudices they have long confronted flow primarily from stereotypes relating to organized crime (the Mafia) and personified in such figures as AL CAPONE. Stories about Mafiosi and other Italian gangsters have long been popular movie and television fare. While criminal ethnic stereotypes are inherently negative, of course, the image was given a certain nobility by the best-selling 1969 Mario Puzo novel *The Godfather* and the highly acclaimed Francis Ford Coppola *Godfather* films that followed in 1972 and 1974 (a less successful third sequel was released in 1990).

See also: IMMIGRANT FOLKLORE.

SUGGESTED READING: Luisa Del Guidice, ed., *Studies in Italian American Folklore* (Logan, Utah, 1993); Joseph Lopreato, *Italian Americans* (New York, 1970); Frances M. Malpezzi and William M. Clements, *Italian-American Folklore* (Little Rock, Ark., 1992); Elizabeth Mathias and Richard Raspa, *Italian Folktales in America: The Verbal Art of an Immigrant Woman* (Detroit, 1985).

Ives, Burl (1909–1995). For many Americans during the forties, fifties, and sixties, Burl Ives was the embodiment of the folksinger-balladeer. While Ives achieved more commercial success and exposure than most traditional singers, he came by his repertoire firsthand. His parents were tenant farmers in Illionis, and Ives learned his first ballads from his grandmother. During the 1930s, he traveled across the United States, picking up many more songs along the way. Becoming a singer and actor in New York late in the 1930s, he was hired by CBS radio as "The Wayfaring Stranger" and introduced a large broadcast audience to traditional American song. In 1944, he starred in a Broadway folk "cavalcade," *Sing Out, Sweet Land,* which solidified his stature as the most visible performer of folk songs in the country.

Although other performers during the folk revival of the late forties, fifties, and sixties were perhaps more sophisticated and presented more obscure as well as more socially challenging material—for example, the protest repertoire—Ives continued to enjoy great success as an exponent of what he called "Native American folk music."

Ives's folksinging success crossed over into commercial country music during the early 1960s, and he won a Grammy in 1962 for his country-western hit "Funny Way of Laughin'." Ives also enjoyed success as a distinguished character actor, both on stage and in film. He created "Big Daddy" in the Broadway production of Tennessee Williams's *Cat on a Hot Tin Roof* in 1958, then went on to re-create the role for the film version.

See also: FOLK MUSIC; LOMAX, ALAN; TERRY, SONNY.

SUGGESTED READING: Burl Ives, *Wayfaring Stranger* (New York, 1948); Burl Ives, *Song in America: Our Musical Heritage* (New York, 1962).

Ives, Charles (1874–1954). One of the most important "classical" American composers of the twentieth century, Ives typically built his music on quotations from and allusions to a vast body of American folk tunes, especially those of his native New England. Even his original melodies often evoke the feeling of folk music, albeit in a strikingly modern, often purposefully discordant, even disconcerting setting.

Ives received his first musical training from his father, a bandleader and music teacher, who was not only devoted to American traditional music, but also experimented with quarter tones, so that, from an early age, Ives became accustomed to the juxtaposition of folk melodies and avant-garde harmonies. Ives's early composition, "Song for the Harvest Season," written about 1894 for voice, trumpet, violin, and organ, put each of the instruments and the voice in different keys, a radical experiment. Ives's highly conventional music professor at Yale University, Horatio Parker, did all he could to transform his student into a classically correct composer.

Ives did not pursue a musical career after graduating from Yale in 1898, but became an insurance clerk. By 1907, he had cofounded his own successful insurance company. He continued composing, however, creating most of his best-known works before 1915. Few were performed during his lifetime; however, his *Third Symphony* (1904–11) received the Pulitzer Prize in 1947.

Ives's contribution to American music—indeed, to music generally—is the extraordinary marriage of traditions deeply rooted in American culture, including folk tunes, popular tunes, hymns, and spirituals, with such highly advanced techniques as tone clusters, microtonal intervals, and aleatoric (chance) elements. With these techniques, he anticipated the course of modern music by thirty to fifty years. While most of his compositions employ folk and traditional elements, many of his *114 Songs* (1919–24) approach the folk material more directly. In some cases, Ives does not quote folk melodies, but creates the feeling of folk music with original compositions.

SUGGESTED READING: Henry and Sidney Cowell, *Charles Ives and His Music* (New York, 1955).

J

Jackalope. The American jackalope combines the body of a jackrabbit with deer antlers or antelope horns. It is a mythical beast, peculiar to the Great Plains and Rocky Mountains, but is often given substance on EXAGGERATED POSTCARDS and by inspired taxidermists. There is a National Jackalope Society in Sheridan, Wyoming, which may be the state of the beast's origin. Taxidermists in Wyoming have been mounting jackalopes since at least the 1930s and, perhaps, as early as the 1920s. It is said that the first jackalope was sighted by a mountain man named Roy Ball in 1829.

The jackalope is a formidable creature. Though not aggressive by nature, it will attack ferociously and at very high speed when provoked. A buffalo gun must be used against it. Jackalopes can imitate the human voice and are known to sing during nocturnal thunderstorms. They mate only during flashes of lightning. Their milk is a sovereign remedy for a host of afflictions.

Analogues to the American jackalope exist in tales of horned rabbits documented from Africa, Mexico, and Mayan Central America.

See also: CRYPTOZOOLOGY; MOTHMAN.

SUGGESTED READING: Richard M. Dorson, *Man and Beast in American Comic Legend* (Bloomington, Ind., 1982).

Jackson, Andrew (1767–1845). One of the most colorful of American military and polit-

Andrew Jackson, from Charles F. Horne, Great Men and Famous Women *(1894).*

ical figures, Andrew Jackson figures in American folklore as a folk hero and a CULTURE HERO, the embodiment of what many Americans saw as the indomitable spirit of the western frontier and a representative as well as champion of the "common man." He was born in Waxhaws, though it is unclear whether on the North or South Carolina side of the settlement. His father, a Scotch-Irish immigrant, died before Andrew was born, and the boy's life was further torn apart in 1780 by the British invasion of the Carolinas during the American Revolution. His brothers, fighting in the Revolution, were captured by the British at the Battle of Hanging Rock on August 1, 1780; one of them, Robert, died. Young Andrew, who had himself enlisted in the patriot cause as a partisan, was captured and, in a scene often retold as a folktale, was severely wounded when a British officer struck him with the flat of his sword after he refused an order to black the man's boots. In the meantime, Jackson's mother had volunteered to minister to American prisoners of war confined on a ship anchored in Charleston Harbor. She contracted prison fever and died, leaving Andrew Jackson an orphan at age fourteen.

After the war, Jackson studied law and was admitted to the North Carolina bar. He moved to Nashville, Tennessee, and became attorney general for the Southwest Territory in 1791, then a circuit-riding solicitor in and about Nashville. As an attorney, Jackson developed a reputation as an opponent of federal tyranny by defending merchant clients who had lost money as a result of the extension of federal authority over the territory. The year 1791 also saw Jackson's marriage to Rachel Donelson Robards. The couple believed that Rachel and her first husband had been legally divorced, but when this proved not to be the case, they remarried in 1794. Nevertheless, the issue would cloud Jackson's private and political life for many years, ultimately becoming the subject of a duel in 1806, in which Jackson killed a man.

Jackson rose quickly through the political ranks, serving as a delegate to the Tennessee constitutional convention in 1796 and a congressman from 1796 to 1797. In 1797, Jackson was appointed to serve out the senatorial term of his political mentor, William Blount, who was expelled from the Senate because of his involvement in a British plan to seize Florida and Louisiana from Spain; however, in 1798, on the verge of

bankruptcy, Jackson resigned from the Senate to return to Tennessee, where from 1798 to 1804, he served as a superior court judge, then stepped down to devote himself full-time to rebuilding his fortune, which he did sufficiently to erect his celebrated plantation, the Hermitage, outside of Nashville.

Jackson did not reenter public life until William Blount, now governor of Tennessee, commissioned him major general of volunteers in the War of 1812. Jackson defeated the pro-British "Red Stick" Creek Indians at the decisive Battle of Horseshoe Bend (March 27, 1814) and was quickly appointed to command of the defense of New Orleans. On January 8, 1815, he defeated British attackers in the Battle of New Orleans, which, ironically, occurred after the Treaty of Ghent had been signed (on December 24, 1814), but before the news reached the commanders in the field. To Americans, this irony hardly mattered. They celebrated Jackson's victory as a vindication of national honor in a war that had consisted of one American military disaster after another. Overnight, Jackson became a legend, the personification of American courage, skill, and righteousness. He continued his military career, fighting the Seminole Indians, mercilessly evicting them from their tribal homelands and pursuing them deep into Spanish Florida through the spring of 1818. After he audaciously deposed Spanish colonial authorities and others in Florida, conservative elements in Congress sought his censure, but failed. Already celebrated as the champion of the "common man," Jackson was beyond the reach of his political opponents. After serving as provisional territorial governor of Florida and U.S. senator for Tennessee (this time elected in his own right), Jackson ran for president in 1824, but was narrowly defeated by John Quincy Adams. He ran again in 1828, winning by a comfortable margin. During his two terms as president, Jackson brought about such profound changes not only in American government, but in the entire American attitude that the era became known as the Age of Jackson.

The tone of the Jackson administration was set by the new president's very first gesture. Disdaining the traditional carriage ride from the inaugural site to the White House, Jackson made the trip on horseback. There was to be no grand inaugural ball, but, rather, a quiet celebration in the executive mansion; however, "the people"— who had put Jackson in the White House— thronged the streets of Washington to cheer their new president and now invited themselves to the private reception, nearly wrecking the White House in the process. There can be no doubt that Andrew Jackson's two terms as president (1829–37) brought a greater degree of democracy to American government—though a very thin line separated democracy from demagoguery. For Jackson's contemporaries, the president assumed his most powerfully symbolic role in doing battle against what Missouri senator Thomas Hart Benton called The Monster, the highly unpopular Second Bank of the United States. With the demise of the Second Bank of the United States, credit became more plentiful and westward settlement proceeded more rapidly (but the economy became less stable).

The first "westerner" elevated to the White House, Jackson ushered in a perceived era of the common man. After him, political candidates of all kinds scrambled to lay claim to humble origins and, if possible, birth in a LOG CABIN. Certainly, it was the Jackson presidency that made the election of another "westerner," ABRAHAM LINCOLN, possible less than a quarter century later.

Jackson's later years, including his final years as president, were plagued by ill health. He retired to the Hermitage after his second term ended, having handpicked his successor, Martin Van Buren.

See also: CROCKETT, DAVY; WEBSTER, DANIEL.

SUGGESTED READING: Burke Davis, *Old Hickory: A Life of Andrew Jackson* (New York, 1977); Arthur M. Schlesinger, *The Age of Jackson* (Boston, 1945).

Jackson, George Pullen (1874–1953).

Jackson collected religious folk songs in the American South and traced their origins. He published *White Spirituals in the Southern Uplands* in 1933 and *White and Negro Spirituals* in 1943. In the second book, Jackson concluded that the African-American spirituals were derived not from African origins, but directly from the white spirituals. This interpretation has now been almost universally rejected by folklorists, who believe that African-American spirituals may be traced to African roots as well as to the interaction with white spiritual traditions.

Jackson was a New Englander by birth, but had been raised in the South, where he was chiefly exposed to the traditions of white religious music. In addition to *White Spirituals in the Southern Uplands* and *White and Negro Spirituals,* he compiled *Spiritual Folk-Songs of Early America* (1937), *Down-East Spirituals* (1942), and *Another Sheaf of White Spirituals* (1952). Generally, Jackson traced the southern spirituals to New England, and, in turn, traced the religious folk songs of New England to Britain.

Jackson was a folk-song scholar and collector by avocation, and a professor of German (at Nashville's Vanderbilt University) by vocation. He also organized singing events and advocated the teaching of American folk music and folk songs in public schools.

See also: APPALACHIA; FOLK MUSIC.

SUGGESTED READING: D. K. Wilgus, "The Negro-White Spirituals," in D. K. Wilgus, *Anglo-American Folksong Scholarship Since 1898* (New Brunswick, N.J., 1959).

Jackson, Mahalia (1911–1972). Dubbed the "Queen of Gospel Song," Mahalia Jackson brought the African-American GOSPEL MUSIC tradition to a wide audience, both black and white. Born in New Orleans, she sang in the choir of the church in which her father preached. Although she was brought up in a strict religious atmosphere and was exposed to African-American sacred song traditions, she also enjoyed listening to such earthy BLUES singers as BESSIE SMITH and Ida Cox. Her religious singing was influenced by the rhythmic inventiveness of those blues vocalists.

Jackson moved to Chicago at age sixteen and worked odd jobs while singing with a gospel quintet. During this period, she carefully husbanded her money, opening a beauty shop, then a flower shop, and investing in Chicago real estate. She did not neglect singing, however, and in the 1930s came to national attention on a cross-country gospel tour singing such songs as "He's Got the Whole World in His Hands." She made her first recording, "I Can Put My Trust in Jesus," in 1934, and her reputation increased steadily from that point. In the 1950s, she debuted at New York's Carnegie Hall, appeared frequently on radio and television, toured internationally, and enjoyed record sales in the millions. In 1961, she was invited to perform at one of the inaugural parties for President John F. Kennedy.

Jackson lent her prestige to the African-American civil rights movement from its beginnings, in 1955, traveling to Montgomery, Alabama, to show solidarity with the momentous bus boycott there, and, in 1963, she sang at the Washington, D.C., rally at which Rev. Martin Luther King, Jr., gave his famous "I have a dream" speech. A number of popular singers, most notably Aretha Franklin, acknowledge a debt of inspiration to Jackson.

See also: FOLK MUSIC.

Jackson, Mary Magdalene ("Aunt Molly") (1880–1960). Jackson was a composer-singer of labor protest songs in the Appalachian coalfields of the 1930s. Her father, Oliver Perry Garland, was a miner, preacher, and union activist, and Molly (as the girl was called) accompanied her father to pickets and union meetings from early childhood. She married Jim Stewart, a coal miner, who died in a 1912 mining accident. She then married another miner, Bill Jackson, and settled in Harlan County, Kentucky, where she made her living as a midwife and earned the sobriquet Aunt Molly Jackson.

Her protest songs from the 1930s include "I Am a Union Woman" (1931), "Kentucky Miner's Wife" (1932), and "Dreadful Memories" (1935), among others. Jackson became nationally known when she performed in New York City in December 1931 and sang to an audience of 21,000 at the Coliseum. She settled in New York after touring and performing at labor rallies through 1936.

SUGGESTED READING: Juila S. Ardery, ed., *Welcome the Traveler Home: Jim Garland's Story of the Kentucky Mountains* (Lexington, Ky., 1983); John Greenway, *American Folksongs of Protest* (1953; reprint ed., New York, 1977).

Jack tales. Jack tales are oral narratives concerning the adventures of a teenage trickster named Jack who searches, in a roundabout way, for maturity and success. Typically, the Jack character leaves home to escape abusive treatment or simply to seek his fortune. Along the way, Jack acquires a magical object, a magical friend, or a magical ability that helps him perform (as a rule) three apparently impossible labors in order to conquer an apparently unconquerable opponent. His reward for success is riches and a beautiful wife with whom he returns to his native community.

American Jack tales have clear European origins—though the European heroes (Hans in Germany, Jock in Scotland, Jack in England and Ireland) tend to be simpletons rather than tricksters. Jack tales are concentrated in the mountains of eastern Kentucky, southwestern Virginia, and northwestern North Carolina, though stories also have been collected elsewhere in the eastern United States. The most influential collection of Jack tales was made by RICHARD CHASE and published in *The Jack Tales* (1943), with additional material included in *The Grandfather Tales* (1948), and *American Folk Tales and Songs* (1956).

See also: WARD, MARSHALL.

SUGGESTED READING: William B. McCarthy, ed., *Jack in Two Worlds: Contemporary North American Taletellers* (Chapel Hill, N.C. 1994); Thomas McGowan, ed., "Jack Tales," *North Carolina Folklore Journal* (Special Issue) 26 (1978), pp. 49–143; Charles L. Perdue, Jr., ed., *Outwitting the Devil: Jack Tales from Wise County Virginia.* (Santa Fe, N.M., 1987).

James, Frank (1843–1915) and Jesse (1847–1882). The most celebrated outlaw brothers in the Old West, Frank and Jesse James were deemed folk heroes in their own time and have continued to figure as legendary characters, frequently portrayed in fiction, dime novels, movies, and television programs.

The boys grew up on a Missouri farm and came of age during the turbulent period leading up to the Civil War. When war broke out in 1861, Frank joined William C. Quantrill's Confederate guerrilla raiders. There he met Cole Younger, who, with his brothers, would become charter members of the James Gang after the war. Jesse followed in his older brother's footsteps by joining the guerrilla band of Quantrill's protégé, "Bloody" Bill Anderson.

The James boys robbed their first bank, at Liberty, Missouri, on February 13, 1866. Over the next ten years, the James Gang robbed banks over a large territory, from Iowa to Alabama, to Texas, and branched out to trains and stagecoaches as well. Eastern dime novelists and newspaper writers reported and embellished the gang's exploits, and in the Missouri Ozark country, the legend of Jesse James spread through oral tales, which portrayed him as a Robin Hood, whose allegiance to the Southern cause had earned him the enmity of Northern and Eastern authorities.

By far the gang's most celebrated raid occurred on September 7, 1876, when they robbed the First National Bank at Northfield, Minnesota. They met with unanticipated resistance, and of the eight gang members, only Frank and Jesse James escaped death or capture. After a hiatus, the brothers formed a new gang in 1879, prompting Missouri governor Thomas T. Crittenden in 1881 to offer a $10,000 reward for their capture, dead or alive. Robert Ford, a young man who insinuated himself into the gang, eager to collect the reward money, assassinated Jesse James as he was adjusting a picture on the wall of his St. Joseph, Missouri, home. Frank James gave himself up to authorities shortly afterward. Tried for murder in Missouri, he was found not guilty by a sympathetic jury. Another jury acquitted him of robbery charges in Alabama, and yet another Missouri jury refused to convict him for armed robbery. He lived the balance of his long life in quiet retirement.

That no jury would convict Frank James attests to his popularity. As to Ford, he was reviled in a popular BALLAD of the period, which told of the "dirty little coward who shot Mr. Howard [James's alias in St. Joseph] and laid poor Jesse in his grave."

See also: CRIME AND CRIMINALS; GUNFIGHTER, WESTERN.

SUGGESTED READING: William A. Settle, Jr., *Jesse James Was His Name* (Columbia, Mo., 1966).

James, Thelma Grey (1899–1988).

With EMELYN ELIZABETH GARDNER, James collected and archived the urban folk traditions of Detroit, beginning in 1923. She was educated at the University of Michigan (B.A., 1920; M.A., 1923) and did additional graduate work at the University of Chicago. She taught on the English faculty of Wayne State University from 1923 to 1967. With Gardner, she founded the Wayne State University Folklore Archive (1939) and collected folklore in Detroit, assisted by her students.

Jameson, R[aymond] D[eloy] (1895–1959).

Jameson is known among folklorists for having initiated and directed an ambitious collecting project of Hispanic folk materials in New Mexico. He also contributed many articles to the landmark *Funk and Wagnalls Standard Dictionary of Folklore, Mythology, and Legend* (1949). Educated at the University of Wisconsin (B.A. and M.A.), Jameson taught literature, philology, and history in the United States, Europe, and at the University of Peking, during 1925–38, where he founded the Orthological Institute of China, for English-language instruction. In 1938, he went to work for the Library of Congress as a consultant in comparative literature, then served during World War II as historical officer of the American Red Cross in the Southwest Pacific. From 1948 until his death, Jameson was a professor of English at Highlands University, Las Vegas, New Mexico.

Jansen, William Hugh (1914–1979).

Folklorist William Jansen is best known for his works on cultural stereotyping and for the formulation of what he termed, in a 1959 publication, the "esoteric-exoteric factor" in folklore. ESOTERIC FOLKLORE is the body of traditional beliefs one group has of itself and supposes others have of itself as well. EXOTERIC FOLKLORE consists of the traditional beliefs one group has of another group and supposes that group has of itself. The esoteric-exoteric factor adds a significant dimension to the understanding of the role of perception and image in folklore and in the study of folklore.

Jansen was born in Stamford, Connecticut, and was educated at Wesleyan University (B.A., 1935) and at Indiana University (Ph.D., 1949). He served on the English faculty of the University of Kentucky from 1949 to 1979 and was well known internationally as a lecturer. He was a distinguished member of numerous professional organizations and was recognized as a key figure in the development of FOLKLORISTICS.

See also: AMOS 'N' ANDY; SMITH, ABRAHAM (OREGON SMITH, SASSAFRAS SMITH).

SUGGESTED READING: William Hugh Jansen, "The Es-oteric-Exoteric Factor in Folklore," *Fabula: Journal of Folklore Studies* 2 (1959), pp. 205–11.

Japanese Americans.

Japanese Americans identify themselves generationally. The *issei* (first people) are first-generation immigrants, who, subject to exclusionary immigration policies, rarely were granted U.S. citizenship. Their children, however, the *nisei* (second people), born in the United States, were citizens by virtue of birth. In addition, Japanese Americans recognize the *sansei* (third generation) and the *yonsei* (fourth generation). Some *issei* were not properly immigrants, but contract laborers, who returned to Japan after their contracts had lapsed. Their children, born in America (and therefore U.S. citizens), often returned to the United States. These are called *kibei*, a coinage from a phrase meaning to "return from America."

Understandably, the *issei* carried with them intact a body of Japanese folklore, including narratives, folk medicine (see MEDICINE, FOLK), and FOODWAYS. Additionally, they placed great value on aspects of "elite" or "classical" Japanese culture, including music, calligraphy, the celebrated tea ceremony, flower arranging, and other visual arts. For the second generation, the *nisei*, the cultural and folkloric heritage was diluted, which was the case to an even greater degree with subsequent generations, who often spoke little or no Japanese. Foodways represent the most strongly preserved aspect of Japanese culture in America, and, indeed, in larger American cities, Japanese restaurants, especially those with sushi bars, have become popular with non-Japanese as well.

All Asian immigrants to the United States were subject to prejudice and de jure as well as de facto discrimination at various times. For the most part, the Japanese did not create the full equivalent of Chinatown communities in American cities, although some cities, including Los Angeles and Chicago, have neighborhoods sometimes informally called Little Tokyo (in San Francisco, "Japantown"). Even during World War II, when Japanese Americans of *issei* as well as *nisei* generations living on the West Coast were summarily interned in "relocation camps," few sought to revive Japanese folkways. The internees regarded their mistreatment at the hands of the United States government as a temporary situation, and they continued to identify themselves primarily as Americans. However, more recently, numbers of young Japanese Americans have been rediscovering aspects of traditional Japanese culture, including the playing of the *taiko* (a festival drum) and participation in the *bon-odori* (or *obon*) festival, which features folk dances performed by traditionally costumed Japanese Americans. Japanese Americans also often celebrate *oshogatsu* (New Year) in traditional ways.

See also: IMMIGRANT FOLKLORE; KOREAN AMERICANS.

SUGGESTED READING: Nancy K. Araki and Jane Horii, *Matsuri: Festival: Japanese American Celebrations and Activities* (Union City, Calif., 1985); John DeFrancis, *Things Japanese in Hawaii* (Honolulu, 1973); Stephen S. Fugita and David J. O'Brien, *Japanese American Ethnicity: The Persistence of Community* (Seattle, 1991).

Jazz.

While such distinguished musicians and students of jazz as Billy Taylor call it "America's classical music," jazz is more immediately rooted in African-American folk music and a combination of American and European popular music traditions. Viewed musicologically, jazz is a highly improvisational form primarily developed by African Americans who combined European harmonic structures with African rhythmic complexities that are, in turn, additionally overlaid with Euro-American dance and march rhythms. Adding to the "feel" of jazz is the use of musical gestures characteristic of BLUES and the intonations and rhythms of speech (in instrumental as well as vocal music).

The musicological literature devoted to jazz is extensive; however, the precise history of the origin and early evolution of this musical form is subject to much debate. While its roots may be traced ultimately, in part, to African traditions, the first recognizable precursor of jazz may be the plantation brass bands of the 1830s and the dissemination of this style to white audiences through the MINSTREL SHOWS of the pre–Civil War period. RAGTIME, an inventively syncopated transformation of the march, emerged late in the nineteenth century and, in New Orleans, developed in an improvisational direction that is widely recognized as early jazz. If Missouri's Scott Joplin (1868–1917) is remembered as the "king of ragtime," New Orleans's CHARLES "BUDDY" BOLDEN (1877–1931) is often called the father of jazz. His band was known for its highly improvisational approach to ragtime. Certainly by the beginning of the twentieth century, many African-American New Orleans bands were playing in an improvisational style that soon became recognized as a style characteristic of the city. It was, however, a white group, the Original Dixieland Jass Band, that first *recorded* in the new style, in 1917.

The origin of the term "jass"—or "jazz"—is even more obscure than the origin of the music. Musicologists speculate that it may be derived from an Afro-Caribbean word meaning "to speed up." It may also be derived from the name of an early performer, Jazbo—or "Chas"—Brown. Most etymologists, however, believe that the clue to the word's origin lies in its early "jass" spelling, which suggests "ass" in the sense of sexual intercourse. Some historical dictionaries of slang define *jazz* as a synonym for intercourse. Additional interpretations abound. Whatever its origin, the word first appeared in print in 1913 in the *San Francisco Bulletin,* but in many places, the older term *ragtime* persisted to describe the music well into the 1920s.

From the 1920s on, jazz developed in many rich directions. The early 1920s were dominated by such New Orleans musicians as Jelly Roll Morton (1890–1941) and King Oliver (1885–1938), but when New Orleans trumpeter and cornetist Louis "Satchmo" Armstrong (1901–71) moved to Chicago in the late 1920s, the locus of jazz shifted to that city and, later, to New York as well. Beginning during this period, large jazz orchestras became popular and, by the 1930s, these ensembles began playing swing, which featured a more regular rhythm and greater emphasis on orchestral color. The popularity of this style came in large part because it was eminently danceable, and through the 1930s and 1940s, swing bands, white and black, such as those led by Fletcher Henderson (1918–52), Count Basie (1904–84), Benny Goodman (1909–86), Artie Shaw (1910–), and the Dorsey brothers—Jimmy (1904–57) and Tommy (1905–56)—created the musical sound that came to define, most especially, the WORLD WAR II era.

Certain African-American musicians took the swing approach beyond the regular dance rhythms and reintroduced improvisational elements of great eloquence, energy, and virtuosity. Leading exponents of this style included pianist Art Tatum (1910–56), trumpeter Roy Eldridge (1911–89), and tenor saxophonist Lester Young (1909–59). The great jazz vocalist Billie Holiday (1915–59) brought jazz singing to a height of expression during this period, combining improvisational sophistication with the soulfulness already associated with the blues. Swing jazz also went in a more symphonic direction beginning at this time, with such ensembles as that led by

Duke Ellington (1899–1974). After World War II, swing underwent a transformation to bop or bebop. As developed by alto saxophonist Charlie "Bird" Parker (1920–55), trumpeter John Birks "Dizzy" Gillespie (1917–93), and others, bebop became a highly energized, driven style characterized by unpredictable accents and very complex cross-rhythms. Partly in reaction against this style, the more relaxed and melodic "Cool School" developed, primarily on the West Coast (bebop was a style associated with New York City), led by white musicians such as saxophonists Stan Getz (1927–91) and Gerry Mulligan (1927–96). Beyond this, jazz developed in a variety of directions, ranging from the introspective piano work of Lennie Tristano and Bill Evans, to the elegant and self-consciously classical Modern Jazz Quartet, to the more intensely idiosyncratic and sometimes avant-garde work of trumpeter Miles Davis (1926–91), bassist Charles Mingus (1922–79), and alto saxophonist John Coltrane (1926–67). Coltrane and others introduced what has been called "free jazz," which often resembles the more aleatoric (random) style of some modern classical music. In the later twentieth century, jazz has also been combined with ROCK 'N' ROLL elements ("fusion") and classical elements ("third stream" music).

In addition to its purely musical relation to folklore, as a form in large part rooted in folk music, jazz is also associated with folklike oral narratives, usually concerning the extravagances of particular musicians, legends (such as those surrounding Buddy Bolden), and contests to demonstrate prowess. "Cutting contests" were public jam sessions popular in the 1940s and 1950s, in which one musician would try to outdo another in feats of virtuosity and improvisation. Finally, what may be called the jazz lifestyle, characterized by late hours, promiscuous sex, hard drinking, narcotic drug use, and premature death, is the subject of both ESOTERIC FOLKLORE and EXOTERIC FOLKLORE. During the 1960s, in part because of the FOLK REVIVAL under way during the period, many young listeners discovered the recordings of the short-lived Charlie "Bird" Parker, a musician who amply satisfied the stereotype. During the 1960s and even into the early 1970s, GRAFFITI proclaiming "Bird Lives" appeared in many American cities.

See also: AFRICAN AMERICANS; ARHOOLIE RECORDS; BLUEGRASS; CAKEWALK; DORSEY, THOMAS A.; FIDDLE; FOLK MUSIC; GIBSON MANDOLIN AND GUITAR MANUFACTURING COMPANY, LTD., THE; RAINEY, MA.

SUGGESTED READING: Imamu Amiri Baraka (Leroi Jones), *Blues People: Negro Music in White America* (1963; reprint ed., New York, 1983); Ted Gioa, *History of Jazz* (New York, 1997); Neil Leonard, *Jazz: Myth and Religion* (New York, 1987); Kathy Ogren, *The Jazz Revolution: Twenties America and the Meaning of Jazz* (New York, 1989).

Jefferson, Blind Lemon (1897–1929).

A seminal blues performer, Jefferson was born blind to a Texas sharecropper family not far from Dallas. Jefferson made a local reputation early in his career, then began touring and, during the 1920s, performed in Texas, Oklahoma, the Mississippi Delta, Georgia, and Virginia. He also performed in the burgeoning blues mecca of Chicago, where he recorded for Paramount Records, laying down more than ninety sides. More than any other performer during this period, Blind Lemon Jefferson brought the rural blues to national attention. He performed both traditional blues songs, including "See See Rider" and "Boll Weevil Blues," as well as his own tunes. One of these, "Matchbox Blues," was the song with which he was most closely identified.

Jefferson's music was "hard core" blues, expressive of pain, poverty, and oppression. The manner of his death fittingly became the stuff of blues legend. In December 1929, he was found dead in a snowdrift, presumably having lost his way after playing at a house party late one night. His body was taken from Chicago back to Texas, where he was buried.

See also: FOLK MUSIC; KING, B. B.; LEDBETTER, HUDDIE (LEADBELLY).

SUGGESTED READING: Bob Groom, *Blind Lemon Jefferson* (Knutsford, Chesire, U.K., 1970).

Jersey Devil.
The Jersey Devil is a mythical monster inhabiting southwestern New Jersey. Legends relating to the Jersey Devil may be traced to the early eighteenth century, when one Jane Leeds, a resident along the Mullica River in the Pine Barrens, learned that she was pregnant with her thirteenth child. In disgust, she prayed to God that this one not be a child, but a devil. In February 1735, the child was born and was apparently normal, but, within a half hour of birth, metamorphosed into a hairy giant (the size of two adult men) with the horned head of a horse, giant bat wings, the legs and feet of a goat or satyr, and a devil's serpentlike tail. The Jersey Devil also possessed great arms and razor-sharp claws, with which it slashed the throat of the midwife and disappeared into the Pine Barrens, which (as legend has it) it continues to haunt to this day.

In 1909, the Jersey Devil became the subject of a hoax in which a kangaroo, painted green and sporting faux wings, was exhibited to the public in southern New Jersey. Today, a sanitized image of the Jersey Devil is seen on T-shirt and postcard souvenirs of southern New Jersey, and the creature has lent its name to a major league hockey franchise.

See also: MOTHMAN.

SUGGESTED READING: James F. McCloy and Ray Miller, Jr., *The Jersey Devil* (Wallingford, Pa., 1976); John McPhee, *The Pine Barrens* (New York, 1968).

Jewish folklore.
The first Jews arrived in New Amsterdam from Curaçao in 1654. Since there were seven Jews among the stockholders of the Dutch East India Company, Jews were allowed to live in the Dutch New World colony and engage in wholesale and retail trades. At first denied the right of public worship, by 1695 they had built a synagogue in Manhattan called Shearith Israel (Remnant of Israel). Before 1789, most American Jews were Sephardim (of Spanish, Portuguese, and Dutch origin). The Sephardic colloquial Jewish language was Ladino, a dialect built on a mixture of Castilian, Spanish, and Portuguese. However, the Jewish immigrants who have had the most impact on American folklore were Ashkenazim, mainly nineteenth-century arrivals from central and eastern Europe, principally from Russia, Poland, Hungary, Romania, and Lithuania, whose colloquial language of the home, the street, business, and social discourse was Yiddish, a blend of medieval German, some Hebrew, and vestiges of the languages of places in which they had lived and generally had been ghettoized and persecuted. They came for the most part between 1880 and 1920, settling mostly in the Northeast. They were regarded with condescension by the Americanized and relatively prosperous German Jews who had settled early in the nineteenth century.

As a people who had been allowed to sink roots for an extended period almost nowhere, faced with slander and persecution in almost every land, the remnants of the tribes of Israel have retained to some degree an ethnic-cultural identity for three thousand years. Their emotional insecurity in the world drove them to a strong dependence on their faith and their religious literature, in which folklore played an important role. The sacred writings, such as the Talmud and the Midrash, contain innumerable legends, myths, and parables.

The strikingly intellectual and sophisticated character of much Jewish folklore stems from an emphasis on learning going back to the public teachings of the Great Assembly in the sixth century B.C. It was a profound conviction that every Jew (the requirements for women were much lighter than those for men) had a religious duty to study Scripture endlessly and argue points of scholarship in hair-splitting detail. Boys in the *shtetls* (Jewish villages of eastern Europe) began their studies at the age of three, and the brightest would continue at a high level for the rest of their lives. A brilliant student could carry on his studies full-time indefinitely, subsidized by the community or a prosperous father-in-law. In their drive to make their teaching vivid and meaningful to the masses, the rabbis of old wove folk stories and sayings into their learned presentations, and other Jews revered the tales as sacred; those who told and retold the tales embellished them with their own fanciful imaginations and practical wisdom.

Jewish folklore tends to be philosophical, witty, ironic, and often didactic. Although there is an underlying universality in the use of most folk motifs, there are important differences in flavor and emphasis. Because of the grimness and tragedy of much of Jewish history, Jews are particularly dependent on the therapy of humor, an ability to laugh through tears. Though the stories are often sad, they achieve an important, ultimately affirmative catharsis, which is defiant of the world's cruelties.

See also: YIDDISH AND YIDDISHISMS.

SUGGESTED READING: Abraham Chapman, ed., *Jewish-American Literature: An Anthology* (New York:

1974); Ellen Frankle, *The Classic Tales: Four Thousand Years of Jewish Lore* (New York, 1993); David C. Gross, ed., *Dictionary of 1000 Jewish Proverbs* (New York, 1997); Steve Koppman et al., *A Treasury of American-Jewish Folklore* (New York, 1997); Syd Lieberman, *Streets and Alleys: Stories with a Chicago Accent* (Chicago, 1995); Barbara Rush, *The Book of Jewish Women's Tales* (New York, 1994); David G. Roskies, *A Bridge of Longing: The Lost Art of Yiddish Storytelling* (Cambridge, Mass., 1995); Josepha Sherman, *A Sampler of Jewish-American Folklore* (New York, 1992); Eli Yassif, *Jewish Folklore: An Annotated Bibliography* (New York, 1986).

Jew's harp. The Jew's harp or jew's harp has no connection with the Jewish people but is probably a corruption of jaw harp or jaw's harp. The most familiar version of the instrument consists of a frame in the shape of horseshoe with a free vibrating tongue attached at one end to the frame. The player holds the instrument in his jaws by the frame, and the tongue is plucked with the finger. The mouth cavity produces the sound, the pitch of which may be changed by changing the shape of the mouth cavity. The instrument is of very ancient origin

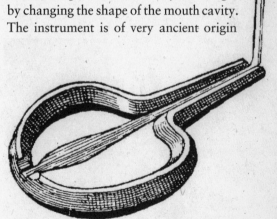

Jew's harp. (From Jim Harter, Music: A Pictorial Archive of Wooducts and Engravings, Dover Books, 1996)

(archaeological evidence of its existence has been dated to Neolithic times) and was highly popular on the American western frontier and in other parts of rural America.

See also: FOLK MUSIC.

Jig. A jig may be a solo dance or a figure dance. As a solo dance, it is an opportunity for virtuoso displays of intricate footwork as the dancer hops repeatedly on one foot while describing patterns in the air with the other foot. The solo jig came to America from Scotland and Ireland, where it is still popular. As a figure dance, the jig is performed in 6/8 time and is typically performed by groups of men and women, always with twice as many women as men, so that one man dances with two women and ends each pattern with a kiss. The figure-dance version was never popular in America.

See also: BREAKDOWN; FIDDLE; REEL; TAP DANCE.

Jiménez, Flaco (1939–). Jiménez is a leading *conjunto* musician, a member of a family that has been performing TEX-MEX music since the early 1900s. Leonardo "Flaco" (Skinny) Jiménez began performing with his father, Santiago, in the 1950s at a club in San Antonio. At the age of sixteen, Flaco was regularly playing with Mike Garza y los Caminantes, a locally renowned *conjunto* group, and by the late 1950s was playing in various Texas towns with his own group. He cut his first records in the 1960s with local San Antonio labels that specialized in *música Norteña,* as *conjunto* music is also called. In the 1970s, Jiménez began to record on national labels as well and gained recognition beyond the Tex-Mex and Hispanic communities.

See also: FOLK MUSIC.

Jitterbug. An improvisational couple dance inviting displays of athleticism, in which the man swings the girl out, across, and in pivot turns and

An 1858 book illustration portraying a jig. (From William E. Burton, Cyclopaedia of Wit and Humor, *1858)*

Two teenagers demonstrate the jitterbug, about 1946.

may even throw her over his shoulder. Danced to swing music, the jitterbug reached the height of its popularity during the heyday of hot swing music, the 1940s. While whites as well as African Americans jitterbugged, it was in the black clubs of Harlem that the most impressive forms of the dance were seen.

See also: DANCE, FOLK.

John and Old Marster. A cycle of African-American folktales; John is a plantation slave on fairly familiar terms with his owner, Old Marster. The stories revolve around John's at-tempts—sometimes successful, sometimes not—to outwit Old Marster.

John Barleycorn. As the personification of liquor (barley is the grain from which many al-coholic beverages are distilled), John Barleycorn in an English ballad of 1620. The personifica-tion was also popular in the United States, and when Prohibition was enacted by constitutional amendment in 1919, various community groups and liquor industry and brewery workers staged plays enacting the interment of John Barleycorn.

"John Hardy." A ballad recounting the crime and punishment of John Hardy, an African-American coal miner who murdered a man in a gambling brawl in West Virginia, was pursued by the law, captured, tried, and hanged (January 19, 1894).

See also: FOLK MUSIC.

John Henry. John Henry is the legendary African-American folk hero celebrated in folktales and a popular ballad for having competed with a steam hammer to lay railroad track. John Henry won the contest, but died of exhaustion. While the historical origins of the John Henry legend are usually traced to the Big Bend Tunnel constructed in West Virginia during the early 1870s, it is impossible to determine the factual basis of the folk hero's exploits. Most of the John Henry material contains five elements in common: John Henry's infant prophecy of his achievement and death; his love for a woman; his contest against the machine; his victory over the machine; his collapse and death. John Henry was not a track layer, but a "steel-drivin' man," a steel driver, a skilled laborer who used a hammer and a steel "drill" to bore holes in rock face for the setting of explosive charges. The steam hammer was designed to do the same job.

The John Henry songs were—and continue to be—compelling and popular. The core story cuts across racial boundaries; the heart of the legend is a contest of human heart and will against inhuman bosses using non-human machinery, which will displace human laborers. The most popular John Henry songs are authentic work songs, which not only celebrate John Henry, but serve to mark rhythm for any number of manual labor tasks.

See also: JOHNSON, GUY BENTON; RAILROAD FOLKLORE.

SUGGESTED READING: Guy B. Johnson *John Henry: Tracking Down a Negro Legend* (Chapel Hill, N.C., 1929).

Johnson, Clifton (1865–1940). Primarily a photographer and writer on local color, Johnson is best known to folklorists for his fairy-tale collections, including *The Oak Tree Fairy Book, The Birch Tree Fairy Book, Mother Goose Rhymes My Children Love Best,* and for his collections of New England folk traditions, including *The Country School in New England, Old-Time Schools and School-Books,* and *What They Say in New England.* Johnson's books are rife with local sayings, beliefs, rhymes, songs, and folktales. In addition, Johnson wrote and/or illustrated numerous volumes of travel and local color.

Johnson was a native of Hadley, Massachusetts, whose formal education was put on hold at age fifteen, but whose self-education continued in the Northampton bookstore he worked in. Johnson studied sporadically at the Art Students League (New York City), then returned to the family farm at Hadley, from which he worked as an artist, illustrator, writer, and photographer for the rest of his life.

SUGGESTED READING: Clifton Johnson, *What They Say in New England and Other American Folklore* (1896; reprint ed., New York, 1963).

Johnson, Guy Benton (1901–1991). A sociologist with an intense interest in folklore, Johnson is best known to folklorists as the editor of HOWARD W. ODUM's collection of African-American folk songs, as the coauthor (with Odum) of two early studies of African-American secular songs (*The Negro and His Songs: A Study* of *Typical Songs in the South* [1925] and *Negro Workaday Songs* [1926]), and as the author of *John Henry: Tracking Down a Negro Legend,* a study of the JOHN HENRY ballad (1929), and *Folk Culture on St. Helena Island* (1930), a study of African-American folk culture on the South Carolina island.

A Texan by birth, Johnson was educated at the University of Chicago and at the University of North Carolina. His later writing and research are more directly concerned with sociology and race relations than with folklore.

See also: BOGGS, RALPH STEELE.

Johnson, Robert (1911–1938).

Johnson was among the most expressive and influential of the Delta BLUES singers, composers, and guitarists. He combined an almost unearthly falsetto singing style with a virtuosic slide guitar technique that influenced his contemporaries as well as later blues and ROCK 'N' ROLL musicians. The child of sharecroppers, he was born in Hazlehurst, Mississippi, and raised in Memphis, Tennessee, and rural Robinsonville, Mississippi. As a youth, he readily absorbed the local Delta blues sounds and was (contemporaries reported) possessed of a "phonographic memory." He heard, either in person or through recording, all of the important Delta blues performers, including SON HOUSE and CHARLEY PATTON. While he was clearly influenced by these musicians and others, he was also brilliantly innovative as an instrumentalist.

Johnson toured throughout Mississippi, Arkansas, Texas, and Tennessee and also played the Chicago and New York clubs. He recorded twenty-nine songs in all, including "I Believe I'll Dust My Broom," "Sweet Home Chicago," "Me and the Devil Blues," "Hellhound on My Trail," and "Love in Vain," each considered a seminal blues performance, either for showcasing his guitar work or (in the case of the last three songs mentioned) for their compelling power as original blues compositions. Johnson's recording career was limited to these twenty-nine sides. In 1938, he died after drinking juke-joint whiskey laced with strychnine.

See also: AFRICAN AMERICANS.

SUGGESTED READING: Samuel Charters, *Robert Johnson* (New York, 1973); Peter Guralnick, *Searching for Robert Johnson* (New York, 1989).

John the Conqueror root.

John the Conqueror root, or High John the Conqueror are alternate names for St. John's Wort, long believed to be a powerful herb useful both for warding off evil spirits and bringing good fortune. In most of the four hundred or so species of St. John's Wort, reddish spots are visible in the leaves when they are held up to the light. Legend holds that these are the blood of the beheaded John the Baptist.

Recently, the herb has enjoyed widespread popularity as "natural Prozac," an antidepressant. Traditionally, it has been used by folk medicine (see MEDICINE, FOLK) practitioners to cure many ills. It may be used in root form, as an infusion in tea, as an oil, or may be chewed. VOODOO practitioners use various dried preparations made from St. John's Wort.

See also: PLANTS AND PLANT LORE; ROOTWORK.

Jokes and joke cycles.

Anyone who doubts that oral folklore is still being produced need look only to the joke. Relatively few jokes are written by professional comedy writers for television comedians; most seem simply to surface anonymously as part of a body of traditional lore. Typically, these humorous narratives are short, concern almost any subject, and are ubiquitous. These days, oral transmission has been augmented by the Internet and e-mail, through which thousands of jokes are sent daily. While the variety of jokes is seemingly endless, they may be classified, like other oral folklore, as to type and MOTIF. Moreover, certain types of jokes are part of joke cycles, examples of which include DUMB DORA JOKES, LITTLE MORON JOKES, LITTLE WILLIE JOKES, and such ethnically offensive cycles as POLACK JOKES.

The humor of jokes may flow from many sources: ridicule, sex, non sequitur (as in the shaggy-dog story), puns, and so on. Often the source of humor may be traced to an exploration of some socially or emotionally forbidden or intimidating subject matter, including castration fears, various "deviant" sexual practices, adultery, sexual dysfunction, withholding of sexual favors, and nymphomania. Often, too, jokes explore social taboos, including racial, religious, or ethnic slurs and so-called sick jokes that mock the infirm or disabled, that make fun of disaster, injury, or death, and that deal with mutilation. Other jokes, known as numskull tales, mock stupidity and foolishness. Sometimes the numskull tale is combined with racial or ethnic slurs. Intoxication is another source of jokes, as is virtually any trait or personality feature that may be absurdly exaggerated for comic effect, such as laziness, gluttony, anger, greed, stinginess, and other human foibles. An important class of jokes deals with occupational groups, such as lawyers (see LAWYER JOKES), physicians, and clergy.

See also: RELIGION, FOLK.

SUGGESTED READING: Alan Dundes, *Cracking Jokes: Studies of Sick Humor Cycles and Stereotypes* (Philadelphia, 1987); James P. Leary, *Midwestern Folk Humor* (Little Rock, Ark., 1991); Gershon Legman, *No Laughing Matter: An Analysis of Sexual Humor* (2 vols., Bloomington, Ind., 1967); Vance Randolph, *Pissing in the Snow and Other Ozark Folktales* (Urbana, Ill., 1976).

Jones, Casey (1863–1900). Famed for a single exploit, John Luther "Casey" Jones is one of those legendary figures, familiar as the hero of BALLADS and tales told to children, who seems the product of fiction, but who was, in fact, a historical person. A locomotive engineer, he was raised in Cayce, Kentucky, and adopted the name "Cayce Jones"; news writers changed the spelling to the familiar "Casey." He went to work for the Illinois Central Railroad in 1888 and, in 1890, earned the coveted position of engineer on the IC's crack passenger train, the Cannonball Express, running between Chicago and New Orleans. All along the line, people became familiar with Jones's signature six-chime locomotive whistle.

On April 29, 1900, Jones and his fireman, Sim Webb, were to pick up the Cannonball in Memphis for an 11:35 P.M. departure. The train arrived 95 minutes late, and Jones was determined to make up the time. He was barreling along at extra-high speed when he approached the town of Vaughan, 175 miles south of Memphis. To his horror, Jones saw that the caboose of a southbound freight, which had pulled over to a passing siding to let the Cannonball by, was still on the main line.

Jones knew that he was moving too fast to stop, but he also knew that, if he stayed on the brakes, he could slow down and reduce the inevitable impact. Jones ordered Webb to jump, which he did, surviving with minor injuries. Jones, refusing to leave, was killed when his engine collided with the freight's caboose.

The most widely known Casey Jones song was written in 1909 by the vaudeville duo of T. Lawrence Seibert and Eddie Newton. Their "Casey Jones (The Brave Engineer)" may have been based on ballads sung by African-American railroad workers after the accident. A complete Casey Jones ballad was published in *Railroad Man's Magazine* in 1908, and field recordings from the 1910s as well as commercial hillbilly records from the 1920s suggest the existence of widely circulated ballads prior to Seibert and Newton's vaudeville hit.

See also: RAILROAD FOLKLORE; "WRECK OF THE OLD 97, THE."

SUGGESTED READING: Norm Cohen, *Long Steel Rail: The Railroad in American Folksong* (Urbana, Ill., 1981).

Jones, Louis Clark (1908–1990).

Jones was a MATERIAL CULTURE specialist, who founded the groundbreaking Cooperstown graduate programs in material culture. In other areas of folklore, Jones was noted as a collector and student of murder tales, ghost stories, and folk art.

He was born on June 28, 1908, in Albany, New York, took his B.A. from Hamilton College (1930) and his Ph.D. from Columbia University (1941). Jones taught at Long Island University (1931) and, subsequently, at Syracuse University and at the State College for Teachers (Albany). He was appointed director of the New York State Historical Association and the Farmer's Museum in 1947 and served until he retired in 1972.

It was Jones's interest in the macabre that brought him into the field of folklore study. He researched and published the factual basis of a popular New York murder ballad in 1936 and, in 1944, he published an important article on the ghostlore of upstate New York. He even had a popular hit with his 1959 collection, *Things That Go Bump in the Night.*

Beginning about 1950, Jones became increasingly interested in American folk art and produced two important books on the subject, *American Folk Art* (with Marshall Davidson; 1952) and *New-Found Folk Art of the Young Republic* (with wife Agnes Halsey Jones; 1960). His 1982 *Three Eyes on the Past: Exploring New York Folklife* is a collection of his articles in three areas: history, folklore, and material culture.

Jones was the guiding spirit behind the Fenimore House Collection at the New York State Historical Association and was a principal founder of the Cooperstown Graduate Programs (1964), which offered master's degrees in museum science and American folk culture, with an emphasis on material culture.

SUGGESTED READING: Louis Clark Jones, *Three Eyes on the Past: Exploring New York Folklife* (Syracuse, N.Y., 1982).

Juba.

An African-American dance, common in the nineteenth century, involving vigorous tap-style steps performed to a clapping accompaniment rather than instruments.

See also: BREAKDOWN; HOEDOWN; RAGTIME; TAP DANCE.

Juke joint.

As originally used by African Americans in the Southeast, a *juke* was a roadhouse purveying liquor and frequented by "loose" women. The word is of Gullah origin, meaning wicked or disorderly. *Juke joint* was used by blacks as well as whites to denote a bar or road-house that offered jukebox entertainment. *Juking around* is the term used to describe the casual dancing style popular in jukes.

See also: THOMAS, JAMES "SON FORD."

Juneteenth. Juneteenth is an African-American folk holiday. On June 19, 1865, Union general Gordon Granger arrived in Galveston, Texas, and read General Order No. 3, which began: "The people of Texas are informed that in accor-dance with a Proclamation from the Executive of the United States, all slaves are free. This involves an absolute equality of rights and rights of prop-erty between former masters and slaves, and the connection heretofore existing between them be-comes that between employer and free laborer." Thereafter, former slaves celebrated June nine-teenth as Juneteenth. The custom began in east Texas, western Louisiana, and southwestern Arkansas, but expanded into other states as African Americans migrated from the South. In 1979, the Texas state legislature made Juneteenth an official Emancipation celebration.

See also: CIVIL WAR.

K

Kachina. Tourists and other non–Native Americans interested in the Indian culture of the Southwest are familiar with the kachina dolls of the Hopi and other Pueblo peoples. The term *kachina* is often broadly applied to these dolls or to the masked dancers they represent. However, to NATIVE AMERICANS, the kachina concept is far more complex, denoting anthropomorphic spirit beings who mediate between the human and spiritual worlds, as well as the masked dancers who personify these beings, and to the doll figures. The Hopi believe that kachinas are the incarnate spirits of departed Hopis who have lived a proper Hopi life. Kachinas live half the year in the San Francisco Mountains (near Flagstaff, Arizona) and, during the other half, live near Hopi villages, where they dance and sing for the people.

Kachina dances are performed by twenty-five to sixty men, who rehearse secretly in the kiva, then perform from sunup to sundown.

See also: KOKOPELLI; WOOD CARVING.

Kachina figure from the Hopi reservation, Second Mesa, Arizona, ca. 1995. (Collection of Alan Axelrod)

Kane, John (1860–1934). Kane is famed as an American folk painter who documented the development of the prototypical industrial cityscape of Pittsburgh. He was born John Cain in West Calder (present-day Glasgow Bank), Scotland, where he had a spotty education. As a nine-year-old boy, Kane went to work in the shale mines of Scotland, leaving at age nineteen for Braddock, Pennsylvania, where other family members had already settled. He earned his living as a manual laborer in many industries, doing (as he said) "almost every kind of work that a man can do" until 1891, when a locomotive struck him, resulting in the loss of his left leg. Thus disabled, Kane worked as a crossing watchman for the B & O Railroad, then as a house and boxcar painter. To make ends meet during slack periods, he enlarged and hand-colored photographs and began making paintings, selling both kinds of items door-to-door. Tragedy struck again in 1904 when his infant son died, and Kane began drinking so heavily that his wife and daughters left him. He drifted from menial job to menial job for some fifteen years, at last settling in an industrial area of Pittsburgh known as "the Strip." It was here that he began painting in earnest and gained a significant measure of recognition, which increased after his death from tuberculosis.

Even as a child, Kane enjoyed drawing and tried to enroll in art schools in Cleveland, Charleston, West Virginia, and Pittsburgh, but he could never afford the tuition. He said that he taught himself how to use color while painting boxcars. He treated the car as a canvas, painting scenes on the cars during his lunch break, only to paint over them before the boss showed up. While he did succeed in selling some paintings door-to-door around 1915, real recognition did not come until 1927. It was during the final seven years of his life that he created the body of Pittsburgh industrial cityscapes for which he is now well known.

Kelley, Lavern (1928–). Lavern Kelley is a carver known for his realistic, polychrome carvings of people and of farm vehicles. He was born in Oneonta, New York, and raised on a farm, which he maintained after his father's death in 1946. He also worked as a logger and was severely injured in a logging accident in 1978, which destroyed his right eye, crushed his leg, and led to a heart attack, from which he never fully recovered. Kelley had begun carving when he was only seven years old and, while recuperating from his accident and illness, began carving again. At first he carved to pass the time, but soon he was commissioned by neighbors to create "portraits" of a prized truck or car. By 1975, local antique dealers began showing Kelley's work, and by the mid-1980s, his work was being shown at galleries.

In addition to trucks, tractors, and other farm equipment, Kelley carves farmers and friends, though he sometimes works from pictures in catalogs and magazines in addition to modeling from life. He uses white pine and sometimes basswood or elm, adding wire, sheet tin, twine, and clear plastic (taken from food wrappers and used for windshields) for his vehicle models. Some of his figures are embellished with bits of ribbon. He paints his work with Rust-o-leum enamel.

King, B. B. (1925–). The BLUES guitarist recognized as one of the creators of rhythm and blues, King was born Riley B. King in the Mississippi Delta between Itta Bena and Indianola, Mississippi. His upbringing was steeped in GOSPEL MUSIC, but was later influenced by such rural blues artists as BLIND LEMON JEFFERSON. Over this foundation of gospel and blues came the influence of the great jazz guitarists Django Reinhardt and Charlie Christian. The result was a virtuoso, lyrical blues guitar style that evolved into R&B.

King entered the music business as a Memphis disk jockey calling himself Beale Street Blues Boy—soon shortened to B. B. His first recording, the 1949 "Three O'Clock in the Morning" was an early R&B hit that launched a two-decade career on the black nightclub circuit. King proved himself a tireless performer, typically playing more than three hundred dates a year. He was repeatedly urged to abandon his allegiance to his blues roots, which, well-meaning friends said, kept him from enjoying big-time popular success. This was especially true by the 1960s, when many African Americans turned their backs on the blues, finding in it uncomfortable reminders of "down home" class and racial oppression. Unlike some other blues performers, King did not benefit from the FOLK REVIVAL of the period. If black audiences found him too "down home," folkies deemed him too commercial. Nevertheless, King persevered. Then, toward the end of the 1960s, the Rolling Stones and other prominent rock musicians began publicly acknowledging King as a major influence. This attention garnered him a 1968 European tour, which brought him acclaim, at last, from American critics, and the white American public was introduced to rhythm and blues in its most authentic form. Since the late 1960s, King has been a consistently popular performer.

SUGGESTED READING: Charles Sawyer, *The Arrival of B. B. King* (New York, 1980).

Kirkland, Edwin Capers (1903–1972). During his lifetime, Kirkland was known to folklorists for the massive bibliography of the folklore of India (published in 1968) he compiled when he was a U.S. cultural officer and consul there. Only after his death did his significant collection of folk songs from the American South, collected by Kirkland and his wife, Mary, become generally known.

Kirkland taught at the University of Tennessee from 1931 to 1946 and did most of his southern folk-song collecting during 1935–39, making many of his field recordings directly to disc. In 1946, Kirkland moved to the University of Florida, where he was instrumental in creating the Florida Folk Festival.

See also: MOSER, ARTUS M.

SUGGESTED READING: Robert Thomson, "Edwin C. Kirkland: The Collector and His Methods," *Tennessee Folklore Society Bulletin* 50 (1984), pp. 95–109.

Kitchen, Tella (1902–1988). Like GRANDMA MOSES, Tella Kitchen was an important memory painter. Her works evoke the Ohio farm country where she was born and raised. Born Tella Gwendolyn Denehue in Londonderry, Ohio, the artist attended school through the eighth grade. She married Noland Dwight Kitchen in 1920 and, with her husband, farmed as well as ran a gas station and sold used cars in Adelphi, Ohio. After her husband died in 1963, Kitchen's son gave her a set of paints "to keep her busy." She did nothing with them for three years, then began painting "the simple things I loved." Her son showed her paintings to folk art historian and curator Robert Bishop, who wrote about and published her work.

Like the paintings of Grandma Moses, Kitchen's works are "homespun" chronicles of daily events in a rural community recalled from early childhood. Most of Kitchen's approximately two hundred paintings are landscapes or town scenes.

See also: MEMORY PAINTING.

SUGGESTED READING: Robert Bishop, *Folk Painters of America* (New York, 1979).

Kittredge, George Lyman (1860–1941). Kittredge was an eminent, even legendary, Harvard University professor of English, who also exerted an important influence on the study of folklore. The range of his interests in the humanities was staggering, encompassing the study of English language and literature, especially Middle English and early modern English authors and, of course, Shakespeare, a major edition of whose works Kittredge edited. In addition, Kittredge was a classicist, Latinist, and student of Old and Middle French. An enthusiastic student of folklore, he worked with material on the BALLAD and on witchcraft, as well as the folklore of early Massachusetts. After taking his undergraduate degree at Harvard in 1882, Kittredge taught Latin at Phillips Exeter Academy (1883–88), then began a forty-eight-year career on the Harvard English faculty.

Kittredge served as president of the Modern Language Association of America and of the American Folklore Society, and he was on the editorial staff of *Journal of American Folklore* from 1909 to 1940. After the death of his mentor FRANCIS JAMES CHILD, Kittredge completed work on the final volume of Child's *The English and Scottish Popular Ballads* (1898) and, throughout his career, wrote widely on the ballad. Kittredge was an encouraging and mentoring influence on the folk-song-collecting work of JOHN LOMAX and ALAN LOMAX, and his own comparative approach to the study of the Middle English romances served as a model of the method to subsequent generations of folklorists.

See also: BARRY, PHILLIPS; EMRICH, DUNCAN B. M.; TAYLOR, ARCHER; THOMPSON, STITH.

SUGGESTED READING: Esther K. Birdsall, "Some Notes on the Role of George Lyman Kittredge in American Folklore Studies," *Journal of the Folklore Institute* 10 (1973), pp. 57–46; Clyde Kenneth Hyder, *George Lyman Kittredge: Teacher and Scholar* (Lawrence, Kans., 1962).

Klezmer music. Klezmer music developed late in the Middle Ages as a special folk form of instrumental music among the Jews of eastern Europe. (The name is derived from the Hebrew *kele zemir,* "instruments of song.") These folk musicians (*klezmorim* in the plural) played in an ensemble that centered on a violin, flute, bass viol, and cymbals, usually including no more than eight instruments. *Klezmorim* played at family festivals, such as weddings, and, although music for orthodox services in the synagogues was performed a cappella, on certain special occasions instrumentalists were welcomed—for joyous events such as the celebrations of Hanukkah and Purim, and also at Hoshanah Rabbah, when a new Torah scroll was dedicated and used for the first time in a service. Many of the musicians were real artists, representative of dynasties of *klezmorim.* Noted outside of Jewish circles as exciting performers, the *klezmorim* often played for the feasts of non-Jews, even the Polish nobility. The *klezmorim* were indeed wanderers between two worlds—or among even more—agents of exchange between peoples. Even early in their history, they were noted for their "hot style," unusual scales, and eccentric rhythms.

Phonograph recording of *klezmer* music began in Europe around 1910, most significantly in Warsaw, Lemberg, and Bucharest. The most featured instruments were the violin, flute, cornet, and accordion, with the cymbalon as the chief instrument for accompaniment. The repertoire was generally of Rumanian origin. With the advent of World War I, the huge Jewish immigration to America, and the rise of the recording industry here, the United States became the center of *klezmer* recording.

See also: ARHOOLIE RECORDS; FOLK MUSIC.

SUGGESTED READING: Henry Sapoznik and Pete Sokolow, *The Compleat Klezmer* (New York, 1998).

Knortz, Karl (1841–1918). This German-American folklorist wrote the first comprehensive study of American folklore, *Zur Amerikanisher Volksunde* (*American Folklore*) in 1905. Knortz was also an avid student of ethnic folklore, and his 1903 *Nachklänge Germanischen Glaubens und Brauche in Amerika: Ein Beitrag zur Volksunde* (*Reminiscences of German*

Beliefs and Customs in America: A Contribution to Folklore) was a pioneering study in ethnic folklore. Except for portions translated in the journal *Folklore Historian,* neither of these works has been translated into English and are therefore relatively little known outside of Germany.

Knortz was born in Prussia, and immigrated to the United States in 1863. He was a very prolific author, writing on literature, education, and German-American relations in addition to folklore. While teaching high school and working as a minister in Michigan, Wisconsin, Ohio, Indiana, New York, and Pennsylvania, Knortz did extensive fieldwork among his German-American neighbors.

SUGGESTED READING: Helga B. Van Iten and James Dow, trans., "American Folklore," *Folklore Historian* 5, no. 1 (1988).

Knots. Knots and knot tying have significance in the folklore and spiritual life of many cultures. Among sailors, for whom tying a variety of knots is essential to their work and their safety, knots may take on an almost mystical significance. Among some African Americans, special knots have had the power of CHARMS or AMULETS. For Boy Scouts, learning how to tie a variety of knots is a kind of rite of passage that is marked by the award of a merit badge.

See also: FISHING LORE.

Knott, Sarah Gertrude (1898–1984).
Knott founded the National Folk Festival in 1934 and served as its program director and producer

through 1971, when she partially retired. (After 1971, Knott served as a consultant to state and local folk arts programs.) Knott was trained in drama rather than folklore, and she was often and widely criticized in academic circles for her emphasis on "big show" theatrics, which (as academic folklorists saw it) were artificial and antithetical to authenticity. Knott believed that the National Folk Festival brought folk performing arts to audiences who would otherwise never come in contact with the performers and their material, and she saw the "big show" format as the only effective means of preserving and perpetuating many folk performance traditions.

Knott staged the first National Folk Festival in 1934 in St. Louis. Thereafter, the annual festivals moved from city to city until 1971, when the festival found a permanent home at Wolf Trap, outside of Washington, D.C.

See also: KORSON, GEORGE.

Knox, George (1862–1892). Knox is the subject of a localized Northern Maine lumber industry legend. This logger was legendary as a malicious trickster who was in league with the devil. He carried with him a "black book" of diabolical tricks.

In the manner of Faust, Knox (it is said) sold his soul to the devil, sealing the bargain with thirty dollars in exchange for three decades of magical power. (The historical Knox, however, succumbed to tuberculosis at age thirty.) Presumably as a result of his diabolical compact, Knox was endowed with superhuman strength, which enabled him to perform prodigious amounts of logging work. It is said that his tools were enchanted, and that Knox could lounge about while his ax chopped down trees. As portrayed and in fact, Knox was not a likable character; on the contrary, he was shunned and avoided by other loggers.

SUGGESTED READING: Richard M. Dorson, *America in Legend: Folklore from the Colonial Period to the Present* (New York, 1973); Roger E. Mitchell, "George Knox: From Man to Legend," *Northeast Folklore* 2 (1969).

Kokopelli. A humpbacked flute player figure, the image of Kokopelli is found on much Southwestern tribal rock art and pottery. The Kokopelli motif is very popular on Native American art and jewelry, including items sold to tourists and other non-Native Americans. Kokopelli is a sexually powerful character, who appears in Hopi stories as a seducer of girls and a bringer of babies. A female version of Kokopelli, Kokopelli Mana, is also highly sexual. In KACHINA dances, she (always impersonated by a man, since all kachina dancers are male) entices another dancer to race with her, overtakes her opponent, casts him down to the ground, and simulates copulation with him—to the great amusement of the audience.

Köngäs-Maranda, Elli (1932–1982). Finnish-born Köngäs-Maranda was a student of Finnish-American verbal traditions. She took a Ph.D. in folklore at Indiana University (1963) and taught at the University of British Columbia, Vancouver, and at Laval University, Quebec. A rigorous structuralist, she was also especially interested in the role of women as the carriers of folklore and as students of their culture's folk-

lore. The Women's Section of the American Folklore Society created an annual Elli Köngäs-Maranda Prize for Contributions to the Study of Women and Folklore.

SUGGESTED READING: Elli Köngäs-Maranda, *Finnish-American Folklore: Quantitative and Qualitative Analysis* (New York, 1980).

Korean Americans. Korean immigration to the United States is a fairly recent phenomenon. Koreans came to Hawaii beginning early in the twentieth century, but did not immigrate to the mainland in substantial numbers until the relaxation of immigration restrictions in 1965. Today, in various American cities (most visibly, perhaps, in Los Angeles's Koreatown), Korean businesses and specialty stores abound. In cities like New York and Los Angeles, small Korean grocery stores, which cater to the general public, not specifically Koreans, are also common. For years, Manhattanites have referred to the small grocery stores on their crowded island as *bodegas* (the Spanish word for such stores), but, more recently, one is apt to hear such a shop generically called a "Korean grocery." To outsiders, the visibility of the Korean community is communicated by such businesses and by distinctive Korean signage. Business concerns provide much community cohesiveness for Koreans themselves, who also focus communal life on Korean Protestant churches. For Koreans as well as non-Koreans, FOODWAYS are another highly visible expression of ethnic identity, although Korean restaurants are not nearly as abundant as Chinese, Japanese, and Thai establishments.

As is true among JAPANESE AMERICANS, active interest in Korean folklore and culture is most evident among young adults. American universities often sponsor Korean-American student associations, which foster the study of Korean culture and history.

See also: IMMIGRANT FOLKLORE.

SUGGESTED READING: Herbert R. Barringer, *Koreans in the United States: A Fact Book* (Honolulu, 1989); Bong-young Choy, *Koreans in America* (Chicago, 1979); Wayne Patterson, *The Koreans in North America* (Philadelphia, 1976).

G.I.s in battle near the 38th Parallel.

Korean War. In contrast to the twentieth century's two world wars, the Korean War did not produce a large body of enduring folklore, perhaps because of a collective desire to suppress memory of the conflict, which was an ambiguous so-called police action rather than a declared war and was judged by many who participated in it as a U.S. military defeat or, at best, a costly stalemate. Commanders and soldiers were caught in what became a typical COLD WAR scenario: a bloody conflict that could be fought only in a limited manner, lest it escalate into thermonuclear World War III. Thus the only alternative to abject defeat was stalemate, and veterans as well as historians often call the Korean conflict "the Forgotten War." Indeed, the most pervasive and enduring popular image of Korean War folklore and folk life was not created until 1970, with Robert Altman's movie *M*A*S*H* and the long-running television sitcom (1972–83) that followed. Moreover, these satirical treatments of day-to-day life in the war zone were motivated less by interest in the Korean War itself than by a desire to use the subject of that conflict as a vehicle to protest the ongoing VIETNAM WAR.

Among the frontline soldiers, there abounded parodic songs and characterizations of themselves as "Harry's police force"—a reference to their participation in a "police action" ordered by President Harry S Truman. Fear of Asian combat tactics, born in part of experience with the Japanese during World War II, of actual experience with the North Koreans and Chinese, and reinforced by racist stereotypes, included belief that the Communist troops were fanatics willing to make suicidal "human wave" assaults. They were also believed to be a dishonorable enemy, who would scruple at nothing, including phony surrender and the torture-extracted collaboration of American POWs, to achieve victory. With regard to capture, American G.I.'s feared physical torture and its psychological equivalent, "brainwashing"—a term that came into general use during the period. It was widely believed that the Communists could, through a combination of physical and emotional means, "break" any man and turn him against his fellow troops. (This became the subject of the 1962 John Frankenheimer film, *The Manchurian Candidate*, adapted from a novel by Richard Condon.) Such demoralizing gossip was further aggravated by the general Cold War atmosphere, in which it was widely believed that not only were Communists taking over much of Asia and Europe, but that they had thoroughly infiltrated the U.S. government as well. Finally, the grim gossip was always balanced by rumors of impending peace and the progress of peace talks.

Both at home and at the front, frustration over the war was often directed personally at President Truman, especially after he dismissed General Douglas MacArthur, overall commander of United Nations forces in Korea, who wanted to press the war into China. Anti-Truman GRAFFITI, the work of G.I.'s, appeared all over Korea. At home, "Oust Truman" and "Punch Harry in the Nose" slogans and BUMPER STICKERS were common. Such outcries were countered, however, by an article of government policy that had attained the popular status of folk belief: that Communism was a plague and had to be "contained" at all costs.

See also: MILITARY FOLKLORE.

SUGGESTED READING: Clay Blair, *The Forgotten War: America in Korea, 1950–1953* (New York, 1987); Donald Knox, *The Korean War: An Oral History* (New York, 1985).

Korson, George (1899–1967).
Korson was an important early collector of anthracite coal-mining folklore in Pennsylvania during the 1920s and 1930s and of lore from the bituminous fields of the South and Midwest during the 1940s. A newspaperman by vocation, Korson started collecting when he was working for newspapers in Pennsylvania and New Jersey. His avocational interest in folklore resulted in five volumes of coal-mining material as well as numerous articles on the subject. Korson also started the Library of Congress archive of miners' songs and ballads, founded and directed the

Pennsylvania Folk Festival, and was instrumental in helping to launch the National Folk Festival (see KNOTT, SARAH GERTRUDE).

See also: KORSON, RAE ROSENBLATT.

SUGGESTED READING: George Korson, *Songs and Ballads of the Anthracite Miner* (New York, 1927); George Korson, *Minstrels of the Mine Patch* (1938; reprint ed., Hatboro, Pa., 1964); George Korson, *Coal Dust on the Fiddle* (Hatboro, Pa., 1965); George Korson, *Pennsylvania Songs and Legends* (1949; reprint ed., Baltimore, 1960); George Korson, *Black Rock: Mining Folklore of the Pennsylvania Dutch* (Baltimore, 1960).

Korson, Rae Rosenblatt (1901–1990).
Korson was the influential head of the Archive of Folk Song at the Library of Congress from 1956 to 1969. A native of Morristown, New Jersey, she was educated at New Jersey College of Law and became interested in folk-song research when she married the collector of coal-mining songs and lore, GEORGE KORSON (1926). Rae Rosenblatt Korson joined the staff of the Library of Congress in 1941 as assistant to archive heads BENJAMIN A. BOTKIN and DUNCAN EMRICH.

As head of the archive, Korson worked effectively to organize the collections more rationally and to provide active assistance to researchers. After her retirement in 1969, she set about directing the organization of the coal-mining material left by her husband, who died in 1967.

Krappe, Alexander Haggerty (1894–1947).
Irascible as he was erudite and prolific, Alexander Krappe was a brilliant student of European as well as American folklore. To American folklorists, he is most familiar—and per-

haps notorious—as the author of *The Science of Folklore* (1930), a survey of the genres of international folk tradition. Krappe argued that American folklore was nothing more than imported European folklore, which soon lost its vitality on these shores. Like FRANCIS JAMES CHILD, he believed that ballads and folk songs "originated anonymously, among unlettered folk in times past."

While Krappe's views of American folklore are hopelessly dated, he is still respected for pioneering work in European folklore and mythology.

A native of Dorchester, Massachusetts, Krappe was educated abroad and at the universities of Iowa and Chicago, where he took his Ph.D. in 1919. He taught primarily at the University of Michigan, Indiana University, and the University of Minnesota.

SUGGESTED READING: Archer Taylor, "Alexander Haggerty Krappe," *Journal of American Folklore* 61 (1948), pp. 201–2.

Kurath, Gertrude Prokosch (1903–1992).

Kurath was a student of folk dance, specializing in Native American dance and the dances of African Americans and immigrants. She was dance editor of the journal *Ethnomusicology* from 1956 to 1971.

Trained in art history and archaeology (Bryn Mawr College, B.A. and M.A.), she held no academic position, but produced many books and articles, as well as an ethnic Folkways record, and a number of performance presentations.

SUGGESTED READING: Gertrude Kurath, *Iroquois Music and Dance: Ceremonial Arts of Two Seneca Longhouses* (Washington, D.C., 1964); Gertrude Kurath, *Dance and Song Rituals of Six Nations Reserve, Ontario* (Ottawa, 1968).

Kwanzaa.

This African-American holiday, created in 1966 by UCLA graduate student and Black nationalist Maulana "Ron" Karenga, begins on December 26 and ends on January 1. Its name is Swahili for "first fruits of the harvest." Observance is marked by the lighting of a candle on each of its seven days and the contemplation of one of the *Nguzo Saba*, the cultural principles that African Americans should live by. The candles are called *Mishumae saba* and are placed in a *Kinara*, a candelabrum symbolizing the African continent and the peoples of Africa. Each candle symbolizes a different quality: on the first day, the candle of *Umoja* (unity) is lit; on the second, that of *Kujichagulia* (self-determination); on the third, *Ujima* (collective work and responsibility); on the fourth, *Ujamma* (cooperative economics); on the fifth, *Nia* (purpose); on the sixth, *Kuumba* (creativity); and, finally, the candle of *Imani* (faith) is lit. The *Kinara* is placed on an altar decorated with a *mazao*, fruits and vegetables symbolizing the produce of unity; a *mkeka*, a straw mat symbolizing respect for tradition; and *vibunzi*, ears of corn symbolizing each of the family's children. Other practices observed during Kwanzaa include exchanging *Zawadi*, simple handmade gifts evocative of African culture, and drinking from a communal cup (*Kikombe cha umoja*) in homage to the past, present, and future. The celebration culminates on December 31 in the *Kwanzaa Karamu*, a feast of African unity, in which characteristic dishes from Africa as well as the diaspora communities are served, cultural traditions are celebrated, the African-American struggle and experience are discussed, the guests rejoice, the names of ancestors and African-American heroes are recited, drumming and dancing take place, and a formal farewell to the guests is spoken.

SUGGESTED READING: Eric V. Copage, *Kwanzaa: An African-American Celebration of Culture and Cooking* (New York, 1991).

L

Lacourcière, Luc (1910–1989). Lacourcière was a French-Canadian folklorist who founded the Archives de Folklore of Laval University, Quebec, Canada. He took his degree at Laval, then studied with MARIUS BARBEAU, whose protégé he became. In 1944, Lacourcière created the first Folklore Department in Canada, at Laval University. From 1942 to 1972, Lacourcière conducted fieldwork in eastern Quebec and in Nova Scotia, New Brunswick, and Prince Edward Island, collecting folktales and folk songs. In 1946, Lacourcière started the journal *Archives de Folklore*.

Laguna Santero (working 1796–1808). An anonymous *santero* (creator of SANTOS, the Hispanic religious folk images of New Mexico), he and his workshop created RETABLOS (altar screens) for churches in Pojaque, Zia, Santa Ana, Acoma, and Laguna, all villages in New Mexico. The style of the Laguna Santero suggests that he was trained in Mexico in the Baroque colonial Spanish style. He and his apprentices simplified this style for use in the churches of the New Mexican frontier.

Lapson, Dvora (1907–). Dvora Lapson is perhaps the foremost American authority on Jewish traditional dance. She was educated at Hunter College, in her native New York City, and studied an array of dance forms with such diverse teachers as Michel Fokine, Irma Duncan, Evelyn Gates, and Doris Humphrey, but her consuming interest was in Jewish folk dance. Lapson's extensive research in this field, particularly in the area of Hassidic dance practices, led to numerous articles and books such as *New Palestine Dances* (1948), *Dances of the Jewish People* (1954), and *Folk Dances of the Jewish People* (1961). In a 1937 article for *The Dance Observer,* Lapson explained that Hassidic dance "was not composed deliberately, nor did it originate as a folk dance. It arose as a conscious attempt to create human joyousness out of misery." Through visiting Hassidic communities in the United States and abroad, she studied the various dance forms, such as those associated with religious occasions and the wedding ceremony, and, through performance, she brought these dance forms to the world beyond the Hassidim.

Lapson's interest in preserving traditional dance inspired her own numerous choreographic works, including the first Hebrew opera, *The Pioneers* (1936). She served as dance critic for the American Yiddish periodical *The Day* (1934–36), and has taught folk dance at the Hebrew Union College–Jewish Institute of Religion and through programs of the Jewish Education Committee of New York.

Larkin, Margaret (1899–1967). Larkin was a collector and performer of cowboy songs. A native of Las Vegas, New Mexico, she grew up among cowboys and cowboy singers. She left

New Mexico to study at the University of Kansas, then returned to Santa Fe, where she gained recognition as a poet, playwright, and journalist. She also became a union activist, and in 1929, while she was press agent for striking textile workers in Gastonia, North Carolina, she met Ella Mae Wiggins, a textile worker who wrote protest "ballets." The subsequent murder of Wiggins radicalized Larkin, who wrote influential articles about her and her songs. Larkin also performed Wiggins's songs in New York.

Larkin's reputation as a singer grew, and she became particularly known as a singer of cowboy songs. She contributed songs to Lynn Riggs's play *Green Grow the Lilacs* and became a member of the road company. In 1931, Larkin published her cowboy repertoire in *Singing Cowboy: A Book of Western Songs*.

Latvian Americans. See BALTIC PEOPLES.

Lawyer jokes. Many Americans have always regarded the legal profession with suspicion, but, during the litigious last quarter of the twentieth century, no profession has been more frequently reviled than the law. Lawyer jokes exist in profusion and are traded with great delight, especially among lawyers themselves. They are almost always in question-and-answer format: *What do you call five hundred lawyers at the bottom of the ocean?* Answer: *A good start.* Or: *How can you tell a lawyer is lying?* Answer: *His lips are moving.*

See also: JOKES AND JOKE CYCLES.

Leach, MacEdward (1892–1967). Leach created the doctoral program in folklore and folklife at the University of Pennsylvania and served the American Folklore Society as its secretary-treasurer (1943–60) and president (1961–62). A native of Bridgeport, Illinois, Leach was educated at the University of Illinois, Johns Hopkins, and the University of Pennsylvania. His faculty appointment at Pennsylvania was in the English Department, where he was a noted medievalist in addition to a student of American folklore.

Ledbetter, Huddie (Leadbelly) (1885?–1949). Born near Mooringsport, Louisiana, where his family owned a sixty-five-acre farm, Huddie Ledbetter was first influenced in music by his mother, who was the leader of her church's choir. He also had two "songster" uncles who forwarded his musical development. At sixteen, he started visiting Fannin Street, the red-light district of Shreveport, and sang about these experiences later in his song, "Fannin Street." He picked up songs and guitar style from the talented black musicians he heard there. He later moved to Dallas, where he sang and played guitar in its red-light district. There he met the great Texas bluesman BLIND LEMON JEFFERSON. He became his leadman and also learned many of his songs, acquiring the nickname of Leadbelly because of his rumbling bass voice.

As he knocked around Texas, Leadbelly ran afoul of the law for several violent crimes, including rape and attempted murder. After escaping from several prisons, he was finally confined, in 1920, to the Central State Farm near Houston, where he worked on labor gangs cutting logs and in the cotton fields, acquiring a reputation for great speed and strength. Famed also for his prowess as a singer and guitar picker, Leadbelly was often summoned to entertain visitors to the prison, among whom was Pat M. Neff, the governor of Texas. Leadbelly took advantage of the moment by singing a plea for mercy to the governor: "[If I] had you, Governor Neff, like you got me, I'd wake up in the mornin', and I'd set you free." The governor was impressed enough to pardon Leadbelly, who had served almost seven years.

Leadbelly returned to Mooringsport in 1926 and continued to develop as a songster and a performer with a wide repertoire of BLUES, BALLADS, spirituals (see SPIRITUALS, AFRICAN-AMERICAN), WORK SONGS, and children's songs, but he again got into serious trouble with the law. In 1930, a group of men pestered Leadbelly for whiskey. The singer stabbed five of them and was condemned to ten years at hard labor for assault with intent to murder. He entered the Louisiana State Penitentiary at Angola and again became leadman on work gangs. When the collecting folklorists JOHN LOMAX and his son ALAN LOMAX visited the prison farm on one of their recording trips for the Library of Congress in 1934, Leadbelly again sang his way to freedom with a song plea the Lomaxes recorded and then played for Governor O. K. Allen. (The original of the later nationally popular "Irene, Goodnight," as performed in the fifties by The Weavers, was recorded at the same session. The substantial royalties came too late for Leadbelly's benefit.)

The Lomaxes took Leadbelly along with them on their collecting trips at other southern prisons and locales rich in African-American FOLK MUSIC. Leadbelly served as a highly effective pump-primer, inspiring informants to sing and play their most characteristic and deeply felt numbers, which were later archived at the Library of Congress. When the trio arrived in New York City after six thousand miles of travel, artistic, literary, and folk music circles received Leadbelly with great fascination. His colorful, vigorous speech and his charismatic performances as "The King of the 12-String Guitar Players of the World" and bearer of a song repertoire of extraordinary diversity and richness were an immediate sensation and remained so until his death in 1949 of myotropic lateral sclerosis. He had become one of the most admired, studied, and imitated of authentic folk performers.

Recordings of Leadbelly interviews and performances are on deposit with the Recording Division of the Library of Congress.

See also: AFRICAN AMERICANS; ASCH, MOSES.

SUGGESTED READING: Richard M. Garvin and Edmond G. Addeo, *The Midnight Special: The Legend of Leadbelly* (New York, 1971); John A. Lomax and Alan Lomax, *The Leadbelly Legend* (New York, 1965); Charles Wolfe and Kip Lornell, *The Life and Legend of Leadbelly* (New York, 1992).

Ledger book drawings. See NATIVE AMERICANS.

Lee, Hector H. (1908–1992). Student of western folklore and folk narrative, Lee is especially well known for his work on Mormon folklore. A native Texan, Lee was raised in Utah, where he was steeped in Mormon pioneer and Paiute lore and narrative. Educated at the University of Utah and at the University of California, Berkeley, Lee took a Ph.D. in American civilization at the University of New Mexico. He taught

English and folklore at the University of Utah and, in 1944, he created the Utah Humanities Research Foundation, a folklore archive, and the quarterly journal *Utah Humanities Review* (later the *Western Humanities Review*).

As a folklore scholar, Lee's most important work was with Mormon material, as evidenced in his *The Three Nephites: Their Substance and Significance in Folklore* (1949). Lee also published four popular folklore collections: *Tales of the Redwood Empire* (1962), *Tales of California* (1974), *Heroes, Villains, and Ghosts* (1984), and *The Bodega War* (1988).

Lee, Robert Edward (1807–1870).

Commander of the Confederate Army of Northern Virginia and, ultimately, general in chief of Confederate forces, Lee is the most universally respected, admired, and beloved military commander in American history. As a figure of folklore, he became the personification of everything perceived as noble about the Southern "cause" and the Southern character. In this regard, he is one of a handful of American CULTURE HEROES.

Lee was born at Strafford, Virginia, the third son of Revolutionary War hero Henry "Lighthorse Harry" Lee and his second wife, Ann Hill Carter. He graduated from West Point, second in the Class of 1829, was commissioned in the Corps of Engineers, and saw service along the southeast coast. During this period, he married another ancestor of the Revolution, Mary Custis, great-granddaughter of Martha Washington. Lee served brilliantly in the Mexican War (1846–48) and, after the war, was appointed superintendent of West Point (1852–55). Lee served in the West for a time, but was back in Virginia when he was ordered to Harpers Ferry to put down the abolitionist John Brown's raid on the armory and ar-

Robert E. Lee, in full uniform. (National Archives and Records Administration)

senal there. He captured Brown on October 18, 1859.

Lee resigned his commission when Virginia seceded from the Union, unwilling to fight against his native state. Given command of Virginia's military and naval forces, Lee also served as personal military adviser to Confederate president Jefferson Davis. He did not fare well in his first field command in western Virginia and was recalled to Richmond to advise Davis. After Gen. Joseph E. Johnston was wounded at Seven Pines during May 31–June 1, Lee was called on to replace him. He created the Army of Northern Virginia and led it from one success to another, almost always against superior Union numbers.

He was, however, defeated by Gen. George G. Meade at the make-or-break Battle of Gettysburg (July 1–3, 1863), which turned the tide of the war finally against the South.

Lee conducted a brilliant defense against Gen. Ulysses S. Grant at the Wilderness (May 5–6, 1864), Spotsylvania (May 8–12), and Cold Harbor (June 3), but was ultimately defeated by siege at Petersburg (June–October). Jefferson Davis named Lee general in chief of the Confederate armies on February 3, 1865, but Lee's forces—and, indeed, the entire Confederacy—were so badly weakened that the general was clearly fighting for a lost cause. Lee surrendered the Army of Northern Virginia to Grant at Appomattox Court House on April 9, 1865, effectively (though not officially) ending the Civil War.

Lee was briefly a prisoner of war, then, in September 1865, accepted the presidency of Washington College (later renamed Washington and Lee University) in Lexington, Virginia. He died five years later of a chronic heart ailment.

SUGGESTED READING: Douglas Southall Freeman, *R. E. Lee: A Biography* (New York, 1949).

Legend. A traditional tale believed to have a historical basis; compare MYTH, which is not believed to be based on history, but instead partakes of the supernatural, religious, and sacred. Most folklorists would agree that a legend is a type of folktale and is transmitted, at least originally, by oral means; however, many folklorists also accept the role of print and other media (such as radio, television, and film) in the creation, transmission, and modification of particular legends.

See also: COLLEGE FOLKLORE; CRIME AND CRIMINALS; LINCOLN, ABRAHAM; LOCAL LEGEND; MASS MEDIA; MEXICAN AMERICANS; MONROE, MARILYN; RAILROAD FOLKLORE; RELIGION, FOLK; REVOLUTIONARY WAR; WEATHER FOLKLORE.

Leutze, Emanuel (1816–1868). Leutze was the painter whose *Washington Crossing the Delaware* (1851) made this scene of the prelude to the battles of Trenton and Princeton an icon of American popular culture. Born in Schwäbisch-Gmünd, Württemberg (now in Germany), Leutze came to the United States as a child, but returned to Germany in 1841 to study painting at the Academy in Düsseldorf. For the next two decades, Leutze lived in Germany, and painted a series of works depicting scenes from American history, the most famous of which is *Washington Crossing the Delaware*. In 1860, a year after he returned to the United States, the U.S. Congress commis-

Emanuel Leutze

Emanuel Leutze, Washington Crossing the Delaware, *1851. (Metropolitan Museum of Art, New York City)*

sioned him to decorate a Capitol stairway. The result was another famed historical work, *Westward the Course of Empire Takes Its Way,* illustrating with mythic intensity the settlement of the far West.

See also: WASHINGTON, GEORGE.

Lincoln, Abraham (1809–1865). The American president most universally admired, at least in the northern states, Lincoln has entered into American folklore, as a folk hero and as a CULTURE HERO, more thoroughly and profoundly than any other political figure. A product of the frontier, he rose from very humble circumstances to become sixteenth president of the United States just before the nation's gravest crisis, the Civil War. Not only has his life story become the stuff of LEGEND, but his unassuming, homespun eloquence has proved a source of folk wisdom and even PROVERBS ("Don't change horses in midstream," "Honesty is the best policy," "You can fool all of the people some of the time, and some of the people all of the time, but you cannot fool all of the people all of the time," and so on). His upbringing in a LOG CABIN, his reputation for prowess as a "rail splitter," his self-education, reading by the light of the hearth, his early career as a circuit-riding lawyer in Salem and Springfield, Illinois—all have provided a trove of folktalelike anecdotes.

Lincoln was born near Hodgenville, Kentucky, and moved to Indiana during December 1816. Fourteen years later, he settled in Illinois. During April–August 1832, he served in the Illinois militia in the war against Chief Black Hawk. Always popular for his sly rural wit, he gained election as captain of his unit, but saw no fighting in the war. In 1836, Lincoln, wholly self-taught, passed the Illinois State bar and set up a law prac-

President Abraham Lincoln. (National Archives and Records Administration)

tice in the state capital, Springfield, in 1837, while serving in the state legislature (1834–40). He was sent to the U.S. House of Representatives in 1847 and served one term. His law practice prospering, Lincoln gained a reputation for honesty and fairness as a circuit lawyer. He is depicted in popular literature and in the 1939 film *Young Mr. Lincoln,* directed by John Ford and starring Henry Fonda, as reticent and rustic in the

The log courthouse in Petersburg, Illinois, where Lincoln tried his first case.

courtroom, but the evidence is that he was shrewd and highly skilled. While he did his share of pro bono work for ordinary citizens, the success of Lincoln's firm was the result of legal work he carried out for the Illinois Central and other railroads. There is probably some historical basis to the popular image of Lincoln's having "kept his office" in the stovepipe hat that became his trademark headgear. Certainly, the stovepipe hat was remarkable even to Lincoln's contemporaries, because, by the time he began his first term as president, the style was already hopelessly old-fashioned.

Lincoln joined the newly formed Republican Party in 1856, losing his bid for a Senate seat to Stephen A. Douglas, whom he engaged in a series of oratorically brilliant debates. While few Americans today have read any of the Lincoln-Douglas debates, folklore has elevated them to a rhetorical clash of two Titans. In truth, the positions of Lincoln and Douglas, even on such monumental issues as slavery, had more similarities than differences.

Despite his loss to Douglas, the debates gained Lincoln national prominence, and he was nominated as the Republican presidential candidate on May 15, 1860. With the Democratic party split over the issue of secession, Lincoln was

elected on November 6, an event that prompted the secession of South Carolina from the Union on December 20. Six other southern states soon followed suit, and the Confederate States of America was created before Lincoln's inauguration on March 4, 1861. The new president's first difficult decision was whether or not to fight to preserve the union. He determined to go to war, if necessary, and, for the next four years, led the Union in its struggle to reunite the nation by force. Although Lincoln was explicit in stating that the object of the war was to save the union and not to free the slaves, he figures in American folklore—and in African-American folklore—as the "Great Emancipator." Lincoln has been frequently and fancifully pictured as literally lifting a black man from his chains. More accurate is the popular image of Lincoln as careworn, his long, homely face bearing upon it the marks of his na-

The presidential box at Ford's Theatre, site of the assassination on April 14, 1865. (National Archives and Records Administration)

tion's suffering. In this, he assumes the role of culture hero, nearly Christlike, as if he willingly took upon himself the pain of his countrymen.

Lincoln was reelected in 1864, when Union victory, long in doubt, seemed a certainty. In his second inaugural speech, he promised to act with "malice toward none and charity for all" in an effort to "bind up the nation's wounds." He was shot on April 13, 1865, by the fanatical southern sympathizer, John Wilkes Booth, while attending a performance of the comedy *Our American Cousin* at Washington's Ford's Theatre. He died the next morning, only days before the war formally ended. The assassination effected the apotheosis of Abraham Lincoln to the status of martyr—and also set off an avalanche of CONSPIRACY LORE relating to the tragedy, echoes of which continue to be heard today.

See also: BOONE, DANIEL; GREENFIELD VILLAGE; JACKSON, ANDREW; QUILTS; SANDBURG, CARL; WARD, ARTEMUS.

SUGGESTED READING: William Hanchett, *The Lincoln Murder Conspiracies* (Urbana and Chicago, Ill., 1983); Abraham Lincoln, *Speeches and Writings 1832–1858* (New York, 1989); Abraham Lincoln, *Speeches and Writings 1859–65* (New York, 1989); Carl Sandburg, *Abraham Lincoln: The Prairie Years and the War Years* (one-volume abridgment of the multivolume biography; New York, 1993); P. M. Zall, ed., *Abe Lincoln Laughing: Humorous Anecdotes from Original Sources by and about Abraham Lincoln* (Knoxville, Tenn., 1995).

Charles A. Lindbergh: the Lone Eagle with an uncharacteristic grin, about 1927.

Lindbergh, Charles A. (1902–1974). The "Lone Eagle," who made the first nonstop solo flight across the Atlantic, from New York to Paris, on May 20–21, 1927, became an instant folk hero and CULTURE HERO. He was born in Detroit and raised in Little Falls, Minnesota, and in Washington, D.C., where his father was congressman for the 6th district of Minnesota. Lindbergh dropped out of the University of Wisconsin to take flying lessons and purchased a World War

I–vintage Curtiss Jenny, in which he "barnstormed" across the South and Midwest. He joined the army as an aviator to take advantage of the flight training offered by the military and served during 1924–25, after which he became an airmail pilot (1926). Lindbergh organized financial backing from a group of St. Louis businessmen to compete for a $25,000 prize offered for the first nonstop flight between New York and Paris. His backers funded modification of a Ryan Aircraft monoplane, which was christened the Spirit of St. Louis. After Lindbergh successfully completed the 33½–hour flight, his plane became one of the most famous in aviation history and its young aviator became perhaps the most famous figure in the world.

Instantly, Lindbergh and Spirit of St. Louis souvenirs became big business, "Lucky Lindy" became a big hit for singer Rudy Vallee, and the Lindy Hop became a popular dance craze.

Lindbergh married Anne Morrow, the beautiful and remarkable daughter of Dwight Morrow, U.S. ambassador to Mexico, in 1929. The activities of the young couple were avidly followed by the public. During this period, Lindbergh, as technical adviser to Transcontinental Air Transport and Pan American Airways, helped to create the modern commercial airline industry.

The Lindberghs were thrust into the headlines again in March 1932, when their two-year-old son was kidnapped from their rural New Jersey home and subsequently found murdered. It was called the "crime of the century," and was the focus of news coverage through April 1936, when Bruno Richard Hauptmann, found guilty of the kidnap-murder, was executed. The Lindberghs left the United States for a long European tour, where Lindbergh created controversy by accepting a decoration from the Third Reich (Nazi Germany). With the outbreak of World War II, he alienated many Americans by his advocacy of neutrality. Nevertheless, once the nation did enter the war, Lindbergh, a civilian, served as a consultant to the Ford Motor Company and to the United Aircraft Corporation, secretly flying fifty combat missions in the Pacific.

After the war, the Lindberghs lived quietly in Connecticut and then in Hawaii, Charles serving as an aviation consultant to industry and government, and Anne Morrow creating an increasing reputation as a writer. Lindbergh's own account of his flight to Paris, The Spirit of St. Louis (1953), received the Pulitzer Prize. Toward the end of his life, Lindbergh became a dedicated environmentalist, campaigning (among other things) for a ban on supersonic commercial passenger flights as excessively harmful to the environment.

SUGGESTED READING: A. Scott Berg, Lindbergh (New York, 1998); Charles A. Lindbergh, Autobiography of Values (New York, 1978); Charles A. Lindbergh, We (New York, 1927); Walter S. Ross, The Last Hero: Charles A. Lindbergh (rev. ed.; New York, 1976).

Lindsay, (Nicholas) Vachel (1879–1931).

The poet Vachel Lindsay is relevant to American folklore not only because he used folklore and legendary material in some of his verse, but because he consciously sought to revive poetry as an *oral* art form of the common people. To this purpose, he attempted to reinvigorate literary poetry with some of the elements of folk poetry.

Lindsay was born in Springfield, Illinois, and spent three years at Hiram College (Hiram, Ohio), leaving in 1900 to study art in Chicago and New York City. Leading the life of a true bohemian, Lindsay supported himself in part by lecturing for the YMCA and the Anti-Saloon League and by traveling throughout the country reciting his verse in exchange for food and shelter. In 1913, the prestigious *Poetry* magazine published his "General William Booth Enters into Heaven," a fiercely rhythmic celebration of the founder of the Salvation Army. The Booth poem was one of several Lindsay based on the lives of popular American icons, including Alexander Campbell (a founder of the Disciples of Christ), JOHNNY APPLESEED, John Peter Altgeld (the Illinois governor who had sacrificed his political career by pardoning three of the Haymarket Square rioters unjustly condemned to execution), and William Jennings Bryan (the Populist politician and orator). In vivid contrast to the genteel manners of most of the period's poets, Lindsay *performed* his verse, stressing its heavily syncopated meters and liberal use of explosive alliteration. His recitations were accented by histrionic gestures.

Lindsay achieved considerable popular success with his verse and his performances, but his literary prowess declined sharply during the late 1920s, as he fell into ill health and depression. Despondent, he committed suicide by swallowing drain cleaner.

See also: HUGHES, (JAMES MERCER) LANGSTON.

SUGGESTED READING: Vachel Lindsay, *To Be Traded for Bread* (New York, 1912); Vachel Lindsay, *General William Booth Enters into Heaven and Other Poems* (New York, 1913); Vachel Lindsay, *The Congo and Other Poems* (New York, 1914); Vachel Lindsay, *The Chinese Nightingale and Other Poems* (New York, 1917); Edgar Lee Masters, *Vachel Lindsay: A Poet in America* (New York, 1935).

Line dance. A dance in which the dancers form a straight line or two straight lines, which

advance and retreat from each other. Country line dancing, which, like the SQUARE DANCE, uses a caller, became a popular dance form among rural and city folk alike beginning in the 1980s.

See also: DANCE, FOLK; FIDDLE.

Linscott, Eloise Hubbard (1897–1978). Linscott was a collector of New England folk songs, ballads, folk dances, and folk music. She is best known for her anthology, *Folk Songs of Old New England* (1939), which was in large part based on the traditions of her own family, and which included a generous selection of tunes as well as text. Linscott was born in Taunton, Massachusetts, and was educated at Wellesley College (B.A., 1920).

SUGGESTED READING: Linda Morely, entry on Linscott in Jan Harold Brunvand, ed., *American Folklore: An Encyclopedia* (New York, 1996).

Lithuanian Americans. See BALTIC PEOPLES.

Little Moron jokes. What the DUMB DORA JOKES were to the 1920s, the Little Moron jokes were to the 1930s. The humor turns on the remarkable stupidity of the Little Moron, who misinterprets simple statements, often by taking them literally yet rendering them nonsensical. For example: *What did the Little Moron do when he was told he was dying?* Answer: *He moved into the living room.* Or this one: *The phone rings in* the middle of the night, and Little Moron gets up to answer it. "Is this one one one one?" the caller asks. "No," Little Moron answers, "it's eleven eleven." "Are you sure this isn't one one one one?" "I'm sure. It's eleven eleven." "Wrong number, then. Sorry to have gotten you out of bed." "Oh that's all right," the affable Little Moron answers, "I had to get up to answer the phone anyway." Little Moron jokes lost their vogue with adults before the end of the thirties, but they remained popular with schoolchildren long afterward.

See also: JOKES AND JOKE CYCLES; POLACK JOKES.

Little Willie jokes.
Black-humor doggerel rhymes popular among urban American schoolchildren during the 1950s and early 1960s. They often involve Little Willie committing mayhem upon his infant sibling and end with their mother's tepid admonitions. The humor turns on a disjointed combination of goriness and deadpan absence of emotion. For example:

> Little Willie with a shout
> Gouged the baby's eyeballs out,
> Stomped on them to make them pop,
> Said his mother, "Now, William, stop."

Or:

> Little Willie, filled with gore,
> Nailed the baby to the door.
> Said his mother with humor quaint,
> "Now, Will, don't mar the paint."

Another Little Willie rhyme involves self-destruction:

> Little Willie was a chemist.
> Little Willie is a chemist no more.
> For what he thought was H_2O
> Was H_2SO_4.

See also: JOKES AND JOKE CYCLES.

Lizzie labels.
Precursor of BUMPER STICKERS, lizzie labels were wisecracks and humorous slogans inscribed or painted on Model T Fords (known as "tin lizzies"), especially those owned by college boys in the 1920s and 1930s. The term "lizzie label" was either coined or first widely reported by the humor magazine *Judge*, which fostered the fad by offering a five-dollar prize for each label its editors deemed clever enough to print. In contrast to later bumper stickers, lizzie labels were rarely didactic or issue oriented, nor did they advertise any product—though they often parodied advertising slogans: "The tin you love to touch" instead of the "The skin you love to touch." Often, the labels punned on the car itself—"Capacity: 4 gals."—or parodied popular song titles: "The Old Chokin' Bucket."

Llorona, La.
This ghost (*espantos*) of the folklore of Mexico and the American Southwest roams the nighttime countryside in search of her lost children. *La Llorona* translates as "the Weeper," and her mournful cry can cause *susto* (mental anguish) in those who hear her. Moreover, heard at one's front door, her weeping portends a death in the household.

The most prevalent legend of *La Llorona* depicts her as the ghost of a widow who drowned her children in a pond or well in order to free herself for remarriage. Legend also holds that she may murder other children she finds in her nocturnal wanderings. She may also cast an evil spell on whomever she encounters.

See also: MALINCHE, LA; MEXICAN AMERICANS.

SUGGESTED READING: Arthur L. Campa, *Hispanic Culture in the Southwest* (Norman, Okla., 1979).

Local-character story.
Anecdote concerning an eccentric person well known in the community. The anecdote may be similar to a LOCAL LEGEND or may describe a brief episode that illustrates the subject's eccentricity. The "local character" is typically disruptive, very clever, offbeat, excessively stingy, highly gullible, or remarkably stupid. Whatever the specific eccentricity, the local character in some significant—usually humorous—way violates the norms of the community.

See also: HARTE, (FRANCIS) BRET[T]; LOCAL-COLOR STORY; MELVILLE, HERMAN; RAILROAD FOLKLORE; THOREAU, HENRY DAVID; TWAIN, MARK.

SUGGESTED READING: Richard M. Dorson, *Buying the Wind* (Chicago, 1964).

Local-color story.
A literary style rather than a folk genre, the local-color story nevertheless often draws on local folklore or deals with local characters (see LOCAL-CHARACTER STORY) or LOCAL LEGENDS. In American literature, the local-color movement emerged after the Civil War and was popular well into the 1890s. Local-color stories focus on the distinctive features, flavor, and characters of a particular region. The object was to create a convincing portrait of an area's character. While some writers of the early republic, most notably WASHINGTON IRVING, might be described as local-color writers, the movement proper begins with BRET HARTE and his stories of the western mining camps, as well as MARK TWAIN and JOAQUIN MILLER, who covered some of the same territory. Prime examples of local-color fiction in its heyday are Sarah Orne Jewett (1849–1909) and Mary Wilkins Freeman (1852–1930), both of whom wrote of New England character and eccentricities, and George Washington Cable (1844–1925) and Kate Chopin (1851–1904), who wrote of New Orleans and Louisiana Cajun country. JOEL CHANDLER HARRIS may also be considered a local colorist. The urban environment also had its local color writers, including the short-story writer O. Henry (1867–1910) and Stephen Crane (1871–1900), in such works as *Maggie: A Girl of the Streets* (1893).

See also: CAJUNS; DIALECT STORIES; FOLKLORE IN AMERICAN LITERATURE; HARTE, (FRANCIS) BRET[T].

Local legend.
A usually brief narrative explaining some local geographical feature, the origin of a local place name, or the story of a local tradition. Typically, the stories are etymological in nature and are believed to be ancient or, in the case of many American local legends, at least very old. Many American localities have a LOVER'S LEAP (often associated with a story of a suicidal lover or couple) and a Dead Man's Curve (usually associated with a tale of a fatal automobile wreck).

This log cabin is part of the reconstruction of Fort Nashborough, Tennessee.

See also: Cobb, Ned; Folklore in American Literature; Legend; Local-character story; Local-color story; Railroad folklore.

The American log cabin is a pervasive cultural icon, as this birdhouse ad from the 1940s suggests. The ad also demonstrates the degree to which the log cabin was associated with Abraham Lincoln, one of a number of important American political figures born and raised in a log cabin.

Log cabin. An important example of VERNACULAR ARCHITECTURE, the log cabin holds a special place in American folklore as a symbol of the pioneers and the pioneering spirit. During the nineteenth century, after the presidency of Andrew Jackson, it became almost de rigueur for presidential candidates to lay claim to having been born in a log cabin. In an association that endures to this day, ABRAHAM LINCOLN became especially identified with this house type. During much of the twentieth century, log cabins were popular as vacation homes and rustic "guest cottages."

Log cabin designs vary widely, but the image that comes to mind when most Americans think

Reconstruction of Abraham Lincoln's birthplace, a log cabin outside of Hodgenville, Kentucky.

of a log cabin is a small, one-room building with a sloping, single-gabled timbered roof and very small, perhaps unglazed, windows. The typical log cabin is built of logs notched at the ends and interlocked one upon another. Spaces between the logs may be filled with plaster, mud, mortar, or even moss or dried manure. Despite the impression created by many movie and television Westerns, log cabins were rarely found on the prairie, because trees were scarce (there the SOD HOUSE predominated). Log cabins are woodland houses, built of locally available materials.

See also: FINNISH AMERICANS; JACKSON, ANDREW.

SUGGESTED READING: C. A. Weslager, *The Log Cabin in America: From Pioneer Days to the Present* (New Brunswick, N.J., 1969).

Lomax, Alan (1915–). Son of folk-song collector JOHN LOMAX, Alan was born in Austin, Texas, and was educated at Harvard University and the University of Texas at Austin, from which he received a B.A. in 1936. He also studied at Columbia University. Lomax accompanied his father on collecting tours of the South, recording folk songs for the Archive of American Folk-Song of the Library of Congress. Together, the Lomaxes discovered and recorded HUDDIE LEDBETTER (LEADBELLY), and, later, Alan Lomax recorded a large number of folk and BLUES performers, among them WOODY GUTHRIE, MUDDY WATERS, and BURL IVES. A collector of wide-ranging materials, Lomax made important recordings of the seminal jazz pianist Jelly Roll Morton in 1938, and, during the 1950s, recorded folk material throughout Great Britain, Italy, and Spain.

Alan Lomax was an active collector as well as a student of folklore, who delved deeply into the emotional, social, historical, and comparative contexts of the material he studied. Not only did he write the standard biography of Jelly Roll Morton (*Mister Jelly Roll,* 1950) and *The Folk Songs of North America in the English Language* (1960), but (with Victor Grauer) he pioneered the field of cantometrics, the statistical analysis of singing styles correlated with anthropological data. Late in his career, he extended statistical analysis to folk and popular dance as well.

See also: ARCHIVE OF FOLK CULTURE; CAJUN MUSIC; FLANDERS, HELEN HARTNESS; FOLK MUSIC; KITTREDGE, GEORGE LYMAN; NYE, PEARL R.; STUBBLEFIELD, BLAINE "STUB"; WALTON, IVAN.

SUGGESTED READING: Alan Lomax, *The Land Where the Blues Began* (New York, 1993); Alan Lomax, *Mister Jelly Roll: The Fortunes of Jelly Roll Morton, New Orleans Creole and "Inventor of Jazz"* (New York, 1950).

Lomax, John Avery (1867–1948). Important collector of American folk songs and the father of folk-song collector and scholar ALAN LOMAX, John Lomax was born to a farming family in Goodman, Mississippi. Lomax was raised in central Texas, where he grew up listening to Methodist camp-meeting hymns and to COWBOY SONGS and cowboy tales. After a year at Granbury College, Lomax taught at Weatherford College for six years, then obtained a B.A. at the University of Texas in Austin (1897). He worked in the administrative office of the university for a time, then taught at Texas Agricultural and Mechanical College, obtaining leave to study at Harvard University, where he earned an M.A. in English (1907). At Harvard, under the tutelage of GEORGE LYMAN KITTREDGE and others, Lomax became interested in folklore and began collecting the cowboy songs that he published in *Cowboy Songs and Other Frontier Ballads* (1910), which was greeted as a major contribution to the celebration and preservation of American heritage. No less a figure than President Theodore Roosevelt contributed a preface to the volume.

Despite the success of his cowboy song collection, Lomax turned to low-level positions in banking and finance to support his family. The onset of the Depression ended these jobs, and, in 1932, armed with a book contract and a grant from the Library of Congress and the American Council of Learned Societies, Lomax returned to fieldwork, this time assisted by his son Alan. He now turned his attention to the folk songs and blues of southern African Americans, amassing some 10,000 recordings for the Library of Congress Archive of American Folk-Song. In 1934, Lomax and his son published *American Ballads and Folksongs* (1934), which was followed by *Our Singing Country* (1941) and *Folk Song U.S.A.* (1947).

In 1935, Lomax introduced to the American public HUDDIE LEDBETTER (LEADBELLY), whom he and his son had discovered in Lousiana's Angola prison, where he was serving a six-year term for having knifed a man. Lomax arranged a singing tour of the Northeast and produced a number of important Leadbelly recordings. In 1936, Lomax was named national folklore editor of the Federal Writers' Project (FWP), from which position he enthusiastically encouraged the collection and study of folklore as living materials rather than nostalgic relics of a bygone age.

See also: BROWN, FRANK CLYDE; DUSENBURY, EMMA HAYS; FOLK MUSIC; NYE, PEARL R.

SUGGESTED READING: John Lomax, *Adventures of a Ballad Hunter.* (New York, 1947); Nolan Porterfield, *Last Cavalier: The Life and Times of John A. Lomax, 1867–1948* (Champaign-Urbana, Ill., 1996).

Henry Wadsworth Longfellow, as pictured in Reuben Post Halleck, History of American Literature, *1911. (Collection of Alan Axelrod)*

Longfellow, Henry Wadsworth (1807–1882).

Without a doubt the most popular American poet in the nineteenth century, Longfellow not only used American folklore and legend as the thematic basis for his most beloved poems, but also consciously used traditional heroic, epic, and saga narrative forms to frame his material. Moreover, many of Longfellow's works have themselves become, if not part of American folklore, then certainly part of American popular culture.

Longfellow graduated from Bowdoin College (1825), where he fell under the influence of Sir Walter Scott's novels and WASHINGTON IRVING's *Sketch Book* (1819–20). He began publishing verse in national magazines and displayed a remarkable facility for literary translation. This prompted the offer of a professorship in modern languages at Bowdoin, on condition that he undertake study abroad. After his tour, he returned to the United States in 1829, became a professor and librarian at Bowdoin, wrote textbooks, and translated literary works. He left the Maine college to accept a professorship at Harvard and toured Germany, England, Sweden, and the Netherlands during 1835–36. Although his collection of travel pieces, *Outre-Mer* (1835), was a popular failure, his 1839 collection of lyric verse, *Voices of the Night*, earned him instant fame. A novel, *Hyperion*, followed, and in 1841 he published *Ballads and Other Poems*, which includes such perennial favorites as "The Wreck of the *Hesperus*" and "The Village Blacksmith."

Longfellow tried his hand at a collection of abolitionist verse, *Poems on Slavery* (1842), but made little impression on the general public. However, his long narrative, *Evangeline* (1847), based on the expulsion of the Acadians from Nova Scotia during the French and Indian War, became a true bestseller. In 1855, Longfellow used HENRY ROWE SCHOOLCRAFT's books on the Indian tribes of North America (in particular his collection of Ojibwa folklore, *Algic Researches* [1839]) as the basis of his *Song of Hiawatha* (1855). Borrowing the trochaic meter of the Finnish epic *Kalevala* as the verse vehicle for his poem, Longfellow created a work of literature that struck ordinary readers and critics alike as the embodiment of heroic legend and myth (see HIAWATHA).

Longfellow turned next to the Puritan past of his native New England for the material of *The Courtship of Miles Standish* (1858), which elevated the figures of the shy John Alden, the vainglorious Standish, and the frank Priscilla to the status of American cultural icons. Yet, tragically, at the height of his popular success, Longfellow's second wife died of severe burns after she accidentally set her dress on fire. Profoundly depressed, Longfellow turned from the material of American history, legend, and lore to the world of Dante Alighieri, whose *Divine Comedy* he translated in masterly fashion, followed by six sonnets on the subject of Dante.

In 1863, Longfellow returned to American matter, publishing *The Tales of a Wayside Inn*, inspired in form by Chaucer's *Canterbury Tales*. This collection includes "Paul Revere's Ride," which, though historically less than accurate, established a niche in legend for the patriot silvermith's ride to alert the Minutemen of the invasion of the British before the battles of Lexington and Concord. The poem's anapestic tetrameter, suggestive of a galloping horse, is a compelling feature of this highly successful attempt to produce, in literature, an imitation of a folk ballad.

Like many other nineteenth-century American writers, Longfellow was restless and wanted to reach beyond national material, and in 1872 published what he believed was his magnum opus, *Christus: A Mystery*, a dramatic verse trilogy dealing with Christianity.

While Longfellow was certainly admired and even loved during and after his lifetime (his bust even occupies a niche in Poets' Corner of London's Westminster), modern literary critics compare him unfavorably to WALT WHITMAN, whose unconventional vigor (they say) more eloquently expressed the spirit of American culture. Nevertheless, Longfellow consciously employed national and regional material in his verse and endeavored to present that material in forms either evocative of ancient oral traditions or folk ballads.

See also: CAJUNS; CURRIER & IVES; CUSTER, GEORGE ARMSTRONG; FOLKLORE IN AMERICAN LITERATURE; HARTE, (FRANCIS) BRET[T]; MORTON, THOMAS; PILGRIMS AND PURITANS; REVERE, PAUL; REVOLUTIONARY WAR; STANDISH, MILES.

SUGGESTED READING: Edward Wagenknecht, *Longfellow: A Full-Length Portrait* (New York, 1955); Edward Wagenknecht, *Henry Wadsworth Longfellow: His Poetry and Prose* (New York, 1986); Cecil Brown Williams, *Henry Wadsworth Longfellow* (1964).

Longways dance. A type of Anglo-American folk dance performed in "longways formation," by lines of men and women facing each other "up and down the hall"—as a dance caller would put it. The longways dance was the most popular social dance form during the colonial era. Well into the twentieth century, it was still danced in rural New Hampshire and Vermont. HENRY FORD, a promoter of what he conceived to be American folklife, encouraged the revival of longways dancing in the 1920s.

See also: DANCE, FOLK.

Loomis, C. Grant (1901–1963). Loomis was editor of *Western Folklore* from 1949 to 1952 and associate editor from 1953 to 1963. Although he was a professor of German at Tufts University, his interest in folklore was great, as evidenced in his *White Magic: An Introduction to the Folklore of Christian Legend* (1948). He was a prime mover behind the California Folklore Society from its inception in 1941 until his death. His essays on the topic of western folklore include "Traditional American Wordplay: The Epigram and Perverted Proverbs" (*Western Folklore* 8 [1949], pp. 248–57), "Traditional American Wordplay: Wellerisms or Yankeeisms" (*Western Folklore* 8 [1949], pp. 1–21), "Bret Harte's Folklore" (*Western Folklore* 15 [1956], pp. 19–22; "Proverbs in the Farmers Almanac" (*Western Folklore* 15 [1956], pp. 172–78; "American Limerick Tradition" (*Western Folklore* 21 [1962],

pp. 153–57), among many other language-oriented studies.

Lopez, Felix A. (1942–). Lopez is a modern *santero*, a carver and painter of the images of saints traditional in Hispanic northern New Mexico, though he does not slavishly reproduce all of the traditional elements, he often modifies traditional positions, gestures, and expressions. His colors are also his own; he makes no attempt to reproduce those used in Spanish colonial times. Lopez carves aspen, cottonwood, and pine, using only hand tools. He makes his own pigments from local minerals, clay, berries, walnut husks, and even his own blood.

Lopez is a college graduate who taught high school Spanish. His father's death in 1975 inspired him to take up traditional carving. He tried sculpting in clay, but, in 1977, "The saints surrounding my father's coffin appeared to me, and I became a *santero*." By the late 1980s, Lopez had gained a national reputation.

See also: SANTOS.

Lopez, José Delores (1868–1937). Recognized as one of the greatest carvers of the *santero* tradition of New Mexico, Lopez was raised in Cordova, New Mexico. With little formal education, he made his living as a carpenter and cabinetmaker, creating furniture that anticipated the much-prized Santa Fe style. He also carved SANTOS and BULTOS—the traditional New Mexican Hispanic religious folk images—in a style marked by great dignity and simplicity. While he was strongly influenced by such santeros as JOSÉ RAFAEL ARAGON, he took a more contemporary approach to carving, and he also left his work largely unpainted—a marked departure from tradition. During the 1930s, the WPA Federal Art Project purchased a number of his saints, and his work began to gain national recognition. Lopez worked with aspen, pine, willow, and juniper, using simple hand tools. Paint, if used at all, was applied sparingly.

Lord, Albert Bates (1912–1991).

With MILMAN PARRY, Lord developed the oral-formulaic theory, a major approach to folklore, folk literature, and anthropology. Often called the Perry-Lord theory, the oral-formulaic theory analyzes formulas (patterned phraseology), themes (typical narrative scenes), and story patterns (overall narrative structures) as the tissue of traditional oral narrative. These elements allow the oral composer to create and maintain fluent, cogent, and intelligible narrative.

Lord was Parry's research assistant in joint fieldwork undertaken among oral epic singers in the former Yugoslavia during 1933–35; Lord continued the fieldwork alone in 1950–51. This research was the basis of the Parry-Lord theory, the fullest expression of which is found in Lord's seminal *The Singer of Tales* (1960).

Lord was educated at Harvard University (A.B. classics, 1934; M.A. and Ph.D. comparative literature, 1936; 1949).

SUGGESTED READING: Albert Bates Lord, *The Singer of Tales* (Cambridge, Mass., 1960).

Loring, Eugene (1911–1982).

A leading American ballet dancer and choreographer, Loring was best known for *Billy the Kid,* which he choreographed and danced (as Billy) in its 1938 premiere. With music composed by AARON COPLAND, *Billy the Kid* was a popular masterpiece based on the life of the youthful folk antihero outlaw.

Loring was born Leroy Kerpestein in Madison, Wisconsin, and was raised in Milwaukee, where he did his first choreography for the Wisconsin Players, a local theater group. In 1933, he moved to New York City to study with George Balanchine and Pierre Vladimirov as well as Anatole Vilzak, Muriel Stuart, and Ludmilla Schollar. His professional stage debut as a dancer came in 1934 with the Mikhail Fokine Ballet, and the following year he appeared as a dancer with the American Ballet (1935–38). Beginning in 1936, he performed as a soloist with Lincoln Kirstein's Ballet Caravan troupe and in 1940–41 soloed with the Ballet Theatre (subsequently American Ballet Theatre). During this period, he also created choreography for the Caravan and the Ballet Theatre. In 1941, Loring founded the Dance Players, for which he created dances and served as principal dancer. At this time, he was also appearing on the Broadway stage as an actor/dancer and was particularly noted for his work in the role of Owen Webster in William Saroyan's 1941 *The Beautiful People.*

With the American Ballet and with Ballet Caravan, Loring danced in many important premieres, including Douglas Coudy's *Folk Dance* (1937). It was for the 1938 season of the Caravan that Loring choreographed and danced the title role in Aaron Copland's *Billy the Kid,* the work for which he was always best remembered.

Loring was a charter member of Ballet Theatre and, in 1944, went to Hollywood, where he appeared in the MGM hit *National Velvet* (as a jockey) and in *Torch Song* (1954), playing a dance director. He also staged dances for a host of musical films, working with Fred Astaire and

Cyd Charisse, among others. Loring also choreographed for the Broadway stage and, in 1958, for the Ice Capades. In addition to his wide range of work as a dancer and choreographer, Loring was highly respected as a teacher. He founded the American School of Dance in Hollywood, specializing in teaching the essentials of ballet and dance technique to film and television actors and actresses. In 1974, he retired from his own school to become the first chairman of the dance department at the University of California, Irvine.

See also: BILLY THE KID.

Lover's leap. In American folklore, the lover's leap is the most frequently encountered form of LOCAL LEGEND. Typically, a rocky outcropping, precipice, or scenic overlook is christened Lover's Leap, the name ascribed to a past incident in which a tragic couple act on a suicide pact, or a lovelorn man or woman, spurned, jumps to his or her death. In many localities, the doomed pair are a boy and girl Indian separated by the mutual hostility of their tribes and who meet a *Romeo and Juliet*–like end at the lover's leap. Sometimes, local legend holds that the area is haunted by the

Loggers at work on a California redwood, 1935.

ghosts of the lovers. In some cases, the name of the lover's leap is particularized with the name of the victim, as in Deborah's Rock, near Reading, Pennsylvania.

Lullaby. Also called a cradle song, the lullaby is known in virtually all cultures as a means of soothing an infant into sleep. A lullaby may be a traditional folk song or may be any song perceived to have a soft, lulling, pleasing effect. Typically, the gist of lullaby lyrics consists of the mother's assurance to her child that all is well and peaceful, so that it is safe to sleep. Some lullabies resort to bribery to coax the child to slumber. In "Bye, Bye Baby Bunting," for example, the child is promised a rabbit skin. (This lullaby also contains elements of reassurance: Daddy has "gone a-hunting"; that is, Daddy is doing what he is supposed to do and, therefore, all's right with the world.) Paradoxically, many lullabies also introduce violent or discordant imagery, as in that most familiar of American lullabies, "Rockabye Baby":

> *When the wind blows, the cradle will rock.*
> *When the bough breaks, the cradle will fall,*
> *And down will come baby, cradle and all.*

SUGGESTED READING: John Minton, "Lullaby," in Jan Harold Brunvand, ed., *American Folklore: An Encyclopedia* (New York, 1996).

Lumberjack folklore. The folklore of lumberjacks, or loggers, presents especially colorful examples of OCCUPATIONAL FOLKLORE. The work is predominantly masculine and always dangerous. Loggers come from a variety of ethnic backgrounds, which adds to the richness of a folklore that is largely verbal. The on-the-job jargon is especially vivid. Loggers call themselves lumberjacks, timberbeasts, brush apes, and shantyboys. They wear "corks," spiked boots, and "tie on the feedbag" or "nosebag" at lunchtime. Personal narratives abound, told about oneself and others, with the emphasis on accidents and close calls, as well as on feats of strength, endurance, and productivity. TALL TALES are common, as are tales of BIGFOOT sightings. In addition to verbal folklore, lumberjack songs have been widely collected. These are frequently ballads of the COME-ALL-YE type. They are not WORK SONGS in the sense of having been sung while working, but were performed in the bunkhouse or wherever loggers gather for a drink or two.

See also: BECK, EARL CLIFTON.

SUGGESTED READING: Robert E. Bethke, *Adirondack Voices: Woodsmen and Woods Lore* (Urbana, Ill., 1981); Richard M. Dorson, *America in Legend: Folklore from the Colonial Period to the Present* (New York, 1973).

Lunsford, Bascom Lamar (1882–1973).
"The Squire of Turkey Creek," Lunsford was a folk musician and folklorist who grew up in Buncombe County, western North Carolina, imbibed the local musical traditions, and, in 1928, organized the Asheville (North Carolina) Mountain Dance and Folk Festival. This festival was the first of its kind and served as a model for many others.

In addition to being a charismatic organizer, Lunsford was a talented fiddler, banjoist, and vocalist. He recorded 303 tunes for Columbia University (1935) and 317 for the Library of Congress (1949) and made a handful of commercial recordings as well.

SUGGESTED READING: Loyal Jones, *Minstrel of the Appalachians: The Story of Bascom Lamar Lunsford* (Boone, N.C., 1984).

Luomala, Katherine (1907–1992).
Luomala was a student of Hawaiian and Oceanic folklore and myth. A native of Minnesota, she took her Ph.D. in anthropology at the University of California, Berkeley, in 1933, basing her dissertation on fieldwork in the Gilbert Islands (Kiribati), Micronesia. Later she did fieldwork among the Diegueno of California and the Navajo in the Southwest. An advocate of the comparative approach, she published *Oceanic, American, and African Myths of Snaring the Sun* in 1940.

Luomala became a professor of anthropology at the University of Hawaii in 1946 and also worked as a researcher for the Bernice P. Bishop Museum in Honolulu. She made intensive studies of Maui, the trickster of Polynesian myth, and of other figures and myths.

SUGGESTED READING: Katherine Luomala, *Maui the Demigod: Factors in the Development of a Polynesian Hero Cycle* (Berkeley, Calif., 1936).

M

Macon, David ("Uncle Dave") (1870–1952). One of the founders of the GRAND OLE OPRY, Uncle Dave Macon was a pioneer of COUNTRY MUSIC and did much to translate southern folk music into commercially viable entertainment. He was an accomplished BANJO player, an appealing singer, and teller of hilarious tales and jokes. His own repertoire was a highly traditional mix of southern BALLADS and PARLOR BALLADS. He was also influenced by middle Tennessee African-American traditions.

Macon was born in Smart Station, Warren County, Tennessee. In 1884, Macon's family moved to Nashville to run a hotel, and the young man fell under the influence of vaudevillian guests. However, his budding passion for the vaudeville stage was cut short by the murder of his father, after which he and his mother retreated to a farm. Macon farmed and did other work until 1923, when the fifty-three-year-old farmer and freight company operator began performing hillbilly songs on the Loew's vaudeville circuit. Two years later, when Nashville's radio station WSM began broadcasting, Uncle Dave became one of its first stars. A short time later, the station began broadcasting the show that became the *Grand Ole Opry,* and Macon became a regular. He also recorded extensively, including topical songs, ballads, and GOSPEL MUSIC. But it was for his late, and long, career on the Opry, which lasted until weeks before his death, that Macon is best remembered.

"Mademoiselle from Armentières." A song of WORLD WAR I (1914–18) originating with the British and eagerly adopted by American doughboys. The song lent itself to the addition of any number of stanzas improvised on any event of significance, such as the peculiarities of one's allies, the quality (or lack thereof) of the food, lice, officers popular and unpopular, the local women, and so on. Doubtless, the printed versions of the song were heavily sanitized and censored.

See also: FOLK MUSIC.

Magarac, Joe. Magarac is a steelworker folk hero, whose last name means *donkey* in Serbo-Croatian. It is not entirely clear whether Magarac is a genuine product of folk process or the 1931 creation of a professional writer named Owen Francis. There is evidence to suggest that the Magarac figure predates 1931.

Magarac is a large man, an immigrant laborer of "solid steel," born in an ore mountain, slag pile, or blast furnace. He works almost nonstop, all shifts, pausing only to consume prodigious quantities of cabbage and other food. His strength is great, and in some stories, clearly superhuman; indeed, Magarac is sometimes depicted as a "superhero," who is able to change size, assuming giant proportions in an emergency—as when a fellow worker requires rescue. Magarac dies by melting himself down in a Bessemer blast oven.

The heyday of Magarac tales came in the 1940s, but the figure reemerged in the 1970s and 1980s, as steelworkers found themselves displaced by general economic recession and specifically the contraction of the United States steel industry. *Magarac (A Steel Sage)* was a mixed-media presentation staged during the 1980s in the rust-belt city of Lackawanna, New York, and in 1991, the union-sponsored Tri-State Conference on Steel created the annual Joe Magarac Award to recognize efforts to reindustrialize southwestern Pennsylvania.

SUGGESTED READING: Walter Blair, "Joe Magarac: Pittsburgh Steel Man," *Tall Tale America: A Legendary History of Our Humorous Heroes* (New York, 1944); Benjamin A. Botkin, "The Saga of Joe Magarac: Steelman," *A Treasury of American Folklore* (New York, 1944); George Swetnam, "Joe Magarac," *Devils, Ghosts, and Witches: Occult Folklore of the Upper Ohio Valley* (Greensburg, Pa., 1988).

Maldonado, Alexander A. (1901–1989).

A folk painter who said of his work, "I paint the impossible," Maldonado was a visionary artist influenced by his interest in astronomy, popular science, and science fiction. His canvases are vividly rendered depictions of futuristic, sometimes utopian worlds, outer space, and extraterrestrial life and landscapes.

Maldonado was born in Mazatlan, Mexico, and moved with his family to San Francisco in 1911. Between 1917 and 1922, he fought as a professional featherweight boxer, then worked in a Western Can Company factory until 1960. Shortly before retiring, he took up painting, and between 1965 and 1980 produced some 250 oils and several watercolors. After he was featured as the subject of a half-hour television documentary in San Francisco in 1973, he began to achieve significant recognition, and his work was the subject of many shows.

Malinche, La.

La Malinche (1502–1527/28) was an interpreter, guide, and strategist to Hernan Cortés, the conqueror of the Aztecs. She is the subject of many legends of Mexico and the American Southwest, and she is often identified with *La Llorona*, "the Weeper," a ghostly apparition who wanders the nocturnal countryside in search of her lost children. Legend holds that La Malinche drowned the son she had with Cortés rather than allow the conquistador to take him away to Spain. Some Hispanics see and have seen La Malinche as the quintessential traitor; others see her as a feminist heroine.

The Spanish called her Doña Marina and the Aztecs Malintzin or Malinal. She was the daughter of an Aztec chief in the Mexican province of Coatzacoalcos. After her father's death, her mother remarried and sent the girl away in order to usurp her inheritance for the son produced by her mother's second marriage. La Malinche was sold to traders, who, in turn, sold her to the chief of the Yucatan Tabasco province. After Cortés conquered the Tabasco province in 1519, La Malinche was one of twenty women presented to him as a gift. The girl quickly learned Spanish and became first an interpreter and, soon, a trusted informer and aide, who advised the conquistador in his dealings with those he conquered. La Malinche helped Cortés win allies among the Mayans, which, in turn, enabled him to conquer the Aztec empire.

La Malinche became Cortés's mistress and

bore him a son. She remained with him even after his Spanish wife joined him in the New World. However, it is not known what became of her after the conquistador returned to Spain. It is believed she succumbed to smallpox at age twenty-five in 1527 or 1528.

La Malinche is the subject of historical debate. Was she a traitor or a rebel and proto-feminist, who collaborated with Cortés not only to improve her lot, but to help him replace the corrupt Aztec society with something better? She also figures in a number of Mexican and southwestern folktales and legends, most notably in her conflation with the figure of *La Llorona*.

See also: *LLORONA, LA*; MEXICAN AMERICANS.

SUGGESTED READING: Arthur L. Campa, *Hispanic Culture in the Southwest* (Norman, Okla., 1979); Cordelia Candelaria, "La Malinche, Feminist Prototype," *Frontiers* 5 (1980), pp. 1–6.

Mammy. Mammy is both a figure of southern folklife and a stereotyped creation of popular culture. Well into the twentieth century, white children belonging to families of some means were often raised by African-American domestics known as mammies, and it is also true that many children so raised looked back in later years on their mammies with the kind of affection expressed in Al Jolson's famous song, "Mammy": "I'd walk a million miles for one of your smiles, my Mammy." It is also true, however, that, by the late nineteenth century, Mammy had developed into an iconic stereotype of great durability. She was a middle-aged African-American woman, maternal and overweight in her calico apron, head wrapped in a kerchief. Her approach to child rearing was no nonsense and guided by a kind of unconscious or inborn wisdom. While she may "sass" the family that employs her, there is never any question of her devotion to that family, to whom she gives everything, while asking almost nothing in return. Her image, the embodiment of old-fashioned, homespun nurturing, adorned the Aunt Jemima line of food products, and her type has been featured in southern fiction ranging from that of William Faulkner to Margaret Mitchell and in many movies depicting white southern families.

Mandolin. The mandolin is a short-necked instrument of Renaissance origin with four courses of two metal strings each, tuned like a violin, e, a, d, g. It sustains long notes by a rapid tremolo achieved with a plectrum. The Neapolitan mandolin with a round lutelike back of many ribs was played in America from the nineteenth century to the early twentieth. In folk circles it has been called the "potato bug" because of its perceived resemblance to the common Colorado potato beetle. The flat-backed form, probably descended from the Portuguese style, which is much more projective and easier to hold, especially in fast passages, has superseded the potato bug, and survives principally as a lead bluegrass instrument as well as for sometimes maintaining a chunky chord rhythm. BILL MONROE's arched-top Gibson F-5 has become the most desired model.

See also: BLUEGRASS; FOLK MUSIC; RINZLER, RALPH CARTER.

SUGGESTED READING: Walter Carter, *Gibson Guitars: 100 Years of an American Icon* (New York, 1996); Paul Sparks, *The Classical Mandolin* (New York, 1995).

Man in the Moon. For untold generations, people have discerned a human face in the crater-scarred markings of the moon. The *man* in the moon is sometimes interpreted as an old woman cooking. Among Native Americans, the face or faces in the moon have been described (for example) as a frog charged with protecting the moon from a bear who would otherwise swallow it.

Manitou. Of all Native American expressions of spirit, manitou is the most familiar to non-Native Americans. Among the Cree and Ojibwa, *manitou* is a general term for the spirits that inhabit and animate all living things ("living things" include virtually all of nature, from plants and rocks to animals and thunder). There are many manitou, classified according to the kind of living thing in which they dwell.

Mardi Gras, Cajun. For most Americans, Mardi Gras brings to mind the somewhat commercialized celebration of New Orleans (see MARDI GRAS, NEW ORLEANS), copied by several other cities in the state, featuring spectacular floats and lavish balls, extending over several weeks and culminating on Shrove Tuesday. There is also, however, a rural celebration of Mardi Gras, which is more traditional and more "folk" than its more sophisticated and gaudier New Orleans cousin. The New Orleans celebration is descended from Mediterranean and Caribbean traditions. The celebration of the Cajun and interrelated Creole black "courir de Mardi Gras" (the running of Mardi Gras or the Mardi Gras maskers) reached southwestern Louisiana with the rural French traditions the Acadians brought with them in the eighteenth century when they were exiled from Acadie (Nova Scotia).

The origin of the custom in southwest Louisiana goes back to the 1780s, when bands of French and Spanish settlers in the Opelousas country gathered together a week or so before Ash Wednesday to make elaborate plans for the Mardi Gras event. Today, as in the eighteenth century, mothers, wives, and sweethearts work feverishly on their men's costumes the week prior to Shrove Tuesday. Favorites still are motley one-piece uniforms, topped with a high conical cap, like a dunce cap, and masks of coarse screen with holes cut out for eyes, nose, and mouth. Currently hideous manufactured rubber masks are supplanting the weird old homemade masks. The uniforms are called "le suit de Mardi Gras," and the headgear, "le capuchon." At the organizing meeting at one of the local bars, men from age eighteen to sixty-five plan the route (sometimes as many as sixty miles in muddy cold), to curry their ponies (a vanishing practice, since few Cajuns still own horses), and to elect the "*capitaine*" and some lieutenants to assist him in maintaining discipline. The *capitaine* is not allowed to mask, for no farmer would tolerate drunken masked riders on his premises unless led by a person of integrity. Hence the *capitaine* and, usually, his lieutenants, do not wear masks, but (in some towns) appear in partial blackface, carrying whips made of braided strips of burlap sackcloth. In Tee Mamou, these lieutenants are a "Negro and Negresse," whites in blackface, wearing elaborate old-time plantation "darky" costumes. In one of the many reversals of role, the Negresse, a white man in drag, whips misbehaving maskers with a rubber chicken, and the Negro bears himself in commandingly aristocratic style.

By five, come Mardi Gras morning, every rider has had a few drinks at the neighborhood bar, has saddled and bridled his horse or mounted a flat-bottomed trailer, which is drawn by a truck. The *capitaine* ceremoniously frisks all the riders to make sure none of them carries a gun or a knife. As the sun comes up, the *capitaine* blows his primitive trumpet—a "corne à vache" (cow's horn)—and "la course de Mardi Gras" is on its boisterous way to visit farmhouses (or, often these days, suburban houses) surrounding the town, which is the hub of their circular route. Neither bad weather nor treacherous, slippery, and muddy dirt roads stop them, and since Shrove Tuesday generally comes around the end of February, many a masker shivers in the cold until he has been warmed by frequent swigs of straight bourbon—or, less colorfully, bottles of Falstaff beer. To protect themselves from the cold, their one-piece uniforms are large enough to cover several layers of clothing. The *"paillasse,"* or clown, nicknamed after a straw mattress, is stuffed with pillows or cotton until he resembles a ball. Like the jester of the Middle Ages, he has the duty to entertain with comic antics and acrobatics. It is not unusual to see him climb a tree, stand on his head, or come riding up on a decrepit mule or donkey.

When the *capitaine* sees a farmhouse or other dwelling he thinks suitable, he rides up to it and asks the master and mistress if they will receive his followers. If they are willing, he waves his white flag, and the maskers come dancing into the yard, singing the weird begging Mardi Gras song (which has a modal melody that is obviously centuries old) and pleading for food for the evening gumbo and masquerade ball. Seizing the people of the house by the arms, the maskers sweep them into their wild dance. The master and mistress usually oblige with rice or a big fat chicken, which they throw into the air; the tipsy maskers have to pursue the chicken through the thick mud—a wild, hilarious chase. Meanwhile, some of the maskers engage in clownish pranks such as hiding, running away, administering arti-

ficial respiration to one of them who is pretending to have fainted, and also seizing on props that "happen" to be on the premises, such as a baby carriage, a tricycle, or a trampoline for more improvised comic business. Stepping in with vigorous punishment when a prank is on the edge of real trouble or danger, such as when maskers start carrying off a young woman, or drunken maskers are on the brink of a fight, the lieutenants apply their whips with stinging force. Morever, if beggars fail to kneel and beg in properly humble style, they are whipped.

In the Mardi Gras procedure of the Grand Marais maskers, at the end of each visit, all the maskers lay themselves facedown on the ground, head-to-toe in a tight formation, and they are all whipped. At a signal from the *capitaine,* a lieutenant blows a blast, and the maskers mount their horses or their vehicles to resume their mission.

"La course" generally ends around four in the afternoon, with the tired, hungry, muddy, drunkenly happy riders parading through the town, bringing their haul for the day (generally forty to fifty assorted chickens, guineas, ducks, or geese, and enough rice to feed a small Chinese army). Before their evening gumbo, many of the saddlesore riders take advantage of the free drinks granted them by all the bars in town. Somehow they manage to arrive at the evening masquerade and even fling themselves into the foot-stamping gyrations of lively dancing until dawn.

There are some significant implied messages in the celebration. Although rebellion against holders of power is partially sanctioned during Mardi Gras, there is a final return to normalcy, acceptance by the beggars (symbolically the underdogs in contemporary society) of the status quo. For example, the evening event of the Grand Marais communal supper includes further whipping of supposedly misbehaving soldiers, but on this occasion, the *capitaine* and some of his lieutenants are also singled out for whipping; they will experience what it feels like to be one of the oppressed. There is a final reconciliation. The *capitaine* praises his crew for their solidity and nobility. Having experienced an emotional catharsis, the maskers leave the occasion in peace of mind, all passion spent, for the beginning of Lent. The participants are relieved to have Mardi Gras over, but are already looking forward to the good fellowship, fun, and Bacchanalia of next year.

It has been hypothesized that the roots of such Mardi Gras celebrations go back to pre-Roman rites of spring, perhaps having Druidic antecedents, as well as to the Roman festivals and ritual celebrations such as Bacchanalia, Lupercalia, and Saturnalia.

See also: CAJUNS.

SUGGESTED READING: Barry Jean Ancelet, "*Capitaine, Voyage to a Flag*": *The Traditional Cajun Country Mardi Gras* (Lafayette, La., 1989).

Mardi Gras, New Orleans.

Mardi Gras, a French phrase meaning *Fat Tuesday*, is celebrated in France on Shrove Tuesday, the day before Ash Wednesday, which marks the beginning of the Lenten season. Mardi Gras is a festive last hurrah before embarking on the austerity of Lent. In the United States, Mardi Gras is a famous aspect of the French heritage of New Orleans.

As a New Orleans event, Mardi Gras is said to have begun in 1837, the year of the first street parade. The festivities associated with Mardi Gras are not confined to Shrove Tuesday, however, but begin on Twelfth Night (the Feast of the Epiphany), January 6, twelve days after Christmas. On this day, a series of masked balls begin. These are private, invitation-only occasions, built around specific themes, which change from year to year. Each ball is sponsored by a club called a krewe, of which there are many associated with New Orleans Mardi Gras activities and parades. Each krewe creates a float and provides marching personnel for the Mardi Gras parades that are held during carnival season and that culminate on Fat Tuesday. The word *krewe* (pronounced "crew") was coined in 1857 by the venerable Mistick Krewe of Comus. Membership in a krewe is an important symbol of social status in New Orleans, and membership in one of the long-established krewes is especially coveted.

While the masked balls are private, the many parades associated with Mardi Gras are very

Mardi Gras parade down St. Charles Avenue in New Orleans, late 1920s.

New Orleans Mardi Gras in the 1880s. (From H. Butterworth, ZigZag Journeys on the Mississippi, *1882)*

public and attract visitors from all over the nation and the world. The parades consist of floats holding the costumed krewe members, who throw "doubloons"—inexpensive strings of beads, plastic doubloon coins, and other souvenir items—to people lining the streets. Many of these onlookers are themselves costumed (or at least wear purple, green, and gold, the colors of Mardi Gras) and scream to the passing krewes, "Throw me somethin'!" or simply "Doubloons! Doubloons!" The Mardi Gras parades are also famed for the participation of the marching jazz bands that are a part of traditional New Orleans music.

Mardi Gras is associated with much drinking and eating, including partaking of the traditional "King Cake." Twelfth Night or The Feast of the Epiphany, as celebrated in France and in other European countries, commemorates the coming of the Magi who brought gifts to the Christ child.

The King Cake represents this event by a cake with a plastic figure of a baby baked inside. New Orleans Mardi Gras tradition dictates that whoever receives the baby in his or her piece of cake must buy the next King Cake or throw the next party. King Cakes are made of a cinnamon-filled dough in the shape of a hollow circle, are glazed, and topped with sugar colored in traditional Mardi Gras hues: purple (representing justice), green (representing faith), and gold (representing power).

Other familiar symbols associated with Mardi Gras include the *Bouef Gras,* the fatted bull or ox, symbolic of the last meat eaten before the Lent. Until 1909, a live animal was featured in the Rex Parade (the parade staged by the Krewe of Rex). A papier-mâché incarnation appeared in the 1959 parade and is now one of the central symbols of Mardi Gras, as are the "flambeaux," the naphtha-fueled torches carried exclusively in the Mardi Gras parades by white-robed black men. Traditionally, these supplied light for nighttime parades.

See also: MARDI GRAS, CAJUN.

Mariachi. The traditional street band of Mexican villages, a mariachi orchestra consists of as few as three string players to as many as a dozen, sometimes augmented by a trumpet or two. Mariachi musicians are influenced by traditional folk tunes as well as contemporary commercial music. Mariachi orchestras are active not only in Mexico, but in Mexican neighborhoods throughout the United States, as well as in many Mexican restaurants, catering to Mexican as well as Anglo clientele. Traditionally, it was believed that the term *mariachi* derives from the French *mariage* and originated during the reign of the French-sponsored Emperor Maximilian (1832–67), who, with his wife Carlotta, was said to be so fond of the musical style that he regularly invited the street musicians to perform at court weddings. Recent scholars suggest that the word is of native origin, perhaps derived from the name of the wood used to make the platform on which people danced to the music of village performers.

See also: ARHOOLIE RECORDS.

Martinez, Maria Montoya (1880s–1980) and Martinez, Julian (1879–1943).

Maria Montoya began making pottery when she was a child on the Tewa Indian pueblo at San Ildefonso. During 1907–09, archaeologists excavated ancient pots near the pueblo, and Maria Montoya, now married to Julian Martinez, a self-taught painter, began to create pots inspired by the ancient pieces. Julian Martinez decorated the pots. The Martinezes combined ancient tradition with innovative, idiosyncratic methods to produce the burnished black-on-black works for which they are best known, decorated with highly stylized geometric birds and serpent figures. Together, they are given credit for reviving a dying tradition of southwestern pottery making. The Martinez family continued to make pots.

See also: NATIVE AMERICANS.

Martin Guitar Company.

After serving as shop foreman for Viennese violin and guitar maker Johann George Stauffer, Christien Friedrich (or Frederick) Martin (1796–1873) moved to New York, where he founded the C. F. Martin Company and a guitar shop at 195 Hudson Street in 1833—the first American guitar manufacturer.

Accustomed to the relatively tranquil atmosphere of the hillside village of his native Markneukirchen, Saxony, Martin soon found New York City disagreeably hectic and intimi-

dating. In 1839, he moved to the Moravian area outside Nazareth, Pennsylvania, where the Martin Company has remained ever since (though it kept the New York source on its label until 1898).

Martin's early guitars followed the design of Stauffer, an almost figure-eight shape, sloping shoulders in the upper bout, pinched in at the waist, with all the tuners on one side of a rounded peg box. By 1840, the shape had shifted to the outlines of the familiar parlor guitar of the nineteenth century. C. F. Martin perfected an X-bracing for the top in the late 1850s, replacing the "ladder" bracing, in which the bars in the top were parallel to the bridge. By 1887, the Martin plant had doubled in size. The company's 1898 catalogue expressed supreme pride in the quality of its instruments: "We can afford to warrant them, not for a year, or a number of years, but for all time. . . . The sizes are recommended as follows: No. 21/2 for young beginners; No. 2 for ladies, or whenever a clear, even tone of moderate loudness is wanted; No. 1, being both strong and well-balanced for general purposes; No. 0 for concert playing and club use; No. 00 for exceptional power."

Before the early 1920s, all Martin guitars were strung with gut (except for a handful of special-order instruments). In 1922, the 2-17 was set up for steel strings, and by 1928 most of their instruments were made strong enough to take metal strings. The most popular Martin today is the Dreadnaught (named for a class of battleship so formidable and strong as to fear naught), quite large in comparison with earlier Martins. It was designed by F. H. Ertis (1865–1948) and Harry L. Hunt, manager of the guitar department of the Charles H. Ditson Company, a prestigious New York retailer. The early Dreadnaughts were labeled *Oliver Ditson & Co., Boston/New York*. By 1937, Martin planned its own series of Dreadnaughts, with the octave where the neck joined the body at the twelfth fret. The fourteenth-fret principal joint became standard in 1934 models. Among the most popular Dreadnaught models was the D-28, which became the favorite BLUE-GRASS guitar, and the Dreadnaught, with its large, flat, almost pear-shaped design and its flat-top X-bracing (scalloped in the more expensive models) was copied for most of the metal-string guitars made by other companies.

See also: FOLK MUSIC.

SUGGESTED READING: Walter Carter, *The Martin Book: A Complete History of Martin Guitars* (New York, 1995); Jim Washburn and Richard Johnston, *Martin Guitars: An Illustrated Celebration of America's Premier Guitarmaker* (Reading, Pa., 1997).

Mason, Otis Tufton (1838–1908).

Mason was curator of ethnology for the Smithsonian Institution and, in 1891, president of the American Folklore Society. He interpreted material culture as evidence of humankind's evolving faculty of invention. Mason was educated at Columbia College (Washington, D.C.), earning his B.A. in 1861. He later was a professor of anthropology at the college. In 1884, he became curator of ethnology at the Smithsonian Institution, serving until his death.

Mason published a number of studies of inventiveness and of American Indian material culture, always stressing production techniques.

SUGGESTED READING: Walter Rough, "Otis Tufton Mason," *American Anthropologist* 10 (1908), pp. 661–67; Otis Tufton Mason, "The Natural History of Folk-Lore," *Journal of American Folklore* 4 (1891), pp. 97–105.

Mass media.

Print, radio, television, audio recording, and film media. Folklore "purists" tend to regard the influence of mass media as a kind of pollution of traditional folklore, which depends on oral transmission and dissemination; however, more recent folklorists see the mass

Radio quickly became pervasive in American life. These women are listening to a radio set on a passenger train, about 1923.

The technology for television was available by the 1930s, but commercial development of the medium was slow until the 1950s. These two photographs show two of the earliest mass-produced sets, from the late 1930s. Note the evening dress one couple wears, and note, too, that it takes a man to handle the complexity of the technology.

media as influenced by folklore even as it influences traditional communication, arts, and beliefs. Mass media often appropriates folk material, including traditional characters, motifs, FOLK SPEECH, PROVERBS, and story lines. This is true not only in dramatic presentations, such as television series, but also in ostensibly nonfiction material. Whereas "serious" newspapers and television and radio news programs pride themselves on journalistic accuracy, "supermarket tabloid" papers and tabloid-style television programs play on folk beliefs, the TALL TALE tradition, and a hunger for contemporary LEGENDS, as well as exploiting that genre of folk speech known as gossip.

If the mass media harvest material from the folk, so the folk freely imbibe folklore as mediated by television, radio, and print vehicles. This is also the case with various folk artists. BLUES traditions, for example, were significantly shaped by blues and other recordings.

See also: ALIEN ABDUCTION; BUFFALO BILL (WILLIAM F. CODY); CUSTER, GEORGE ARMSTRONG; FOLK MUSIC; FRIDAY THE THIRTEENTH; GUNFIGHTER, WESTERN; MONROE, MARILYN; POPULAR CULTURE; WORLD WAR I POSTERS; WORLD WAR II POSTERS.

SUGGESTED READING: Hermann Bausinger, *Folk Culture in a World of Technology* (Bloomington, Ind.,

1990); S. Elizabeth Bird, *For Enquiring Minds: A Cultural Study of Supermarket Tabloids* (Knoxville, Tenn., 1992); John Fiske, *Television Culture* (London, 1987).

Material culture. The expression of cultural ideas, motifs, and traditions through human-made physical objects and structures. Students of *folk* material culture seek culturally meaningful patterns in such physical objects as the products of traditional crafts, VERNACULAR ARCHITECTURE, costume, FOODWAYS, folk medicine (see MEDICINE, FOLK), and folk decorative arts.

See also: ANGLO AMERICANS; CAJUNS; CHINESE AMERICANS; COLONIAL WILLIAMSBURG; FORD, HENRY; GHOST TOWNS; GREENFIELD VILLAGE; JONES, LOUIS CLARK; MEXICAN AMERICANS; POTTERY; SCANDINAVIAN AMERICANS; SCOTTISH AMERICANS; SHAKER FOLK ART AND CRAFTS; VIETNAM WAR; WEATHER FOLKLORE; WHALING; WORLD WAR II.

Mather, Cotton (1663–1728). One of the most famous of American Puritans, Mather combined extreme conservatism, religious mysticism, and a belief in witchcraft with scientific curiosity and the powers of a keen observer. The author of some five hundred books and pamphlets, he is among the most prolific of all American writers. Many of his literary works were conscious attempts to bolster the mythology of American Puritanism—the idea that the Puritans were God's new "chosen people," who had been brought to the "New Jerusalem," America. His monumental *Magnalia Christi Americana* (1702) merges history, folklore, and theology to reveal the Puritan experience in this light. In addition, the *Magnalia*

and other works record much colonial American folklore, especially relating to folk medicine (next to theology, medicine was Mather's most consuming interest), supernatural beliefs, and witchcraft. His writings on witchcraft, especially *Wonders of the Invisible World,* are treasure troves of folk material concerned with witchcraft.

Born in Boston, Cotton Mather was the son of Increase Mather and the grandson of John Cotton and Richard Mather—the constituents of the so-called Mather dynasty of Puritan preachers and leaders. Cotton Mather enrolled in Harvard at age twelve and received his M.A. at eighteen. He was ordained in 1685. A believer in witchcraft well after most other Puritan leaders had renounced the notion, Mather also advocated some of the most advanced scientific ideas of his

Cotton Mather, as pictured in Reuben Post Halleck, History of American Literature, 1911. (Collection of Alan Axelrod)

time, including smallpox inoculation, and won membership in the prestigious Royal Society of London.

See also: CAPTIVITY NARRATIVES; FOLKLORE IN AMERICAN LITERATURE; MEDICINE, FOLK.

SUGGESTED READING: Kenneth Silverman, *The Life and Times of Cotton Mather* (New York, 1984).

Maypole of Merry Mount. Best known through NATHANIEL HAWTHORNE's short story of the same name (1837), the historical maypole was erected about 1627 near the fur-trading post of THOMAS MORTON at Mount Wollaston (modern Quincy), Massachusetts, which Morton renamed Ma-re-Mount or Merry Mount. In defiance of his Puritan neighbors, Morton invited the local Indians, male and female, to dance around this traditional pagan symbol of sexuality and merrymaking. Morton was tried on charges of selling guns to the Indians by MILES STANDISH, and shipped back to England. The Puritan authorities tore down the maypole.

Through Morton's own story about the maypole, in his *The New English Canaan or New Canaan* (Amsterdam, 1637), and through Hawthorne's transformation of that story, the Maypole of Merry Mount entered American folklore generally and the folklore of New England in particular as a traditional tale expressing a central bifurcation in American culture: between conformity-enforcing authority and libertine abandon.

The folk symbol of the maypole is descended from ancient Roman and contemporary English rural traditions. In some parts of England and North America, a maypole dance is performed on May Day. Long streamers are tied to the top of the maypole. Two opposing circles of dancers each take hold of the free end of a streamer, then dance in a weaving manner so as to intertwine and braid the streamers.

Mazurka. A Polish folk dance that became popular in American ballrooms late in the nineteenth century. In its folk form, the mazurka is a round dance, and as a ballroom dance it is for couples, danced in 3/4 time, with the accent falling on the middle beat.

See also: DANCE, FOLK; TEX-MEX MUSIC.

McCoy, Minnie ("Memphis Minnie") (1897?–1973). The foremost female BLUES vocalist, Memphis Minnie was also a fine guitarist and an important blues composer. She recorded 212 sides between 1929 to 1959 and greatly influenced diverse ROCK 'N' ROLL musicians. Born Minnie Douglas in Algiers, Louisiana, she was raised in Walls, Mississippi, and began performing in Memphis well before World War I. In the 1920s, while she toured the South, she met blues singer "Kansas Joe" McCoy, with whom she made several recordings and whom she married.

Memphis Minnie was celebrated for the frank sexuality of her lyrics—not unusual in the blues, of course, but very innovative for a female vocalist. Her 1929 "Bumble Bee" is considered a classic of the hokum blues genre, which combines sly humor and double-entendre in a most delectable manner.

By 1935, Memphis Minnie and Kansas Joe had gone their separate ways, and, settling in Chicago, she teamed up with Memphis guitarist Ernest "Little Son Joe" Lawlers on a number of recordings. She made her last recordings at the end of the 1950s, suffered a disabling stroke about 1961 and lived out her life in a nursing home.

SUGGESTED READING: Lawrence Cohn, *Nothing but the Blues: The Music and the Musicians* (New York, 1993).

McTell, Blind Willie (1901–1959). Born blind in Thomson, Georgia, McTell learned guitar from his mother and, in his early teens, left home to join a series of carnivals and minstrel shows. When he was not working with the traveling shows, he earned what money he could performing on the street, making a precarious living from this as well as from a long, but (as with many early blues musicians) not lucrative recording career spanning 1927 to 1956.

McTell's high-pitched, plaintive vocal style was both distinctive and moving, and he was a virtuoso performer on the twelve-string guitar. His many recordings reveal a great range of versatility, from the dancelike "Atlanta Strut" to the bleak "Death Cell Blues" and to such BLUES BALLADS as "Chainey and Delia."

McTell stopped recording and performing in 1956 to take up duties as pastor of Atlanta's Mt. Zion Baptist Church from 1957 until his death from a stroke in 1959.

SUGGESTED READING: Lawrence Cohn, *Nothing but the Blues: The Music and the Musicians* (New York, 1993).

Medicine and medicine man. "Medicine" and "medicine man" are terms familiar to non–Native Americans, but usually poorly understood by them. In most Native American cultures, "medicine" refers to the power of persons, objects, or actions, which may be used for such benevolent purposes as healing and divination, or for such malevolent ends as sorcery. The term "medicine man" is non–Native American in origin, having been applied by missionaries and others to describe Indian healers, priests, wise elders, and even storytellers—in short, anyone of charismatic power within the tribe or group. Non–Native Americans generally understand "medicine man" to be an Indian folk physician.

See also: CORN; SITTING BULL.

Medicine, folk. Folk medicine is a complex system of folk beliefs and practices involving the use of herbs, roots, commercially available drugs, and folk medicine practitioners to maintain or to recover health. In the United States, folk medicine has been practiced widely and is still prevalent, especially in the rural South. Folk medicine may be broadly divided into knowledge and use of home remedies; herbalism and root medicine; and magical medicine or conjuration. Folk healers are called hoodoo doctor, voodoo doctor, herb doctor, root doctor, conjurer, or just plain healer. The practice of VOODOO includes much folk-medical lore and is concentrated along the coastal regions of Georgia and South Carolina and especially southern Louisiana. Healers are also sought for expertise in particular ailments.

Most Americans resort to home remedies from time to time, ranging from adhering to the maxim "feed a cold, starve a fever," to drinking various concoctions to combat a hangover, to putting moistened tobacco on a bee sting. Herbalism requires greater knowledge of folk-medical tradition and is less widespread than it once was, although it is still widely practiced in the rural South. However, herbs and natural remedies are widely available in urban "health food" stores, and while the traditional practice of herbalism may be on the wane, many people read about, purchase, and use "natural medicines" as alternatives to over-the-counter and prescription drugs. This modern phenomenon is rarely called a folk practice, but instead is referred to as "alternative medicine."

In traditional folk medicine, good health is generally regarded as the result of successfully maintaining a balance between the good and bad forces. A person must establish and maintain harmony with these forces. Disharmony can come about through natural causes, in which case traditional practitioners generally employ herbal medicines (usually in the form of teas) as remedies; or disharmony may result from "unnatural" causes—that is, spells and curses. Traditional practitioners may treat these cases with CHARMS and AMULETS and with incantations or magical rhymes ("Sty, sty, in my eye, go to someone passing by!"), as well as with ROOTWORK, conjuration with the roots of certain plants.

See also: BUNIONS AND CORNS; CHILDBEARING FOLKLORE; CURANDERO; FINNISH AMERICANS; FOXFIRE; HAIR OF THE DOG THAT BIT YOU; JAPANESE AMERICANS; JOHN THE CONQUEROR ROOT; MATERIAL CULTURE; MATHER, COTTON; MEXICAN AMERICANS; MIDWIVES; NUTMEG; PLANTS AND PLANT LORE; POWWOW; RELIGION, FOLK; SASSAFRAS; TONGUE TWISTERS; WARTS.

SUGGESTED READING: Norman Genitz, ed., Other Healers: Unorthodox Medicine in America (Baltimore, 1988); Wayland Hand, ed., American Folk Medicine: A Symposium (Berkeley, 1976); Wayland Hand, Magical Medicine: The Folkloric Component of Medicine in the Folk Belief, Custom, and Ritual of the Peoples of Europe and America (Berkeley, Calif., 1980).

Melville, Herman (1819–1891). One of the giants of American literature, Melville is best known for his novel *Moby-Dick* (1851), a complexly symbolic work woven around the central drama between the great white whale Moby-Dick and Captain Ahab, who, having lost a leg in a previous encounter with the whale, is consumed with vengeance against him. Whatever else *Moby-Dick* means—and the critical literature on the novel is fittingly gargantuan—the novel is a trove of WHALING lore and may be considered, on one level, a valuable document for those interested in OCCUPATIONAL FOLKLORE. The novel Melville published the year before *Moby-Dick* appeared, *White-Jacket; or, The World in a Man-of-War* (1850), which concerns a young sailor's life on a U.S. Navy vessel, also contains much occupational folklore about the seafarer's life (see SAILOR AND SEAFARING LORE). Melville's earliest novels, *Typee: A Peep at Polynesian Life* (1846) and *Omoo: A Narrative of Adventures in the South Sea* (1847), while in many ways conventional romances of the period, also offer rich whaling and seafaring material.

In addition to his seaborne novels, Melville is also of interest to students of folklore for two landlocked works of fiction. "Bartleby the Scrivener," a long short story published in *The Piazza Tales* (1856), is a literary example of an extended LOCAL-CHARACTER story or what might now be called an URBAN LEGEND. It concerns a mysterious Wall Street law-office clerk, a copier of legal documents (a "scrivener"), whose passive resistance to authority mystifies and bedevils his employer in a way that is both darkly humorous and ultimately tragic. Melville's late novel *The Confidence-Man: His Masquerade* (1857) explores the CON ARTIST AND CONFIDENCE MAN motif, which, by the mid-nineteenth century, was emerging as an important theme in American folklore and POPULAR CULTURE.

Melville was born into a prosperous New York family, which fell on hard times when the family import business collapsed in 1830. The Melvilles left New York City for Albany, and in 1832, the death of Herman's father brought the family into desperate straits. Herman took a clerical job, then joined his brother in business while attending Albany Classical School. Melville briefly taught school. After the family went bankrupt in 1837, Melville, in 1839, went to sea as a cabin boy. He set out again in 1841, this time on a whaling voyage to the South Sea. He and a companion jumped ship in the Marquesas Islands (present-day French Polynesia) and spent some four months among cannibals (the subject of the novel *Typee*). Melville portrayed the Typee people as NOBLE SAVAGES.

Melville served aboard another whaler and then signed as an ordinary seaman on the U.S. Navy frigate *United States,* which became the basis of *White-Jacket.* Returning to New York, he wrote *Typee* and *Omoo,* which were received with considerable acclaim. His third book, *Mardi* (1849), was a strangely disjointed allegory that critics dismissed as incomprehensible. Melville responded with *Redburn* (1849) and *White-Jacket* (1850), both much more straightforward and both critically approved. After Melville read NATHANIEL HAWTHORNE and became his friend and neighbor in Pittsfield, Massachusetts, he turned again to allegory and wrote, in a fury of composition, *Moby-Dick* (1851). The epic effort, which Melville recognized as his masterpiece, was a critical and popular failure. Melville turned to another strange story, *Pierre* (1852), and was once again met with indifference. *Israel Potter* (1855) was simpler and met with modest success, but was an artistic disappointment for Melville.

In 1856 Melville sought solace in a tour of Europe and the Levant. He returned to America, wrote *The Confidence-Man* (1857), and gradu-

ally began to withdraw from the world of letters. He wrote some poetry, including the fine *Battle Pieces* (1866), Civil War poems, then secured an appointment as a customs inspector on the New York docks. For the next nineteen years, he wrote only in his spare time, producing verse and a short novel masterpiece, *Billy Budd,* left unpublished at his death.

See also: FOLKLORE IN AMERICAN LITERATURE; POCAHONTAS; THORPE, THOMAS BANGS; WHITMAN, WALT.

SUGGESTED READING: Jay Leyda, *The Melville Log: A Documentary Life of Herman Melville, 1819–1891* (2 vols., 1951; reprint ed., New York, 1969); Herschel Parker, *Herman Melville: A Biography* (Baltimore, MD, 1996). Many editions of Melville's work are available.

Memory painting. Folk painting depicting disappearing ways of life or lifestyles. Typically, memory painting shows peaceful rural scenes before the use of mechanized farm implements. GRANDMA MOSES is the most famous of American memory painters.

See also: KITCHEN, TELLA; O'KELLEY, MATTIE LOU.

Mencken, H[enry] L[ouis] (1880–1956). Best remembered as a witty and acerbic social and literary critic and journalist, creator and editor of *The Smart Set* magazine, Mencken is also recognized by linguists and folklorists as a great student of American English, including FOLK SPEECH. *The American Language* appeared as a

H. L. Mencken in the early 1920s.

witty foe of cant, provincialism, prudery, and, generally, the American middle class, which he called the "booboisie."

See also: PILGRIMS AND PURITANS.

SUGGESTED READING: George H. Douglas, *H. L. Mencken, Critic of American Life* (New York, 1978); H. L. Mencken, *The American Language* (1919; 4th ed., abridged, New York, 1977).

single substantial volume in 1919 and brought together examples of American expressions and idioms. Instantly recognized as an important work, it enjoyed significant success. Mencken continued to develop *The American Language,* revising and adding to it several times. In 1945 and 1948, he published ambitious supplements to the original. The volumes are a trove of colloquial eloquence, slang, folk idioms, ethnic idioms, and folk speech.

Mencken was born and raised in Baltimore, where he attended private schools before becoming a newspaper reporter. From 1914 to 1923, he coedited (with George Jean Nathan) *The Smart Set* and in 1924 he and Nathan founded the *American Mercury,* which Mencken edited until 1933. During the 1920s and 1930s, Mencken became the nation's most influential literary and social critic, the champion of the likes of Theodore Dreiser and Sinclair Lewis and the caustically

Mercer, Henry Chapman (1856–1930). Mercer was the founder of the Moravian Pottery and Tile Works and of the Bucks County (Pennsylvania) Historical Museum. He was a pioneering student of American material culture, publishing some thirty books and articles on the subject, beginning with *Tools of the Nation Maker* (1897). Mercer was educated at Harvard University and was certified to practice law in 1881, but turned instead to the study of the folk culture of Pennsylvania, with particular emphasis on the objects and artifacts of everyday life. The large collection of artifacts Mercer gathered were the basis of the Bucks County Historical Museum he founded in Doylestown. While best known to folklorists for his important work in material culture, Mercer was even better known during his lifetime as a decorative-tile maker.

Mexican Americans. Persons of Mexican descent live in all parts of the United States, but the largest Mexican-American communities are found nearest the Mexico–United States border, in the American Southwest. While Mexican-American communities show much regional diversity, those in the Southwest often reveal greater affinity with Mexican folk culture than with that of North America. This is especially true with regard to VERNACULAR ARCHITECTURE, FOODWAYS, language, and entertainment. Indeed, identity is often a major issue with Mexican Americans, some of whom (usually those of wealthier means) refer to themselves as Spanish, Latino, or Hispanic, and some (usually those of the working class) call themselves *mejicanos*. Mexican Americans in Texas call themselves *tejanos*. In New Mexico and Colorado, the usual term is *hispanos*, and in California it is *californios*. (Most Mexican Americans reject the term *chicano*.) The most familiar term Mexican Americans apply to Anglos is *gringo*—though this is only used when a pejorative is required.

Folklorists have studied Mexican-American folklore extensively, focusing on folktales, FOLK MUSIC, FOLK SPEECH, folk medicine (see MEDICINE, FOLK), FOLK ART, handicrafts, vernacular architecture, foodways, dress, and other areas. Additionally, folk LEGENDS relating to certain saints play an important role in Mexican American folklore (most Mexican Americans are Catholic). Mexican Americans have also created "folk saints," individuals recognized as holy by the community, but not canonized by the church. In addition to religion, spiritual folklore extends to GHOST STORIES and other supernatural beliefs, such as the pervasive southwestern legends of LA LLORONA and LA MALINCHE. Folk heroes and CULTURE HEROES are of importance, including the Mexican revolutionary bandit Pancho Villa and the social bandit Joaquin Murietta.

While Mexican-American folk music is rarely heard any longer in Mexican-American communities, such popular commercial genres as CONJUNTO MUSIC and TEX-MEX MUSIC are widely broadcast. Other Mexican-American popular forms developed from the CORRIDO (folk ballad).

Folk medicine is one of the most tenacious features of Mexican American FOLKWAYS. A majority of Mexican-American families continue to make use of traditional herbal cures and many consult CURANDEROS (folk healers).

The MATERIAL CULTURE of Mexican Americans includes a variety of adobe structures in the Southwest and a rich heritage of folk arts and handicrafts. Leather work (boot and saddle making) is a common traditional craft, as are textile weaving and the making of folk instruments. Religious folk art is extensive (see BULTOS, RETABLOS, and SANTOS), and such artworks are not limited to the Mexican-American villages of the Southwest, but are also found in urban neighborhoods, often in the form of *nichos* and *grutas,* private shrines erected in yards. Travelers along southwestern highways may still find roadside monuments and crosses (*crucitas*) marking the site of traffic fatalities or other deaths. Mexican-American urban communities also often exhibit communal artworks, especially large-scale murals on the sides of buildings, usually conveying a message of community spirit or community political activism. "Low-rider" automobiles (older cars that have been lovingly restored and customized and equipped with special hydraulic shock absorbers that allow the car to ride very low to the ground, but also jump up and down at the flick of a switch) have attracted much attention outside of the Mexican-American community. In some neighborhoods, owners proudly cruise their low riders, park them together, then enjoy an outdoor party.

Perhaps the most visible of all Mexican-American folkways are foodways. Mexican restaurants are popular with Anglos as well as Mexicans, and many fast-food chains offer attenuated versions of tacos, enchiladas, burritos, and tamales. In all sorts of restaurants and bars, Mexican American or otherwise, Mexican beers and tequila are popular drinks.

Many Mexican-American communities mount periodic festivals to celebrate their heritage.

Of these, *Cinco de Mayo* (May 5) is the most popular and widely known beyond the Mexican-American community. Ostensibly, *Cinco de Mayo* commemorates the May 5, 1862, victory of Mexican partisans led by Benito Juárez over the French forces sent by Napoleon III to establish a French puppet state in Mexico; however, the day is now observed as an occasion for general ethnic celebration.

See also: IMMIGRANT FOLKLORE.

SUGGESTED READING: Bainbridge Bunting, *Of Earth and Timbers Made: New Mexico Architecture* (Albuquerque, N.M., 1974); Elaine Miller, *Mexican Folk Narrative from the Los Angeles Area* (Austin, Tex., 1973); John D. Robb, *Hispanic Folk Music of New Mexico and the Southwest: A Self-Portrait of People* (Norman, Okla., 1980); John O. West, *Mexican-American Folklore* (Little Rock, Ark., 1988).

"Michigan I-O." A lumberman's COME-ALL-YE from the end of the nineteenth century, the song tells of the heroic life of the logger. Its name changes to suit the singer's state of origin. The song has been traced most directly to "Canaday-I-O," a Canadian lumberman's song apparently composed by one Ephraim Braley about 1854. That song may have descended from an English sailor come-all-ye called "Caledonia."

See also: FOLK MUSIC; WORK SONGS.

Mickey Mouse. A WALT DISNEY animated cartoon character so universally known as to have entered into American popular culture folklore, Mickey debuted in "Steamboat Willie" (1928), the first animated cartoon with sound.

Although Disney created the character (whom he intended to call Mortimer Mouse, until Mrs. Disney suggested Mickey) and also provided the rodent's high-pitched voice, the actual figure was drawn by Ub Iwerks, a Disney associate. Mickey's girlfriend was Minnie Mouse. Mickey (often together with Minnie) starred in well over a hundred cartoon shorts; his likeness has been licensed to innumerable manufacturers of toys and other products, most notably for the Mickey Mouse watch, now a highly prized and highly priced collectible.

Midwives. Midwives attend and assist women in childbirth and have been doing so at least from Old Testament times and, doubtless, even much earlier. A formal movement to train midwives did not get under way in Europe until the seventeenth century and by the eighteenth, maternity hospitals in major cities were staffed by and trained midwives. In the nineteenth century, many European nations regulated midwifery by law.

Midwives were active in America since the seventeenth century, but, by the end of the eighteenth century, upper-class and urban women resorted increasingly to male physicians to attend delivery. By the nineteenth century, physicians actively campaigned against midwives as incompetent anachronisms. For a long period, midwifery fell into disrepute and was generally regarded as a dangerous and outmoded example of folk medicine (see MEDICINE, FOLK). However, in the 1920s, a professional midwifery movement began, and, in 1928, the Kentucky State Association of Midwives was founded. It subsequently became the American Association of Nurse-Midwives. The American College of Nurse-Midwives was founded in 1955, but it was not until 1971 that midwives received official recognition by the College of Obstetricians and Gynecologists. Midwifery has increased in popularity since the counterculture movement of the 1960s, which inspired many people to seek alternatives to mainstream medical care.

SUGGESTED READING: Cecilia M. Benoit, *Midwives in Passage: The Modernization of Maternity Care* (St. John's, Newfoundland, 1991); Fran L. Buss, *La Partera: Story of a Midwife* (Ann Arbor, Mich., 1980); Jane Donegan, *Women and Men Midwives: Medicine, Morality and Misogyny in Early America* (Westport, Conn., 1978); Judy Barrett Litoff, *American Midwives, 1860 to the Present* (Westport, Conn., 1978).

Military folklore. Military folklore may be regarded as a kind of OCCUPATIONAL FOLKLORE or as the folklore of a folk group, since the military profession is both a distinctive way of life and a community. Military folklore involves indoctrination rituals and procedures, rituals and routines to enforce conformity, narrative folklore to share experiences, narrative and other kinds of folklore to reduce anxiety, folklore to cope with authority, and massive quantities of FOLK SPEECH. The latter may be the most important feature of military folklore, since a command of the group's folk speech is essential to admission to full membership within the group. Some military folk speech is familiar almost exclusively to the troops. A "shit screen," for example, is a fall guy, the person who takes the blame for some foul up or infraction. A "jar head" is an enlisted marine. A "boot" is a recruit in basic training. Other elements of military vocabulary have become part of general folk speech. For example, official military jargon is replete with acronyms. During WORLD WAR II, soldiers invented some of their own, the most popular of which was *snafu*

(situation normal, all fucked up). The word, without its obscene connotation and, indeed, without a sense of its even being an acronym, is now in general speech. Variants on *snafu* never entered general speech and have vanished from military folk speech as well. These include: *fubar* (fucked up beyond all recognition), *tarfu* (things are really fucked up), *janfu* (joint army-navy fuck up), *fubis* (fuck you, buddy, I'm shipping out), *fta* (fuck the army), and *gfu* (general fuck up). Arguably as popular as snafu was SOS, which had been adopted in 1908 as the international radiotelegraph Morse code signal for distress and, some time during World War II, was adopted in the enlisted men's mess as a signal of specifically gustatory distress. A staple of World War II military cuisine was creamed chipped beef on toast, unofficially and universally dubbed shit on a shingle: SOS. The utility of this acronym rapidly increased as the expression came to signify any old lies, chores, or routines the army dished up day after day: same old shit. In this latter sense, it, too, has entered general folk speech, as have such expressions as *grunt*, which means an ordinary G.I. or enlisted marine, but, in the general population, means any working stiff, and *scut work,* which originated in military folk speech as a label for any disagreeable task (such as cleaning latrines) and is now found outside the military as well. Other items of military folk speech were borrowed *from* general folk speech. *Bogey,* for example, is a term for an unidentified air contact that is assumed to be hostile. The word seems to have come into general use during the early years of jet and electronic air combat— that is, during the KOREAN WAR—and is usually used to describe radar-screen blips interpreted as hostile aircraft, though bogies can also be sighted visually, usually on one's tail (or *six,* as pilots call a jet fighter's tail). The word recalls the BOGEY of fairy tale and nightmare. Finally, military folk speech also borrows words from general standard English. World War I produced the term *dogfight* to describe aerial combat between two or more fighter planes. During the Persian Gulf War (1990–91), American pilots often used *fur ball* to describe the same situation. This term aptly evokes the visceral effects of high-speed jet combat, an amalgam of pumping adrenalin, blackout-inducing G-forces, an urge to kill, and ever-churning fear. It is almost certainly descended from pilot slang dating back to the Army air force of World War II, when a close call or frightening situation was referred to as "hairy."

Much military folklore is intended to transform the recruit from a civilian into a soldier, to sever him from his former life, and to turn his affection from his girl to his rifle. (Which is emphatically *not* to be called a gun. Recruits who make this mistake may have to strip naked and repeat this chant: "This is my rifle. / *This* is my gun. / This is for shooting. / *This* is for fun.") As much as boot camp training is intended to desensitize soldiers, to make them (at least to some degree) obedient killers, so some military folklore has a toughening effect. New arrivals to Vietnam (see VIETNAM WAR) were sometimes greeted with this verse, sung to the tune of "Camptown Races": "You're going home in a body bag, / Do dah, do dah! / You're going home in a body bag, / O do dah day!"

Soldiers in combat are, of course, under great stress, and such emotionally intense circumstances often produce folklore intended to bring luck or explain things that are essentially irrational and terrifying. Thus much military folklore resembles TALL TALES or miracle narratives and includes stories of near-misses, brushes with death, miraculous escapes, and even GHOST STORIES (in the form of the returning spirits of fallen comrades).

SUGGESTED READING: Paul Holsinger and Mary Anne Schofield, eds., *Visions of War: World War II in Popular Literature and Culture* (Bowling Green, Ohio, 1992).

Millennialism. Millennialism is important in several Protestant religions (especially the Seventh-Day Adventists and the Jehovah's Witnesses) practiced in America and is of interest to students of folk religion (see RELIGION, FOLK). Millennialism interprets the Book of Revelation as foretelling a time in which Satan would be cast down into a bottomless pit and the Christian martyrs would be raised from the dead to reign with Christ for a millennium—a thousand years. At this time, evil would cease to exist and righteousness would rule on earth.

Miller, Joaquin (1837–1913). This poet and writer of LOCAL-COLOR STORIES is probably best remembered for his poem "Columbus" (1896), memorized by several generations of schoolchildren and a reinforcement of the image of CHRISTOPHER COLUMBUS as a CULTURE HERO. Miller's poetry and prose set in the West did much to create excitement about the region and to elaborate and affirm popular romantic images of the West.

Born Cincinnatus Hiner Miller in rural Indiana, Miller migrated west with his family and enjoyed an adventurous life in California among miners and gamblers. He was briefly exposed to college (at Columbia College in Eugene, Oregon) during 1858–59, was admitted to the Oregon bar (1860), then ran both a pony express and a newspaper in Eugene (1862–66). After writing an article in defense of the Mexican social bandit Joaquin Murietta, Miller adopted his first name cepted as a nostalgic, romantic vision of the American West.

SUGGESTED READING: Martin S. Peterson, *Joaquin Miller: Literary Frontiersman* (Palo Alto, Calif., 1937).

●

Mining folklore. Like other groups involved in difficult and hazardous work, miners of all minerals have developed a rich body of OCCUPATIONAL FOLKLORE, the emotional intensity of which is often heightened by an *us versus them* attitude prevalent among many mining groups, which traditionally have been embattled against mine company management.

Much mining folklore is very basic in that it concerns safety and hazards. Certain ritual taboos may be observed (such as not whistling in the mine shaft), or as RICHARD M. DORSON reports, refraining from killing rats found in the mine. A rationale applies to the latter taboo: rats are believed to hear advance signs of ground breaking up, and their actions, therefore, provide warning of a possible cave-in. Some mining SUPERSTITIONS revolve around subterranean trolls or tommy knockers.

Once back on the surface, miners during the late nineteenth and early twentieth centuries might gather to swap stories and sing songs, which include BALLADS about the routine of the job as well as about celebrated mining disasters (see DISASTER FOLKLORE). With its history of turbulent relations between management and labor, mining has also produced a substantial body of protest and labor songs, such as those composed by and composed about mining labor activist JOE HILL (1879–1915).

SUGGESTED READING: Richard M. Dorson, *Bloodstoppers and Bearwalkers: Folk Traditions of the Upper*

Joaquin Miller, late in life.

as his own pseudonym when he published his first two volumes of verse, *Specimens* (1868) and *Joaquin et al.* (1869). While neither he nor his verse drew much attention in America, he created a minor sensation when he traveled to Europe, sporting colorful western garb. His next two volumes of verse, *Pacific Poems* (1871) and *Songs of the Sierras* (1871), were published in Europe and praised there, but disparaged in the States as overly romantic. Yet *Songs of the Sierras* gradually insinuated itself into favor on this side of the Atlantic, as did his later verse and prose. His work and, no less, his own posturings became ac-

Peninsula (Cambridge, Mass., 1952); Archie Green, *Only a Miner: Studies in Recorded Coal-Mining Songs* (Urbana, Ill., 1972); George Korson, *Minstrels of the Mine Patch: Songs and Stories of the Anthracite Industry* (Philadelphia, 1938); George Korson, *Coal Dust on the Fiddle: Songs and Stories of the Bituminous Industry* (Philadelphia, 1943); George Korson, *Black Rock: Mining Folklore of the Pennsylvania Dutch* (Baltimore, 1960); Dennis Richard Preston, *Bituminous Coal Mining Vocabulary of the Eastern United States* (Tuscaloosa, Ala., 1975).

a number of African-American minstrel troupes were formed; often, these groups, although black, performed in blackface makeup.) The shows were tremendously popular in the United States as well as in England, especially during the years 1850–70, the decades bracketing and encompassing the Civil War. Racially offensive by modern standards, the minstrel show was nevertheless the first in a very long line of popular entertainments peculiar to America, catering to national sentiment and a nostalgia for an ideal-

Minstrel show. The first wholly indigenous form of mass popular entertainment in America, the minstrel show originated with three performers, THOMAS "DADDY" RICE (1808–60), DANIEL DECATUR EMMETT (1815–1904), and EDWIN P. "NED" CHRISTY (1815–62). In 1829, Rice created and performed "Jim Crow," a song and dance supposedly inspired by a crippled African-American stable boy Rice encountered in Louisville, Cincinnati, or Pittsburgh. Rice, a white man, "jumped Jim Crow" in blackface, and evolved the simple routine into a stand-alone act by 1832. Probably inspired by "Daddy" Rice's "Jim Crow," composer Daniel Decatur Emmett (playing fiddle and rendering the vocals) and three others organized the Virginia Minstrels in New York City in March 1843. This was the first true minstrel show troupe. Three years later, Ned Christy, of Buffalo, New York, created the seven-man Christy Minstrels, which established the pattern for hundreds of imitators throughout the nineteenth century and into the early part of the twentieth.

The basis of the minstrel show was white performers, in blackface, caricaturing the singing and dancing of African-American slaves. (Later,

A nineteenth-century minstrel show, depicted in a book illustration from the 1940s.

ized rural past. The minstrel stage provided a showcase for popular dance freely synthesized from English and American folk origins, including genuine African-American "breakdowns" and "shuffles." In addition to the original "Jim Crow" step, blackface minstrelsy produced the enormously popular cakewalk. These shows also served as the vehicle through which a large number of now-familiar songs reached the public in the days before the phonograph and radio: "Polly Wolly Doodle," "Buffalo Girls," "The Old Folks at Home," in addition to Rice's own "That Long-tail'd Blue," Emmett's "OLD DAN TUCKER" and "Dixie," as well as many others written for minstrel shows. Many of STEPHEN FOSTER's most popular songs were written for minstrel shows.

The "classic" format of the minstrel show, usually in two parts, was established by the Christy company and changed little thereafter. In part one the performers were arranged in a semicircle, with the interlocutor in the center and the end men—Mr. Tambo, who played the tambourine, and Mr. Bones, who rattled the bones—at the ends. The interlocutor, in whiteface, usually wore formal attire; the others, in blackface, wore gaudy swallow-tailed coats and striped trousers. The program opened with a chorus, often as a grand entrance, and at the conclusion of the song the interlocutor gave the command, "Gentlemen, be seated." Then followed a series of jokes between the interlocutor and the end men, interspersed with ballads, comic songs, and instrumental numbers, chiefly on the banjo and violin. The second part, or olio (mixture or medley), consisted of a series of individual acts that concluded with a hoedown or walk-around in which every member did a specialty number while the others sang and clapped. Occasionally there was a third part consisting of a farce, burlesque, or comic opera.

Minstrelsy influenced later popular forms, including vaudeville, as well as radio, television, and film. It was also the earliest instance of interaction between a form of mass popular entertainment and folk material.

See also: AFRICAN AMERICANS; BALL THE JACK; "BLUE-TAIL FLY"; BUCK-AND-WING; "BUFFALO GIRLS"; HAYS, WILL; JAZZ; PLAY PARTY; RAGTIME; RAINEY, MA; TAP DANCE.

SUGGESTED READING: Russel Nye, *The Unembarrassed Muse: The Popular Arts in America* (New York, 1970); Constance Rourke, *American Humor: A Study of the National Character* (New York, 1931); Carl Wittke, *Tambo and Bones: A History of the American Minstrel* (New York, 1930).

Mistletoe. This plant (*Viscum album*), long prized in Europe for its medicinal and magical powers, is best known in America as a Christmastime decoration. If a man and woman step under a sprig of mistletoe, they are permitted to kiss—some believe they are obliged to do so. African Americans in the southern states have boiled mistletoe to make a decoction useful for drying up mother's milk, and in the bayou country of Louisiana, mistletoe is hung over doors to ward off the EVIL EYE and other actions of malevolent conjurors.

Mobile homes. The mobile home may be considered a feature of American folklife because, within a decade of its introduction into the marketplace (the first mobile home was manufactured by the Covered Wagon Company of Detroit in 1929), it often served relatively poor

Early mobile homes from the 1920s and from the late 1930s.

families as a permanent home, taking the place of traditional houses considered examples of VER-NACULAR ARCHITECTURE, especially the SHOT-GUN HOUSE.

Mojo. *Mojo* is a rather amorphous term applied to a charm object associated with VOODOO or to all of voodoo as it is known by some contemporary African Americans. In this latter sense, *mojo* is synonymous with *voodoo, hoodoo, fixing, tricking,* and *rootworking.* It may be a term applied to an abstract system of magic, powers, and influences or very specifically to a love potion or amulet.

The system and/or objects of mojo operate in many aspects of African-American belief systems. Infatuation and infidelity are often attributed to mojo. Good or ill fortune may be similarly ascribed to the influence of mojo. Likewise illness and cure and general luck.

Some people seek advice on securing an effective mojo (charm) or realizing favorable mojo (good fortune). For such advice, the counsel of a *mojo doctor* or *hoodoo doctor* is sought. In some

modern African-American communities, these counselors are called more generically spirtual-ists, psychics, or *readers*.

See also: HOODOO HAND; ROOTWORK.

SUGGESTED READING: Zora Neale Hurston, "Hoodoo in America," *Journal of American Folklore* 44 (1931), pp. 317–417; Harry M. Hyatt, *Hoodoo, Conjuration, Witchcraft, Rootwork* (Hannibal, Mo., 1970–75).

Monroe, Bill (1911–1996). The father of BLUEGRASS music, William Smith Monroe was born in Rosine, Kentucky, and began playing professionally in 1927 with his older brothers Birch and Charlie. Unable to support themselves by music alone, the brothers moved to northern Indiana in 1930 to work in the oil refineries. They also played on local radio stations in the oil and steel towns just outside of Chicago. In 1932, the band toured with a "barn dance" show, but Birch, disliking life on the road, dropped out. Bill and Charlie Monroe continued to tour as a duet, making their first recordings in 1936.

After a period of intense recording during

1936–38, Bill and Charlie went their separate ways, Bill Monroe forming the Blue Grass Boys—a name intended both to honor his native "bluegrass state" of Kentucky and to make reference to the BLUES, an important influence on Monroe. The band auditioned for the GRAND OLE OPRY radio show with "Muleskinner Blues." The studio audience demanded an encore—the first ever in the history of the show. Monroe's "bluegrass sound" established itself very quickly. It would never take COUNTRY MUSIC by storm, but it would prove very durable and enduring. Monroe skillfully programmed a combination of Appalachian folk songs, popular commercial country tunes, and his own compositions.

Monroe was known as a strict taskmaster, unsparing in the level of musicianship he demanded from his "boys." Lester Flatt and EARL SCRUGGS, among others, were Blue Grass Boys alumni who went on to develop the bluegrass style with their own ensembles and in their own directions.

See also: FOLK REVIVAL; GIBSON MANDOLIN AND GUITAR MANUFACTURING COMPANY, LTD., THE; MANDOLIN; RINZLER, RALPH CARTER.

SUGGESTED READING: Country Music Foundation, *Country: The Music and the Musicians* (New York, 1988).

Monroe, Marilyn (1926–1962). Many

film actors and actresses have become pop culture icons, but a few, like Marilyn Monroe, achieved substantially more, becoming the object and subject of folklore. In the simplest sense, Monroe was a "sex symbol," a term that came into vogue during the 1950s specifically to describe her and such Marilyn wanna-be's as Jayne Mansfield. Like Jean Harlow (1911–37) before her, Monroe was called a "blonde bombshell." Such phrases were the invention of press agents, but they were quickly and universally incorporated into everyday language, becoming part of the fabric of modern FOLK SPEECH and excellent examples of the ongoing dialogue between folklore and MASS MEDIA. Beyond this, though, many have come to see Marilyn Monroe as more deeply symbolic, a LEGEND, even. Her life seems to sum up much about American attitudes toward sexuality and fame—and the price that both may exact.

Certainly, Marilyn Monroe's rise to stardom seems a modern female version of the HORATIO ALGER story. Born Norma Jean Mortenson (also called Norma Jean Baker) in Los Angeles, she grew up in orphanages and foster homes before becoming a photographer's model. Late in the 1940s, her nude photograph appeared on a wall calendar, which caused a sensation and led to her film debut in *Scudda-Hoo! Scudda-Hay!* (1948). After several bit and minor roles, she starred in *Gentlemen Prefer Blondes* (1953), *How to Marry a Millionaire* (1953), and *The Seven Year Itch* (1955), all of which were highly successful and brought the young actress much attention—albeit as yet another cultural stereotype, which might be considered a modern folklore motif: the Dumb Blonde. Seeking to take herself beyond the stereotype, Monroe enrolled in the prestigious Actors Studio under Lee Strasberg and then, indeed, starred in better and more serious films, including *Bus Stop* (1956), *The Prince and the Showgirl* (1957), *Some Like It Hot* (1959), and *The Misfits* (1961).

Monroe's romantic life was always a subject of fascination and speculation. She was married briefly to baseball great Joe DiMaggio in 1954 and to playwright Arthur Miller from 1956 to 1961. Apparently credible rumors have connected her romantically to President John F. Kennedy as well as his brother, Robert F. Kennedy, then attorney general of the United States.

Monroe's emotional condition declined during the early 1960s, and she became difficult to work with. Her death, apparently from an overdose of sleeping pills, not only shocked the nation (and the world), but augmented her status as a contemporary legend. Monroe's romantic connection with the Kennedy brothers has evoked much CONSPIRACY LORE suggesting that Monroe was murdered.

SUGGESTED READING: Norman Mailer, *Marilyn: A Biography* (New York, 1987); Donald Spoto, *Marilyn Monroe: The Biography* (New York, 1994).

Monza, Louis (1897–1984). Monza was a folk painter best known for his allegorical depictions of the horrors of the two world wars. His works are often gory, replete with gruesome details of battle carnage. Monza was born in Turate, Italy, but immigrated to the United States on the eve of World War I. He worked as a railroad hand until 1917, when he joined the army and was stationed in Panama during the war. After his discharge, he settled in New York City and worked as a housepainter. A 1938 fall from a scaffold injured his spine, and he started painting shortly afterward. He received some recognition during the 1940s, and in 1946 moved to Redondo Beach, California. He married the following year and settled into a life of painting while his wife supported them both. Major recognition of Monza's work did not come until after his death in 1984.

Mooney, James (1861–1921). Mooney was an important early collector of Native American folklore. He met John Wesley Powell (the great geologist and ethnologist who was the first director of the U.S. Bureau of Ethnology) in 1885. Mooney, a schoolteacher and journalist, had studied Native American culture on his own and had acquired so vast a store of knowledge that Powell hired him as a Bureau of Ethnology researcher. Mooney continued in this position until his death. He carried out extensive fieldwork among the Cherokee and the Sioux. Mooney's best-known book is *The Ghost-Dance Religion and the Sioux Outbreak of 1890* (1896; reprint ed., 1965), but his most important contribution to folklore study is *Myths of the Cherokees* (1900; reprint ed., 1982), a large collection of material gathered from 1887 to 1890.

Morgan, Gib (1842–1909). An early oil-well driller, Gib Morgan earned more than local fame for his tall tales of oil-field adventures. Morgan has often been compared to PAUL BUNYAN and is to the oil industry what Paul Bunyan is to logging. Morgan, however, was a historical figure, while Paul Bunyan was fiction. Morgan was a native of Callensburg, Pennsylvania, served in the Union army during the Civil War, then worked as an itinerant driller in Pennsylvania and elsewhere on the East Coast. He retired in 1892.

The tales Morgan spun are mainly wildly exaggerated accounts of fantastic oil-drilling exploits, such as working on a derrick so big that it had to be hinged to allow the moon to pass, or acquiring a pet boa constrictor so long that it served as a drilling cable, or drilling in Fiji through layers of buttermilk, champagne, and sweet cream. Morgan failed to locate the peppermint he had been hired to find, and he missed realizing a fortune from ice cream made out of the cream he struck because the cream soured by the time he had built an ice cream factory.

Morgan originally told his tales in local bars, achieving considerable fame in the decade before his death.

SUGGESTED READING: Mody C. Boatright, *Gib Morgan: Minstrel of the Oil Fields* (Dallas, 1945); Richard M. Dorson, *America in Legend: Folklore from the Colonial Period to the Present* (New York, 1973).

Morgan, Sister Gertrude (1900–1980).

Sister Gertrude Morgan was an African-American religious folk painter, a preacher, and a singer. Born and raised in Lafayette, Alabama, she received there in 1937 a divine inspiration to preach "to the world." Two years later, she moved to New Orleans, where she became a street preacher and, with two other women, founded an orphanage, a chapel, and child-care facility in the New Orleans suburb of Gentilly. After a hurricane destroyed the Gentilly orphanage in 1965, Sister Gertrude increasingly devoted herself to painting, which she had begun in 1956. She continued to sing gospel music and to preach on the street.

Sister Gertrude Morgan's paintings are both naive in imagery and complex in composition. Her subject matter is chiefly apocalyptic and visionary, combining biblical imagery with the artifacts of the modern world, as in visual realizations of a line from one of her gospel chants, "Jesus is my airplane." A number of her paintings are autobiographical.

See also: VISIONARY ART.

SUGGESTED READING: Jane Livingston and John Beardsley, *Black Folk Art in America: 1930–1980* (Jackson, Miss., 1982).

Mormons.

As a religion of relatively recent vintage, created by persons of colorful character, and closely tied to the frontier and the expansion of westward settlement, the Church of Jesus Christ of Latter-Day Saints, the Mormon church, is rich with folklore. That body of folklore begins with the story of Joseph Smith (1805–44) and how he received the revelation that moved him to found the church. Beyond this are many stories concerning the Mormon Trek, the series of migrations from eastern and midwestern Mormon settlements to Utah during the mid-1800s. These stories concern hardships of the trail, endurance of persecutions at the hands of the "gentiles" (non-Mormons), struggles with Indians, and battles against the harsh elements of the desert West. Often, these stories are related by pattern and analogy to incidents narrated in *The Book of Mormon*, the holy writ said to have been revealed to Joseph Smith. Tales of modern, even contemporary, Mormon experience are also often patterned after or paralleled with *Book of Mormon* narratives.

Another motif central to Mormon folklore is polygamy. More than any other feature of Mormon "separateness," plural marriage (as the Mormons called it) provoked—or perpetuated and rationalized—persecution. Mormon folklore relating to this issue is often humorous, consisting of anecdotes of the dodges and tricks used to dupe federal and state authorities. In this respect, some of the tales resemble the folklore of African-American slavery, which often deals with "puttin' on ol' massa."

The foremost writer on the subject of Mormon folklore was AUSTIN E. FIFE (1909–86).

SUGGESTED READING: Austin and Alta Fife, *Saints of Sage and Saddle: Folklore among the Mormons* (Bloomington, Ind., 1956); Hector Lee, *The Three Nephites: Substance and Significance of Legend in Folklore* (Albuquerque, N.M., 1949).

Morton, Thomas (ca. 1579–ca. 1647).

Thomas Morton was the author of a single book, *The New English Canaan or New Canaan* (Amsterdam, 1637), which is an account of Indian life and manners, a history of early New England told from an unusual non-Puritan perspective, a tract promoting settlement of the region, and, most memorably, the story of bitter rivalry between the saintly settlers of Plymouth and the reveling Morton of Merry Mount. This latter narrative, charming, yet acidly satiric, develops a theme that figures in much subsequent American folklore and literature and, especially, literature drawn from folklore: a pointed conflict between piety and wildness. Morton also tells the story of the Maypole of Merrymount, which became a feature of New England folklore and received literary expression in NATHANIEL HAWTHORNE's nineteenth-century short story, "The Maypole of Merrymount."

Morton was born about 1579, possibly in the West Country of England. He became an attorney, and his marriage in 1621 to a widow named Alice Miller almost immediately embroiled him in a series of lawsuits over property rights. Shortly after the conclusion of litigation, in 1624, he left for New England, establishing a fur-trading post at Mount Wollaston (modern Quincy), Massachusetts, which he renamed Mare-Mount or Merry Mount. In 1627, with the trading post prospering, Morton invited the local Indians, male and female, to dance around the maypole he had erected. This pagan symbol and the revelry associated with it greatly offended the Pilgrims of Plymouth (according to Morton) almost as bitterly as did the financial success of the Merry Mount trading post. In the spring of 1628 Plymouth and other plantations charged Morton with selling guns to the Indians; he was arrested in June by Miles Standish, tried, and shipped back to England in August. Acquitted there, he returned to Merry Mount in 1629. Plymouth

Thomas Morton, author of The New English Canaan or New Canaan *(1637), a source of New England folklore mined by numerous writers of the nineteenth century. (Courtesy the British Museum)*

governor John Endecott, who had chopped down the offending maypole while Morton was abroad, arrested the reveler again in 1630 and, again, banished him to England, also confiscating his goods and burning down his house.

In response to this, Morton prevailed on the anti-Puritan Anglican Archbishop of Canterbury, William Laud, to nullify the Massachusetts Bay Company patent. (The judgment, however, proved unenforceable.) As part of his campaign against the Massachusetts Bay Company, Morton wrote *New English Canaan*. Book One contrasts the Indians of New England, portrayed as naturally noble, with the greedy and mendacious white Puritan settlers of Plymouth. Book Two is an example of the popular colonial literary genre, the promotion tract. Morton writes of New England's natural resources, drawing on his own observations as well as on John Smith's *A Description of New England* (1616) and blending biblical and Renaissance traditions to depict the new land as both a biblical Canaan and a classical Arcadia. Book Three draws on Renaissance literary conventions—especially the anti-masque (as developed by Ben Jonson)—to relate Morton's misadventures among the Plymouth Separatists, contrasting his good-natured revelries around the maypole with the Puritans' sour and life-denying efforts against him.

Thomas Morton returned to New England in 1643, after an absence of thirteen years. He was arrested by Boston authorities in September of 1644 and was convicted of slander. Imprisoned during the winter of 1644–45, on his release he settled in Agamenticus (modern York), Maine, and died there about 1647.

While *New English Canaan* is biased and suspect as history, it articulated what proved to be enduring cultural stereotypes and was used as a source of folk history by such later American writers such as WASHINGTON IRVING, Nathaniel Hawthorne, JOHN GREENLEAF WHITTIER, HENRY WADSWORTH LONGFELLOW, STEPHEN VINCENT BÉNET, and Robert Lowell.

See also: FOLKLORE IN AMERICAN LITERATURE; MAYPOLE OF MERRY MOUNT.

SUGGESTED READING: Charles Francis Adams, Jr., Introduction to *The New English Canaan of Thomas Morton* (Boston, 1883); Alan Axelrod, entry on Morton in *Dictionary of Literary Biography* 24 (Detroit, 1984); Donald F. Connors, *Thomas Morton* (New York, 1969); Thomas Morton, *New English Canaan or New Canaan. Containing an Abstract of New England, Composed in Three Books* (Amsterdam, 1637; reprinted in Peter Force, ed., *Tracts* 2, no. 5 Washington, D.C., 1838.

Moser, Artus M. (1894–1992).

Moser was a collector of ballads and folktales from Swannanoa, North Carolina. He was introduced to the study of folklore by EDWIN C. KIRKLAND, for whom he served as an informant. An educator by vocation, Moser taught in Knoxville, Tennessee, then worked in western North Carolina. In this region, he collected widely from local singers and storytellers, making more than a hundred field recordings during the late 1930s and early 1940s. In 1945, DUNCAN EMRICH of the Library of Congress loaned Moser a state-of-the-art portable disk recorder and commissioned him to rerecord his informants. The result was several hundred recordings for the Archive of American Folk Song.

Moser himself was a performer, who was recorded in a 1955 session that was subsequently released by FOLKWAYS RECORDS.

See also: RITCHIE, JEAN.

Moses, Grandma (1860–1961).

Anna Mary Robertson Moses, better known as Grandma Moses in tribute to her remarkable longevity, was the most famous of American "outsider artists" or "folk painters." Her naive depictions of rural America as it appeared to her at the turn of the century achieved great popularity.

Moses left her parents' farm when she was twelve, and married Thomas Moses in 1887. They farmed in Staunton, Virginia, then moved in 1905 to a farm at Eagle Bridge, New York, near the place of her birth. After her husband died in 1927, Anna Moses continued to farm, finally retiring to live with her daughter in 1936.

At about this time, Moses began painting. As a child, she had liked to draw, and after the death of her husband, she embroidered, but when arthritis made it difficult for her to ply her needle, she turned to painting. At first, Moses copied CURRIER & IVES prints and picture postcards, but then began to reflect on her own memories of farm life in New York and Virginia. The titles she gave her paintings were as simple and nostalgic as the naive images themselves: *Catching the Thanksgiving Turkey, Over the River to Grandma's House, Sugaring-Off in the Maple Orchard,* and the like. She sold her first painting in a local Hoosick Falls, New York, drugstore, but her work was discovered about 1939 by art dealer Otto Kallir. He exhibited her paintings in 1940 at his Gallerie Saint Etienne in New York City, and the following year Grandma Moses received the New York State Prize for *The Old Oaken Bucket* (1941). After this, her work was exhibited nationally and even internationally. In 1949, President Harry S Truman presented Moses with the Women's National Press Club Award for outstanding accomplishment in art. Moses continued to paint, exhibit, and sell her work until she died at 101, by which time she was as famous for her advanced age as for her paintings, and the expression "as old as Grandma Moses" was commonly used as a synonym for extremely old.

See also: KITCHEN, TELLA; MEMORY PAINTING; "Naive" ART; O'KELLEY, MATTIE LOU.

SUGGESTED READING: Grandma [Anna Mary Robertson] Moses, *My Life's History* (New York, 1952).

Mothman.

Mothman is perhaps the latest in a line of paranormal creatures that appear from time to time in American folklore, including BIGFOOT, the JACKALOPE, and the JERSEY DEVIL. Mothman was allegedly sighted near Point Pleasant, West Virginia, between mid-November 1966 and mid-December 1967. No one has succeeded in photographing the creature, which (according to "eyewitness accounts") stood six to seven feet tall and sported huge, featherless wings ten feet in span. Mothman's eyes are said to have been huge, red, and glowing, set into an otherwise entirely featureless face. Some reports hold that Mothman is actually headless, his striking eyes actually in the shoulder area in place of a neck and head. It is also said that Mothman can fly without flapping his wings, and can match the speed of an automobile fleeing from it at one hundred miles an hour. Mothman floats airborne, then speeds through the air silently and without effort.

That the "legend" of Mothman has survived in and around Point Pleasant (and beyond) since the late 1960s suggests some significance as folklore; however, the "legend" is also kept alive by a marketing and design firm, based in Point Pleasant, which produces glow-in-the-dark "Lair of Mothman" and the "Classic 30th Anniversary" Mothman T-shirts. *The Mothman Prophecies,* by John A. Keel (New York, 1991), is a fairly objective account of the rash of UFO reports and Mothman sightings around Mount Pleasant.

Motif.

A definable element, constituent, or building block of folklore that may be analyzed to assess relationships among various features of folklore or relationships among the folklores of various groups or cultures. A motif may be a step in folk dances, a pattern in folk narrative, a character or plot type or narrative pattern in folktales, an architectural feature in a folk building type, and so on. To be valid for analysis, a motif must be out of the ordinary, distinctive, and clearly salient; it must also demonstrably recur.

See also: JOKES AND JOKE CYCLES; NOBLE SAVAGE; PRESLEY, ELVIS.

Muddy Waters (1915–1983). BLUES singer Muddy Waters was born McKinley Morganfield in Rolling Fork, Mississippi, and, in early youth, made a name for himself as a blues guitarist and harmonica player as far as Memphis. He was recorded in the 1940s by ALAN LOMAX and other folklorists, then cut his first commercial record in 1946. Muddy Waters then moved to Chicago, where he performed with his own band that included Willie Dixon, Otis Spann, Pat Hare, James Cotton, and Little Walter Jacobs. It was also during the 1940s that Muddy Waters introduced the electric guitar to the Delta blues. Thus he was responsible for transforming the blues into an ensemble music, for helping to bring the rural Delta blues into the national mainstream, and, with his use of electric instruments, he set up the blues as a major influence on rock 'n' roll. Indeed, the most enduring of the British rock groups formed in the 1960s, the Rolling Stones, took their name from one of Muddy Waters's most famous songs, "Rolling Stone." Waters is often called "Godfather of the Blues."

See also: FOLK REVIVAL.

Mummers. The origin of mummers is obscure. They are people who don distinctive costumes and, in Newfoundland, make house-to-house visits at Christmastime, and, in Philadelphia, stage a large parade on New Year's Day. Presumably, both of these traditions are related to the English practice of "mumming," which involves the performance of folk plays during the season of winter solstice.

In Newfoundland, mummers are a group of adults who disguise themselves and call on people in the community. The homeowner answers the door, invites the mummers inside, asks ritualized questions about their identities, then requests a musical performance, often offering refreshment in return. Mumming (also called "mummering" or "janneying") may be related to a similar practice, "belsnickling," found in German-American communities as late as the beginning of the twentieth century.

Most people associate mummers with the Mummers Parade, which has been an official Philadelphia function since 1900, based on some two hundred years of mummers' parades in the

Mummers' parade in Philadelphia, 1920s.

city's neighborhoods. This is a massive event, involving many thousands of marchers, who dress in elaborate costumes that may consume a full year in the making. The parade lasts twelve hours and involves displays of ethnic entertainment, usually with a comic slant and focused on particular skitlike theme. Groups of ethnic mummers form clubs to organize preparation for the play. In this respect, the mummer clubs are similar to the "krewes" who prepare for and participate in New Orleans Mardi Gras parades and balls. For many years, the Mummers Parade excluded African Americans from participation, an issue that created increasing controversy and bitterness.

See also: MARDI GRAS, NEW ORLEANS.

SUGGESTED READING: Herbert Halpert, and G. M. Story, eds., *Christmas Mumming in Newfoundland: Essays in Anthropology Folklore, and History* (Toronto, 1990); Charles E. Welch, *Oh! Dem Golden Slippers: The Story of the Philadelphia Mummers* (Philadelphia, 1991).

Musica Tejana. See TEX-MEX MUSIC.

Musick, Ruth Ann (1897–1974). Musick was best known as a collector of ghostlore and immigrant legends in the coalfields of West Virginia. Her "The Old Folks Say" folklore column, which ran from 1948 to 1954 in the *Fairmont*

Times-West Virginian, was highly popular, and she also founded the *West Virginia Folklore Journal* in 1951. Musick earned a Ph.D. in English from the University of Iowa, and she spent her academic career as a professor of English at Fairmont State College, West Virginia. Her early folklore collecting began in 1946 with ballads and folk songs, but she began increasingly to concentrate on folktale and legend. Her publications include numerous articles and the books *Ballads, Folk Songs, and Folk Tales from West Virginia* (1960), *The Telltale Lilac Bush* (1965), *Green Hills of Magic* (1970), and the posthumous *Coffin Hollow and Other Ghost Tales* (1977).

Myth. A narrative of characters having lived and events having occurred in an earlier age, which explains the cosmology of a people, including their gods, heroes, traits, religious beliefs, and, often, basic identity. Often, myth has been described as the science of a prescientific age. The purpose of myth is etiological: it accounts for origins. In a myth, the main characters are gods or demigods, and the background of the story is essentially religious. In these qualities, a myth differs from a folktale, which may or may not be etiological, but which does not include gods or demigods and is not, in essence, religious. There is interchange between myth and folklore, as when certain folktales take their inspiration from myth.

See also: LEGEND; SUPERMAN.

N

"Naive" art. Simple, childlike, artistic expression. The term is most often applied to formally trained European artists such as Henri Rousseau (1844–1910) rather than American folk artists; however, such artists as GRANDMA MOSES, whose works are simple and direct, are sometimes described as "naive" as well.

See also: WOOD, GRANT.

Nampeyo (ca. 1860–1942). A Hopi-Tewa Indian from First Mesa, Arizona, Nampeyo was a potter, who learned her art from her grandmother and who specialized in designs emulating ancestral patterns unearthed at the Sityatki archaeological site between 1895 and 1900. Her work, polished but unslipped vessels painted with the ancestral motifs, initiated the Sikyatki Revival, a twentieth-century rebirth of Hopi folk pottery traditions. By the 1920s, Nampeyo's pottery was nationally known, and her family has continued to create works in the Sikyatki style.

Nasby, Petroleum V. (1833–1888). The "V" stood for Vesuvius, and the entire name was the invention of David Ross Locke, a journalist born in Binghamton, New York, and, in 1861, employed as editor of the *Findlay* (Ohio) *Jeffersonian*. While working for the *Jeffersonian*, Locke-Nasby published the first of what would be a long-running series of satirical letters signed Petroleum V. Nasby. For more than two decades, "Nasby Letters" appeared in the *Toledo Blade*, of which he became editor. In large part because of the letters, the newspaper gained national circulation. Locke collected the letters in such books as *The Nasby Papers* (1864) and *The Diary of an Office Seeker* (1881).

Locke-Nasby was an abolitionist, who, unlike the overwhelming majority of those with similar convictions, had a sense of humor. His Nasby character was a crude and vicious "Copperhead"—a so-called Peace Democrat, a Northerner with Southern sympathies. With comical illiteracy, Nasby "argued" the Southern position in the Civil War in order, of course, to expose it to ridicule. Nasby became folk antihero/scoundrel, a figure of fun everyone loved to hate, and President Abraham Lincoln would regularly read Nasby letters aloud to his cabinet.

Petroleum V. Nasby was adopted by the nation, even well after the Civil War years, as a folk figure. Certainly, he was far more than a one-dimensional caricature. He took on a life of his own, expressed through his letters. Drafted into the Union army, he escapes to Canada and then to the South, only to be drafted into the Confederate army. (He justified his evasion of the Northern draft by pointing out, among other things, that he is "bald-head'd, and hev bin obliged to wear a wig these 22 years" and that "I hev dandruff in wat scanty hair still hangs around my venerable temples.") Nasby makes another es-

Petroleum Vesuvius Nasby, in profile and with his literary friends, Josh Billings (left) *and Mark Twain* (standing).

cape and becomes a founder of churches in the North, then, after the war, obtains the political patronage position of postmaster of "Confedrit X Roads," Kentucky. Later, this founder of churches opens a tavern in New York, which fails because he drinks up the profits. Nasby finally retires to fulminate in Kentucky.

Massachusetts senator Charles Sumner reported that Lincoln once said of Nasby: "For the genius to write these things I would gladly give up my office."

See also: FOLKLORE IN AMERICAN LITERATURE.

Native Americans. The folklore of Native Americans is a subject at least as vast as the folk-lore of non–Native Americans. This entry is a very brief outline of the major subjects and issues encompassed by Native American folklore.

Several theories have been offered concerning the origin of Native American peoples. The most widely accepted speculates that Asian peoples began migrating, during the later stages of the Ice Age, across a land bridge connecting Asia and North America where the Bering Strait is today. The migration and dispersion throughout the continent probably consumed at least 20,000 years. However, some theorists suggest that migrations may have taken place as early as 155,000 years ago, while others place the first migrations as recently as 9,000 years ago. Native American populations declined after extensive European contact from the sixteenth through the eighteenth centuries, then plummeted again during the nineteenth century, a period of continual warfare with whites and a period of other hardships, including widespread poverty and disease. By the beginning of the twentieth century, however, Native American population was on the rise and it is now growing rapidly.

Native Americans are not a single people, but an array of culturally and geographically diverse peoples. In many cases, "community," built of family and tribal units, is quite different from non–Native concepts of community. In the case of Native Americans, it is also often much more difficult, even impossible, to separate mythology and religion from folklore. Generally, in non–Native American groups, folklore is an active force in daily life, while mythology is dead, fossilized in history and literature, and religion, while it overlaps folklore in various areas, is more formally organized and institutionalized. Among many Native American groups, however, and at various times in history, mythology, religion, and folklore may or must be viewed on a continuum. It is usually misleading to attempt to divide one of these cultural aspects from another. This said, the difficulty of making a meaningful study of Native American "folklore" may be appreciated; for such study requires a thorough understanding of the groups' religious and mythological beliefs. Indeed, the task is even more complicated, because many Native American groups relate to nature—the natural environment—differently from non–Native groups. At least at various times in their histories, most Native peoples have felt a seamless connection to the natural world, which, as is true of human beings, is animated by a variety of spirits. This connection is a fact of daily life and informs, to some degree, all actions, utterances, and artifacts. Thus, as it is impossible to divide Native American folklore from religion and mythology, so it is at the very least a distortion to separate any of these things from such activities as hunting, planting, warfare, food preparation, handicrafts, music, dancing, storytelling, and various ceremonies. In short, the study of Native American "folklore" is a profound anthropological enterprise.

Of great interest to students of Native American folklore (the term we will use, with the understanding that it encompasses religion and mythology as well) is storytelling, the oral narration of story and tradition. Typically, storytelling creates bonds, reaffirms identity, explains the cosmos, and entertains. Native American stories may be anecdotal; may relate to the origins of various animals, spirits, and so on; may be improvised, may be fictional, or may be precise components of prescribed ritual. Among some groups, stories are regarded as the "property" of the teller and may not be taken without permission, but may be given as gifts. Some stories are appropriate only to men, others only to women, some are restricted to certain occasions or seasons. The subject matter of traditional Native American stories is rich, but some of the most important origin stories involve complex TRICKSTER characters (such as COYOTE), which, in much Native American lore, function as creators.

If storytelling is important to Native American folklore, dance is even more central. Much ritual involves dance, and occasions for dance range from great public ceremonies to private healing rites, such as the Iroquois "False Faces" dance. Dancers are typically attired in special ceremonial clothing and often wear masks (see KACHINA). Many Native Americans perform animal dances, such as the "Bear Dance," versions of which are performed by many tribes. Dances related to agriculture and to hunting are also common. Best known to outsiders—by reputation and report—is the Sun Dance, a summer ceremony that lasts for three to four days and that is performed by the Lakota, Dakota, Cheyenne, Ponca, Kiowa, Mandan, Hidatsa, Arapaho, Blackfoot, Crow, Shoshone, Ute, and Comanche tribal groups. The ceremony, believed to be central to the health and strength of participants and their families, came into being early in the nineteenth century, but was suppressed by U.S. government authorities. In the course of the Native American civil rights movement of the 1960s, however, it came back into prominence as an important ethnic and spiritual ceremony. Another nineteenth-century ritual dance became notorious among non–Native Americans. The GHOST DANCE was part of a spiritual and religious movement among reservation Sioux and other tribes, which alarmed government officials and ultimately triggered the last major armed conflict of the American Indian Wars, the "battle" at Wounded Knee, Dakota Territory, on December 29, 1890.

In the area of material culture, folklorists have been interested in such things as weapons, housing, and handicrafts, including, especially, southwestern POTTERY, southwestern silverwork, BASKETMAKING, beadwork, and WEAVING. In large part because of the frequently hostile relations between Native Americans and non–Native Americans, weaponry has been the focus of much study and collecting. Common to virtually all tribes are bows, arrows, lances, clubs, and knives. Weapons are an important nexus of contact between Indian and white culture, for Indians avidly sought from white traders metal to improve the effectiveness of their weapons. This became both the basis of profitable trade and the basis of much conflict. In the area of housing, adobe structures and the HOGAN have drawn the most attention. Silverwork, pottery, baskets, weaving, and beadwork have attracted collectors (and acquisitive tourists) as much as they have folklorists. Most tribes created baskets of woven or coiled grasses, sticks, tree bark, and leaves— whatever materials were available—and those produced in the Southwest, often highly decorative, have been widely sought by collectors. Thus basketmaking became an important source of in-

come for many of Native Americans. The same holds true for weaving, especially the blankets and mats of the Navajo, Hopi, and Zuni. The creation of Native American pottery dates to great antiquity, and modern re-creations of ancient pottery, such as those by MARIA MONTOYA MARTINEZ (1880s–1980) and JULIAN MARTINEZ (1879–1943) of the Tewa Pueblo at San Ildefonso, New Mexico, have been recognized as masterworks of folk art.

The Navajos began working silver about 1868, melting down American silver dollars and Mexican pesos, at first to create such utilitarian objects as tobacco containers, bridles, and so on. By the later nineteenth century, however, Navajo and other tribes of the southern Plains began fashioning jewelry. The Fred Harvey Company, famous as railroad concessionaires, bought much of this jewelry and retailed it to tourists, thereby spreading its fame to the East. Today, Navajo, Zuni, and Pueblo jewelry is regarded as highly collectible.

Beadwork was also central to white-Indian trade, in the form of WAMPUM and the wampum belt, but it also continues to figure as a pervasive form of adornment among the Native Americans themselves. Shells, stone, deer hooves, animal teeth, bones, nuts, and seeds—all were used to create beautifully beaded designs. Native Americans also freely traded with whites for commercially manufactured beads to decorate clothing, saddlebags, weaponry, and other items.

A special class of Native American material artifact is the ledger drawing, which maintained the Native American tradition of storytelling through visual art, yet developed that form of expression on a medium resulting from contact with Anglo-Americans. In many tribes, momentous events, such as a hunt or battle, were memorialized by more-or-less schematic narrative drawings or paintings made on large animal skins. About 1860, Plains Indians, particularly the Sioux peoples, began using crayon and ink on paper in accountant's ledger books they purchased from white traders. Gradually, these ledger drawings supplanted works on animal hides, which had become scarce as Anglo-Americans hunted the BUFFALO to near-extinction. The small size of the ledgers limited the narrative scope of the art, so that, instead of depicting on a single sheet several scenes detailing a biography or a great battle, an entire book might be filled with individual scenes "told" in chronological order. Typically, too, ledger-book artists provided more distinguishing detail in the individual drawings. This, combined with the use of perspective, made the ledger drawings appealing to non–Native Americans, who sometimes purchased the books from the artists.

While, as a group, Native Americans today suffer disproportionate economic and social hardships, they also have developed a variety of cultural programs to foster and celebrate their heritage, and the literature on Indian folklore increases year by year.

See also: FOLKLORE IN AMERICAN LITERATURE; NOBLE SAVAGE; SITTING BULL.

SUGGESTED READING: Bertha P. Dutton, *Indians of the American Southwest* (Englewood Cliffs, N.J., 1975); Christian F. Feest, *Native Arts of North America* (London, 1992); Nancy Fox, *Pueblo Weaving and Textile Arts* (Santa Fe, N.M., 1978); Sam D. Gill, *Native American Religions: An Introduction* (Belmont, Calif., 1982); Robert Hofsinde (Gray-Wolf), *Indian Warriors and Their Weapons* (New York, 1965); A. J. Jaffe, *The First Immigrants from Asia: A Population History of the North American Indians* (New York, 1992); Thomas E. Mails, *Mystic Warriors of the Plains* (New York, 1991); William C. Orchard, *Beads and Beadwork of the American Indians* (New York, 1929); Frank W. Porter, III, ed., *The Art of Native American Basketry: A Living Legacy* (Westport, Conn., 1990); Joyce Szabo, *Howling Wolf and the History of Ledger Art* (Albuquerque, N.M., 1994); Marta Weigle and Peter White, *The Lore of New Mexico* (Albuquerque, N.M., 1988).

Needlework. A catchall term for all work done with needle and thread. Folklorists study ornamental work ("fancy work") as well as utilitarian work ("plain work"), although more early specimens of fancy work survive, since these were displayed rather than used and worn out. In colonial America and even well into the nineteenth century, needlework served as a creative, expressive outlet for women, who were typically debarred from such "masculine" pursuits as writing. Needlework also provided occasions for bonding among women (in the case of quilt making, for example) and for mothers to pass on treasured skills to daughters.

Among the earliest examples of American needlework is crewelwork, embroidery of a two-ply worsted wool yarn ("crewel") on linen. Colonial examples are generally copied from the English work the women knew. Crewelwork was decorative.

Canvaswork is embroidery of thin wool or silk yarn on a canvas background, typically with very small stitches used to create works of great detail and durability. Whereas crewelwork was used to create such items as bed drapery, canvaswork was sufficiently durable to serve as seat covers and fireplace screens. Decorative motifs resemble tapestries, with outdoor scenes among the most popular.

By the nineteenth century, girls no longer learned needlework exclusively from their mothers, but also acquired skill with a needle at girls' academies. The nineteenth century introduced the SAMPLER, a strictly decorative exhibition of a girl's repertoire of stitches. The sampler was an intermediate step along the way to mastering needlework. Beyond this, a girl graduated to silk-on-silk pictorial embroidery, which involved the rendering of scenes rather than the alphabets and designs of the sampler. A variety of motifs were popular, including mourning scenes, classical scenes, classical-pastoral scenes, and biblical scenes. Printwork is an advanced form of silk-on-silk pictorial embroidery, in which black and gray silk thread is worked on a white background to achieve the look of an engraved print.

Academic instruction in needlework was in full decline by final third of the nineteenth century. Nevertheless, the Victorian household, in the United States as well as England, continued to feature a variety of fancy work stitched decorative items, ranging from pillow covers to bookmarks to wall hangings.

In the middle of the nineteenth century, Berlin work—fine embroidery—enjoyed a vogue, but as the Victorian period yielded to the Edwardian, crazy work became popular. The most familiar form of crazy work is the crazy QUILT, which consists of irregularly shaped patches of variously colored and variously patterned cloth stitched together in fantastic patterns. In addition to the crazy quilt, crazy work was used for screens, for pillow covers, and for other decorative items. Creation of crazy work might be communal, girls or women passing the piece from one to another for the addition of a new patch. The mass appeal of needlework would begin to decline as the twentieth century neared. Increased educational and work opportunities for women took them away from the home in larger numbers. Technological advances such as the sewing machine made social calls with needlework in tow—a popular convention during the nineteenth century—impossible. Soon it ceased being a social activity. Affordable manufactured clothing and household linens also eliminated the need for women to make these items themselves.

SUGGESTED READING: Georgiana Brown Harbeson, *American Needlework: The History of Decorative Stitchery and Embroidery from the Late Sixteenth to the Twentieth Century* (New York, 1938); Susan Burrows Swan, *Plain and Fancy: American Women and Their Needlework, 1700–1850* (New York, 1977).

Ness, Eliot (1903–1957). This "G-man" (federal agent) became a popular cultural icon in his own time as head of a nine-man team of law officers whose incorruptibility during the thoroughly corrupt Prohibition era earned them the sobriquet "The Untouchables." Charged with enforcing Prohibition, The Untouchables' chief target was AL CAPONE and his Chicago gangland network. Later, Capone lieutenant Frank Nitty was the prime adversary. The name of Eliot Ness became permanently enshrined in the pop culture lexicon as a result of *The Untouchables* television series, which aired from 1959 to 1963, with Robert Stack as a steely-eyed, square-jawed Eliot Ness, and the distinctive machine-gun staccato voice of columnist WALTER WINCHELL narrating each episode. In 1987, the Ness story was again told, this time on the big screen, with Kevin Costner as Ness and Sean Connery as the tough Chicago Irish cop who shows him the ropes. Another Ness movie was released in 1998, starring Robert DeNiro and Connery.

The TV series was inspired by *The Untouchables: The Real Story,* a book on which Ness collaborated with ghostwriter Oscar Fraley (a UPI reporter). It was published in 1957, shortly after Ness's death, and contains much exaggeration and self-conscious legend making—almost certainly the work of Fraley.

Eliot Ness was a graduate of the University of Chicago, and was hired in 1929 as a special agent of the U.S. Department of Justice to head the Prohibition bureau in Chicago, primarily to investigate and harass Al Capone. The Untouchables staged well-publicized raids (reporters were invited along) on Chicago breweries and speakeasies. Despite this grandstanding, Ness's unit was effective in obtaining the financial evidence that secured Capone's conviction on charges of federal income tax evasion. Later in his career, Ness headed the alcohol-tax unit of the U.S. Department of the Treasury (1933–35), then served as director of public safety in Cleveland, Ohio (1935–41). During World War II (1941–45), he was director of the Division of Social Protection of the Federal Security Agency in Washington, D.C. He went into private-sector business after the war.

SUGGESTED READING: Eliot Ness, *The Untouchables: The Real Story* (1957; reprint ed., New York, 1993); Paul W. Heimel, *Eliot Ness: The Real Story* (New York, 1997).

Newell, William Wells (1839–1907).
Newell founded the AMERICAN FOLKLORE SOCIETY at Harvard University on January 4, 1888. Newell was a wealthy native of Cambridge, Massachusetts, who was educated at Harvard and at the Harvard Divinity School. When he came into his inheritance in 1883 after his father's death, he set up as an independent scholar, concentrating on folklore and publishing four books, *Games and Songs of American Children* (1883; reprint ed., 1963), the first systematic collection of children's folklore, and three books on Arthurian legend. After founding the American Folklore Society, Newell served as its secretary from 1888 to 1906 and as editor of the *Journal of American Folklore* from 1888 to 1899. Newell was determined that the society would adhere to

and promote high scholarly standards and, to this end, he secured the participation of such distinguished students of folklore and anthropology as FRANZ BOAS.

See also: GAMES.

SUGGESTED READING: Michael J. Bell, "William Wells Newell and the Foundation of American Folklore Scholarship," *Journal of the Folklore Institute* 10 (1973), pp. 7–21.

New Year.
Celebration of the passing of the old year and the beginning of the new are found in many cultures. In America, New Year's Eve is marked by parties, by the consumption of alcoholic beverages, and by the drinking of toasts, preferably with champagne. At the stroke of midnight, couples kiss, noise is made with various noisemakers, the celebrants wish one another a Happy New Year, and the group breaks into a

The traditional personification of the New Year: an infant.

chorus of "Auld Lang Syne," the traditional Scottish song by Robert Burns (1759–96). The origin of the noisemaking, most authorities believe, may be traced to ancient practices of making noise at the start of the year to frighten away malevolent spirits. Among Americans, especially urban Americans, New Year's Eve tends to evoke a need to celebrate en masse. In many cities, large groups congregate at some designated public space to count down the seconds as the clock approaches midnight. Television networks broadcast the usually massive assembly in New York's Times Square, where many thousands gather to celebrate and to watch a giant lighted ball descend from a mast atop the old *New York Times* building, coming to rest at the bottom precisely at midnight. Revelers nationwide typically participate in this observance by watching the broadcast together.

See also: CHRISTMAS; FATHER TIME.

John Jacob Niles singing to the accompaniment of his mountain dulcimer. The photo is from the late 1940s.

Niles, John Jacob (1892–1980). Niles was a folksinger, folklorist, and composer. He is best known as a collector of Appalachian BALLADS and as a composer of ballads (including the Christmas favorite "I Wonder as I Wander" and "Black Is the Color of My True Love's Hair") inspired by the ballads he collected. His books include *Songs My Mother Never Taught Me* (with Douglas Moore; 1929), *Songs of the Hill Folk* (1934), *The Shape Note Study Book* (1950), *The Ballad Book of John Jacob Niles* (1961), and a 1972 collection of Thomas Merton poems he set to music.

Niles was born into a musical family, which included a great-grandfather who was a composer, organist, and cello maker, and a mother who taught music theory, but it was while working as a surveyor in the Appalachians that Niles

found what would become his life's work. There he heard the ballads and folk songs of the mountains and, after flying with the U.S. Army Air Service during World War I, he studied in music conservatories in Cincinnati, Ohio, and Lyons, France, as well as at the famed Schola Cantorum of Paris. Niles worked during 1921 as the master of ceremonies at the Silver Slipper nightclub in New York, then teamed up with Marion Kerby to tour internationally as a folksinger, typically performing on lutes and Appalachian DULCIMERS he made himself.

From 1928 to 1933, Niles made four trips through the southern Appalachians with photographer Doris Ulmann, photographing performers and collecting their music. Niles also served briefly as music director of the John C. Campbell Folk School in Brasstown, North Carolina. During the 1930s, at the height of his popularity,

Niles gave some fifty concerts a year and recorded for RCA, FOLKWAYS RECORDS, and Tradition. He did not retire from the stage until 1978 and was always active in original composition, creating art songs inspired by folk traditions.

See also: FOLK MUSIC.

SUGGESTED READING: David F. Burg, "John Jacob Niles," *Kentucky Review* 2 (1980), pp. 3–10; John Jacob Niles, *The Ballad Book* (1960; reprint ed., New York, 1970).

Noble savage. More a literary concept than a folklore MOTIF, the idea of the noble savage nevertheless has influenced both folklore study and popular perceptions of "simple" or "primitive" people, including NATIVE AMERICANS. The noble savage is an idealization of uncivilized man as a kind of universal Adam symbolizing the innate goodness of one uncorrupted by civilization. The concept was crystallized in the works of Jean-Jacques Rousseau, primarily in his *Émile* (1762), *Confessions* (composed 1765–70), and *Reveries of a Solitary Walker* (composed 1776–78). Rousseau had drawn on the Greeks, including Homer, Pliny, and Xenophon, and the Romans, Horace, Virgil, and Ovid, for the basic concept, and examples of the noble savage can be found in a wide variety of literature, both before and after Rousseau. *American Adam: Innocence, Tragedy and Tradition in the Nineteenth Century* (1959), by literary historian Richard Lewis, was highly influential in translating the idea of the noble savage to the interpretation of nineteenth-century American literature and culture. However, long before Lewis's analysis, François-René de Chateaubriand had treated Native Americans as noble savages in his novels *Atala* (1801), *René*

(1802), and *Les Natchez* (1826), as did JAMES FENIMORE COOPER in the "Leatherstocking" cycle of novels (1823–41). Much of the nineteenth- and early twentieth-century interest in folklore, not only of Native Americans, but of all supposedly "simple" folk (such as Appalachian southerners), was motivated by ideas of the noble savage. Folklore was seen as survival of a culture before it was sophisticated by the corrupting forces of civilization.

See also: FUNK, MIKE; HILLBILLY FIGURE; MELVILLE, HERMAN.

SUGGESTED READING: Richard Lewis, *American Adam: Innocence, Tragedy and Tradition in the Nineteenth Century* (Chicago, 1959).

Nutmeg. Nutmeg is a spice made from the kernel of the fruit of trees of the genus *Myristica*. In folk medicine (see MEDICINE, FOLK.), nutmeg is used to cure a variety of ills. It may be brewed in a tea, taken in powdered form, or simply carried, depending on the locality and the malady. Connecticut was traditionally called the Nutmeg State (and, sometimes, its citizens Nutmegs) apparently because shrewd Yankee traders carved wooden nutmegs, painted them gold, and sold them as the true gilt nutmegs traditionally exchanged on Christmas in some parts of England.

See also: YANKEE TRADER OR TRICKSTER.

Nye, Pearl R. (1872–1950). Nye was a colorful captain of an Ohio Canal boat, who sang and composed traditional canal ballads, which JOHN LOMAX recorded in 1937. Nye was one of eighteen children in a family that was devoted both to song and to canal boating. Nye himself was born on a canal boat near Chillicothe, Ohio. Nye was well aware of the value of the song collection he had amassed, and during the early 1930s corresponded with archives and libraries about it. Lomax learned of Nye and his collection in 1936 and recorded thirty-three songs in June 1937, after which ALAN LOMAX recorded thirty-nine more in November of that year. Shortly after this, in a burst of creative energy, Nye wrote out hundreds of songs for the collections of the Library of Congress and, in 1938, performed at Philadelphia's Constitution Hall. In 1946, Ohio State University recorded more of his canal songs.

Toward the end of his life, Nye composed numerous original canal songs, including "The Old Canal," which catalogues every town, lock, store, and mill along the canal between Akron and the Ohio River.

See also: CANALS.

SUGGESTED READING: John A. Lomax, *Adventures of a Ballad Hunter* (New York, 1941).

O

Ocarina. Also called a sweet potato because of its oblong, globular shape, the ocarina is finger-stopped flute (with whistle mouthpiece) that may be made of earthenware, wood, gourd, or molded plastic. Ocarinalike flutes have been made and played in many cultures, probably beginning well before recorded history; however, the modern ocarina was developed in the mid-nineteenth century from traditional Italian earthenware carnival whistles. Popular as a folk instrument, the ocarina enjoyed a commercial renaissance in America during the 1930s when ocarinas of various sizes and pitch ranges were manufactured, allowing the formation of ocarina bands that could play in harmony.

See also: FOLK MUSIC.

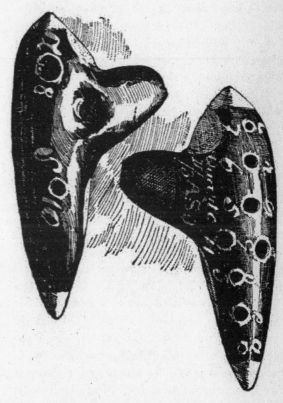

These ocarinas are made from terra-cotta.

Occupational folklore. The folklore of the workplace, including the FOLK SPEECH, songs, and traditional crafts and craft practices involved in various occupations. Some of the earliest collections of American occupational folklore focused on COWBOYS, LUMBERJACKS, farmers and other agricultural workers, fishermen (see FISHING LORE), miners (see MINING FOLKLORE), and sailors (see SAILORS AND SEAFARING LORE). More recently, folklorists have turned their attention to a wider variety of occupations, including many urban industrial occupations and even the world of white-collar office worker and professional (especially lawyers and medical professionals).

The boom folklore collecting enjoyed during the Depression of the 1930s, when the WPA's Federal Writers' Project funded widespread collection efforts, was especially strong in the area of occupational folklore, with emphasis on the industrial and urban sectors. Also beginning in the 1930s, folklorists extensively collected labor-related folklore, especially protest songs.

See also: BOTKIN, BENJAMIN A.; COLLEGE FOLKLORE; GREENWAY, JOHN; HAND, WAYLAND D.; LUMBERJACK FOLKLORE; MELVILLE, HER-

MAN; MILITARY FOLKLORE; OLD JOHN; RAIL-
ROAD FOLKLORE; SLAPPY HOOPER; WHALING;
WORK SONGS.

SUGGESTED READING: Mody Boatright, *Folklore of the Oil Industry* (Dallas, 1963); R. Serge Denisoff, *Great Day Coming* (Urbana, Ill., 1971); Archie Green, *Wobblies, Pile Butts, and Other Heroes: Labor-Lore Explorations* (Urbana, Ill., 1993); Richard Reuss, *Songs of American Labor, Industrialization, and the Urban Work Experience: A Discography* (Ann Arbor, Mich, 1983); Jack Santino, *Miles of Smiles, Years of Struggle: Stories of Black Pullman Porters* (Urbana, Ill., 1989).

Odum, Howard Washington (1884–1954).

Sociologist Howard Odum was an important collector of southern African-American folk songs. In 1920, Odum became the first chairman of the Sociology Department at the University of North Carolina, and his *Southern Regions of the United States* (1936) is considered a classic of American sociology. Odum's interest in African-American folk songs came early in his career, while he was studying for his master's degree at the University of Mississippi. He earned two doctorates, in psychology (Clark University, 1909) and sociology (Columbia University, 1910), and his Ph.D. dissertation in psychology was based on songs he had collected in Mississippi. Indeed, throughout his career, Odum held that folklore study was essential to understanding African-American culture and, ultimately, to improving race relations in the troubled South. With GUY BENTON JOHNSON, he wrote two books on folk songs as the products of and index to culture. Odum also wrote three novels based on the repertoire of one of his African-American informants.

SUGGESTED READING: Wayne Douglas Brazil, *Howard W. Odum: The Building Years, 1884–1930* (Cambridge, Mass., 1975); Guy Benton Johnson and Howard Washington Odum, *The Negro and His Songs: A Study of Typical Songs in the South* (Chapel Hill, N.C., 1925); Guy Benton Johnson and Howard Washington Odum, *Negro Workaday Songs* (Chapel Hill, N.C., 1926).

Ohrlin, Glenn (1926–).

Orhlin is a singer of traditional cowboy songs. Although raised in Minneapolis, Ohrlin early on developed a love of horses and horsemanship and soon after his family moved to California in 1940, Ohrlin became a cowboy in Nevada. In 1943, he began a rodeo riding career, which endured into the 1960s.

Ohrlin's early musical training came from his musically talented family, and, during military service in World War II, he learned flamenco guitar from a Mexican-American G.I. This gave Ohrlin a perspective on the Spanish traditions of much cowboy music. After the war, Ohrlin resumed his rodeo career and also performed for informal cowboy audiences. It was not until 1963, when he met folklorist Archie Green, that he became known to a wider audience, during the heyday of the folk music revival. Orhlin recorded widely and also collected a hundred cowboy songs in his *The Hell-Bound Train: A Cowboy Songbook* (1973).

O'Kelley, Mattie Lou (1908–).

Like GRANDMA MOSES, Mattie Lou O'Kelley is a memory painter. Her works are idyllic landscapes reflecting her childhood in rural northwest

Georgia. The landscapes are populated with an array of colorful people and animals in bucolic settings that emphasize the fruitfulness of nature. Her works are typically highly detailed and are often as large as three by four feet.

While O'Kelley's memory paintings are idealized and romanticized visions, she did grow up on a Georgia farm, until the death of her father in 1943 sent her packing to the town of Maysville, Georgia, where she struggled to earn a living as seamstress, waitress, and factory worker. It was after her retirement in 1968 that she began painting. Her work was exhibited in the gift shop of Atlanta's High Museum of Art in 1974 and came to the attention of Robert Bishop, director of the Museum of American Folk Art in New York City. He connected her with a New York gallery, and her paintings were immediately in demand.

See also: MEMORY PAINTING.

"Old Dan Tucker." Composed about 1830 or 1831 by DANIEL DECATUR EMMETT for his MINSTREL SHOWS, "Old Dan Tucker" may have been based on a folk song Emmett's mother had taught him. The Old Dan Tucker character partakes of the frontier TALL TALE tradition: Dan combs his hair with a wagon wheel and dies of toothache—in his heel. Long after the demise of the minstrel shows, the song remained a favorite SQUARE DANCE tune and is often played by BANJO pickers and fiddlers.

See also: FOLK MUSIC; PLAY PARTY.

Old John. A character from American OCCUPATIONAL FOLKLORE, Old John was a tramp printer or, more precisely, typesetter (compositor). An itinerant, Old John was said to hire on at a paper, work for a time, then quit. He would finish his last job with a sweep of his hand, whereby the types would magically fall into place. Printers said that Old John and his like were sent to compositor's heaven when they died, a pristine print shop with all new type.

"Old Smoky." A popular folk song of lost love, "Old Smoky" is an amalgam of elements from a number of other folk songs, including "The Wagoner's Lad," "Courting Too Slow," "Loving Nancy," "The Forsaken Girl," "The Inconstant Lover," among others. It shares its tune with "The Little Mohee."

See also: FOLK MUSIC.

Opossum. The only marsupial native to the Americas, the odd-looking opossum (pronounced and often spelled *possum*) has given rise to a number of folk beliefs. Its distinctive habit of "playing dead" when confronted by a predator meshes with a well-established folktale motif and has also inspired the expression "playing possum"—a well-known piece of FOLK-SAY. Opossum characters are found in Native American, African American, and southern white American folktales. Its long, hairless, prehensile tail has inspired origin stories in Cherokee lore as well as in the folklore of southern blacks. The Cherokee story says that the opossum originally had a furry white tail, wanted a brown one, and was tricked by a raccoon into browning it in a fire; the result was the opossum's characteristic hairless tail.

The Opossum Didelphis virginiana, as illustrated in Chambers' Encyclopedia, 1875.

The African-American story depicts the opossum as an accomplice of the FOX and the rabbit, stealing corn from a field adjacent to a graveyard. A ghost appears, catches the opossum by the tail, and, although the creature escapes the ghost, he skins his tale in the process.

The opossum has also inspired a number of folk beliefs, the most common of which is a belief that the male opossum copulates into the snout of the female, who then blows the semen into her marsupial pouch, where the young are conceived and gestate.

Ouija board. According to the current owners of the patent for the Ouija board, Parker Brothers, Inc., Ouija is nothing more or less than a board game. For many, however, it is a serious tool of divination, akin to such practices as DOWSING, Tarot reading, and crystal gazing. The Ouija board was invented in 1892 by an American named Elijah J. Bond, who combined the French and German words for *yes* to get the name of his product. He sold his patent to William Fuld, whose company manufactured Ouija boards for many years before selling the patent to Parker Brothers in 1966.

Ouija apparatus consists of two items: a hand-sized table, often called a planchette, with a miniature window in the top, and a board printed with the letters of the alphabet, the numbers zero through nine, and the words *yes* and *no*. Players lightly place their fingers on the planchette, which moves around the board, spelling out messages. It seems as if the planchette has a will of its own and is not moved by the players' fingers.

The Ouija board enjoyed popularity from the beginning, but became even more popular—and the subject of some controversy—after the celebrated spiritualist Pearl Curran began using it during the 1910s and 1920s. Scientists protested that there was nothing magical or mystical about the apparatus, and religious fundamentalists decried it as a tool of Satan. For the majority of Americans, Ouija remained a popular parlor amusement and is still enjoyed today.

SUGGESTED READING: Gina Covina, *The Ouija Book* (New York, 1979).

Outsider art. A term that achieved currency beginning in the 1980s and that is generally applied to works by artists outside of the mainstream (in the U.S., this is defined in large part by residency in New York City), *outsider art* is sometimes used as a synonym for modern FOLK ART.

See also: WOODCARVING.

Owen, Mary Alicia (1850–1935). Owen collected folktales principally among African Americans and Native Americans in Missouri. She was the author of *Old Rabbit the Voodoo and Other Sorcerers* (1893; reprint ed., 1969), a collection of African-American folktales, and *Folk-Lore of the Musquakie Indians of North America and Catalog of Musquakie Beadwork and other Objects in the Collection of the Folk-Lore Society [of England]* (1904).

Owen was active in the Folk-Lore Society of England and the American Folklore Society and was a charter member of the Missouri Folk-Lore Society (1906), serving as president of the organization from 1908 to 1935.

See also: BELDEN, HENRY MARVIN.

SUGGESTED READING: Mary Elizabeth Alleorn, "Mary Alicia Owen: Missouri Folklorist," *Missouri Folklore Society Journal* 8–9 (1986), pp. 71–78; William K. McNeil, "Mary Alicia Owen: Collector of Afro-American and Indian Lore in Missouri, *Missouri Folklore Society Journal* 2 (1980), pp. 1–14.

P

Parler, Mary Celestia (1905–1981). Parler was a collector of Ozark folklore and a professor at the University of Arkansas. She actively collaborated with her husband, Ozark folklorist Vance Randolph. Born in South Carolina, Parler earned an M.A. in English at the University of Wisconsin (1925) and completed all Ph.D. requirements except for her dissertation there as well. She joined the University of Arkansas faculty in 1948. She was one of the founders of the Arkansas Folklore Society (1950) and was the editor of *Arkansas Folklore*. She also undertook a great deal of fieldwork in the state and, after 1950, contributed to the publications of Vance Randolph.

Parlor ballad. With the CHILD BALLAD, the BLUES BALLAD, and the BROADSIDE, the parlor ballad is one the four types of Ango-American BALLADS folklorists recognize. The parlor ballad is also called the sentimental ballad and was popular in the late nineteenth century. Generally performed in a genteel domestic setting (hence the name), parlor ballads were often sung from sheet music and were popularized by professional entertainers on stage. In contrast to the other ballad types, the typical parlor ballad is not of anonymous origin—the composer is usually known and credited—and the sentiments conveyed in the narrative lyrics tend to be conventional and solidly middle class, even pious, often moralizing in spirit and tone. The motive behind most parlor ballads is moral uplift.

See also: ANGLO AMERICANS; COWBOY SONGS; FOLK MUSIC; FOSTER, STEPHEN; HAYS, WILL; MACON, DAVE (UNCLE DAVE); REVIVAL SONGS.

Parry, Milman (1902–1935). Parry is best known for the work he did with ALBERT BATES LORD in creating the oral-formulaic theory, also known as the Parry-Lord Theory. Seeking to prove that Homeric epics were the product of centuries-old oral traditions rather than the work of a single author, Parry undertook field study among the preliterate epic singers, the *guslari,* of the former Yugoslavia, in the belief that these folk artists were analogous to the epic singers of ancient Greece. Parry concentrated on a range of formulaic phrases found in epic poetry, concluding that these were, in fact, a kind of specialized language, inherited as part of a heroic oral tradition, and that, furthermore, such formulas were essential to oral composition.

The work of Parry and Lord provided a valuable tool for the comparative analysis of oral traditions, both current as well as ancient.

SUGGESTED READING: Milman Parry, *The Making of Homeric Verse: The Collected Papers of Milman Parry* (Oxford, Eng., 1971).

Parsons, Elsie Clews (1875–1941). Parsons was a prolific folklorist, specializing in African-American folklore and the folklore of the Pueblo Indians of the American Southwest. She was trained as sociologist (Ph.D., Columbia University, 1899), but began working in the related fields of anthropology and folklore about 1912. Her fieldwork took her to the Southwest, the Caribbean, Nova Scotia, the East coast, and the southern United States. Beginning in 1915, she worked closely with Franz Boas. Parson's later fieldwork took her to Mexico (1930) and Ecuador (1945), but she also traveled to Spain (1923) and to Egypt and Sudan (1926) in search of the origins of certain African-American folktales.

Parsons published numerous collections of folklore, as well as a book on Pueblo Indian religion (1939), and was president of the American Folklore Society (1919), president of the American Ethnological Society (1923–25), and president of the American Anthropological Association (1941).

SUGGESTED READING: Rosemary Levy Zumwalt, *Wealth and Rebellion: Elsie Clews Parsons, Anthropologist and Folklorist* (Urbana, Ill., 1992).

here, he toured New Orleans, Memphis, St. Louis, Chicago, and elsewhere.

Patton, whose racial heritage was part Native American, part white, and part African American, was a flamboyant individual who married eight times or more. He was celebrated for his magnetic personality and his ability to have a very good time all of the time, but most of all he was highly regarded for his musical talent. He recorded in 1929, 1930, and, shortly before his death, in 1934, fifty-six sides in all, mostly blues, but also African-American folk songs, including ten spirituals (Patton was a part-time preacher).

While his life was short and his recording career brief, Patton was the most influential of the Delta blues artists and was looked to as a role model by aspiring performers. His recordings were also influential on later ROCK 'N' ROLL musicians.

See also: JOHNSON, ROBERT.

SUGGESTED READING: Stephen Calt and Gayle Wardlow, *King of the Delta Blues: The Life and Music of Charley Patton* (Newton, N.J., 1988); Lawrence Cohn, *Nothing but the Blues: The Music and the Musicians* (New York, 1993); John Fahey, *Charley Patton* (London, 1970).

Patton, Charley (1891–1934). A Delta BLUES singer and guitarist who was born in the Mississippi hills, Charley Patton was raised on the Dockery Plantation, near Cleveland, Mississippi, where his father had settled to farm. Dockery's boasted an array of sharecropping families with extraordinary musical talent. It was, in effect, the seedbed of much Delta blues, and Patton, who had already learned the basics of guitar, honed his licks there. By about 1910, he began performing locally, and, within a decade, he was renowned throughout the Delta. From

Patton, George Smith (1885–1945). Except for GEORGE ARMSTRONG CUSTER, perhaps no American military figure has figured more vividly as popular cultural icon than George Patton. In part, this is the result of George C. Scott's powerful portrayal of the World War II commander in the 1970 film *Patton,* directed by Franklin Schaffner and written by Francis Ford Coppola and Edmund H. North. Scott, a bigger-than-life actor, played Patton as a bigger-than-life figure, which, in fact, he was. However, Patton was a folk hero—or, perhaps, folk anti-hero—long be-

General George S. Patton with the four stars of a general, 1945, and years earlier, before the outbreak of World War II, in the green uniform and gold football helmet he designed for use by tank corpsmen. The press mocked the uniform, calling Patton "The Green Hornet," and the design was rejected by the army.

fore the appearance of the film. During WORLD WAR II, his brilliant victories over German general Erwin Rommel in North Africa, his lightning invasion of Sicily, his epoch-making drive from Normandy across France, and his relief of Bastogne during the Battle of the Bulge would be enough to make a national hero of any man. But Patton was possessed of a compulsively outspoken, intolerant, poetic, vulgar, and brutal temperament that made headlines as big as his victories. If those victories entered into history, it was the notorious "slapping incident" that entered even more forcefully into the popular image of Patton. On the August 3, 1943, while visiting wounded soldiers in a field hospital in Sicily, Pat-

ton encountered a private suffering from battle fatigue. Patton accused the man of cowardice and slapped him in the face. On August 10, he threatened another victim of battle fatigue with execution, unholstering his revolver and waving it in front of the soldier's face. (That revolver was in itself legendary. It had an ivory handle, and when a reporter referred to it as pearl-handled, Patton indignantly corrected him, pointing out that pearl-handled guns were for New Orleans pimps.) The public and Patton's superiors were scandalized by the two incidents (which, in the reporting, were usually telescoped into one), and Patton was sent to England in disgrace on January 22, 1944. He returned to fully active duty only after the D-Day landings and the general Allied invasion of France.

The slapping incident was part of the picture of a courageous, wily, but brutal commander, whose nickname was "Blood and Guts." The origin of the sobriquet is obscure, but the press loved it (Patton hated it), and it stuck.

Patton was born in San Gabriel, California, the son of a family with a strong military tradition. Patton was educated at Virginia Military Institute (1904) and at West Point, graduating in 1909 after a difficult four years. A superb horseman, Patton was commissioned a 2d lieutenant in the cavalry and represented the army on the U.S. pentathlon team at the 1912 Stockholm Olympics. An expert swordsman, Patton wrote the army's saber manual. In 1916, Patton served under Gen. John J. Pershing in pursuit of Pancho Villa, then was appointed to Pershing's staff during World War I.

Patton was the first American officer to receive tank training and became an enthusiastic convert to the potential of mechanized warfare.

After a distinguished record in World War I, Patton rose steadily through the ranks of the interwar army and, shortly after U.S. entry into World War II, was named commander of I Armored Corps. He was instrumental in the conquest of North Africa, but a dispute with his British colleagues prompted his temporary relief from command. Patton's arrogance and ungovernable bluntness would plague him throughout the war. Friction with Allies, the press, and with his superiors became legendary not only within the army, but with the public at large.

Following Patton's spectacular advance across Europe and his heroic relief of Bastogne during the Battle of the Bulge, his Third Army crossed the Rhine at Oppenheim on March 22, 1945. But with the war in Europe won, the indiscreet expression of political opinions once again got Patton into deep trouble. He outspokenly criticized the Soviet allies and, even worse, as military governor of Bavaria, opposed de-Nazification policies because (he said) they left the conquered territories without qualified officials to maintain order. Yielding to public and diplomatic pressure, the Allies removed Patton from command of the Third Army and from the governorship of Bavaria. Patton had an "usoldierly death," the victim of an otherwise trivial automobile accident near Mannheim, Germany, on December 9, 1945. He died from his injuries on December 21.

SUGGESTED READING: Carlo d'Este, *Patton: A Genius for War* (New York, 1995).

Paulding, James Kirke (1778–1860). The literary reputation of James Kirke Paulding is justly overshadowed by that of his friend WASHINGTON IRVING, with whom he founded *Salmagundi* (1807–8), a literary periodical. Like Irving, Paulding was concerned with creating an original or indigenous American literature, distinct from that of England and the rest of Europe. To this end, he explored and exploited, with mixed success, "native" American subjects, many drawn from folk stereotypes. His *Diverting History of John Bull and Brother Jonathan* (1812), written during the War of 1812, satirizes English attitudes and manners by contrasting them with those of the stereotypical Yankee, BROTHER JONATHAN. His 1,600-line epic poem *The Backwoodsman* (1818), is rich with frontier stereotypes, though its appeal to a modern audience is considerably dimmed by its uninspired use of heroic couplets. In the novel *Koningsmarke, the Long Finne: A Story of the New World* (1823), Paulding paints a vivid picture of life in the Swedish colonies of Delaware, and two other novels, *Westward Ho!* (1832) and *The Old Con-*

tinental, or, the Price of Liberty (1846), are also notable as early efforts to portray the fabric of American life in American fiction. More effective are the short stories of *The Dutchmen's Fireside* (1831), which contains sketches of Dutch life in early New York. Paulding's play, *The Lion of the West* (1831), is the first instance of frontier humor presented onstage, in the person of a character strikingly similar to DAVY CROCKETT.

Like most authors of the early American republic, Paulding was a part-time writer. He was involved in the government of New York and later served as secretary of the navy.

SUGGESTED READING: James G. Wilson, "James K. Paulding," *Bryant and His Friends* (New York, 1886).

Paw Paw Patch. A pantomime-dance-song PLAY PARTY activity. Dancers line up in couples and sing "Where, oh where is sweet little [name of a woman present]?" She, the named woman, dances around the dancers, and, as the male dancers sing "Come on, boys, let's find her," the male dancers dance around the women's line. Next, to the lyrics "Pickin' up Paw Paws, puttin' 'em in her pocket . . . way down yonder in the Paw Paw Patch," all of dancers mime the action of picking the fruit of the paw paw (or papaw) tree. At the end of the song, the head couple slides down between the two lines of dancers to the end of the line.

Payne, Leslie (ca. 1907–1981). An African-American folk artist, Leslie Payne was born in rural Virginia on the Chesapeake Bay's Northern Neck. Formally educated through the fourth grade, he worked as a fisherman and crabber and may have also worked for a time in a New Jersey junkyard. Payne had become fascinated with airplanes since he attended an air show in 1918. Beginning about 1947, he started building large metal replicas of World War I–vintage aircraft and of CHARLES LINDBERGH's *Spirit of St. Louis*. At least one of his aircraft was equipped with an engine, but failed to fly (though it was apparently drivable on the highway!). Payne's engagement with his airplanes went beyond their creation; he embarked on imaginary flights in the craft—journeys he dutifully recorded in a logbook.

While Payne's most spectacular works are the large airplane replicas, he was also a sculptor who worked on a smaller scale with painted wood and metal. He created model fishing vessels, fishing-related tableaus, and one-dimensional figure works depicting such subjects as a pair of World War I doughboys (*Two Soldiers*) and *Hitler,* both from the 1970s. Payne's work was known only locally until it was exhibited at the Corcoran Gallery of Art, Washington, D.C., in 1982.

SUGGESTED READING: Jane Livingston and John Beardsley, *Black Folk Art in America: 1930–1980* (Jackson, Miss., 1982).

Peace pipe. See CALUMET.

Pecos Bill. Pecos Bill is a fictitious cowboy hero with superhuman abilities. While Bill resembles the kind of folk hero often created in the oral tradition, he is actually the creation of a journalist, Edward O'Reilly, writing in a 1923 *Century*

A 1945 book illustration by Everett G. Jackson of Pecos Bill wrestling a rattler and a cougar.

Magazine article. The folklorist MODY BOATRIGHT elaborated on Bill's adventures in his *Tall Tales from Texas Cow Camps* of 1934. Although Boatright explicitly credited O'Reilly as his source, Bill's appearance in his book was evidence of—even as it bolstered—the perception of Pecos Bill as a famous figure of folklore. The character appeared in many subsequent stories, including a number written for children. His character appeared in *Melody Time*, a 1948 WALT DISNEY film, and his image was featured on the back of a Kellogg's Cocoa Krispies cereal box.

Pecos Bill is the Texas cowboy–as–SUPERMAN. Like another well-known "invented" folk hero, PAUL BUNYAN, he is the embodiment of superlatives: strongest, meanest, greatest. Attributed to him is the *invention* of calf roping, the practice of branding, and the six-shooter. He could ride any horse, but he also rode a panther, and not just any panther, but one that weighed as much as three steers—and a yearling. He managed the animal by using a convenient rattlesnake as a quirt. Pecos Bill was fond of riding cyclones, while rolling a cigarette with one hand, and when drought hit, it was he who excavated the Rio Grande to bring water up from the Gulf of Mexico to the Pecos.

SUGGESTED READING: Mody Boatright, *Tall Tales from Texas Cow Camps* (Dallas, 1934); Benjamin A. Botkin, "The Saga of Pecos Bill," *A Treasury of American Folklore* (New York, 1944).

Peer, Ralph Sylvester (1892–1960).

Ralph Peer may be the closest thing to a "father" that commercially recorded blues and COUNTRY MUSIC have. He was born in Kansas City, Missouri, and went to work for the Columbia Phonograph Company as soon as he graduated from high school. He left Columbia in 1918 to became director of recordings (an "A & R man") for the new, and diminutive, Okeh label. Peer was uniquely open to new markets, and, in 1920, commissioned a recording of Mamie Smith, an African-American singer who commanded a small but loyal following in Harlem. The success of her "Crazy Blues" encouraged Peer to record more African-American music and, then, to find music that would appeal to other "minorities" who were unserved by the commercial recording industry. In 1923, Peer launched the first of his regional expeditions in search of local talent with commercial recording potential. He discovered FIDDLIN' JOHN CARSON in Atlanta, then, over the years, recorded many hillbilly musicians, black musicians, and other performers in the rural South, including, most famously, the CARTER FAMILY and JIMMIE RODGERS. Later, Peer began recording Latin American music and may be considered the pioneer in introducing this ethnic music to a broader audience.

SUGGESTED READING: Country Music Foundation, *Country: The Music and the Musicians* (New York, 1992).

Penitentes. Los Penitentes or Los Hermanos Penitentes (The Brotherhood of the Penitents) are a lay brotherhood of Christian flagellants in the Southwest. Inspired by Franciscan missionaries during the Spanish colonial period, but little supervised by the clergy, these Native Americans developed their own liturgy and ceremonies, which included extreme penances such as flagellation during Lent (in order to achieve mystical union with Christ) and, on occasion, even hanging a penitent from a cross on Good Friday until pain and exhaustion induced a loss of consciousness. The Penitentes also conducted charitable works, including minstering to the sick and indigent. Although flagellation is neither new nor unusual in the spectrum of Christian practice, the Penitentes attracted much attention from travelers.

Members of the Penitentes are divided into two classes: "*La Luz,*" the Light, which consists of the *Hermano Mayor* (Chief Brother) and other titled individuals, and "*De las Tinieblas,*" Of the Darkness, consisting of common brothers. Meetings are held in the "*morada,*" or private meeting

hall, and public processions take place every Friday during Lent and on the last three days of Holy Week. Methods of public flagellation include scourging with rough pads or prickly pear cactus, rubbing the skin with flint to draw blood, and actually lashing the flesh.

Officially, the Catholic Church considered the Penitentes practitioners of "criminal extravagances," and the archbishop responsible for New Mexico caused the excommunication of entire *moradas* during the mid-nineteenth century. Still, the Penitentes survived, flourished, and exist to this day. Rumors about the Penitentes have circulated for centuries. No outsider has witnessed Penitente crucifixions, and there have been periodic accusations of violence against those who have opposed Penitente practices.

Suggested Readings: Arthur L. Campa, *Hispanic Culture in the Southwest* (Norman, Okla., 1979); Marra Weigle, *Brothers of Light, Brothers of Blood: The Penitentes of the Southwest* (Albuquerque, N.M, 1976).

Pennsylvania Germans. For many years, the Pennsylvania Germans were better known as Pennsylvania Dutch, though they immigrated to Pennsylvania from Germany and not the Netherlands. "Dutch" was a term most non–German Americans applied to Germans, probably because the Germans referred to themselves as *Deutsch*. The Pennsylvania Germans settled during the seventeenth and eighteenth centuries primarily in Lehigh, Berks, Lebanon, Lancaster, and York counties, where many of their descendants continue to live. The Pennsylvania Germans were originally distinguished, first and foremost, by the "Pennsylvania Dutch" German dialect (*Pennsylfawnish Deitsch*) they spoke, but they retained their cultural separateness long

Decorated Pennsylvania-German wedding chests are coveted by collectors, but are out of the reach of all but a few museums. This is an eighteenth-century example from Lancaster county, Pennsylvania.

after the dialect fell into disuse. This was the result of distinctive FOODWAYS (Pennsylvania cooking includes, shoofly pie, scrapple, funnel cakes, *fastnacht cakes* [fried doughnuts], and so on), distinctive decorative motifs (including HEX signs on barns and characteristic floral stenciling on furniture and housewares), and *FRAKTUR* illumination of legal and family documents. Folklorists are also especially interested in Pennsylvania German VERNACULAR ARCHITECTURE, which includes distinctive styles of farmhouse and barn.

While Pennsylvania German furniture and housewares, whether as antiques or reproductions, continue to be highly valued, and scrapple, funnel cakes, and other Pennsylvania German foods continue to be enjoyed, and hex signs are still painted on many Pennsylvania barns, most Pennsylvania Germans are now thoroughly assimilated into mainstream American culture. The exception to this are certain Pennsylvania German religious groups, most notably the Amish, whose plain, old-fashioned dress, horse-drawn buggies, and quasi-communal lifestyle sets them apart.

See also: CRAFTS, AMERICAN FOLK; DUTCH AMERICANS; GERMAN AMERICANS; IMMIGRANT FOLKLORE; REGIONAL FOLKLORE.

An example of a traditional Pennsylvania-German stencil motif. Such patterns were used to apply decorations to a wide variety of furnishings.

SUGGESTED READING: Thomas R. Brendle and William S. Troxell, *Pennsylvania German Folk Tales, Legends, Once-upon-a-Time Stories, Maxims, and Sayings* (Norristown, Pa., 1944); Thomas R. Brendle and Claude W. Unger, *Folk Medicine of the Pennsylvania Germans: The Non-Occult Cures* (1935; reprint ed., New York, 1970); Albert F. Buffington, *Pennsylvania German Secular Folksongs* (Breinigsville, Pa., 1974); Robert F. Ensminger, *The Pennsylvania Barn: Its Origin, Evolution, and Distribution in North America* (Baltimore, 1992); Edwin M. Fogel, *Beliefs and Superstitions of the Pennsylvania Germans* (Philadelphia,

1915); Scott Swank et al., *Arts of the Pennsylvania Germans* (New York, 1983); Don Yoder and Thomas E. Grave, *Hex Signs: Pennsylvania Dutch Barn Symbols and Their Meaning* (New York, 1989).

Peyote. Peyote is a cactus plant that is also known as mescal or mescal button. Native to the Southwest, especially Mexico, it has been and is still used by Native Americans as part of religious ceremonies. Ingestion of peyote produces hallucinogenic effects, which some Native Americans believe are expressions of a tutelary spirit, who provides knowledge of the spirit world. Peyote became widely known to non–Native Americans during the wave of interest in "mind-altering" drugs in the 1960s.

Pilgrims and Puritans. Puritans were members of a sixteenth- and seventeenth-century religious reform movement that sought to "purify" the Church of England, purging from it elements of Roman Catholicism. Persecuted in England before and after the Civil Wars of the seventeenth century, a small group of Puritans (called Separatists) fled first to Holland and then to America. The first group to set sail for America were called Pilgrims, a name applied to them by William Bradford, one of their early leaders and their earliest historian. The Pilgrims settled at a place they called Plymouth, in present-day Massachusetts, having landed on November 21, 1620 (though tradition fixes this date as December 26). Only the first contingent of Separatist Puritans are properly called Pilgrims, though the term is often applied indiscriminately to any of New England's early colonists.

A 1920 ad for "Pilgrim Pictures" to decorate the home.

Folklore relating to the Pilgrims and Puritans developed primarily during the nineteenth century, in part as a nativist or xenophobic reaction to the influx of immigrants throughout the latter half of the century. Tradition holds that the Pilgrims landed on "Plymouth Rock," which was first identified in 1741 and was first celebrated as a symbol of freedom in 1774, after it was fractured when it was hauled to the town of Plymouth's "Liberty Pole Square." In 1889, Plymouth Rock was returned to what is believed to be its original waterfront site, and a granite portico was erected over it. It is inscribed with the year 1620.

Throughout the nineteenth and early twenti-

In 1644 the first American "public school" was established at Dedham, Massachusetts.

eth centuries, the Puritan or Pilgrim "fathers" were held up as exemplars of courage, justice, faith, and hard work. As the twentieth century unfolded, however, many progressive writers (such as Van Wyck Brooks, H. L. MENCKEN, and William Carlos Williams) painted Puritanism in much less flattering colors, seeing in it the roots of meanness and intolerance rather than admirable achievement. Nevertheless, while intellectuals might question and even reject the Puritan "fathers," generations of American schoolchildren were exposed to the folkloric images of the Pilgrims and Puritans that first appeared in the nineteenth century. Schoolchildren heard the story of the "first THANKSGIVING," they read HENRY WADSWORTH LONGFELLOW's "Courtship of Miles Standish," they learned about the Puritans' willingness to make sacrifices to achieve and protect their religious freedom, and they also formed an image of Pilgrims as men and women in severe black clothes with broad white collars; the women wore plain bonnets, while the men wore stiff, high-crowned hats with broad brims and wide, buckled hatbands. The

Pilgrims and Puritans were taken as "pure" examples of America at its "purest," and they figured as the stern, unsmiling, and inflexible yardstick against which all subsequent Americans were to be measured.

See also: ANGLO AMERICANS; CAJUNS; QUAKERS.

SUGGESTED READING: Alan Axelrod, ed., *The Colonial Revival in America* (New York, 1985); Van Wyck Brooks, *The Wine of the Puritans* (1908), reprinted in Claire Sprague, ed., *Van Wyck Brooks: The Early Years* (New York, 1968).

Pippin, Horace (1888–1946). Pippin became one of the best-known African-American painters of the twentieth century. He painted with a social consciousness, often exploring themes of social and political injustice. He also created landscapes, portrayed biblical subjects, and painted interiors reflecting turn-of-the-

The Holy Mountain *(Oil on canvas, 1944), by Horace Pippin.*

Shell Holes and Observation Balloon, Champagne Sector *(Oil on canvas, 1938), by Horace Pippin.*

century African-American home life. His palette is distinctive. Characteristically, Pippin contrasted broad areas of muted, somber colors with vivid concentrations of bright color. The result was paintings of powerful, moving atmosphere. In addition to oils on canvas, Pippin experimented with pyrography, using a white-hot poker to burn lines into wood, then sometimes adding painted detail to these works.

Pippin was raised in poverty and dropped out of high school in 1903 to help support his widowed mother. Pippin worked as a hotel porter and a warehouseman, as well as in a factory. He served in the army during World War I, was severely wounded in France (an injury that permanently crippled his right arm), and was decorated with the French croix de guerre. It was not until 1945 that the U.S. government finally awarded him a Purple Heart. His war experience transformed Pippin. He returned to his hometown of West Chester, Pennsylvania, where, having learned to support his injured arm so that he could work, he labored obsessively over a small number of canvases while his wife took in laundry to help make ends meet. Pippin studied

Horace Pippin, late 1930s or early 1940s.

briefly at the Barnes Foundation in Philadelphia, but he made the conscious decision to pursue his own vision rather than follow academic traditions. In 1937, more than fifteen years after he had started painting seriously, Pippin entered two works in the West Chester County Art Association's annual invitational show. His work was hailed, and he was immediately given a one-man show. In 1938, he was included in "Masters of Popular Painting" at the Museum of Modern Art in New York, and the Robert Carlen Galleries of Philadelphia became his dealer in 1939. For the remainder of his life, Pippin enjoyed significant creative and financial success. His posthumous reputation became even greater. Pippin's relatively small oeuvre of little more than twenty paintings is included in important museum and private collections.

SUGGESTED READING: Mary E. Lyons, *Starting Home: The Story of Horace Pippin* (New York, 1993); Selden Rodman, *Horace Pippin: The Artist as a Black American* (Garden City, N.Y., 1972).

Plants and plant lore. The folklore associated with plants is rich, encompassing beliefs and practices relating to care and use (including use in folk medicine), as well as interpretation; some plants, for example, bring or betoken good fortune. With regard to edible plants, folk beliefs tend to relate to perceived health benefits or liabilities. Many groups, for example, value dandelion greens as a general tonic (not too many years ago, the sight of elderly Italian women picking dandelions along urban expressways and streets was common), while, until recently, it was widely believed that raw fruit was unhealthy for children, and until the 1840s, many believed tomatoes to be downright poisonous. Of course, the lore devoted to the medicinal use of plants is extensive, and modern medicine, which once scorned traditional herbal remedies, is increasingly researching the folklore relating to medicinal plants.

Planting customs and rituals have traditionally been important. Many American farmers believed that potatoes had to be planted by SAINT PATRICK'S DAY and peas by Good Friday. Planting flowers on May Day morning was believed to be conducive to the most beautiful blooms. Certain crops, such as potatoes and tomatoes, were believed to be incompatible if planted in proximity to one another.

Another substantial body of plant lore relates to plants as bringers of good or bad luck. Finding a four-leaf clover, everybody knows, brings good luck, but giving a friend sage will precipitate a quarrel. Beyond bringing good or ill fortune, plants may convey symbolic meaning. The Victorians, on both sides of the Atlantic, developed extensive guidebooks to the symbolism of plants, and, in some spheres of activity, such symbolism remains strong today. Roses, for example, are appropriate to convey affection or congratulations, but would be offensive if presented as a funeral flower. Plants also figure in a variety of divination rituals (see JOHN THE CONQUEROR ROOT and ROOTWORK).

See also: FAIRIES; FOLKLORE IN AMERICAN LITERATURE; MEDICINE, FOLK; THOREAU, HENRY DAVID.

SUGGESTED READING: Charles F. Millspaugh, *American Medicinal Plants* (1892; reprint ed., New York, 1974).

Play party. A social gathering of young people, especially in the eastern mountain region and the rural West, for dancing and singing and for the playing of singing games. Play parties were "safe" social gatherings from which liquor was barred. The play party offered a kind of dancing that was acceptable to the straitlaced morality of rural Protestantism. In "swinging play," the dancers swung one another by the hand instead of holding one another around the waist. For reasons of morality as well as economy, the play party rarely included musicians; participants accompanied themselves with a capella song. Nor was a SQUARE DANCE–style caller present. Any number of traditional songs were popular in play parties, including "Skip to My Lou," "Weevily Wheat," "Old Joe Clark," and "Old Brass Wagon," as well as MINSTREL SHOW songs such as "BUFFALO GALS," "Little Brown Jug," and "OLD DAN TUCKER."

See also: HONKY-TONK MUSIC; PAW PAW PATCH; QUADRILLE; VALENTINE'S DAY.

Portrait of Pocahontas in the fancy dress of an Englishwoman, about 1616, after she had arrived in England with her husband, John Rolfe.

Pocahontas (ca. 1595–1617).

The daughter of Powhatan, the powerful chief of the so-called Powhatan Confederacy, Pocahontas befriended the settlers of Jamestown, Virginia, and eventually married an important settler, John Rolfe, who took her with him back to England. An extraordinarily intelligent and perceptive young woman, Pocahontas appears in various works of American literature and entered American folklore largely because of her intercession to save the life of Jamestown settler Captain JOHN SMITH. The story of this event was originally narrated by Smith himself in his 1624 *Generall Historie of New England, Virginia, and the Summer-Isles* and tells how the Indian maiden laid her head upon Smith's as it lay positioned on the sacrificial stone, awaiting the blow of a club. From this kernel of a tale, much oral folklore and literary production has developed.

The literary critic Philip Young calls the Pocahontas story "one of our few, true native myths."

She and her story figure in *Staple of News* (1625), by the British playwright Ben Jonson; in John Davis's *Travels of Four Years and a Half in the United States of America* (1798); in such nineteenth-century plays as *The Indian Princess* (James Nelson Barker, 1808), *Pocahontas* (George Washington Parke Custis, 1830), *The Forest Princess* (Charlotte Barnes Conner, 1844), and many more into the early twentieth century. Of more importance is the treatment of Pocahontas in William Carlos Williams's *In the American Grain* (1925) and by Hart Crane in his modern American epic, *The Bridge* (1930). But Young points out that, in a deeper sense, Pocahontas prefigures the many "Dark Ladies" of American literature, the heroines of NATHANIEL HAWTHORNE, JAMES FENIMORE COOPER, HERMAN MELVILLE, and others.

Unfortunately for the historical Pocahontas, her life was brief. Her personal name was Matoaka ("lively one"), "Pocahontas" ("my favorite daughter") was a sort of nickname, and the English called her Rebecca. After she saved Smith (an episode some believe Smith invented) and after Smith returned to England in 1609, relations between the settlers and Powhatan deteriorated. One Captain Samuel Argall kidnaped Pocahontas, holding her hostage as a means of negotiating a favorable peace. During her captivity, she converted to Christianity and grew close to the English, having fallen in love with John Rolfe before her father ransomed her. Powhatan consented to her daughter's marriage to Rolfe, and this act sealed a peace between the settlers and the Indians that endured during Powhatan's lifetime. This was of great importance to preserving the fledgling English colony, which was in a precarious state of survival.

Pocahontas accompanied Rolfe to England, where she was feted at court and in society. Tragically, however, she contracted smallpox and died. She had borne Rolfe a son, Thomas, who was educated in England, but later immigrated to the Virginia colony.

See also: CRANE, (HAROLD) HART; CUSTER, GEORGE ARMSTRONG.

SUGGESTED READING: Philip L. Barbour, *Pocahontas and Her World* (New York, 1970); Frances Mossiker, *Pocahontas: The Life and the Legend* (1976; reprint ed., New York, 1996); Philip Young, "The Mother of Us All," *Three Bags Full* (New York, 1967).

Poetry, folk. Folk poetry is vernacular verse, usually using rhyme and meter, and including such genres as children's rhymes, COUNTING-OUT RHYMES, SKIP-ROPE RHYMES, peddlar's cries, military marching cadences, TOASTS, cowboy poetry, and various examples of GRAFFITI. Typically, the verse is doggerel and the purpose is often humorous.

See also: RAILROAD FOLKLORE.

SUGGESTED READING: Roger deV. Renwick, *English Folk Poetry: Structure and Meaning* (Philadelphia, 1980).

Polack jokes. Jokes premised on the assertion that POLISH AMERICANS are stupid, Polack jokes, most popular in the 1960s, are ethnically offensive latter-day incarnations of the DUMB DORA JOKES popular in the 1920s and the LITTLE MORON JOKES popular in the 1930s. Polack jokes typically begin, "Did you hear about the Polack who . . ." (". . . thought his typewriter was pregnant because it skipped a couple of periods"), but another type of Polack joke asks questions like "How many Polacks does it take to screw in a lightbulb?" (Answer: Three. One to hold the bulb and two to turn the ladder.)

See also: JOKES AND JOKE CYCLES.

Polish Americans. Most Polish immigrants came to the United States between 1860 and 1929 as unskilled mining and industrial laborers. A second major wave of immigration, consisting of political refugees, came in the aftermath of World War II. More recently, immigrants have come during the period of the collapse of Poland's Soviet-controlled Communist government. Many of the later immigrants tended to settle in the Polish communities established during the nineteenth and early twentieth centuries, primarily in New England, the Mid-Atlantic region, and the northern Midwest. Chicago claims the largest Polish community outside of Warsaw; and New York, Detroit, Buffalo, Pittsburgh, Philadelphia, and Milwaukee also boast large Polish-American communities. In such urban locales, the Polish-American community is typically centered on the local Catholic church, which is not only the spiritual but the social heart of the neighborhood.

While Polish immigration to America was numerically insignificant before 1860, Polish Americans celebrate the memory of two REVOLUTIONARY WAR heroes, Tadeusz Kościuszko and Kazimierz Pulaski, both of whom aided GEORGE WASHINGTON and his army. A number of U.S. towns and counties are named for Pulaski (but few for Kościuszko, probably because it is difficult to pronounce), as are streets, bridges, and highways. Although Polish Americans cherish and foster the image of the Pole as courageous and liberty-loving, an image enhanced by anti-Communist political activity in Poland during the 1970s and 1980s, Polish Americans have also suffered under ethnic stereotyping, which portrays them as dumb, crude working-class stiffs. For many years, primarily during the 1960s through the 1980s, Polish Americans have been the unwilling butt of POLACK JOKES, ethnic modifications of the numskull joke type.

Among Polish Americans themselves, the oral folktales and anecdotes brought by the first wave of immigrants from the "old country" are still cherished and preserved. Various religious holidays, such as Christmas, are occasions for display of folk costumes, folk customs, traditional dances, and traditional foods.

Probably the most familiar aspects of Polish folklore, as far as outsiders are concerned, are the POLKA dance and the music associated with it. Around the polka, Polish Americans have built many celebratory occasions, including weddings, picnics, and informal group get-togethers. Many large Polish restaurants maintain in-house polka bands and a dance floor. The Polish polka as danced in the United States is roughly divided into New York (or Eastern) and Chicago styles. The former is rather more sophisticated in terms of orchestration and, often, also in the level of the musicians' professionalism, but the Chicago style, which draws more directly on Polish village roots, is now more popular, albeit less polished.

See also: ANGLO AMERICANS; IMMIGRANT FOLKLORE; SLAVIC AMERICANS.

SUGGESTED READING: John J. Bukowczyk, *And My Children Did Not Know Me: A History of the Polish Americans* (Bloomington, Ind., 1987); Sophie Hodorowicz Knab, *Polish Customs, Traditions, and Folklore* (New York, 1993); Eugene E. Obidinski and Helen Srankiewicz Zand, *Polish Folkways in America* (Lanham, Md., 1987).

Polka. The polka originated as a Bohemian folk dance associated with courtship. A couple dance, it is characterized by three quick steps and a hop danced in 2/4 time and covering considerable space as couples whirl around the dance floor. This folk dance made its way from Bohemia to Paris by the 1840s and was immediately transformed into a popular ballroom dance. It swept Europe as well as the Americas and was subject to many variations. Although its popularity as a ballroom dance diminished by the early twentieth century, it remains extremely popular as an ethnic dance, particularly among German, Czech, and Polish communities in the United States, and it enjoyed a leap into the popular mainstream after World War II, especially through the recordings of the "Polka King," Frankie Yankovic (1915–1999).

See also: DANCE, FOLK; POLISH AMERICANS; SCHOTTISCHE; TEX-MEX MUSIC.

SUGGESTED READING: Robert Dolgan, *The Polka King: The Life of Frankie Yankovic* (Cleveland, Ohio, 1977); Victor Greene, *A Passion for Polka: Ethnic Old Time Music in America, 1880–1960* (Berkeley, Calif., 1992).

Poole, Charlie (1892–1931) and the North Carolina Ramblers. The two finest early hillbilly bands were the SKILLET LICKERS and Charlie Poole and the North Carolina Ramblers. Born in Alamance County, North Carolina, in 1892, Poole was a rolling stone when he was not working at the Haw River textile mills before he established a career as a musician. His authentic hill dialect, the tight nasal quality of his singing voice, and the traditional songs that he often sang, were stamped with his local origins, but he actually had relatively eclectic tastes, including in his shows many of the popular songs of RAGTIME and vaudeville. He and the band liked to do tunes drawn from such well-known numbers such as "Milwaukee Blues," "Leaving Home," and "Goodbye Sweet Liza Jane." Poole's favorite singer was Al Jolson, who had some impact on his style.

Five-string banjoist Poole, fiddler Posey Rorer, and guitarist Norman Woodlieff started their part-time musical careers about 1917 in and around Spray and Leadville, North Carolina, playing at dances and the occasional fiddlers' conventions. However, when the trio started recording for Columbia in New York in 1925, they began to earn enough as performers to make a final break with working in the textile mills. At their first session they recorded "Don't Let Your Deal Go Down," which became their most often requested number. The trio format continued, but Roy Hervey took the place of Woodlieff in their Columbia session of 1926, and Rorer, who left the group in 1928 was followed by Lonnie Smith and then Odell Smith in the fiddle slot.

When the group was invited to play background music in a Hollywood movie in 1931, it looked as though national fame might be ahead, but Poole, a heavy drinker, died of a heart attack at the age of thirty-nine, becoming one of the first COUNTRY MUSIC legends to die young.

"Pop Goes the Weasel." Although most familiar today as a traditional children's song, "Pop Goes the Weasel" was long a popular SQUARE DANCE tune derived from an English original song and dance of the same name.

See also: FOLK MUSIC.

Popular culture. Most students of folklore define popular culture as mass-mediated culture, the commercial products of film, television, radio, recordings, and print, in contrast to FOLKLORE, which is unmediated popular, but essentially non-commercial, expression. Thus a "folk song" rendered by JOAN BAEZ becomes an artifact of popular culture, while a folk song sung by an Appalachian miner's wife becomes an artifact of folklore. Increasingly, students of folklore have tended to (more or less) deliberately blur the distinction between popular culture and folklore, mainly because, in an age saturated by mass communication, it has become difficult if not impossible to keep "small group," orally transmitted folk traditions separate from mass-mediated popular culture. A good example of this is the BLUES, a folk form strongly influenced by such MASS MEDIA as radio and recording.

See also: FORD, HENRY; MELVILLE, HERMAN; PRESLEY, ELVIS.

Portuguese Americans. Portuguese Americans are immigrants and descendants of immigrants from Portugal as well as Portuguese possessions, including the Cape Verde Islands, Brazil, and Portuguese enclaves in China. The earliest set of immigrants arrived during 1820–70, primarily through the WHALING trade, and settled mainly in New England and Long Island. The next wave arrived during 1870–1920 and were employed principally in the New England textile industry. Additional immigrants have been arriving since the late 1950s. The middle group of immigrants were the least culturally assimilated and, therefore, most deeply involved with Portuguese FOLKWAYS.

Some of the most vivid folklore among Portuguese Americans was brought by emigrants from the Azores and includes SUPERSTITIONS related to natural disasters (the Azores are prone to earthquakes) and to farming and FISHING LORE. Traditional dances, such as the Chama Rita (*chambritza*) are still performed among older descendants of this middle group. Paramount among cherished musical traditions is the *fado*, the doleful folk-song style popular on the Portuguese mainland and chiefly performed among the working class in Lisbon. Other forms of folk song, some from the Azores, are still performed as well, many with a nostalgic, melancholy cast. Another style of folk song, more satirical and locally topical, continues to be improvised by Portuguese folk musicians in New England.

Folklorists report few or no folktales current among Portuguese Americans, but, instead, a rich heritage of saints' legends and stories about miracles. Also preserved are personal anecdotes and narratives concerning the trials of immigration. The Catholic Church is the center of life in most Portuguese-American communities, and feast days honoring the saints (typically organized by the Portuguese Holy Ghost Society) are important community events. The best known of such feast days is that dedicated to Our Lady of Fatima, which memorializes the appearance of the Virgin to peasant children in mainland Portugal. Feast days are occasions for the preparation and consumption of traditional foods, which many Portuguese and non-Portuguese alike enjoy in a small but growing number of ethnic restaurants in New England and in some Middle Atlantic cities, such as the Ironbound neighborhood of Newark, New Jersey.

See also: IMMIGRANT FOLKLORE.

SUGGESTED READING: Stephen Leonard Cabral, *Tradition and Transformation: Portuguese Feasting in New Bedford* (New York, 1992); Hans Howard Leder, *Cultural Persistence in a Portuguese-American Community* (New York, 1980); Leo Pap, *The Portuguese Americans* (Boston, 1981).

Potlatch. One of a handful of Native American ceremonies with which non–Native Americans have some familiarity, the potlatch is the purposely extravagant ritual distribution of property and wealth practiced among tribes of the Northwest Pacific coast. The demonstration of wealth potlatch affords enhances the social status of the giver. Politically, potlatch may function to assert superiority over a neighboring group or tribe.

Pottery. Pottery—vessels made from fired clay—are among the most familiar and numerous of MATERIAL CULTURE artifacts. The most highly regarded of these folk objects combine homely utility with graceful, inventive beauty. Pottery is found among the earliest archaeological evidence in NATIVE AMERICAN archaeological sites, and potters were among the earliest European settlers. The ceramic traditions the early settlers brought with them were chiefly English and, somewhat later, Germanic as well. While the early English-style ceramics tended to be plain and utilitarian, much of the work of the German communities, in Pennsylvania, Virginia's Shenandoah Valley, and the Moravian communities of North Carolina, was highly decorative by the end of the seventeenth century. While both English- and German-style ware used lead-based glazes through much of the eighteenth century, the fancier German products employed multicolored slips (mixtures of clay, water, and other materials to create design and color), sgraffito decoration (ornament produced by scratching through a layer of slip to expose the contrastingly colored clay body beneath it), and decorative molded forms applied to the body of the work. By the turn of the eighteenth century, most American potters had abandoned lead glazes and had begun working with stoneware and associated nonlead salt glazes. The resulting product was not only stronger, but also nontoxic. In some parts of the South (chiefly the Edgefield district of North Carolina), an alkaline glaze, compounded of wood ashes or lime, resulted in pots with a distinctive dark brown or dark green color marked by beautiful thick veins produced by the alkaline flux in the glaze. A later development, from the early nineteenth century, was Albany slip, compounded from clay found near Albany, New York, which was used on the interiors of salt-glazed wares made in the Northeast and on some exterior surfaces of midwestern pots, producing a characteristic chocolate brown color. In the South, Albany slip was sometimes mixed with ordinary salt glaze to produce "frog skin," a yellow-green color.

In slip as well as form, traditional pottery tends to be highly regional. It is also very conservative. Styles, passed down from one generation of potters to another, are slow to change. Typically, too, the folk potter was very much a part of his community, producing vessels for sale, but only as a sideline to farming or some other common livelihood. Pots were produced mainly for sale in the fall, when people needed containers to put up their crops. Most folk ceramics through the nineteenth century functioned to preserve food. A smaller number of products, bowls and the like, were used in the preparation of food, and an even smaller proportion of the typical potter's output was devoted to food consumption—cups, plates, teapots, and so forth. The latter function was more commonly served by wooden, tin, and pewter vessels and by imported ceramics. By the mid-nineteenth century, however, local potters were turning out increasing numbers of more decorative work, ornamented not only with colorful slips, but also with such molded features as animal and flower figures, especially on flowerpots and ceramic grave markers, as well as playful "face vessels"—mugs adorned with typically comical human faces.

It was in the nineteenth century that the folk potter came into his own as a folk artist. Competition from mass-produced pottery from factories all over the Northeast, had greatly reduced the demand on the potter for strictly utilitarian wares. Valued now were the virtues of handicraft, and potters were expected to be inventive. By the close of the nineteenth century, however, the competition from mass production and the use of glass and tin for food-preservation purposes put most folk potters out of business, except in parts of the South. In North Carolina and Georgia, folk potters began turning out wares intended to appeal to tourists, and that industry continues to flourish today.

See also: WEAVING.

SUGGESTED READING: John Bivins, Jr., *The Moravian Potters in North Carolina* (Chapel Hill, N.C., 1972); John A. Burrison, *Brothers in Clay: The Story of Georgia Folk Pottery* (Athens, Ga., 1983); Georgeanna H. Greer, *American Stonewares: The Art and Craft of Utilitarian Potters* (Exton, Pa., 1981); John Spargo, *Early American Pottery and China* (Rutland, Vt., 1974); Nancy Sweezy, *Raised in Clay: The Southern Pottery Tradition* (Washington, D.C., 1984); Charles G., Zug, III, *Turners and Burners: The Folk Potters of North Carolina* (Chapel Hill, N.C., 1986).

Pound, Louise (1872–1958).

Pound collected Nebraska folklore and folk songs and was a BALLAD scholar. A native of Nebraska, the daughter of early settlers, she took her undergraduate degree at the University of Nebraska, then studied abroad, earning her doctorate from the University of Heidelberg. In 1900, she joined the faculty of the University of Nebraska English Department, inaugurating programs in philology and folklore. Pound began by studying the American language, with emphasis on word origins, uses, and euphemisms. She also collected and encouraged others to collect regional folklore, and in 1915 published *Folk-Songs of Nebraska and the Central West: A Syllabus.* Six years later, she published her most provocative and influential book, *Poetic Origins and the Ballad,* in which she attacked the theory advanced by FRANCIS JAMES CHILD (and generally accepted at the time) that

ballads were the products of communal origin. Pound demonstrated that ballads were the work of individuals rather than the result of communal inspiration and improvisation.

Pound was a member of numerous professional societies and was president of the American Folklore Society (1925–27) and of the American Dialect Society. She was the first woman elected president of the Modern Language Association of America (1955). Her last book, *Nebraska Folklore,* appeared posthumously, in 1959.

See also: BELDEN, HENRY MARVIN.

SUGGESTED READING: Benjamin A. Botkin, "Louise Pound," *Western Folklore* 18 (1959), pp. 63–65; Louise Pound, *Selected Writings* (Lincoln, Nebr., 1949).

Powwow.

This term is used by non–Native Americans as an informal synonym for a meeting or gathering. In the past, it was used by European Americans as a label for any Native American gathering or ceremony, and its connotation was typically negative or demeaning. The original word, *pauwaw, po'wah,* or *pow'waw,* is from the Narragansett and Natick Algonquian dialects and denotes a person skilled in the practice of divination, especially for the purpose of healing. Non–Native Americans extended this meaning, which is applied to a key celebrant in healing ceremonies, to the ceremony itself and, indeed, to any Indian ceremony or gathering. By the early twentieth century, Native Americans reclaimed the word and used it to denote an intertribal social dance based on the dance styles of the Plains Indians.

Modern powwows are popular social events

among Native Americans. Music is provided by singers grouped around large drums. Each grouping of singers is called "a drum," and each drum, consisting of five to ten singers, alternates with other drums to produce a variety of dance rhythms. Dances include a variety of traditional steps and range from communal circle dances to "war dances" performed individually. War dance performers combine improvisation and idiosyncratic steps with traditional movements learned by watching others. Other features of modern powwows include ritualized entrances of the participants and a variety of customs and traditions that combine and modify folk practices and beliefs of various participating tribes.

Powwow is also a term traditionally used in the Pennsylvania-German community for a folk healer who practices magical medicine in an occult tradition called *brauche* in the Pennsylvania-German dialect. The powwow primarily uses verbal CHARMS to cure illness.

See also: MEDICINE, FOLK.

SUGGESTED READING: Vanessa Brown and Barre Toelken, "American Indian Powwow," *Folklife Annual* 1987 (Washington, D.C., 1988); George Horse Capture, *Pow Wow* (Cody, Wy., 1989).

Presley, Elvis (1935–1977). The single most famous of all American ROCK 'N' ROLL singers, Elvis Presley created an enduring sensation that significantly influenced American popular music and POPULAR CULTURE. Moreover, in the process of becoming a superstar, Elvis Presley was transformed into what may be described as a folk hero and, for some people, a demigod. His untimely death in 1977 immediately brought many thousands of mourners to Graceland, his home in Memphis, Tennessee, which has since become the most visited home in the United States after the White House. As they do in the case of many legendary heroes (one thinks of King Arthur, if not Jesus Christ), traditions persist that Elvis is not dead at all, but has simply disappeared or gone into hiding. "Evidence" of this continually surfaces in the tabloid press, and "Elvis sightings" have become a kind of folk MOTIF, taken seriously by some, the stuff of jokes to others. A great many people regard Elvis as a kind of deity, "the King," and even a kind of personal savior or patron saint, whose memory renders aid in time of need.

Certainly, Presley's humble birth and upbringing fit religious molds as well as the HORATIO ALGER mold conducive to the creation of an American folk hero. He was raised in Memphis, where he was influenced by the music of the Pentecostal Church, the GRAND OLE OPRY, and local African-American musicians. He made his first recordings in 1954 for the brilliant rhythm-and-blues record producer Sam Phillips, who wanted to expand the appeal of R&B to white audiences by finding a white singer who sounded black. Late in 1955, Phillips sold Presley's contract to RCA Victor for $35,000, and the recording giant quickly made Presley a star. Not that it was ever recordings alone that accounted for the Presley phenomenon. His onstage masculine sexuality was unlike anything else in the 1950s, and he was dubbed "Elvis the Pelvis" for the fluid use he made of his hips in gyrating to his songs. Elvis also projected an appealing hint of outlawry and rebellion at a time when these qualities were both feared and valued. Yet, withal, he also conveyed a becoming modesty, courtesy, and even vulnerability. Finally, he was, quite simply, an extraordinarily accomplished singer, with a beautiful, rich baritone voice. This formidable package of qualities was effectively marketed by his manager, promoter Colonel Tom Parker.

Presley's early hits helped shape rock 'n' roll,

not only by winning fans to the genre, but by influencing the next generation of singers. These first hits included "Heartbreak Hotel," "Hound Dog," "All Shook Up," "Don't Be Cruel," and "Burning Love." They led to his appearance in thirty-three movies and many national television appearances (though, early on, network self-censorship decreed that he could be televised only from the waist up).

Presley's career was interrupted in 1958, when he was drafted into the U.S. Army, but it resumed upon his discharge in 1960. Through the 1960s, a decade in which rock 'n' roll changed radically in the wake of the "British invasion" of the Beatles and other groups, Presley retained his original fans and added legions of new ones by transforming himself into a big-scale, glittering Las Vegas–style act. During this period, Elvis-related merchandise—souvenirs and the like—became a major industry. Yet, amid the adulation, Presley himself became increasingly depressed and withdrawn, depending more and more on prodigious doses of prescription drugs and narcotics. He battled weight gain, ill health, depression, and exhaustion until he succumbed to a heart attack in 1977.

SUGGESTED READING: Neal Gregory and Janice Gregory, *When Elvis Died: Media Overload and the Origins of the Elvis Cult* (New York, 1992); Peter Guralnick, *Careless Love: The Unmaking of Elvis Presley* (New York, 1999); Peter Guralnick, *Last Train to Memphis: The Rise of Elvis Presley* (New York, 1994); Ted Harrison, *Elvis People: The Cult of the King* (London, 1992); Greil Marcus, *Dead Elvis: A Chronicle of a Cultural Obsession* (New York, 1991).

Primitive art. Traditionally, this term has been used to describe the art of "primitive" peoples in Africa, Asia, and Oceania; however, most

Hogman Maxey in the Louisiana State Penitentiary at Angola. (Photo by Harry Oster)

students of the art and culture of these peoples now avoid the term. It has also been used loosely to describe the work of many American folk artists, but is not used by students of this art and is generally disdained by the artists themselves.

Prison work songs. Among the most eloquent and powerful folk songs in the American tradition are the group of WORK SONGS that developed on prison work farms such as those at Angola in Louisiana and Parchman in Mississippi. Songs made group labor easier and more efficient, served as a means of expressing resentment and frustration, and were vehicles for amusement. Work songs were not a practical ne-

Andy Mosely in the Louisiana State Penitentiary at Angola. (Photo by Harry Oster)

flourished is evoked by the colorful words of Roosevelt Charles, an African American in his early forties who had been in and out of Angola four times in twenty-two years:

> Back in 1937, times was hard and work was hard, the boss was very hard, the inmates they were very cruel themselves. You get out on the job, some time early in the mornin'; we'd be drowsy, feelin' bad. The leader of Number One would go to hollerin', "John Henry!" That mean pick up your tools high an' let them fall together. Boys, then the life would hit the gang an' they would start to rollin' on.
>
> Every now an' then you'd call the water

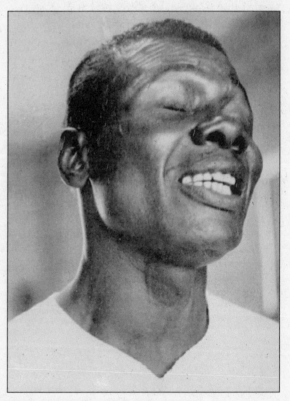

Roosevelt Charles in the Louisiana State Penitentiary at Angola. (Photo by Harry Oster)

cessity after machinery replaced much hand labor, but on prison farms manual labor cost nothing and therefore survived the onslaught of the machine. Besides, it was important to exhaust the prisoners' pent-up energy and to get them out of their claustrophobic cells in order to avert bursts of violence. Group labor by hand was also lucrative for the state. Work songs, then, were encouraged for such activities as reaping and sowing, chopping cane, laying rails and repairing track on the prison railroad system, and picking cotton.

To understand the intense bitterness, anguish, and desperation of the black prison work songs, which used to be sung constantly at Angola and similar prisons, one must picture the vicious practices of prison administrations, circa 1940 and earlier. The world in which the work song boy, and the water boy he'd look around at the boss. The boss would tell him you can carry him water if ya wanta, and if you don't ya don't hafta because they get water outa the tools. They mean you'd hafta drink the sweat from yo' top lip.

So then you'd roll on until about half-past eleven; you'd go out an' you'd strike a track, run all the way. That means run. Run maybe sometimes five and six miles. To get yo' food. Then yo' would sit down to eat. You'd find a fly in yo' plate an' guess what would be applied to ya. Ya shouldn't-a said nothn' about it. Ya better break it in half and give yo' partner half. Ya know it was kinda hard then. An' then if you'd raise too much bug about that, the boss'd take yo' plate an' give it to yo' partner, an' then you'd have to work on before you'd get anythin' else.

Then you'd go in an' ya just might find a rat in yo' plate. Then if ya said anythin', better not breathe above a whisper—ya might have trouble with the man.

So by an' by, trouble lightly, lighten up. The boys they would start to singin', still in the spirit along the way.

Go in the cellroom sometime yo'd be feelin' bad. Somebody across the cellroom would holler, "John Henry." The back water on the levee'd begin risin'. You know what that would call for—plenty work! Some time twelve o'clock at night yo' raise out yo' bed, workin' from then until twelve o'clock the next night. In a track, an' if yo' fall, hmm, yo' better not fall in the way, yo' better roll to the side when yo' fall. . . . The man'd holla to the water boy, "I got ten for the water cart, nine for the hospital, two for the graveyard." An' so that would cause a very mis'rable thing when he got to hollerin' that. Make ya feel bad! And then otherwise, ya do

Robert Pete Williams in the Louisiana State Penitentiary at Angola. (Photo by Harry Oster)

mo' better if ya get a few lines from home for consolation, but a great deal of time, ya can't get no mail from home. Everybody at home turned their back on ya. An' then ya feel like ya is in the world all alone.

Some of the boys they try to take Lawyer Green and Lawyer Bushes, that mean the woods up on the hillside. That's after ya get off the river an ya be makin' the hilltop, crossin' over into the Mississippi woods. That's Lawyer Green. An' Lawyer Bushes, that's a tree top. That's when ya jumpin' from limb to limb, crossin' them ravines and gulleys. An' the Mississloppy—that the Mississippi when ya been tryin' to swim across. That's too much water to try to drink. So ya got to try to swim. But ya can't go round—it ain't no end. In the meantime some would make it, an' some wouldn't. Some would get shot down an' some would get caught. But of course the warden, he would holla, "Don't bring back none alive. Say, I got a carload o' leather [whips]; I got two carloads o' buckshot, an' I ain't issuin' my buckshot so I can cripple a man, 'cause I can't use him when he's crippled . . ."

The official records at Angola show that between 1929 and 1940 more than 10,000 floggings occurred. The whip consisted of two belts of sole leather five feet long, three to four inches wide, attached to a heavy wooden handle. Three or four blows vigorously applied to a convict's bare back broke the skin. Few prisoners failed to start screaming by the fifth or sixth blow. As many as thirty-five could put a convict in the hospital. Punishments of fifty lashes, however, were not uncommon.

A typical work song is "Take This Hammer." In his usually eloquent and colorful style, Roosevelt Charles described the sort of situation which must have originally goaded a prisoner into making up this song:

> This was when the train was rollin' down the track of Angola. They had a railroad runnin' around about. They had a railroad gang there, and they had quite a few hammers on the line. There was a boy he had been roll and roll, sometime he'd be up through the night, through the day. The sun was shinin' hot in the month of August, an' the sweat was beginnin' to roll along, and he call the water boy, and the water boy he refuse. He call for the boss, and the boss turned his back. So the boy he laid his hammer on the spike, and he begin to strike on the spike and these are the words he said:

1. This old hammer, most too heavy
   Lightweight, Lawdy, light man.
2. Take this hammer, take it to the sergeant;
   Tell him I'm gone, Lawdy, tell him I'm gone.
3. If he asks you what got the matter,
   Had too long, Lawdy, had too long.
4. I'm gonna roll on a few days longer, (2)
   I'm gonna roll on few days longer, (2)
   I'm goin' home, Lawdy, I'm goin' home.

This song is an ironic wish-fulfilment fantasy in which the overworked prisoner pictures himself boldly announcing to the authorities that he's giving them back their hammer and headed for home.

As can be seen from the texts of the work songs, in addition to their basic function of making work go more smoothly and easily, they served as an outlet for the violent resentments of prisoners under the cruelty of captains and guards. Improvements in the treatment of prisoners—including better food, shorter work hours, a better system of pardon and parole, attempts to rehabilitate prisoners by teaching them trades—were factors in the decline of the work songs. In addition, younger prisoners jeered at the old songs, which they associated with slavery times; they would say "it's modern days now. We're not interested in that old John Henry stuff, because that was slavery times."

See also: CRIME AND CRIMINALS; FOLK MUSIC.

SUGGESTED READING: Harry Oster, *Living Country Blues* (Detroit, 1969).

Proverbs. Pithy, traditional, memorizable sayings passed orally from generation to generation and regarded as concise statements of wisdom and truth, proverbs are typically quite brief. They have a fixed structure; that is, form is inseparable from content. Structure is frequently oppositional or parallel: "To err is human; to forgive, divine" and "Easy come, easy go." They are rich in metaphor. They are typically poetic, using rhyme and alliteration: "Haste makes waste." They tend to be economical, even elliptical grammatically: "In for a penny, in for a pound." They often turn on paradox: "The shoemaker's children go unshod." Finally, and of great significance, proverbs gain meaning only when applied in context. "Nothing ventured, nothing gained" is a statement of little interest until it is issued as advice to timid friend deciding whether or not to ask his boss for a raise.

Where do American proverbs come from? Proverbs go back as far as evidence of written language itself, to the Sumerian cuneiform writings of 3000 B.C. Many proverbs still current in the United States have their origin in classical times and in the Bible, Old and New Testaments. The works of William Shakespeare are another popular source of American proverbs. But proverbs are continuously coined (witness "Garbage in, garbage out," coined by computer programmers) and continuously parodied ("Every silver lining has a cloud"). With America's diverse ethnic population, the proverbs of many cultures and nationalities have been introduced into current American usage.

Paremiology is the study of proverbs, and *paremiography* is the collection of proverbs.

See also: FRANKLIN, BENJAMIN; LINCOLN, ABRAHAM; MASS MEDIA; VIETNAM WAR; WEATHER FOLKLORE; WEDDINGS; WORLD WAR I POSTERS.

SUGGESTED READING: Jan Harold Brunvand, *A Dictionary of Proverbs and Proverbial Phrases from Books Published by Indiana Authors before 1890* (Bloomington, Ind., 1961); Margaret Bryant, *Proverbs and How*

An advertising image showing a boy carving the traditional Halloween jack-o'-lantern. (From L. Cabarga et al., 1,001 Advertising Cuts from the '20s and '30s, *1996)*

to Collect Them (Greensboro, N.C. 1945); Francis A. De Caro and William K. McNeil, *American Proverb Literature: A Bibliography* (Bloomington, Ind., 1971).

Pumpkin. This large yellow-orange or orange squashlike fruit (family *Cucurbita*) functions in modern American folklore as an ingredient in the traditional THANKSGIVING pumpkin pie and as a jack-o'-lantern decoration for HALLOWEEN. The traditional jack-o'-lantern is made by cutting around the stem to make a removable lid, scooping out the seed and fibrous pulp of the pumpkin (the seeds are often dried, salted, and eaten), carving a grotesque and menacing face into it (usually featuring jagged or squared-off teeth), and placing a lighted candle inside the hollowed-out pumpkin to illuminate the face from within. The idea is to create a ghostly, supernatural effect.

Pyramidal house. An example of VERNACULAR ARCHITECTURE, the pyramidal house has a high, pyramidal roof, with a chimney on either side of its abbreviated ridge. The basic first-floor plan includes four rooms, two on either side of a broad central hall. This building type was popular on the Georgia-Carolina coast.

Q

Quadrille. The quadrille began as an aristocratic court dance in Europe during the eighteenth and nineteenth centuries, involving four couples moving in square formation and intertwining figures.

As practiced in France and England, the quadrille was composed of several formal sections, each with prescribed combinations of figures. (A variation on the quadrille, lancers, was danced well into the twentieth century.) Quadrilles were danced in the refined ballrooms of the United States during the nineteenth century and were also translated into the more rural New England singing quadrille and, in the Appalachians as well as parts of the rural West, it became the basis for more improvisatory dancelike PLAY PARTY games.

See also: SQUARE DANCE.

Quakers. More properly called the Society of Friends or the Friends Church, the Quakers are a Protestant religious denomination founded in seventeenth-century England by George Fox (1624–91) and brought to America by William Penn (1647–1728), proprietor of the Pennsylvania colony. Quakers advocate an unmediated, direct relation with God and therefore eschew creeds, clergy, and dogma. The persecution with which Quakers typically met motivated their settlement in America. Quaker community practice and worship have been traditionally characterized by extreme austerity. Members of the

William Penn's Treaty with the Indians When He Founded the Province of Pennsylvania 1661. *Print by Currier & Ives, undated. (Collection of Walton Rawls)*

monthly meeting, as the worship service is called, speak out as the spirit moves them. Traditional observance is without prayer, hymns, or prepared sermons, but, today, some of these elements do figure in some meetings. The Quakers espoused an ideal of "plainness," which proscribed many forms of art and folk art, including painting, music, and drama. The Quaker folk painter EDWARD HICKS (1780–1849) continually struggled with feelings of guilt about his avocation. The Quakers have traditionally fostered advanced education, however, and have numbered among their ranks prominent scientists and inventors.

In American folklore, Quakers figure most prominently as the objects of EXOTERIC FOLKLORE, much of it focused on the sect's pacifism, an extreme belief in the Christian principle of turning the other cheek and an absolute opposition to bearing arms. During times of war, this has led to persecution and other conflicts. Aside from this, the folkloric perception of Quakers is as founding fathers, rather like the PILGRIMS AND PURITANS, soberly garbed in plain black dress, in the manner of the portrait on containers of Quaker Oats oatmeal. For many Americans, this antique perception is the image of the American Quaker, whose ideals and pacific way of life are highly regarded, but also considered to lie outside of the American mainstream.

SUGGESTED READING: Hugh Barbour and J. William Frost, *The Quakers* (Philadelphia, 1994).

Quilts. The patchwork quilt, widely regarded as the most beautiful form of American folk art, reached its highest artistic development in the period 1800–1900, when women all over the country chose it as their prime vehicle for artistic expression. Requiring a great deal of talent, imagination, and needlework dexterity, the quilt had to be conceptualized for overall effect well in advance of execution; its shapes had to be designed for pleasing integration and its color combinations planned for best effect; therein lay the artistry. As a folk craft, quilting went into decline at the end of the nineteenth century when machine-made blankets came within economic reach of most Americans. Since then there have been periodic revivals, by necessity in the Great Depression, and, in the twentieth century, as interest in American folk crafts has grown.

"Quilting" properly refers to the final stage of creating a quilt, after the top cover has been created by piecing, that is, sewing pieces of fabric together at their edges, or by appliqué, where individual patches are sewn onto a background fabric. Both techniques are often embellished by embroidery where the pieces are joined. At this point, the top is attached to the backing by stitching through the inner padding in a decorative pattern, although quilting stitches are expected to be virtually invisible; quilters pride themselves on infinitesimal stitches.

Quilting is known from artifacts to predate written history, for it was discovered early that two layers of fabric stitched together over an inner core of padding, or bombast, provided extra warmth for combating winter cold in clothing, curtains, and bed furnishings. The earliest surviving bed quilt dates from the end of the fourteenth century.

By the time America was colonized, quilt making was highly developed in most of Europe, and NEEDLEWORK skills were an important asset to immigrants, who brought only bare necessities. Every scrap of clothing was worn as long as possible and then reused in some other way, particularly in bedding. As patches, fabrics were appliqued to tattered quilt tops or saved as remnants to be pieced together to make new quilts.

No quilts survive from the earliest period of settlement because of constant use and the natural fragility of aging fabric. The oldest American quilt dates from the beginning of the eighteenth century, and it is not until the late eighteenth century that there are many survivors; by then at least some settlers were prosperous enough to have "best quilts" carefully stored away and brought out only for special occasions.

Although thrift and economy remained significant factors in American life, in the late eighteenth century well-to-do quilters were no longer confined mostly to secondhand fabrics. American textile printing got under way in the Revolutionary period as patriots began to boycott British goods and support local industry. This led to the introduction of printed fabric panels in quilts.

Most early crafts in rural areas were carried on as family undertakings, and both girls and boys were taught the rudiments of sewing, with boys going on to mechanical duties such as tracing designs on backgrounds, preparing templates for cutting component pieces, and then the actual cutting of fabric. Girls went on to master ever finer techniques of sewing and to learn the intricacies of popular quilt designs. Needlework was an integral part of the school curriculum on into the mid-nineteenth century, for young ladies were expected to produce a hope chest full of linens and bed coverings for their future families. Initially a young girl would just piece together the tops and not actually quilt until it was certain that a marriage was taking place. Harriet Beecher Stowe, in *The Minister's Wooing*, spoke of "those pretty bits, which, little in themselves, were destined, by gradual unions and accretions, to bring about at last substantial beauty, warmth, and comfort." Some quilts might be made of as many as 60,000 pieces, but the big effort was thought to come in providing the wadding and backing and quilting everything together. It was a family effort up to a certain point, when the neighbors were called in for the quilting bee.

As important in rural areas as the church social or barn raising, the quilting bee brought people together and was a source of socializing, news, and gossip. Neighbors expected to help each other, and it was regarded as a slight not to be asked. There might be twenty to thirty bees in a winter, and when not actually taking a turn at sewing a housewife would be baking cookies and brewing tea for the others. The men built a sewing frame, which could be hoisted to the ceiling when the quilt was not being worked on, and it provided a way to roll up the finished parts and give the quilters easier access to their work. The number of stitches in a quilt, both in the piecing and appliquéing, as well as in the quilting, was beyond calculation.

Certain patterns for quilt tops became well established, although they bore several names, but no two quilts were ever alike. The dominant forms chosen were readily understood in an era before literacy was widespread. Rings and hearts suggested love and marriage, the pineapple stood for hospitality, and the swastika brought good luck. Many symbols had national connotations, as in the popular Pine Tree pattern, which had figured on the first colonial coins and flags. There were religious associations as well to the tree, which symbolized the Garden of Eden. Some of the most frequently used patchwork patterns were based on the star shape, and the most beautiful of them is the Star of Bethlehem. Originally a single central shape with eight points, it went into numerous geometric variations. As subjects, flowers and plants appear in astonishing variety, which probably was stimulated by the interest of settlers in collecting and classifying the local flora. The rose was most often represented, appearing as centers or borders in bouquets, wreaths, and arranged in pretty baskets. Oddly, vegetables rarely appear on quilts.

Many of the strongest patterns were well known everywhere by name, but given possible variations, a quilter often christened her work something new. From the 1850s to the 1880s, one of the most popular patterns was known as Log Cabin, but in variants it was also called Courthouse Steps and Barn Raising. In the period of western expansion, certain similar patterns might be known as "Rocky Road to California," "Wagon Trail," or "Wandering Foot." Mothers were careful never to use the latter on a young boy's bed, lest it incite wanderlust. Certain patterns became identified with the maiden's hope chest and were called by names like "Bridal Stairway," "Honeymoon Cottage," and "Double Wedding Ring," which persists today as a popular pattern for machine-made quilts.

Besides the patterns, there were certain thematic innovations that developed in the mid-nineteenth century: the Album Quilt featured random figures of people and animals as well as village scenes, and whatever struck the quilter's fancy. The Presentation Quilt usually was developed along a single theme and commended some person, institution, or event. The Victorian Crazy Quilt carried patchwork to excess and offered a collage of odd shapes and materials, including beads, spangles, fancy embroidery, and satin ribbons. In the period between 1880 and the turn of the century, there was a fashion for quilts pieced together with wool patches created as premiums for tobacco products—among them patriotic emblems, flags, and Indian rug designs. Some quilts were even made from silk ribbons used to tie up bunches of cigars. The most unusual fad of the period was the Autograph Quilt. Famous people were asked to contribute bits of their clothing, which were to be autographed. Among those known to participate were ABRAHAM LINCOLN and the actress Ellen Terry. A variation on this was the Quotation Quilt, which was embroidered with Scripture or everyday advice meaningful to the quilter, such as "Learn to be useful, not fanciful."

SUGGESTED READING: Robert Bishop, *The Romance of Double Wedding Ring Quilts* (New York, 1989); Myron and Patsy Orlofsky, *Quilts in America* (New York, 1974); Florence Peto, *American Quilts and Coverlets* (New York, 1949).

R

Rabbit's foot. A very popular CHARM or AMULET used in specific VOODOO rituals as practiced by African Americans and also carried by non–African Americans to bring good luck. Often, the rabbit's foot is used as a key-chain ornament. Those most frequently seen nowadays are artificial, specifically made to be attached to a key chain, and, indeed, bearing little resemblance to an actual rabbit's foot. Artificial rabbit's feet are frequently dyed pink.

See also: HOODOO HAND.

A rabbit's foot.

Ragtime. One of the most significant forms of African-American music is ragtime, which is especially well suited to the piano, with the left hand playing a steady bass in a duple rhythm (a dance-orchestra regular beat) and the right hand playing in a highly syncopated triple rhythm, with a frequently syncopated melody. The first ragtime musicians were wanderers from dive to dive in the Mississippi countryside and on the eastern seaboard who tickled the ivories in honky-tonk joints, cheap restaurants, bordellos, and saloons. They were usually paid a meager wage or depended solely on tips. W. C. HANDY described such a "piano thumper" in a visit to Memphis in the late 1880s.

There is some logic in rooting the origins of the music in antebellum African-derived slave danc-ing to FIDDLE and BANJO accompaniment over percussive foot-stomping and "JUBA patting" by the crowd. In ragtime, the left hand assumed the role of the stomping and patting while the right hand played syncopated melodies often derived from fiddle and banjo music.

Circulating for a long time only in black communities, ragtime made the leap onto the national scene in 1896 when vaudeville impresario Tony Pastor's Fourteenth Street Variety House in New York City featured a black BUCK-AND-WING dancer named Strap Heel, accompanied by Ben Harney of Kentucky, a white pianist. Linked to the CAKEWALK, a popular MINSTREL SHOW act in which dancing couples competed for a cake, ragtime spread all over the country.

The black actor and songwriter Ernest Hogan composed a song in 1896, "All Coons Look Alike to Me," a ragtime number that swept the country and also reached audiences abroad. It was used as the piece the finalist pianists played in the Ragtime Championship of the World Competition at Tammany Hall in New York City in 1900.

One of the most popular ragtime songs, "My Ragtime Baby" (1898) won a prize for John Philip Sousa and his band at the Paris Exposition in 1900, and also gave Europeans their initial exposure to ragtime.

A concentration of black pianist-composers settled in and around St. Louis, Missouri, between 1890 and 1910, the most notable of them being Scott Joplin (1865–1917), originally from Texarkana, Texas, and universally recognized as the "King of Ragtime." His "Mapleleaf Rag," published in 1890 by the white firm of John Stilwel Stark, was widely popular and helped make Stark the country's leading publisher of ragtime music.

Ragtime was almost wholly supplanted by JAZZ by the 1920s, but interest in the music never entirely died. Ragtime—and especially the music of Joplin—received renewed popular interest following the release of the popular Paul Newman and Robert Redford film *The Sting* (1973), which featured a score by Marvin Hamlisch, who had adapted Joplin's rags. Many recordings of Joplin's music followed.

See also: AFRICAN AMERICANS; BOLDEN, (CHARLES) BUDDY; FOLK MUSIC; FULLER, BLIND BOY; JAZZ; POOLE, CHARLIE AND THE NORTH CAROLINA RAMBLERS.

SUGGESTED READING: Edward A. Berlin, *King of Ragtime: Scott Joplin and His Era* (New York, 1994); David A. Jasen and Trebor Jay Tichenor, *Rags and Ragtime: A Musical History* (New York, 1989); Terry Waldo and Eubie Blake, *This Is Ragtime* (New York, 1991).

Railroad Bill. Called the "Robin Hood of Alabama," Railroad Bill is an African-American folk hero. Born Morris Slater in Escambia County, Alabama, he gained local notoriety after he shot a deputy sheriff who had arrested him for possession of a gun. He escaped by hopping a freight train and thereafter rode the rails, getting his living by looting freight, part of which he distributed to the poor. He successfully evaded all efforts to capture him, and it was said that he had the power of a SHAPE SHIFTER, assuming the form of a black dog to escape his pursuers. Railroad Bill is celebrated in a number of BALLADS.

Railroad folklore. Space has always been a defining quality of America, and the ability to traverse that space rapidly and at will is, for many Americans, a measure of liberty. The nation's railroads were the first truly efficient means of moving across the vast American spaces, and this fact alone would be sufficient to imbue America's railroads with the collective emotional significance that is productive of folklore. Add to this, however, the adventure, effort, and enterprise required to build the railroads and the colorful characters associated with operating the railroads, and the subject becomes even more intensely romantic. Railroading has inspired folk songs, folktales, personal narratives, folk poetry (see POETRY, FOLK), LEGENDS, LOCAL LEGENDS, and LOCAL-CHARACTER STORIES. The vocation of railroading has also produced OCCUPATIONAL FOLKLORE, including WORK SONGS and occupation-specific FOLK SPEECH.

Much of the romance of railroading is associated with the era of steam, which extended into the 1940s, before steam locomotives were generally supplanted by diesel-electric power. The steam locomotive seemed more a living thing than a machine, and railroaders worked with these machines in much the same way that COWBOYS worked with animals, managing, taming, and caring for them. Many engineers personalized the locomotives they operated by installing special signature whistles, which they "played" in a distinctive way. Thus people who lived along the right of way learned to recognize the whistle of this or that engineer as his train passed through.

The ESOTERIC FOLKLORE of railroading included the occupational hierarchy among train crews. There was much debate as to whether the engineer or the conductor was in charge of the train, and relations between the two were sometimes strained. The fireman stoked the firebox and generally looked after the boiler. He also functioned as an apprentice engineer. Answering to the conductor was the brakeman, who had the hazardous jobs of operating track switches, coupling and uncoupling cars, and, before the advent of the Westinghouse air brake, also had to climb along the tops of cars to set and release each car's brakes. A brakeman could aspire to become a conductor—if he lived long enough. It is said that a brakeman who sought employment would show his hands. An amputated finger or two was ample proof that the job applicant was an experienced brakeman. While engineers (such as CASEY JONES) were traditionally the most romantic figures—the railroaders celebrated in BALLADS— brakemen were often the most intriguing. They had a reputation as drifters and hard drinkers, whose raucous, loud, and violent ways earned them the nickname of "boomer" during the nineteenth century. Conductors, in contrast, were typically embodiments of authority and were depicted in popular lore as the implacable enemy of the HOBO seeking to "ride the rails" for free.

Telegraphers were also vital personnel in nineteenth-century rail operations. A telegrapher who demonstrated sufficient accuracy and responsibility might gain promotion to train dispatcher, the controller of rail traffic. Dispatcher errors could easily have disastrous results, especially on long stretches of single-track western lines, where mistakes could easily result in head-on collisions. Legends about dispatchers committing suicide after bearing the responsibility for such catastrophes were common.

The work of building the railroads has produced many songs and legends, the best known of which is the story of JOHN HENRY. Work songs were an essential adjunct to the labor of laying rails. Gandy dancers, the men who set down and aligned the individual rail sections, used chants to synchronize their movements in order to achieve the necessary accuracy, and the laborers who spiked the rails measured their sledgehammer strokes to their own songs. Nineteenth-century railroading was not only hazardous as an occupation, it was a dangerous way to travel. Train wrecks were endemic and, often, epidemic. Many folk ballads commemorate wrecks.

SUGGESTED READING: B. A. Botkin and Alvin F. Harlow, eds., *A Treasury of Railroad Folklore* (New York, 1953).

Rainey, Ma (1886–1939). Born Gertrude Malissa Nix Pridget, Ma Rainey became the first notable female BLUES singer. Although the first recording of blues was made by Mamie Smith ("Crazy Blues," 1920), Ma Rainey began performing as early as 1902 and was accepted and esteemed by blues and JAZZ musicians throughout her life. She was a singer, comedienne, MINSTREL SHOW performer, gifted songwriter, a dancer, and one of the blues recording stars of the 1920s. Signed by Paramount Records, she recorded her first eight songs in Chicago in 1923 at the age of thirty-seven. She made at least ninety-two recordings in her career. With some justice, Ma has been called "Mother of the Blues."

Ma Rainey was a leading exponent of classic blues, which dealt with romantic and sexual relationships much more centrally and frequently than did country blues. Rainey's style was sensual, characterized by slurs, moans, and the skillful use of blue notes. In addition to Ma Rainey, the major recorders of classic blues in the twenties were several unrelated Smiths—Bessie, Clara, Mamie, and Trixie—as well as Ethel Waters, Alberta Hunt, Bertha "Chippie" Hill, Sippie Wallace, Ida Cox, Lucille Hegamin, Rosa Henderson, and Victoria Spivey. The noted African-American composer of blues and gospel songs THOMAS A. DORSEY served for some years as Ma's pianist arranger, and band director. Many legends have sprung up about the relationship between Ma and Bessie Smith (1895–1937), a younger artist destined to eclipse Ma's popularity. Certainly Smith was influenced by Rainey when they worked together in two traveling shows early in Smith's career. They remained lifelong friends.

Rainey stopped performing by the Depression, when jazz and swing had largely displaced classic blues.

See also: SMITH, BESSIE.

SUGGESTED READING: Sandra Lieb, *Mother of the Blues: A Study of Ma Rainey* (Cambridge, Mass., 1981).

Rap.

Outside of the African-American community, "rap" is best known as a popular musical genre, which emerged from the Bronx during the early 1970s. Rap began with African-American disc jockeys who worked parties and who mixed prerecorded music alternately on two turntables while reciting "rap" phrases to the crowd. By the late 1970s and into the 1980s, rapping over music or over a beat came into its own as a form of musical expression.

The term "rap" predates the music, however. For some African Americans it describes a highly stylized manner of speech, using braggadocio, double entendre, and DIRTY DOZENS. As a style of speech, rap evolved from jive talk, a feature of African-American urban speech that emerged during the 1930s and 1940s. Jive is highly metaphorical, witty, improvisational, and typically fast paced. It gained currency through its use by popular jazz musicians. The "militant" civil rights leader H. "Rap" Brown energized his fiery political speeches with a more barbed form of jive, which became rap. Today, some rap music conveys an angry political message and even exhortations to violence (in "gangsta rap").

See also: AFRICAN AMERICANS; BREAKDANCING; FOLK MUSIC; SOUNDING; TOASTS.

SUGGESTED READING: Cheryl L. Keyes, *Rappin to the Beat: Rap Music as Street Culture among African Americans* (Ann Arbor, Mich., 1992).

Redneck.

An epithet describing a working-class white southerner, usually pejorative, and usually connoting a man (less often a woman) both generally ignorant and specifically racist. The term first appeared in the 1930s and has its origin in the sunburned neck of the farmer or laborer who bends in outdoor toil all day. By mid-century, the term had taken on many connotations of EXOTERIC FOLKLORE; redneck characteristics included a distinctive manner of speech, always larded with double negatives, mispronunciations, and malapropisms; a fondness for greasy southern diner food, whiskey, beer, and country music; and an uncanny penchant for tearing apart a car to repair it, but never getting around to putting it back together, so that it sits, stripped of tires, on blocks in his ramshackle front yard. Rednecks also have distinctive names, such as Bubba or Slick or some combination of diminutives, such as Billy Bob. Sometimes initials suffice: T.J., for example. More recently, some southern men have taken to calling *themselves* rednecks as a matter of pride, deeming a redneck an honest, forthright, hardworking, fun-loving "good ol' boy." Southern politicians have long applied the term to themselves in order to identify themselves with the electorate.

See also: APPALACHIA; CRACKERS.

Reel. A figure dance similar to a JIG, but danced in 2/4 rather than 6/8 time. The most elaborate reels are those of Ireland; however, the reels of New England and the Virginia Reel, which featured a multitude of fancy turns, are also celebrated. Southern African Americans of the nineteenth and early twentieth centuries used the term reel to denote nonchurch music or even music deemed sinful, the tunes of which were most often derived from Scottish and Irish sources.

See also: FIDDLE; TAP DANCE.

Regional folklore. Folklore peculiar to a given region of the United States and believed to be especially characteristic of the region. Regional folklore develops in response to environmental and geographical conditions, to political conditions, or to the occupational situation dominant in an area. It is often a means of expressing or affirming regional identity and of excluding outsiders. Generally, folklorists recognize the following regions as productive of distinctive folklores: APPALACHIA, the Great Basin, the Great Lakes, the Great Plains, Middle Atlantic, Midwest, New England, Pacific Northwest (including Alaska), Ozarks, PENNSYLVANIA GERMAN region

(or Pennsylvania Culture region), Piedmont, Rocky Mountains, the South, and the Southwest.

See also: SCANDINAVIAN AMERICANS.

SUGGESTED READING: Barbara Allen and Thomas J. Schlereth, eds., *Sense of Place: American Regional Cultures* (Lexington, Ky., 1990).

Religion, folk. Religious beliefs, practices, and material artifacts that exist among people separately from and in addition to "official" theological doctrine, dogma, practices, and material artifacts. Folk religion often encompasses folk medicine, folk beliefs, and SUPERSTITIONS. It often includes traditional beliefs and practices that are "outmoded" in conventional or orthodox religious practice. Typically, such beliefs and practices are found in rural communities or among poor or ethnically isolated urban dwellers —any group of worshipers who are apart from the cultural mainstream. It is often difficult, however, to determine whether a particular set of beliefs and practices should be called folk religion or the products of religious dissenters or both. The concept of folk religion also takes in the beliefs, practices, and artifacts of conventional religions as these religions are actually practiced by a given group. Finally, some students of folk religion study the folklore (for example, LEGENDS, folktales, jokes, and so on) associated with religion, whether in the cultural mainstream or outside of it.

See also: JOKES AND JOKE CYCLES; MEDICINE, FOLK; MILLENNIALISM; SERMON, FOLK; SNAKE HANDLERS.

SUGGESTED READING: Larry Danielson, "Religious Folklore," in Elliott Oring, ed., *Folk Groups and Folk-*

lore Genres: An Introduction (Logan, Utah, 1986); Don Yoder, "Toward a Definition of Folk Religion," in Western Folklore 33 (1974), pp. 2–15.

Retablos. Sacred images painted on wood or tin and often used as altar screens in Hispanic churches. Smaller *retablos* also served as religious images to adorn private chapels and homes in Hispanic New Mexico. The earliest *retablos* date from the end of the eighteenth century.

See also: ARAGON, JOSÉ RAFAEL; LAGUNA SANTERO; MEXICAN AMERICAN; TRUCHAS MASTER.

Reuss, Richard August (1940–1988). Reuss was a historian of the folk-revival movement and a student of the relationship between the American folklore movement and radical politics, which was the subject of his unpublished (yet widely read) Ph.D. dissertation, "American Folklore and Left-wing Politics, 1927–1957" (Indiana University, 1971). Active in the folk-revival movement of the late 1950s and a contributor to *Sing Out!* and *Broadside* (two folk-revival magazines), he became the movement's historian.

Reuss taught at Wayne State University (Detroit), at Indiana University, and elsewhere before becoming a social worker in 1981. He retained his passion for folklore, however, founding in 1983 *Folklore Historian*, a journal dedicated to the history of folklore study. Reuss was also a nationally famous collector of baseball cards. He died of Huntington's disease.

Revenant. As used by folklorists, a synonym for ghost.

See also: GHOST STORIES.

Revere, Paul (1735–1818). A colonial silversmith, Paul Revere was among the greatest practitioners of the art of metalworking, but he is best remembered as a folk hero of the American Revolution, the man whose "Midnight Ride" of April 18, 1775, to warn the citizens in and around Boston of the approach of the British "Redcoats," was commemorated in verse by HENRY WADSWORTH LONGFELLOW. In "Paul Revere's Ride" (1863), the poet takes a number of liberties with history, not the least of which is ignoring the fact that Revere was only one of three riders on that night. The other two were William Dawes and Samuel Prescott, of whom only Prescott made it all the way to Concord; British patrols captured Revere and Dawes.

What is true is that Revere was a prominent Patriot, a spokesman for Boston's artisan and "mechanic" class, a participant in the 1773 Boston Tea Party, and, for some years, the princi-

Early twentieth-century book illustration depicting Paul Revere's ride.

pal rider for Boston's Committee of Safety. In this capacity, he carried messages to revolutionaries in New York and Philadelphia. On April 16, 1775, he rode from Boston to Concord to warn the Patriots to move their military stores, which were a target of approaching British troops. Revere also arranged to signal the Patriots of the manner of the British approach by putting lanterns in Boston's Old North Church steeple—as Longfellow famously records, "One if by land and two if by sea." Two days later, he rode out to alert the countryside that the British were on the march. His object, and that of the other two riders, was in particular to alert the Minutemen and the revolutionary leaders John Hancock and Samuel Adams, both of whom were subject to imminent capture. Both Revere and Dawes reached Lexington separately and issued timely warning to Hancock and Adams. With Prescott, the two riders set out for Concord. Only Prescott got through; Revere and Dawes were captured and soon released. The ride of Revere and his compatriots succeeded in alerting the Minutemen, who were ready the next morning to meet the Redcoats on Lexington green in the opening battle of the Revolution.

Revere was the son of a Huguenot refugee, Apollos De Revoire (the father later Anglicized his surname), who taught Paul the silversmith's art. During the Revolution, Paul Revere built a gunpowder mill and commanded Boston Harbor's defenses. After the war, he built a rolling mill to produce sheet copper, which was used to sheathe the hulls of many American ships, including "Old Ironsides"—the U.S.S. *Constitution*—and the dome of the Massachusetts statehouse.

See also: REVOLUTIONARY WAR; WORLD WAR I POSTERS.

SUGGESTED READING: Esther Forbes, *Paul Revere and the World He Lived In* (1942; reprint ed., New York, 1988).

Revival songs. Revival songs came into being around 1800, when the first camp meetings were being held, particularly in the South. The leading spiritual theme of the revivalist camp meetings was the individual struggle toward salvation, and that was a subject inadequately addressed by traditional hymns. "Camp-meeting songs," also called "spiritual songs," described and narrated the stages of religious conversion. The verse was typically set to folk songs and other familiar secular tunes. In addition to camp-meeting songs, "choruses" or "revival spiritual songs" followed call-and-response patterns and were written in rhyming couplets, which could be easily learned and committed to memory. By 1810, "camp-meeting songsters," books of revival poetry, began to appear, as did tunebooks such as *The Sacred Harp* by the 1840s. The popularity of the revival songs faded with the rise of urban America after the Civil War and were largely replaced by so-called gospel hymns, which partook of the Victorian PARLOR BALLAD tradition.

See also: FOLK MUSIC; SACRED HARP MUSIC; SHAPE-NOTE SINGING; SPIRITUALS, AFRICAN-AMERICAN; SPIRITUALS, WHITE.

SUGGESTED READING: Dickson D. Bruce, Jr., *And They All Sang Hallelujah: Plain-Folk Camp-Meeting Religion, 1800–1845* (Knoxville, Tenn., 1974); George Pullen Jackson, *White Spirituals in the Southern Uplands* (1933; reprint ed., New York, 1965).

Revolutionary War. Folklore associated with the Revolutionary War (1775–83) is of four major types: folktales, BALLADS, folk songs, and LEGENDS familiar to the participants (American and European); lore and ballads growing out of actual events in the war; and figures later regarded as folk heroes. Tristram Potter Coffin (see Suggested Reading) cites a contemporary TALL

TALE of Patriot scout Tim Murphy shooting an Indian hiding behind a rock by bending his rifle, so that the bullet fires in a curve. Coffin points out that this is a well-documented European folktale type transplanted into an American context. (It is also a folktale that turns up later in WORLD WAR II folklore.) Another tale about Murphy, in which he shoots British general Simon Frazer from behind a tree, is based on an actual Revolutionary War incident. Yet Murphy can no longer be considered a folk hero, because few people, other than historians, know of him. Modern Americans regard as folk heroes the likes of PAUL REVERE and Nathan Hale, whose fame was created not directly through the vehicles of folklore, but through the vehicles of literature. Revere's ride was celebrated in a nineteenth-century poem by HENRY WADSWORTH LONGFELLOW, and the story of Nathan Hale has appeared in print hundreds of times, always in deliberate efforts to fashion him into the folk-hero patriot who uttered "My only regret is that I have but one life to give for my country." In truth, Revere was only one of three who rode to rouse the Minutemen, and Hale was an inept secret agent who arrived in Manhattan to begin his spying only after it was too late for the information to do Washington any good. He did nothing to make himself inconspicuous, and he even carried notes of his observations on his person, a fact that ensured his execution on September 22, 1776. Hale's amateurishness was in marked contrast to most of Washington's network of spies, who were typically quite capable and successful—but who play no role in American folklore.

ETHAN ALLEN is rare among Revolutionary heroes because he is a genuine folk hero, a figure originally celebrated primarily in oral tradition, rather than a literary creation after the fact. It is surprising how little Revolutionary folklore survives in other than an antiquarian context.

See also: POLISH AMERICANS.

Nineteenth-century advertising art freely appropriated A. M. Willard's famous painting, The Spirit of '76.

SUGGESTED READING: Tristram Potter Coffin, "Revolutionary War," in Jan Harold Brunvand, ed., *American Folklore: An Encyclopedia* (New York, 1996); Tristam Potter Coffin, *Uncertain Glory: Folklore and the American Revolution* (Detroit, 1971); Kenneth Silverman, *A Cultural History of the American Revolution* (New York, 1976).

Rice, Thomas "Daddy" (1808–1860).

Thomas "Daddy" Rice, a nineteenth-century

blackface entertainer, created a dance step he called "Jim Crow," which enjoyed extraordinary popularity in the United States and abroad and became a central feature of America's earliest form of popular mass entertainment, the MIN-STREL SHOW. Rice was born in New York City, but little is known about his life before he surfaced in a number of traveling stage companies, first as a property handler, then as an actor and writer. In 1829, he was cast as a comic African-American field hand in a Louisville production of Henry Morton Robinson's *The Rifle*, a backwoods play. He injected into this otherwise minor role a dance set to lyrics he wrote and music he either composed or arranged. The step has never been accurately reconstructed, but it was apparently based on a combination of a shuffle and a jump. Rice called the song and dance "Jim Crow," and his lyrics provide the only description of the step extant:

> First on de heel tap, den on de toe,
> Eberty time I wheel about I jump Jim Crow.
> Wheel about and turn about and do jis so,
> And eberty time I wheel about I jump Jim
> Crow.

Most authorities believe that Rice learned the step from a crippled African-American stable boy he met in Louisville, Cincinnati, or Pittsburgh while he was traveling with a stage company. Whatever its precise origin, "Jim Crow" produced such a sensation in *The Rifle* that Rice made it into a separate act and took it to New York in 1832. For the next three decades, until he died in 1860, Daddy Rice continued to "jump Jim Crow," earning wide popular acclaim, a handsome living, and an army of imitators, among them the popular entertainers Barney Williams, Jack Diamond, Bill Keller, Barney Burns, Bob Farrell, and, most notably, DANIEL DECATUR EMMETT, one of the early developers of

the blackface minstrel show. Although Emmett and his Virginia Minstrels developed and popularized the classic minstrel show, it was Rice who laid the foundation. He appropriated and adapted African-American folk tunes and lyrics and costumed himself in the red-and-white striped trousers and long blue "Yankee" coat that became the subject of one of Rice's most popular songs, "That Longtail'd Blue." Rice always appeared in blackface, continuing a tradition of the popular stage that may be traced at least as far back as 1769, when the English comedian Lewis Hallam played a "drunken darky" in a widely imitated theatrical afterpiece. (One of the leads in the first American comic opera, *The Disappointment* [1767] is a black character named Raccoon, played by a white actor in blackface.)

The "Jim Crow" routine became so pervasive a fixture of American popular culture that the phrase was used after the Civil War to describe any of the repressive racist laws enacted by southern state legislatures beginning during the 1870s, in the wake of Reconstruction.

See also: AFRICAN AMERICANS.

SUGGESTED READING: Russel Nye, *The Unembarrassed Muse: The Popular Arts in America* (New York, 1970); Constance Rourke, *American Humor: A Study of the National Character* (New York, 1931); Carl Wittke, *Tambo and Bones: A History of the American Minstrel Stage* (New York, 1930).

Richmond, W. Edson (1916–1994). A student of the BALLAD, Richmond was a leading folklore professor at Indiana University. A native of Nashua, New Hampshire, he was educated at Miami University of Ohio (B.A.), earning an M.A. and Ph.D. at Ohio State, where he also taught briefly until he joined the English faculty of Indiana University. Richmond served in many official positions within the folklore community and was editor of *Hoosier Folklore*, later renamed *Midwest Folklore*, and of the *Journal of Folklore Research*. His *Ballad Scholarship: An Annotated Bibilography* (New York, 1989) is considered a standard reference in the field.

Rickaby, Franz (1889–1925). Rickaby was an important early student and collector of logging and other occupational folk songs. A native of Rogers, Arkansas, Rickaby grew up in Springfield, Illinois, and was educated at Knox College (B.A., 1916) and at Harvard (M.A., English, 1917). He taught at the University of North Dakota from 1917 to 1923 and at Pomona College (Claremont, California) from 1923 until he succumbed to rheumatic heart failure in 1925. At North Dakota, he taught what he called "comparative balladry" and, with his students, embarked on numerous field trips, collecting at least 243 songs in North Dakota, Minnesota, Wisconsin, and Michigan. Fifty-one of these, all lumbercamp songs, were published in his posthumous *Ballads and Songs of the Shanty Boy* (1926).

SUGGESTED READING: Franz Rickaby, *Ballads and Songs of the Shanty Boy* (Cambridge, Mass., 1926).

Riddle, Almeda (1898–1986). Riddle was a well-known Ozark folksinger, who was popular on the folk-festival circuit and made a number of well-received commercial recordings. She was born in Arkansas and learned much of her early repertoire from her father, J. L. James, her uncle John Wilkerson, and other family members. Her mature repertoire of traditional Ozark folk songs numbered over six hundred. Married in 1916 to Price Riddle, she was widowed in 1926 when a cyclone killed her husband and the youngest of her four children. Struggling as a single parent through the Depression, she sang, she said, to preserve her sanity. But it wasn't until 1952 that folk-song collector JOHN QUINCY WOLF, JR., learned of her and recorded her. Later in the decade, as the folk-song revival picked up momentum, Riddle began to perform, and, by the 1960s and early 1970s, she was touring extensively.

SUGGESTED READING: Roger D. Abrahams, *A Singer and Her Songs: Almeda Riddle's Book of Ballads* (Baton Rouge, La., 1970).

Riddles. Among the oldest types of folklore known, riddles are questions or propositions requiring thought to answer or solve; typically, the riddle poses a "trick question"—one that is deliberately designed to trip up the respondent. The scholarly literature on riddles is extensive and often subtle in making distinctions among various riddle styles, but, generally, the following types of riddles are commonly encountered:

1. Description riddles: "What's black and white and red all over?" Answer: A newspaper. (Pun on red/read.) Alternate answer: A nun who has fallen down the stairs.
2. Comparison riddles: "Why is a fish like a piano?" Answer: Both have scales.
3. Contrast riddles: "What is the difference between a dog and a flea?" Answer: A dog can have fleas, but a flea can't have dogs.

4. Definition riddles: "What do you call 500 lawyers at the bottom of the ocean?" Answer: A good start.
5. Visual riddles: The riddler holds his hand out, palm up, the fingers pointing upward. "What do you call this?" Answer: A dead one of these. (The riddler turns his hand palm down, so that the fingers resemble the legs of an animal or insect.)

See also: TONGUE TWISTERS.

SUGGESTED READING: Elli Köngäs-Maranda, ed., *Riddles and Riddling* in *Journal of American Folklore* (Special Issue) 89, pp. 127–265; W. J. Pepicello and Thomas A. Green, *The Language of Riddles* (Columbus, Ohio, 1984); Archer Taylor, *English Riddles from Oral Tradition* (Berkeley, Calif., 1951).

Ringtailed roarer. Sometimes called a screamer, snorter, squealer, Mississippi roarer, or Salt River roarer, the ringtailed roarer is a backwoods and frontier stereotype, a bully and a loudmouthed braggart who typically picks fights and makes claims about his supernatural prowess that partake of the frontier's TALL TALE tradition. The roarer is also given to strutting about like a rooster and crowing in the manner of same, or neighing like a stallion while shaking his mane, or simply leaping into the air and clicking his heels together. The legendary flatboatman MIKE FINK was a ringtailed roarer. The epithet suggests a resemblance to some fantastic wild animal.

See also: BOASTING.

Rinzler, Ralph Carter (1934–1994). Rinzler was founding director of the SMITHSONIAN INSTITUTION's Festival of American Folklife (begun in 1967), and he also created the Office of Folklife Programs. The festival, which became an annual event, drew together many scholars, folk artists, and others interested in folklore and folklife.

Educated at Swarthmore College in Pennsylvania and at the Sorbonne, Paris, Rinzler was himself an accomplished performer on the MANDOLIN, BANJO, and other stringed instruments. Rinzler was associated with musicians of the 1960S FOLK REVIVAL, including BOB DYLAN, JOAN BAEZ, and Mary Travers, and he was, for a time, manager for Arthel "Doc" Watson and BILL MONROE. He also did extensive fieldrecording work. In 1987, Rinzler was instrumental in the Smithsonian's acquisition of FOLKWAYS RECORDS and began producing recordings for the newly acquired label.

Rip Van Winkle. The most popular of WASHINGTON IRVING's literary creations, Rip Van Winkle appeared in *The Sketch Book* (1819–20) as a simpleminded, good-natured, perpetually henpecked resident of a New York Dutch village in the Catskills. Accompanied by his faithful dog, Rip takes to the mountains one day, ostensibly to hunt, but mainly to gain respite from the shrewish Dame Van Winkle. Rip encounters a curiously dressed dwarfish figure, whom he helps to carry a keg up the mountain. Rip watches from a distance a group of similarly quaint figures playing ninepins. Rip then gives in to the urge to drink from the keg and falls into a deep sleep, only to awaken to a world transformed. His gun is rusted beside him. His dog is no more. He himself sports a long, long beard. Venturing back to his village, he discovers it is transformed as well; for one thing, the village inn that had borne a likeness of

The popular nineteenth-century American actor Joseph Jefferson built a career on his portrayal of Washington Irving's Rip Van Winkle.

King George III on its sign now sports a portrait of George Washington. He has slept for twenty years—slept through many events, including the American Revolution. No trace of Dame Van Winkle is to be found, and Rip is accepted by his grown children.

While Irving identifies the band of dwarfs as the spirits of the explorer Henrik Hudson (after whom the river is named) and his men, he drew on diverse material for his story, including the legend of Thomas the Rhymer (the English poet said to have lived for seven years in fairyland) and various German folktales, primarily the story of Peter Klaus, a Thuringian goatherd who, like Rip, witnesses a ritualistic game and falls into a sleep of many years' duration. Indeed, part of the enduring power of the Rip Van Winkle tale re-sults from its having tapped into a folk motif—the magical sleep—that appears in the tales of many traditions.

SUGGESTED READING: Philip Young, "Fallen from Time: Rip Van Winkle," in *Three Bags Full: Essays in American Fiction* (New York, 1967).

Ritchie, Jean (1922–). Folksinger and folksong collector Jean Ritchie was educated at Kentucky's Hindman Settlement School, Viper (Kentucky) High School, and Cumberland College. After graduation, Ritchie became a social worker at the Henry Street Settlement on New York City's Lower East Side and used traditional Kentucky ballads as part of her curriculum. In 1946, ARTUS MOSER recorded Ritchie at the Renfro Valley Folk Festival and Ritchie was soon part of the folk revival that began in the late 1940s and intensified through the 1950s and 1960s. During 1952, Ritchie, backed by a Fulbright grant, embarked on a folk-song-collecting trip to England, and in 1955 published her autobiography and song anthology, *Singing Family of the Cumberlands*.

Ritchie was married to filmmaker George Pickow, with whom she made several film documentaries about ballad and other folk traditions of the Appalachians.

See also: DULCIMER.

Robb, John Donald (1892–1989). Robb was a composer and professor of music at the University of New Mexico. He became acting dean of the institution's College of Fine Arts in 1942 and dean from 1946 to 1957. His contributions to folklore include numerous modern "classical" compositions based on folk music as well as his fieldwork throughout New Mexico, recording Hispanic and Native American folk songs. (He also recorded folk music in Latin America, Nepal, and Japan.) To the university, he left some three thousand recordings, which are housed in the John Donald Robb Archive of Southwestern Music in the Fine Arts Library at the University of New Mexico, Albuquerque.

Robb wrote extensively on southwestern folk music, including *Hispanic Folk Songs of New Mexico* (1954) and *Hispanic Folk Music of New Mexico and the Southwest: A Self-Portrait of a People* (1980). Robb was a founder and president of the New Mexico Folklore Society.

Roberts, Leonard Ward (1912–1983).

Born in rural Floyd County, Kentucky, one of eleven children, Roberts became an important collector of Appalachian folklore. He was educated at Berea College, the University of Iowa's Writer's Workshop, and at Indiana University, from which he earned a Ph.D. in 1953 with a dissertation published in 1955 as *South from Hell-fer-Sartin: Kentucky Mountain Folk-tales*. He issued another collection in 1969, *Old Greasy-heard: Tales from the Cumberland Gap,* and in 1978, *In the Pine. Sang Branch Settlers: Folk-songs and Tales of a Kentucky Mountain Family* (1974) documented and studied the oral history and folklife of the Couch family of Hardin County, Kentucky. In addition to his published work, Roberts amassed a large number of Appalachian legends, which are on deposit at the Southern Appalachian Archive, Hitchins Library, Berea College (Berea, Kentucky).

At Pikeville College, Kentucky, Roberts founded the Appalachian Studies Center and the Pikeville College Press (neither of which endured after his death), and he was also president of the National Folk Festival Association (1954–68).

Robinson, Rowland E. (1833–1900).

Robinson was a nature writer and an amateur collector of Vermont folklore. He wrote realistic local-color fiction based on genuine dialect speech, local proverbs, and traditional riddles, rhymes, games, and beliefs. His fiction presented folk material so meticulously that it is valued by folklorists as documentation.

SUGGESTED READING: Rowland E. Robinson, *Works of Rowland E. Robinson* (7 vols., Rutland, Vt., 1934–38).

Rock Candy Mountain.

Generations of American hoboes have imagined and sung about their version of the Land of Cockaigne (a medieval land of limitless plenty, luxury, and pleasure), the Rock Candy Mountain or Big Rock Candy Mountain. Here beer flows in streams, and cigarettes grow on trees, as do dollar bills—though these are left unplucked since, here, there is no need of money. Atop the Rock Candy Mountain is ice cream, and, nestled in the underbrush along the mountain's slopes, are fried breakfasts.

Rock 'n' roll.

A style of music, also called "rock," that developed in the United States beginning in the mid-1950s to become the dominant form of popular music through the balance of the century and, one may assume, for some time to come. Rock is not rooted in mainstream popular music—the song tradition of the 1950s and earlier—but, most immediately, in rhythm and blues and COUNTRY MUSIC, and, through these, African-American FOLK MUSIC. (In the mid-1960s, BOB DYLAN and others developed a subgenre of "folk rock," which had more to do with the FOLK REVIVAL of the period than with any direct reconnection to folk roots.)

Rock 'n' roll began as a very basic, straightforward style and was primarily dance music intended to appeal to teenagers, whose chief interests were romance, rebellion, and automobiles. The term *rock 'n' roll* was popularized in 1953 by Cleveland disc jockey Alan Freed, who applied it to the rhythm and blues recordings he broadcast. Freed was among the first disc jockeys to offer to white listeners what had been an exclusively African-American form of popular music. This paved the way for the rapid emergence of rock 'n' roll proper (at first little more than a quick-tempo version of R&B), performed in the mid-1950s by such musicians as Chuck Berry, Bill Haley and the Comets, Buddy Holly and the Crickets, and, paramountly, ELVIS PRESLEY.

It was Presley who was responsible for much of the music's early development, by adding into the mix a strong element of country music, creating a rock subgenre that was subsequently termed "rockabilly." Far more important to acceptance of the music was Presley's rich baritone voice, his musical savvy, his energy, his sexuality, and what must be described as his boundless charisma.

Rock burst on the rather complacent landscape of 1950s popular music with raw energy, which nevertheless flagged by the end of the decade as record companies sought to commercialize and homogenize the music. It took the so-called British Invasion, heralded by the ap-

pearance of the British group calling itself The Beatles, to rekindle rock's early promise. The Beatles and other British groups, including the Rolling Stones, had taken inspiration from rock's R&B roots as well as the early American rockers, and then brought that music back to America. By the mid-1960s, a host of important and original American groups achieved popularity and developed rock 'n' roll in many, often quite complex directions. The early seventies brought the music into another interval of commercial blandness and also saw the emergence of disco, highly stylized, heavily orchestrated, and (in the judgment of its detractors) fundamentally superficial dance music. Disco, while very popular, mobilized the opposition of those who longed for rock's earlier energy, and urban walls soon sported such GRAFFITI dialogues as "Death to Disco" versus "Disco Lives" and "Disco Forever." But, during the 1970s, a number of highly original and durable composers did emerge—among them Elton John, David Bowie, and Bruce Springsteen—and rock tended to divide into a more serious stream on the one hand and, on the other, "pop rock" or "bubble gum music," fare intended to appeal to young and unsophisticated listeners. The "serious" stream evolved into "art rock," a more intellectual, acerbic, ironic, and sometimes minimalist style. Art rock frequently incorporated elements of theater or performance art, and from this, the "rock video" or "music video"—a brief, elaborately produced video program—developed and achieved great popularity.

See also: AFRICAN AMERICANS; FOLK MUSIC; GIBSON MANDOLIN AND GUITAR MANUFACTURING COMPANY, LTD., THE; HONKY-TONK MUSIC; JAZZ; JOHNSON, ROBERT; McCOY, MINNIE (MEMPHIS MINNIE).

SUGGESTED READING: Art Fein and John Tobler, *The Greatest Rock & Roll Stories* (New York, 1996); Gary

J. Katz, *Death by Rock 'n' Roll: The Untimely Deaths of the Legends of Rock* (New York, 1994); Patricia Romanowski et al., eds., *The New Rolling Stone Encyclopedia of Rock & Roll* (New York, 1995); Irwin Stambler, *Encyclopedia of Pop, Rock, and Soul* (New York, 1990); Nick Tosches, *Country: The Twisted Roots of Rock 'n' Roll* (New York, 1996).

Rockwell, Norman (1894–1978). Norman Rockwell was an accomplished and very popular commercial illustrator, not a folk artist; however, his illustrations, especially those for *The Saturday Evening Post,* effectively evoked a world of Americana, usually contemporary, yet nostalgic, and typically focusing humorously on the idealized everyday events of small-town life. As far as the general public was concerned, Rockwell portrayed "folklife."

He had studied at the Art Students League and began illustrating for Condé Nast magazines when he was only seventeen. He sold his first cover to *The Saturday Evening Post* in 1916, and during almost half a century illustrated 317 *Post* covers. Rockwell was also the official illustrator of the Boy Scout calendars from 1926 to 1976. While no folk artist, Rockwell was regarded as "the people's" artist, in that he was continually condemned by critics but admired by millions of *Post* readers.

See also: WORLD WAR II POSTERS.

Rodgers, Jimmie (1897–1933). A highly pivotal figure in the history of COUNTRY MUSIC, Jimmie Rodgers was the first country singing star and is often called the father of country music.

James Charles Rodgers was born on September 8, 1897, in Pine Springs, just north of Meridian, Mississippi. His father, Aaron Rodgers, was an extra gang foreman on the Mobile and Ohio Railroad. Since Jimmie's mother died of tuberculosis when he was four or five years old, Jimmie was raised mostly by his father, a closeness he recognized later in the sentimental song "Daddy and Home."

When he left school for good at the age of thirteen, already showing early signs of the illness that had taken his mother, he traveled with his father on his various assignments. In one of the extraordinary twists in his life, he became a water boy on the railroad for which his father worked. Since water boys were almost always young African Americans, Jimmie had a rare opportunity to hear and absorb BLUES, WORK SONGS, HOLLERS, and the verbal idiom and patterns of expression of the African-American railroad gangs. The men among whom Jimmie worked took a liking to the motherless boy, and during the lunch breaks, they taught him to pick out melodies on BANJO and GUITAR as well as to sing moaning chants, crooning lullabies, blues, and work songs. He would draw on these early experiences throughout his performing career.

In the tough times after World War I, Jimmie was often out of work and also very vulnerable to bad weather. Colds would leave him with a persistent cough. By the end of 1925 his health had become too delicate for railroading, so he decided to become a full-time entertainer in order to support his wife and two little girls. Most of his early professional experience was performing in schoolhouses, in beer joints, and even on street corners. On one school appearance he started singing:

T for Texas. T for Tennessee,
T for Thelma, the gal made a wreck out
of me.

At the close of each verse he added a yodeling stanza, introducing a unique combination of blues and yodeling that would become the trademark of "America's Blue Yodeler."

In 1926, Rodgers moved to Asheville, North Carolina, where he hooked up with a hillbilly band. Putting himself on tenor banjo, he persuaded the band to call itself the Jimmie Rodgers Entertainers. It was jobless in only six weeks and barnstormed across the southeastern states in search of engagements until Rodgers's wife learned that Victor talent scout RALPH PEER was setting up a portable recording studio in Bristol, on the Virginia-Tennessee border, to audition country talent. A genius at judging salable talent, Peer decided that Rodgers had a perfect voice for popular recordings and got down two numbers, "The Soldier's Sweetheart" and an old lullaby of unknown origin, "Sleep, Baby Sleep." They were released in October 1927. In his next session, which took place in New York, Jimmie recorded four songs, including "T for Texas," the first of the "blue yodels," a form that proved to have great popular appeal. Jimmie began numbering these tunes; "T for Texas" became "Blue Yodel No. 1," the first of thirteen he would record. By 1928, he was known as America's Blue Yodeler as well as The Singing Brakeman.

Since Peer wanted original material, Jimmie enlisted the collaboration of his musical sister-in-law, Elsie McWilliams. Together, they produced numerous excellent songs, including "The Sailor's Plea," "I'm Lonely and Blue," and "Mississippi Moon." Although he was broadly inclusive in his recording output, and sang a significant number of Tin Pan Alley hits and popular standards, his creative instincts were deeply rooted in his native southern environment and manifested themselves in numerous songs such as "My Carolina Sunshine Girl," "My Little Old Home Down in New Orleans," "Dear Old Sunny South by the Sea," "Mississippi River Blues," "Peach Pickin' Time Down in Georgia," "Memphis Yodel," "In the Hills of Tennessee," and others.

Through the warmth of his personality and his performing gifts, he established the role of country music star, later having an impact on such artists as Gene Autry, Hank Williams, Ernest Tubb, George Jones, and Willie Nelson. His career, like his life, was brief. He recorded 110 sides before he died at age thirty-five, like his mother, of tuberculosis.

See also: BLUEGRASS; CARTER FAMILY, THE; GUTHRIE, WOODY (WOODROW WILSON); TUBB, ERNEST.

SUGGESTED READING: Nolan Porterfield, *Jimmie Rodgers: The Life and Times of America's Blue Yodeler* (Urbana, Ill., 1979).

Rodia, Simon "Sam" (1875–1965).

Rodia was the builder of *Watts Towers,* the most celebrated work of ENVIRONMENTAL FOLK ART in the country. Rodia built the structure, single-handedly, in the Watts section of Los Angeles during 1921–54. The tallest tower is almost one hundred feet, and the mixed-media environment includes complex mosaic inlays consisting of cement, bottles, dishes, seashells (72,000 of them), and mirrors. The principal structural elements are cement and steel rods. An engineering as well as aesthetic marvel, the towers contain no welds and are nowhere bolted or riveted together.

It was not until late into its construction that *Watts Towers* attracted attention. In 1951, art critic Jules Langsner, wrote about it, and in 1952 William Hale, a filmmaking student at the University of California, filmed Rodia at work. Despite this degree of attention, the structure was essentially abandoned after Rodia left Watts, and in 1959 was about to be torn down by the city.

Although the artist himself disavowed interest in his work, the public protested, and the *Towers* were restored and preserved. They are now the property of the State of California.

Watts Towers is a true environment. A scalloped mosaic wall faces the street and encloses three large towers and four smaller ones, in addition to fountains, birdbaths, decorated walkways, a ship model, and a gazebo. The work proclaims its connection with the community by the words "*Nuestro Pueblo*" ("Our Town" or "Our People") etched repeatedly into the tallest tower.

Rodia was born in Italy, probably near Naples, and came to America when he was ten or eleven years old. He lived with an older brother in Pennsylvania and educated himself, largely by reading the *Encyclopedia Britannica*. As a young adult, Rodia supported himself with a series of jobs, including logger, miner, and, most significantly, tile setter. He moved to Long Beach, California, in 1919, then, in 1921, moved to 107th Street in Watts, at the time a predominantly Spanish-speaking neighborhood. Rodia worked eight hours, every day, on *Watts Towers* until 1954, when he suddenly left Watts, deeding his property to a neighbor for the price of bus fare to Martinez, California. He dropped out of sight until 1959, but never said anymore about the *Towers,* and never returned to Watts to visit them.

SUGGESTED READING: Bud Goldstone, *The Los Angeles Watts Towers* (Los Angeles, 1997); Daniel Franklin Ward, *Simon Rodia and His Towers in Watts* (Monticello, Ill., 1986).

Rogers, Roy (1911–1998) and Evans, Dale (1912–). For many moviegoers, radio listeners, and young television viewers, this husband-and-wife team created the image of the American cowboy and, in particular, the American *singing* cowboy. Rogers, who was billed as "The King of the Cowboys," was a founding member of the great western swing group Sons of the Pioneers before he went solo as an actor and singer. On December 31, 1947, Rogers married Dale Evans, "Queen of the Cowgirls," and the pair recorded more than five hundred songs, some as duets, some separately. They also appeared together in twenty-six of Rogers's 104 films, starred on radio together, and, beginning in 1951, costarred on a popular children's television series that ran to one hundred episodes. In addition to being highly appealing "cowboy" stars, Rogers and Evans were acute businesspeople, who marketed their fame through extensive merchandising of toys, clothing, lunch boxes, and the like. Many of these items—such as the garishly embossed Roy Rogers wallet and Roy Rogers–Dale Evans lampshades (for children's bedrooms)—have entered the realm of kitsch and pop culture.

Roy Rogers was born Leonard Slye in Cincinnati, Ohio, and first adopted the stage name Dick Weston. Republic Studios signed him as a contract player in 1937, and the following year he was joined by his trademark palomino named Trigger, an animal that became about as famous (and popular) as Rogers himself. The star rode Trigger, in films, on television, and in innumerable public appearances, for three decades. Through the taxidermist's art, Trigger has been preserved and is on display at the Roy Rogers Museum in Victorville, California.

During the early 1940s, Rogers was second only to GENE AUTRY in popularity, and he surpassed Autry after the latter entered military service during World War II. While Rogers was at the height of his matinee film popularity, he premiered his radio show in 1944, the year he first

Franklin Delano Roosevelt created a strong personal bond with the American people, which was reflected in the Roosevelt ballads.

appeared (in *The Cowboy and the Señorita*) with Dale Evans. Born Frances Smith in Uvalde, Texas, Dale Evans was "girl singer" at the Chez Paree Night Club in Chicago in 1940, then became a Twentieth Century–Fox featured performer and a regular on ventriloquist Edgar Bergen's radio show. The Rogerses created a museum dedicated to their careers and personal lives in Victorville, California.

See also: COUNTRY MUSIC; COWBOYS; COWBOY SONGS.

SUGGESTED READING: David Rothel, *The Roy Rogers Book* (Madison, N.C., 1987).

Roosevelt ballads. The day following the death of Franklin D. Roosevelt, a printed ballad honoring him was offered for sale on the streets of a Mexican town. Composed overnight by Manuel Delgadillo, it was a traditional *CORRIDO*, which incorporated such details as the late president's "good neighbor policy" with Latin Amer-

ica and expressed on behalf of the Mexican people sorrow and sympathy at Roosevelt's passing. A short time after this, an African-American gospel or jubilee singing group recorded "Tell Me Why You Like Roosevelt." "Everybody knowed he was the poor man's friend," the lyrics ran, and "Only two presidents that we ever felt / Was Abraham Lincoln and Roosevelt." Other African-American ballad or gospel tributes appeared as well.

See also: FOLK MUSIC.

Rootwork. Also called root conjuring, rootwork is the practice of using the roots of various plants as AMULETS and CHARMS to counteract ailments brought on by malevolent spells or curses. Rootwork was traditionally common among African Americans in the rural South. Root doctors—the practitioners of rootwork—may also use roots to cast spells, a practice sometimes called *rootin'*. Both cures and spells may be effected by mere sight of the root (especially powerful is St. John's Wort, called JOHN THE CON-QUEROR ROOT), or by chewing a bit of the root, or by drinking the liquid yielded by boiling certain roots.

See also: MEDICINE, FOLK; PLANTS AND PLANT LORE.

Ross, Betsy (1752–1836). Born Elizabeth Griscom in Philadelphia, this seamstress earned a local reputation for fine needlework and helped her husband John Ross (whom she married in 1773) in his upholsterer's shop, a business she carried on after he was killed in 1776 while serving in the militia. Writing in 1870, her grandson, William Canby, said that she was visited in June 1776 by GEORGE WASHINGTON, Robert Morris, and her uncle, Gen. George Ross, who asked her to make a flag for the nation that, the next month, would declare its independence. The men handed her a rough sketch, which she improved and (according to Canby) Washington himself redrew, incorporating her suggestions, chief among which was replacing easy-to-make six-pointed stars with more technically demanding five-pointed ones, which Ross insisted would look better. It is said that Betsy Ross then sewed the flag, secretly, in her back parlor. There is no evidence either corroborating or confuting Canby's story, but it is known that Betsy Ross did sew flags for the navy of Pennsylvania. Betsy Ross has become as much a figure of folk legend as of historical fact.

Roswell incident. In July 1947, rancher William "Mac" Brazel reported to the sheriff in Roswell, New Mexico, that wreckage from an explosion was scattered across part of his property. The sheriff, in turn, reported this to the Roswell Army Air Base, whereupon (according to reports) Brazel was detained by military authorities while a team under Maj. Jesse A. Marcel collected the debris from the ranch. The debris was then loaded onto a B-29 bomber and transported to Wright-Patterson Air Base near Dayton, Ohio. Subsequently, stories circulated that the debris was from a flying saucer, a large portion of the "flying disc" was recovered intact, and (according to some stories) either dead or injured extraterrestrial beings were recovered from the wreckage. Marcel, however, repeatedly informed the press that, while debris was recovered, there was no "flying disc" or aliens. Nevertheless, an initial press release from the Roswell Army Air Base confirmed the recovery of a flying disc; later, this report was "corrected," and air base officials stated that the material recovered was from a weather balloon. When base officials exhibited weather balloon wreckage to the press, however, Marcel reported that the exhibited debris was not like what he had recovered, which, he said, was thin and foil-like, but could not be dented or permanently deformed. He further claimed that the wreckage included a light material resembling balsa wood, but was completely fireproof. Most astoundingly, Marcel described the presence of strange hieroglyphics on some of the debris.

The Roswell incident is one of the central stories of UFO FOLKLORE. It is the subject of many books, including *Alien Landing* (Terry Deary, 1996), *Beyond Roswell: The Alien Autopsy Film, Area 51, and the U.S. Government Coverup of UFOs* (Michael Hesemann and Philip Mantle, 1997), *Roswell Incident* (Charles Berlitz and William L. Moore, 1991), *The Roswell Message* (René Coudris, 1997), *The Roswell UFO Crash: What They Don't Want You to Know* (Kal K. Korff, 1997), *The Truth About the UFO Crash at Roswell* (Kevin D. Randle and Donald R.

Schmitt, 1997), *UFO Crash at Roswell: The Genesis of a Modern Myth* (Benson Saler et al., 1997), *The Day After Roswell* (Philip J. Corso and William J. Birnes, 1997), *The Real Roswell Crashed Saucer Coverup* (Philip J. Klass, 1997), *The Roswell Report: Case Closed* (James McAndrew, 1997), and *The Roswell Report: Fact vs. Fiction in the New Mexico Desert* (James McAndrew, 1995), to name only a few. In addition to the books, those interested in the Roswell incident can build a plastic model of the Roswell saucer (manufactured by the Testors company), the design of which is supposedly based on information supplied by an insider in the original investigation. In 1996, a purported film record of an autopsy performed on the alien corpses recovered from the downed disc was aired on Fox Network television. While some UFOlogists believe the film is genuine, most have concluded that it is a hoax, the latest in the many artifacts that make up the folklore of the Roswell incident. Strong evidence published in 1996–97 suggests that the debris recovered at Roswell did, in fact, come from a balloon—not a conventional weather balloon, but a balloon of an advanced secret design intended to detect Soviet atmospheric atomic-bomb tests.

Rounder Records. In 1970, Ken Irvin, Marian Leighton Levy, and Billy Nowlin, all Boston-area college students, carried their common interest in traditional music and its contemporary offshoots into founding Rounder Records, headquartered in Cambridge, Massachusetts. Their first release was the performance of the seventy-six-year-old traditional North Carolina BANJO player George Pegram. The passion for putting out recordings of folk artists drove them to document and nurture musical styles that include BLUEGRASS, CAJUN MUSIC, ZYDECO, New Orleans rhythm and blues, Memphis blues and soul, reggae, and TEX-MEX. Their work has been honored with Grammy Awards for recording bluegrass singer-fiddler Alison Krauss (twice), Professor Longhair, and Clarence "Gatemouth" Brown, and the company has received various other awards and honors as well.

After a a slow beginning—two releases in the founding year of 1970 and three more in 1971—Rounder expanded steadily and now averages more than a hundred new albums released each year, with many distributors supplying Canada, western Europe, Japan, Australia, and New Zealand, in addition to the United States. Their current catalogue includes more than 1,500 records, and the company's offerings are especially strong in bluegrass. Leading Rounder artists include such traditional performers as D. L. Menard, Eddie LeJeune, John Delafose, and the internationally popular Beausoleil.

Rourke, Constance Mayfield (1885–1941). Rourke was a cultural and literary historian who is best remembered for her *American Humor: A Study in the National Character* (1931), which identified folk humor (see HUMOR, FOLK) as the key influence on American literature. Rourke's was the first study of American folk humor to step beyond classification and conduct genuine analysis.

Rourke was born in Cleveland, Ohio, and took her A.B. at Vassar College in 1907, then studied at the Sorbonne, Paris. She returned to Vassar as a professor of English, stepping down in 1915 to work as an independent scholar. In addition to *American Humor,* Rourke wrote many magazine articles and book-length works on American cultural history.

SUGGESTED READING: Constance Rourke, *American Humor: A Study in the National Character* (New York, 1931); Joan Shelley Rubin, *Constance Rourke and American Culture* (Chapel Hill, N.C., 1980).

Ruth, Babe (1895–1948).

Born George Herman Ruth in Baltimore, Babe Ruth remains the most famous baseball player in history. Long-time holder of a record of sixty home runs in a major-league season (1927), Ruth became legendary as the "Sultan of Swat" and was the quintessential sports hero, whose feats seemed the stuff of TALL TALES, but were fact.

An unruly child, Ruth was deposited in St. Mary's Industrial School, Baltimore, where he became interested in baseball. He began his career in 1914 in the Baltimore minor league team and played with the Boston Red Sox until he was sold to the New York Yankees in 1920. He was a Yankee outfielder through 1934. Ruth led the American League in home runs for a dozen years, accumulating a lifetime home run total of 714 in twenty-two seasons of play, a record unbroken until Hank Aaron hit his 715th home run in 1974. Other Ruth records include 2,056 bases on balls and 2,211 runs batted in. Ruth played his last season in 1935 with the Boston Braves and ended his baseball career as a coach of the Brooklyn Dodgers in 1938. He was one of the first five players elevated to the Baseball Hall of Fame in 1936.

Ruth was purchased by the Yankees for the highest price ever paid for a player, and he became the highest paid player. When a reporter told him that he was making more money than President Herbert Hoover, Ruth replied, "I had a better year than him." This was an example of Ruth's instinctive talent for rendering himself a popular legend. He also owned a factory that turned out Babe Ruth cigars, featuring his face on every band—although Ruth had no part in the introduction of the Baby Ruth candy bar, which predates his fame. According to some sources, the candy had been named for President Grover Cleveland's daughter; others report that Baby Ruth was the granddaughter of candy company owner George Williamson. Like PAUL BUNYAN and any number of other folkloric giants, Ruth, at six-two and 215 pounds, had a gargantuan ap-

Babe Ruth's fame was international. Here Britain's Lord Louis Mountbatten and his wife, Lady Edwina, meet the Babe, 1927.

Ruth played himself in the 1942 film about his Yankee teammate and rival, Lou Gehrig in Pride of the Yankees. *During a break in shooting, he shakes hands with the film's star, Gary Cooper.*

petite, regularly wolfing six hot dogs and an equal number of sodas or beers at a sitting. He was renowned for his all-night binges with the boys—and for his ability to whack out home runs the next day nevertheless. He was held in such universal esteem that Japanese soldiers fighting in the Pacific jungles during World War II would yell out "To hell with Babe Ruth!" in response to GI's denigration of Emperor Hirohito.

Of the many legends (usually founded on fact) surrounding Babe Ruth, the most famous is that of the Indicator Home Run during the 1932 World Series against the Chicago Cubs. The thirty-seven-year-old Ruth had two strikes against him at the hands of Charlie Root in the fifth inning. Before the third pitch, Ruth solemnly pointed with his bat (some say it was his finger) toward the bleachers, then promptly connected with the next pitch and sent it flying into the spot indicated. Although Root insisted that Ruth's gesture was meant for him, telling him that he "still need[ed] one more, kid!" reporters claimed that Ruth had indeed called the shot, and Ruth did his best to confirm that impression. Almost equally famous is the story that Ruth visited a sick child, Johnny Sylvester, in a hospital and promised to hit three home runs for him in a World Series game—if he promised to get better. The legend was given the air of fact by its depiction in the 1948 film, *The Babe Ruth Story.* There is more than a grain of truth in the highly embellished story. During the 1926 World Series, young Sylvester was desperately ill and did receive autographed balls from players on the other team before the fourth game of the series, in which Ruth did hit three home runs, each longer than the one that had come before. It was a radio announcer who had heard about the sick boy and the baseballs and quickly improvised the story of Babe Ruth's promise. It, in turn, spawned another legend Ruth himself later told, about a crippled boy in Tampa who miraculously rose from his bed just to catch a glimpse of Ruth as he paraded through town with the Yankees en route to an exhibition game.

See also: BASEBALL FOLKLORE.

SUGGESTED READING: Robert W. Creamer, *Babe: The Legend Comes to Life* (1974; reprint ed., New York, 1992); Marshall Smelser, *The Life That Ruth Built* (1975; reprint ed., New York, 1993); Kal Wagenheim, *Babe Ruth: His Life and Legend* (1974, reprint ed., New York, 1992).

S

Sacred Harp music. *The Sacred Harp* is a religious tunebook published in Georgia (but printed in Philadelphia) in 1844 and compiled by two Georgia Baptist singing school teachers, Benjamin Franklin White (1800–79) and Elisha J. King (c. 1821–44). It was very popular, having been used in Georgia, Florida, Alabama, Tennessee, Mississippi, and Texas, and was based on the SHAPE-NOTE system of musical notation. The musical texts are primarily DR. WATTS HYMNS (hymns by Isaac Watts, 1674–1748) and the work of other hymnists.

Sacred Harp "singings" were informal gatherings for religious song. They were popular in the South before the Civil War, but can still be found today. The singers are seated facing one another in a square formation, grouped by four voice parts: tenor (melody), bass, treble, and alto. Each person who wished to do so might lead a song, which was first sung by the shape note syllables and then repeated, sung to its words. The Sacred Harp singing style is hard-edged, almost harsh, and, to those unaccustomed to it, sounds whining and nasal.

A "singing" typically begins late in the morning, is followed by a lunch for all, and then the singing resumes until midafternoon, when all sing a final tune, traditionally "Parting Hand" by Jeremiah Ingalls.

See also: FOLK MUSIC.

SUGGESTED READING: Buell E. Cobb, Jr., *The Sacred Harp: A Tradition and Its Music* (Athens, Ga., 1978).

Saddlebag house. An example of VERNACULAR ARCHITECTURE, the saddlebag house is based on a rectangular plan, sports a central chimney and two front doors, and is one room deep. Only after a second room was added to the chimney end of the original building (saddlebag fashion) did the structure become a saddlebag house. The American saddlebag house is modeled on English prototypes and was first imported into Pennsylvania, and had spread to the South by the nineteenth century.

Sailor and seafaring lore. Sailors work and struggle with unpredictable elements and forces of nature. Much of the folklore associated with seafaring, therefore, attempts to assert some degree of control over these elements and forces, even as it reinforces procedures and work habits designed to minimize risk and maximize efficiency. Seafaring is also an inherently romantic and heroic occupation, which has given rise to many legends and songs.

In confronting nature, sailors are aided by SUPERSTITIONS and folk beliefs. To outsiders, the best known of these holds that women aboard a ship bring ill fortune. Another superstition, made widely known through Samuel Taylor Coleridge's *Rime of the Ancient Mariner* (1797–98), proscribes the killing of sea birds. Sailing lore is full of stories about the consequences of violating these and myriad other taboos, such as embarking on a Friday, changing a vessel's name, and whistling at sea. Good-luck superstitions and rituals are less numerous than those intended to avert bad luck, but the most familiar good luck superstition is the christening ritual, in which a new vessel is launched by breaking a champagne bottle against her bow and declaring "I christen this ship *Titanic* [or whatever name]," just before she slides down the ways. Generally, a women is accorded the honor of christening a vessel.

The central uncontrollable element in seafaring is the weather, and much sailing is rich with WEATHER FOLKLORE, the most familiar of which is the rhyme, "Red sky in the morning, / Sailor take warning. / Red sky at night, / Sailor's delight." Sailors also look for such signs as a halo around the moon, which bodes stormy weather, the presence of sun dogs (small haloes or rainbows, near the horizon, on either side of the sun), the behavior of fish and birds, the look of the waves, and the shape and color of clouds.

While many individual mariners observe a variety of idiosyncratic personal rituals, most share in common an insistence on maintaining a highly ordered vessel—a shipshape ship. This not only enforces discipline and morale in a crew, it makes the ship efficient, something critical in dangerous situations, such as bad weather. Another seagoing ritual common on U.S. Navy and Coast Guard vessels is the good-natured hazing of "pollywogs"—neophyte sailors who cruise across the International Dateline, the Equator, or the Arctic Circle for the first time. On crossing the Dateline, pollywogs are initiated by being given a haircut (of indifferent quality), being subjected to questioning by King Neptune (a senior enlisted crew member), and finally being drenched with seawater. The initiated crew members are then pronounced members of the "Order of the Golden Dragon." Those who cross the Equator become "sons of Neptune," and those who cross the

Arctic Circle, members of the "Order of the Bluenose."

Seafaring is also replete with legends, TALL TALES, and DISASTER FOLKLORE, as well as WORK SONGS, the most familiar of which is the CHANTEY.

See also: MELVILLE, HERMAN; OCCUPATIONAL FOLKLORE.

SUGGESTED READING: Fletcher S. Bassett, *Sea Phantoms; or, Legends and Superstitions of the Sea and of Sailors* (Chicago, 1892); Horace P. Beck, *Folklore and the Sea* (Mystic, Conn., 1973); Joanna Colcord, *Songs of American Sailormen* (New York, 1938); Joanna Colcord, *Sea Language Comes Ashore* (New York, 1945).

St. John's Wort. See JOHN THE CONQUEROR ROOT.

Saint Patrick's Day. The March 17 feast day of the patron saint of Ireland who lived during the fifth century, Saint Patrick's Day is ostensibly an ethnic and religious festival. In the United States, it is an occasion for Irish-Americans to exhibit national and ethnic pride; however, this "great day for the Irish" is sometimes referred to as a day when "everyone is Irish." On this day, Irish and many non-Irish alike wear some conspicuous article of green clothing. Bars offer green-dyed draft beers, and many restaurants serve such items as green-dyed mashed potatoes. Urban politicians, regardless of ethnic or even racial background, eagerly participate in Saint Patrick's Day parades. Roman Catholic churches often serve dinners of corned beef and cabbage,

Two St. Patrick's Day chromolithographed greeting cards from the late nineteenth century.

traditional Irish fare, the proceeds going to charity. In Chicago, under Mayor Richard J. Daley (1902–76), the Chicago River was dyed bright green and a green center stripe was painted down State Street. Both traditions have continued, years after Daley's death.

See also: IRISH AMERICANS; PLANTS AND PLANT LORE.

Sainte-Marie, Buffy (1941–).
Buffy Sainte-Marie was born on a Cree reservation in the Qu'Appelle Valley, Saskatchewan, Canada, and was adopted and raised in Maine and Massachusetts. A college student during the 1960s, she began to write protest songs and love songs for such singers as Janis Joplin, Bobby Darin, Donovan, The Highwaymen, Barbra Streisand, ELVIS PRESLEY, Roberta Flack, Neil Diamond, among others. Sainte-Marie also began to perform on the folk music circuit during the FOLK REVIVAL of the period. She sang few traditional folk songs, preferring to perform her own compositions, the best known of which, "Universal Soldier," became one of the protest anthems of the decade. Sainte-Marie was particularly active on behalf of Indian rights and environmental issues. Other well-remembered Sainte-Marie protest songs in-

clude "Now That the Buffalo's Gone" and "Bury My Heart at Wounded Knee." She continues to write music, to perform, and to record. She is also a noted visual artist, who holds a Ph.D. in Fine Art from the University of Massachusetts.

See also: FOLK MUSIC.

Salem witch trials. During May through October 1692, a Court of Oyer and Terminer was convened in Salem, Massachusetts Bay Colony, to investigate accusations of witchcraft in and about the town. Ultimately, nineteen persons were convicted as witches and hanged. Others were imprisoned. The round of accusations began when a group of girls, having heard VOODOO stories told by a West Indian slave named Tituba, claimed they had been possessed by the devil. They accused Tituba and two other women of having bewitched them. The accused, fearing for their lives, incriminated others, and the hysteria thus spread. By the fall, some 150 persons were imprisoned and awaiting trial. In October, Governor Phips dissolved the special court and released all remaining prisoners. Later, all convictions were annulled.

The Salem trials are evidence of the intensity with which folklore relating to witches was experienced in colonial New England. The episode itself informed the folklore of New England for many years afterward and served writers as diverse in temperament and time as NATHANIEL HAWTHORNE and Arthur Miller as inspiration for short stories and, in the case of Miller, an allegorical play, *The Crucible* (1953).

See also: SEWALL, SAMUEL; WITCHES AND WITCHCRAFT.

SUGGESTED READING: Marion L. Starkey, *Devil in Massachusetts: A Modern Inquiry into the Salem Witch Trials* (New York, 1973).

Sambo. An example of EXOTERIC FOLKLORE, Sambo was a stereotyped character created by whites to denigrate African Americans. The Sambo image was crudely humorous, a thick-lipped, broadly smiling, shuffling, slow-witted, simian figure, which became pervasive in American folklore and popular culture until well into the twentieth century.

Some linguists believe that *sambo* may ultimately be derived from the Fulani (Senegalese) word for uncle or a Hausa word meaning "second son," but it is more immediately Hispanic deriving from *zambo,* a sixteenth-century word describing a monkeylike person with bowlegs. Depictions of Sambo appeared in British North

The Sambo figure used in an 1860 southern political cartoon, portraying Abraham Lincoln as "Sambo Agonistes," attempting to bring down the pillars of the Constitution. During the bitter election contest of 1860, pro-slavery newspapers frequently referred to candidate Lincoln as "black Lincoln."

America as early as the seventeenth century and were pervasive in the United States, in popular illustrations, on sheet music, calendars, social and political cartoons, CURRIER & IVES prints, and on advertisements for a variety of products, by the nineteenth century. Particularly popular in the later nineteenth century were painted cast-iron coin banks featuring the Sambo character, and, later, any number of items included representations of Sambo: place mats, souvenir pillows, and the cast-iron lawn jockey figures that once adorned many suburban homes. Well into the 1970s, a national restaurant chain, founded after World War II, called itself Sambo's and, for many years, used the racially offensive image as its logo. The Sambo type also appeared in literature, most famously as the Uncle Tom of Harriet Beecher Stowe's *Uncle Tom's Cabin* (1851), but also in such "subliterary" vehicles as newspapers, magazines, dime novels, and children's bedtime stories. Although JOEL CHANDLER HARRIS is generally affectionate and respectful in his treatment of African-American lore, even his UNCLE REMUS may be seen as a literary incarnation of Sambo. Movies and television exploited the Sambo type in many supernumerary roles, typically as a chauffeur, bellhop, shoeshine "boy," or Pullman porter. By the 1950s, as the civil rights movement came into its own, the Sambo stereotype fell under sustained attack. Helen Bannerman's popular children's book *Little Black Sambo* (1923) was removed from library shelves during this period although the central character is an East Indian child, not an African. In 1981, the Equal Employment and Opportunity Commission, a federal agency, found that "Sambo's Restaurants," a popular fast-food chain, violated public accommodation laws because its name was offensive to black customers. During the course of two to three decades, 1950s–80s, the image of Sambo gradually disappeared from mainstream American popular culture.

SUGGESTED READING: Joseph Boskin, *Sambo: The Rise and Demise of an American Jester* (New York, 1986).

Samplers. Embroidered panels of linen on which various types of stitches are demonstrated, samplers are the most familiar American examples of decorative folk NEEDLEWORK. European samplers date from at least as early as the sixteenth century, and their purpose has always been to demonstrate an individual's repertoire of embroidery stitches, either as an exhibition of skill and accomplishment or as a reference for onself or other needleworkers. By the 1600s,

An elaborate American sampler from New England, 1747.

A modern sampler, by an eleven-year-old Girl Scout, 1941.

samplers were being produced by girls as needle-work exercises and were typically signed and dated. American samplers featuring such motifs as alphabets, border designs, flowers, and even landscape scenes are found from the eighteenth, nineteenth, and twentieth centuries. Samplers were usually done in silk thread on a natural linen background, and the activity was begun as early as age five. By the teenage years, a girl was ex-pected to be able to complete quite complex sam-plers, with landscape scenes and decorative borders. Often, biblical text or proverbial sayings were integrated into the design.

SUGGESTED READING: Mary Jane Edmonds, *Samplers and Samplermakers: An American Schoolgirl Art, 1700–1850* (New York, 1991); Tandy Hersh and Charles Hersh, *Samplers of the Pennsylvania Germans* (Birdsboro, Pa., 1991).

Sandburg, Carl (1878–1967).

At one time, Carl Sandburg was perhaps the best-known poet in the United States, one of a handful of *living* poets whose works entered schoolbook an-thologies. Sandburg was also well known as a performer of folk songs. In addition, he was a col-lector of folk songs and other folk material, and was the author of a monumental six-volume biography of ABRAHAM LINCOLN (1926–39), a Pulitzer Prize–winning masterpiece of the genre. Sandburg's 1950 *Complete Poems* was also awarded a Pulitzer.

Sandburg was a native of Galesburg, Illinois, the son of Swedish immigrants. He was at loose ends as a youth, going to work at age eleven and spending his teen years hopping freight trains from one city and odd job to another. Beginning in the 1890s, he used his travels to transcribe folk songs in the journal he kept, listening to the hoboes and laborers he met. With the outbreak of the Spanish-American War in 1898, he enlisted in the 6th Illinois Infantry. On his return to Illi-nois, Sandburg became a door-to-door salesman, another peripatetic occupation that afforded op-portunities for learning new folk songs.

During 1910–12, Sandburg worked as an organizer for the Social Democratic Party and secretary to the mayor of Milwaukee, Wisconsin, then moved to Chicago in 1913, where he be-came an editor of *System*, a business magazine, and, later, a writer for the *Chicago Daily News*. He also began writing poetry, publishing his *Chicago Poems* in *Poetry* magazine in 1914 (they appeared in book form two years later). The best known of these poems—and perhaps the most fa-miliar of all Sandburg's verse—is "Chicago," in which the city itself becomes a veritable folk fig-ure: "Hog Butcher for the World, / Tool Maker, Stacker of Wheat, / Player with Railroads and Freight Handler to the Nation; / Stormy, husky, brawling, / City of the Big Shoulders." Critics saw Sandburg as the inheritor of WALT WHIT-MAN's mantle, except that, in contrast to Whit-man, Sandburg enjoyed rapid popularity with a general audience. People found his free-verse po-etry appealing.

Carl Sandburg in the 1920s and in the early 1940s.

While working for the *Chicago Daily News* from 1917 to 1932, Sandbrug embarked on research for his Lincoln biography, also using his research expeditions to collect more folk songs. In order to support himself during extended research trips, Sandburg lectured, presented poetry readings, and performed folk songs. He developed a strong rapport with his audiences, from whom he often collected variant versions of the songs and ballads he sung. Sandburg combined his historical research with his folk-song studies in another way as well, using the songs as windows into history, into the lives, thoughts, and dreams of "average" American people.

When the first two volumes of the Lincoln biography were published in 1926, Sandburg released a phonograph album of songs from Lincoln's era. This was followed the next year by his book *American Songbag*, a pioneering collection of 280 folk songs spanning all social strata and all of America's history, from colonial times to the twentieth century. In 1936, Sandburg published American folk sayings, slang, and proverbs, many of which he collected during his Lincoln research, in *The People, Yes*, and in 1950 issued the *New American Songbag*. This was his last significant contribution to American folklore; he spent the remainder of his long life in more literary pursuits and in semiretirement on his farm near Flat Rock, North Carolina.

See also: BUNYAN, PAUL; FOLKLORE IN AMERICAN LITERATURE; FOLK MUSIC.

SUGGESTED READING: Penelope Niven, *Carl Sandburg: A Biography* (New York, 1991); Helga Sandburg, *Sweet Music: A Book of Family Reminiscence and Song* (New York, 1963).

A Navajo sandpainting depicting the Sky Father and
Earth Mother.

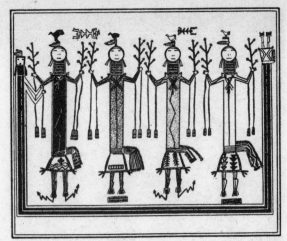

A Navajo sandpainting depicting the spirits of the
four directions, North, South, East, West.

Sand Man. The Sand Man seems to have originated in the nursery lore of western Europe, but
became very popular in the United States by Victorian times and has continued to figure in the
lore of American childhood. The Sand Man carries a sack of magical sleep sand, which he sprin-
kles on the eyes of children to make them sleep
and give them happy dreams.

Sandpainting. While non–Native Americans
collect framed examples of Navajo sandpainting
as prized folk art, it is, for the Navajo themselves,
a rite performed in healing ceremonials. The
sandpainting itself is an object made in preparation for this rite. During the final four days of an

eight-day, nine-night healing rite, a base of clean
sand is prepared in the center of the ceremonial
HOGAN. Colored crushed minerals are strewn
over this base to create images and patterns associated with the mythology of the ceremonial. The
finished sandpainting is blessed by strewing corn-
meal or pollen over it from the four cardinal directions. The person for whom the healing
ceremonial is being performed walks on the
painting and sits in the middle of it. The person is
identified with the figures of the sandpainting by
having the painting applied to his or her body, beginning with the feet, legs, trunk, and, finally, the
head. In the process of this application, the sandpainting is destroyed. By identification with the
painting, the suffering of the subject of the ceremonial is identified with the suffering of the
Navajo heroes and is thereby purged. At the conclusion of the ceremonial, the sand is gathered
and removed from the hogan.

SUGGESTED READING: F. J. Newcomb, *Hosteen Klah:
Navaho Medicine Man and Sand Painter* (Norman,

Three modern American images of Santa Claus: from a 1950s greeting card (flying over a town on Christmas Eve, presumably with a list of good boys and girls who will receive gifts), as a Christmas tree ornament, and as a Christmas Day parade float.

Okla., 1964); F. J. Newcomb and G. A. Reichard, *Sandpaintings of the Navajo Shooting Chant* (New York, 1937).

Santa Claus. Known as Father Christmas in Britain, Santa Claus came to America chiefly through the Dutch of New Amsterdam (modern New York). Dutch folklore included Sante Klaas—the incarnation of St. Nicholas, a bishop of Myra, Asia Minor, who was canonized some time after the fourth century, when he saved three sisters from enforced prostitution by giving each a dowry gift of bags of gold. In this way, St. Nicholas, Sante Klaas, Santa Claus, or Father Christmas became popularly associated with the ritual of gift giving, which, in turn, recapitulated the bestowal of gifts upon the Christ child at the Nativity. In this roundabout way, the jolly, rotund, white-bearded figure of Santa Claus, adorned in a white-fur-trimmed outfit of bright red, came to share the CHRISTMAS holiday with the central figure of the Christ child.

American popular culture has celebrated Santa Claus in ways ranging from the poem "A Visit from St. Nicholas," beginning "'Twas the night before Christmas . . . ," written in 1822 by the American Hebrew scholar Clement Clark Moore to amuse his children and first published anonymously in the Troy (New York) *Sentinel* on December 23, 1823, to the Santa Claus actor or emulator who sits on a throne in department stores and shopping malls across the United States at Christmastime, with children perched on his knee, taking note of their requests for gifts. Children seem to have little difficulty reconciling the commercial and fairy-tale aspects of Christmas, though adults often agonize over when, how, and whether to admit to their children that "there is no Santa Claus."

For American children, the Santa Claus story includes his residency at the North Pole, where he keeps house with Mrs. Claus (we do not know her first name) and where he runs a workshop assisted by elves or "Santa's Helpers"; his keeping of a roll of children who are "naughty or nice" (naughty children get no Christmas gifts—or, at best, receive a lump of coal in their Christmas stocking); and his annual magical rounds on an airborne, reindeer-drawn sleigh to deliver gifts. Santa lands on the roof of each house, which he enters by sliding down the chimney. Thoughtful children leave milk and cookies for the nighttime visitor. Some zealous, if literal-minded, fathers dress up as Santa Claus and distribute presents on Christmas Eve. An URBAN LEGEND tells of such a father who "actually" attempted to slide down his own chimney, became stuck, and suffocated (or succumbed to a heart attack). He was discovered by his family later that evening when they try to light a fire.

See also: TOOTH FAIRY.

Santo Niño Santero (working 1830–1860). An anonymous *santero* (creator of SANTOS, the Hispanic religious folk images of New Mexico) is named for his representations of the Christ child (the Santo Niño). He also probably created a number of BULTOS (three-dimensional representations of saints). His painting is characterized by simple, flat composition, bright colors, and careful outlining. The *bultos* attributed to him are prized for their grace and beautiful detail and are considered the high point of the nineteenth-century *bulto* in New Mexico. It is believed that he was a student of JOSÉ RAFAEL ARAGON.

Santos. Religious folk images carved and/or painted in the Hispanic tradition of the American Southwest, particularly in northern New Mexico. The earliest examples date to the end of the eighteenth century, and the tradition is continued today by such *santeros* as FELIX A. LOPEZ.

See also: ARROYO HONDO CARVER; ARROYO HONDO PAINTER; LAGUNA SANTERO; LOPEZ, JOSÉ DELORES; MEXICAN AMERICANS; SANTO NIÑO SANTERO; TRUCHAS MASTER.

Sassafras. This tree (*Sassafras albidum*), native to North America, produces leaves, flowers,

The Native American practice of scalping was reported by some of the earliest European explorers of North America. This engraving from Theodor de Bry's Collectiones peregrinationum in Indiam orientalem et Indiam occidentalem (1590–1634) depicts a battle scene in Florida.

berries, and bark and has roots that have long been used in Native American remedies, as well as non–Native American folk remedies borrowed from the Indians. Because parts of the sassafras tree are traditional remedies for ague, the tree is sometimes called the ague tree. Oil of sassafras, extracted from the roots, was the original flavoring agent for root beer.

See also MEDICINE, FOLK.

Saxon, Lyle (1891–1946). A native of Bellingham, Washington, Saxon was raised in Baton Rouge, Louisiana, and, as an adult, grew to consider New Orleans as his home. A journalist, Saxon was an enthusiastic advocate of the historic preservation and restoration of the French Quarter and of such New Orleans traditions as Mardi Gras. His popular histories of Louisiana, *Fabulous New Orleans* (1928) and *Old*

Louisiana (1929), included much folklore and gained him sufficient reputation so that he was tapped in 1935 to be head of the WPA's Federal Writers' Project in Louisiana. In this capacity, Saxon supervised a major folklore collecting effort, which was published in 1945 as *Gumbo Ya-Ya: A Collection of Louisiana Folk Tales* (coedited with Edward Dryer and Robert Tallant).

Scalping. No feature of Indian warfare is better known than scalping, or subject to more folkloristic speculation. Traditionally, many non–Native Americans have pointed to scalping as evidence of the Indian's incorrigible barbarity, while others have attributed to it special religious significance, claiming that the act of taking a scalp was intended to release the "spirit" or "soul" of the slain. Still other non–Native Americans assert that scalping was unknown among Indian tribes before the arrival of Europeans.

Scalping was, in fact, practiced among North American Indians before the advent of the Europeans: Jacques Cartier reported it in 1535, Hernando de Soto in 1540, Tristan de Luna in 1559, and others subsequently. It was not, however, universal among Indians, and it spread generally from east to west with the migration of eastern tribes and contact with whites who had adopted the custom from eastern Indians. Thus, while whites did not introduce scalping to the Indians of North America, they did contribute to the proliferation of the custom, both by pushing eastern Indians westward and by their own example. As to the non–Native American belief that scalping was meant to be of spiritual benefit to the victim, the evidence suggests the contrary. The act of scalping was meant as an insult to the defeated, and the scalp itself served as a battle trophy. Colonial and later authorities added a profit motive to the practice by offering scalp bounties, rewards paid for the scalps of "hostiles."

Different tribal groups practiced various methods of actually taking the scalp. Some tribes took the whole skin of the upper head, ears included; others removed only the crown. After Europeans introduced sharper, sturdier steel knives and hatchets among the Indians, many tribes practiced a more expedient method of scalping, which involved grasping the forelock, making a single gash in the front of the head, and popping the "scalp lock" trophy out with a sharp tug. As the "scalp lock" method was an abbreviated technique for taking scalps, so the practice of scalping seems to have originated in the first place as a substitute for decapitation. The scalp trophy stood for the head, even as the head represented the entire person of the victim. In some tribes, particularly among certain Plains groups, whole decapitation persisted in tandem with scalping—a severed head was considered a greater trophy than a scalp or scalp lock.

Scandinavian Americans. Scandinavian Americans are immigrants and the descendants of immigrants from Norway, Denmark, Sweden, and (far less numerous) Iceland. While Finland is geographically part of Scandinavia, its language is very different from that of the other countries, and FINNISH AMERICANS are therefore treated in another entry. While Scandinavians have been present in America since early colonial days, most came during the nineteenth century, primarily in search of economic opportunity. Scandinavian Americans produced distinctive oral and material folklore, but they also were assimilated rather rapidly into the American cultural mainstream. For that reason, little in the way of lengthy or complex narrative folklore from the Old Country survives among contemporary Scandinavian Americans. However, several museum collections preserve lore from the first two or three generations of immigrants. This includes oral narratives as well as examples of MATERIAL CULTURE, such as WEAVING, traditional dress, furniture, WOODCARVING, boats, and so on.

The REGIONAL FOLKLORE of the upper Midwest is dominated by Scandinavians, and much of the oral folklore in this region deals with the hardships of immigration and settlement. Many nineteenth-century oral accounts of starting a farm, raising a church, surviving the cold, hunger, disease, and hostile Indians, found their way into local newspapers. The nineteenth-century landscape of the upper Midwest was also marked by Scandinavian VERNACULAR ARCHITECTURE. Boats and boatbuilding (see BOATS, VERNACULAR) were also important Scandinavian-

American folk crafts. On a smaller scale, Scandinavian craftspeople produced beautiful examples of woodcarving, the most characteristic of which is furniture work ornamented with acanthus designs and other elaborate scroll carving. Furniture was also traditionally decorated with painted roses (*rosemaling*), and numerous Scandinavian-American families today treasure such pieces in their households.

In urban as well as rural communities, Scandinavian Americans celebrate traditional holidays, including Danish Constitution Day (June 5) and Norwegian Independence Day (May 17). As with the celebrations of other national and ethnic groups, these festival days are open to non-Scandinavians and Scandinavians alike and feature traditional foods, handicraft exhibitions, dances, and costume.

See also: IMMIGRANT FOLKLORE.

SUGGESTED READING: Philip J. Anderson and Dag Blanek, *Swedish-American Life in Chicago: Cultural and Urban Aspects of an Immigrant People, 1850–1930* (Urbana, Ill., 1992); Darrell D. Henning et al., *Norwegian-American Wood Carving of the Upper Midwest* (Decorah, Iowa, 1978); Barbro Sklute Klein, *Legends and Folk Belief in a Swedish American Community* (New York, 1980); Philip Martin, *Rosemaling in the Upper Midwest: A Story of Region and Revival Mount* (Horeb, Wis., 1989); Dorothy Burton Skaardal, *The Divided Heart: Scandinavian Immigrant Experiences through Literary Sources* (Lincoln, Nebr., 1974).

Scarborough, Emily Dorothy (1878–1935).

"Aunt Dot" Scarborough was primarily a scholar, novelist, and a teacher of creative writing (at Columbia University), but she also pub-

Henry Rowe Schoolcraft, as pictured in the 1856 edition of Algic Researches.

lished two important folk-song collections, *On the Trail of Negro Folksongs* (1925) and *A Song Catcher in the Southern Mountains* (1937). She also published the first scholarly article on W. C. HANDY (1923), which was based on firsthand interview material. Scarborough was president of the Texas Folklore Society (1914).

Scarborough was educated at Baylor University (B.A., 1896; M.A., 1899) and at Columbia University (Ph.D., 1917); she also studied at Oxford University (1910).

Schoolcraft, Henry Rowe (1793–1864).

Schoolcraft was an explorer and ethnologist. As an explorer, he is best known for having discovered the source of the Mississippi River; as an ethnologist, he is remembered for his valuable writings on the Plains Indians. He was the first to collect and systematically study a significant body of Native American folklore. Of great significance was his reliance on native informants. His two-volume *Algic Researches* (1839) is a collection of narrative folklore from the Ojibwa and formed the principal basis of HENRY WADS-WORTH LONGFELLOW's *Song of Hiawatha* (see HIAWATHA). The bulk of his contributions to Native American ethnology was published in his six-volume *Historical and Statistical Information Respecting the History, Condition, and Prospects of the Indian Tribes of the United States* (Washington, D.C., 1851–57).

Schoolcraft made his first expedition into the American frontier during 1817–18, on a mineralogical survey of the present states of Missouri and Arkansas. In 1820, he was a topographer attached to an expedition to the upper Mississippi and Lake Superior region, and he was subsequently appointed as federal agent to the Indian tribes of the Lake Superior region. In 1822, he married a woman who was part Ojibwa, and this relationship gained him access to the tribe he most closely studied.

In 1832, Schoolcraft traveled to the upper Mississippi, locating its source at Lake Itasca (in the present state of Minnesota). He became superintendent of Indian affairs for Michigan (1836–41), concluding a treaty with the Ojibwa in 1836, by which the tribe ceded much of northern Michigan to the United States.

SUGGESTED READING: Rosemary Zumwalt, "Henry Rowe Schoolcraft, 1793–1864: His Collection and Analysis of the Oral Narratives of American Indians," *Kroeber Anthropological Society Papers* 53 (1978), pp. 44–57.

Schottische.

Like the POLKA, the schottische is a social folk dance for couples. Probably Scottish or German (or imported from Scotland through German sources) in origin, the schottische was popular in American as well as European ballrooms during much of the middle to late nineteenth century. The form appears in diverse folk dance traditions, including Scottish, Scandinavian, and Mexican dances. Schottische rhythm is 2/4 or 4/4, and the step is typically a variation on a basic three rapid steps and a hop. Dancing couples circle the room, promenade forward, and turn round each other. The dance has many variations.

See also: DANCE, FOLK; FIDDLE; TEX-MEX MUSIC.

Scottish Americans.

Scots were among the most numerous of early colonial immigrants, most of them settling in the southern colonies during the seventeenth and eighteenth centuries. By the nation's first census of 1790, some 6 percent of the U.S. population was Scottish or Scotch-Irish. The Scotch-Irish are descendants of Scots Protestants who colonized Ulster, in Northern Ireland, during the seventeenth century. Immigrants of Scotch-Irish descent typically settled on the Appalachian frontier, bringing with them many of the BALLADS that drew the attention of early students of American folklore and that influenced COUNTRY MUSIC, BLUEGRASS, and the music of the FOLK REVIVAL.

Evident in modern southern and western dialects are many characteristics of Scotch-Irish pronunciation, patterns of speech (for example, the southerner's "I might could" for "I could"), and vernacular vocabulary (including *pinky* for little finger, and even the exclamation *wow!*). Also still in evidence throughout parts of the South and West are the Scots' Calvinist religious, moral, and social attitudes that prevailed in the eighteenth and nineteenth centuries. In terms of MATERIAL CULTURE, these attitudes find expression in the plain architecture of many southern Protestant churches.

Today, those who identify themselves as being

of Scottish descent organize and participate in such ethnic cultural festivals as the Highland Games (in New York) and the Caledonian Games (in various areas) and may also participate in a wide variety of Scottish-American clan societies, "Scottish societies," and bagpipe bands. Despite the variety of Scottish-American cultural and heritage organizations, Scottish Americans are still subject to an EXOTERIC FOLKLORE, which reduces the salient Scottish characteristic to a single trait: thrift (if positively interpreted) or stinginess (if negatively interpreted). Scottish names and iconic images of tartans, bagpipes, and figures in kilts and tam-o'-shanters adorn the logos of cut-rate furniture stores, bargain car rental companies, cheap household movers, and so on. Allusions to Scots and things Scottish often serve, in vernacular speech, as synonyms for stinginess: "Don't expect a loan from him. Where money's concerned, he's Scotch!"

See also: IMMIGRANT FOLKLORE.

SUGGESTED READING: Emily Ann Donaldson, *The Scottish Highland Games in America* (Gretna, La., 1986); David Hackett Fischer, *Albion's Seed: Four British Folkways in America* (New York, 1989); Clayton Jackson, *A Social History of the Scotch Irish* (Lanham, Md., 1993).

Scrimshaw. See WHALING.

Scruggs, Earl (1924–). A virtuoso five-string BANJO player, Scruggs was largely responsible for reviving popular interest in the instrument. Born in Flint Hill, North Carolina, Scruggs started playing his father's banjo when he was only five and, by age fifteen, was performing on the radio. At this time, he developed an idiosyncratic picking technique using the thumb and first two fingers of the right hand. This, now called the "Scruggs style," allowed him to play with great velocity and accuracy. He auditioned for and was hired by BILL MONROE for his Blue Grass Boys band in December 1945. He was the group's first banjoist. As one of the Boys, Scruggs gained national exposure on tour and over the air, on the *GRAND OLE OPRY*.

With Blue Grass Boys guitarist and tenor singer Lester Flatt, Scruggs left the Monroe ensemble, and the two became a duet, the Foggy Mountain Boys—also known simply as Flatt and Scruggs. By the 1950s and 1960s, the pair's bluegrass recordings challenged those of the Blue Grass Boys in popularity. Scruggs's instrumental compositions, especially "Foggy Mountain Breakdown," "Flint Hill Special," and "Earl's Breakdown," became substantial and enduring hits.

The Flatt and Scruggs partnership ended in 1969, and Scruggs joined his sons in creating a country-rock band, the Earl Scruggs Revue. Scruggs retired as a stage performer in 1980, but continued to record. He was inducted into the Country Music Hall of Fame in 1985.

See also: BLUEGRASS; COUNTRY MUSIC.

SUGGESTED READING: Country Music Foundation, *Country: The Music and the Musicians* (New York, 1988).

Seeger, Charles Louis (1886–1979). Seeger was an important American musicologist, composer, and musical educator. He was educated at Harvard University and, after graduating in 1908, studied composition in Europe. He returned to the United States in 1912, when he joined the faculty of the University of California, Berkeley.

Seeger became interested in folk music during the 1930s and created a number of New Deal–era programs using folk music as a means of addressing social tensions and creating a sense of community. He extended this work beyond the United States during 1941–53, when he worked with the Pan American Union to create a community of musicians throughout the Americas. From 1961 to 1971, Seeger worked the Institute of Ethnomusicology at UCLA. Seeger's interest in and commitment to folk music was transmitted to his children Pete, Michael, and Peggy, all of whom played roles in the folk revival of the 1950s and 1960s.

See also: PETE SEEGER.

SUGGESTED READING: Charles Seeger, *Studies in Musicology, 1935–1975* (Berkeley, Calif., 1977).

Seeger, Pete (1919–). A leading figure in the folk music revival of the 1940s, 1950s, and 1960s, Pete Seeger is among the nation's best-known social activist folksingers and songwriters. Seeger consistently used folk music to further social ends, including the rights of labor, freedom from government oppression, civil rights, ending the Vietnam War, promoting environmental responsibility, and, by the 1990s, living with, rather than for, technology.

Born in New York City to musicologist and social activist CHARLES SEEGER and avant-garde classical composer Ruth Crawford Seeger, Pete Seeger was educated at Harvard. Unable to find employment in his chosen field, journalism, Seeger began performing on a four-string BANJO and, later, a five-string banjo, for local groups, schools, and summer camps. The five-string instrument, which had been largely supplanted by the four-string banjo in modern performance, became Seeger's trademark, and, in homage to WOODY GUTHRIE, whose guitar bore the legend "This machine kills Fascists," Seeger inscribed on his, "This machine surrounds hate and forces it to surrender." Seeger toured with Guthrie in 1940.

With Lee Hays and Millard Lampell—and, later, Woody Guthrie and others—Seeger formed the Almanac Singers, who performed mainly to labor audiences. At this time, Seeger also joined the Communist Party. World War II interrupted his musical career, as Seeger did a stint in the army, then, after the war, reunited with Hays and added Ronnie Gilbert and Fred Hellerman to form the Weavers. Unlike the Almanac Singers, the Weavers appealed to popular audiences, although much of their material was still distinctly political and social. But it is for such mainstream folk hits as "Wasn't That a Time," "Kisses Sweeter Than Wine," the ethnic Yiddish song "Tzena, Tzena," "Michael, Row the Boat Ashore," and their signature "Goodnight, Irene" that the Weavers are best remembered.

Like many other artists in the McCarthy-era 1950s, Seeger was blacklisted—from 1952 to 1962—because of his Communist ties. While the career of the Weavers was, therefore, limited by the effect of the blacklist, they exerted a formative influence on such late 1950s and 1960s "folkie" groups as the Limelighters, the Kingston Trio, and Peter, Paul, and Mary, as well as on Woody Guthrie's son Arlo.

After Seeger left the Weavers in 1957, he continued to perform, compose, and engage in social activism. Extensively recorded, Seeger has performed some 300 songs on approximately fifty albums. His "Where Have All the Flowers Gone?" became the veritable anthem of the Vietnam War protest era.

See also: ASCH, MOSES; FOLKWAYS RECORDS; HILL, JOE; TERRY, SONNY.

SUGGESTED READING: Pete Seeger, *Where Have All the Flowers Gone: A Singer's Stories, Songs, Seeds, Robberies* (Bethlehem, Pa., 1993); Pete Seeger and Jo Metcalf Schwartz, eds., *The Incompleat Folksinger* (New York, 1972).

Sermon, folk. A spontaneous, extemporaneous sermon given by a folk preacher. Folk sermons are most common among certain groups of Baptists, Methodists, and Pentecostals, as well as other, nonaffiliated faiths and are especially prevalent among African-American religious assemblies. Typically, the folk sermon is intensely emotional and histrionic, chanted rather than spoken, and often building to a crescendo of expressiveness. Usually, there is a considerable degree of give and take, question and response (antiphonal structure), between preacher and congregation. Like other forms of oral performance, the folk sermon usually contains much repetition and much that is formulaic, including many phrases typical of oral folklore and bardic recitation. During the 1960s, the folk sermon, in the form of the eloquent civil rights "speeches" of Dr. Martin Luther King, Jr., reached what was certainly its widest audience ever.

See also: RELIGION, FOLK.

SUGGESTED READING: Bruce A. Rosenberg, *Can These Bones Live?* (Urbana, Ill., 1989).

Sewall, Samuel (1652–1730). Sewall was born at Bishopstoke, Hampshire, England, and

Samuel Sewall in a portrait by John Smibert, 1792. The original is at the Museum of Fine Arts, Boston.

immigrated with his family to the Puritan Massachusetts Bay Colony. A prosperous and prominent New England merchant, he served as a judge in the SALEM WITCH TRIALS, for which he later publicly apologized. Historians and folklorists value his extensive, candid, and detailed *Diary* for the insight it gives into daily life in the New England colony. The *Diary* is a rich source of folklore and folklife information for the period.

Sewall was educated at Harvard College (graduated 1671) and was manager of the colonial printing press (1681–84), member of the colonial Council (1684–1725), and chief justice of the Superior Court (1718–28). In 1692 Governor William Phips appointed Sewall one of the commissioners to try the Salem witchcraft cases. Sewall was the only judge to admit the error of having condemned nineteen persons to death.

See also: FOLKLORE IN AMERICAN LITERATURE.

Shakers Near Lebanon, *an undated print by Currier & Ives. (Collection of Walton Rawls)*

SUGGESTED READING: Samuel Sewall, *Diary of Samuel Sewall, 1674–1729* (New York, 1973); Ola Winslow, *Samuel Sewall of Boston* (New York, 1964).

Shaker folk art and crafts.

Formally known as the United Society of Believers in Christ's Second Appearing, the Shakers were a celibate millenarian sect, originally derived from an extreme sect of the Quaker faith, that established communal settlements in the United States beginning in the eighteenth century. The sect believed in living a life of perfect simplicity combined with productive labor. Small Shaker communities flourished in the nineteenth century, but declined by the end of the century, largely the result of their adherence to celibacy.

The first Shaker community in the United States was established at New Lebanon, New York, in 1787. From here, Shaker groups fanned out to create communities ("villages") in Kentucky, Ohio, and Indiana. By 1826, eighteen Shaker villages had been established in eight states, and the sect attained its high-water mark in the 1840s, when some 6,000 members were enrolled. Like the Quakers and the Mormons, the Shakers were often persecuted for differing from the mainstream; however, they were also widely admired for the ingenuity of their inventions and the simple beauty of their crafts. These also brought them a considerable degree of economic prosperity. Shaker technological innovations include a version of the marine screw propeller, Babbitt metal, a rotary harrow, a turbine waterwheel, a new type of threshing machine, the circular saw, and the common clothespin. They also created a flourishing packaged seed industry (a marketing and merchandising innovation) and a medicinal herb industry.

Music was an important part of Shaker life and worship. Hymns original to the sect were transmitted from member to member by letter until the first Shaker hymnal was published in 1813. The hymn "Simple Gifts" became widely known outside of the Shaker communities as a traditional song, and the tune gained international prominence after AARON COPLAND adapted it in his popular 1944 ballet score *Ap-*

palachian Spring. Even more widely known and admired outside of the communities were and are the Shakers' extraordinary architectural design, pottery, quilts, rugs, bonnets, silk scarves, brooms, cedar pails, churns, and furniture. All examples of Shaker MATERIAL CULTURE are characterized by austerity of decoration and truth to materials, aesthetic ideals that emanated from the sect's religious convictions. Coincidentally, the religiously inspired ideal of an object's form following its function, without extraneous ornament, anticipated concepts of functionalism, which entered mainstream American architecture, industrial design, and art beginning in the early twentieth century. The single most representative Shaker craft object is the Shaker chair. Elegant and beautifully crafted, it was very sturdy, yet also very light, so that it could be hung on wall pegs when a room was being cleaned or when the space was required for communal dance or religious services. The chair, like other examples of Shaker furniture, relies little on European models and is truly innovative.

By 1905, only about a thousand Shakers remained. Today the sect is virtually extinct. However, its culture and crafts are well represented in American museums, most notably at the Fruitlands Museum in Harvard, Massachusetts, and in the Shaker Museum at Auburn, Kentucky.

SUGGESTED READING: Julia Neal, *The Kentucky Shakers* (Lexington, Ky., 1982); Edward Andrews, *People Called Shakers: A Search for the Perfect Society* (New York, 1994); Julie Nicoletta and Bret Morgan, *The Architecture of the Shakers* (Woodstock, Vt., 1995); June Sprigg, *By Shaker Hands* (Boston, 1990).

Shape-note singing. Shape notes, also called patent notes, are the elements of a system of musical notation using four distinctively shaped note heads to indicate the four syllables of the musical scale (*fa, sol, la,* and *mi*) employed at the time in vocal teaching. This simple system made it unnecessary to learn key signatures. It opened scored music to far more performers. The system was invented by William Little and William Smith in *The Easy Instructor,* published in Philadelphia in 1801. While shape-note notation found a chilly reception in New England and the Northeast generally, it was widely adopted in the South and West for sacred music. *The Sacred Harp* (1844), by B. F. White and E. J. King, was the most popular and successful of the numerous shape-note tunebooks published in the early nineteenth century (see SACRED HARP MUSIC), and shape-note singing was taught in singing schools throughout the South. (The singing school was an important early American institution and was especially popular in the South, from the early eighteenth century through the antebellum period.) The REVIVAL SONGS sung at camp meetings were typically drawn from shape-note tunebooks.

Shape-note singing persisted in the South even after the Civil War, although a more flexible seven-shape system supplanted the original four shapes. A few shape-note singing schools still exist in the South.

See also: FOLK MUSIC; GOSPEL MUSIC; VAUGHAN, JAMES D.

SUGGESTED READING: Buell E. Cobb, Jr., *The Sacred Harp: A Tradition and Its Music* (Athens, Ga., 1978); George Pullen Jackson, *White Spirituals in the Southern Uplands* (1933; reprint ed., New York, 1965).

Shape shifting. A power associated with malevolence and witchcraft in certain Native

American folk cultures, shape shifting is the ability to change appearance. The Navajo Yenaldooshi (Skinwalker) and COYOTE are examples; both have the ability to trade skins with hunters in order to sleep with their wives. Occasionally, shape shifting has a positive association and may be an attribute of a CULTURE HERO.

See also: RAILROAD BILL; STAGOLEE.

Sharp, Cecil James (1859–1924).

Sharp was a pioneering collector of English and Anglo-American folk song and dance. In addition to work in his native England, where he revived the English Folk-Song Society and founded the English Folk-Dance Society (later merged the Folk-Song Society), Sharp, assisted by Maud Karpeles, traveled widely in the southern Appalachians during 1914–16, collecting a massive amount of American folk songs. His chief interest was in the American incarnations of English material, a collection of which was published after his death in *English Folk Songs from the Southern Appalachians* (1932).

See also: APPALACHIA; CAMPBELL, OLIVE DAME; CHASE, RICHARD; FOLK MUSIC; IMMIGRANT FOLKLORE.

SUGGESTED READING: Maud Karpeles, *Cecil Sharp: His Life and Work* (Chicago, 1967).

Shaw, Lloyd "Pappy" (1890–1958).

Shaw was a pioneer popularizer of folk dance and was responsible for bringing square dancing to a broad audience. A native of Denver, Colorado, Shaw earned his B.A. at Colorado College in 1913 and taught at Cutler Academy and in a Colorado Springs high school. From 1916 until his retirement in 1951, Shaw was superintendent of Cheyenne Mountain School, a system of three schools and a kindergarten near Colorado Springs. Under Shaw's direction, the school became internationally famous for its creative programs, which seamlessly joined in-school with extracurricular activities. Among the many subjects Shaw taught was American folk dancing, with particular emphasis on the square dance. His lectures and writings are credited with bringing about a widespread revival of square dancing. Especially influential was his work on the role of the square-dance "caller."

From 1929 to 1951, Shaw was director of the Cheyenne Mountain Dancers, made up of high school students, and from 1940 to 1957 he conducted the Lloyd Shaw Summer Session in the American Square Dance, at Colorado Springs, for teachers and recreation leaders. Shaw served as technical dance adviser on several motion pictures, most notably the 1945 *Duel in the Sun,* and he founded Lloyd Shaw Recordings, Inc., in 1950, to produce records meant to accompany American round dances, quadrilles, folk dances, and the like, complete with spoken instructions. Among Shaw's several books is *Cowboy Dances* (1939), which includes the first—and still most complete—discussion of the evolution of the American square dance and *The Round Dance Book* (1948) is a thoroughgoing study of American couple dances.

See also: SQUARE DANCE.

Sheepman stories.

Although less picturesque than the COWBOY, the sheepman played an important role in the agriculture of the American

West. Sheepmen and cattlemen feuded, often violently, because they were in competition for precious grazing land. Cattle and sheep could not share the same pasturage, and whereas the grazing habits of cows left the root structure of the grass intact, sheep grazing destroyed the grass, roots and all, threatening to denude vast tracts of cattle range. The most violent feuds erupted into full-scale "range wars," which produced stories as well as FOLK-SAY in addition to mayhem. Expressions such as "crazy as a sheepherder" and "there ain't nothing dumber than sheep except the man who herds 'em" became common, as did tales about the sheepherder living so long among his sheep that he forget how to speak or speaks in sheep-inflected English: A traveling salesman took a seat beside a sheepherder on a train. "Where are you from?" the salesman asked. "Montanaa-aa-aa!" came the bleating reply. "Where are you going?" "Baa-aaaack!"

"Shenandoah." A majestic sea CHANTEY of haunting beauty, "Shenandoah" is of American origin and may have been composed by a *voyageur* (a fur company boatman working the far West). In earlier versions of the song, Shenandoah is an Indian chief whose daughter is wooed and won by a fur trader, but the later (and more familiar) versions sing of homesickness for the Shenandoah Valley. The song was popular with immigrants to the West, who doubtless identified with the emotions of leaving the lush green valleys of the East for the harsh prairies of the Midwest and West. The song was frequently heard during the FOLK REVIVAL of the 1960s and has always been a favorite in choral and glee club performances.

See also: FOLK MUSIC.

Shine. Shine is the principal character in a cycle of African-American TOASTS. He is a TRICKSTER, who defies authority—typically *white* authority—to come out on top at the conclusion of the tale. Most famously, Shine is depicted as the sole survivor of the *Titanic* sinking (1912). He is on board as a stoker and repeatedly warns the captain and others of danger, but, because he is black, he is ignored. The ship strikes the iceberg, Shine swims all the way to the United States, and relaxes in a Philadelphia bar as the ship finally disappears below the surface. Shine is a survivor, who not only defies white society, but triumphs over it.

The word *shine* is a derogatory epithet used by blacks as well as whites to describe a very dark black man. It is unclear whether the name comes from a perception of the dark skin's sheen or from the African American's stereotypical occupation as a shoeshine "boy." Shine tales were once prevalent in Louisiana and Mississippi.

See also: AFRICAN AMERICANS.

Shivaree. A raucous serenade to newlyweds, the shivaree is a kind of rite of passage. The "serenaders" gather outside the new couple's home in the evening and make as much noise as possible with an array of "instruments" (mainly pots and pans). They keep up the racket until they are offered money or invited into the house for food and drink. Once invited in, it is customary for the revelers to play practical jokes, including placing some sort of booby trap on the bed. Bride, groom, or both may also be hazed by being tossed into a pond or by having water or some other benign substance dumped on them.

The word *shivaree* is derived from the French *charivari* (meaning crude music). In France and throughout much of Europe, the *charivari* was not a rite of passage for newlyweds, but an expression of community disapproval of adulterous unions, wife beaters, or "unnatural" unions (marriages in which the couple is mismatched by age or social rank, for example). In effect, the *charivari* was a form of vigilantism and ranged from simple harassment to mob violence. When the custom came to North America as the shivaree, it was almost wholly transformed into a good-natured hazing ritual for all newlyweds.

The shivaree was popular in rural parts of the United States and Canada during the nineteenth century and is still practiced in some remote Canadian communities. The custom of tying shoes and other noisemakers to the back of the newlyweds' car before it departs from the site of the wedding ceremony may be seen as a vestige of the shivaree.

See also: FRENCH AMERICANS; WEDDINGS.

SUGGESTED READING: Monica Morrison, "Wedding Night Pranks in Western New Brunswick," *Southern Folklore Quarterly* 38 (1974), pp. 285–97.

Shmoo. A ghostly, ham-shaped, all-providing, magical creature from the *L'il Abner* COMIC STRIP by Al Capp (1909–79), the Shmoo shares many features with the magical characters of TALL TALES and may also be seen as the satirical embodiment of an American (or maybe just human) desire to get something for nothing. The Shmoo always smiles, demands nothing, eats nothing, reproduces rapidly and in abundance, and obligingly drops dead in an ecstasy of joy when a person so much as eyes it hungrily. The Shmoo lays eggs, gives milk (always Grade A), and even produces creamery butter. Broil a Shmoo, and it is a steak; fry or boil it, and it is a chicken; its eyes

may be used as suspender buttons, and its hide as top-grain leather. The name is derived from *schmo,* a term for a stupid, dopey individual, which, in turn, is a corruption of the Yiddish *shmok* or *schmuck,* literally penis and, figuratively, a clod, dumbell, oaf, or "prick."

Shoemaker, Alfred L. (1913–?). Shoemaker established the first college department of folklore in the United States, at Franklin and Marshall College (Lancaster, Pennsylvania) and was cofounder of the Pennsylvania Folklife Society. He joined the faculty of Franklin and Marshall in 1948, having studied at Muhlenberg College (B.A., 1934) and, in Europe, at Munich, Heidelberg, Uppsala, and Lund. He earned a doctorate in German at the University of Illinois in 1940, then, following service in World War II, studied at the Irish Folklore Commission and the Folklore Institute in Basel, Switzerland.

Shoemaker's approach to folklore study emphasized material culture and folk life, and he was especially active in studying and teaching Pennsylvania German folk culture. With Don Yoder and William Frey, he founded the Pennsylvania Dutch Folklore Center at Franklin and Marshall College. The center became a very successful public outreach facility, largely through publication of its popular journal, *Pennsylvania Dutchman* (later called *Pennsylvania Folklife*), and sponsorship of the Pennsylvania Dutch Folk Festival (later called the Kutztown Folk Festival), which evolved into the nation's largest folk festival. In 1959, the center became the Pennsylvania Folklife Society.

Shoemaker suffered a mental breakdown in the 1960s, was institutionalized for a time, then dropped out of sight. His subsequent whereabouts are unknown.

SUGGESTED READING: Simon J. Bronner, "A Prophetic Vision of Public and Academic Folklife: Alfred Shoemaker and America's First Department of Folklore," *Folklore Historian* 8 (1991), pp. 38–55.

Shoemaker, Henry Wharton (1882–1958).

Shoemaker, an early collector of Pennsylvania folklore, was especially interested in legends from the Pennsylvania mountain region, as well as folk narratives from lumbermen, hunting camps, and coal miners. A journalist by trade, Shoemaker published the material he collected in Pennsylvania newspapers, then issued a collection in book form as *Pennsylvania Mountain Stories* (1908). Eleven other volumes followed in what became the *Pennsylvania Folklore Series* (1908–24).

While Shoemaker not only pioneered folklore collecting in Pennsylvania as well as relating folklore study to efforts at conserving and preserving other "natural" resources, he is often criticized by academic folklorists for embellishing and even fabricating legend material. This notwithstanding, the sheer volume of the Shoemaker's publications, over a hundred book-length works and many more pamphlets and articles, makes a him a formidable and valuable figure in American folklore studies. In addition to his work on legends, he published collections of songs and ballads, folk speech, and crafts. He cofounded the Pennsylvania Folklore Society with Bishop J. H. Darlington in 1924 and served as its president from 1930 until 1957. Shoemaker served on various state folklore commissions.

From 1930 to 1933, Shoemaker was U.S. minister to Bulgaria and informally studied the Bulgarian government's effort to preserve the nation's folklore. When he returned to the States, Shoemaker became an advocate for government-sponsored preservation, and, in 1937, was appointed state archivist of Pennsylvania—the first appointment of its kind in the United States. He served until 1948 and was also director of the State Museum in Harrisburg during 1939–40. After supervising the creation of the Division of Folklore, he became, in 1948, Pennsylvania's first state folklorist, a post in which he drew criticism from academic folklorists for distorting folk material through popularization. Shoemaker retired in 1956.

See also: FINK, MIKE.

SUGGESTED READING: Simon Bronner, *Popularizing Pennsylvania: Henry Shoemaker and the Progressive Uses of Folklore and History* (University Park, Pa., 1995).

Shotgun house.

An example of VERNACULAR ARCHITECTURE, the shotgun house is a familiar sight in the mill towns and working-class city neighborhoods of the South. In New Orleans, this house form evolved rather more elegantly, and the city retains numerous surviving examples. Its basic plan is one-room wide and three-rooms long, with a gable roof that has eaves to the sides. Examples that add a second row of rooms to one side are called a double shotgun. As with the BUNGALOW, the shotgun house became commercially quite successful, and what began as folk housing evolved by the late nineteenth century into a house type offered by various southern lumber companies. The style is well suited to narrow urban lots and to dependent housing situations—for example, situations in which mill workers live in company-owned houses.

See also: MOBILE HOMES.

SUGGESTED READING: Henry Glassie, *Pattern in the Material Folk Culture of the Eastern United States* (Philadelphia, 1968).

Shout. Probably derived from the Arabic word saut, which was current on the West Coast of Africa, meaning "to walk or run around," the "shout" is a ritual in which, against a background of drums and rattles, participants dance and sing, moving in a circle counterclockwise, following a leader. The dancing and singing gradually mount in intensity and wildness until a state of possession occurs; that is, each dancer "merges his identity in that of the god, losing control of his conscious faculties and knowing nothing of what he does until he comes to himself" (Melville J. Herskovits, *The Myth of the Negro Past* [New York, 1941], p. 215). The singing, dancing, and drumming of the crowd are usually the necessary background for possession; possession does not occur in private. In possession, the spirit of the god enters the participant, who "loses consciousness, becomes the deity, and until his release dances or performs after the fashion of the spirit who has taken possession of him" (Herskovits, p. 215). Such manifestations have been observed in Christian religious ceremonies of African Americans in northern Louisiana and in the Georgia Sea Islands. Several fundamentalist Christian churches achieve similar states of possession.

See also: AFRICAN AMERICANS.

Simmons, Philip (1912–). Born on Daniel Island, South Carolina, Simmons is an important American BLACKSMITH. He moved to Charleston in 1919 and apprenticed himself to a smith in 1925, taking over the shop in the early 1930s and producing his first piece of ornamental ironwork about 1939. By the 1960s, Simmons had designed and fabricated more than two hundred of the decorative iron gates that are greatly prized in Charleston.

Sitting Bull (ca. 1831–1890). Sitting Bull (Tatanka Yotanka) is probably the most famous Native American leader of the nineteenth century. He led through a combination of religious and moral force, achieving fame as a CULTURE HERO legendary not only among the Sioux, but also among a vast number of whites. He was so well known and revered that BUFFALO BILL (WILLIAM F. CODY) recruited him as a performer in his Wild West Show during 1885–86. This exposed the leader to a wide audience of non–Native Americans, who were impressed by his dignity and quiet strength, as well as his skill as a horseman. In part based on his general reputation and in part on his appearances with Buffalo Bill, Sitting Bull became an important influence on the EXOTERIC FOLKLORE relating to NATIVE AMERICANS.

Sitting Bull was a member of the Hunkpapa branch of the Teton Sioux, born on the Grand River in South Dakota, the son of a distinguished chief. Among his people, Sitting Bull acquired fame as a hunter by age ten and as a warrior by fourteen. During the 1860s, he fought in numerous important engagements against the U.S. Army, and when, in 1874, prospectors began to invade the Black Hills, land sacred to the Sioux, Sitting Bull became chief of the war council of combined Sioux, Cheyenne, and Arapaho in Montana. While Sitting Bull did not actually fight against GEORGE ARMSTRONG CUSTER at the Battle of the Little Bighorn on June 25, 1876, he "made the medicine" that (according to the Indian warriors' belief) made the triumph possible. However, after Little Bighorn, Sitting Bull led most of the Hunkpapa to Canada to avoid reprisals. The tribe suffered from hunger and disease in their exile and, at length, Sitting Bull brought those who remained back to the United States, where he and 170 followers surrendered at Fort Buford, North Dakota, in July 1881. Sitting Bull was held at Fort Randall, South Dakota, from 1881 to 1883 and was then placed at Standing Rock Reservation, North Dakota. During this period, Sitting Bull became an advocate of traditional Sioux culture, which he struggled to maintain against the inexorable incursions of white culture. He was a supporter of the GHOST DANCE movement during 1889–90, which government authorities saw as a threat. An order was given for Sitting Bull's arrest, in the course of which, on December 15, 1890, he was slain with two of his sons.

See also: CRAZY HORSE; GERONIMO; MEDICINE AND MEDICINE MAN.

SUGGESTED READING: Robert M. Utley, *The Lance and the Shield: The Life and Times of Sitting Bull* (New York, 1993).

Sitting Bull in the full ceremonial regalia of a chief. The photograph was taken while he was a featured act in Buffalo Bill's Wild West Show, during 1885–86.

Skillet Lickers, The. The Skillet Lickers were among the first significant groups to record old-time string band music, usually called "hillbilly" music (a term that soon took on a pejorative connotation). Much of the music the group performed, as well as their musical style, reached back into the wellsprings of southern folk tradition before the recording industry became a commercializing force.

On March 7, 1924, a hillbilly duo made their first recordings for Columbia Records in New York. These first hillbilly performers were a chicken farmer and old-time fiddler from Georgia, James Gideon (Gid) Tanner, and George Riley Pucket, a blind guitarist from Alpharetta, Georgia. The duo had been popular locally as regulars on station WSB, Atlanta. By the time they recorded again in 1926, the duo had become a quartet with the addition of two more Georgia performers, also popular on WSB, fiddler Clayton McMichen and five-string BANJO player Fate

Norris. It was at this time that the group took on the humorous name of Gid Tanner and his Skillet Lickers.

Recording for Columbia from 1926 to 1931, they played in a catchy, often raucous style, including a diversified repertoire of traditional BALLADS, BREAKDOWNS, humorous skits, and even recent hits from Tin Pan Alley. Tanner and McMichen provided virtuoso fiddling, and singer-guitarist Riley Pucket furnished a driving rhythm. Pucket's style significantly influenced other guitarists. By 1931, the group was including more jazz and pop numbers. After 1931, McMichen left the group to start several other bands; after 1934, Tanner joined a reorganized Skillet Lickers band; and Riley continued to play as a soloist and, on occasion, with an instrumental group. He died in 1946.

See also: HILLBILLY FIGURE; POOLE, CHARLIE AND THE NORTH CAROLINA RAMBLERS.

Skinner, Charles M. (1852–1907). Skinner was a collector of myths and legends. A writer for the *Brooklyn Daily Eagle, Century, Outlook, Atlantic Monthly,* and other magazines, he turned to folklore topics in 1896, publishing that year a two-volume collection titled *Myths and Legends of Our Own Land,* based on printed sources. Two years later came *Myths and Legends beyond Our Borders* (1898), followed by *Myths and Legends of Our New Possessions and Protectorates* (1900), *American Myths and Legends* (1903), and *Myths and Legends of Flowers, Trees, Fruits, and Plants, in All Ages and in All Climes* (published posthumously, 1911). Skinner's popular works have been generally criticized by the few folklorists who have made reference to them, because they were compiled from unidentified printed sources and because

Skinner often altered texts to make them more appealing. Nevertheless, Skinner's volumes did much to bring the myth and legend aspect of folklore to a greater public.

SUGGESTED READING: John Bealle, "Another Look at Charles M. Skinner," *Western Folklore* 53 (1994), pp. 99–123; Richard M. Dorson, "How Shall We Rewrite Charles M. Skinner Today?" in Wayland D. Hand, ed., *American Folk Legend: A Symposium* (Berkeley, Calif., 1971).

Skip-rope rhymes. Children's rhymes, similar to COUNTING-OUT RHYMES, which are used as accompaniment to jump-rope games and to bouncing-ball games. The rhymes are strongly rhythmical, often allow for acceleration as the verse progresses, and typically contain non sequiturs as well as nonsense rhymes. Probably the most universally known American skip-rope rhyme is EENY-MEENY-MINY-MO, which doubles as a counting-out rhyme.

See also: POETRY, FOLK.

SUGGESTED READING: Charles Francis Potter, "Skip-rope rimes," in Maria Leach, ed., *Funk and Wagnalls Standard Dictionary of Folklore, Mythology, and Legend* (1949; reprint ed., New York, 1984).

Slappy Hooper. An OCCUPATIONAL FOLKLORE character, Slappy Hooper is to the profession of billboard painting what PAUL BUNYAN is to logging. He painted bigger billboards faster than anyone else, creating images so lifelike that (for example) birds broke their beaks on his painted loaves of bread; ultimately, the humane society made him paint the loaf out. In the dead of winter, he painted a stove that looked so hot it caused dandelions and weeds to sprout in January and attracted hoboes looking for a place to warm up. Hooper's magnum opus was a sky painting commissioned by the Union Pacific Railroad, which stretched from one end of the line to the other. During the composition of the sign, Hooper used "sky hooks" to hold up his scaffold. The Slappy Hooper lore was apparently invented and transmitted by old-time sign painters.

Slavic Americans.

This group of immigrants and their descendants includes Slavs other than Poles, whose folklore is treated in a separate entry (see POLISH AMERICANS). Non-Polish Slavic Americans include those of Russian, Ukrainian, Czech, Slovak, Slovene, Croatian, Serbian, Bosnian, Macedonian, and Bulgarian origin or descent, most of whom immigrated during the latter half of the nineteenth century and the first quarter of the twentieth. Like the Polish immigrants of this period, these Slavs were mainly of peasant stock and found work in urban heavy industry as well as mining, though a significant minority (most notably the Czechs of the upper Midwest) entered into farming as well.

Slavic Americans are an ethnically diverse group, but they share variations on traditional FOODWAYS, FOLK MUSIC, folk dances, and peasant costume. Many Slavic-American communities are organized around the local church, which also sponsors liturgical choirs, in which the community takes an active interest. As a group, too, Slavic Americans are the victims of EXOTERIC FOLKLORE in the form of a prejudiced perception of Slavs as ignorant laborers given to crude tastes and coarse habits.

See also: DANCE, FOLK; IMMIGRANT FOLKLORE.

Smith, Abraham (Oregon Smith, Sassafras Smith) (1796–1893).

Smith achieved enduring fame as a storyteller and folk physician. He was born in Tennessee, but settled in the Midwest in 1821, then migrated to Oregon in 1852, returning to Indiana in 1859, then retiring to Chrisman, Illinois. Smith's repertoire is known to have encompassed at least seventy legends, tall tales, jokes, and folktales, many relating to Oregon. Smith was the subject of an important analysis by WILLIAM HUGH JANSEN, which has served as a model for later students of traditional storytelling and storytellers.

SUGGESTED READING: William Hugh Jansen, *Abraham "Oregon" Smith: Pioneer, Folk Hero, and Tale-Teller* (New York, 1977).

Smith, Bessie (1894–1937).

"Empress of the Blues," Smith was born in Chattanooga, Tennessee. Orphaned in 1902, she survived by singing on the streets, and, in 1903, sang at Chattanooga's Ivory Theater. She then toured with blues artist MA RAINEY as one of the Rabbit Foot Minstrels. Smith's first issued sides were "Downhearted Blues" and "Gulf Coast Blues," which sold an incredible 800,000 copies and catapulted the young singer to stardom. Her recording career spanned from the 1920s into the early 1930s. She recorded some 160 sides. Smith's life was cut short on September 26, 1937, when she succumbed to injuries suffered in an auto accident in Coahoma, Mississippi. (A 1937 article by record producer John Hammond reported that Smith had died after having been denied admission to a hospital because of her color. This information was later proved untrue.)

Smith's repertoire encompassed the entire range of traditional blues and other songs. Her performances are prized for their skill and nuance, especially her trademark phrasing, in which she often held a word or syllable into the next bar.

SUGGESTED READING: Chris Albertson, *Bessie* (New York, 1970).

Smith, Fred (1886–1976). From about 1950 until he was disabled by a stroke in 1968, Fred Smith was engaged in the creation of *Concrete Park,* a mixed-media work of ENVIRONMENTAL FOLK ART consisting of more than two hundred sculptures of animals and people spread over more than sixteen acres in the northwestern Wisconsin hamlet of Phillips. The sculptures are of concrete into which pieces of stained glass, colored glass bottles, power pole insulators, mirrors, and other items are inlaid. All of the sculptures are larger than life size, including a thirteen-foot-tall representation of PAUL BUNYAN, and all were created to last, set on concrete footings, like a house. Although many of the pieces have a blocky, stylized look, Smith was concerned with realism, even modeling the heads of his horses over real horses' heads obtained from a butcher. Smith never charged admission to his park, which he said was "for the American people."

Born in Price County, Smith had no formal education, worked as a logger, then opened up the Rock Garden, a tavern, which he operated after his retirement as a logger in 1949.

Smith, Grace Partridge (1869–1959). Smith was a collector of the folklore of "Little Egypt," the area of extreme southern Illinois, where the Ohio and Mississippi Rivers converge at Cairo. Smith was a prime mover behind the creation of the Illinois Folklore Society in 1946 and was also active in the American Folklore Society. She published articles on proverbs, folk songs, children's folklore, slang, and folk speech, but was especially interested in tales of the supernatural. She was also among the first folklorists to devote attention to folk elements in popular comic books.

Smith, John (1580–1631). English soldier of fortune and explorer who helped found the first permanent English settlement in North America at Jamestown, Virginia, and who wrote extensively about the New World. His writings, including *The Generall Historie of Virginia, New England, and the Summer Isles* (1624); *A Description of New England* (1625); and *The True Travels, Adventures, and Observations of Cap-*

Captain John Smith, as depicted in John Clark Ridpath, History of the World, *vol. 6 (1909).*

taine John Smith in Europe, Asia, Africa, and America (1630), were in some measure promotion tracts for American settlement. Certainly, the natural abundance they portrayed did much to excite interest in New World exploration and settlement and helped foster an Edenic vision of America. To many generations of Americans, however, Smith is best known as the man who was saved from death at the hands of Chief Powhatan by the intervention of the chief's daughter, POCAHONTAS. In briefly telling that story in his *Generall Historie*, Smith created the basis for a wealth of subsequent folklore and literature developed around Pocahontas.

Smith was born and raised on a farm in Willoughby, Lincolnshire, England. He chafed under apprenticeship to a wealthy merchant, and, at age twenty, fought as a mercenary against the Turks in Hungary. Captured, he eventually escaped and offered his services to a group intent on establishing an English colony in North America. Smith and the others landed on May 14, 1607, at what was to become Jamestown. Smith is at pains, in his writings, to present himself as a CULTURE HERO, and it is probably true that the settlers looked to Smith to lead them. Smith was much occupied with gathering the means of survival, and it was while he was exploring the Chickahominy River in December 1607 that he was captured, taken to Chief Powhatan, and saved at the last minute by the thirteen-year-old Pocahontas.

Smith continued to lead the colony, until September 1609, when a powder explosion injured him and necessitated his return to England. He returned to America again in 1614, exploring the area he himself named New England. In 1615, on another exploratory trip, he was captured by pirates, but managed to escape.

See also: CRANE, (HAROLD) HART; CUSTER, GEORGE ARMSTRONG; FOLKLORE IN AMERICAN LITERATURE.

SUGGESTED READING: Everett H. Emerson, *Captain John Smith* (New York, 1971).

Smithsonian Institution. Popularly called the "nation's attic," the Smithsonian Institution

The original buildings of the Smithsonian Institution in a photograph from 1886.

is a group of museums and scientific and cultural institutes. Except for the Cooper-Hewitt Museum, a branch of the Museum of the American Indian in New York City, and the Smithsonian Tropical Research Institute in Panama, all of the Smithsonian group is located in Washington, D.C. It includes the Anacostia Museum, the Joseph H. Hirshhorn Museum and Sculpture Garden, the Arthur M. Sackler Gallery (of Asian Art), the National Museum of African Art, the National Air and Space Museum, the National Museum of American Art, the Archives of American Art, the National Museum of American History, the National Portrait Gallery, the National Zoological Park, the Freer Gallery of Art, the National Museum of Natural History, and, administered separately, the John F. Kennedy Center for the Performing Arts, the Woodrow Wilson International Center for Scholars, and the National Gallery of Art. A Washington, D.C., branch of the National Museum of the American Indian is scheduled to open in 2002. The Smithsonian was created by an act of Congress in 1846, and was funded by a bequest of the British scientist James Smithson.

The Smithsonian has long played a key role in scholarship and collecting devoted to Native American culture and to general folklife in the United States. Beginning in 1967, the Festival of American Folklife has been held, in Washington, D.C., on the National Mall, under the aegis of the Smithsonian. In 1976, the Office of Folklife Programs was established under the directorship of RALPH RINZLER, and in 1992 this Smithsonian unit became the Center for Folklife Programs and Cultural Studies. In 1987, the Smithsonian acquired FOLKWAYS RECORDS. The Folklife Center produces Smithsonian museum and traveling exhibits based on American folklife; it continues to produce and release recordings of folk music and folklife-related videos and books. The center also sponsors and funds a variety of folklife research projects and educational programs.

See also: FOLK REVIVAL.

Snake handlers. Certain members of some independent Pentecostal Holiness churches in the South interpret Mark 16:18, "They shall take up serpents," as an instruction to use poisonous snakes in religious services. Twice weekly— sometimes more often—they gather in their one-room churches and handle rattlers, copperheads, and other poisonous snakes without showing any signs of caution, confident that their faith will protect them. The snakes are often manhandled—tossed and trod upon or wrapped around the worshiper's neck. The handling is performed to the accompaniment of loud music. Bites, which are infrequent, are interpreted as evidence of a lapse in faith. If bitten, few victims seek medical assistance, but prefer to trust in faith for a cure.

See also: RELIGION, FOLK.

Sod house. Nineteenth-century settler dwellings constructed entirely or primarily of prairie sod. The western prairie offered few trees for building houses, but had no end of another building material, sod. Prairie earth was typically rootbound, highly resistant to the settlers' plows, but strong enough to be cut into sturdy bricks for building either a temporary or permanent dwelling. Typically, a settler would first quickly build a "dugout," a sod house sited on the side of a hill or ravine. A "hollow" was cut from this site, the face of the hill or ravine serving as the building's rear wall and the sides of the hollow serving as the side walls. The front portion of the house was then closed off with sod bricks. These bricks, usually a yard long, twelve to eighteen inches wide, and about three inches thick, were cut out from the plowed furrows of the earth. These bricks were laid into the walls just as fired clay bricks are.

The dugout usually served as a shelter while the farmer built a freestanding sod house—although, often, a hill or rise still served as a rear wall. Most sod houses consisted of one large room, perhaps as large as twenty feet long by sixteen or seventeen feet wide. Doors, door frames, windows, and window frames of wood were fitted into apertures in the sod. Few early sod-house dwellers could afford more than a single glass window. If this was beyond financial reach, both window and door openings were sealed with blankets or Indian buffalo robes.

Sod houses, especially larger structures, were internally reinforced with hickory stems driven into the bricks like tie rods. Roofs might be made of nothing more than brush spread across precious wooden rafters, over which a layer of prairie grass was laid and then a top layer of prairie sod. If lumber and tar paper were available and within financial reach, these were used as roofing materials. Even in these cases, however, sod formed the top layer of the roof. Roof bricks were cut thinner than wall bricks, and were laid with the grass-side down.

The interiors of sod houses varied. In some, the sod walls were smoothed as much as possible, while, in others, the interior walls were plastered. Some sod houses had interior walls to separate rooms, but most settlers achieved privacy by hanging quilts or rag carpeting as dividers.

Although sod houses were easy to repair—just apply more sod—they required continual maintenance. They leaked and were filthy. Many sod dwellers hung cheesecloth from the rafters to catch falling fragments of earth. Despite the drawbacks, however, the sod house was remarkably well insulated and was fireproof, though its life expectancy was at most eight years.

The heyday of the sod house came with the Homestead Act of 1862, and most were built in the years following the Civil War, though they appeared in Kansas as early as the 1850s.

See also: LOG CABIN; VERNACULAR ARCHITECTURE.

SUGGESTED READING: Everett Dick, *The Sod-House Frontier: 1854–1890* (Lincoln, Nebr., 1954).

Solstices. There are two moments each year when the apparent path of the sun is farthest north or south from the equator. In the Northern Hemisphere, the summer solstice occurs on June 21 or 22 ("Midsummer Day") and the winter solstice on December 21 or 22 ("Midwinter Day"). The situation is the opposite in the Southern Hemisphere because the seasons are reversed. These days have been celebrated in many cultures and in all ages. In pre-Christian Europe and pre-Columbian North America, fire-making and dancing rituals were common. In Europe, Christianity absorbed and diluted pagan celebrations, and the winter solstice festivals were supplanted by Christmas traditions, such as burning the Yule log, while the midsummer festival became the Feast of John the Baptist (June 24), which may include the lighting of bonfires ("St. John's fires").

St. John's Day was brought to North America primarily by Scandinavian immigrants, and other North American midsummer rituals seem to have developed from observation of the solstice. These include fortune telling and divination rituals in the Midwest, a June 23 snake-dance ritual observed by some in New Orleans, and water-related rituals among some Hispanic groups (public bathing) and Slavic groups (blessing of the water on June 24 prior to swimming). A number of public or civic festivals coincide with the solstice, including *Svenskarnas Dag* (Swede's Day) in Minneapolis and Vasa Day in Seattle.

Sounding. Sounding is a BOASTING duel in which the "combatants" try to best one another by skillfully hurling formulaic taunts and brags. The practice was found among young African-American men and is the direct precursor of modern RAP and of rapping and capping.

Spectral ships. Spectral ships are ghost vessels, lost at sea, that return, apparently doomed to sail eternally without ever touching port. The most famous of these revenant ships was the *Flying Dutchman*, subject of a Germanic legend, which the composer Richard Wagner (1813–83) used as the basis for his opera *The Flying Dutchman* (*Der fliegende Holländer*, 1843). American sea lore tells of at least fifteen spectral ships reported along the northeastern coast. Typically, spectral ships are without crew or are manned by ghosts and sail, at top speed, *against* the wind. Music is sometimes heard from on board, but the ships never acknowledge when hailed. Sightings of the *Titanic* as a spectral ship have been reported on the anniversary of its loss. To see a spectral ship is considered a bad omen, a sign of an impending storm at best and of catastrophe at worst.

Spirituals, African-American. Colonial American slaves typically responded to Christian instruction with enthusiasm, but there were too few missionaries from England available to minister to the widely scattered white population, let alone to blacks and Indians. By 1750, a few Presbyterian ministers, led by Samuel Davies of Hanover, Virginia, worked to convert blacks, using Watts hymnbooks (*see* DOCTOR WATTS HYMNS) imported from England. But planters were of divided opinion about conversions of slaves; many felt that exposing them to Christianity made revolt more likely, and the conversion effort was hampered as a result.

Nevertheless, interaction between whites and blacks occurred on a large scale during the camp meetings that were a special feature of the "Second Great Awakening," a revival movement that took place among the frontier communities of the United States from 1780 to 1830. Those who took part were members of various Protestant denominations, common people, both whites and blacks. During this period, a camp meeting was a continuous religious service that went on for days, sometimes for a whole week. Although the camp meetings were interracial, they were also segregated, with rows of seats set up so that the blacks were on one side, the whites on the opposite side. In some instances, a portion of the circle to the rear of the preacher's stand was set apart for black people. Three to five thousand worshipers would be assembled in the huge main tent.

Although the two races influenced each other, the blacks tended to take an Africanized approach to what they picked up from white hymns, improvising on both the melodies and texts they heard, syncopating the melodies, and sometimes shocking the more conservative white church fathers. A Reverend Watson complained:

In the black's quarter, the coloured people get together, and sing for hours together, short scraps of disjointed affirmations, pledges, lengthened out with long repetition choruses. These are all sung in the merry chorus-manner of the southern harvest field, or husking frolic method of the slave blacks . . . the example has already visibly affected the religious manners of some whites. From this cause I have known in some camp meetings from 50 to 60 people croud [sic] into one tent, after the public devotions had closed, and there continue the whole night, singing tune after tune (though with occasional episodes of prayer) scarce one of which were in our hymn books.

This is a significant description of the spontaneous improvised creation of African-American spirituals.

African Americans continued to make up spirituals, drawing on colorful dramatic human interest stories in the Bible and transmuting these into vivid images. To make the drama more intense, the black bards freely drew on whatever parts of the Bible seemed appropriate, as well as on aspects of contemporary life that seemed suitable. Often elements from the New Testament were interpolated into events in the Old and vice versa. One spiritual might include Job, Jesus, Judas, and Joshua, for example. The songs are also marked by an economy of statement and rich, fresh dramatic scenes. The complex story of Jonah, for example, is told in a highly visual and dramatic fourteen lines. Many of the songs allude to events in a poetically elliptical fashion rather than describing them fully, and some standard images are evoked again and again. For example, the chariot of Elijah appears in different contexts, in some instances dealing with Elijah's transportation to heaven, and in some symbolizing the heavenly ascent of everyone who is saved. As the puffing, snorting steam locomotives with their stirring wailing whistles increasingly appealed to nineteenth-century African-American song

makers, the train became a favorite image, a modern substitute for the chariot. Old Testament, New, contemporary life—all was fair game for the spiritual.

Among recent generations of scholars and others there has been a great deal of speculation that many of the spirituals were full of hidden meanings, signals for slaves planning to escape or dreaming of an end to slavery. Spirituals that lend themselves readily to this approach include "Steal Away to Jesus," seen as a disguised invitation to steal away to freedom; "Go Down, Moses," interpreted as an invocation of Harriet Tubman, the female Moses of the slaves, a great leader trying to end slavery, and the unofficial "conductor" of the Underground Railway for the black equivalents of the enslaved Israelites; "Crossing the Jordan" could be interpreted as escape to the North; all the references to Elijah's chariot or the gospel train could be interpreted as references to the Underground Railroad; trumpet blasts could be representative of the day of emancipation; the epic of Samson and Delilah in "If I Had My Way (I'd Tear This Old Building Down)" lends itself to the symbolism of the destruction of the institution of slavery. Yet the probability appears to be that the songs were created originally as *religious* songs, though no doubt some slaves interpreted them as cries for freedom on earth.

Some scholars classify spirituals by type, including:

- Lyrics of Sorrow, Alienation, and Desolation, in which the slaves' experience is said to be identified with that of Christ.
- Lyrics of Consolation and Faith, which emphasize healing and redemption.
- Lyrics of Resistance and Defiance, which are interpreted as conveying a valiant message of struggle.

- Lyrics of Deliverance, which emphasize deliverance, perhaps through physical escape or, spiritually, through death and resurrection.
- Lyrics of Jubilation and Triumph, which are ceremonial in nature.
- Lyrics of Judgment and Reckoning, emphasizing retribution in a day of reckoning.
- Lyrics of Regeneration, which sing of the rejuvenating virtues of religion.
- Lyrics of Spiritual Progress, which narrate a spiritual journey toward salvation.
- Lyrics of Transcendence, which look beyond present woes to eternal peace and transcendent values.

Whether or not one discerns a political agenda in these religious songs, the African-American spiritual is intensely poetic and was one of the means of expression through which enslaved African Americans not only maintained a sense of identity, purpose, and hope, but also, after the Civil War, a venue through which African-American culture became known to white America. Performances of spirituals became popular with white audiences, some of whom were particularly moved by the religious-political significance of the songs, while others insisted that spirituals were never anything more than adaptations of European musical traditions.

See also: AFRICAN AMERICANS; FISK JUBILEE SINGERS; FOLK MUSIC; LEDBETTER, HUDDIE (LEADBELLY); REVIVAL SONGS; SPIRITUALS, WHITE.

SUGGESTED READING: Samuel A. Floyd, Jr., *Index to Negro Spirituals* (Chicago, 1991); James Weldon Johnson, *The Books of American Negro Spirituals: Including the Book of American Negro Spirituals and the Second Book of Negro Spirituals* (reprint ed., New York, 1988); Richard Newman et al., *Go Down,* *Moses: A Celebration of the African-American Spiritual* (New York, 1998).

Spirituals, white. Less well known than African-American spirituals (see SPIRITUALS, AFRICAN-AMERICAN), white spirituals derive from the "lined-out" psalm singing of the seventeenth-century Protestant Church. A leader would sing a line of the psalm, and the congregation would follow, often in harmony; the singing would proceed this way, line after line. By the eighteenth and nineteenth century in America, the rather staid tradition of line singing was replaced by more spirited revivalist hymns. Today, the white spiritual tradition draws liberally on the African-American tradition, incorporating elements of jazz and blues and using such instruments as the banjo, guitar, accordion, electric guitar, and electric piano to accompany the singers.

See also: APPALACHIA; FOLK MUSIC; REVIVAL SONGS.

Squanto (ca. 1580–1622). Squanto, whose Wampanoag Indian name was Tisquantum, became part of American folklore as much as history by befriending the Plymouth Pilgrims and saving them from starvation by showing them how to fertilize their cornfields with fish. First mentioned by the early chroniclers of the Plymouth colony, most notably William Bradford, in his *Of Plimoth Plantation* (written by 1650), the story of Squanto has been passed down to generations of American schoolchildren. He is both the archetypal "good" or "friendly" Indian and, like JAMES FENIMORE COOPER's Mohican Chingachgook, the last of his tribe (the Patuxet band of the Wampanoags).

A 1930s schoolbook illustration of Squanto's first meeting with the Pilgrims.

Squanto is believed to have been kidnapped by Captain George Weymouth in 1605 and taken to Malaga, Spain, where he was sold into slavery. Ransomed by a sympathetic Englishman, he was taken to England and returned to the Cape Cod, Massachusetts, area in 1618–19. Few Patuxets were alive when he returned; most had succumbed to smallpox brought by the Europeans. Samoset, an Abnaki guest of the Wampanoags, presented Squanto as well as the Wampanoag sachem Massasoit to the Pilgrims in March 1621. Squanto, conversant in English, instructed the imperiled settlers in the arts of wilderness survival, including, most famously, the use of fish fertilizer. With Massasoit (for whom he acted as interpreter), Squanto helped make possible the first THANKSGIVING (1621).

Squanto ran afoul of Corbitant, a rival of Massasoit, and was imprisoned until MILES STANDISH intervened with Corbitant to secure his release. In 1622, Squanto offered to act as interpreter for the Pilgrims, who wanted to establish a trading relation with the Narraganset tribe. In the course of the journey to the Narragansets, Squanto contracted smallpox and died.

SUGGESTED READING: Samuel Eliot Morison, ed., *Of Plymouth Plantation 1620–1647, by William Bradford* (New York, 1976).

Square dance. A dance for four couples or groups of four couples arrayed in square forma-

This photograph from about 1944 shows two square dancing couples executing a step called "Wringing Out the Dish Rag."

tion, the square dance is the most popular type of folk dance (see DANCE, FOLK) in the United States. The square dance is, in effect, an American form of QUADRILLE and first appeared as the "Kentucky running set" (a dance style adapted from English group folk dances) and from the *cotillon,* a precursor of the French quadrille dating to the court of Louis XV.

The classic American square dance progresses smartly in well-ordered patterns within squares formed by sets of four couples, one set making up each side of the square. The dancers are accompanied by banjo and fiddle, often guitar and accordion as well, and are prompted by a singsonging "caller," who announces the steps. Movement is a kind of shuffle; no great skill in stepwork is required in this style of dance, which emphasizes instead smoothly coordinated cooperative movement.

The name "square dance" arose to distinguish this American style from such European folk dances as the contradance (also called the longways dance), which features a double file of couples, and from the round dance, in which couples are arranged in a circular pattern.

Traditionally, square dancing has been a rural pastime, the staple of the BARN DANCE and 4-H Club activities; however, square dance clubs exist nationwide, and many city dwellers enjoy it as a social activity. A number of square dance organizations even maintain informational sites on the Internet's World Wide Web, and several of these organizations offer for-fee training not only in square dance basics, but in the art of calling.

See also: "BUFFALO GALS"; "CINDY"; CLOGGING; HOEDOWN; LINE DANCE; "OLD DAN TUCKER"; PLAY PARTY; "POP GOES THE WEASEL."

Stagolee. Variously called Stagger Lee, Stackerlee, and Stackalee, Stagolee was the outlaw subject of an African-American ballad and of a number of blues versions and variants on that ballad. He shot and killed one Billy Lyon (sometimes spelled Lion or Galion) in a barroom brawl either in Memphis or St. Louis because Lyon had stolen his "magic Stetson." Legend has it that Stagolee bought this hat from the Devil in exchange for his soul, that it transformed him into a shape shifter (see SHAPE SHIFTING) as well as gave him the ability to eat fire and to walk on red-hot slag. Stagolee was so bad, so mean, so ornery that the Devil himself became disgusted and used Billy Lyon to purloin the hat, thereby depriving Stagolee of his magic. Stagolee ultimately ended up in hell.

Stagolee, who is said to have worked as a steamboat stoker or roustabout, is often confounded with Stacker Lee, son of a steamboat captain and famed along the Ohio and Mississippi Rivers for his prowess among the ladies. At one time in the early twentieth century, Stacker Lee was a popular name for African-American children living along the rivers.

See also: AFRICAN AMERICAN; BLUES BALLAD.

Standish, Miles (ca. 1584–1656). Standish became a figure of American folklore largely through his appearance in HENRY WADSWORTH LONGFELLOW's immensely popular narrative poem *The Courtship of Miles Standish* (1858), in which Standish, depicted as rather foppish and shy where women are concerned, induces John Alden to ask on his behalf for the hand of the fair Priscilla. "Speak for yourself, John," Priscilla replies, and Standish loses the lady.

The historical Standish was born in England and served with the Dutch as a soldier of fortune before 1620, when he was hired by English Puritans living in Holland to serve as a military adviser in their project to resettle in America.

Miles Standish as illustrated in an 1882 edition of Henry Wadsworth Longfellow's Courtship of Miles Standish.

Standish sailed to Massachusetts on the *Mayflower* with the Pilgrim founders of the Plymouth colony. It was Standish who acted as the colony's primary negotiator with the Indians, and he was the first of the Pilgrim group to learn the Algonquian dialects. He established a valuable friendship with the Wampanoag sachem Massasoit, who provided much useful advice on military threats to the fledgling settlement. During 1625–26, Standish served as agent for the colonists in England, successfully negotiating clear title to the Pilgrim's lands and, in 1627, assisting in the buyout of non-Pilgrim interests in Plymouth colony. Standish also led an attack against THOMAS MORTON, a rival to the Plymouth colony for trade with the Indians. It was with John Alden that Standish founded Duxbury, Massachusetts, in 1631. He lived the remainder of his life there, serving the Plymouth colony in various government posts.

See also: SQUANTO.

Stubblefield, Blaine "Stub" (1896–1960).
Stubblefield was a singer of traditional songs of the Northwest and the primary organizer of the Northwest Mountain Fiddlers' Contest, which, in 1963, became the National Old-Time Fiddlers' Contest. Educated at the University of Idaho, Stubblefield worked as a publicist for the Spokane, Washington, Chamber of Commerce, the American Automobile Association, Varney Air Lines (predecessor company of United Air Lines), and, later, served as aviation editor for the McGraw-Hill publishing company. In 1949, he became a riverman, operating through the Snake River Canyon.

As with the National Old-Time Fiddlers' Contest, Stubblefield's Northwest Mountain Fiddlers' Contest evolved into a major national folk festival, which continues to be held the third full week of June in Idaho. Stubblefield personally recorded a number of songs for ALAN LOMAX at the Library of Congress during the late 1930s.

Superman.
Progenitor of all popular "superheroes," Superman, the "Man of Steel," debuted in Action Comics in June 1938 and appeared as well in a newspaper COMIC STRIP in January 1939. The character was the creation of Jerry Siegel (who wrote the stories) and Joseph Shuster (who created the art). The story of Superman contains many elements that smack of folktale traditions. He was sent to Earth as an infant when his parents realized that their planet, Krypton, was disintegrating. His spacecraft crash-landed in the rural Midwest and was discovered by a farm couple, Martha and Jonathan Kent, who adopted the boy and named him Clark. Growing into young manhood, Clark Kent discovered that he possessed secret powers, including phenomenal strength, X-ray vision, and the ability to fly, all the result of an interaction be-

tween the earth's sun and his physical makeup. Young Clark resolves to use his superpowers for the good of mankind, but to do so, he decides to live a double life as Clark Kent, a mild-mannered newspaper reporter for *The Daily Planet,* transforming himself into Superman (complete with blue tights and red cape) whenever the need arises. It arises frequently, as Superman is called on to fight crime, effect impossible rescues, and, most often, retrieve girl reporter Lois Lane from the clutches of assorted evildoers. As Superman shares an origin story that is at least as old as Moses and has superpowers that recall the world of MYTH as well as of the TALL TALE, so he has a vulnerability that recalls Achilles and his infamous heel. Exposure to Kryptonite, a substance from his shattered home planet, not only deprives him of his powers, but is ultimately lethal. Students of American popular culture have also commented on the historical context of Superman's creation—on the edge of World War II. As Americans were feeling the impending menace of Hitler and Mussolini, as they witnessed the apparent triumph of terror and injustice in Europe, they welcomed an all-but-invincible crusader for "truth, justice, and the American way."

Superman has proved an extremely durable character and has not only inspired and spawned a legion of comic book superheroes, but has appeared on a radio show, in animated cartoons, in book-length fiction, in a Broadway musical, in a television series, and in motion pictures ranging from cheap serials to a multimillion-dollar string of elaborate features.

Superstition. A folk belief or practice, for which there appears to be no rational substance,

intended to explain some phenomenon, predict some causal relationship, or produce some desired result, superstitions may constitute the most voluminous body of all folklore, not only in America, but worldwide. WAYLAND D. HAND, for example, assembled and classified over one million superstitions (archived at UCLA). The subject is of great interest to folklorists and to folklore theorists, who continually debate the significance of folk belief for what it says about human behavior. For most contemporary Americans, however, the word *superstition* suggests nothing more than the ignorant beliefs of naive, backward, or uneducated people.

See also: FISHING LORE; FRIDAY THE THIRTEENTH; GREEK AMERICANS; HUNTING; MINING FOLKLORE; PORTUGUESE AMERICANS; RELIGION, FOLK; SAILORS AND SEAFARING LORE; VIETNAM WAR.

SUGGESTED READING: Wayland D. Hand and Donald J. Ward, *Encyclopedia of American Popular Belief and Superstition* (Berkeley, Calif., 1994).

Sweat lodge. In several Native American cultures, the sweat lodge is an enclosure—constructed either of bent withe rods covered with skins or blankets or of mud-daubed stacked wood—in which a fire is built for the purpose of administering a sweat bath. The sweat lodge is the province of males and is used as a place of teaching, consulting, praying, and otherwise communing with one another. The sweat lodge is often used as a place either to prepare for or to return from important rituals and ceremonials.

T

Talley, Thomas Washington (1870–1952). By profession a chemistry professor at Nashville's Fisk University, Talley was by avocation a collector of the African-American folktales and songs with which he had grown up in middle Tennessee. While still a student, he sang with the famed Fisk Jubilee Singers and, during the 1890s, began collecting songs. As a professor at Fisk, he met folklorist John Work II, whose 1915 *Folk Songs of the American Negro* concluded that black folk music was entirely religious. In 1922, Talley published *Negro Folk Rhymes* (*Wise or Otherwise*), a collection of distinctly *secular* songs from rural black Tennessee. *The Negro Traditions*, a collection of black folklore, was completed in 1923 or 1924, but was not published until 1993.

See also: AFRICAN AMERICANS.

SUGGESTED READING: Thomas Washington Talley, *The Negro Traditions* (Knoxville, Tenn., 1993); Charles K. Wolfe, ed., *Thomas W. Talley's Negro Folk Rhymes: A New, Expanded Edition, with Music* (Knoxville, Tenn., 1991).

Tall tale. The extravagant, outlandish, and exaggerated narrative, usually centered on a larger-than-life hero, is common to the folklore of many cultures, including those of the United States, and is especially prevalent in folktales associated with the western frontier. The western tall tales are typically characterized by the great inventiveness of the storyteller, a dry delivery that is an effective foil to the extravagance of the story content, vivid vernacular idiom, fanciful rhetoric, and, often, either an overt or implied nationalistic bombast. As with tall tales generally, western tall tales partake of certain conventions. The hero of the tale cannot be expected to offer proof of veracity; usually, no one else is present at the fantastic event. Sometimes, the issue of credibility is sidestepped by the teller's attribution of the tale to someone else, now dead or living far away and unavailable.

The matter of tall tales ranges from fishing stories (the classic "one that got away" tale), to hunting, to farming (the cultivation of gigantic vegetables is a common motif), to the kind of fantastic feats of strength and size related in the PAUL BUNYAN tales. Cowboy lore is replete with tall tales, usually related in a dry, deadpan manner, such as this one recalled by Edward Everett Dale, in his *Cow Country* (1942):

The usual Saturday afternoon crowd of loafers was gathered about a crossroads store in western Arkansas. Looking up the road toward the west, they saw a little cloud of dust approaching and as it came nearer they saw a most astonishing spectacle—a man in a two-wheeled cart to which was hitched a pair of mountain lions. The man himself was an unkempt, bearded individual with two six-shooters buckled about his waist and a bowie knife in his belt. A huge wild cat with a spiked collar about its neck sat on the seat beside him and the man was driving his fearsome team with a live rattlesnake for a whip. He pulled up in front of the store with a loud Whoa! laid down his rattlesnake, and asked: "Has anybody here got anything to drink?" There was a moment's silence and then one man diffidently stated that he had a little corn whisky "Corn whisky is no sort of drink for a man," roared the newcomer, "ain't you got no sulphuric acid?" After another pause someone remarked that there was some in the store. "Bring me a quart of it," cried the newcomer. It was brought and, draining the liquid in a few gulps, the visitor picked up his rattlesnake, gathered up the lines and said: "Well, cats, we've got to be goin'. Much obleeged, men." Then one of the goggle-eyed crowd summoned up the courage to ask: "Stranger, whare be ye frum? We ain't seen anybody like you in these parts afore. Whare do you live at anyhow?" "I'm frum Oklahomy," said the stranger. "To tell you th' truth, men, th' damned Ku Klux is gettin' so bad out there it's runnin' all of us sissies out."

See also: BENÉT, STEPHEN VINCENT; COW-BOYS; DEATH VALLEY; DISASTER FOLKLORE; EDISON, THOMAS ALVA; EXAGGERATED POST CARD; FISHING LORE; FRENCH AMERICANS; GREAT DIAMOND HOAX; HUMOR, FOLK; HUNTING; LUMBERJACK FOLKLORE; MASS MEDIA; MILITARY FOLKLORE; "OLD DAN TUCKER"; REVOLUTIONARY WAR; RINGTAILED ROARER; RUTH, BABE; SAILORS AND SEAFARING LORE; SHMOO; SUPERMAN; TRICKSTER; TRUCKING AND TRUCKERS; TWAIN, MARK; URBAN LEGEND; WEBSTER, DANIEL; WORLD WAR II; YARN.

SUGGESTED READING: Carolyn S. Brown, *The Tall Tale in American Folklore and Literature* (Knoxville, Tenn.,

1987); Vance Randolph, *We Always Lie to Strangers* (New York, 1951).

Tamaris, Helen (1905–1966). Tamaris was one of the major figures of "traditional" modern American dance and developed as a staple of her repertoire dance based on American folk music and African-American spirituals. She was born Helen Becker in New York City and began her dance career as a member of the children's chorus of the Metropolitan Opera Company. As a teen, she studied with Mikhail Fokine, then went on to study modern dance at the Neighborhood Playhouse from 1918 to 1920. Tamaris appeared on Broadway, in at least one show, *The Music Box Revue of 1924–25.* But it is as a concert dancer that Tamaris is best remembered. She debuted on October 9, 1927 in New York, presenting a program of solos she had choreographed. The next year, she introduced dances based on American folk music and spirituals, the material with which she became most closely associated.

During the period of her most intense concert activity—from 1927 to 1944—Tamaris was instrumental in the creation of the Dance Repertory Theater (1930–32), the American Dance Association, and the Federal Dance Project (created under the auspices of the WPA). She choreographed a vast number of short works, for herself, her own company, or in conjunction with such contemporaries as MARTHA GRAHAM, Doris Humphrey, Sophie Maslow, and Anna Sokolow. In addition to her concert work, Tamaris choreographed for the stage, at first for experimental theater groups, including the Provincetown Players and the Group Theater (whose cast included the likes of John Garfield and Clifford Odets), and the Federal Theatre Project. After 1944,

Tamaris entered the Broadway mainstream as the choreographer of such major hits as *Annie Get Your Gun* (1946) and *Plain and Fancy* (1955).

SUGGESTED READING: *Studies in Dance History* 1 (Fall/Winter 1989–90), an issue devoted to Tamaris's life and work.

Tamburitza music and orchestra. Tamburitza instruments and the music traditionally played on them was brought to the United States and Canada by emigrants from Croatia, Bosnia, and the Vojvodina region of Serbia. This ethnic music is heard mainly in western Pennsylvania and in the urban Great Lakes region, especially at such family gatherings as weddings and reunions, as well as in ethnic restaurants and taverns. A tamburitza orchestra consists of five fretted stringed instruments: *prima, brac, celo brac, bugarija,* and *berde*. The *prima* is smaller than a mandolin, and the *berde* larger than a double bass, with the rest of the instruments ranging in size and register between these extremes.

The ultimate origin of tamburitza is Turkish. The Ottomans brought the precursors of the modern instruments to the Balkans in the fourteenth century. Over the years, tamburitza traditions developed as folk symbols of opposition to cultural domination of the Balkans by the Austro-Hungarian Empire. Professional and semiprofessional tamburitza orchestras appeared in Balkan villages and towns by the end of the nineteenth century, and it is primarily this tradition that Balkan immigrants brought with them to North America.

By the 1910s, U.S. recording companies began issuing tamburitza discs by recognized tamburitzans. A few orchestras (such as Zvonimir and the Elias Serenaders) toured on the vaudeville circuits, bringing tamburitza to nonethnic audiences. Today, Duquesne University (Pittsburgh) sponsors a touring tamburitza ensemble, and the Tamburitza Association of America sponsors an annual Tamburitza Extravaganza.

See also: FOLK MUSIC.

SUGGESTED READING: Walter Kolar, *A History of the Tambura* (Pittsburgh, 1975).

Tap dance. Historically the most popular style of theatrical dance, tap derives from such folk forms as JIGS, REELS, and flings brought to America by emigrants from the British Isles, combined with the complex rhythmic foot-stamping characteristic of African-American folk dance traditions. The synthesis of these two folk streams came in the MINSTREL SHOWS of the nineteenth century. As the minstrel show gave way to vaudeville, tap dancing continued to develop, and while

Tap dancing is a folk form that found great commercial favor. From the 1920s through the 1940s, untold legions of youngsters and would-be entertainers saw tap as a ticket to a stage or film career. This photograph shows Eleanor Powell, tap-dancing star of MGM musicals of the late 1930s and early 1940s.

individual performers created distinctive styles of their own, two basic techniques emerged. BUCK-AND-WING was a fast, rhythmically precise and percussive dance performed in stiff, wooden-soled shoes. Soft-shoe was slower and more relaxed, danced in soft-soled shoes. The styles merged by the mid-1920s, at which time, metal taps were attached to the heels and toes of leather-soled shoes to produce sharp, clean, and distinctly audible percussion—an effect that was often augmented and counterpointed by hand clapping and body slapping. From the mid-1920s through the 1930s, the first great tap performers emerged, including George M. Cohan and Bill ("Bojangles") Robinson, regarded as among the very greatest dancers in the genre.

Beginning in the 1940s, some tap performers introduced elements of ballet and modern dance into tap, creating especially expressive and virtuosic dances, which were featured in a series of movie musicals produced primarily by the MGM and Warner Bros. studios. Leading tap dancers during this period were often the stars of these films and included the Nicholas Brothers, Fred Astaire, Ray Bolger, Eleanor Powell, Paul Draper, Gene Kelly, and others. Although the films of Astaire and Kelly, in particular, remain popular, tap faded after the 1940s. It is still popular in dancing schools, however, but gone are the days when would-be "stage parents" packed off their sons and daughters to take tap lessons in the hope of their becoming child film stars like Shirley Temple, Judy Garland, and Mickey Rooney.

See also: DANCE, FOLK; JUBA.

SUGGESTED READING: Rusty E. Frank, *Tap: The Greatest Tap Dance Stars and Their Stories, 1900–1955* (New York, 1995); Mike Seeger, *Talking Feet: Buck, Flatfoot and Tap: Solo Southern Dance of the Appalachian, Piedmont and Blue Ridge Mountain Regions* (Berkeley, Calif., 1993).

Tar Baby. Most familiar as the sticky black tar effigy BRER FOX uses to exact revenge on BRER RABBIT in "The Wonderful Tar-Baby Story" told by JOEL CHANDLER HARRIS's UNCLE REMUS, the tar baby motif is, in fact, common to many TRICKSTER folktale cycles. The tar baby plot, as used by Harris and as found in his folktale precursors, involves a figure made from a sticky material (tar, wax, or gum) fashioned by an enemy of the trickster. When the trickster passes the effigy, he greets it, and is increasingly disturbed by the doll's apparent refusal to return the greeting. The trickster threatens the tar baby on account of his insolence, and when silence continues to prevail, he throws a punch. The trickster's hand becomes embedded in the figure. Enraged, he hits the tar baby with his other fist. With both hands now stuck, he kicks, and first one foot and then the other gets stuck. In some versions of the tale, the trickster's head and stomach are similarly held fast as well. Eventually, the trickster's adversary happens by and administers punishment to the helpless trickster.

In the African stories, including those brought to the New World, the trickster-spider, ANANSI, falls victim to the tar baby. The spider's flat shape is the result of the beating Anansi takes while he is held fast by the tar baby. Native American folklore also features tar baby figures. An Apache tale tells how the trickster COYOTE became stuck in a figure of pitch. Tales from other tribes tell of a thieving skunk similarly trapped and of a BUFFALO becoming stuck in a tree while in pursuit of prey. Most scholars believe that the Native American motif was derived from the African motif.

"The Wonderful Tar-Baby Story" is by far the most popular of the Uncle Remus tales and that the sticky motif continues to have appeal is made evident by a number of URBAN LEGENDS involving such powerful instant-adhesive products as "Super Glue" or Krazy Glue.

See also: AFRICAN AMERICANS.

SUGGESTED READING: Florence Baer, *Sources and Analogues of the Uncle Remus Tales* (Helsinki, Finland, 1980).

Tarzan. Tarzan first appeared in the short fiction of American novelist EDGAR RICE BURROUGHS in 1912 and soon became one of the most durable figures of popular fiction and film. The first full-length Tarzan novel, *Tarzan of the Apes,* appeared in 1914 and spawned a series of sequels, which, during the lifetime of the author (1875–1950) sold at least 25 million copies in some fifty-six languages. Tarzan, the son of an English nobleman, is abandoned in the jungles of Africa, but is saved by apes who adopt and raise him. Later, grown to muscular and scantily clad manhood, he meets and falls in love with Jane, the daughter of an American scientist, and eventually recovers his noble English title. The first Tarzan silent film was made in 1918, with Elmo Lincoln in the title role, but of the dozen or so actors who have portrayed Tarzan, the most popular was former Olympian Johnny Weissmuller, who, learning English from his newfound love, utters a phrase that instantly entered into American popular culture: "Me Tarzan, you Jane."

The appeal of Tarzan is manifold. He combines animal virility and innocent but compelling sexuality with superhuman strength, yet he also has a connection to civilization. Moreover, his story partakes of profound folk motifs, including infant abandonment and the motif of the animal nurse, which is at least as old as the story of Romulus and Remus, the legendary founders of Rome, who were raised by a she-wolf.

See also: COMIC STRIPS.

Tattooing. Tattooing is the process of creating permanent marks or designs on the body by in-

As late as the close of the nineteenth century in the United States, the tattoo was popularly associated with Native Americans and other so-called primitive peoples rather than as personal adornment appropriate to "civilized" folk. This drawing is reproduced from an 1890 volume, Adventures with Indians, by J. E. Potter.

troducing pigment through ruptures in the skin. The design is permanent (or can be removed only by specialized dermatological procedures). The practice of tattooing is found in most parts of the world, except for most of China. Motives for undergoing the pain and disfigurement of tattooing include decoration as well as a belief (among some peoples) that tattooed designs provide magical protection against sickness or misfortune. In some cultures, including various criminal subcultures (such as American street gangs and prison inmate populations), tattoos identify rank, status, or group membership. In the Americas, many Indian tribes customarily tattooed the body or the face, or both. Tattooing was rediscovered by Europeans during the Renaissance age of exploration, and the word *tattoo* was borrowed into English (and other European languages) from Tahiti.

The practice of tattooing seems to have begun in the United States during the 1850s, when tattooed sideshow freaks commonly toured with traveling circuses. The first professional tattooists in the United States practiced during the Civil War, and mainly tattooed military insignia on soldiers. By the beginning of the twentieth century, the port city of New York became a center of tattooing, with sailors constituting a principal clientele. Most "tattoo artists" have remained relatively anonymous, but a few gained reputation and recognition among sailors and others. At the turn of the nineteenth century, New Yorker Lewis "Lew the Jew" Alberts gained a high degree of recognition, in large measure because he distributed his designs in the form of wall charts (called "flash") to other tattoo artists.

Tattooing has always been popular with military personnel, and, during wars, patriotic designs and slogans abound. At all times, pop culture figures, such as Popeye and Mickey Mouse, have been much in demand. During the 1960s, the "hippie" movement brought revived interest in tattooing, and designs incorporating peace signs, marijuana leaves, and astrological signs became popular.

In the United States, tattoos have been traditionally associated with delinquent and antisocial attitudes and individuals, as well as "tough guy" statements. "Outlaw" motorcycle gang members frequently adorn themselves with tattoos, as do prison inmates. (Long-term inmates may tattoo an emblematic teardrop below one eye.) Beginning in the 1980s, however, tatooing became, for some, a fashion statement rather than a declaration of social outlawry. Popular designs have become more self-consciously artistic, more decorative, and less threatening in nature. Once exclusively a male adornment, women have increasingly adopted the practice.

SUGGESTED READING: Fred Fried and Mary Fried, *America's Forgotten Folk Arts* (New York, 1978); Clinton Sanders, *Customizing the Body: The Art and Culture of Tattooing* (Philadelphia, 1989).

Taylor, Archer (1890–1973). A major folklorist, Taylor is especially remembered for his classification system of formula tales, which STITH THOMPSON used in his seminal *The Types of the Folktale* (1961 revision). Many of Taylor's contributions to the historic-geographic study of folktales are still considered authoritative, and his pioneering work on proverbs and riddles is definitive. Taylor's approach was comparative rather than parochially American, but his impact on American folklore studies was great.

Taylor was educated at Swarthmore College and at Harvard, where he earned a Ph.D. in German in 1915 and where he studied with GEORGE LYMAN KITTREDGE. He was professor of German at the University of California, Berkeley, from 1939 until his retirement in 1958. Principal founder of the California Folklore Society, he edited its journal, *California Folklore Quarterly* from its first issue in 1942 through 1954.

See also: BOGGS, RALPH STEELE; HAND, WAYLAND D.

SUGGESTED READING: Wayland D. Hand, "Archer Taylor, 1890–1973," *Journal of American Folklore* 87 (1974), pp. 2–9.

Terry, Sonny (Sanders Turell) (1911–1986). Blues singer and harmonica player Sonny Terry was best known as the partner of guitarist Brownie McGhee. Terry was born Sanders Turell near Greensboro, North Carolina, and learned harmonica from his father. Two accidents, one at age eleven and another at sixteen, left Terry blind. During the Depression, he performed with medicine shows and as a street musician in Durham, North Carolina, along with blind guitarists Gary Davis and BLIND BOY FULLER. Terry came to the attention of the mainstream in 1939, when he performed at Carnegie Hall with BIG BILL BROONZY and with such swing musicians as Benny Goodman and Count Basie. Within a few years, he settled permanently in New York, where he participated in the folk-music revival of the 1940s through the 1960s. He recorded with such folk musicians as WOODY GUTHRIE, PETE SEEGER, and BURL IVES, and with his old partner, Brownie McGhee, with whom he also toured internationally.

See also: ASCH, MOSES.

Tex-Mex music. Also called *Música Tejana,* Tex-Mex is the music of the *Tejanos,* the Texas-Mexicans living in the southern part of the state. A distinct and distinctive Tex-Mex music has existed since the eighteenth century. It traditionally combined Spanish and Mexican music with French-European styles, then took on influence from Latin-Caribbean music, and, into the twentieth century, from Mexican and American popular music as well. By the middle of the nineteenth century, especially during the reign of Emperor Maximilian in Mexico, European salon music (including such dance forms as the POLKA, WALTZ, MAZURKA, and SCHOTTISCHE) became popular in Mexico and were eagerly adopted by *Tejanos.* By the end of the nineteenth century, Tex-Mex music was essentially European salon music with a Hispanic frontier accent. During the early twentieth century, Tex-Mex traditions diversified into the music of the *guitarreros,* the singing guitarists, who specialized in narrative BALLADS sung over waltz and polka tunes. Beginning in the 1920s, another Tex-Mex tradition appeared in *orquesta tipica,* a small band of musicians who specialized in instrumental music built around the accordion. At about this time, from the working class, CONJUNTO MUSIC came into its own, together with a softer tradition more suited to the middle class, the *orequestra Tejana.*

The Tex-Mex musical traditions are still very much alive, as *Tejano* rock, jazz, and country, and as *música Tropical,* Tex-Mex Carribean-influenced music.

See also: ARHOOLIE RECORDS; FOLK MUSIC; JIMÉNEZ, FLACO; MEXICAN AMERICANS; ROUNDER RECORDS.

SUGGESTED READING: Manuel Peña, *The Texas-Mexican Conjunto: History of a Working-Class Music* (Austin, Tex., 1985).

Thanksgiving. Believed to have originated in the fall of 1621 when William Bradford, governor of Plymouth Plantation, Massachusetts, invited neighboring Indians to join the Pilgrim settlers in a three-day feast in thanksgiving for the bounty of the season, Thanksgiving was officially proclaimed a national holiday in 1863 by President Abraham Lincoln, who responded to popular enthusiasm for the holiday. This enthusiasm had been orchestrated in large part by Sarah J. Hale, longtime editor (1837–77) of *Godey's*

A popular image of Thanksgiving: a 1925 book illustration portraying The First Thanksgiving.

Thanksgiving dinner at the Labor Temple, New York City, 1910.

Lady's Book, the leading women's periodical of the time, who, as early as 1837, began agitating for the proclamation of a national holiday, supposedly in emulation of the Pilgrim-Indian feast. It was annual articles in *Godey's* that established many of the food traditions associated with the holiday, including the turkey, dressing, pumpkin pie, and apple cider.

Thanksgiving was traditionally celebrated on the last Thursday of November until 1939, when business interests succeeded in persuading President Franklin D. Roosevelt to move it from the last Thursday of the month to the second-to-last; the holiday had come to mark the opening of the Christmas shopping season, and the businessmen felt that moving the holiday up would add a week of shopping nationwide. This change proved short-lived. In 1941, observance of the holiday was established by an act of Congress as the fourth Thursday in November. Canada adopted Thanksgiving as a national holiday in November 1879 and celebrates it on the second Monday in October.

Thanksgiving is in the tradition of harvest festivals that have been celebrated at least since classical and biblical times. Before Lincoln proclaimed it an official holiday, Thanksgiving was generally observed at least throughout New England, and, in 1858, eight southern governors proclaimed the holiday as well.

The centerpiece of today's Thanksgiving celebration is a dinner with TURKEY as the main course. The assumption is that turkey was consumed by the Pilgrims and Indians at the first Thanksgiving, although there is no record of this, except for Governor William Bradford's mention, in his *Of Plimoth Plantation,* that wild turkeys abounded during that first Thanksgiving autumn. During the late nineteenth century, turkey growers actively promoted the notion of the turkey dinner, and they were aided in this effort by popular artists and printmakers who portrayed the "traditional" Thanksgiving table as centered on the turkey. Combining, then, folk traditions, federal law, and commercial interests, Thanksgiving has become a nonsectarian holiday and, perhaps, the most universally and uniformally celebrated of American national holidays.

See also: PILGRIMS AND PURITANS; PUMPKIN; SQUANTO.

Thomas, James "Son Ford" (1926–).

"Son Ford" Thomas is an African-American Delta blues musician and sculptor. He was born in rural Yazoo County, Mississippi, and picked up the guitar by imitating his uncle. As a teenager, he began performing in JUKE JOINTS near Leland and Greenville, Mississippi. By the 1970s, he was working the college blues circuit and has participated in the Smithsonian Festival of American Folklife on several occasions.

Thomas is also a sculptor, working in clay. He produced so many models of Ford tractors that he was nicknamed "Son Ford." As a mature sculptor, he creates idiosyncratic works, most notably heads and skulls that are open at the top so that they can be used as containers or ashtrays.

Thomas, Jeannette Bell (1881–1982).

Calling herself the "Traipsin' Woman," Thomas wrote local-color stories drawing on folklife along the Kentucky–West Virginia border. She was also director of the American Folk Song Festival, held annually near Ashland, Kentucky, from 1930 to 1972. Born Jeannette Bell in Ashland, Kentucky, she worked as a circuit court stenographer after graduating from high school. In this itinerant position, she became acquainted with the folk music of the eastern Kentucky mountains. After a brief marriage to businessman Albert Hart Thomas (1913–14), Thomas attended Hunter College and the Pulitzer School of Journalism in New York, and began writing folklore-oriented features for magazines and newspapers between 1925 and 1930. She also became active as a folk music promoter, bringing Kentucky fiddler J. W. Day to New York's Roxy Theatre in 1928. In 1930, she published a story in the *American Magazine* portraying herself as "The Traipsin' Woman," and, with this, her career as a folklife-oriented writer began in earnest. This year, too, she presided over the beginnings of the American Folk Song Festival in Ashland, Kentucky, which she incorporated the next year. Thomas published her first book, *Devils' Ditties,* in 1931, a collection of mountain folk songs. Her other folklore-focused books were fiction, the most famous of which was *The Singin' Fiddler of Lost Hope Hollow* (1938).

Roundly criticized by academic folklorists as the commercial entrepreneur that she, indeed, was, Thomas nevertheless produced books and a music festival that made many people aware of folklore and folklife.

SUGGESTED READING: Jeanette Bell Thomas, *Traipsin' Woman* (New York, 1933).

Thompson, Harold W. (1891–1963).

Thompson was a collector of New York State folklore and was a founder of the New York Folklore Society in 1944, serving as its president from 1945 to 1950. He taught at Albany State University from 1915 to 1940 and at Cornell University from 1940 to 1959. Both a scholar and a popularizer, he hosted a monthly radio show on folklore from 1935 to 1943.

Thompson, Stith (1885–1976).

Stith Thompson was one of the great American folklorists. He was born near Springfield, Kentucky, and was educated at Butler University and the University of Wisconsin, then at the University of California, Berkeley, where he earned an M.A. (1912) and at Harvard (Ph.D., 1914). He was a student of GEORGE LYMAN KITTREDGE. Thompson held several teaching posts before joining the English Department faculty of Indiana University in 1922 and offering one of the first folklore courses taught in any American university. He later established at Indiana the nation's first Ph.D. program in folklore.

As a scholar, Stith Thompson specialized in the folktale, and his seminal work in this area is his series of surveys and indexes, most importantly *The Motif Index of Folk-Literature* (1932–36; revised ed., 1955–58).

See also: BAUGHMAN, ERNEST WARREN; DORSON, RICHARD M.; TAYLOR, ARCHER.

Thoreau, Henry David (1817–1862).

Celebrated as an essayist, poet, naturalist, champion of civil disobedience, and Transcendentalist philosopher, Henry David Thoreau was also an informal student of Native American folklore, of PLANTS AND PLANT LORE, and of FOLK SPEECH. His *Journals* as well as many of his works published during his lifetime are replete with folklore notes gleaned both from reading and observation, mostly relating to nature and to Native American nature lore. Thoreau also earns a place in American folklore for having fashioned himself into a local character (see LOCAL-CHARACTER STORY), adopting an acerbic, curmudgeonly, stubborn, and argumentative attitude as a way of living in a society that (as Thoreau saw it) continually demands compromise of personal liberty and integrity.

Thoreau was born in 1817 in Concord, Massachusetts, and was educated at Harvard College, graduating in 1837. After an abortive attempt at teaching school, he worked in his father's pencil factory, then, with his brother, founded a school in 1838, which lasted through 1841. Inspired by a canoe trip on the Concord and Merrimack Rivers in 1839, Thoreau determined to become a nature poet. During this period, he developed a friendship with Ralph Waldo Emerson, already recognized as a poet, essayist, and Transcendentalist philosopher, who mentored the younger man and who published Thoreau in *The Dial*, the Transcendentalist magazine Emerson edited. During extended periods, Thoreau lived with the Emersons in their Concord house. In 1845, he

Henry David Thoreau.

Site of Thoreau's cabin at Walden Pond, Massachusetts. Photograph published in Reuben Post Halleck, History of American Literature, *1911. (Collection of Alan Axelrod)*

acted on an idea offered earlier by a Harvard classmate, to build a shed by a lake or pond and simply live. Thoreau chose Walden Pond, just south of Concord, and erected his shelter on land Emerson owned. He set about learning everything he could about Walden Pond and its environs and recorded the natural and human lore associated with the area. The literary result of this experience, published in 1854, was *Walden; or, Life in the Woods,* a work that combines the practical application of Transcendental philosophy with an account of the realities of nature at Walden.

Thoreau lived at Walden Pond from 1845 to 1847, returning to the town of Concord to spend a night in jail in July 1846, when he refused to pay a poll tax to support a government that upheld slavery and prosecuted an unjust war against Mexico. Although Thoreau's incarceration was brief, "Civil Disobedience," the essay he wrote as a result of it, has profoundly influenced civil libertarians ever since, including Mahatma Gandhi and Martin Luther King, Jr. As far as the citizens of Concord were concerned, however, Thoreau had simply added to his growing reputation as a local character.

After his Walden sojourn, Thoreau worked as an amateur naturalist and as a professional surveyor. He took over his father's pencil business and wrote more essays, many of which were gathered together in *The Maine Woods* (1864). Thoreau also became an ardent abolitionist and an eloquent supporter of the raider of Harpers Ferry, John Brown. Thoreau succumbed to tuberculosis in 1862. Thoreau's books were not popular during his lifetime. His first effort, *A Week on the Concord and Merrimack Rivers,* sold a mere two hundred copies, and *Walden* sold about two thousand over a five-year period.

See also: Folklore in American Literature; Hawthorne, Nathaniel; Whitman, Walt.

suggested reading: Walter Harding, *The Days of Henry Thoreau* (expanded ed., Boston, 1982); Sherman Paul, *The Shores of America: Thoreau's Inward Exploration* (Urbana, Ill., 1958). Thoreau's works are available in many modern editions.

Thorp, Nathan Howard ("Jack") (1867–1940).

Thorp was the nation's first collector of cowboy songs. His cowboy songbook, *Songs of the Cowboy*, was published in 1908. Thorp was a New Hampshire–educated New Yorker, but he came into contact with life in the West working on his brother's Nebraska ranch during summers. In 1886, he settled in New Mexico to make his living as a horse trader specializing in polo ponies. It was during this period that he came into close contact with cowboys and cowboy culture and began collecting songs in New Mexico, Texas, and Indian Territory (Oklahoma). His first collection, of twenty-three songs, was published in New Mexico in an edition of two thousand paperbacks in 1908. He enlarged the collection to 101 songs in 1921.

Thorp was also a cowboy poet and storyteller, who influenced the better-known teller of western tales J. Frank Dobie.

See also: Cowboy songs.

SUGGESTED READING: Nathan Howard Thorp, *Songs of the Cowboy* (1921; reprint ed., Lincoln, Nebr., 1984).

Thorpe, Thomas Bangs (1815–1878).

A minor American writer, Thorpe was the author of well-received literary versions of frontier TALL TALES, the most famous of which was "The Big Bear of Arkansas" (1841). A literary representation of an oral tale told on a Mississippi riverboat, "Big Bear" is "narrated" by one Jim Doggett, an Arkansas backwoodsman, who tells of his hunt for a "creation b'ar," a mammoth creature born of the limitless fertility of the Arkansas forests. The comic narrative rings with echoes of myths (such as St. George's combat with the dragon) and prefigures such great literary works as HERMAN MELVILLE's *Moby-Dick* and William Faulkner's long short story *The Bear*. It also contains a great deal of highly creditable dialect writing.

Born in Westfield, Massachusetts, Thorpe was the son of a Methodist minister. His father died when the boy was four, and Thorpe grew up with his mother's family in Dutch Albany. In New York City, he studied painting with John Quidor, an early illustrator of scenes from the works of WASHINGTON IRVING. Through his contact with Quidor, Thorpe developed an interest in literature. This first bore fruit in 1837, when, while living in the South, he published a literary sketch about Louisiana, which was widely reprinted not only in the United States, but also abroad. Two years later, he published "The Big Bear of Arkansas," which created a sensation. In 1845, Thorpe published *Mysteries of the Backwoods; or, Sketches of the Southwest: Including Character, Scenery, and Rural Sports*, then pursued a journalistic career during the Mexican War (1846–48). In 1854, he expanded *Mysteries* as *The Hive of "The Bee-Hunter": A Repository of Sketches, Including Peculiar American Character, Scenery, and Rural Sports*. During the Civil War, Thorpe served in the military government of occupied New Orleans. After the war, in 1869, he worked in the New York City Custom House while writing occasional articles for *Appleton's Magazine*.

See also: FOLKLORE IN AMERICAN LITERATURE.

T house.

An example of VERNACULAR ARCHITECTURE, the T house is also called a "cross-plan" or "gable-front-and-wing" house. It is found throughout the United States, but is especially prevalent in the South, where it flourished toward the close of the nineteenth century and the early years of the twentieth. The T house is generally a frame dwelling consisting of a gable or projecting wing two-rooms deep, straddled by a side wing one-room deep.

Toasts.

To non–African Americans, a toast is a brief salute honoring a person, event, or thing, recited with a raised glass containing liquor, beer, or wine and followed by the assembled party raising their glasses in return and all taking a drink by way of affirming the honor bestowed in the toast. Many toasts are mock serious. Some are simple formulas, such as "Here's to you!" or "To your health!" or "Let's drink to the happiness of the bride and groom!" Some toasts are personalized to a greater degree, the individual who offers the toast giving what amounts to a short speech. Some toasts are miniature rhymes, usually doggerel: "Over the teeth, over the gums, / Look out, stomach, here it comes!" Other toasts are memorized bits of verse from literary poets such as Robert Burns or William Butler Yeats.

In African-American folklore, a toast is often something more in the nature of folk poetry (see POETRY, FOLK) or a prose recitation. Usually, these toasts are accompanied by drinking. Some toasts, intended for an all-male audience, are humorously obscene, others are more moralistic in tone and fit to be presented in mixed company. Sometimes toasts are exchanged in toast contests. The best known of the toasts in the African-American tradition is the tale of SHINE's survival of the *Titanic* disaster.

See also: AFRICAN AMERICANS; RAP.

SUGGESTED READING: Roger Abrahams, *Deep Down in the Jungle: Negro Narrative Folklore from the Streets of Philadelphia* (1963; reprint ed., Chicago, 1970); Bruce Jackson, *"Get Your Ass in the Water and Swim Like Me": Narrative Poetry from Black Oral Tradition* (Cambridge, Mass., 1974).

Tobacco.

Tobacco is of the genus *Nicotiana* and is native to the Americas and West Indies. Before European contact with the New World, tobacco was "cured" (dried), then smoked, sniffed, and chewed by Native Americans. By the sixteenth century, Europe had discovered the pleasures of this plant, which became the basis of much New World trade.

Among Native Americans, tobacco plays a role in religious ceremony as the gift of a Promethean CULTURE HERO. It functions as a means of facilitating communication with the spirit world by inducing a trancelike state in the smokers, and it is also used to solemnize and ratify a range of important events, such as the conclusion of treaties. Indians also smoke or chew tobacco recreationally.

Among non–Native Americans, tobacco has had a somewhat checkered cultural reputation. Some groups condemn its use as a vice only slightly less objectionable than the consumption of alcohol. Boys have traditionally viewed their first cigarette as a rite of passage into manhood, while smoking among teenage girls—and among women generally—was once considered daring, naughty, unseemly, or even obscene. By the 1910s and 1920s, cigarette smoking marked a woman either as liberated or as a libertine, depending on one's preconceptions. Cigarettes have served as symbols of romantic sophistication in relations between men and women, as well as of comradeship among men. In the culture of American prisons, cigarettes serve as a kind of currency. Among young people especially, cigarette smoking has been viewed as a badge of sophistication—or "cool"—and also as a token of rebellion. A song lyric from the 1957 Broadway musical (and, in 1961, film) *West Side Story* tells of the meaning of membership in a street gang: "When you're a Jet, you're a Jet all the way, / From your first cigarette, to your last dying day."

The status of pipe and cigar smoking always differed from that of cigarette smoking. Although among rural folk, pipe smoking was an activity enjoyed by both sexes, in urban culture, it was exclusively male and conveyed an aura of calm and thoughtfulness on the smoker. A pipe was often seen as a mark of intelligence and sophistication. Cigar smoking, in contrast, was frequently regarded as aggressively masculine to the point of boorishness, although the savoring of a fine cigar has been regarded traditionally as a mark of prosperity and as a token of the good life. During much of the nineteenth and early twentieth centuries, the use of so-called smokeless tobacco products—chewing tobacco—was so widespread that spittoons or cuspidors were furnished in such public places as saloons and hotel lobbies. By the 1920s, chewing was becoming increasingly confined to rural areas and was chiefly an outdoor activity, popular among farmers and professional baseball players. By the 1970s, chewing became popular among teenaged boys, especially college students, in some urban as well as rural areas.

Beginning in the 1960s, concern over the effects of tobacco use on health, particularly as a contributing cause of cancer and heart disease, has gradually diminished the near-universal popularity of cigarette smoking, although, during the 1990s, the smoking of expensive "gourmet" cigars enjoyed a resurgence of popularity, among young men as well as women.

Tolson, Edgar (1904–1984). Many students of folk art consider Tolson the most impor-

tant Kentucky carver of the twentieth century. He carved mainly biblical and religious scenes, creating figures of stark simplicity, from which all nonessential elements had been stripped. His medium of choice was poplar, carved with a pocketknife, and very sparingly painted. His output ran to some two thousand figures, all small, ranging from two inches to two feet high, and highly prized by collectors and museums alike.

Born and raised in the Kentucky mountains, Tolson worked as a farmer, laborer, chair maker, and a "called preacher." Beginning in 1921, he served as pastor of the Holly, Kentucky, Baptist Church, but in 1935 or 1936, dismayed by what he perceived as the hypocrisy of his flock, he blew the church off its foundation with a stick of dynamite. Fortunately, no one was injured, and Tolson even continued preaching in the repaired building for the next quarter century, until he stepped down in 1961.

Tolson began creating Appalachian toy pieces during the 1910s, but it wasn't until the mid-1960s that the Smithsonian Institution's Museum Shop took some of his work on consignment. It proved popular, and more of Tolson's work was shown at the Smithsonian's 1968 and 1973 Festival of American Folklife. Today, his work is in many collections.

SUGGESTED READING: Chuck and Jan Rosenak, *Museum of American Folk Art Encyclopedia of Twentieth-Century American Folk Art and Artists* (New York, 1990).

Tongue twisters. A popular form of oral tradition in many cultures, a tongue twister is a phrase or rhyme purposely contrived to trip the tongue or, at least, to challenge the elocutionary skill of the speaker. The difficulty of tongue twisters typically lies in difficult successions of consonants or unusual changes in otherwise regular consonant patterns, and the challenge is to negotiate these difficulties smoothly and rapidly. "Peter Piper picked a peck of pickled peppers" is to be recited at a fast clip, not leisurely. For the most part, tongue twisters, like RIDDLES, are meant to be enjoyed in and for themselves; however, they sometimes serve as charms or incantations useful in folk medicine (see MEDICINE, FOLK), especially as a remedy for hiccups.

Tooth Fairy. The tooth fairy is a fictive spirit who is said to appear at night to remove a shed baby tooth, which has been placed under the child's pillow, and leave in its place a gift—usually a coin. Like SANTA CLAUS, the tooth fairy is a figure of popular culture and is not taken seriously by adults (who, nevertheless, faithfully play the role of tooth fairy, surreptitiously removing the tooth from beneath the sleeping child's pillow, and leaving a coin). The pop culture trivialization of the tooth fairy notwithstanding, the figure and the ritual of exchange associated with it are related to ancient rites of passage marking the transition from infancy to childhood. In various folk cultures, baby teeth were thrown to the sun, to an animal, over the roof, or placed in a tree. Other rituals involved having a person—not the child—swallow the tooth, hide the tooth, or burn it.

SUGGESTED READING: William Carter et al., *Ethnodentistry and Dental Folklore* (Overland Park, Kans., 1987).

Totem pole. Among non–Native Americans, totem poles are associated with Indians generally; in fact, they are peculiar to the Native American peoples of the Northwest coast. They are large poles, often spectacular in dimension, into which are carved and painted animal figures emblematic of the lineage of prominent families in the area. It is the belief of the Northwest coastal tribes that, in prehistoric times, all beings were animals, some of whom assumed human form.

See also: WOODCARVING.

These totem poles were photographed in 1926 at Alert Bay, British Columbia, a settlement of Haida people.

Toys, folk. Folk toys are traditional playthings made by hand. Some are made by children (such as hats and sailboats fashioned from newspaper), but most enduring folk toys are made by adults for children. Simple toys are made by parents, and more complex toys by craftspeople. Among the most common of folk toys are a wide array of dolls, including those with faces carved from apples (a popular folk craft item in APPALACHIA) and those with corncob bodies dressed in scraps of fabric simulating clothes. Skill toys are also common, such as the cup and ball (in which the ball is tied to the cup, and the object is to toss the ball and catch it in the cup), puzzles of various sorts, wheeled toys, imitation rifles carved from wood, and so on. Surprisingly, folk toys have held little interest for folklorists, in part, perhaps, because they tend to be ephemeral. However, in the years since the general FOLK REVIVAL of the 1960s, commercially handmade wooden toys patterned after folk traditions have become increasingly popular as alternatives to the mass-produced plastic toys of major manufacturers. While this has increased the number of folklike toys in existence, it has also tended to obscure some of the distinctions between folk toys and toys that are merely handcrafted in the manner of folk toys.

See also: WOODCARVING.

SUGGESTED READING: Simon Bronner, *American Children's Folklore* (Little Rock, Ark., 1988); Linda Garland Page and Hilton Smith, eds., *The Foxfire Book of Toys and Games: Reminiscences and Instructions from Appalachia* (New York, 1985).

Travis, Merle Robert (1917–1983). Travis was a country-music-style folk musician who specialized in "Travis picking," a "thumb style" guitar technique in which the thumb and index finger play melody with harmonic and bass accompaniment. The technique was brought to Travis's native Muhlenberg County, Kentucky, by an African-American folk musician named Arnold Shulta, but Travis learned it from white coal miners Mose Rager and Ike Everly. Subsequent commercial country musicians adopted the technique from Travis. As a singer, Travis leaned toward the folk repertoire and also composed folk-style songs (usually focused on the lives of Kentucky coal miners) as well as songs in the country-western vein. Travis's best-known coal-mining song is "Sixteen Tons," which was a very big hit for the slick country star Tennessee Ernie Ford in 1955.

SUGGESTED READING: Charles K. Wolfe, *Kentucky Country: Folk and Country Music of Kentucky* (Lexington, Ky., 1982).

Traylor, Bill (1854–1947). Born a slave on the plantation of George Traylor, near Benton, Alabama, Bill Traylor continued to work as a hired hand of the Traylor farm after emancipation, then, in 1938, at the age of eighty-four, with his wife deceased and his twenty children gone off on their own, he moved to Montgomery, Alabama. There he worked in a shoe factory for a time until he was crippled with rheumatism. Living in the back room of a funeral parlor, he began, in 1939, at the age of eighty-five, to draw for his amusement. He typically began by creating geometric shapes, which he then developed into human or animal figures. His work typically reflected his rural background, depicting farm animals and simple farm scenes with vivid, even violent use of color and a naive yet oddly graceful approach to form that may bring to mind prehistoric drawings found on cave walls. In a short time, Traylor worked intensively, filling his days and nights with drawing. With the encouragement of a Montogmery artist named Charles Shannon, Traylor began selling some of his work and soon developed a local following and reputation. However, with the advent of World War II, Traylor moved north, living with children in Washington and Detroit, before returning to Montgomery in 1946. Apparently he did not draw during this period (at least, no work survives), but he resumed his art when he returned to Montgomery. Traylor's work was seen outside of Montgomery once during his lifetime, when it was exhibited at New York City's Fieldston School in 1941. The work was "rediscovered" in 1979, when it was again exhibited in New York, at the R. H. Gosterom Gallery.

SUGGESTED READING: Jane Livingston and John Beardsley, *Black Folk Art in America: 1930–1980* (Jackson, Miss., 1982).

Trickster. Trickster figures are among the most basic and universal characters in folklore, including that of NATIVE AMERICANS and African Americans. In Native American folklore, such characters as COYOTE and Rabbit, as well as others, appear as tricksters. Indeed, the most powerful mythic figures in Native American lore typically have an aspect of the trickster about them. In African-American folklore, BRER RABBIT is the trickster par excellence. European folklore is likewise replete with trickster characters, including the Greek god Hermes and the Scandanavian demigod Loki; however, one is hard-pressed to find godlike tricksters in Euro-American lore—though American literary folklore does offer examples of CON ARTISTS AND CONFIDENCE MEN, who seem to have an affinity with European godlike archetypes, and certainly, JOEL CHANDLER HARRIS, in introducing BRER FOX as a foil to Brer Rabbit in his UNCLE REMUS versions of African-American trickster tales, imported a European trickster into American popular culture, if not folklore. It is also possible to see the TALL TALE, a popular American folk genre, as related to the trickster tale.

See also: AFRICAN AMERICANS; ALLIGATOR; ANANSI; COMPUTER FOLKLORE; FOX; GREEK AMERICANS; SHINE; TAR BABY.

SUGGESTED READING: Richard M. Dorson, *American Negro Folktale* (Bloomington, Ind., 1958); Paul Radin, *The Trickster* (New York, 1956).

Trolls. In Scandinavia, trolls were originally depicted as gigantic monsters, but, in later folklore, evolved into dwarflike creatures, especially in southern Scandinavia. From Scandinavia, troll lore spread into much of the rest of continental Europe, where they figured as a race of malevolent little beings who live under bridges, demanding a heavy toll—perhaps even the life—of anyone who would pass. Trolls entered American folklore via a commercial route, when U.S. children and adults eagerly bought the long-haired fleshy plastic troll dolls, which appeared on the market beginning in the 1960s. The dolls came in many sizes and were also adapted to such uses as key-chain ornaments and decorations to hang from automobile rearview mirrors. The trolls sold in the U.S. were smiling, ugly-cute figures, which were often touted as good-luck charms, to be carried like a rabbit's foot.

See also: AMULET.

Truchas Master (working 1780–1840). Also called the "Calliographic Santero" because of his free-flowing, linear drawing style, the Truchas Master is named for his two major works, RETABLOS (altar screens) that decorate the church of Nuestra Señora del Rosario de las Truchas, forty miles north of Santa Fe, New

Mexico. This painter of SANTOS (the religious folk imagery of Hispanic New Mexico) is unique in his idiosyncratic style and obscure iconography, which are unrelated to other *santeros* of the period. Most likely, he was inspired by religious paintings and sculptures imported from Spain into the New Mexican colony during the latter eighteenth century. That he was rather more sophisticated than his fellow *santeros* is suggested by the handwritten inscriptions found on some of his panels; literacy among the folk painters of this period was rare.

Trucking and truckers. For some Americans—and for some American truckers as well—the truck driver is a latter-day COWBOY, freely ranging the highways, a knight of the road. For many years, truckers were known as the "gentlemen of the road," skillful, courteous drivers, who were always ready to help motorists in distress. More recently, this EXOTERIC FOLKLORE has faded, and has been replaced by a popular image of the typical trucker as overworked, keeping himself awake by popping pills and drinking gallons of coffee, often endangering the lives of innocent motorists in the process.

The facts of the trucker's life have always been hard. Hours are typically long, monotonous, and lonely. The life is particularly grueling for the independent trucker, who works for himself or herself rather than for a larger trucking company. The independent must at times drive almost continuously to make a living. At truck stops and rest stops, the company and conversation of other truckers is sought. Important information relating to weather, road conditions, traffic, and the presence of highway patrol officers is exchanged, as are personal narratives and TALL TALES, often involving scrapes with the law and adventures with hitchhikers. Drivers also exchange cautionary tales concerning accidents and other road disasters.

The informal folklore network among truckers develops not only around the truck stop, but over the airwaves via citizens band (CB) radio. During the 1970s, truckers' CB lingo swept the nation, as did a fad for the purchase and use CB radios. Today, few nontruckers use CB radios for recreational purposes, but truckers still rely on their CBs and often hold extended conversations with one another; however, most of the CB jargon of the 1970s has been ditched, and "good buddy," the ubiquitous form of CB address in that decade, is now used only as an insult. "Handles"—radio nicknames—are still important and the subject of considerable invention. Often, truckers' CB handles express their own feelings about the lore of trucking: "Lone Wolf" and "Outlaw," for example, are common.

SUGGESTED READING: Ron Kowalke and John Gunnell, *Trucking in America: Moving the Goods* (New York, 1995); Lawrence J. Ouellet, *Pedal to the Metal: The Work Life of Truckers* (Philadelphia, 1994).

Tubb, Ernest (1914–1984). Tubb was a major force in COUNTRY MUSIC and, in particular, was a leading exponent of the HONKY-TONK MUSIC style. Born in Crisp, Texas, not far from Dallas, he was influenced by the music of JIMMIE RODGERS, whom he emulated. With help from Carrie Rodgers, widow of Jimmie, Tubb obtained a recording contract with the Victor Company in 1936, though it wasn't until the 1940s that Tubb's recordings—for Decca—began to score hits. In 1943, he joined the cast of the

GRAND OLE OPRY and was among the first musicians to bring an electric guitar to the stage of the Opry.

Tubb was not only a fine performer, he was a talented promoter, who helped to reshape the image of country music to appeal to a wider audience. He advocated the replacement of the term "hillbilly music" with "country music," and promoted the development of fresh, new country talent, including Hank Williams, Johnny Cash, Loretta Lynn, and Willie Nelson. Tubb was inducted into the Country Music Hall of Fame in 1965.

Turkey. The common domestic turkey is native to North America and enjoys special status among many Americans as the meal of choice for THANKSGIVING dinner and, to a lesser extent, CHRISTMAS dinner. In partaking of turkey at Thanksgiving, many believe they are reenacting the Pilgrims' first Thanksgiving meal; in fact, the promotion of turkey as the Thanksgiving bird was the work of poultry growers during the 1930s. Before approximately 1935, there was little special association between turkey and Thanksgiving.

Shortly after independence was won, BENJAMIN FRANKLIN proposed the gorgeously plumed wild turkey as the national bird emblematic of the United States; eventually, the bald eagle was adopted instead. In many Native American cultures, the turkey figures as a CULTURE HERO in certain folktales, and some tribes incorporate a "turkey dance" in their ceremonials—though it is uncertain what special or sacred significance, if any, this dance has. A ballroom dance called the turkey trot was popular among non–Native Americans during the early twentieth century. While quite unrelated to the Indian dance, it features a similarly humorous strutting step, imitative of the turkey's ungainly gait.

"Turkey in the Straw." A favorite FIDDLE and BANJO tune, "Turkey in the Straw" shares a melody with "Old Zip Coon," a minstrel show song. Although "Turkey in the Straw" strikes a modern ear as quintessentially rural, the song was first heard in New York's Bowery Theatre in 1834 and may be rooted in some traditional English songs.

See also: FOLK MUSIC.

Turnbo, Silas Claiborn (1844–1925). Turnbo was an early collector of Ozark folklore and oral history, beginning in 1866 and working through approximately 1913. Turnbo was a determined amateur folklorist, who published the material he collected as nostalgia features in a number of Arkansas and Missouri newspapers between 1898 and 1907. He privately published two book-length collections, both titled *Fireside Stories of the Early Days in the Ozarks,* in 1905 and 1907. Disappointed by the public's lack of interest in his work, Turnbo sold his collection to William Elsey Connelley, secretary of the Kansas State Historical Society. From here, portions of the collection surfaced in libraries in Arkansas and Missouri. Six volumes of Turnbo's material were privately printed in 1987.

SUGGESTED READING: Desmond Walls Allen, ed., *Turnbo's Tales of the Ozarks* (Conway, Ark., 1987).

Twain, Mark (1835–1910). Greatest of the nation's local color writers (see LOCAL-COLOR STORY), Mark Twain was born Samuel Langhorne Clemens in Florida, Missouri, and was raised in nearby Hannibal. He would become an author who made great use of local lore and whose best literary works, in turn, would have the feel and texture of genuine folklore.

Growing up in the Mississippi River town of Hannibal, Clemens was exposed to the colorful, rough-and-tumble world of those who made their living on the river. Clemens's father died in 1847, compelling eleven-year-old Samuel to help support the family. After working odd jobs, he became a printer's apprentice and, with his older brother Orion, founded and ran the *Hannibal Journal,* publishing his first humorous sketches in that paper. In 1853, Clemens became an itinerant printer, working on newspapers in St. Louis, New York City, and Philadelphia, then rejoined his brother for a time and published more sketches. In 1856, Clemens became an apprentice Mississippi steamboat pilot, a vocation he pursued for four years, cultivating an intimate familiarity with the river and the array of humanity associated with it.

The Civil War cut short Clemens's career as a pilot, and after a brief stint in the Confederate militia, he joined Orion on a trip to the Nevada Territory. After failing as a prospector, Clemens became a writer for the *Virginia City Territorial Enterprise* and was the author of several delightful hoaxes of the TALL TALE genre. One travel sketch written for the paper, on February 3, 1863, Clemens signed "Mark Twain," the Mississippi leadsman's term for water "two fathoms deep" and, therefore, navigable. It became his pseudonym thereafter and was later trademarked.

Twain moved to San Francisco in 1864, where he associated with the writers BRET HARTE and ARTEMUS WARD, then went on to do a little prospecting at Angels Camp in the Tuolumne Hills. Here he heard a folktale about a jumping frog, which he transformed into "The Celebrated Jumping Frog of Calaveras County," his first literary hit—and one that proved so enduring that jumping frog contests, inspired by the story, are still annual events at Angels Camp. The story launched Twain's literary career and set the pattern for his most characteristic works, which either drew on folklore or invented something very much like it to create a gallery of frontier types and situations.

In 1866, Twain went on a world cruise as a correspondent for *The Sacramento Union,* producing a series of hilarious letters later published as *The Innocents Abroad; or, The New Pilgrim's Progress* (1869). While the scenes Twain described were foreign, he did so in the persona of the shrewd American westerner—yet another folklore type he depicted with consummate skill. The book also showcased Twain's ability to write

Mark Twain, photographed in bed, late in life.

in imitation of southwestern oral narratives and tall tales, a technique he would develop in later books, most notably *Adventures of Huckleberry Finn.*

His next book-length work, *Roughing It,* appeared in 1872, another volume filled with the lore of the West, and in 1873, with coauthor Charles Dudley Warner, he wrote *The Gilded Age,* a satire on the business and political corruption of the era. The post–Civil War years have been known as "the gilded age" ever since.

Throughout the 1870s, Twain toured with tremendous success as a lecturer, both in the United States and in England. He published a long series of sketches, "Old Times on the Mississippi," in the *Atlantic Monthly* during 1875, a marvelous account of life and folklife along the river as seen through the eyes of a young steamboat pilot. (An expanded version of the sketches was published in book form as *Life on the Mississippi* in 1883.)

The Adventures of Tom Sawyer, published in 1876, drew on Twain's own boyhood recollections as well as those solicited from friends. The character of young Tom Sawyer was delineated so vividly that he has assumed the universal stature of a figure of American folklore and such episodes as the one in which Tom tricks his friends into whitewashing his Aunt Polly's fence for him are told and retold as if they were tales from anonymous oral tradition.

The Adventures of Tom Sawyer included a ragtag friend of Tom's named Huckleberry Finn. Twain made him the hero of *Adventures of Huckleberry Finn* (1884), certainly the author's masterpiece and a novel at once so delightful, moving, disturbing, and profound that Ernest Hemingway once remarked that all American literature began with it. Through *Huck,* Twain, with remarkable sensitivity and skill, records the FOLK SPEECH of the people of the Mississippi and

portrays an array of folk types, from roarers to confidence men, while spinning a story about a youngster's initiation into a world both wondrous and evil.

Twain created an extended tall tale in *A Connecticut Yankee in King Arthur's Court* (1889), exploiting in the process an entirely different American folklore stereotype, the Yankee, whose native ingenuity is tested to its utmost when he is brought back in time to the days of King Arthur.

During all of this period, Twain cultivated his own persona as a kind of local character (see LOCAL-CHARACTER STORY), a cynical curmudgeon, yet one with infinite sympathy for the foibles of what he later called "the damned human race." During the 1880s, a series of disastrous financial investments bankrupted Twain, who wrote a number of works, some quite undistinguished, in an effort to recoup his fortune. He also embarked on a lecture tour around the world, which was financially very successful and enabled him to pay his many creditors. However, the tour exhausted the aging writer, who was emotionally devastated by the news of his eldest daughter's death in 1897. During this period, it also became clear that his youngest daughter was suffering from mental illness as well as severe epilepsy, and Twain's wife, his beloved Olivia—Livvy—now drifted into terminal illness. The works of Twain's later years are bitter and melancholy. The most famous of these, *The Man That Corrupted Hadleyburg* (1900), is an extended, cynical portrait of an enduring American folk type, the con artist or confidence man.

See also: BASS, SAM(UEL); CON ARTIST AND CONFIDENCE MAN; DIALECT STORIES; FOLKLORE IN AMERICAN LITERATURE; HARTE, (FRANCIS) BRET[T].

SUGGESTED READING: Bernard Devoto, *Mark Twain's America* (New York, 1932); Justin Kaplan, *Mister*

Clemens and Mark Twain (New York, 1966). Twain's works are available in many editions.

Tyler, Royall (1757–1826). Born William Clark Tyler in Boston, Royall Tyler was educated at Harvard and became a lawyer. After meeting Thomas Wignell, a comic actor with New York City's American Company, Tyler was inspired to write *The Contrast* (premiered in New York's John Street Theater on April 16, 1787), generally considered the first American comic play. While this still quite fresh, readable, and eminently stageworthy play is stylistically imitative of British light comedy as practiced by the likes of Oliver Goldsmith and Richard Sheridan (*The Contrast* is clearly modeled on Sheridan's *The School for Scandal*), *The Contrast* also presents a vivid portrayal of a seminal American folk type: the Yankee known as BROTHER JONATHAN. The honest, straightforward, but shrewd Jonathan is contrasted with the foppish and devious Englishman, Colonel Manly, whom Jonathan ultimately bests by winning the hand of the wholesome American girl toward whom both have romantic aspirations. Not only does the play develop an emerging national folk figure, it is replete with local references and even features a patriotic rendition of "YANKEE DOODLE."

Tyler's subsequent plays lack both the humor and the folkloric significance of *The Contrast*, but his 1797 novel, *The Algerine Captive*, has the

Scene from Royall Tyler's The Contrast, *1787.*

distinction of being one of the first American novels to be published in England.

SUGGESTED READING: G. Thomas Tanselle, *Royall Tyler* (Cambridge, Mass., 1967); Ada Lou Carson and Herbert L. Carson, *Royall Tyler* (Boston, 1979).

u

UFO folklore. People have been reporting Unidentified Flying Objects (UFOs) at least since biblical times (see, for example, the spectacular visions of Ezekiel, 1:4–28, also Ezekiel 10), and "UFOlogists" have found numerous references scattered through all the ages of recorded history. The first widely publicized encounter with UFOs took place between November 1896 and May 1897, when thousands of people in Alabama, Arkansas, California, Colorado, Illinois, Indiana, Iowa, Kansas, Kentucky, Michigan, Minnesota, Missouri, Nebraska, Oklahoma, South Dakota, Tennessee, Texas, West Virginia, and Wisconsin reported sightings of a cigar-shaped "mysterious airship." Many recent authorities suggest that the airship sightings were inspired by the popularity of Jules Verne and other early science-fiction writers and also suggest that tabloid-style journalism embellished (perhaps even fabricated) the sightings. The reports sparked widespread panic and controversy, however, foreshadowing a national fascination with UFOs that became an obsession in the two decades following WORLD WAR II and, then, during the 1970s and 1980s, matured among some groups into various forms of popular religion, systems of ad hoc mythology, "New Age" philosophies, and even scientifically grounded belief. Despite many—some apparently government-sanctioned—efforts to dismiss UFO phenomena as everything from "swamp gas," to mass hallucination, from individual psychosis to brilliantly orchestrated hoaxes, sightings continue to be reported, not only by the public at large but by such highly credible spe-

cialist witnesses as astronauts, astronomers, pilots, and military and law enforcement officials.

Since the 1960s, there have been at least five

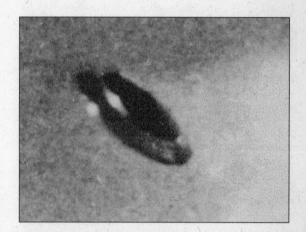

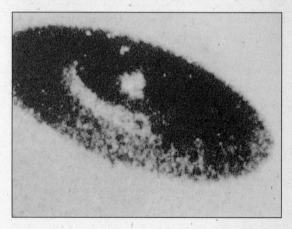

These two undocumented photos of "flying saucers" are typical of the grainy UFO images Americans (and others) have been looking at since the late 1940s. The disc or saucer is the most common UFO shape reported.

hundred reports of something more than mere sightings, as UFO investigators continue to encounter individuals who, usually during the course of regressive hypnosis, relate accounts of having been abducted and medically examined by the alien occupants of landed UFOs (see ALIEN ABDUCTION). Even more recently, mysterious CROP CIRCLES have been reported with increasing frequency, mostly in England, but also in the United States (and elsewhere). Some have suggested that these large-scale, often complex geometric patterns impressed into crop fields are massive hieroglyphics of extraterrestrial origin, perhaps an attempt to communicate. Others have claimed definitive proof that the crop circles have all been hoaxes.

Gallup polls indicate that almost all Americans have heard of UFOs, and several million claim to have sighted one. About half of the U.S. population believes UFOs are real. This reflects the division existing between proponents and opponents of the reality of UFOs. Proponents include mildly interested believers, eccentric cranks, cultists (as, for example, the cultists of the Heaven's Gate commune, who committed mass suicide in 1997, apparently believing that this would allow their spiritual deliverance by extraterrestrial visitors), and serious UFOlogists, amateur and professional investigators who attempt to apply scientific methods to the study of UFO phenomena. UFOlogists often organize societies to carry on UFOlogical research, and the societies publish periodicals intended to be read by their membership.

UFO opponents argue that all sightings and encounters may be explained conventionally and may be ascribed to terrestrial causes. Some opponents believe that purported UFO encounters are expressions of archetypes from a collective unconscious that has also produced stories, lore, and legends about ghost lights, demonic encounters, and fairy kidnapings.

See also: AREA 51; BLUE BOOK, PROJECT; FOO-FIGHTERS; Fort, Charles; HILL, BETTY AND BARNEY; ROSWELL INCIDENT.

SUGGESTED READING: Jerome Clark, *UFOs in the 1980s* (Detroit, 1990); Jerome Clark, *The Emergence of a Phenomenon: UFOs from the Beginning through 1959* (Detroit, 1992); J. Allen Hynek, *The UFO Experience: A Scientific Inquiry* (Chicago, 1972); David Michael Jacobs, *The UFO Controversy in America* (Bloomington, Ind., 1975); Curtis Peebles, *Watch the Skies! A Chronicle of the Flying Saucer Myth* (Washington, D.C., 1994); John Spencer, ed., *The UFO Encyclopedia* (New York, 1991); Gordon Stein, *The Encyclopedia of the Paranormal* (New York, 1996); Jacques Vallee, *Passport to Matgonia: From Folklore to Flying Saucers* (Chicago, 1969).

Uncle Remus. The fictional creation of JOEL CHANDLER HARRIS, Uncle Remus was the avuncular old black narrator of Harris's famous series of African-American folktales. It is said that Harris based the character on an aged freedman who frequently visited the offices of the *Atlanta Constitution,* for which Harris was a writer. The first Uncle Remus tale, "The Story of Mr. Rabbit and Mr. Fox as Told by Uncle Remus," appeared in the July 20, 1879, *Atlanta Constitution.* Harris drew Uncle Remus with considerable respect, portraying him as a kindly, gently good-humored, wise old man who told his stories to a white boy. The Uncle Remus character was adapted by WALT DISNEY in his studio's 1946 animated feature *Song of the South.*

See also: AESOP'S FABLES; AFRICAN AMERICANS; ANANSI; BRER FOX; BRER RABBIT; COYOTE; FOX; SAMBO; TAR BABY; TRICKSTER.

SUGGESTED READING: Stella Brewer Brookes, *Joel Chandler Harris, Folklorist* (Athens: University of Georgia Press, 1950).

A. B. Frost's illustration of Joel Chandler Harris's Uncle Remus telling one of his tales.

Uncle Sam. This popular symbolic personification of the United States is usually depicted as a cartoon figure with long, stringy white hair, a long face with prominent cheekbones, and goat-like chin whiskers. Uncle Sam, whose initials are those of the United States, is typically dressed in a blue swallow-tailed coat, vest (often with a star pattern like that of the American flag), tall hat, and red-and-white striped trousers. His appearance is clearly derived from two earlier personifications of the nation, BROTHER JONATHAN and YANKEE DOODLE. As to the name "Uncle Sam," most authorities believe it originated with a Troy,

New York, businessman named Samuel Wilson, familiarly known as "Uncle Sam" Wilson. A purveyor of beef to the U.S. Army during the War of 1812, he stamped "U.S." on the barrels of rations he sold. While this stood for "United States," to denote government property, the initials were also identified with "Uncle Sam," which subsequently evolved into a nickname for the nation. While this origin of the name has been often disputed, Congress passed a resolution in 1961 officially recognizing Wilson as the namesake of the Uncle Sam symbol.

The Uncle Sam figure, like Brother Jonathan before it, was frequently rendered by American cartoonists, but it was the British satirical magazine *Punch* that popularized the portrayal both of Brother Jonathan and of Uncle Sam as rawboned and lean, adorned with a top hat and striped trousers. The prevailing modern image of Uncle Sam was developed by the American political cartoonist Thomas Nast in the 1870s, and this was further elaborated by James Montgomery Flagg's famed World War I recruiting poster of 1917 (later used in World War II), which depicted a stern Uncle Sam pointing his finger directly at the viewer above the caption "I Want You." (The Uncle Sam figure in this poster may have been inspired by the American Nast, but its design was derived from a British recruiting poster of 1914 by artist Alfred Leete that featured a uniformed and familiarly mustached Lord Kitchener pointing his finger above the caption "Your Country Needs You.")

See also: WORLD WAR I POSTERS; WORLD WAR II POSTERS.

Urban legend. A concept largely pioneered by the American folklore scholar Jan Harold Brunvand, an urban legend is an apocryphal contemporary story, told as true, but displaying features characteristic of "traditional" folklore. Urban folklore narratives may be transmitted orally—and, as such, are typically attributed to the "friend of a friend" (so commonly that Brunvand coined the acronym FOAF to denote this)—or disseminated by the mass media. Unlike the TALL TALE common on the western frontier during the nineteenth century, the urban legend, despite its fantastic or supernatural elements, always contains a tantalizing grain of plausibility. Characteristically of all folk narrative, urban legends are usually embellished with each retelling and are liberally larded with specific geographical and historical references. Again in common with many other folk narrative forms, the urban legend serves a somewhat didactic purpose. For example, the widespread story that a group of alligators dwell in the sewers of New York City, occasionally emerging from toilets to attack unsuspecting sitters, includes an explanation that the alligator population was born of pet baby alligators flushed down the toilet. The morals possible here are several: don't be cruel to animals, respect the environment, what goes around comes around, and so on. Beginning in the 1980s, with growing awareness of the burgeoning AIDS epidemic, chilling and cautionary AIDS TALES became a recognizable subgenre of the urban legend, underscoring the fact that urban legends tend to be spawned from society's fears and obsessions. While urban legends partake of elements of traditional folk narrative, they often strongly resemble the horrific stories published in urban newspapers or heard on TV's local evening news. This is especially true of any number of "maniac tales," such as the story of the couple who park their car in a lonely lover's lane one night, then hear on the radio that an escaped maniac is on the loose. Alarmed, they decide to leave, but the car won't start, and the man decides to walk to the nearest gas station, leaving his terrified girlfriend alone in the car. Her boyfriend fails to return, and she hears a scraping on the car roof. She endures this until dawn, when a policeman speaking through a loudspeaker tells her to get out slowly from the car and walk toward him. "Don't look back!" But, of course, she *does* look back—and beholds her boyfriend, headless, swinging from a tree above the car, his shoes scraping the roof. In a world apparently populated by amply documented maniacs such as the "Son of Sam" killer, child sodomizer and murderer John Wayne Gacey, and cannibal killer Jeffrey Dahmer, urban legends such as this are all too plausible.

Urban legends are not merely horrific. Like fairy tales, they often turn on a strong element of irony or poetic justice. The bully who delights in beating up gay men abrades the knuckles of his fist as he delivers a punch and, as a result, contracts AIDS. Nor do the horrific elements of urban legends merely draw on contemporary news stories. Timeless taboos such as incest and cannibalism are often plot features. EXOTERIC FOLKLORE (based on ethnic or racial stereotypes and prejudice) sometimes figures in urban legends as well, as in stories about a rash of disappearances of neighborhood cats in the vicinity of Chinese restaurants.

Much as nineteenth-century American ALMANACS harvested, broadcasted, and even manufactured folktales and other lore, supermarket tabloid newspapers feed off and create urban legend material. But urban legends also can be sufficiently compelling to take on more credible lives of their own. Brunvand cites what he calls "The Unsolvable Math Problem," a narrative about an undergraduate student who solves three problems his professor puts up on the blackboard as part of a test. Actually, only two of the problems were intended to constitute the test. The third had been offered as an example of an "unsolvable" problem. Astoundingly, the student solves it. This story, Brunvand points out, was offered as a true-life anecdote by television preacher Robert H. Schuller on his television and radio programs and in a 1983 autobiography.

See also: ALLIGATOR; CRIME AND CRIMINALS; MELVILLE, HERMAN; SANTA CLAUS; TAR BABY.

SUGGESTED READING: Gillian Bennett and Paul Smith, *Contemporary Legend: A Folklore Bibliography* (New York, 1993); Jan Harold Brunvand, "Dorson and the Urban Legend," *Folklore Historian* 7 (1990), pp. 16–22.

Utley, Francis Lee (1907–1974). Utley spent most of his professional career in the English Department of Ohio State University, where he founded its folklore program in the 1930s. Utley was instrumental in the establishment of the Folklore Archives. While Utley contributed to the study of American folklore and to the study of folklore in America, he published primarily on Europe in the Middle Ages and Renaissance. Utley served as president of the American Folklore Society during 1951–52.

SUGGESTED READING: Francis Lee Utley, *The Crooked Rib: An Analytical Index to the Argument about Women in English and Scots Literature to the End of the Year 1568* (Columbus, Ohio, 1944).

V

Valentine's Day. Celebrated on February 14, Valentine's Day (or St. Valentine's Day) has been associated with love and courtship since the fourteenth century. The modern holiday is entirely secular, but it coincides with the feast day of two Christian martyr saints, one a Roman priest and physician who was martyred by the Roman emperor Claudius II Gothicus, and the other, the bishop of Terni, Italy, also martyred by the Romans. There is no discernible connection between the saints' lives and deeds and the role of Valentine's Day as a lovers' festival. Most likely, this meaning of the holiday derived from the Roman festival of Lupercalia, during which young men drew the names of young women—potential lovers or wives—from an urn. In the fourteenth century, February 14 was also regarded as the day on which birds begin to mate.

In the United States, during the nineteenth century, young men drew names of prospective sweethearts from a hat during PLAY PARTIES. At about the time of the Civil War, commercial valentine cards became common in America and were, in fact, the first commercial greeting cards. (Handmade paper valentines date from as early as the sixteenth century, and by the beginning of the nineteenth century, copperplate-printed valentines were available, either sold hand-painted or painted by the giver.) Today, Valentine's Day is celebrated by school parties, with the exchange of candies and cards, and adults

Commercial Valentine's Day greeting cards like these two became popular by the end of the nineteenth century.

often regard it as an occasion for gift giving, usually items of a precious and loving nature, such as jewelry, presented by a man to his sweetheart or wife. For those embarrassed by frank confessions of affection, the greeting-card industry offers an array of humorous and satiric greeting cards.

The holiday took on unexpected new significance in 1929 when members of AL CAPONE's gang lined up and gunned down seven members of the George "Bugs" Moran gang in a commercial garage owned by Moran at 2122 North Clark Street in Chicago. Instantly infamous as the "St. Valentine's Day Massacre," the incident turned the tide of public opinion against Capone (hitherto seen by many as a kind of Robin Hood figure) and gangsterism and became an icon of popular culture that was frequently re-created on film and in other mass media.

SUGGESTED READING: Hennig Cohen and Tristram Coffin, eds., *The Folklore of American Holidays* (Detroit, 1987).

Vampires. Vampires are monsters of popular legend, supposedly the restless souls of heretics, criminals, or suicides, which take on human form or the form of a bat, and leave their burial places at night, in search of human blood. The victim of a vampire, once bitten, becomes a vampire him- or herself after death. Vampires must return to their graves or to a coffin filled with earth from their native place before daybreak. Belief in vampires occurs over much of Asia and Europe, but is especially prevalent in Slavic and Hungarian regions. These legends may ultimately be based on the historical figure of Vlad III Dracula, known as Vlad the Impaler, who lived from about 1431 to 1476 and was prince of Wallachia. He ruled by terror, impaling on wooden stakes large numbers of Transylvanian merchants, together with their wives and children. Whether or not this figure inspired the Middle European legends, Vlad certainly served as a model for the Irish-born novelist Bram Stoker (1847–1912), whose 1897 *Dracula* tells the story of a Transylvanian vampire who ultimately travels to England, where he preys upon innocent people until the novel's hero, Jonathan Harker, and his friends manage to destroy him. Immensely popular, the novel was adapted for the stage and, numerous times, for the cinema, beginning with the classic version directed by Tod Browning in 1931 and starring the Hungarian-born actor Bela Lugosi.

The film-born American image of the vampire includes a pallid face, seemingly drained of blood, vacant, staring eyes, and prominent incisors, with which the monster bites his victim's neck. A vampire can be recognized by the fact that it neither casts a shadow nor is reflected in mirrors; the creature may be warded off by displaying a crucifix or sleeping with a wreath of garlic around one's neck, and it may be killed only by driving a stake through its heart, by burning it, or by finding and destroying its daytime place of refuge.

The image of the vampire in American folklore and popular culture has gone through many transformations. In a Broadway play of the 1970s, actor Frank Langella portrayed Dracula as a sensual, even sexy presence and reprised this performance on film in 1979. Dracula has also been trivialized in the form of symbols and trademark logos for any number of products, including a chocolate-flavored children's breakfast cereal (*Count Chocula,* from General Mills), and is even a character on Public Television's *Sesame Street* ("The Count," whose obsession is not drinking blood, but *counting*).

See also: WITCHES AND WITCHCRAFT.

SUGGESTED READING: Paul Barber, *Vampires, Burial, and Death* (New Haven, Conn., 1988); Norine

Dresser, *American Vampires: Fans, Victims, and Practitioners* (New York, 1989).

Vaughan, James D. (1864–1941).

Vaughan was a promoter and popularizer of GOSPEL MUSIC. He ran a singing school in Lawrenceburg, Tennessee, and published a songbook, *Gospel Chimes,* in 1900. In 1912, he founded the James D. Vaughan Company, which published gospel-related books, magazines, and songbooks. Vaughan dispatched male vocal quartets to churches across the country to promote his materials, established one of the earliest commercial radio stations in Tennessee, and produced gospel recordings. Vaughan not only helped preserve and popularize the gospel tradition, he was also important in preserving SHAPE-NOTE SINGING.

Vernacular architecture.

Vernacular architecture is especially interesting to folklorists and students of MATERIAL CULTURE, who seek to "read" community beliefs, traditions, and values in the buildings members of the community create. Vernacular—or folk—architecture consists of buildings constructed according to traditional customs and without the aid of professional architects. Generally, vernacular architecture expresses identifiable patterns of national, ethnic, and especially regional character. By studying how certain of these characteristics evolve through time, folklorists can make generalizations about the community's developing interaction with the world at large. The most salient characteristic examined is the structure's form, which includes its plan, elevation, and general layout. Also significant are construction techniques.

The American landscape exhibits a wide variety of vernacular architecture, among which the most familiar are the BUNGALOW, I HOUSE, LOG CABIN, PYRAMIDAL HOUSE, SADDLEBAG HOUSE, SHOTGUN HOUSE, SOD HOUSE, and the T HOUSE. While these types are all "American," in that they exist on the American landscape, they often express the ethnic background of the builders as that heritage acts on available materials, environment, the elements, and financial resources. Most of the vernacular forms are based on European traditions, with the notable exception of the shotgun house, the origins of which may be traced to West Africa.

Available materials also greatly influence vernacular building. In forested areas, log structures are common. On the thinly forested western and midwestern plains, sod houses were numerous during the nineteenth century. In the Southwest, adobe was often the building material of choice.

The study of vernacular architecture is by no means limited to house types. Barns have long been an object of interest among folklorists, who have identified distinct barn types, including the English type, found chiefly in the East; the transverse-crib type, familiar in the Midwest; and the southern type. Church types and the architecture of commercial structures—especially the false front stores of many American Main Streets—have also been extensively studied.

See also: APPALACHIA; COLONIAL WILLIAMSBURG; DOGTROT HOUSE; DUTCH AMERICANS; FINNISH AMERICANS; FOLKWAYS; GHOST TOWNS; MEXICAN AMERICANS; MOBILE HOMES; PENNSYLVANIA GERMANS; SCANDINAVIAN AMERICANS.

SUGGESTED READING: Thomas Carter and Bernard L. Herman, eds., *Perspectives in Vernacular Architecture* (3 vols., Columbia, Mo. 1989–91); Henry Glassie, *Folk Housing in Middle Virginia: A Structural Analysis of Historical Artifacts* (Knoxville, Tenn., 1975); Thomas Hubka, *Big House, Little House, Back House, Barn* (Hanover, N.H., 1984)..

Vietnam War. Like the KOREAN WAR, the conflict in Vietnam (1965–75) was an undeclared war motivated, in part, by a combination of policy and folk belief relating to the necessity of "containing" the spread of communism. As all American wars since at least the CIVIL WAR have done, Vietnam added to the vocabulary of FOLK SPEECH with new military jargon, some of which filtered to the home front, such as "VC" for Vietcong, the enemy forces, which were often also called "Charlie" because "VC" in radio alphabet designation is "Victor Charlie." The Vietnam War has been called the nation's first televised war, with frontline images beamed to American homes for a decade of dinnertime news hours. American soldiers and civilians became familiar with terms like "body count" and "pacification" and soon used them in everyday speech. Indeed, during the Vietnam period, public speech came into increasing doubt and disrepute, as Americans were alternately horrified and amused by such terms as "pacification," which really meant annihilation, and such Pentagon-generated phrases as "the vertical deployment of explosive devices," which meant bombing. Bitterest of all

words was "Vietnamization," the process of turning over prosecution of the war to the South Vietnamese, an elusive and illusory process pro-war politicians ("Hawks") frequently cited as their goal. As to the soldiers themselves, the most cherished and elusive goal was summed up in "the world," the phrase used as a synonym for the United States. Typically, soldiers counted the days: "I'll be back in the world in sixty more days."

"Countdown calendars," photocopied calendar pages with each passing day colored in and the DEROS (date of estimated return from overseas) starred and otherwise decorated, were common features of soldiers' MATERIAL CULTURE. Some of these calendars were adorned with patriotic or sexually explicit images—or both. Because so much emphasis was placed on the countdown, SUPERSTITIONS relating to being "short" (having a short time left on one's tour of duty) abounded. "Short-timer calendars" were often traded among troops. Another ubiquitous feature of material folklore among Vietnam War troops were decorated helmets. Soldiers inserted good-luck charms, military patches, souvenirs,

An image typical of the Vietnam War: ground assault supported by armed Huey helicopters. This U.S. Army photograph is from 1968.

cigarettes, and others items in the standard-issue helmet's chin strap or camouflage net. Military personnel who flew helicopters—the "Huey" attack helicopter was the most numerous—often decorated their aircraft with personal and political slogans as well as fierce animal images. (Compare the nose art on WORLD WAR II bombers.)

The countdown and images of home were among the few things in which troops could take comfort. The war had escalated insidiously and had quickly lost popular support on the home front. Like the Korean War, it was fought with limited and poorly defined objectives, which made it a war that could not be won. As a result, troop morale was low, and cynical "PROVERBS" were commonly heard: "Murphy was a grunt." ("Murphy" refers to "Murphy's Law," the proposition that if anything can go wrong, it will go wrong; and a "grunt" is a lowly infantryman.) Or: "The only thing more accurate than incoming fire is incoming friendly fire." Or: "Peace is our profession. Mass murder is just our hobby." (The first part of the "proverb" is the motto of the Strategic Air Command.) As U.S. troop strength was reduced in Vietnam by President Richard Nixon during the 1970s, morale among those who remained behind deteriorated even more sharply. Infantry patrols officially designated "search and destroy" missions were now informally dubbed "search and avoid" missions, the sole object being to put in one's time and get back to "the world" in one piece. (Officers who were overly zealous in leading their men into harm's way risked being "fragged"—assassinated by their troops.) As in any war, narratives, rumors, and gossip were widespread, with many anecdotes told about "million-dollar wounds"—relatively minor wounds (often self-inflicted) just serious enough to warrant a ticket back home.

The Vietnam War also produced what might be called EXOTERIC FOLKLORE about the "Vietnam vet," who was stereotyped as an emotionally damaged, drug-addicted individual rendered unfit for civilian life and expected to go berserk at any moment, perhaps opening up on innocent bystanders with an automatic weapon the U.S. Army had taught him to use.

See also: MILITARY FOLKLORE.

SUGGESTED READING: Timothy Corrigan, *A Cinema without Walls: Movies and Culture after Vietnam* (New Brunswick, N.J., 1991); Bernard Edelman, ed., *Dear America: Letters Home from Vietnam* (New York, 1988); W. D. Ehrhart, *Carrying the Darkness: The Poetry of the Vietnam War* (Lubbock, Tex., 1989); Tim O'Brien, *If I Die in a Combat Zone: Box Me Up and Ship Me Home* (New York, 1992); William Appleman Williams et al., *America in Vietnam: A Documentary History* (New York, 1989).

Visionary art. Much American folk art may be described by this term, which denotes art, often of a religious nature, that is inspired by dreams, visions, or voices. Often, explicit religious messages are part of the artwork. Among the best-known visionary American folk artists are HOWARD FINSTER and SISTER GERTRUDE MORGAN.

Voodoo. The national religious folk cult of Haiti, voodoo also influences African-American folk religion in parts of the southern United States, especially in portions of Louisiana. Traditionally, some African Americans used the word *voodoo* or *hoodoo* to signify any malevolent magical force, and a *hoodoo* man was a conjurer. True voodoo, however, is a blend of Roman

Catholic ritual with elements of African religion and magic. It was brought to Haiti by slaves drawn from the Yoruba, Fon, Kongo, and other peoples. The word *voodoo* is derived from the Fon *vodun,* god or spirit.

Voodoo is a complex religion, which also involves magical rituals and sorcery, and is the subject of much sensational discussion in popular culture and folklore, both among African Americans and whites. The most sensational aspect of voodoo involves the creation of zombis. A zombi may be the disembodied soul of a dead person used for magical purposes, or corpse raised from the grave and reanimated as a will-less automaton.

See also: AFRICAN AMERICANS; JOHN THE CONQUEROR ROOT; MEDICINE, FOLK; MOJO; RABBIT'S FOOT; SALEM WITCH TRIALS.

W

Walton, Ivan H. (1893–1968). Walton collected Great Lakes folklore, specializing in sailors' songs. He was raised in the Lake Michigan port town of Ludington, Michigan, where he became enthralled with the stories and songs of the freshwater sailors. He began actively collecting in the 1920s, after graduating in 1919 from the University of Michigan. In 1940, Walton founded the Michigan Folklore Society and, in 1955, created the first folklore course at the University of Michigan. With EARL CLIFTON BECK, Walton collected songs for a Library of Congress project directed by ALAN LOMAX. Walton's collection of Great Lakes folklore is housed at the Bentley Historical Library at the University of Michigan.

SUGGESTED READING: George M. McEwen, "Ivan H. Walton: A Pioneer Michigan Folklorist," *Michigan Academician* 2 (1970), pp. 73–74.

Waltz. Most familiar as the rapid 3/4-time Viennese ballroom dance, which swept Europe and America during the nineteenth century (thanks in large part to the music of "Waltz King" Johann Strauss), the waltz is also a folk form in many nations, including the United States. Some of the most distinctive American folk waltzes are found in the Southwest, where they were adapted from Mexico during the reign of Napoleon III's Austrian puppet Maximilian (reigned 1864–67). These include the celebrated *vals de la escoba,* the broom waltz, in which the odd man out waltzes a broom down the center of the room, snatches the girl of his choice, and is then pursued by the other male dancers.

See also: DANCE, FOLK; FIDDLE; TEX-MEX MUSIC.

Wampum. The word *wampum* may be considered a specimen of FOLK-SAY when used as a jocular and general synonym for money. To the various Indian tribes of the East Coast, however, *wampum,* an Anglicized version of the Algonquian word *wampompeag,* had a more precise meaning, denoting cylindrical seashells strung on strings or beaded into belts, which were used in trade like money, but also served a more important diplomatic purpose as tokens of good faith. Wampum strings or belts were exchanged by tribes, by bands within tribes, or (as early as the seventeenth century) by Indians and whites to seal a variety of bargains and alliances. Especially elaborate belts of wampum served as "war belts," which were passed from tribe to tribe or band to band to solemnize alliances in preparation for large-scale warfare.

See also: NATIVE AMERICANS.

Ward, Artemus (1834–1867). Born Charles Farrar Browne in Waterford, Maine, this Ameri-

Artemus Ward vied with Mark Twain to be the nation's most popular humorist. The photograph is from the 1860s.

Ward was tremendously popular and befriended the young MARK TWAIN, helping to publicize Twain's breakthrough story, "The Celebrated Jumping Frog of Calaveras County."

See also: FOLKLORE IN AMERICAN LITERATURE.

SUGGESTED READING: Don C. Seitz, *Artemus Ward (Charles Farrar Browne): A Biography and Bibliography* (New York, 1919).

Ward, Marshall (1906–1981). Ward was an Appalachian storyteller specializing in JACK TALES. He was the informant of folklorist RICHARD CHASE, who introduced Chase to the "Jack tale" genre. Ward's tales were gathered from his extended family, and he performed them not only for his own elementary school students, but on tours of other schools and in folk festivals.

SUGGESTED READING: Richard Chase, *The Jack Tales* (Boston, 1943); Vivian Shipley, *Jack Tales* (Greenfield Center, N.Y., 1982).

can humorist took Artemus Ward as his pseudonym when he wrote satirical articles and sketches for the *Cleveland Plain Dealer* and other periodicals, including the Toledo *Commercial, Vanity Fair* in New York, and other periodicals. His humor is replete with puns, malapropisms, and backwoods misspellings. Ward's fame spread most widely through his lecture tours, which began in 1861. His book-length works include *Artemus Ward: His Book* (1862), *Artemus Ward: His Travels* (1865), and *Artemus Ward in London* (1867). His pseudonym was, in fact, his principal character, a sharply drawn version of the Yankee type, a kind of backwoods cracker-barrel philosopher, whose command of the English language was badly—and hilariously—fractured.

Warner, Frank (1903–1978) and Warner, Anne Locher (1905–1991). These collectors and interpreters of the American folk song worked extensively in North Carolina and in the Northeast, collecting songs, lecturing on folksong traditions, and performing folk songs.

Frank Warner was a native of Selma, Alabama, who was raised in Tennessee and Durham, North Carolina. He studied at Duke University, then became an executive in the YMCA organization in New York City. There he met and married Anne Locher in 1935. She was born in St. Louis, but was raised in St. Paul, Minnesota, and in Chicago. The couple made their first collecting trip, to North Carolina, in 1938. Frank Warner performed in the style of his informants, recording seven albums of traditional songs and making various television and radio appearances. In 1963, he published a series of his lectures as *Folk Songs and Ballads of the Eastern Seaboard: From a Collector's Notebook,* and Anne Warner published widely in the folklore journals.

SUGGESTED READING: Kristin Baggelaar and Donald Milton, entry on the Warners in *Folk Music: More Than a Song* (New York, 1976); Frank Warner and Anne Warner, "Frank Noah Proffit: A Retrospective," *Appalachian Journal* 1 (1973), pp. 163–93.

Warts. Warts (medical name, *verruca vulgaris*) are small, well-defined growths on the skin. They are composed of an abnormal proliferation of cells of the epidermis caused by a virus. Warts have been the object of much folk-medical lore (see MEDICINE, FOLK). In some parts of the United States, folk healers attempt to "talk off" warts, others tie knots in a piece of string, the number of knots corresponding to the number of warts to be cured, then throw the knotted string into running water or bury it in a damp place, so that it—and the warts it represents—will decompose rapidly. Another folk practice is to rub a wart with a coin, then drop the coin in the street; the wart will be transferred to the person who picks up the coin. In a practice called "nailing," the wart is pricked with a nail, which is then hammered into a tree in the hope of transferring it to that natural object. In "plugging," a small piece of cloth is rubbed on the wart and stuffed into a hole bored in a tree, which is then plugged with a piece of wood.

Perhaps the most widespread folk belief concerning warts is that they may be acquired from handling toads (whose bumpy skin is thought to resemble warts).

Washington, George (1732–1799). Given Washington's status as the commander in chief of the Continental army during the Revolutionary War and as our nation's first president, a figure of incalculable historical importance, surprisingly little folklore has grown up around him. The appellation "Father of His Country" is less a folklore motif than it was the product of the eighteenth century's reverence for classical, particularly Roman, culture; *Patris Patriae* was an official honor the Roman Senate conferred upon great heroes. Indeed, Washington is associated with only three distinct iconic anecdotes of folklore. Everyone is familiar with the image of Washington, wrapped in a cloak, foot mounted on the thwart of the rowboat in which he leads his troops across the Delaware to victory at the battles of Trenton and Princeton. This vignette achieved the status of folklore exclusively through the heroic 1851 painting, *Washington Crossing the Delaware,* by the immigrant artist EMANUEL LEUTZE. On a less heroic level, everyone has likewise heard about Washington's false teeth, allegedly made of wood, and this bit of lore has been the source of jokes and humorous drawings. (In fact, dentures of the period were partly wooden and partly ceramic.) Finally, the most famous legend tells of six-year-old George's having chopped down his father's prized cherry tree with his brand-new ax. When his furious father confronts him, little George replied "I cannot tell a lie, Pa; you know I cannot tell a lie. I did cut it down with my hatchet." The parent, overwhelmed with pride in the child's honesty, forgets

Grant Woods's Parson Weems' Fable *illustrates the popular legend in which young George confesses to having chopped his father's favorite cherry tree: "I cannot tell a lie."*

his anger and clasps the boy to his breast. This episode first appeared in print in the fifth edition (1806) of MASON LOCKE WEEMS's *The Life and Memorable Actions of George Washington*, first published in 1800. (Weems does not depict Washington as having chopped the tree down, but as having damaged it, so that it dies.) Weems claimed to have heard the tale from a distant female relation of Washington. The scene was depicted in *Parson Weems' Fable*, a mordantly ironic painting by GRANT WOOD in 1939.

See also: CULTURE HERO; POLISH AMERICANS; ROSS, BETSY.

Weather folklore. Folklore is often about dealing with elements beyond human understanding or control. Such is the case with weather folklore, which encompasses beliefs, rituals, and other actions related to predicting, understand-

ing, and even controlling the weather. Weather folklore includes PROVERBS, rituals, LEGENDS, narratives, and various aspects of MATERIAL CULTURE.

Most weather folklore is intended to predict rainfall or cessation of rain. "When there's a ring around the moon, rain is coming soon" is a well-known proverb, and even people unfamiliar with the proverb as such "know" that a ring around the moon means rain. Other rain-predictive folklore interprets the actions of animals and birds or the presence of sun dogs—parahelic halos—that may be on one or both sides of the sun. Many people are familiar with the sailor's proverb—"Red sky in the morning, / sailor take warning. / Red sky at night, / sailor's delight"—but there are many less well-known beliefs concerning the color of the sky as a predictor of rain. Cloud patterns are also important. A "mackerel sky" is one in which the clouds lie in parallel bands. The proverb goes: "Mackerel sky, mackerel sky, three days wet and three days dry." Another sure predictor of rain is aching bunions (see BUNIONS AND CORNS) or rheumatism that acts up at the approach of a storm. Old people are generally considered better weather forecasters than young people. The old "feel the weather in their bones."

"Everybody talks about the weather, but nobody does anything about it" is a familiar proverbial expression (widely attributed to MARK TWAIN). In fact, the work of "rainmakers" is a subject of primarily nineteenth-century folklore, especially in arid parts of the United States. Rainmaking methods range from prayer to setting off gunpowder charges or building huge bonfires. Modern people also have rainmaking rituals. Many are convinced, for example, that a causal relationship exists between washing and waxing one's car and subsequent rainfall.

Rain is also often seen as an omen. Traditionally, rainy days are associated with bad luck, especially on one's wedding day—though in some places (especially where farming is important), a rainy wedding day bodes good fortune (see WEDDINGS).

A substantial body of folklore deals with predictions concerning the seasons: a hot summer, for example, or a severe winter. The behavior of animals is often scrutinized as a predictor of the severity of the approaching winter, and, of course, GROUNDHOG DAY (February 2) is a well-known predictor of winter's longevity.

Much folklore concerning severe weather may be classified as DISASTER FOLKLORE, but the predictive signs of severe weather are passed from generation to generation, especially in the Midwest, where tornadoes abound, and in the Southeast, which is vulnerable to hurricanes.

See also: FISHING LORE; FRANKLIN, BENJAMIN; SAILORS AND SEAFARING LORE.

SUGGESTED READING: Richard M. Dorson, *Buying the Wind: Regional Folklore in the U.S.* (Chicago, 1964).

Weaving. While weaving has been produced in a great variety of patterns, styles, and forms, all weaving is basically the same process: an interlacing of two sets of yarns so that they cross each other at right angles. The yarns running lengthwise constitute the warp, while those running crosswise are called the weft. A loom is a device that holds the warp in tension so that the weft can be passed over and under it.

Folk weaving began as a so-called household art, primarily practiced by women. Even the weaving of plain, humble, and utilitarian objects requires considerable skill, while ornamental work draws heavily on the imaginative power, manual dexterity, and taste of the weaver. Wide variation in pattern and complexity is possible.

In Arizona's Monument Valley with a Native American rug loom, 1944.

A seventeenth-century spinning wheel and loom in the John Balch House (1636), Beverly, Massachusetts.

The "plain weave" is a simple over-one-thread-and-under-the-next pattern. A relatively simple variation is the diamond pattern, which is created by varying the number of threads passed over and under. Interlacing threads create a gridlike waffle weave, which is both decorative and utilitarian, since it is both strong and absorbent. Damask patterns may be highly elaborate and ornamental, playing on contrasts between warp-faced and weft-faced satin effects. By introducing elements of patterned color, the woven fabric may become even more ornate and complex, with striped, checked, and plaid patterns possible, as well as other geometric designs.

The looms on which folk weavers work are themselves fascinating objects of material folklore. They range from large frames to handheld devices. If any loom may be deemed the standard American hand machine, it is the foot-powered, four-harness jack loom. Although more complex looms allow for more harnesses, which determine the complexity of the pattern, many thousands of patterns may be woven with only four harnesses. Another aspect of the material culture of weaving is the draft—the paper patterns used to indicate

A class of young spinners and weavers, about 1935.

the positioning of the warp threads on the harnesses in order to create the desired design.

Weaving is among the very oldest of humankind's crafts, predating even POTTERY. Certainly, weaving was practiced by the earliest colonists, and many of the ethnic groups that have immigrated since then have introduced their own distinctive styles of woven goods. In the Southwest, Navajo weaving is particularly prized. By the end of the nineteenth century, the craft of weaving in the Anglo-American tradition was being revived and nurtured in APPALACHIA by teachers and administrators in the settlement schools in the region. Soon, Appalachian weavers were selling their goods to tourists and others. In Appalachia and elsewhere, local weavers have organized guilds, which hold regular meetings, sponsor workshops, and mount exhibitions. Many of the local organizations are affiliated with the national Handweavers Guild of America, which sponsors a major conference, Convergence, annually. It and other organizations publish periodicals devoted to techniques and to presenting patterns and projects.

See also: NATIVE AMERICANS; SCANDINAVIAN AMERICANS.

SUGGESTED READING: Mary Meigs Atwater, *The Shuttle Craft Book of American Handweaving* (New York, 1961); Allen H. Eaton, *Handicrafts of the Southern Highlands* (1937; reprint ed., New York, 1973); Beverly Gordon, *Shaker Textile Arts* (Hanover, N.H, 1980).

Webster, Daniel (1782–1852). Webster is one of very few nonpresidential American politicians who has entered into popular consciousness and folklore. Born in Salisbury, New Hampshire, he was educated at Phillips Academy (in Exeter) and Dartmouth College, where he quickly earned a reputation for eloquence. After graduation, he became a lawyer in Portsmouth, New Hampshire, and spoke on behalf of Portsmouth

Daniel Webster's feats of oratory became the subject of popular legend.

shipowners and merchants, who were opposed to Thomas Jefferson's embargo and, later, the War of 1812 against Britain. In 1812, Webster was elected to the first of three terms in the House of Representatives and eloquently opposed the war, even to the point of advocating states' rights over federalism.

In 1816 Webster moved with his wife and two children to Boston, where he became the nation's leading lawyer, successfully arguing key cases before the Supreme Court, including the groundbreaking *McCulloch* v. *Maryland* (1819), which greatly strengthened the power of the federal government—despite Webster's earlier states' rights position. Webster did remain opposed to federally imposed tariffs and expressed his idea that individual enterprise was essential to the emerging American way of life. His most famous expression of this position came in his 1820 address on the occasion of the bicentennial celebration of the landing of the Pilgrims at Plymouth. Widely reported, his oration gained him national fame as an orator—a reputation that soon grew to legendary proportions. As senator from Massachusetts during the era of ANDREW JACKSON, in 1830, Webster eloquently argued against South Carolina senator Robert Y. Hayne, who presented Vice President John C. Calhoun's doctrine of nullification (the proposition that a state could nullify an obnoxious and unconstitutional law and, if need be, secede from the Union), concluding his speech with a cry of "Liberty and Union, now and forever, one and inseparable!" The speech made Calhoun a Southern nationalist hero.

Although Webster made himself unpopular by his support for the Second Bank of the United States, he served in the cabinet of President William Henry Harrison and (after Harrison's sudden death) that of John Tyler. In the 1840s, he opposed the U.S.-Mexican War and, in the 1850s, advocated Henry Clay's Compromise of 1850 in an effort to avoid civil war. He served President Millard Fillmore as secretary of state.

Politically, the reputation of Webster has been the subject of dispute. Some saw him as unprincipled and guided by overweening ambition, while others regarded him as an effective advocate of nationalism and union. In folklore, however, he became the archetypal persuader, the silver-tongued orator who could persuade anyone of anything. His fame in this regard receded by the twentieth century until STEPHEN VINCENT BENÉT resurrected traditional material and shaped it into a literary TALL TALE in his 1939 play *The Devil and Daniel Webster,* which depicts the legendary orator outdoing the ultimate adversary: Satan.

SUGGESTED READING: Stephen Vincent Bénet, *The Devil and Daniel Webster* (New York, 1939); Claude M. Fuess, *Daniel Webster,* (2 vols., 1930; reprint ed., New York, 1968); Walker Lewis, ed., *Speak for Yourself, Daniel: A Life of Webster in His Own Words* (New York, 1969).

Weddings.

The wedding ceremony is an occasion rich with folklore—that is, traditional rituals and superstitions believed to promote the good fortune and happiness of the couple. The wedding date is of great importance, with many women choosing to become "June brides," probably because this generally pleasant spring month suggests renewal and fertility. However, in agricultural communities and in an era dominated by agriculture, winter weddings were favored. The weather that prevails on the wedding day may be interpreted as an augury of the couple's life together. Some believe a sunny wedding day betokens good fortune, while rain bodes sadness, and a thunderstorm predicts a childless marriage. However, many people insist that a rainy wedding day brings good luck. Most people also believe that the site of the wedding is of great importance. For both religious reasons as well as reasons of custom, a church is often chosen, and, short of a church, a "wedding chapel"—a commercial enterprise that has some of the trappings of a church.

Weddings abound in taboos, including a proscription against the groom seeing the bride, in her gown, before the ceremony and a belief that it is bad luck for the bride to bake her own wedding cake or to sew her own gown. Wearing the gown (other than for a fitting) before the ceremony is typically considered a jinx. Social custom generally prescribes formal wear for the wedding party and a veiled white gown (token of virginity) for the bride; however, the PROVERB or proverbial rhyme "Something old, something new, something borrowed, something blue" is also usually invoked, and the bride incorporates into her wedding-day wardrobe elements that satisfy each of these requirements. In addition, the bride may put a coin in her shoe to ensure prosperity. It is also often considered important to "start the marriage off on the right foot"—literally: the couple is supposed to begin walking toward the altar right-foot first. The family of the bride as well as the groom often cry during the ceremony (the individuals excusing themselves by explaining, "I always cry at weddings"), but tears from the bride may also be encouraged—to ward off future sadness.

On emergence from the church, the bride and groom are typically showered with rice thrown by the wedding guests who line the church steps. This ensures fertility. Additionally, cheering and noisemaking have their origin in ancient rituals of protective magic intended to frighten away evil spirits. The same function is served by the old shoes and cans that may be tied to the automobile that whisks the couple off, either to their honeymoon or to the wedding reception (see SHIVAREE).

Much of the actual ceremony at the altar or before a justice of the peace is dictated by religious practice and the law—though some couples write their own vows. The wedding reception, however, is shaped more by custom, although, in modern weddings, "custom" is often defined by the commercial motives of enterprising caterers and the wallet of the father of the bride. Most couples attach significance to the manner in which the wedding cake is cut. Usually, the bride cuts the cake first, as the groom places his hand over hers. The couple then feed each other a piece of the cake. This ritual is meant to propitiate a cooperative marriage and fertility. Most cultural traditions endorse dance—popular dances or appropriate ethnic dances—as a way to celebrate and validate the union. Before the bride and groom depart the reception, the bride tosses her bridal bouquet. This is done over her head while facing away from the unmarried women guests, who scramble to catch the bouquet; whoever captures it will be the next to marry.

The wedding day is memorialized in anniversaries, on which friends or family may present gifts to the couple—and the couple may exchange gifts with each other. Many people attach importance to giving a gift appropriate to the anniversary, and they may consult books of etiquette to ensure that they choose a gift of the "correct" material. The first-year anniversary is to be observed with a gift made of paper. The five-year anniversary warrants wood; the ten-year, tin; the fifteen-year, crystal; the twenty-year, china; the twenty-five-year ("silver anniversary"), silver; the fifty-year ("golden anniversary"), gold; and the seventy-five-year ("diamond anniversary"), diamond. Custom, as described in etiquette books, also prescribes appropriate gifts for the intermediate-year anniversaries. On the occasion of their first anniversary, some couples consume a piece of the wedding cake, which had been preserved by freezing after the reception.

See also: WEATHER FOLKLORE.

SUGGESTED READING: Margaret Baker, *Wedding Customs and Folklore* (Vancouver, 1977).

Weems, Mason Locke (1759–1825).

Known as Parson Weems, this clergyman, bookseller, and author of popular biography (mainly intended for the edification of youth) was the author of *The Life and Memorable Actions of George Washington,* first published in 1800, the year following the president's death, and to which, in the fifth edition of 1806, Weems added the story of six-year-old GEORGE WASHINGTON's chopping down his father's prized cherry tree. (Weems does not depict Washington as having actually chopped the tree down, but as having damaged it, so that it dies.) In this, one of the few folkloristic icons associated with Washington, the boy, confronted by his enraged father, confesses that he "cannot tell a lie" and admits having brought to bear against the tree his brand-new ax. Filled with pride in his son's honesty, the father's anger instantly dissolves, and he clasps the boy to his bosom. Weems claimed to have heard this story from an elderly woman, a distant relative of Washington, but most scholars believe that it is simply a fiction created by Weems, a shrewd author. In 1809, Weems also wrote a biography of Francis Marion, the legendary "Swamp Fox," much of which contained appealing, though apocryphal, anecdotes.

Weems was an Anglican minister who served as a pastor in Maryland until 1792. Beginning in 1794, he worked as an "agent" (itinerant salesman) for the publisher Mathew Carey. His career as an author began in 1800 with the volume on Washington.

See also: WOOD, GRANT.

SUGGESTED READING: Lewis Leary, *The Book-Peddling Parson: An Account of the Life and Works of Mason Locke Weems* (Chapel Hill, N.C., 1984).

Welsh Americans.

Welsh-American folklore may be said to have begun with the story of Madog ab Owain Gwynedd (fl. 1170), legendary voyager to America. According to legend, Madog, son of Owain Gwynedd (d. 1170), prince of Gwynedd, argued with his brothers over the distribution of their father's lands. This prompted Madog to sail to Ireland, thence westward to America at about this time. He returned to Wales, put together a group of would-be colonists, set sail again, and disappeared. The legend continues: the colonists survived and intermarried with Indians. As late as 1841, the painter George Catlin wrote in his *Letters and Notes on the Manners, Customs, and Condition of the North American Indians* that Madog's party had reached the upper Missouri River, and that the Mandan Indians were descendants of the Welsh. Folklore has long held that there was a Welsh Indian settlement at Louisville, Kentucky, and anecdotal reports exist from the seventeenth and eighteenth centuries of encounters with Welsh-speaking Indians. The adventures of Madog were given their most permanent literary expression in the English poet Robert Southey's epic *Madoc* (1805) and were first reported, in print, in Richard Hakluyt's *Voyages* (1582) and David Powel's *The Historie of Cambria* (1584). Few anthropologists or historians believe that Madog ever voyaged here, and many doubt his existence at all; however, his story was important in the sixteenth century as support for England's claims versus Spain's claims to the New World, and even Lewis and Clark were ordered to investigate the presence of Welsh Indians.

What is undeniable is that Welsh settlers were among those who came to Virginia in 1607 and that a significant number of Welsh Baptists settled near Rhode Island in 1667 in search of religious freedom. A few years later, other Welsh Baptists settled in Pennsylvania and Delaware. During the eighteenth and nineteenth centuries, more immigrants arrived, most of these settling west of the Alleghenies, in western Pennsylvania, Ohio, Kentucky, and Wisconsin. Whereas early Welsh immigrants had been chiefly farmers, many in the nineteenth century were miners, metalworkers, and slate quarry workers.

Welsh communities were almost always marked by Welsh chapels and by distinctive ethnic festival activities. The *eisteddfod* is a poetic competition dating to medieval times and, as practiced in the nineteenth-century United States, celebrated Welsh literature, music, and the arts generally. While the *eisteddfod* has largely disappeared from Welsh-American communities, the *gymanfa ganu*, traditional hymn singing, continues to be actively performed.

See also: IMMIGRANT FOLKLORE.

SUGGESTED READING: Elwyn T. Ashton, *The Welsh in the United States* (Hove, Eng., 1984); Edward George Hartmann, *Americans from Wales* (Boston, 1967); Gwyn A. Williams, *Madoc* (Oxford, Eng., 1987).

Whaling. The folklore of whaling is of at least two kinds: the lore and rituals of Eskimo and Inuit whalers and the OCCUPATIONAL FOLKLORE of primarily nineteenth-century commercial whalers.

Whales have been hunted for food and/or oil since prehistoric times. In the nineteenth century, the demand for whale products, especially whale oil for lubrication and illumination purposes, was very great, and the whaling industry was quite large and active. Some species of whales were hunted nearly to extinction. The replacement of whale oil with petroleum products greatly reduced the demand for whales by the close of the nineteenth century. This, coupled with stringent international environmental regulation, has reduced the twentieth-century whaling industry to a fraction of its former importance.

Evidence of Eskimo and other Native American hunting of whales dates to at least as early as A.D. 100. The hunt and capture of whales developed into a cult along the Alaskan coast, with whalers taking on some of the role of shamans. Rituals included such rites of preparation and initiation as bathing with human mummies, miming a successful hunt, sprinkling the ice with ashes to ward off evil spirits, singing special songs and reciting incantations, performing ceremonial dances, and so on. Among some groups, a ritual mourning period was observed to placate the spirits of the animals about to be killed.

Among Europeans, the systematic hunting of whales dates to the late Middle Ages and may have taken Basque whalers as far as Newfoundland and Iceland as early as the fourteenth century. The Dutch and the English built large whaling fleets by the seventeenth and eighteenth centuries, including those operating in British North America. By the late eighteenth century, whaling vessels were evolving into factory ships, equipped with large brick ovens called tryworks, in which whalers boiled the whale blubber into oil, which could be stored in barrels on board the ship instead of hauling the entire whale or its blubber to onshore rendering facilities. This meant that whaling vessels could remain at sea for extended periods—usually up to four months—harvesting several whales. Factory-ship operations also multiplied the hazards of whaling and the variety of skills required.

By the mid-nineteenth century, the United States dominated the world whaling industry, with a fleet of more than seven hundred vessels, most of them sailing out of such New England ports as New Bedford and Nantucket, Massachusetts. Aboard these ships, crew members shared

Whalers "cutting in" on a sperm whale, about 1928.

in the profits of the voyage according to their se-
niority and level of skill. Senior harpooners,
whose work required the greatest skill and was
the most hazardous, received larger shares than
the junior men whose work involved rendering
the blubber.

Lookouts on board the ship watched for
whales breaching the surface or spouting water
from their blowholes. On seeing this, the cry of
"There she blows!" would go up, and a crew of
six would be launched in a "whaleboat," an
oared craft about twenty-eight feet in length. The
harpooner on the whaleboat was armed with
barbed harpoons tied to long ropes. The whaleboat had to be maneuvered very close to the
whale (which might attack it and "stove it in"—
break it apart), so that the harpooner could hurl
his weapon into the mammal's flesh. Once
wounded, the whale would run with the rope
until it was exhausted. Typically, the whale
would then surface, where it could be finished off
with a long harpoon called a lance. The whale
carcass was towed to the factory vessel and
lashed to its side, where other crewmembers
would "cut in" to it in an operation called flens-
ing. Using large blades mounted on pikes, they
stripped off the animal's blubber in great slabs
called bible leaves. These were rendered in the
tryworks. Stripped of its blubber, the carcass was
unlashed and abandoned.

All aspects of nineteenth-century whaling
were hazardous and, as with any activity on the
sea, required great skill, courage, and coordination on the part of the crew. Crew members developed a rich store of personal narratives,
anecdotes, and legends—many of them similar to
the lore of HUNTING. HERMAN MELVILLE's 1851
masterpiece Moby-Dick is not only a vast compendium of whaling lore, it is an epic literary example of a whaling legend.

The vocation of whaling also produced many
WORK SONGS, including CHANTEYS and COME-
ALL-YE's, and a rich heritage of MATERIAL CUL-
TURE. Of special interest in the latter regard is
scrimshaw, the decoration of whale "ivory"
(whale teeth) with carved designs. Scrimshaw
was chiefly an Anglo-American practice, and was
executed with a jackknife or a sail needle. The
etched designs were blackened to heighten contrast. Typical scrimshaw designs include whaling
scenes, ship portraits, and portraits of sailors'
wives and sweethearts, as well as floral designs
and such emblems as Masonic devices. While
scrimshaw examples can be found as early as the
late 1600s, the craft flourished in New England
between 1830 and 1850.

In Moby-Dick, Melville depicted whaling as a
great primal and heroic undertaking. To be sure,
the occupation has those elements, yet its folklore
and popular mythology never became as widely
known as that of the COWBOY. Nevertheless, the
occupational folklore of commercial whaling is
well served by a number of East Coast museums,
including the New Bedford Whaling Museum in
New Bedford, Massachusetts, and the Kendall
Whaling Museum, in Sharon, Massachusetts.

See also: FOLKLORE IN AMERICAN LITERA-
TURE; PORTUGUESE AMERICANS.

SUGGESTED READING: Briton Cooper Busch, "Whaling
Will Never Do For Me": The American Whaleman in
the Nineteenth Century (Lexington, Ky., 1994);
Richard Ellis, Men and Whales (New York, 1991);
Charles H. Carpenter, Jr. and Mary Grace Carpenter,
The Decorative Arts and Crafts of Nantucket (New
York, 1987).

White, George (1903–1970). George White
was a Texas folk artist, whose ancestry was

African American, Native American, and Mexican, the influence of all of which may be found in his relief paintings and sculptures. Many of his works are colorful scenes of the Old West and include rodeos, logging, hunting, and fights with Indians. Such scenes reflect White's own experience as a Texas farmhand, an oil-field roughneck, a cowboy and a bronco rider, a veterinarian, and a soldier. White also worked as a barber and a peace officer. In 1945, White went into business for himself, selling his home-brewed "White's New Discovery Liniment." After a dozen years hawking this cure-all on the street, he had a dream and woke up determined to become a full-time artist.

Although White had always amused himself with carving small objects, his art career began in earnest in 1957 when he painted a rodeo scene. From this beginning, he produced a large output of paintings and sculptures, and he had plans to open up his own museum to exhibit his work. Although the museum never materialized, White eventually came to refer to his house, which was collaged in paintings and filled with carved mechanical figures, as his museum. In 1967, his work came to the attention of Dallas art dealer Murray Smither, who aggressively promoted the artist.

White developed two approaches to his work: painted relief carvings and freestanding sculptural dioramas or assemblages. The paintings tend to reflect romantic action scenes—hunting, Wild West adventure—while the sculptures often depict more homely (though often emotionally freighted) scenes of black experience, including slavery and emancipation, field labor, and shoe shining.

SUGGESTED READING: Jane Livingston and John Beardsley, *Black Folk Art in America: 1930–1980* (Jackson, Miss., 1982).

White, John I. (1902–1992). White was a collector, singer, and student of cowboy songs. Although he was raised in Washington, D.C., his family spent summers on the Arizona dude ranch of Romaine Loudermilk, a cowboy singer, who taught young White some of his repertoire. In 1926, while he was a graduate student at Columbia University, White sang cowboy songs on New York radio station WEAF. From 1929 to 1931, he recorded twenty sides, including five cowboy songs, and, during 1930–36, he was the "Lonesome Cowboy" on radio's *Death Valley Days* series.

From 1936 to 1965, White worked as a cartographer, then returned to the realm of cowboy songs, using material he had collected thirty and forty years earlier as background for articles on various cowboy poets and singers. The articles are published in book form as *Git Along Little Dogies: Songs and Songmakers of the American West* (Champagne-Urbana, Ill., 1975), which is highly valued by folklorists for its material on the origins of cowboy songs.

White, Newman Ivey (1892–1948). White collected African-American and North Carolina folklore. He was educated at Trinity College (now Duke University) and earned his doctorate at Harvard University. While he taught English at Auburn University, he collected African-American songs from his students, from townies, and from local singers. Later, after he returned to teach at Trinity, he collaborated with Walter Clinton Jackson on *An Anthology of Verse by American Negroes* in 1924 and, four years later, published *American Negro Folk-Songs,* a major publication in the field. In 1943, White became general editor of the *Frank C. Brown Collection of North Carolina Folklore,* but had completed only the first volume at the time of his death.

Whitman, Walt (1819–1892).

Best known for his *Leaves of Grass,* a monument of American poetry, Walt Whitman presents a puzzle to the folklorist. Is he a "folk poet" or a literary poet? Certainly, Whitman himself aimed to be a poet of the people—more specifically, a poet of democracy—and his extraordinary verse exhibits many of the hallmarks of folk poetry. It is unconventional and even idiosyncratic. It is the product of a self-taught man and a self-educated poet. It incorporates colloquial language in a variety of characteristic idioms. It often takes as its subject matter the everyday and the homely; one of the great strengths of Whitman's poetry is that, while steeped in the activities, sounds, sights, and artifacts of mid-nineteenth-century American life, it also possesses a quality apart from any particular time and place. While Whitman had a profound feeling for nature, most of his poetry partakes of bustling urban working-class culture rather than any conventional pastoral traditions. Finally, Whitman's poetry is bardic, and the "speaker" of many of the poems adopts the voice and persona of the bard, the spiritual-poetic voice of the folk.

Despite these "folk" qualities in Whitman's personality and work, his poetry owes as much to distinctly literary traditions as it does to folk traditions. If, for example, "Song of Myself" contains a wealth of urban folklore and is filled with the details of contemporary material culture, its opening line (in the first, 1855 edition), "I celebrate myself, and sing myself," seems a self-conscious variation on the opening of Virgil's *Aeneid,* the prototypal epic: "Arms and the man I sing." And if Whitman had limited formal education, he had thoroughly educated himself, read-

Walt Whitman at the end of the Civil War. The photograph was made in the studio of Mathew Brady. (Courtesy National Archives and Records Administration)

ing voraciously and attending the many public lectures by educators, philosophers, scientists, and theologians, which were popular in his day. Not only was Whitman well aware of the literary poetry of his own age and earlier, but by the end of his life, he had received recognition from the literary world, both in the United States and abroad. He was regarded as an important poet, not a folk curiosity, and shortly after his death, his works became a regular part of school and university curricula. Literary scholars put Whitman in company with the other writers of what critic F. O. Matthiessen called the American Renaissance: Ralph Waldo Emerson, HENRY DAVID THOREAU, NATHANIEL HAWTHORNE, and HERMAN MELVILLE. Perhaps it is best, then, to see Whitman as a hybrid, rooted firmly both in folk and literary traditions.

He was born Walter Whitman in rural West Hills, Long Island, but the family settled in

Brooklyn in 1823, where his father, inept in business, struggled to support nine children. Whitman attended public school in Brooklyn, then left at age twelve to apprentice with a printer. He worked as a journeyman printer in Brooklyn and New York City, taught in rural schools on Long Island, and, at twenty-three, became a newspaper editor in New York, then, in 1846, edited the *Brooklyn Daily Eagle*. His vocal support of the abolitionist Free Soil Party provoked his discharge from the paper in 1848. He worked briefly for the New Orleans *Crescent*, then returned to New York, where he was active in the abolitionist cause. During 1850–55, Whitman dabbled in New York real estate. Whitman was an enthusiastic theatergoer and opera lover, and he spent much time in the libraries of New York City, reading omnivorously. Quietly, on his own, he developed a revolutionary style of free verse (yet powerfully rhythmical) poetry, at once intimate in nature and epic in scope. By the spring of 1855 Whitman had written enough poems to make up a slender volume. Since no publisher would take on his work, Whitman printed the first edition of *Leaves of Grass* at his own expense. The volume received little notice, except from the remarkably perceptive Ralph Waldo Emerson (to whom Whitman had sent a copy), who wrote to the poet that his book was "the most extraordinary piece of wit and wisdom [America] has yet contributed." Whitman revised *Leaves of Grass* continually and added new poems to it. The second edition (1856) included the hauntingly celebratory "Crossing Brooklyn Ferry" (at first called "Sun-Down Poem"), but this second edition was, like the first, a financial failure. In 1860, however, a Boston publisher brought out the third, much enlarged, edition of *Leaves of Grass*, which added some more overtly autobiographical masterpieces, including the "Calamus" poems (covert expressions of the poet's apparently latent homosexuality) and

"Premonition" (better known from a later edition as "Starting from Paumanok," a hint of Whitman's often tormented and lonely childhood). "A Word out of the Sea" (later called "Out of the Cradle Endlessly Rocking") is introspective and almost melancholy, while such pieces as "Chants Democratic," "Enfans d'Adam," and "Messenger Leaves" continued to develop the upbeat tone of the poems in the first edition.

When his brother was wounded at Fredericksburg (December 13, 1862), Whitman went to care for him, then took a temporary job in the army paymaster's office in Washington. In his spare time, he visited and looked after wounded soldiers in the Washington hospitals. He became a clerk in the Department of the Interior in January 1865, but was dismissed in June because the secretary of the Interior deemed *Leaves of Grass* indecent. Whitman's friend, journalist William O'Connor, wrote a vindication of Whitman and his work in an 1866 essay titled "The Good Gray Poet," and because of this, Whitman was able to obtain a post in the attorney general's office. The "good gray poet" label also proved to have considerable popular appeal, and Whitman's work began to come to the attention of a wider public.

The Civil War prompted Whitman to write a collection of war poems, *Drum Taps* (1865), and the *Sequel to Drum Taps* (1865), which included the sublimely moving elegy on President Abraham Lincoln, "When Lilacs Last in the Dooryard Bloom'd." The war also produced a great collection of brief prose sketches and descriptions of battle and its aftermath, *Specimen Days & Collect* (1882–83).

A fourth edition of *Leaves of Grass* was published in 1867, and the poet's fame slowly broadened, aided by John Burroughs's *Notes on Walt Whitman as Poet and Person* (1867) and a British edition of *Leaves of Grass*, edited in 1868 by William Michael Rossetti, brother of the poet

Dante Gabriel Rossetti. Whitman suffered a partially paralytic and debilitating stroke in 1873, after which he lived with his brother in Camden, New Jersey. An 1881 Boston edition of *Leaves of Grass* was condemned by the Society for the Suppression of Vice as immoral, but Whitman was undaunted and created yet another revision, which was published in 1888 and brought Whitman modest but gratifying financial return. The ninth—or "authorized" edition—of *Leaves of Grass* appeared in 1892, the year of Whitman's death.

See also: FOLKLORE IN AMERICAN LITERATURE; LONGFELLOW, HENRY WADSWORTH; SANDBURG, CARL.

SUGGESTED READING: Gay Wilson Allen, *The Solitary Singer* (1955; reprint ed., New York, 1985); Gay Wilson Allen, *The New Walt Whitman Handbook* (1975; reprint ed., New York, 1986); Justin Kaplan, *Walt Whitman, a Life* (New York, 1980).

John Greenleaf Whittier, poet.

Greenleaf Whittier, *The Supernaturalism of New England* (1847; reprint ed., Norman, Okla., 1969).

Whittier, John Greenleaf (1807–1892).

Best known as a genteel American poet, the author of the perennial favorite *Snow-Bound* (1866), Whittier was also an amateur folklore collector, who gathered traditional oral material for use in his literary work. He delved into printed sources, but also collected from live informants, as his *Legends of New England in Prose and Verse* (1831) and *The Supernaturalism of New England* (1847) attest. Both books should be considered pioneering works of American folklore scholarship.

See also: FOLKLORE IN AMERICAN LITERATURE; MORTON, THOMAS.

SUGGESTED READING: John Greenleaf Whittier, *Legends of New England* (Hartford, Conn., 1831); John

Wilgus, D. K. (1918–1989).

Wilgus was a student of the folk song and the author of a definitive study of early folk-song scholarship. A native of West Mansfield, Ohio, he was educated at Ohio State University (B.A., M.A., and Ph.D.) and taught at Western Kentucky State College (now Western Kentucky University) and UCLA, where he was instrumental in creating the institution's folklore program. He was president of the American Folklore Society during 1971–72. His scholarhsip ranges from ballad classification to "hillbilly" records and the relationship of folklore and mass media.

See also: COMBS, JOSIAH H.

SUGGESTED READING: D. K. Wilgus, "Folksong and Folksong Scholarship: Changing Approaches and Attitudes. IV: The Rationalistic Approach," in Mody C. Boatright et al., eds., *A Good Tale and a Bonnie Tune* (Dallas, 1964).

Williams, Hank (1923–1953). Born Hiram King Williams in Georgiana, Alabama, Hank Williams is considered by many the greatest singer-composer in COUNTRY MUSIC. The son of a sawmill and railroad worker, he began playing guitar when he was eight and made his radio debut at thirteen. The very next year, he formed his first band, Hank Williams and his Drifting Cowboys. Popular legend has it that he learned his early songs and guitar chords from an African-American street singer, Rufus "Teetot" Payne.

During World War II, Williams worked in the shipyards at Mobile and sang in the rough honky-tonks there (see HONKY-TONK MUSIC). After the war, in 1947, he began recording on the MGM label the songs that earned him national and worldwide fame. His 1949 "Lovesick Blues" was not only a hit, it got him an invitation to join the cast of the GRAND OLE OPRY. There followed during the balance of his brief life such classic country songs as "Cold, Cold Heart," "Your Cheatin' Heart," and "Hey, Good Lookin'." He brought to country music a combination of intense sincerity and a fresh commercialism. His singing and his composition were unmistakably "country," but also "pop." They spoke to rural folk on the farm as well as in the factory, and they also appealed to the urban dweller who enjoyed the likes of Tony Bennett and Frankie Laine, both of whom recorded Hank Williams tunes.

Williams's brilliant career was cut short by a heart attack early in 1953. His untimely death was almost certainly hastened by alcoholism.

SUGGESTED READING: Roger M. Williams, *Sing a Sad Song: The Life of Hank Williams* (New York, 1981).

Wills, Bob (1905–1975). Billed as the "King of Western Swing," Wills and his "Texas Playboys" group were the genre's leading exponents. He was born near Kosse, Texas, to a family that included some of the most renowned Texas fiddlers, and Wills early on learned to play the fiddle. After 1929, when he moved to Fort Worth, his rural fiddling became influenced by urban blues genres, and Wills soon evolved western swing's distinctive blend of country-western and urban blues and small-band swing jazz sounds. While Wills never abandoned his rural roots, he was determined to "raise" his music above the level of "hillbilly music" and freely combined traditional tunes and techniques with current commercial sounds.

See also: COUNTRY MUSIC.

Winchell, Walter (1897–1972). Born Walter Winchel in New York City, this onetime vaudevillian essentially invented the profession of gossip columnist, bringing gossip (which folklorists define as moralistic, speculative talk about persons not present) into a highly public forum and fashioning it into an instrument not only of great popularity but of significant power. While he was still appearing onstage, Winchell began publishing a single-page Hollywood gossip sheet, which secured him a job as West Coast correspondent for the *New York Vaudeville News*. After Winchell moved from Los Angeles back to New York in 1922 as a full-time writer for the *Vaudeville News*, his career quickly prospered.

The powerful Walter Winchell at work. His sign-on trademark, taps on a telegraph key followed by "Hello, Mr. and Mrs. America and all the ships at sea," became familiar to millions of radio listeners.

tional news of President Franklin D. Roosevelt's decision to seek a third term in 1940, and his following included figures from all walks of life, such as FBI director J. EDGAR HOOVER and many high-profile members of organized crime. In August 1939, Winchell persuaded Louis "Lepke" Buchalter, the founder of Murder, Inc., and the FBI's Public Enemy Number One for more than two years, to surrender. Mob officials arranged a meeting in which Winchell, whom Lepke trusted, would pick up Lepke and take him directly to Hoover.

Winchell's popularity waned as the public's infatuation with gangsters and gangster culture diminished during the 1940s. By the 1950s, Winchell, once a champion of liberal causes, had become an arch-conservative who publicly supported the Red-baiting senator Joseph McCarthy and who used his radio program to broadcast the names of those blacklisted as communist sympathizers during McCarthy's reign of terror in the early part of the decade. In 1959, he was introduced to a new generation when he became the voice-over narrator of the popular television crime series *The Untouchables* (1959–63).

SUGGESTED READING: Walter Winchell, *Winchell Exclusive: "Things That Happened to Me—and Me to Them"* (Englewood Cliffs, N.J., 1975).

He wrote a syndicated newspaper column and then, in 1932, earned a syndicated radio program as well. A national audience of twenty million listeners eagerly anticipated his famous sign-on: the staccato burst of a radio-telegraph key and Winchell's equally staccato voice greeting, "Hello, Mr. and Mrs. America and all the ships at sea. Let's go to press. . . ." The millions who read and heard him learned to equate Winchell's racy Broadway idiom with absolute authority. He was widely quoted, and although he had many detractors, he was a prolific phrasemaker whose pronouncements could (and did) make or break reputations. His power and influence extended far beyond the entertainment industry. It was Winchell, for example, who broke the sensa-

Wiseman, Lulu Belle (1913–) and Wiseman, Scotty (1909–1981) (Lulu Belle and Scotty). This folk-country duo introduced to a popular audience traditional Appalachian folk music during the early Depression. Lulu Belle and Scotty were longtime stars of radio's *National Barn Dance* program. Lulu Belle played guitar and Scotty played the banjo; together, they sang two-part harmony renditions of a repertoire ranging from folk to sentimental commercial country songs.

Scotty Wiseman was raised in North Carolina's Blue Ridge Mountains and was a folk-song collector as well as composer before he married Lulu Belle (born Myrtle Cooper) in 1934. Both were stars of WLS radio, Chicago, before they married and performed together.

Witches and witchcraft.

Most Euro-Americans, African Americans, and Native Americans understand the term "witchcraft" to mean the malevolent practice of magic to cause harm; however, those who practice the religion known as Wicca—neo-Pagan witchcraft—interpret witchcraft more broadly as the practice of magic, period.

Witches and witchcraft enter into American folk culture most dramatically during the period of the SALEM WITCH TRIALS of 1692, but they were hardly an aberration; belief in witchcraft was a central feature of the prescientific worldview and continued to figure as an issue in America well into the eighteenth century. While not common, witchcraft trials (and executions) were not unknown in America both before and after the events at Salem. In New England, the first execution of a woman for witchcraft occurred in 1647.

Typically, witches are blamed for any number of misfortunes, including illness, crop failure, the faithlessness of a spouse or lover, and so on. That such instances of misfortune may be attributed to witchcraft is supported by physical evidence, including the presence of balls of hair or feather crowns left on the pillow of the bewitched; frequently, the bewitched individual suffers seizures, convulsions, or a trancelike state; often, too, the victim feels as if he or she is being pinched, stabbed, or burned by invisible forces.

Actually identifying witches and bringing them to trial—as happened at Salem—is an extreme and relatively rare occurrence. More typically, groups who believe in witches and witchcraft employ any number of remedies to ward off the effects of witchcraft. These include such AMULETS as iron knives, horseshoes, and silver coins. Placing a pin in a chair should paralyze any witch who happens to sit there, and objects containing many small parts (such as sieves with many holes or brooms with many straws) will transfix a witch, who must compulsively count the parts. As ordinary lead bullets are believed to be powerless against the werewolf and VAMPIRE, who will, however, succumb to a silver bullet, so it is with witches.

For the most part, today, witches and witchcraft have moved from the realm of folk belief to popular culture, where they are frequently caricatured in children's literature and in such films as *The Wizard of Oz* (1939). Television's popular situation comedy, *Bewitched* (1964–72) overturned the stereotype of the ugly, mole-afflicted, hook-nosed crone and depicted a pert, pretty witch, married to a mortal and trying to live a "normal" life in suburbia. Despite the general trivialization of witches and witchcraft in recent popular culture, news reports of apparently senseless murders and multiple murders sometimes suggest links to so-called satanic cults and, possibly, contemporary witches' "covens." Despite, then, the general dilution of witches and witchcraft in contemporary popular culture, there remains an undercurrent of genuine terror, often linked to a persistent belief in the presence of the devil.

See also: FAMILIAR; FINGERNAILS; HEX.

SUGGESTED READING: John Demos, *Entertaining Satan: Witchcraft and the Culture of Early New England* (Oxford, Eng., 1982); Rosemary Ellen Guiley,

The Encyclopedia of Witches and Witchcraft (New York, 1989); Wayland Hand, *Magical Medicine* (Berkeley, Calif., 1980).

Wolf. While the wolf figures in various European folktales and in AESOP'S FABLES, he appears in American folklore mainly in Native American mythology and lore. Wolf appears in the role of the creator in Paiute lore and as a CULTURE HERO in Ute stories. The Lakota identify Wolf as the spirit of the hunt and of war. Wolf also figures prominently in Cree, Shoshone, Aleut, and Nootka folklore and mythology.

Wolf, John Quincy, Jr. (1901–1972). Wolf collected folk music from his native Ozarks. He grew up in Batesville, Arkansas, the son of a banker. Wolf was educated at Arkansas College (Batesville) and at Johns Hopkins University, from which he earned a Ph.D. He then taught at Rhodes College, in Memphis. Beginning in 1941, with his wife, Bess Millen, a classical musician, he recorded the music of the southeastern Ozarks, and, later, also recorded African-American folk music in northern Mississippi and regional shape-note singing. Wolf's recordings are housed at Arkansas College.

See also: RIDDLE, ALMEDA.

Wood, Grant (1892–1942). Iowa-born and Paris-trained (Académie Julian, 1923) Grant Wood was not a folk artist, but a leader of the Midwestern Regionalism movement, which flourished during the Depression years. His often geometrically simplified style ("lollipop trees"), however, has a strong affinity with folk art, and his subject matter often draws on material folk culture and themes generally suggestive of folk culture. It is for these qualities that Wood was and is both praised and denigrated.

Wood's "folksy" style owes as much to the sharply delineated technique of the sixteenth-century Flemish and German masters as it does to any conception of an American folk style. After young Wood spent a year in Paris, he returned to Iowa, settling in Cedar Rapids, where in 1927 he was commissioned to do a stained-glass window. He traveled to Germany to consult stained-glass craftsmen to assist him and, while there, fell under the influence of the German and Flemish style. Up to this point, Wood had emulated the soft Impressionist style, but now he began to paint in the hard-edged, geometrically stylized, but quasi-realistic manner for which he is best known. He made his first national sensation in this style with his 1930 *American Gothic,* a witty image of a stern farmer-preacher and his dour daughter in front of their farmhouse (the models were actually Woods's sister, Nan, and his dentist, Dr. B. H. McKeeby). The painting has entered American popular culture as one of its most enduring icons and has been frequently satirized and adapted, often as advertising artwork for a wide range of products. In 1939, Wood illustrated the legendary scene in which six-year-old GEORGE WASHINGTON confesses to having chopped down his father's prize cherry tree; with a touch of irony, Wood depicts the figure of MASON LOCKE WEEMS, who first wrote about the incident in the fifth edition (1806) of his 1800 biography of Washington, drawing aside a window curtain to reveal the tableau. Less overtly iconic are Woods's many midwestern landscapes, rolling, rounded vistas painted with a deceptive simplicity suggestive of "NAIVE" ART and identi-

Grant Wood, photographed about 1945.

Grant Wood, American Gothic (Oil on canvas, 1930, Art Institute of Chicago).

fied as such by many nonprofessional, casual observers.

In 1934, Wood joined the fine arts faculty of the University of Iowa and lived the remainder of his life in Iowa City.

SUGGESTED READING: Wanda Corn, *Grant Wood: The Regionalist Vision* (New Haven, Conn., 1983); James M. Dennis, *Grant Wood: A Study in American Art and Culture* (New York, 1975).

Woodcarving. The traditional craft and art of creating objects in wood. Such objects range from toys (see TOYS, FOLK) to tools, to kitchen and other household utensils, to furniture, to hunting decoys, to religious sculptures, to Native American TOTEM POLES, and to sculptures intended as nothing more or less than works of art. Almost any carved object can be considered an example of folk woodcarving if it has been created by a person who has learned to carve not from books or through formal training, but by watching other carvers in the community—"community" defined in terms of region, ethnicity, race, or religion. A folk carving thus typically bears a strong family resemblance to work created before it and in the same general region. Some folklorists would not consider certain so-called folk art pieces examples of folklore if these were merely eccentric works of OUTSIDER ART, created by untrained individuals, and without meaningful relation to the work and traditions of the community.

During most of the nineteenth century, folk carvers produced work not only of the community, but for the community. By the early twentieth century, however, interest in folk crafts grew, and many carvers were induced to create objects for sale. This trend has increased in proportion to the number of various folklife festivals held throughout the country. Many folk carvers rent kiosk space at such festivals and some even advertise, selling their work by mail order. Some folklorists express regret over this practice, suggesting that it introduces a mediating element into the relationship between carver and community. Others, however, see the marketplace as a means of preserving at least some aspects of folklore and folk art.

See also: AARON, JESSE; ARAGON, JOSÉ RAFAEL; BULTOS; CRAFTS, AMERICAN FOLK; KACHINA; SCANDINAVIAN AMERICANS.

SUGGESTED READING: Charles L. Briggs, *The Wood Carvers of Cordova, New Mexico: Social Dimensions of an Artistic "Revival"* (Knoxville, Tenn., 1980); Simon Bronner, *Chain Carvers: Old Men Crafting Meaning* (Lexington, Ky., 1985); Susan W. Fair, ed., *Alaska Native Arts and Crafts* (Anchorage, 1985).

Work songs. Some time in prehistory laborers discovered that if they moved in rhythm to the beat of a song, the work would go more easily and efficiently. Also, quite probably, they found out that with the help of a song leader, they could find catharsis for their woes by expressing their resentments and frustrations in improvised verses ridiculing those who exploited them. The best-known work songs from the eighteenth century on have been CHANTEYS and PRISON WORK SONGS.

See also: ARHOOLIE RECORDS; BLUES; CANALS; COME-ALL-YE; COWBOY SONGS; FOLK MUSIC; FOSTER, STEPHEN; FRENCH AMERICANS; LEDBETTER, HUDDIE (LEADBELLY); LUMBERJACK FOLKLORE; "MICHIGAN I-O"; OCCUPATIONAL FOLKLORE; RAILROAD FOLKLORE; RODGERS, JIMMIE; SAILORS AND SEAFARING LORE; WHALING.

World War I. America's participation in the war to end all wars was presented to her people as a great moral crusade. In his war message to Congress, President Woodrow Wilson pledged that the United States would be fighting for "the rights of nations great and small," that "the world must be made safe for democracy." Following the reported horrors of the "Rape of Little Belgium" and the great loss of innocent lives (including Americans) in the sinking of the British liner *Lusitania*, America was finally ready to tackle "the Hun at civilization's gate." As one poster proclaimed: "We can do no otherwise." With the war set upon this moral pedestal, it is no wonder that much of what is folkloric in the period reflects an Armageddon where Good eventually triumphs over Evil.

But many Americans, not content to wait as their country debated whether to undertake this crusade, had already gone to help save France as ambulance drivers, as soldiers with the British and French armies, and even as pilots with the famous all-American Lafayette Escadrille. Victor Chapman, the first of the Escadrille to die, said he enlisted in the French Foreign Legion "for the cause of humanity, the most noble of all causes." When Chapman transferred to the French air service, he wrote home that it was "like being made a knight." Indeed, many of the pilots saw themselves as modern-day knights, going out in single combat to challenge the forces of evil. They held to a code of chivalry that would have done Lancelot proud, and when the Red Baron, Manfred von Richtofen, was shot down over Allied territory he was buried with full military honors; his enemies sent wreaths with tributes such as, "To Our Gallant and Worthy Foe." When America's top ace, Eddie Rickenbacker, returned home after the armistice, he was hailed by the secretary of war as "one of the real crusaders of America—one of the truest knights our country has ever known." While in France, like many who wanted to prove they were "100 percent American," he had changed the spelling of his name from the more Germanic original Rickenbacher. One newspaper duly noted this: "Rickenbacker has taken the Hun out of his name." He was hardly the only one leery of links to German *Kultur*. Back home, in the Midwest, a high percentage of the population was first- or second-generation German and active subscribers to publications in the language of their fatherland—which quickly lost all circulation. Towns named for places in Germany were rapidly renamed "Liberty" or some other more acceptable American prototype. The old favorite sauerkraut suddenly had to be called liberty cabbage. Indeed, food became a great concern for Americans, who were feeding not only themselves and their million-man army in Europe but starving refugees in places they had never heard of. Posters appealed for food conservation: "Little Americans do your bit. Leave nothing on your plate," proclaimed a poster appealing to children. "Don't waste food while others starve," another pleaded (see WORLD WAR I POSTERS).

Shortly after American forces arrived in France, they paraded up the Champs-Elysees in Paris, on July 4, 1917, singing, true to form, "Onward Christian Soldiers." They went on to lay a wreath at Lafayette's tomb, to honor the French general who helped America win her independence. A colonel, on behalf of the American Expeditionary Force, announced, "Lafayette, we are here," a statement often misattributed to Gen. John J. Pershing, commander of the AEF. It was one of those evocative phrases that captured the American imagination at the time and imbedded itself into the collective consciousness. Among others were the stirring "Over the Top!" which ordered men to charge their enemy, since they first had to climb up out of their trenches; and "No-man's-land," the contested territory between opposing lines of trenches, a phrase already filled with sinister overtones, since it had indicated a place outside medieval London's walls set aside for executions. To cloak his whereabouts from the enemy, General Pershing marked all of his official correspondence as coming from "Somewhere in France." Among other phrases well known to the military were "Hurry up, and wait," and "40 & 8"—what the troops called the small French freight cars they were transported in; they held forty men or eight horses. "Three on a match," which continues to be very unlucky, came about through sad experience in the trenches. You might strike a "lucifer" to light your "fag" in the darkness, and perhaps that of your buddy, too, but if you held a flaming match long enough to light a third cigarette, a German sniper might sight in on it and kill you.

Among the legendary heroics that captured the most attention in the American press was the plight of the "Lost Battalion." During the Meuse-Argonne offensive in the fall of 1918, a brigade of the 77th Division advanced so boldly through a gap in the German lines that it found itself cut off in a ravine and surrounded with little hope of reinforcement or retreat. The Germans lobbed in grenades with impunity as the troops settled in to defend their position. Eventually facing starvation and running out of ammunition, the brigade steadfastly refused to surrender, even when a plane that finally spotted them attempted to drop supplies and was shot down. Unaware of their presence, American artillery began to shell the area. The only possibility for contacting the outside was to let loose their last carrier pigeon, Cher Ami, who finally got through to division headquarters with a message that gave the unit's exact location. However, in making this heroic flight through shot and shell, Cher Ami arrived with only one eye and one leg. Awarded the croix de guerre, he became the mascot of the Signal Corps and now resides, stuffed, in the Smithsonian Institution. The battalion ultimately was rescued, but only 252 of the 679 men who went in survived.

Among those who rescued the Lost Battalion was the greatest hero of them all, Serg. Alvin C. York. Supreme commander Marshal Ferdinand Foch personally decorated this American doughboy with the croix de guerre for what he said was the "greatest thing accomplished by any private soldier of all the armies of Europe." York was typical of many soldiers of the AEF in that he had never traveled before, was barely educated, and, as a churchgoer, was troubled by the prospect of killing another man. He tried to avoid the war by declaring himself a conscientious objector, but was drafted anyhow. By the time he reached France he had come to terms with his country's noble mission. God had assured him that as long as he was "right in his own soul," he remained "a righteous man." His Bible by his side, he was divinely confident that he would not be harmed. So, on October 8, 1918, when his unit, trapped within the range of several enemy machine-gun nests, was decimated, York calmly set about killing Germans. Like many backwoodsmen he was a good shot; indeed he was known as the best shot in the Cumberland Mountains. His skills had been tested in many a turkey shoot, and that's what he later compared this action to. He gobbled like a turkey to get a German to stick his head up, and then he shot him—"I just tetched him off." Single-handedly he killed no fewer than 25 of the enemy and forced 132 more to surrender.

The loneliness of the doughboys, so far from home and their loved ones, and the anxiety of those left behind produced a wide variety of popular songs. Perhaps the favorite was "Keep the Home Fires Burning," which ended, "till the boys come home." At the other end of the scale was that snappy recognition of innocence lost: "How're you gonna keep 'em down on the farm after they've seen Paree?" And then there were the soldiers' own inventions of countless bawdy refrains to "MADEMOISELLE FROM ARMENTIERES."

As the war's most famous song promised when the Yanks went over, they wouldn't be back "till it's over, Over There." Armistice finally established that it would be over at the eleventh hour of the eleventh day of the eleventh month of 1918.

SUGGESTED READING: Hans Christian Adamson, *Eddie Rickenbacker* (New York, 1946); Newton Diehl Baker, *Why We Went to War* (New York, 1936); Arthur Guy Emprey, *"Over the Top" by an American Soldier Who Went* (New York, 1917); Walton Rawls, *Wake Up, America! World War I and the American Poster* (New York, 1988).

World War I posters. The United States had reluctantly entered WORLD WAR I, the kind of foreign entanglement with militaristic and obsolete governments that George Washington had warned against in his farewell address of March 1797. However, once committed, it became necessary to quickly mobilize Americans for the task of ridding civilization of militarism, of wresting France from Germany's clutches, and of making the world safe for democracy. Within a week of declaring war on Germany, President Woodrow Wilson created the Committee on Public Information and named journalist George Creel to head what would be a new venture in MASS MEDIA. The major instrument chosen to reach the American public, in an era before radio broadcasting and in the infancy of film, was a variant of the colorful advertising sheet: the propaganda poster. America was already blessed with experienced commercial illustrators eager to serve their country, and among them were some of the most prominent artists of the period: Charles Dana Gibson (1867–1944), J. C. Leyendecker (1874–1951), James Montgomery Flagg (1877–1960), Howard Chandler Christy (1873–1952), and N. C. Wyeth (1882–1945). They produced about 2,500 dramatic posters in support of the war effort: from military recruiting to European war relief to Liberty Bond drives to food and fuel conservation.

A poster by its very nature has to play upon broad ideas and feelings already current, for it has to be instantly understandable to be effective. The poster succeeds by relying upon a common tradition of ideas, beliefs, and even folk sayings (see PROVERBS) that are shared by the people it intends to influence. As in many cultures, even in one as young as America, the common traditions and beliefs can be summoned through symbols. The folkloric content, in this case, may be no more than a common awareness that the symbol is significant to being American, despite the country's wide variety of national and cultural backgrounds. It is what people identify with. In World War I, the majority of posters made use of a rather select repertory of American folkloric symbols: UNCLE SAM, Columbia, the Liberty Bell, the Stars and Stripes, the American EAGLE, and the Statue of Liberty. All of them were tied to our earliest history as a nation, except the Statue of Liberty, which reached our shores in the late nineteenth century as a gift of the people of France. It was especially poignant as a symbol in World War I, since Americans felt that they were repaying Lafayette's support of American independence by fighting to restore France's liberty. However, Liberty had long been an American symbol. She appears in 1792 on the first coins issued by the U.S. Mint, challenging America's earlier personification, Columbia (a feminization of the name Columbus), who appeared on earlier coins marked *Immune Columbia,* or, "Columbia, fortify us." France and her revolution are saluted in the Liberty cap, now decorated in stars and stripes, that is worn by both Columbia and Liberty in these posters. Along with the eagle, Liberty, in bust, seated, standing, and walking, is the most persistent symbol in American coinage. In these posters, the bald eagle represents America's strength and is also the emblem of the Army Air Corps; the bald eagle first appeared as a symbol in Massachusetts on a coin of 1776 and made its way onto the Great Seal of the United States shortly afterward. Right from the first, on U.S. Mint coins, the eagle took the obverse to Liberty.

The most persistent male figure in the posters is Uncle Sam, who came into being as the American counterpart to England's John Bull in the War of 1812. Legend has it that he developed as an interpretation of the letters "U.S." stamped on barrels of rations supplied to the U.S. Army by a meatpacker named "Uncle" Sam Wilson. His characterization seems to have been based on BROTHER JONATHAN, a shrewd Yankee type in the first American play on current social life, ROYALL TYLER's *The Contrast* (1787). However, he was not given visual representation in his

A U.S. government–sponsored propaganda machine of unprecedented scope sought to shape not only the perception, but the folklore of the war. These government-produced posters demonize the German kaiser Wilhelm II and seek to involve even schoolchildren in the war effort, through the "U.S. School Garden" program. (Collection of Walton Rawls)

trademark outfit of Stars and Stripes until 1832. In all of the posters, especially in the famous "I Want You," Uncle Sam is the stern, upright, caring, decent human being that Americans think represents themselves and the United States.

In propaganda especially, the enemy needs to be identified symbolically as well. In these posters, the German soldier, also representing Militarism, is linked to his savage forebear, the

Hun, as well as to an earlier ancestor, the subhuman ape, in one startling poster. Even in his uniform, the German is pictured with the hulking shoulders, forward slouch, and the too-long arms of the ape. He is also recognized even in silhouette, in a poster titled "Remember Belgium," by the spiked helmet, the *Pickelhaube,* as he leads a young girl off to "a fate worse than death." By contrast, American men and women, and the Allies, are pictured as wholesome, earnest, dedicated, and eager.

Another frequent poster image is the loving, nurturing, sympathetic woman: the Red Cross nurse caring for the wounded, the Salvation Army lass ministering to soldiers' needs, the mother entrusting her son to Uncle Sam, the

Raised 'em myself in my **U.S. School Garden**

One poster, "Wake Up America Day," appears to say it all symbolically, as Columbia, draped in the Stars and Stripes, takes on the persona of PAUL REVERE by wearing a three-cornered hat and holding out the "one if by land . . ." signal lantern.

See also: WORLD WAR II POSTERS.

SUGGESTED READING: Walton Rawls, *Wake Up, America!: World War I and the American Poster* (New York, 1988); Maurice Rickards, *Posters of the First World War* (New York, 1968); George Theofiles, *American Posters of World War I* (New York, 1973).

woman defense worker, the YMCA girls in France handing out coffee and doughnuts, and the members of the Woman's Land Army growing vegetables for victory. One poster goes farther back for its symbolism; "The Greatest Mother in the World" shows a seated Red Cross nurse cradling a wounded soldier still lying on his battlefield stretcher, a tableau certainly intended to call to mind Michelangelo's *Pietà* of the Virgin Mary holding the crucified Christ in her lap. Another poster pictured Joan of Arc in shining armor and appealed to American women to be like her and help save France.

Finally, elements of the Stars and Stripes are used liberally throughout the posters, on Uncle Sam but also on representations of Columbia, Liberty, and the Red Cross lady, as well as grasped proudly in soldiers' hands as Old Glory.

World War II. Often referred to as "the last good war," World War II is unique among America's twentieth-century conflicts in having drawn almost universal support from civilians and soldiers alike. It was the only twentieth-century war in which all Americans had reason to feel directly and immediately threatened. The Japanese had attacked the U.S. military installation at Pearl Harbor, Hawaii (then a U.S. territory), and the Nazis clearly intended to achieve nothing less than domination of the world. Probably in no other American war did the general feeling that "we are in this thing together" more strongly prevail.

If the war produced some larger-than-life commanders, including some of mythic proportions, such as GEORGE S. PATTON, it was above all a "soldiers' war," in which the "G.I." or "dogface," as the enlisted man was called, became the collective hero. The typical G.I. was depicted as a kind of antihero, cynical but spirited, a "wise guy," but sincere in his devotion to protecting his loved ones at home, maybe lacking in spit-and-polish, but courageous and capable of great endurance. The G.I.'s military life began, if he was drafted, with a telegram or letter conveying "Greetings from the President." Through a course of basic training, all inductees were democratically leveled, and the barracks became a place to spin YARNS and tell TALL TALES, some of which are recognizable as common tall-tale types. For example, stories about killing hidden Japanese soldiers by firing around obstructions with a bent rifle have analogues in the REVOLUTIONARY WAR and in European folktales. World War II barracks life was also the origin of the term "snow job," which was a tall-tale type intended to terrify raw recruits and usually involved a description of some draconian punishment meted out by a drill instructor for the most trivial of infractions. World War II soldiers did not gather around the campfire to sing folk songs, but instead listened to the radio in the barracks. To an unprecedented degree, popular commercial music—primarily big band swing (see JAZZ)—marked the era and helped define its mood.

Although the dogface was popularly celebrated precisely because he was not glamorous, World War II aviators—"fly boys"—certainly captured public attention. Gone, however, were the chivalric myths of the World War I dogfight—one-on-one combat between fighter planes. The celebrated World War II aviators were the bomber crews, who delivered retributive destruction directly to the enemy people. Among themselves, aviators developed a host of superstitions and rituals, many intended to promote survival to twenty-five missions—the "magic number" bomber crews were required to complete in order to be "rotated Stateside" (returned home). Aircrews also exchanged stories about GREMLINS—demons responsible for inexplicable mechanical failures—and FOO-FIGHTERS, an early form of UFO (see UFO FOLKLORE). Fighter and bomber crews named their aircraft, often after a wife or girlfriend, and they stenciled bombs, swastikas (emblem of Nazi Germany), or rising suns (national emblem of Japan) on the fuselages of their craft, either to count the number of bombing missions flown or to record the number of enemy fighters downed. Nose art was a popular manifestation of MATERIAL CULTURE on bombers. Typically, nose art consisted of pinup girl images artfully painted beneath the cockpit and near the nose of the aircraft, usually incorporating into the design the plane's name.

As in most wars, folklore relating to the enemy was important. Both the Nazis and the Japanese were depicted as fanatics utterly careless of life. The Japanese in particular were seen as an enemy of incredible tenacity and cruelty, quite willing to commit suicide in order to inflict casualties. Such folklore, regrettably, was well founded in fact.

Although many—perhaps most—troops were highly motivated to fight to victory, they often spoke of doing anything to get back home, and even longed for a "million-dollar wound," a relatively trivial injury that was nevertheless sufficiently serious to warrant return to the States and even discharge. Some soldiers inflicted such wounds on themselves. If it was impossible to return home, troops brought many reminders of home with them, in the form of recorded music and pinup pictures, and all branches of the armed forces made special efforts to bring familiar items of popular culture even to the most remote locations. USO shows toured the front, bringing favorite radio and movie stars to the troops. Armed Forces Radio broadcast popular music and other programs. A special V-mail system enabled relatively rapid delivery of letters to and from loved ones. The troops themselves emblazoned familiar "Kilroy Was Here" GRAFFITI on countless walls in Europe, Asia, and North Africa.

World War II consumed the American home front as no other war (save the CIVIL WAR) had before or since. The "V for Victory" sign that was British prime minister Sir Winston Churchill's trademark was universally adopted in the United States. Civilians eagerly bought war bonds and scratched out victory gardens in their backyards for the purpose of growing vegetables to help conserve food for "our boys." They also readily submitted to a complex system of rationing—although black market activity was not uncommon. Women, who had played an important part in war production during World War I, served even more extensively in the second war. Rosie the Riveter, clad in denim overalls and brandishing a rivet gun, became a universal icon of the "war effort."

See also: MILITARY FOLKLORE; VIETNAM WAR.

SUGGESTED READING: John Morton Blum, V Was for Victory: Politics and American Culture during World War II (New York, 1976); Studs Terkel, The Good War: An Oral History of World War II (New York, 1984).

World War II posters. In the spring of 1941, well before America was at war, the government called upon leading illustrators in advertising and public relations to create a bond drive campaign in support of countries already fighting Germany. Among those who flocked to the colors were several well-known illustrators who had done some of the best posters of World War I (see WORLD WAR I POSTERS), artists such as James Montgomery Flagg (1877–1960), Joseph Christian Leyendecker (1874–1951), Adolph Treidler (1886–1981), and N. C. Wyeth (1882–1945). Naturally a great many of the early World War II posters took their themes, symbols, and overall design from earlier precedents. Flagg's UNCLE SAM reappears with frequency, but now with whiter hair, since (as in World War I) he continues to be the artist's self-portrait. Wyeth, the era's top adventure-book illustrator, did at least two war bond posters similar to what had worked in the earlier war. A superhuman Uncle Sam points the way to victory as over his shoulder Old Glory billows in the wind, flights of bombers pass overhead, and tanks and soldiers charge in the foreground. Leading magazine illustrator NORMAN ROCKWELL (1894–1978), who, in his early twenties, had painted at least one Liberty Loan poster during World War I, concentrated strictly on home-front issues in his World War II posters. His work would be highly regarded in the "Four Freedoms" series—"Freedom from Fear," "Freedom from Want," "Freedom of Speech," and "Freedom of Worship"—which Franklin D. Roosevelt had enumerated in his 1942 State of the Union Address. They showed clearly what it was the United States was fighting for—practical, everyday stuff that all Americans treasured as their heritage, rather than the abstract, ideal images that were presented in the earlier war. Far fewer evocative symbols are made use of in these posters than in those created during World War I; as a matter of fact, Uncle Sam is almost the only one we see with any regularity. There are a few Statues of Liberty and Liberty Bells, but virtually no Columbias swathed in Stars and Stripes. The focus of most World War II posters is the American serviceman himself, in portraits and close-ups of handsome and determined soldiers, sailors, and marines just doing their duty and expecting the viewer's wholehearted support; "Keep 'Em Flying" is a frequent refrain. As in the earlier war, with almost the lone exception of a poster showing a "Black Eagle" in the African-American Tuskeegee Squadron, they are all tough yet photogenic Anglo-Saxons. And for the first time, glamorous women are presented in their own smart WAVE, WAC, and Nurse Corps uniforms, rather than dressed, as Flagg earlier had them, in the military outfits of their brothers and boyfriends, or as Miss Liberty.

Posters were created for recruitment in all the military services, and, as before, for war bonds, food conservation, war production, and other urgent needs. The newer posters reflect an increased sophistication in the American public and respond to the practical immediacy Americans had become conditioned to from the swelling barrage of photographic "buy images" they were exposed to in advertising. The artists for a high percentage of the posters remain unknown, but the names of some of the most famous illustrators of the period often appear on the artwork: Albert Dorne (1905–1965), Peter Helck (b. 1893), Jon Whitcomb (b. 1906), and Stevan Dohanos (b. 1907).

The later posters rely less on folk sayings and stirring historical legends than the World War I pieces, but we do see representations of The Minute Man and The Spirit of '76; their messages are direct—"Let's Go," "Let's Hit 'Em," "Let 'Em Have It!"—rather than vaguely conceptual, like "Protect Your Child from Autocracy and Poverty." The conservation posters have virtually the same message as before: "Food Is a Weapon; Don't Waste It." Also reflecting great strides in rapid communication since the earlier war are the numerous posters that carry the message: "Loose Talk Can Cost Lives" and "The Enemy Is Always Listening."

Posters of the Second World War differ from those of the First World War not only in their subject matter but in the way they were produced. Unlike the earlier posters, which were created as lithographs by artists who had to plan the process step by step, those of the 1940s were truly products of MASS MEDIA, created in huge quantities by modern four-color-process high-speed presses and machine-folded for distribution. Although the original artwork was, as before, in most cases a painting, the printing plates were made photomechanically, with no further participation of the original artist.

SUGGESTED READING: G. H. Gregory, ed., *Posters of World War II* (New York, 1993); Derek Nelson, *The Posters That Won the War: The Production, Recruitment, and War Bond Posters of World War II* (Osceola, Wis., 1991); Peter Paret, Beth Irwin, and Paul Paret, *Persuasive Images: Posters of War and Revolution* (Princeton, N.J., 1992).

"Wreck of the Old 97, The." Since the appearance of the Baltimore and Ohio in 1826, the first steam railway in the United States, Americans have been fascinated by trains—more so before the advent of regular commercial air travel. Yet it is curious that only three railroading ballads have been widely sung, "Casey Jones" (see JONES, CASEY), "The Wreck of the Old 97," and "The Wreck of the C&O." In all three, the engineer is killed as a result of trying to make up time in a fast train.

The folk audience is much more intrigued by a disaster that centers on a single hero rather than one in which many are killed. The typical pattern in the composition of songs like "The Wreck of the Old 97" is part of a process we can call new wine in old bottles. When a creative folk observer of a sensational event has the impulse to make up a song about it, he or she tends to write to the tune of an already existing melody, attached often to a similar sensational event, in this case a ballad composed in 1865 by the popular professional songwriter of the latter half of the nineteenth century, Henry Clay Work. The first stanza of his "The Ship That Never Returned" runs:

*On a summer's day, when the waves were
  rippled
By the softest, gentle breeze,
Did a ship sail with its cargo laden
For a port beyond the seas.*

*Chorus: Did she ever return?
No, she never returned,
And her fate is yet unlearned,
Tho' for years and years there were fond ones
  waiting
For the ship that never returned.*

This popular work inspired a folk parody, "The Train That Never Returned," using the same melody and embodying the same central theme. Then, when the Fast Mail of the Southern Railroad crashed on its run between Monroe and Spencer, Virginia, on September 27, 1903, engineer Joseph A. (Steve) Broady and twelve others died in the wreck. Several ballads were composed about the incident. "The Wreck of the Old 97," which later became prodigiously popular in a host of country music recordings, was first recorded by Henry Whitter, a Virginia textile worker and hillbilly singer in New York in March 1923; it was released in December 1923. But the first hit recording was made by Texasborn VERNON DALHART for Victor in 1924 and became the first great country music hit, catapulting Dalhart to national popularity.

The variant Dalhart sang used the original tune by Work, and the text had a chorus with similar lyrics, showing some influence from Work's song and also possibly the parody. In 1927, one David Graves George filed a claim of authorship, asserting that he had been at the scene of the wreck in 1903 and had been so struck by the tragedy that he made up the song that Dalhart and others had recorded. The Circuit Court of Appeals decreed that Graves was not the composer and had in fact copied his version from Dalhart's recordings. The legitimate author of the song has never been determined.

See also: COUNTRY MUSIC; FOLK MUSIC.

Y

Yankee Doodle. As a caricature of a citizen of colonial America, especially of the New England colonies, Yankee Doodle was born in the early years of the Revolution, the invention of snobbish Britishers and equally snobbish colonial sophisticates. Yankee Doodle was an image of a bumpkin or hayseed, and the popular song "Yankee Doodle" or "Yankee Doodle Dandy" was intended to mock the ineptitude and pretension of the officers and soldiers of the Continental army. The Patriots, however, co-opted the Yankee Doodle figure and turned it into an emblem of national identity, associated with such characteristics as shrewdness, thrift, ingenuity, and stubborn determination. From the figure of Yankee Doodle there developed even more vivid American national caricatures, most notably BROTHER JONATHAN and UNCLE SAM.

As to the term *Yankee,* its origins remain obscure. It may come from the Dutch *Janke,* a diminutive of Jan (John). *Janke* was used by British soldiers as early as 1775 as a term of derision. As early as the 1680s, Yankee Doodle was used as a nickname or personal name. Historical records reveal a slave in Brooklyn known as "Yankee Doodle" in 1725, and Gen. James Wolfe used it in 1758, during the French and Indian War. During the 1760s, the Dutch freely used it as a term for the English colonists. Despite historic precedents, numerous and often fantastic folk etymologies (see ETYMOLOGIES, FOLK) have been suggested, including a theory that an Indian tribe called the Yankos (a name said to mean "Invincibles") relinquished their name to the New Englanders who defeated them, who then some-how assumed the name. There never was such an Indian tribe, however. Certain southerners have argued that *Yankee* is derived from the Cherokee word *eankke,* meaning coward; however, no such word exists in the Cherokee language. Still others have suggested that Indians in New York observed Dutchmen (generically called Jan) frequently eating cheese; from this evolved the Indian term for any Euro-American, Jan Cheese or Jan Kees. There is, however, no evidence that any Indian ever referred to white colonists as Jan Kees.

See also: TYLER, ROYALL.

SUGGESTED READING: Hugh Rawson, *Devious Derivations: Popular Misconceptions and More Than 1,000 True Origins of Common Words and Phrases* (New York, 1994).

Yankee trader or trickster. Since the eighteenth century, the Yankee has had a reputation for sharp dealing; by the nineteenth century, the verb to *yankee* meant to cheat. The Yankee sharper grew out of early portrayals of the Yankee "type" as a bumpkin; in truth, the Yankee was a sharper in bumpkin's clothing. Yankee tricksters indulged in "skunking" and "skinning," both terms for deceiving someone or playing a practical joke, often to the end of giving a deserving victim his comeuppance. Late nineteenth- and early twentieth-century stories about slick traveling salesmen probably originated in the traditional contest between the backwoods-man and the Yankee peddler, who somehow always succeeded in selling the yokel things he didn't want, including such items as hollow wooden clocks without works and wooden NUTMEGS painted to simulate gilded ones.

In some stories, the Yankee trickster masks his chicanery behind the pious mask of the church deacon or elder. "John, have you wet down the tobacco?" the deacon peddler asks his clerk. "Yes, sir," he answers. "Have you sanded the sugar?" Again: "Yes, sir." "Then come in to prayers!"

The Yankee horse trader was another traditional trickster stereotype. One persuades his mark to buy a worthless nag by admitting that the animal does have two faults. He agrees to reveal one fault before trading and the other after the deal is concluded. The trader admits: "He is awful hard to catch." That's sufficient to prompt the trade, whereupon, after taking the money, the trader reveals the second fault: "He ain't good for nothin' when you catch him."

The Yankee trickster was given literary expression in *The Clockmaker*, an 1836 novel by Thomas Chandler Haliburton. The protagonist of his book, Sam Slick, was a sharper and a rustic sage or cracker-barrel wit.

See also: CON ARTIST AND CONFIDENCE MAN.

Yarn. In the sense of a long-winded, hyperbolic, episodic oral story of fantastic or semi-fantastic adventure, yarn came into the language about 1812. Tellers of yarns are called "yarn spinners," and their stories are typically first-person narratives; often, yarns are sea stories told by sailors ("old salts"). While the term is well enough defined in dictionaries, its use in folklore studies is loose. BENJAMIN A. BOTKIN called it a humorous

(not comic or witty) story that "may be spun out to great length." As the definition of yarn is loose, so the form itself is informal, and yarns are typically spun in such casual social settings as taverns or other traditional informal gathering places. Sometimes a corner of a tavern or other establishment is unofficially devoted to yarn spinning and may be called a "liars' bench." The yarn may be considered a subgenre of the TALL TALE.

See also: WORLD WAR II.

Yiddish and Yiddishisms. Hebrew is the language of the Bible, used in prayers and religious ceremonies, and the language Jews spoke from about 4,000 B.C. until the destruction of Solomon's Temple in 586 B.C. It has been resurrected as the official and actual spoken language of the state of Israel. About a thousand years ago, one major group of Jews moved from the north of France to settlements along the Rhine. There, another language, Yiddish, crystallized. It is a mixture of Hebrew, medieval German, the Romance languages, and, ultimately, contains elements from the languages of the various countries in which Jews have lived. (In Russia, for example the Yiddish word for window was *fenster*, which in America has been supplanted by *vinder*—a Yiddish pronunciation of window.) Written Yiddish continues to use the letters of the Hebrew alphabet.

As the colloquial tongue of Jews, Yiddish is a colorful, earthy, highly expressive language with a special flair for comic expression, and witty, evocative figures of speech. It has a great range of psychological subtlety, and a large repertoire of the nuances of insult, mockery, irony, sarcasm, satire, and paradox.

Before World War II, many Yiddish newspapers, magazines, and books were published in the

United States, and a rich theatrical tradition flourished on Second Avenue on the Lower East Side of New York, where there were as many as a dozen Yiddish shows appearing at the same time. Yiddish-language films were also produced for an international market.

The children of Jewish immigrants from about 1880 to 1920 grew up hearing and understanding—though not always speaking—Yiddish. The Nazis killed six million European Jews, most of them Yiddish speakers. Surviving Jews who spoke Yiddish on a regular basis in the United States, Western Europe, Latin America, and pre-Israel Palestine gradually died out, and, for a time, it appeared that the language would disappear with them. But in the wake of the Holocaust, a modest but significant movement developed among young Jews to study Yiddish. The most eloquent defender and romanticizer of Yiddish is Leo Rosten, whose major works on the subject are *The Joys of Yiddish* (1968), *Hooray for Yiddish* (1982), and *The Joys of Yinglish* (1990). He traces the impact of Yiddish on American humor and culture to the strikingly large presence of Jews in American media. Jews are creators of comic strips, and are also comedians, actors, writers and producers in vaudeville, radio, movies, television, and Broadway shows, and they were songwriters on Tin Pan Alley, not to mention working as nationally syndicated gossip columnists, magazine cartoonists, and authors of popular novels and short stories.

The following are a few of the approximately five hundred Yiddish words that have entered the American vernacular. In America, *gonif* literally means "America, thief," but early Jewish immigrants used it to express their general disappointment about some aspect of American life. Similar in meaning is a *klug zu Columbus*—a curse on Columbus. *Bubbe meise* is a grandmother's tale, a comforting but flawed account or explanation. *Gelt* is money; *glitch*, an error, a slip; *kosher*, lit-erally, approved by the Jewish dietary laws, has become a synonym for on-the-up-and-up, legal, proper; *kvech* is to gripe, or a griper; *l'chayim* means to life—a frequent toast at Jewish functions and the title of a key song in the popular musical *Fiddler on the Roof*. A *luftmensch*, literally, a person who lives on air, is an impractical person who lives on the bounty of others, or has no visible means of support, but a *mensch* is a thoroughly admirable person. In a synagogue, the *shamus* is the sexton, but the word has come to mean a private detective. A *shlemiel* is a clumsy bungler or a chronic misfit, while a *shlimazel* is someone for whom nothing turns out well. A classic description of the *schlimazel* was penned by the twelfth-century poet, Abraham ibn Ezra (Robert Browning's "Rabbi ben Ezra"):

If I sold lamps,
The sun,
In spite,
Would shine
At night.

Other popular Yiddishisms include: *alter kocker* (crotchety, ineffectual old man); *klutz* (a clumsy oaf); *meshugana* (a crazy person); *momzer* (a bastard or simply an unworthy person); *nebbish* (a Sad Sack, a loser); *nudnik* (a pest, bore); *schlep* (to lug; also a long, tedious journey or job; also an unimaginative person, a hack or drudge); *schlock* (cheap, inferior merchandise or art); *schnook* (a dope); *schnorrer* (a beggar or freeloader); and *zhlub* (a boor).

In addition, there are many idiomatic expressions and verbal constructions that are now not only part of the vernacular of the United States, but they have also made their mark on British English. Examples of common Yiddishisms include such expressions as *could be* (in the sense of possibly or it might be so); *eat your heart out; get lost!; you should live so long; you should excuse* the expression; *I need it like a hole in the head; a dummy he's not; that's not chopped liver; that no-goodnik!; go do her something; that's like putting ham on a bagel;* and *go fight City Hall.*

Not only are Yiddish words and phrases common in English, so are Yiddish linguistic devices. For example: dismissal and scorn through repetition and the addition of the syllable *sh:* "fat-shmat." Reversal of syntax for mordant effect: "Intelligent, he's not." Reversal of word order to convey scorn: "One year of college and already you're an expert?" The use of a question to answer a question: "Will fifty dollars cover expenses?" "Will fifty dollars cover expenses?"—uttered incredulously.

See also: DIALECT STORIES.

SUGGESTED READING: Leo Rosten, *The Joys of Yiddish* (1968; reprint ed., New York, 1970).

Yoakum, Joseph (1886–1972). Yoakum was a Navajo–African-American folk artist who created strikingly organic mountain landscapes, working chiefly in ink, watercolor, and pastel. He was born into a large family on a Navajo reservation in Arizona and was raised in Kansas City, Missouri, and on a farm near Walnut Grove, Missouri. Yoakum had almost no formal education and left home in his early teens to join a trav-eling circus as a handyman. He claims to have worked in Buffalo Bill's Wild West Show, among other circuses, and, in 1903, became the personal valet of John Ringling. Yoakum traveled the nation and the world, not only with the circuses, but as a hobo, and his artworks sometimes depict landscapes on every continent except Antarctica—the single continent Yoakum reported never having visited. Yoakum served in France during World War I and began at that time to draw and paint, achieving some recognition, but still working mainly in other occupations, including sailor, railroad porter, and janitor in various parts of the country, finally buying an ice cream parlor on the South Side of Chicago.

Yoakum's work has been widely exhibited at Chicago's Sherbeyn Gallery (1968), Pennsylvania State University Art Museum, University Park (1969), the School of the Art Institute of Chicago (1971), the Whitney Museum of American Art, New York (1972), and the University of Rhode Island, Kingston (1973). His work was included in the important "Outsider Art in Chicago" exhibit at Chicago's Museum of Contemporary Art in 1979 and in "Transmitters: The Isolate Artist in America" at the Philadelphia College of Art in 1981.

SUGGESTED READING: Jane Livingston and John Beardsley, *Black Folk Art in America: 1930–1980* (Jackson, Miss., 1982).

Z

Zydeco. Zydeco, a currently popular type of music, is an eclectic blend of Cajun traditions, black Creole and Afro-Caribbean influences, and African-American rhythm-and-blues. The name of the music evolved out of the line of a Cajun song describing poverty so extreme that the performer couldn't afford salt for his snap beans: "Les haricots sont pas sale." The first two words are pronounced like "Layzareeco," which modulated into Zydeco. The chief developer and popularizer of the style, which evolved in Louisiana over the last 150 years, was CLIFTON CHENIER (1925–88), who started performing professionally early in his life on a piano accordion given to him by his father. While the principal instrument in white Cajun music is a one-key diatonic instrument with only a tonic and dominant chord for the right hand, the piano accordion can play in any key and has a set of 120 chords. Famous as a rhythm-and-blues performer in the early 1960s, Chenier signed up with ARHOOLIE RECORDS in 1964 and returned to his south Louisiana roots, recording such zydeco albums as *Louisiana Blues and Zydeco, Bon Ton Roulet, King of the Bayous,* and *Bogalusa Boogie.* Acclaimed as the "Black King of the South" and the "King of Zydeco," Chenier became an international star, appearing at the Berkeley Blues Festival (1966), the Newport Folk Festival (1969), and touring Europe (1967–69) with his exciting combo, the Louisiana Hot Band.

The frequent interactions between Cajun and Creole cultures in southwest Louisiana have caused many fans outside the state to confuse the music of the two groups. Cajun music emphasizes the melodic line more strongly, while zydeco musicians play faster and hotter; the latter play highly syncopated rhythms with frequent shifts of the placement of the accented beats. They have a strong preference for Cajun or Afro-Caribbean blues tunes in an Afro-Caribbean framework.

Although there are evidences of many cultural influences from the West Indies in Louisiana life and music, there is no musical form in the French West Indies resembling zydeco. Evidently the interchange between Cajuns and black Creoles has created a style of music native to Louisiana.

See also: ROUNDER RECORDS.

SUGGESTED READING: Philip Gould, *Cajun Music and Zydeco with Companion (Special Edition)* (Baton Rouge, La., 1992); Pat Nyhan et al., *Let the Good Times Roll: A Guide to Cajun and Zydeco Music* (Portland, Maine, 1998).

FOR THE BEST IN PAPERBACKS, LOOK FOR THE

In every corner of the world, on every subject under the sun, Penguin represents quality and variety—the very best in publishing today.

For complete information about books available from Penguin—including Puffins, Penguin Classics, and Compass—and how to order them, write to us at the appropriate address below. Please note that for copyright reasons the selection of books varies from country to country.

In the United Kingdom: Please write to *Dept. EP, Penguin Books Ltd, Bath Road, Harmondsworth, West Drayton, Middlesex UB7 0DA.*

In the United States: Please write to *Penguin Putnam Inc., P.O. Box 12289 Dept. B, Newark, New Jersey 07101-5289* or call 1-800-788-6262.

In Canada: Please write to *Penguin Books Canada Ltd, 10 Alcorn Avenue, Suite 300, Toronto, Ontario M4V 3B2.*

In Australia: Please write to *Penguin Books Australia Ltd, P.O. Box 257, Ringwood, Victoria 3134.*

In New Zealand: Please write to *Penguin Books (NZ) Ltd, Private Bag 102902, North Shore Mail Centre, Auckland 10.*

In India: Please write to *Penguin Books India Pvt Ltd, 11 Panchsheel Shopping Centre, Panchsheel Park, New Delhi 110 017.*

In the Netherlands: Please write to *Penguin Books Netherlands bv, Postbus 3507, NL-1001 AH Amsterdam.*

In Germany: Please write to *Penguin Books Deutschland GmbH, Metzlerstrasse 26, 60594 Frankfurt am Main.*

In Spain: Please write to *Penguin Books S. A., Bravo Murillo 19, 1° B, 28015 Madrid.*

In Italy: Please write to *Penguin Italia s.r.l., Via Benedetto Croce 2, 20094 Corsico, Milano.*

In France: Please write to *Penguin France, Le Carré Wilson, 62 rue Benjamin Baillaud, 31500 Toulouse.*

In Japan: Please write to *Penguin Books Japan Ltd, Kaneko Building, 2-3-25 Koraku, Bunkyo-Ku, Tokyo 112.*

In South Africa: Please write to *Penguin Books South Africa (Pty) Ltd, Private Bag X14, Parkview, 2122 Johannesburg.*